PAGE
28

# ON THE ROAD

YOUR COMPLETE DESTINATION GUIDE
In-depth reviews, detailed listings
and insider tips

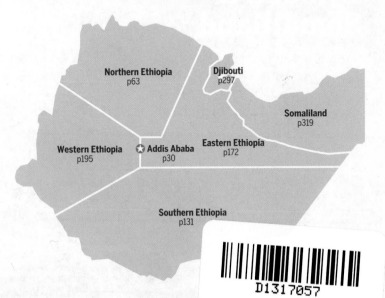

**Northern Ethiopia** p63

**Djibouti** p297

**Somaliland** p319

**Western Ethiopia** p195

⭐ **Addis Ababa** p30

**Eastern Ethiopia** p172

**Southern Ethiopia** p131

D1317057

**Health**

THIS EDITION WRITTEN AND RESEARCHED BY

**Jean-Bernard Carillet,
Tim Bewer, Stuart Butler**

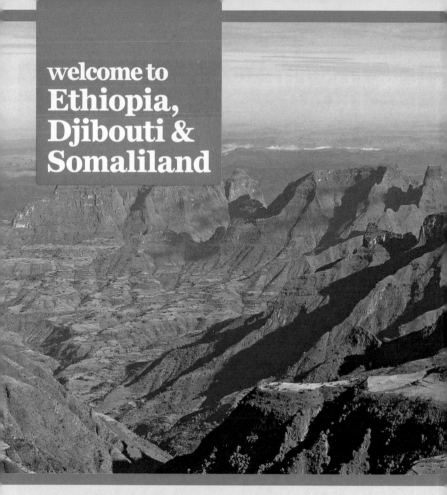

# welcome to Ethiopia, Djibouti & Somaliland

## A Land-Lover's Dream

Ethiopia's landscape impresses in both scale and beauty. Travellers are thrilled by the amazing backdrop of canyons, chasms, lakes, savannah plains and high plateaus – not to mention the mesmerisingly desolate Danakil Depression, peppered with an astonishing 25% of Africa's active volcanoes. Lying at the convergence of three tectonic plates, Djibouti offers a unique geological landscape. The vast salt lake of Lac Assal and the bizarre lunarscape of Lac Abbé are strangely unforgettable. Somaliland wows visitors with its natural beauty, from the superscenic Daallo Escarpment to the seemingly endless beaches that are strung along the coast.

## Outdoor Adventures

These countries beg outdoor escapades with their larger-than-life, hallucinatory landscapes. Hiking and trekking in Ethiopia's Simien and Bale Mountains or Djibouti's Goda Mountains are obvious choices. Then there are those must-do-before-you-die moments, such as swimming with whale sharks in Djibouti's Gulf of Tadjoura or diving amid coral-encrusted wrecks off Djibouti City. Last but not least, Ethiopia and Somaliland rank among Africa's best birdwatching destinations, with plenty of endemic species. One thing is sure: you'll be rewarded with memorable experiences.

*In Ethiopia, Djibouti and Somaliland, you'd be hard-pressed to find a better combination of nature and culture. The best part: there'll be no crowds to hinder the experience.*

(left) Simien Mountains (p87)
(below) Karo (p163) woman and child

## Peoples with Proud Traditions

Peopling these landscapes is a wide variety of African peoples, including the Afar, the Mursi, the Karo, the Hamer, the Nuer and the Anuak, whose ancient customs and traditions have remained almost entirely intact. Staying with these communities is a great introduction to a way of life once followed by all of humankind. A highlight of any trip to the Horn is witnessing one of the many ceremonies and festivals that are an integral part of traditional culture in the region. They may be Christian, Islamic or animist festivals, or village events, such as a wedding, a rite-of-passage celebration or a local market day.

## Historical Wonders

Ethiopia, almost the only African country to have escaped European colonialism, has retained much of its cultural identity. Its sovereign story has left its wide-ranging and fertile highlands laden with historical treasures ranging from ancient Aksumite tombs and obelisks to 17th-century castles. And it's not dubbed the Cradle of Humanity for nothing; archaeologically speaking, Ethiopia is to sub-Saharan Africa what Egypt is to North Africa. In neighbouring Somaliland, you'll have the chance to marvel at the fantastic site of Las Geel, replete with exceptionally well-preserved rock paintings. Djibouti also boasts superb rock engravings hidden in the mountains.

# › Ethiopia, Djibouti & Somaliland

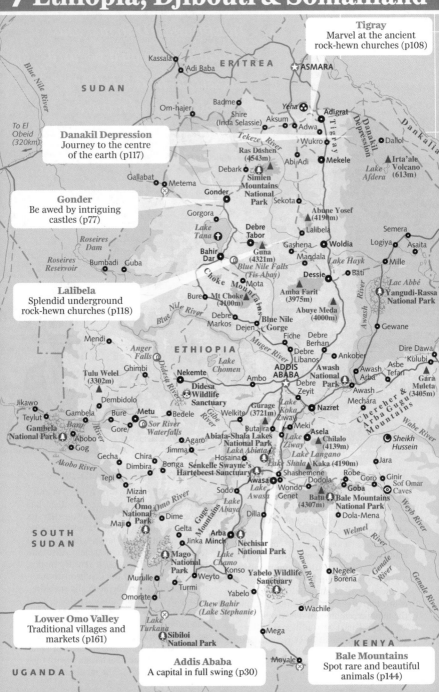

**Tigray**
Marvel at the ancient
rock-hewn churches (p108)

**Danakil Depression**
Journey to the centre
of the earth (p117)

**Gonder**
Be awed by intriguing
castles (p77)

**Lalibela**
Splendid underground
rock-hewn churches (p118)

**Lower Omo Valley**
Traditional villages and
markets (p161)

**Addis Ababa**
A capital in full swing (p30)

**Bale Mountains**
Spot rare and beautiful
animals (p144)

# Top Experiences ›

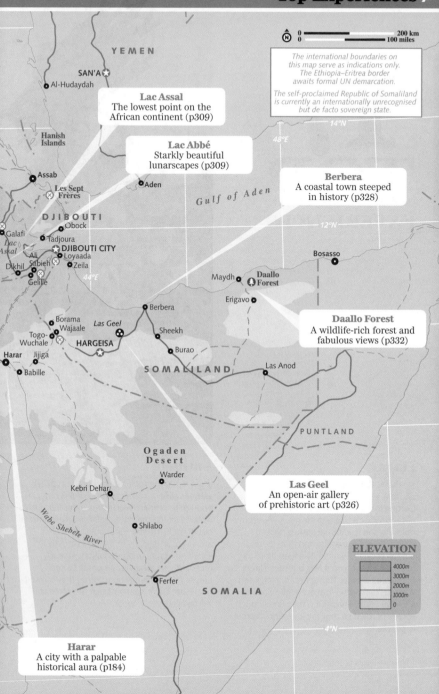

**Lac Assal**
The lowest point on the African continent (p309)

**Lac Abbé**
Starkly beautiful lunarscapes (p309)

**Berbera**
A coastal town steeped in history (p328)

**Daallo Forest**
A wildlife-rich forest and fabulous views (p332)

**Las Geel**
An open-air gallery of prehistoric art (p326)

**Harar**
A city with a palpable historical aura (p184)

The international boundaries on this map serve as indications only. The Ethiopia–Eritrea border awaits formal UN demarcation.

The self-proclaimed Republic of Somaliland is currently an internationally unrecognised but de facto sovereign state.

0   200 km
0   100 miles

YEMEN

SAN'A
Al-Hudaydah

Hanish Islands

Assab
Les Sept Freres

DJIBOUTI

Galafi
Obock
Lac Assal
Tadjoura
DJIBOUTI CITY
Loyaada
Ali Sabieh
Dikhil
Zeila
Gelille

Aden

Gulf of Aden

Bosasso

Maydh   Daallo Forest

Erigavo

Berbera

Borama   Las Geel
Wajaale
Togo-Wuchale
HARGEISA
Sheekh
Harar   Jijiga
Babille
Burao

SOMALILAND

Las Anod

PUNTLAND

Ogaden Desert

Warder

Kebri Dehar

Wabe Shebele River

Shilabo

Ferfer

SOMALIA

**ELEVATION**

4000m
3000m
2000m
1000m
0

# 17 TOP EXPERIENCES

## Harar

**1** By far the most intriguing city in Ethiopia, Harar (p184) is a joy to explore. Getting lost in its crooked alleyways is just as fascinating as visiting the many museums, markets and traditional homes packed inside the old city walls. And then there are the hyenas. Two families feed them by hand, and let you do it too, but these large carnivores wander throughout the city and you may just bump into one while walking about at night. Thankfully, they find enough scraps of meat so that they have no interest in people.

## Lalibela

**2** Seeing the rock-hewn churches (p119) of Lalibela on TV and in books is not enough to prepare you for the experience of walking inside them for real. Carved entirely out of rock, the still-functioning churches are large, artistically refined and mostly in excellent states of preservation. An early morning visit, when locals come to seek blessings and inspiration, shows their mystical side. The longer you visit the more you will be filled with wonder. Bet Giyorgis (p119)

## Timkat

**3** Timkat, the feast of Epiphany, celebrates the baptism of Christ with a three-day festival starting on 19 January. Join the procession behind regalia-draped priests as the church *tabots* (replicas of the Ark of the Covenant) are taken to a nearby body of water on the afternoon of the eve of Timkat. Next morning, the *tabots* are paraded back to the church accompanied by much singing and dancing. Easily Ethiopia's most colourful festival.

## Las Geel (Somaliland)

**4** Gaping at the rock paintings at Las Geel (p326) feels like taking a time machine into the prehistoric past. This enigmatic site was known only to locals until late 2002 when a team of French archaeologists undertook a field mission in Somaliland. What to expect? Quantities of rock paintings that are striking both for their rich complexity and their incredible state of preservation. As if that wasn't enough, the site is easily accessible from Hargeisa.

ANGELO CAVALLI/GETTY IMAGES ©

ARIADNE VAN ZANDBERGEN/GETTY IMAGES ©

ANDREW MCCONNELL/GETTY IMAGES ©

PIPER MACKAY/GETTY IMAGES ©

GAVIN HELLIER/GETTY IMAGES ©

## Lac Abbé (Djibouti)

**5** There is nothing else on earth quite like the large, spikelike calcareous chimneys of Lac Abbé (p309). Hot springs dot the landscape, and fumaroles can also be found. These surreal-looking formations are a geological work of art, the result of millennia of volcanic activity and wind erosion. Experiencing this eerie landscape at dawn or at sunset is truly exhilarating.

## Lower Omo Valley Ethnic Groups

**6** The Lower Omo Valley (p161) is a remarkable cultural crossroads. From the Mursi people and their lip plates to the Banna with their calabash hats to the body painting Karo, tradition runs deep here. While the commonly held notion that the more than a dozen ethnic groups residing here live completely outside modern society is wrong, walking through the markets and villages or attending one of the many ceremonies really is a bit like stepping back in time. Surmi woman (p206)

## Simien Mountains

**7** With deep canyons and bizarrely jagged mountains sculpting scenery so awesome that if you saw it in a painting you might question whether it was real or not, the Simien Mountains (p87) are one of the wonders of the natural world. They're an important preserve for some of Ethiopia's endemic wildlife, and sitting amid a troop of tame gelada monkeys at Sankaber is an experience you'll never forget. This is terrific trekking territory but also easily accessible by car.

GAVIN HELLIER/GETTY IMAGES ©

## Gonder

**8** Gonder (p77) preserves a treasure trove of history. The walls of the Royal Enclosure contain a half-dozen medieval palaces and a host of legends; you can easily imagine the grand feasts they held here as you walk among them. Further out are peaceful and atmospheric sites, including Fasiladas' Bath, the Kuskuam complex and Debre Berhan Selassie Church, saved from the marauding Sudanese Dervishes by a swarm of bees. Fasiladas' Palace, Royal Enclosure (p77)

## Rock-Hewn Churches of Tigray

**9** Hidden like jewels in the arid Tigrayan countryside, the old rock-hewn churches of Tigray (p108) will wow you. Partially carved and partially constructed, most sit on remote cliffsides requiring long walks (and sometimes steep climbs) and the sense of discovery upon arrival is a big part of their appeal. But they also delight on their artistic and historic merits alone. Mikael Imba (p112)

## Bale Mountains

**10** The Ethiopian wolf is the rarest canid in the world, but on the 4000m-high Sanetti Plateau in the Bale Mountains (p144) you are almost guaranteed to see them. And when you're not watching wolves hunt giant molerats, your eyes will be drawn to the fairy-tale forests draped in 'old man's beard' and the sheer drop of the Harenna Escarpment. Though the mountains are prime trekking territory, there's no need to step out of your car to enjoy them since you can drive right through on the highest all-weather road in Africa. Ethiopian wolves (p146)

## Lac Assal (Djibouti)

**11** Djibouti's version of the Dead Sea, Lac Assal (p309), at -155m, ranks as the world's third-lowest point. Like most of Djibouti's lakes, which are saline and host incredible crystal formations, Lac Assal's shore is carpeted with spheres of halite and angular gypsum. For visitors, nothing beats a walk on the salt crust or a dip into the briny waters of the lake. It's encircled with volcanic mountains, which adds to the appeal. Salt extraction by the Afar people is still practised; the salt is taken to Ethiopia for barter trading.

## Whale-Shark Spotting (Djibouti)

**12** Don't know what a *Rhincodon typus* is? It's time to get an education in the Bay of Ghoubbet (p301). Expect your flippers to be blown off by an interaction with one of Mother Nature's most impressive creatures – the whale shark. Several individuals move through the Gulf of Tadjoura annually between November and January, and are a guaranteed wildlife experience.

11

ANDREW MCCONNELL/GETTY IMAGES ©

12

FERGUS KENNEDY/GETTY IMAGES ©

## Danakil Depression

**13** The actively volcanic Danakil Depression (p117) features a permanent lava lake and a vast field of yellow and orange sulphuric rocks. Just as interesting are the hearty Afar people who eke out a living from the baking, cracked plains. Though there are regular tours into its depths, travel here is not easy due to the lack of roads, services and normal temperatures. The Danakil Depression may feel inhospitable, but the sense of exploration is real. The best way to visit this territory is with a well-established tour operator.

## Food

**14** Culinary delights in the Horn of Africa? Yes, it's possible. It's easy to travel here with the thought that the region subsists on rice or pasta and sauce. But hunt around, and you'll be positively surprised. Ethiopian food (p259), and the myriad ways it's prepared, is some of the most diverse on the continent. Djibouti is a feast for the tastebuds, with savoury seafood dishes, elegant French cuisine and superb Yemeni-influenced dishes. In Somaliland, why not grab the opportunity to sample camel meat?

## Addis Ababa

**15** Addis Ababa (p30) is evolving at a fast pace. The noisy, bustling capital of Ethiopia is blessed with a balmy climate, with cloudless blue skies for about eight months of the year. It offers plenty of cultural highlights, including the Ethnological Museum and the National Museum. Addis is also famed for its buzzing restaurant scene and nightlife, with lots of eateries, bars, galleries and clubs. Delve in!

Musicians playing drums at a local wedding celebration

## Berbera (Somaliland)

**16** Berbera (p328) feels impossibly exotic. Although only 150km to the east of Hargeisa, this coastal city could not be more different from the capital. The history, climate, architecture and atmosphere of the town seem to come from another world. Though in dire need of rehabilitation, the various historic buildings in the centre give an engaging character to the city, as do the big cargo ships in the port. What's more, Berbera boasts miles of deserted beaches that are great for swimming, relaxing and enjoying fiery sunsets.

## Daallo Forest & Lookout (Somaliland)

**17** One of East Africa's last frontiers, the Sanaag is the largest, most sparsely populated and least developed province of Somaliland. Getting there is half the fun and involves a gruelling 4WD trip from the capital. But the rewards are exceptional. The Daallo Forest (p332) is noted for its abundant wildlife. Cross the forest and you'll reach a lookout at the edge of the escarpment, with mesmerising views down into the valley. If you're armed with a sense of adventure and have a taste for rugged travel, you'll love this area.

# need to know

**Djibouti & Somaliland**

» See p297 and p319 for Need to Know information for Djibouti and Somaliland, respectively.

**Currency & Money**

» Ethiopian Birr; sometimes US dollars.

» ATMs in large towns. Credit cards (Visa and MasterCard) only useful in Addis Ababa.

## When to Go

- **Aksum** GO Oct–Apr
- **Addis Ababa** GO Year-round
- **Harar** GO Oct–Apr
- **Gambela** GO Dec–Mar
- **Jinka** GO Jan–Apr

Desert, Dry Climate
Tropical Climate, Wet & Dry Season
Warm to Hot Summers, Mild Winters

### High Season
(Jan–Mar)

» Expect sunny skies and warm days.

» These months are good for wildlife watching.

» Ethiopia's most colourful festivals, including Timkat and Leddet.

### Shoulder Season
(Oct–Dec)

» The country is green, skies are sunny and there are fewer visitors. Trekking during this time is particularly sublime.

» Good for birding.

### Low Season
(Apr–Sep)

» The rainy season in southern Ethiopia and the scorching hot temperatures in the lowlands can make travel difficult.

## Your Daily Budget

### Budget less than US$30

» Basic double with private facilities: US$5–20

» Travel between cities by bus; chartered taxi for day trips

» Local-style meals are tasty and cheap

### Midrange US$30–80

» Double room in a comfortable hotel: US$20–40

» At the upper end, hire a car and driver

» Dinner with alcohol at a midrange restaurant: around US$10

### Top End more than US$80

» Accommodation in a full-board resort or an upmarket hotel room: from US$100

» Travel by private 4WD with driver; internal flights to save time

» Fine dining at an upmarket restaurant

## Language
» Amharic, Tigrinya, Oromo, Somali, Afar, Arabic, French

### Visas
» Required by most travellers; single-entry, one-month visas available on arrival at Addis Ababa's airport or in advance from an Ethiopian embassy overseas.

### Mobile Phones
» Local SIM cards are widely available and can be used in most international mobile phones. Coverage is extensive but service unreliable.

## Transport
» Buses, rental 4WDs and internal flights are the main ways of getting around.

# Websites
» **Lonely Planet** (www.lonelyplanet.com/ethiopia) Destination information, travel forum, photos.

» **Selamta** (www.selamta.net) Travel information.

» **Ethiopian Treasures** (www.ethiopiantreasures.co.uk) Categorised information on history and culture.

» **Tourism Ethiopia** (www.tourismethiopia.gov.et) Ministry of Culture and Tourism.

» **All Africa** (www.allafrica.com) Collates daily news and sorts it into country profiles.

# Exchange Rates

| Australia | A$1 | Birr19 |
|-----------|------|--------|
| Canada | C$1 | Birr18 |
| Eurozone | €1 | Birr24 |
| Japan | ¥100 | Birr21 |
| New Zealand | NZ$1 | Birr15 |
| UK | UK£1 | Birr29 |
| USA | US$1 | Birr18 |

For current exchange rates see www.xe.com.

# Important Numbers
You need to drop the first zero from the number when calling Ethiopia from abroad.

| Country code | ☎251 |
|--------------|------|
| International access code | ☎00 |
| Police | ☎991 |

# Arriving in Ethiopia

» **Bole International Airport**
Minibus – to Piazza, Mexico Sq and Meskal Sq from 6am to 8pm
Taxi – from US$20 to US$35; 20 to 30 minutes to the centre

# Ethiopia Transport Tips
Ethiopia is a huge place, and you're likely to spend a considerable portion of your stay travelling. Here are some tips to maximise comfort and safety:

» Internal flights can be huge time savers. The national carrier has an extensive domestic route service and a solid safety record. It's cheaper to book your flight once in Ethiopia.

» If travelling by bus, opt for the newer companies, which offer better service and more comfortable buses.

» Though expensive, it's not a bad idea to hire a 4WD with a driver, especially for southern and western Ethiopia. Having your own car allows you to stop wherever you want and saves time. The driver can also act as a guide-cum-interpreter. Note also that some national parks can only be entered with a 4WD. Shop around and hire through a reputable agency.

# if you like...

## Wildlife Watching

The region is a nature-lover's dream. Ethiopia, Djibouti and Somaliland offer superb wildlife-viewing opportunities. A variety of charismatic species, some of which are found nowhere else in the world, can easily be approached under the supervision of a knowledgeable guide.

**Gambela National Park** Migrating herds of antelope a million strong (p212)

**Bale Mountains National Park** You're almost guaranteed to see Ethiopian wolves here (p144)

**Babille Elephant Sanctuary** Bushwhack through thick, thorny brush for an up-close elephant encounter (p193)

**Nechisar National Park** There are some zebra and other big mammals here, but it's the massive gathering of crocodiles that attracts the crowds (p156)

**Bay of Ghoubbet** Swim alongside massive whale sharks between November and January (p301)

**Decan** This small wildlife refuge near Djibouti City shelters various species, including cheetahs, that have been illegally caged for trafficking purposes (p308)

## Birdwatching

Ethiopia and Somaliland are major birdwatching destinations, and you never have to venture too far to get some shiny feathers in front of your binoculars. In Ethiopia, twitchers benefit from a relatively well-organised network of guides and tours.

**Gibe Sheleko National Park** All the classic highland species can be spotted in this park (p209)

**Gambela National Park** Some of the birds here are seen nowhere else in Ethiopia (p212)

**Bale Mountains National Park** Offers easy access to both highland and lowland habitats and their associated species, including nine Ethiopian endemics (p144)

**Rift Valley Lakes** The string of large lakes, from Ziway to Chamo, are surprisingly diverse, leading to a great variety of possible encounters over many days (p135)

**Yabelo Wildlife Sanctuary** The locally endemic Ethiopian bush crow and white-tailed swallow are the major drawcards here (p151)

**Daallo Forest** At the eastern end of Somaliland, this unique forest hosts a wealth of avian species (p332)

## History & Culture

The Horn of Africa offers a wealth of attractions for culture buffs, from exceptional rock-art sites and centuries-old, rock-hewn churches to atmospheric, historical towns and grand castles.

**Ethnological Museum** One of the best if its kind in Africa, this museum in Addis Ababa gives a great insight into the many different Ethiopian peoples and their rich cultures (p32)

**Harar** The labyrinthine, walled old city is a pleasure to explore, and close encounters with wild hyenas add to its magic (p184)

**Lalibela** Subterranean churches, gorgeously carved into the rock, rarely fail to wow visitors (p119)

**Gonder** The various ruined castles in and around the city are exceptionally evocative (p77)

**Berbera** Historical buildings document sleepy Berbera's long and fascinating history (p328)

**Las Geel** Africa's most significant Neolithic rock-painting site is striking both for its vibrant colours and rich complexity (p326)

**Abourma** It's a tough hike to get here, but you'll be rewarded with eye-catching rock engravings (p310)

ARIADNE VAN ZANDBERGEN/GETTY IMAGES ©

» Burchell's zebras, Nechisar National Park (p156)

# Festivals

Visitors are often over-whelmed by the sense of devotion that emanates from the incredibly colour-ful festivals held throughout the region. Some are so impressive that it's worth timing your trip around them.

**Meskel** One of Ethiopia's most colourful festivals, Meskel is famous for its cross-topped bonfires and elaborately dressed clergy (p20)

**Great Ethiopian Run** Join thousands of joggers in Africa's biggest running race in Addis Ababa (p42)

**Jumping of the Bulls** This coming-of-age ceremony is usually a highlight of visitors' time in Ethiopia for anyone lucky enough to see one (p169)

**Timkat** Ethiopia's most impor-tant holiday celebrates Jesus' baptism with a lot of splashing of water and parading of replica Arks of the Covenant (p19)

**Leddet** During Leddet (Christ-mas) the faithful attend all-night church services, often moving from one church to another. Priests don their full regalia (p19)

# Trekking & Hiking

For an unforgettable taste of Ethiopia and Djibouti, grab your kit, lace up your boots and head into the landscape that covers all the geological highs and lows.

**Bale Mountains** The combina-tion of wildlife, scenery and quality facilities makes this a fantastic wilderness destination (p144)

**Menagesha National Forest** Follow the trails through this wildlife-filled forest (p209)

**Lalibela & Tigray** The commu-nity trekking programs in these areas offer both lovely scenery and a chance to get to know the locals (p111 and p125)

**Simien Mountains National Park** This very popular park holds some of the most stun-ning mountain scenery in Africa and trekking is easily organised (p87)

**Menz-Guassa Community Conservation Area** This seldom-visited spot protects one of the most pristine high-alpine habitats in Ethiopia (p130)

**Goda Mountains** Waterfalls, forests, canyons – what the little-known Goda Mountains lack in size is more than made up for in diversity, with walks of various lengths (p309)

# Dramatic Scenery

The Horn of Africa is brim-ming with natural wonders, from geological oddities to powerfully majestic mountainscapes. Ethiopia, Djibouti and Somaliland have countless places to ready your wide-angle lens for some shutter-blowing compositions.

**Danakil Depression** Truly unique in the world, the sub-sea-level volcanic landscape here is eerily beautiful (p117)

**Simien Mountains National Park** Huge cliffs, oddly formed mountains and unusual Afro-alpine habitat create one of the most stunning spots in Africa (p87)

**Rock-hewn churches of Tigray** Though it's the churches that draw people in, the soaring mountain pinnacles are equally mesmerising (p108)

**Lac Abbé** Spikelike calcareous chimneys make for apocalyptic landscapes (p309)

**Lac Assal** The great salt lake and black volcanic terrain of Lac Assal are truly photogenic (p309)

**Daallo Lookout** Peering over the vertigo ledges of the Daallo Escarpment is a Somaliland highlight (p332)

» *Waga* (carved wooden sculptures), Konso (p159)

# Traditional Cultures

An anthropologist's dream, the Horn of Africa is home to numerous ethnic groups, each with their own language and customs. The 200 dialects spoken in Ethiopia give an indication of the country's incredible diversity.

**Kibish and southwest Omo Valley** Meet the fierce Surmi people, who are known for their white body paintings (p205)

**Itang** Mingle with the ritually scarred Nuer and Anuak peoples around Gambela (p212)

**Lower Omo Valley** This awesome region is home to 16 ethnic groups, many of which have not strayed far from their ancient cultures (p161)

**Konso Villages** The fortresslike villages here, built of stone and sticks, and terraced fields are World Heritage listed (p159)

**Danakil Depression** The Afar residing in this scorching hot desert still walk their camel caravans to the highlands to sell salt (p117)

**Dorze** The woven houses are just one of the many fascinating things about this proud culture (p158)

# Offbeat Travel

There's no shortage of opportunities in Ethiopia, Djibouti and Somaliland to get off the beaten path. You'll find countless places where you'll be the only visitor.

**Kibish** Venture to the forgotten side of the Omo Valley and arrange a village stay to experience some of the most traditional cultures of Ethiopia (p205)

**Nejo** This is a special place: it is said to shelter the oldest gold mines in the world (p202)

**Awra Amba** Witness a small Utopia in the making (p72)

**Asaita** When you reach this remote town in the Danakil Desert, your first impression may well be: 'Have I reached another planet?' (p180)

**Abi Adi** This is the rock-hewn churches of Tigray's least visited cluster, and all the better for it (p113)

**Sof Omar Cave** Follow the Web River straight through a limestone ridge (p149)

**Maydh** This hard-to-reach coastal village feels like the world's end (p332)

# Creature Comforts

Rejoice! If you've had enough of trekking, wildlife seeking and bumping around in a 4WD, put your bags down for a few days at one of these wonderful places to stay.

**Negash Lodge** Wake up to the sing-song of birds in this great-value lodge (p209)

**Sheraton Hotel** If you really want to chill, book a room at this plush resort and enjoy its splendid swimming pool (p43)

**Gheralta Lodge** An unexpected splash of style and comfort in the midst of a remote region (p113)

**Debre Zeyit** Home to several lakeside lodges, this town makes a fine final night alternative to staying in Addis Ababa (p174)

**Djibouti Palace Kempinski** (p301) It may not feel very Djiboutian, but this sprawling resort has a prolific list of amenities, including two superb pools and excellent restaurants

**Ambassador Hotel Hargeisa** (p322) Somaliland's best and most secure hotel is a great base if you need to recharge the batteries. Good news: it's affordable.

# month by month

## Top Events

1. **Leddet** January
2. **Timkat** January
3. **Meskel** September
4. **Great Ethiopian Run** November

## January

**This is the most vibrant and busy time to visit, with Ethiopia's most colourful festivals, and the weather is usually cool and dry. It's also the best time to explore Djibouti and Somaliland.**

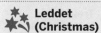 **Leddet (Christmas)**

Being in Ethiopia for Leddet (6 to 7 January) is a dramatic throwback to a time when Christmas still had real meaning. The faithful attend all-night church services, often moving from one church to another. Lalibela is one of the best places to experience Leddet; Addis Ababa is also good.

 **Timkat (Epiphany, celebrating Christ's baptism)**

This three-day festival is the most colourful of the year. Join the thousands of white-robed faithful in Gonder as they sing and dance behind a solemn procession of regalia-draped priests. Other good places to be for Timkat are Addis Ababa and Aksum.

## February

**The heart of the dry season is the easiest time to travel around the region, including Djibouti and Somaliland.**

 **Trekking**

The Simien Mountains (p87) are at their best – now is your chance to scale up Ras Dashen, Ethiopia's highest peak, and snap pictures of gelada monkeys.

 **Antelope Migration**

Herds of migrating white-eared kob and Nile lechwe over a million strong move through Gambela National Park (p212) – magic.

## March

**March marks the end of the high season. Days are warm and dry, and there's excellent wildlife watching around waterholes in the national parks.**

 **Bull-Jumping Ceremony**

Head to the Lower Omo Valley (p169) to witness a young man run across the backs of cattle to be initi-

ated into the responsibilities of manhood, while, in a show of solidarity and stoic allegiance, women volunteer to be whipped with slender canes. Ceremonies typically take place between late January and early April.

## April

**April is a transition month. Increasing temperatures in the Ethiopian lowlands are mitigated by heavy showers. It's still a pleasant travel time, before the heavier rains and the increasing heat of the following months.**

 **Good Friday**

From Thursday evening before Good Friday, the faithful fast until the Easter service, which ends at 3am on Easter Sunday. Held in March or April.

**Fasika (Orthodox Easter)**

Fasika marks the end of a vegetarian fast of 55 days. Stay up on the night of Easter Saturday in Lalibela (p118) to see hundreds of white-robed pilgrims crowd the courtyards of the churches and pray under the moonlight.

# May

**Pessimists call this the beginning of the rainy season, but the region is green and lush. If you're planning a trip to visit the people of the Lower Omo Valley, you should avoid this month, when many roads are impassable.**

# August

**The big annual rains continue to batter Ethiopia. Getting around is difficult. The hot season sends lowland temperatures in the three countries up to 45°C. Avoid visiting now.**

# September

**The rains usually continue well into September; when they stop and you can see the horizon, Ethiopia is lush. By late September, rains may have subsided.**

### ✦ Kiddus Yohannes (New Year's Day)

At Ethiopian New Year (11 September), new clothes are traditionally bought for the occasion, particularly for children, and relatives and friends are visited.

### ✦ Meskel (Finding of the True Cross)

Starting on 27 September, this two-day festival is the most colourful after Timkat. Bonfires are built, topped by a cross to which flowers,

most commonly the Meskel daisy, are tied. Priests don their full regalia. Addis Ababa, Gonder and Aksum are good places to be.

# October

**Mid-October, just after the rains, is a great time to visit. The countryside glows green, the wildflowers are in bloom and there are few visitors.**

### ✦ Irecha

On the first Sunday following Meskel, the Oromo people celebrate Irecha on the shores of Lake Hora (p174). Devotees gather around ancient fig trees to smear perfume, butter and *katickala* (a distilled drink) on the trunks and share ceremonial meals of roasted meat, coffee and alcohol.

# November

**A great time to visit; expect plenty of wildlife in the national parks, and migratory birds begin arriving in great numbers.**

### ✦ Great Ethiopian Run

This 10km race takes over Addis Ababa on the last Sunday of November and attracts over 20,000 runners (p43). Whether running or watching, it's a fun time and it's a great chance to see some of East Africa's elite athletes in action.

### ✦ Festival of Maryam Zion

This vibrant festival is held only in Aksum (p103). In the days leading up to the event on 30 November, thousands of pilgrims head towards

Aksum. Celebrations start in front of the Northern Stelae Field, where the monarchs of the Orthodox church line the steps.

# December

**The weather is mostly dry throughout the region and it's a fine time for wildlife watching. Temperatures are also at their best – warm but not stifling. This is a great time to explore the Danakil Depression.**

### ✦ Kulubi Gabriel

Although not on the official religious holiday list, large numbers of Ethiopians make a pilgrimage to the venerated Kulubi Gabriel church (p184), near Dire Dawa in the east (28 December).

### 🏃 Trekking

This is an ideal month for trekking in the Bale Mountains (p142). It's dry and the skies are clear – perfect for capturing scenic landscapes.

### 🏃 Birdwatching

Calling all birders! Some 200 species of Palae-arctic migrants from Europe and Asia join the already abundant African resident and intra-African migrant populations.

### 🏃 Whale-shark spotting

Whale sharks migrate annually from their usual feeding grounds to the warm waters of the Gulf of Tadjoura (p301) to mate and give birth. They can be observed from November to January.

# itineraries

*Whether you've got six days or 60, these itineraries provide a starting point for the trip of a lifetime. Want more inspiration? Head online to lonelyplanet.com/thorntree to chat with other travellers.*

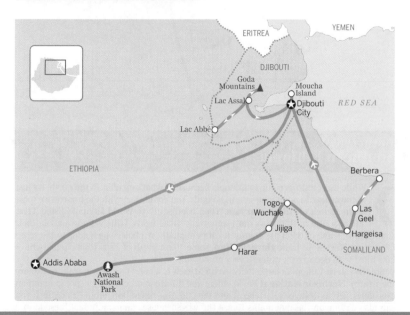

Three Weeks
## The Grand Tour

Start by spending two full days in fascinating **Addis Ababa**. Once you've had your fill of Addis' joys, forge east to **Awash National Park** for some great wildlife watching. Spend a day in the park and continue on to the eastern belle of **Harar**, whose attractive architecture, active markets and unique and unforgettable ambience deserve at least two days. You might make a half-day stop in **Jijiga** to recharge the batteries before hopping on a bus to **Togo-Wuchale**, at the border with Somaliland. From the border it's an easy taxi ride to **Hargeisa**. After a day or two recuperating in the laid-back capital of Somaliland, arrange for a car and driver to take you to the fantastic archaeological site of **Las Geel** and the atmosphere-laden coastal town of **Berbera** – you'll need at least two days to do the area justice. Back in Hargeisa, fly to **Djibouti City**, which merits at least several days for relaxing and exploring. Sign up for a three-day tour taking in **Lac Abbé**, **Lac Assal** and the **Goda Mountains**. Stop for a night on the island of **Moucha** before flying back to Addis Ababa.

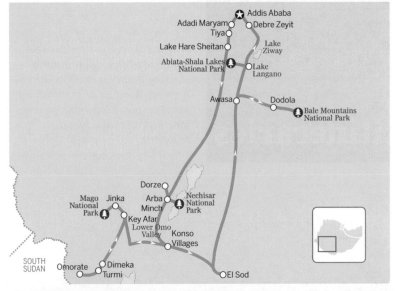

Two to Three Weeks
# Southern Ethiopia

While most visitors come to Ethiopia because of what's on offer in the north, it's just as rewarding to point your compass south. You could start with the impressive rock-hewn church of **Adadi Maryam**. Then head south to World Heritage–listed **Tiya**, one of southern Ethiopia's most important stelae fields. Little is known about their significance; some of them are engraved with enigmatic symbols, which adds to the sense of mystery. Next stop: **Lake Hare Sheitan**, some 50km south of Tiya. It's a circular crater lake filled with deep-green waters – very photogenic.

Southwestern Ethiopia's largest city, **Arba Minch** is a good base if you want to explore the nearby **Nechisar National Park**, where you'll have good chance to spot gargantuan crocodiles, zebras, Swayne's hartebeest and the odd Abyssinian lion. From Arba Minch you can also detour up the mountains to see the woven houses and traditional lifestyle in a **Dorze** village and then continue south and visit the amazing, fortresslike **Konso** villages, at the gateway to the cultural riches of the **Lower Omo Valley**.

In Omo, visits to ethnic villages such as those of the Mursi above **Mago National Park**, the Karo northwest of **Turmi** and the Daasanach along the mighty Omo River at Omorate will transport you to another world; as will the important markets in **Jinka**, **Dimeka** and **Key Afar**. If you're lucky, a Jumping of the Bulls ceremony will be happening during your visit.

Slip east for a look at the 'House of Salt' and a 'singing well' at **El Sod** before turning north for a night lakeside in modern and orderly **Awasa**. Then it's time for some remote trekking amid Ethiopian wolves and superb scenery in **Bale Mountains National Park** and around **Dodola**.

See the hot springs and flamingo flocks in **Abiata-Shala Lakes National Park** before unwinding in a lakeside resort and doing a bit or birdwatching at **Lake Langano**. Stop at **Lake Ziway** to see hippos, birdlife and island monasteries. You could spend another night on a lake at **Debre Zeyit** before returning to the chaos of capital Addis Ababa.

» (above) *Agelgil* (goat-skin lunch boxes) for sale, Bahir Dar (p68)
» (left) Marabou storks, Lake Ziway (p135)

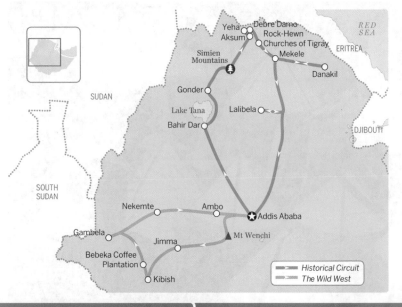

## Two Weeks
# Historical Circuit

The historical sights along this loop north of Addis Ababa are monumental in both scale and detail.

After a few days revelling in the chaos of **Addis Ababa**, head north to palm-fringed **Bahir Dar** for a day. Spend the next day at **Lake Tana** exploring some of the lake's centuries-old island monasteries. Next wander the extensive ruins of crenulated 17th-century castles in **Gonder**. Looming 100km north, the **Simien Mountains** are one of Ethiopia's most stunning national parks – spend a couple of days trekking in this sensational massif and spotting wildlife.

Push on to **Aksum** where pre-Christian tombs underlie splendid 1800-year-old stelae (obelisks). After two days, venture to the 3000-year-old ruins of Ethiopia's first capital, **Yeha**, and to the cliff-top monastery of **Debre Damo**. Then head south and search out Tigray's precarious and stunning **rock-hewn churches**. A short hop to the south is **Mekele**, which is the obvious launching pad for the desolate expanses of the **Danakil**. Back in Mekele, drive south to **Lalibela**. Its 11 astounding rock-hewn churches and myriad tunnels have poignantly frozen 12th- and 13th-century Ethiopia in stone. After three or so days here, it's back to Addis Ababa.

## 12 Days
# The Wild West

A journey out into the lush, green west is one for trail blazers. Leaving Addis it's a short and easy drive to **Mt Wenchi** where a crater lake and a beautiful day walk awaits. Next head past fields of golden tef (an indigenous grass cultivated as a cereal) and sunshine-bright meskel flowers to the bustling town of **Jimma** where you can soak up some culture in the museums. A long day's driving will take you deep into Surma country and the village of **Kibish**. After a few days of swapping stories with Surmi warriors, head up to the **Bebeka Coffee Plantation** where you'll probably be happy to just relax and watch tropical birds in the guesthouse gardens. Drive along misty mountain ridges, and through dense forests and descend into the steamy lowlands to fascinating **Gambela**, home of the Nuer and Anuak peoples as well as herds of antelopes. From Gambela you have two options – complete the loop by heading back to Addis via the low-key towns of **Nekemte** and **Ambo**, which makes for a scenic ride blessed with superb mountain vistas, or flying back to Addis from Gambela.

# regions at a glance

## Addis Ababa

**Museums** ✓✓✓
**Food** ✓✓
**Nightlife** ✓✓

### Museums

From your great-great-(repeat endlessly) aunt Lucy in the National Museum to the cultural insights of the Ethnological Museum or the bold and distinctive art of the capital's numerous art galleries, Addis is home to a collection of museums almost unrivalled in sub-Saharan Africa.

### Food

Arriving in Addis Ababa is like stepping into one giant food feast. Superb Italian restaurants dishing up perfect thin-crust pizzas, Indian-run eating houses serving spicy delights from southern Asia and a stash of old-fashioned cafes brewing up what some might say is the best coffee in the world. But good as all that is, it pales compared to the opportunity to dip your fingers into some seriously delicious Ethiopian dishes. Oh yes, your tummy will be happy.

### Nightlife

Addis Ababa is one of the most underrated nightlife capitals of Africa. Sure, there are bars and clubs like those at home by the dozen, but Ethiopia is nothing if not exotic so why not try a night out with a difference? A *tej bet,* a bar serving *tej* or honey wine, is a good place to begin. When you're done, catch some live music (and a deeply Ethiopian cultural immersion) at an *azmari bet* (a bar). Whatever you opt for, Addis will have you up half the night.

p30

## Northern Ethiopia

**History** ✓✓✓
**Landscapes** ✓✓✓
**Trekking** ✓✓✓

### History

They don't call it the Historical Circuit for nothing! Lake Tana, Gonder, Aksum, Yeha and Lalibela are legendary among historians while even lesser known sites, such as Debre Libanos, Gorgora and Mekele, offer antique intrigue.

### Landscapes

Staring down a massive cavern in the Simien Mountains, up one of the soaring pinnacles around Hawzien; or out across the volcanic creations in the Danakil Depression – Northern Ethiopia's scenery will wow you.

### Trekking

It's not just the scenery that makes the trekking in Northern Ethiopia world-class, it's also the variety. There are high-alpine landscapes in the Simien Mountains and little-known Menz-Guassa Community Conservation Area, and treks through farms and villages around Lalibela and Tigray. If you're truly hardcore, join the camel caravans out of the Danakil.

p63

# Southern Ethiopia

**Culture** ✓✓✓
**Trekking** ✓✓✓
**Lakes** ✓✓

## Traditional Cultures

The Omo Valley isn't just the most fascinating cultural melange in Ethiopia, it's tops of the entire continent. Most of its multitude of ethnic groups haven't strayed noticeably far from their past, and the opportunity to meet them is truly special. The unheralded Konso and Dorze cultures are less exotic, but even more interesting.

## Trekking

Though the Simien Mountains in the north get all the attention, most trekkers consider the Bale Mountains more satisfying due to better facilities, fewer people and near-guaranteed sightings of Ethiopian wolves. Lephis, Dorze, Konso and the Omo Valley also offer the chance to hoof it.

## Lakes

The Rift Valley runs the length of this region and along its path are various lakes; home to crocodiles (Chamo), hippos (Awasa), flamingos (Abiata and Chitu) and luxury resorts.

**p131**

# Eastern Ethiopia

**History** ✓✓
**Exploration** ✓✓
**Wildlife** ✓

## History

Eastern Ethiopia wouldn't be a historical destination if it weren't for World Heritage–listed Harar. Its old walled city centre, full of crooked cobblestone alleys and symbolically designed stone homes, is captivating.

## Exploration

Relatively few travellers venture east, and those who do rarely get off the Addis–Harar highway. This leaves places like Asaita and the caves and villages around Harar and Dire Dawa to the truly intrepid.

## Wildlife

There's a very good chance of meeting the elephants of Babille Elephant Sanctuary, although you'll probably have to bushwhack to do it. And though it's of more interest for its geology than wildlife, a game drive in Awash National Park will take you past oryx and gazelle; plus the birding is excellent. And, of course, don't forget about the urban hyenas of Harar.

**p172**

# Western Ethiopia

**Cultures** ✓✓✓
**Adventure** ✓✓✓
**Wildlife** ✓✓

## Traditional Cultures

Western Ethiopia is populated by an impressive mix of ethnic groups. The Nuer and Anuak people are around Gambela, and the Gurage people are near Jimma. For the ultimate adventure, journey to the wild land of the Surmi people in southwest Omo.

## Adventure

Even a country as little known as Ethiopia has to have its last frontier and that title goes to the west. With so few tourists venturing here, any journey is a guaranteed trailblazing adventure that will reward you a hundred times over.

## Wildlife

Ethiopia lacks the stellar reputation of Kenya when it comes to big animals, but that's only because people don't know what's hiding in the bush out west! Gambela National Park is witness to a migration of white-eared kob and Nile lechwe up to a million strong, and the birdlife everywhere is out of this world.

**p195**

# Djibouti

**Outdoors** ✓✓
**Geological Wonders** ✓✓
**Ecotourism** ✓

## Diving & Hiking

There's superb diving in the Gulf of Tadjoura and top snorkelling off Plage des Sables Blancs and Moucha Island. From November to January you can swim alongside gigantic whale sharks near the Bay of Ghoubbet. The Goda Mountains offer great hiking options, and fabulous multiday treks led by Afar nomads can be arranged.

## Epic Scenery

Djibouti offers unparalleled scenery. You might think you're walking on the moon at Lac Abbé or approaching Dante's *Inferno* at Lac Assal. The eerie, desertlike expanses of Grand Barra are no less impressive.

## Staying in Nature

Take a few days upcountry to explore the Goda Mountains and Forêt du Day, staying in traditional huts, spending your days hiking, enjoying mountain vistas and learning about traditional Afar culture.

**p297**

# Somaliland

**Archaeology** ✓✓✓
**Exploration** ✓✓✓
**Landscapes** ✓✓

## Rock Paintings

The most compelling attraction in Somaliland, the superb rock art at Las Geel is unique, with hundreds of the finest polychrome paintings ever discovered on the African continent – and this is one of the few places in the world where it's possible to see them up close.

## Remote Places

Somaliland is tailormade for adventure travellers. Once you leave Hargeisa, the capital, it's virtually uncharted territory. For serious offroad exploration, consider making it to Zeila, near the border with Djibouti, or to Maydh, at the far eastern corner of the country.

## Scenic Scenery

Immense arid plains, endless stretches of deserted beaches, vast plateaus, majestic mountain ranges, awesome escarpments and pristine environments: one of the main draws of Somaliland is its diverse landscapes.

**p319**

**Every listing is recommended by our authors, and their favourite places are listed first**

**Look out for these icons:**

 Our author's top recommendation

 A green or sustainable option

 No payment required

See the Index for a full list of destinations covered in this book.

# Ethiopia On the Road

For Djibouti see p297

For Somaliland see p319

# Addis Ababa

POPULATION: 3,384,569  ALTITUDE: 2300M

## Includes »

## Best Places for Culture

» Ethnological Museum (p32)

» National Museum (p33)

» St George Cathedral & Museum (p36)

» Bole Rd restaurants & bars (p51)

» 'Red Terror' Martyrs Memorial Museum (p36)

## Best Places to Stay

» Stay Easy (p49)

» Itegue Taitu Hotel (p43)

» La Source Guest House (p48)

» Addis Regency (p44)

## Why Go?

Since its establishment in the 19th century, Addis Ababa (አዲስ አበባ) has always seemed like a magical portal, a gateway to another world. For the rural masses of Ethiopia it was, and is, a city whose streets are paved in gold; and for a foreign visitor, the portal of Addis Ababa is at the verge of an ancient and mystical world.

For both these groups, Addis – Africa's fourth-largest city and its diplomatic capital – is a place of contrasts: the shepherd from the countryside bringing his flock to a city market; the city priest with the business investments; the glossy nightclubs with the country-girl prostitutes. Despite this merging of worlds, many foreign visitors try to transit Addis as quickly as possible. But take note: by skipping out on the contradictions of this happening city you run the risk of failing to understand Ethiopia altogether.

## When to Go
### Addis Ababa

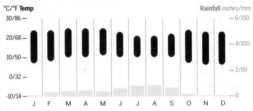

**Jan** The festivals of Leddet and Timkat add colour and pomp to any visit to Addis.

**Sep** Light a bonfire during the Meskel festival on September 27th.

**Nov** Bring your running shoes for the Great Ethiopian Run held in late-November.

## Addis Ababa Highlights

① Delve into the treasure trove that is the astounding **Ethnological Museum** (p32)

② Peer back through the ages at the **National Museum** (p33), home of Lucy, one of our oldest ancestors

③ Stare in silent contemplation at the moving

**'Red Terror' Martyrs Memorial Museum** (p36)

④ Tickle your tongue with your first *injera* (flatbread) and *wat* (tripe stew) and satisfy your rumbling tummy in Ethiopia's best restaurants (p50)

⑤ Throw back a *tej* (honey wine) or sip on a cool cocktail

as you kick-start a night on the tiles Addis style (p53)

⑥ Visit one of the most interesting religious museums in Ethiopia: **St George Cathedral & Museum** (p36)

⑦ See the final resting place of Emperor Haile Selassie in the **Holy Trinity Cathedral** (p36)

## History

Unlike Addis Ababa's numerous predecessors as capitals, the locations of which were chosen according to the political, economic and strategic demands of the days' rulers, Addis Ababa was chosen for its beauty, hot springs and agreeable climate. Why the drastic (and pleasant) change of convention in the late 19th century? Perhaps it was because it was the first time a woman had any say in the matter! Yes, it was the actions of Taitu, the consort of Menelik II, which led to the birth of Addis Ababa.

Menelik's previous capital, Entoto, was in the mountains just north of present-day Addis Ababa and held strategic importance as it was easily defended. However, it was unattractive and sterile, leading Taitu to request a house be built for her in the beautiful foothills below, in an area she named Addis Ababa (New Flower). In the following decade, after Menelik's power increased and his need for defence waned, he moved his court down to Taitu and Addis Ababa.

A lack of firewood for the rapidly growing population threatened the future of Addis Ababa in 1896 and Menelik even started construction of a new capital, Addis Alem (New World), 50km to the west. In the end, it was the suggestion of a foreigner (thought to be French) to introduce the rapidly growing eucalyptus tree that saved the new capital.

Since 1958 Addis Ababa has been the headquarters of the UN Economic Commission for Africa (ECA) and, since 1963, the secretariat of the Organisation of African Unity (OAU). Many regard the city as 'Africa's diplomatic capital'.

## ⊙ Sights

Most sights are scattered throughout the city centre and Piazza, though there is a concentration of major museums and other sights in the vicinity of Arat Kilo and Siddist Kilo, which sit east of Piazza and north of the city centre.

**TOP CHOICE** **Ethnological Museum**                          MUSEUM
(Map p34; Algeria St; adult/student Birr50/30; ⊗8am-5pm Mon-Fri, 9am-5pm Sat & Sun) Set within Haile Selassie's former palace and surrounded by the beautiful gardens and fountains of Addis Ababa University's main campus is the enthralling Ethnological Museum. Even if you're not normally a museum fan, this one is worth a bit of your time – it's easily one of the finest museums in Africa.

The show starts before you even get inside: look for the intriguing set of stairs spiralling precariously skyward near the palace's main entrance. Each step was placed by the Italians as a symbol of Fascist domination, one for every year Mussolini held power (starting from his march to Rome in 1922). A

---

### ADDIS ABABA IN...

#### Two Days

Start in Piazza with a steaming espresso at **Tomoca**, before visiting **St George Cathedral & Museum**. Next, get ready to say hello to Auntie Lucy, your long-lost ancestor, in the **National Museum**. From there, stroll north and absorb the magnitude of the **Yekatit 12 Monument**.

After lunch, explore the massive **Merkato** and, after checking you still have all your belongings, finish the day dining and drinking *tej* (honey wine) at a traditional Ethiopian restaurant, while enjoying a show of song and dance.

Day two, and the morning kicks off with more culture when you marvel at the brilliant **Ethnological Museum**. In the afternoon, pay your respects to Emperor Haile Selassie at the **Holy Trinity Cathedral** and then be moved to tears by the powerful displays in the new **'Red Terror' Martyrs Memorial Museum**. Finish your day off on a more cheerful note at the wonderful **La Mandoline restaurant**.

#### Four Days

With four days, you could complete the two-day itinerary at a slower pace (more espressos!), squeezing in extra sights like the **Bete Maryam Mausoleum** and **Asni Gallery**. Another well-worthwhile alternative is to head out of town to the extraordinary **Washa Mikael Church** or get some fresh air walking in the **Entoto Mountains** and visit the **Entoto Maryam Church**.

## NAVIGATING ADDIS

Addis Ababa is massive and incoherent. To navigate the city, it's best to break it down into distinct districts.

The **city centre** is at the end of Churchill Ave, the southern section of which is named Gambia St. Here you'll find many government and commercial buildings.

To the north is **Piazza**, a district whose legacy and architecture is owed to the Italian occupation. Piazza is found atop the hill at Churchill Ave's north end and houses budget hotels, as well as many cafes and bars.

To the east of Piazza is **Addis Ababa University**, several museums and the landmark roundabouts of **Arat Kilo** and **Siddist Kilo**. South from there is **Menelik II Ave**, which boasts the National Palace, Africa Hall, a series of new urban parks and, at its southern end, the huge **Meskal Sq**.

Thanks to the ring road, the southeast of the city, on and around **Bole Rd** between Meskal Sq and the airport, is thriving with exciting development, such as high-quality restaurants, bars, cafes and shopping centres, that contrasts sharply with the rest of the city.

small Lion of Judah (the symbol of Ethiopian monarchy) sits victoriously atop the final step, like a jubilant punctuation mark at the end of a painfully long sentence.

Within the entrance hall you'll find a small exhibition dedicated to the history of the palace, and the doorway to the Institute of Language Studies library (p42).

This contemporary museum truly comes into its own on the 1st floor, where superb artefacts and handicrafts from Ethiopia's peoples are distinctively displayed. Instead of following the typical static and geographical layout that most museums fall into, these displays are based upon the life cycle. First comes Childhood, with birth, games, rites of passage and traditional tales. We particularly enjoyed the 'Yem Tale', a story of selfishness, dead leopards and sore tails! Adulthood probes into beliefs, nomadism, traditional medicine, war, pilgrimages, hunting, body culture and handicrafts. The last topic is Death and Beyond, with burial structures, stelae and tombs. The exhibition gives a great insight into Ethiopia's many rich cultures.

Other rooms on this floor show the preserved bedroom, bathroom and exorbitant changing room of Emperor Haile Selassie, complete with a bullet hole in his mirror courtesy of the 1960 coup d'état.

The 2nd floor plays home to two drastically different, but equally delightful displays. The vibrant hall focuses on religious art, with an exceptional series of diptychs, triptychs, icons, crosses and magic scrolls. Magic scrolls, like the Roman lead scrolls, were used to cast curses on people or to appeal to the gods for divine assistance. The collection of icons is the largest and most representative in the world. Senses of another sort are indulged in the small cavelike corridor that sits next to the hall. Inside, traditional music gently fills the air and the black surrounds leave you nothing to look at besides the instruments – brilliant.

It's well worth coming to this museum twice; once at the start of your journey through Ethiopia and once at the end when you'll be able to put everything into context.

After you've lapped up the treasures in the museum, stop by the double-decker London bus next to the university entrance gates. Brought to Addis by Haile Selassie it's now a cool bar and packed with students.

**National Museum**  MUSEUM

ብሔራዊ ሙዚየም (Map p34; ☑0111-117150; King George VI St; admission Birr10; ◔8.30am-5pm) The collection on show at the National Museum is ranked among the most important in sub-Saharan Africa, but sadly many of its exhibits are poorly labelled, lit and displayed, particularly in the upper levels of the museum.

The palaeontology exhibit on the basement level contains fossilised evidence of some amazing extinct creatures, like the massive sabre-toothed feline *Homotherium* and the gargantuan savannah pig *Notochoerus*. However, the stars of the exhibit are two remarkable casts of Lucy (see p218), a fossilised hominid discovered in 1974. One lays prone, while the other stands much like she did some 3.2 million years ago, truly hitting home how small our ancient ancestors

# Addis Ababa & Around

To Muger Gorge (53km);
Debre Libanos (104km);
Blue Nile Gorge (200km);
Bahir Dar (588km);
Gonder (771km)

Panoramic
Viewpoint

🔼 3

Entoto
Mountains

Entoto Rd

**ENTOTO**

🏛 Kidane
Mehret
Church

**GEFERSA**

To Ambo (125km);
Nekemte (327km);
Gambela (790km)

Dejazmach Belay Zeleke St

**KECHENE**

13

22

26

Botswana St

Entoto Ave

Arbeynoch St

**GULELE**

18

17

2

Senegal St

Algeria St

**ABA
KORAN**

4

Addis Ababa
University
10

Siddist
Kilo

9

Jan Meda
Sports
Ground

Central African
Republic St

Autobus Terra
(Long-distance
Bus Station)

See Piazza
Map (p44)

6

Russia St

**KOLFE**

Fitawrari Habtegyorgis St

Fitawrari
Gebeyehu St

Arat Kilo

7

**MERKATO**

5

Lorenzo Tezaz St

See Central
Addis Ababa
Map (p38)

Congo St

Dejazmach Mekonen
Demisaw St

Uganda St

**GEJA
SEFER**

Churchill Ave

**GOLA
SEFER**

**AWARE**

**KAZANCHIS**

Dejazmach Balt
Cha Abanfeso St

Burundi St Sudan St

Yohanis St

Josif Tito St

Chad St

Ras Mekonen Ave

Haile Gebreselassie Rd

1

24

Ring Rd

La Gare

**URAEL**

To Weliso (100km);
Welkite (142km);
Jimma (342km);
Gambela (722km)

Mauritania St

**LIDETA**

23

Roosevelt St

Ras Lulseged St

**KIRKOS**

Ras Biru Wolde Gebriel St

Menelik II Ave

Bole Rd (Africa Ave)

14

South Africa St

Seychelles
St

16

**MEKANISA**

**KERA**

Alexander Puskin St Beyene Merid St

Dejazmach
Beyene Merid St

Ethio-China Ave

12

Lesotho St

To Nazret (99km);
Lake Ziway (159km);
Lake Langano (185km);
Shashemene (248km)

To Awasa (274km);
Arba Minch (500km);
Dire Dawa (544km)

# Addis Ababa & Around

were. The real bones are preserved in the archives of the museum.

The periphery of the ground floor focuses on the pre-Aksumite, Aksumite, Solomonic and Gonder periods, with a wide array of artefacts, including an elaborate pre-1st-century-AD bronze oil lamp showing a dog chasing an ibex, a fascinating 4th-century-BC rock-hewn chair emblazoned with mythical ibexes, and ancient Sabaean inscriptions. The middle of the room hosts a collection of lavish royal paraphernalia, including Emperor Haile Selassie's enormous and rather hideous carved wooden throne.

On the 1st floor, there's a vivid display of Ethiopian art ranging from early (possibly

14th-century) parchment to 20th-century canvas oil paintings by leading modern artists. Afework Tekle's massive *African Heritage* is one of the more notable pieces. Another painting depicts the meeting of Solomon and Sheba. Note the shield of the soldier next to Solomon, which is engraved with the Star of David *and* a Christian Cross. The artist must have forgotten that this meeting is said to have occurred long before the birth of Christianity.

The 2nd floor contains a collection of secular arts and crafts, including traditional weapons, jewellery, utensils, clothing and musical instruments.

English-speaking guides are available for free (they should be tipped afterwards) and help to bring things alive.

**Holy Trinity Cathedral** CHURCH
ቅዱስ ስላሴ ቤተክርስቲያን (Map p38; ☑0111-233518; admission Birr50; ⊗cathedral 8am-1pm & 2-6pm, museum 8am-12pm & 2-5pm) Off Niger St, this massive and ornate cathedral is the second-most important place of worship in Ethiopia (ranking behind the Old Church of St Mary of Zion in Aksum). It's also the celebrated final resting place of Emperor Haile Selassie and his wife Empress Menen Asfaw. Their massive Aksumite-style granite tombs sit inside and are a sight indeed.

The cathedral's exterior, with its large copper dome, spindly pinnacles, numerous statues and flamboyant mixture of international styles, provides an interesting and sometimes poignant glimpse into many historical episodes of Ethiopia's history.

Inside, there are some grand murals, the most notable being Afework Tekle's depiction of the Holy Trinity, with Matthew (man), Mark (lion), Luke (cow) and John (dove) peering through the clouds. There are also some brilliant stained-glass windows and two beautifully carved imperial thrones, each made of white ebony, ivory and marble.

The entrance fee also includes admission to a small but impressive **museum** of ecclesiastical artefacts.

To the south of the cathedral is the **memorial** and graves of the ministers killed by the Derg for opposing them in 1974 (see the History chapter, p234). Due to the prime minister's compound being behind this memorial, photographs are strictly forbidden.

The **churchyard** also hosts the graves of many patriots who died fighting the Italian occupation, including the great Resistance fighter Ras Imru. To the west of the cathedral is the tomb of the famous British suffragette Sylvia Pankhurst. Sylvia was one of the very few people outside Ethiopia who protested Italy's occupation; she moved to Addis Ababa in 1956.

Purchase tickets at the administration office 20m west of the main gate. Self-appointed guides charge Birr10 to Birr15 per person.

**TOP
CHOICE ❭ St George
Cathedral & Museum** CHURCH
ቅዱስ ጊዮርጊስ ቤተክርስቲያን (Map p44; Fitawrari Gebeyehu St) Commissioned by Emperor Menelik II to commemorate his stunning 1896 defeat of the Italians in Adwa, and dedicated to St George (Ethiopia's patron saint), whose icon was carried into the battle, this Piazza cathedral was completed in 1911 with the help of Greek, Armenian and Indian artists. Empress Zewditu (in 1916) and Emperor Haile Selassie (in 1930) were both crowned here.

Thanks to its traditional octagonal form and severe neoclassical style, the grey stone exterior is easily outdone by the interior's flashes of colour and art. Sections of ceiling glow sky-blue and boast gilded golden stars, while the outer walls of the Holy of Holies are covered in paintings and mosaics by artists such as the renowned Afework Tekle.

In the grounds just north of the cathedral is the **museum** (admission Birr50; ⊗9am-noon & 2-5pm Tue-Sun). It's well presented and contains probably the best collection of ecclesiastical paraphernalia in the country outside St Mary of Zion in Aksum. Items include beautiful crowns, hand crosses, prayer sticks, holy scrolls, ceremonial umbrellas and the coronation garb of Zewditu and Haile Selassie. Entry includes a **guided tour** of both the museum and church. Try to get Archdeacon Mebratu to be your guide. He's very entertaining – maybe the most amusing and informative church guide we've had anywhere in Ethiopia – and liable to burst into song and dance, and get you to do likewise, at the drop of a hat.

**TOP
CHOICE ❭ 'Red Terror' Martyrs
Memorial Museum** MUSEUM
(Map p38; Meskal Sq; admission by donation; ⊗8.30am-6.30pm) 'As if I bore them all in one night, They slew them in a single night.' These were the words spoken by the mother, whose four teenage children were all killed on the same day by the Derg, who officially

opened the small but powerful 'Red Terror' Martyrs Memorial Museum in 2010. Over the space of a couple of rooms the museum reveals the fall of Emperor Haile Selassie and the horrors of life under Mengistu's Derg regime. The museum is well laid out and incredibly moving. Nothing more so than the walls of photos and names of just some of the estimated half a million killed under the Derg, or the display cabinets filled with human remains dug out of mass graves. Some of the skulls and other bones are displayed alongside a photo of the victim and personal artefacts they had on them when they died. The watch hanging in one display case was given by the victim to his wife with the words 'Keep this safe. One day you will need it', just as he was led away by the soldiers of the Derg. When the museum opened she brought it here.

Excellent English-speaking guides are often available, although you may prefer to just look on in silence.

The museum is funded by donations only.

### Yekatit 12 Monument                MONUMENT
የካቲት 12 መታሰቢያ ሐውልት (Map p34; Siddist Kilo) Rising dramatically from the roundabout Siddist Kilo is this moving monument to the thousands of innocent Ethiopians killed by the Italians as retribution for the attempt on Viceroy Graziani's life on 19 February 1937. 'Yekatit 12' is a date in the Ethiopian calendar roughly equivalent to 19 February.

### Derg Monument                MONUMENT
የድል ሐውልት (ድላችን) (Map p38; Churchill Ave) Nothing in the capital is as poignant a reminder of the country's painful communist rule as the towering Derg Monument. Topped by a massive red star and emblazoned with a golden hammer and sickle, the cement obelisklike structure climbs skyward in front of Black Lion Hospital.

### Merkato                MARKET
መርካቶ (Map p34; ⊗6am-7pm Mon-Sat) Wading into the market chaos known as Merkato, just west of the centre, can be as rewarding as it is exasperating. You may find the most eloquent aroma wafting from precious incense. You may also find that your wallet has been stolen and that you've got stinky excrement on your shoe.

Some people say it's the largest market in Africa, but as its exact boundaries are as shady as some of its characters, this is a little hard to verify. What should be noted, however, is that this isn't one of those nicely photogenic markets with goods laid out on the ground or in little stalls. Most vendors now have permanent tin shacks in which to house their wares, so in many eyes this changes the market from a scene of exotica to just a slum.

The mass of stalls, produce and people may seem impenetrable, but on closer inspection the market reveals a careful organisation with different sections for different products. You can spend your birr on pungent spices, silver jewellery or anything else that takes your fancy. There's even a 'recycling market', where sandals (made out of old tyres), coffee pots (old Italian olive tins) and other interesting paraphernalia can be found.

### Natural History Museum                MUSEUM
የተፈጥሮ ታሪክ ሙዚየም (Map p34; ☑0111-119496; Queen Elizabeth II St; admission Birr20; ⊗9-11.45am & 1.30-4.30pm Tue-Sun) Go eye to eye with a bloated leopard and other wildlife wonders of Ethiopia in this natural history museum. Sometimes the stuffers just don't know when to stop stuffing!

### Addis Ababa Museum                MUSEUM
አዲስ አበባ ሙዝየም (Map p38; Meskal Sq; admission Birr10; ⊗8.30am-12.30pm & 1.30-5.30pm Tue-Fri, 8.30-11.30am Sat) Despite only

---

## MENELIK BUYS A NEW CHAIR

If Emperor Menelik II (r 1889–1913), the founder of Addis Ababa, was alive today he'd have been the first in the queue for the latest mobile phone or other technological gadget. If it was new and flashy he just had to have one. So, when he first heard about a new invention in America called the electric chair, he decided that Ethiopia just had to have a couple of these ingenious death machines. After months of waiting, the new contraptions arrived in Addis. When he first saw them the emperor was delighted with the craftsmanship that had gone into them and asked for a demonstration. It was only then, and no doubt to the great relief of the chosen 'demonstrator', that Menelik's technicians suddenly realised that electricity hadn't yet been turned on in Ethiopia…

# Central Addis Ababa

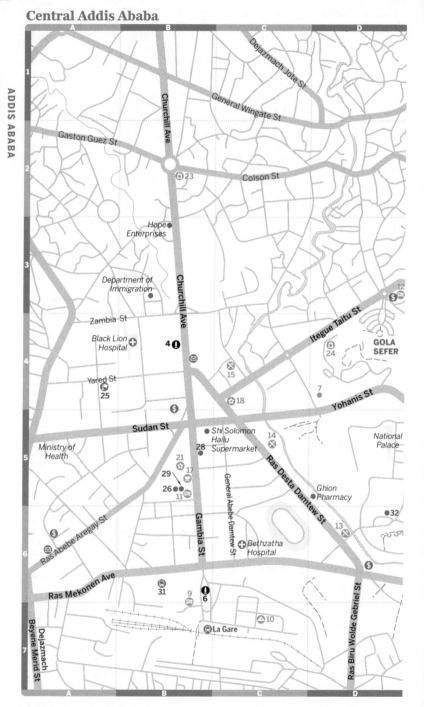

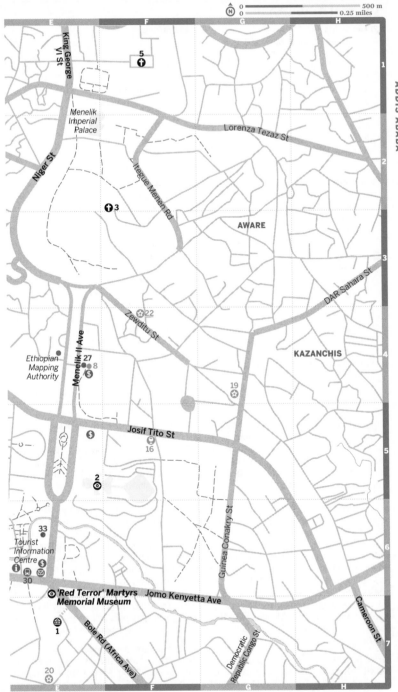

ADDIS ABABA

0    500 m
0    0.25 miles

King George VI St

Menelik Imperial Palace

Lorenza Tezaz St

Niger St

Itegue Menen Rd

5

3

AWARE

DAR Sahara St

Zewditu St

22

KAZANCHIS

Menelik II Ave

Ethiopian Mapping Authority

27

8

19

Josif Tito St

16

2

33

Guinea Conakry St

Tourist Information Centre

30

'Red Terror' Martyrs Memorial Museum

Jomo Kenyetta Ave

Cameroon St

1

Bole Rd (Africa Ave)

Democratic Republic Congo St

20

# Central Addis Ababa

being founded on the centenary of the city in 1986, the Addis Ababa Museum is the town's scruffiest museum. That said, perusing candid portraits of the redoubtable Empress Taitu, rakish Lij Iyasu and the very beautiful Empress Zewditu, along with pictures of the capital in its infancy, is still worth an hour or so. It's unbelievable that the raucous city outside was nothing more than tents on a hill just over a century ago.

There's also a 'first-in-Ethiopia' room, with a picture of the first telephone in Ethiopia (which was brought from Italy by Ras Makonnen in 1890; it's said that local priests, when they first heard the disembodied voices, thought telephones the work of demons) and another of Menelik with Bede Bentley in Addis Ababa's first motor car (1907).

**Africa Hall**                    NOTABLE BUILDING
አፍሪካ አዳራሽ (Map p38; ☎0115-517700; Menelik II Ave; ⊙8am-1pm & 2-5pm Mon-Fri) Built

in 1961 by Emperor Haile Selassie, Africa Hall, near Meskal Sq, is the seat of the UN's ECA. The Italian-designed building isn't very interesting, apart from the friezelike motifs that represent traditional Ethiopian *shamma* (shawl) borders.

Far more interesting is *Africa: Past, Present and Future,* a monumental stained-glass window inside by the artist Afewerk Tekle. Measuring 150 sq m, it fills one entire wall and is one of the biggest stained-glass windows in the world. During some hours of the day, the white marble floor of the foyer is flooded with colour. It's well worth a visit, but this is only possible by prior appointment (call the number above). You'll need to bring your passport and they generally prefer it if you visit as part of a group.

**Bete Maryam Mausoleum**         CHURCH
ቤተ ማርያም መቃብር (Map p38; Itegue Menen Rd; admission Birr30; ⊙9am-6pm) Also known as Menelik's Mausoleum, the Bete Maryam

Mausoleum is located just south of Menelik's palace and offers an enchantingly eerie experience for travellers. After the priest has rolled up the carpet and pried open the large metal door in the floor, you will descend into the thick air of the creepy crypt. There you will find the four elaborate marble tombs of Empress Taitu, Emperor Menelik, Empress Zewditu and Princess Tsehai Haile Selassie.

At least that's how a visit should go. The reality is that thanks to the Prime Minister's residence being next door the whole complex is guarded by an inordinate number of very surly and unhelpful soldiers, who, if our last visit was anything to go by, try to make visiting the church as problematic as they possibly can.

On Wednesdays and Fridays it closes for prayers between 12.30pm and around 2pm.

**FREE** Asni Gallery                    GALLERY
አስኒ ጋለሪ (የስእል አዳራሽ) (Map p34; ☎0911-206697; ⏰10am-7pm Tue-Sat, closed Jul & Aug) Housed in the 1912 villa of Lij Iyasu's minister of justice, the Asni Gallery annually hosts six or seven splendid contemporary-art exhibitions of emerging and established Ethiopian artists. Other events include workshops and lectures; look for announcements in the *Addis Tribune* or *What's Up!*

The turn-off is about 4km northeast of the town centre, just north of the French embassy. Take a minibus from Arat Kilo heading to 'Francey' and get off at the Total petrol station. It's a short walk from there.

Afewerk Tekle's Home & Studio    GALLERY
የአፈወርቅ ተክለ ቤት እና ስቱዲዮ (Map p34; www.maitreafewerktekle.com) A member of

several international academies and with a drawer full of international decorations – about 100 at last count, including the British Order of Merit – Afewerk Tekle is considered among Africa's greatest artists.

It used to be possible to organise a 90-minute tour of Villa Alpha, Afewerk's home and studio, led by the artist himself. However, after his death in 2012 the house was closed to the public. At the time of writing, renovations were taking place and plans are afoot to re-open the house, though when, and in what form, is not yet known.

Lion of Judah Monument        MONUMENT
ጥቁር አንበሳ ሐውልት (Map p38; Gambia St) Long the symbol of Ethiopia's monarchy, the Lion of Judah is ubiquitous throughout the country. Although images of the almighty animal abound in Addis Ababa, it's the storied history of the Lion of Judah Monument that makes this statue significant.

After being erected on the eve of Haile Selassie's coronation in 1930, it was looted by Italians in 1935 and placed in Rome next to the massive Vittorio Emanuelle Monument. In 1938, during anniversary celebrations of the proclamation of the Italian Empire, Zerai Deress, a young Eritrean, spotted the statue and defiantly interrupted proceedings to kneel and pray before it. After police verbally and physically attempted to stop his prayers, he rose and attacked the armed Italians with his sword while screaming 'the Lion of Judah is avenged!' He seriously injured several officers (some reports say he killed five) before he was shot. Although he died seven years

**ADDIS ABABA SIGHTS**

---

### AFEWERK TEKLE

Born in 1932, Afewerk Tekle was one of Ethiopia's most distinguished and colourful artistic figures. Educated at the Slade School of Art in London, he later toured and studied in continental Europe before returning to work under the patronage of Emperor Haile Selassie. A painter as well as a sculptor and designer, he was also a master fencer, dancer and toastmaster.

Proud to have 'survived three regimes' (when friends and peers did not), his life was hardly without incident. In almost cinematic style, a 'friendly' fencing match turned into an attempt on his life, and a tussle over a woman led to him challenging his rival to a duel at dawn. In the royal court of the emperor, he once only just survived an assassination attempt by poisoned cocktail.

The artist famously made his own terms and conditions: if he didn't like the purchaser he wouldn't sell, and his best known paintings must be returned to Ethiopia within a lifetime. He even turned down over US$12 million for the work considered his masterpiece, *The Meskel Flower*.

In April 2012 the artist died in Addis Ababa at the age of 80.

later in an Italian prison, his legend lives on in Ethiopia and Eritrea.

The Lion of Judah Monument was eventually returned to Addis Ababa in the 1960s.

**Institute of Ethiopian Studies**      LIBRARY
(Map p34; ☑0111-239740; Addis Ababa University, Algeria St) This institute boasts the world's best collection of books in English on Ethiopia. It's free for a half-day's casual use. At the time of research they were in the slow process of building a new home for the collection.

**National Archives &**
**Library of Ethiopia**      LIBRARY
(Map p38; www.nala.gov.et; ☺closed morning Mon) Shelves groan under the weight of 20,000 books on Ethiopia. The English-language section is quite good. It is located off Sudan St.

# 🏃 Activities

Thanks to hosting the UN's ECA, activities are more catered to business people than backpackers. Though, after returning from a tough slog out on the Ethiopian roads, many travellers indulge in a heavenly massage, steam bath or sauna. Cooling swims are also justifiably popular.

### Massage, Steam Bath & Sauna

**Boston Day Spa**      SPA
(Map p46; ☑0116-636557; Bole Rd; ☺8.30am-8.30pm) The Boston Day Spa has a great reputation. Massages start at Birr184. A session in the sauna, steam bath and jacuzzi is Birr210 and includes a free foot massage. It also provides a waxing service and has a hairdresser.

**Sheraton Hotel**      MASSAGE
(Map p38; ☑0115-171717; Itegue Taitu St; ☺9am-9pm) A sublime massage at the Sheraton Hotel starts at Birr350. There's a full range of reflexology, Swedish, deep-tissue and neck and shoulder massages, as well as mineral body scrubs.

**Addisu Filwoha Hotel & Hot Springs**      SPA
(Map p38; ☑0115-519100; shower Birr60, sauna Birr170; ☺6am-10pm) While certainly not as sophisticated as the previous two options, the Addisu Filwoha Hotel & Hot Springs complex is powered by Addis Ababa's original raison d'être: its natural hot springs. At the time of research only the showers were operating, but the sauna is expected to start operating again 'soon'. You don't have to be in Ethiopia long to realise that sexual attitudes are fairly free and easy and this place

is no exception (for heterosexual couples, anyway). In fact, if you go as a couple it's expected that you will have sex in the bath. Make sure you follow the rules, which say that you must use a condom, which you then have to leave neatly in the corner! The complex is off Yohanis St.

### Running

If you want to run with the best of the best, head to Meskal Sq before dawn (5am is a good time) where you'll find household-name runners going through their paces as they jog up and down the square along the concrete, terraced seating. If you complete the entire circuit, running up and down each aisle, you'll have sweated through 42km. Note that the standard is high and weekend-warrior runners will be considered an obstacle – if you fall into this category then it's best to just watch!

### Swimming

Beat the heat with some underwater action. The sweetest swims in town are to be had at the **Sheraton Hotel** (Map p38; Itegue Taitu St; nonguest admission weekday/weekend Birr200/250) and the **Hilton Hotel** (Map p38; Menelik II Ave; nonguest admission Mon-Thu/Fri-Sun Birr144/220).

# 🎓 Courses

**Institute of**
**Language Studies**      LANGUAGE CLASS
(Map p34; ☑0111-239702; Addis Ababa University, Algeria St) Institute of Language Studies teaches three Ethiopian languages (Amharic, Tigrinya and Orominya). Classes last four months and cost US$100.

Head immediately left after entering the main university gates. The office is on the 2nd floor, room 210.

# 👉 Tours

There are no scheduled tours of Addis Ababa itself; however, if you contact one of Addis Ababa's many travel agencies (see p295), most can usually arrange something.

# 🎆 Festivals & Events

Although Addis doesn't boast any major festivals of its own, it's a great place to catch some of the national festivals. For Leddet and Timkat, head to Jan Meda Sports Ground, in the north of the city, where the most exuberant celebrations take place. During Leddet the festivities also include a traditional game of *genna* (hockey without boundaries). When the festival of Meskel is underway, Meskal Sq is one of the best places to be in the country. For more details on these festivals, see the Month by Month chapter.

For minor festivals and upcoming cultural events, check out www.addisallaround.com.

### Great Ethiopian Run                    RACE

Inaugurated in 2001, the 10km run is now the biggest mass-participation race on the continent. It takes over the city on the last Sunday of November and attracts over 20,000 runners. Whether running or watching, it's a fun time and it's a great chance to see some of East Africa's elite athletes in action.

## 🛏 Sleeping

Accommodation runs the gamut in Addis – brandish your flip-flop and do battle with almighty insects, or sink into a sumptuous suite. It's all up to you, your budget and the strength of your flip-flops.

For many years, budget travellers have congregated around the Piazza; however, with hotels there starting to look a bit creaky, more and more travellers are moving out to the brighter and newer options around the more salubrious surrounds of Bole and Haile Gebreselassie Rds.

Hotel owners in Addis quote their rates in a mixture of birr or US dollars, though all accept payment in birr. We have quoted prices using the currency the hotel uses. All hotels listed here have hot water unless otherwise indicated.

### CENTRE

**Sheraton Hotel**          BUSINESS HOTEL $$$

(Map p38; ☎0115-171717; www.luxurycollection.com/addis; Itegue Taitu St; d from US$295, ste from US$775; ✳@🛜🏊) One of Africa's most elite hotels, the Sheraton is astounding and, in a country like Ethiopia, almost obscene. Actually just about anywhere spending well over US$7000 a night on a room (which is what the best ones start at) would still be considered obscene! Needless to say, it's an absolute treat to stay here.

**Ras Hotel**                HOTEL $$

(Map p38; ☎0115-517060; Gambia St; d incl breakfast Birr305-587, tw incl breakfast Birr372-690) Set squarely in the town centre, this government-run hotel might be fading a little and feel a bit like a sanatorium, but it's a real institution and has a constant buzz of

people coming and going. The large rooms are a fair deal though some have views over the slums. Aside from the location, the best assets are the numerous facilities, including a decent bar and restaurant, internet cafe and travel agent.

**Buffet de la Gare**          HOTEL $

(Map p38; d Birr250) Once upon a time the chuff-chuffing of passing steam trains would have soothed you to sleep here. With the trains no longer functioning, peace and quiet prevails. Even today the atmosphere harks back to the age of rail travel – the attached bar looks like a train carriage. The handful of rooms, set around a garden, are old but clean and come with some character, but noise from said bar can be a problem.

**Holland House**          CAMPSITE $

(Map p38; ☎0911-608088; wims_hollandhouse@ethionet.et; campsites Birr50, jeep Birr150, motorbike Birr70; ⊚) Hidden in the maze of lanes to the east of the train station (look for the big yellow Shell signs), this campsite, the sole overlanders' party in the city, is a cramped area normally overflowing with hardened road warriors talking about oil filters. There's a busy bar, frequent party nights, and a kitchen for guest use.

### PIAZZA & THE NORTH

At all of the following budget hotels, keep your eyes peeled for dodgy individuals who hang about the streets outside waiting for gullible tourists to fall into whatever contrap they've set that day (see Dangers and Annoyances, p57, for an idea of what these traps might be).

**TOP CHOICE Itegue Taitu Hotel**          HISTORIC HOTEL $$

(Map p44; ☎0111-560787; www.taituhotel.com; r without bathroom Birr129-345, r with bathroom Birr297-492; ℗🛜) Appear in the dream of an empress! Built at the whim of Empress Taitu in 1907, this is the oldest hotel in Addis, and the main building, which has recently been tastefully renovated, is virtually a museum piece full of beautiful old furniture and high ceilings. The newer block contains a wide range of rooms, including some very jolly doubles. There are plenty of facilities, a lovely garden in which breakfast is served and lots of other travellers to hang out with. All up it offers a cash-strapped overlander a classy experience for very little coin.

# Piazza

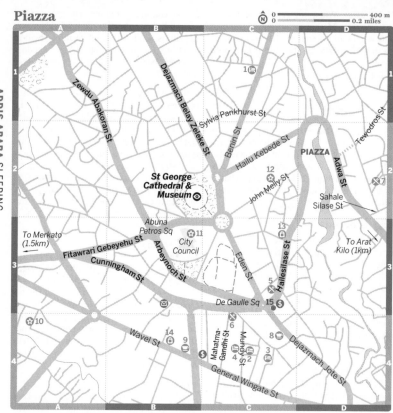

## Addis Regency Hotel HOTEL $$$

(Map p44; ✆0111-550000; www.addisregency.
com; off Benin St; incl breakfast d US$75-95, tw
US$90, ste US$150; ⓟ🛜) Friendly, immaculately well-kept, supremely comfortable
with beds that seem custom designed to
give sweet dreams, endless piping-hot water
and a quiet side-street location make this
place a cut above the competition. The only
drawback is that it's quite far from all the
more interesting dining and nightlife options, so it's a good job they have a reasonable in-house restaurant.

## Ankober Guest House HOTEL $

(Map p44; ✆0111-12350; Mundy St; d/tw US$20/30;
🛜) The most salubrious of the cheap Piazza-
area hotels, this place has smart, spacious
rooms with polished wood floors and good
showers. On the flip side, the echoey corridor means sound travels and the wi-fi never
seems to work.

## Baro Hotel HOTEL $

(Map p44; ✆0111-551447; barohotel@ethionet.et;
Mundy St; s from Birr170, d Birr225-330; ⓟ🛜) One
of the great backpacker hangouts of Ethiopia; the cheaper rooms at the Baro are decidedly skanky, but opt for one of the more
expensive options and you'll be the proud
resident of a large and fairly well-maintained
room (some with a bath tub). The garden is a
fantastic place to meet other travellers.

## Wutma Hotel HOTEL $

(Map p44; ✆0111-562878; wutma@yahoo.com;
Mundy St; d Birr210; 🛜) The backpacker hotel
of choice for years; the smallish grey-walled
rooms at the Wutma are simple but satisfying. The downstairs restaurant is popular
with travellers.

## BOLE RD & EAST ADDIS

## Desalegn 2 Hotel BUSINESS HOTEL $$$

(Map p46; ✆0116-624524; desalegn2@gmail.com;
Cape Verde St; s/d/tw incl breakfast US$80/95/95;

## Piazza

**ADDIS ABABA** SLEEPING

@🛜) Ohh, there have been changes for the better here since our last visit. Not just has this large hotel been refurbished, it's been virtually reconstructed. The result is a plush business-class hotel offering rooms for an exceptionally good rate.

**TDS Hotel** BUSINESS HOTEL **$$$**
(Map p46; ☎0116-635816; www.tdstravel.com; Cameroon St; r US$66-88; 🛜) This impressive hotel has a manic cleaner who stalks the corridors hunting down every speck of dirt and wiping it out; dark-wood furniture that's been polished until it shines like a mirror; super-comfortable beds; and piping-hot showers. On top of all that, there's a decent restaurant and friendly service.

**Weygoss Guest House** HOTEL **$$$**
(Map p46; ☎0115-512205; d incl breakfast US$45-65; 🛜) Lacking a sign and hidden up an alley just north of Ethio Supermarket, this five-storey guesthouse is well looked after and friendly. It's very popular with foreigners looking to adopt a local child. If you can overlook the annoying fact that it's one of the only hotels in Addis to charge for internet usage then you'll probably agree that it's a solid deal.

**Selam Pension** HOTEL **$**
(Map p46; ☎0910-511083; selampension2@yahoo.com; Gabon St; incl breakfast d Birr250-328, tw Birr 530) This shining white place offers one of the better deals in Addis. It's all very clean, though the bathrooms are a little cramped. It's also well run and far enough from the

road to mean honking horns won't interrupt your sleep – too much! The sign is in Amharic only, so ask someone to point it out.

**Mr Martins Cozy Place** HOTEL **$**
(Map p46; ☎0116-632611/0910-884585; Mike Leyland St; d/ste Birr220/340) This colourful little German-run backpackers has gained a name for itself as one of the better-value cheapies in the city. All the rooms are impeccably clean, though some are a little poky, and there's a pleasant courtyard restaurant to hang out in. All rooms share clean common bathrooms. Be warned that there are lots of prostitutes in the vicinity of the hotel.

**Meridian Hotel** HOTEL **$$$**
(Map p46; ☎0116-615050; meridian-hotel@ethionet.et; Zimbabwe St; s/d/tw incl breakfast US$60/74/85; 🛜) It's a little dated, but still represents reasonably good value. Discounts are also easy to come by. Oh, and no, it's not part of the worldwide hotel chain!

**Rita's Guest House** HOTEL **$$**
(Map p46; ☎0115-530979; Democratic Republic Congo St; d US$25-27, tw US$40; 🛜) Cosy (read: small) rooms in an excellent central location. Even though the rooms are tiny they are well cared for and contain everything you might require. It's down a little dirt track off the main road.

**Tina Pension & Guest House** GUESTHOUSE **$$**
(Map p46; ☎0115-549090; tinapension@yahoo.com; d incl breakfast US$25-60; 🛜) On a dusty back lane off Bole Rd and surrounded

# Bole Road Area

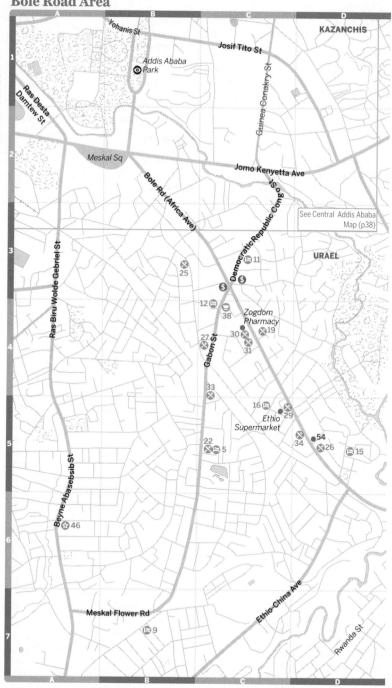

See Central Addis Ababa Map (p38)

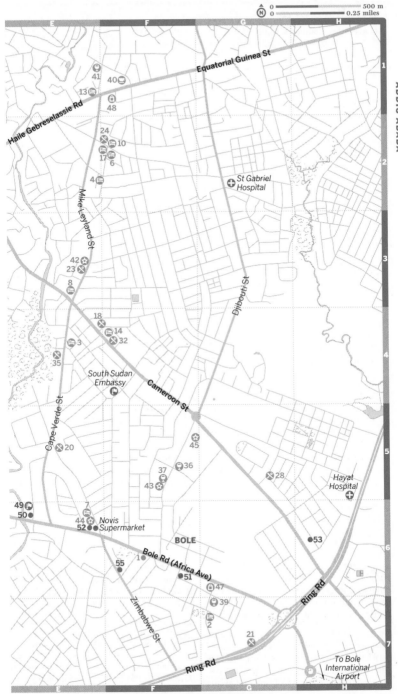

## Bole Road Area

by flowering trees, this clean and secure guesthouse offers somewhat overpriced but otherwise reasonable rooms with frilly bedspreads and hot-water showers. It feels far removed from the hustle of the city centre.

### Ceasars Court     HOTEL $$$
(Map p46; ☎0116-189600; off Bole Rd; d/ste incl breakfast US$60/80; @🖥) It's hard to know what to make of this place. The fake columns and plastic statues of Roman Caesars

are tacky indeed, but the rooms are quiet and comfortable and come with extras such as computers and printers (yeah, ok, so none of these actually seemed to work…).

### SOUTHWEST

⭐**TOP CHOICE** La Source Guest House GUESTHOUSE $$
(Map p46; ☎0114-665510; lasourceguesthouse@ gmail.com; Meskal Flower Rd; incl breakfast d US$25-35, tw US$35-40, ste US$45; @🖥) Finally, Addis has produced a guesthouse with

style. It's sparkling clean with constant hot water and it even has that rare thing – character, in abundance. All the rooms have loud and lovely African art and masks adorning the walls, rainbow-tainted bedspreads and furnishings made of twisted tree branches. There's a pleasing communal area with a big-screen satellite TV. The front-facing rooms can be very noisy, though, thanks to the proximity to the road and a loud bar.

### Adot-Tina Hotel
BUSINESS HOTEL $$$

(Map p46; ☑0114-673939; www.adottinahotel.com; Meskal Flower Rd; s/d incl breakfast from US$100/125; @🛜) The small and plush rooms of this intimate business-class hotel, which come with either a deep, relaxing bath or a space-age shower that was far too complicated for us to work out, are really good value. However, the seal on the deal might be the free sauna and gym. It's a popular choice with tour groups and people coming to Ethiopia to adopt a child. Discounts are common.

### Palm Pension
HOTEL $

(Map p46; ☑0114-162606; off Meskal Flower Rd; d Birr250) If this wasn't so far out it would be a great deal – it's very peaceful, has a pocket-sized garden, safe parking for exhausted jeeps, and large, tidy rooms kept polished and smart. To get here cross the railway tracks at the end of Meskal Flower Rd and walk down the dirt road for 100m.

## NORTHEAST ADDIS

Around Mike Leyland St and Haile Gebreselassie Rd are some of the best budget and midrange hotels in Addis. In addition you'll find plenty of restaurants and bars and none of the touts or hustlers of the Piazza.

### TOP CHOICE Stay Easy
BUSINESS HOTEL $$

(Map p46; ☑0116-616688; www.stayeasyaddis.com; off Haile Gebreselassie Rd; r US$40-50; @🛜P) With its minimalist and utterly modern design, this budget business-class hotel is hands down the best place to stay in Addis at the moment. It has glittery art on the walls, high-quality mattresses, sound-proofed rooms, flat-screen TVs with satellite channels, great service and a decent in-house restaurant.

### Polaris Pension
GUESTHOUSE $

(Map p46; ☑0920-224499; off Mike Leyland St; r from Birr200) Holy moly Batman, this new guesthouse is a scorching-hot deal! Peach-pink rooms; inviting bathrooms: some with showers, some with bath tubs; art on the walls; cupboards for your gear; a TV; and a safe and quiet location. Oh yes, we like this one.

### Yahoo Pension
HOTEL $

(Map p46; ☑0913-103562; off Mike Leyland St; d Birr160-200, tw Birr250) Basic but well-kept and clean, which is all that really matters. Unusually for this price all rooms have attached bathrooms. The staff is ever smiling

## ADDIS SCAMS

One scam that still seems to be snagging tourists is the 'siren scam'. It takes various forms, including offering you a 'cultural show' or a traditional coffee ceremony.

The venue is usually somebody's living room, where a hostess will promptly dish out copious quantities of *tej* (honey wine) and, perhaps, traditional dancers and musicians will perform.

Suddenly the 'entertainment' comes to an end and an amount upwards of 1500Birr is demanded. Approaches are made to couples or groups, as well as to single males. Most commonly, the person approaching you is a young, well-dressed Ethiopian male, often claiming to be a student.

If you end up in a situation like this, offer to pay for anything you've consumed (a litre of quality *tej* shouldn't be more than Birr65), and if it's not accepted, threaten to call the police. The area around the hotels in the Piazza and Churchill Ave seem to be prime hunting grounds for potential victims.

Another increasingly popular pocket-emptying scam involves a passer-by 'accidently' spitting on you. He then makes a big fuss trying to wipe it off and in the process relieve you of your wallet.

Another one involves someone waving a packet of tissues in your face pretending to sell it to you. As you're distracted the accomplices pilfer the contents of your pocket or bag. Still, at least you'll have some tissues with which to wipe off the spit!

and it's on a tranquil side street. For the price, it's hard to find fault.

### Lana Pension
HOTEL $

(Map p46; ☑0910-170680; off Mike Leyland St; d Birr165) With oversized rooms, not a speck of muck in sight, hot-water showers and a pleasant and safe location, this is a mighty fine place to bed down for the night. The only drawback might be that the owner only speaks Amharic and two travellers of the same sex are not allowed to share a room.

### Henok Guest House
HOTEL $

(Map p46; ☑0116-624234; off Mike Leyland St; r Birr165-330) The rooms here are set around a sun-baked courtyard and are clean and as well-cared for as you can hope to find in this price range. It's tucked away up a maze of dusty tracks, so it stays nice and quiet.

### Melat Pension
GUESTHOUSE $

(Map p46; ☑0118-951287; off Mike Leyland St; r without bathroom Birr150, r with bathroom Birr200-250) This smart, new guesthouse has well-cared-for rooms; the larger ones are kitted out almost like miniature suites.

## ✗ Eating

You lucky, lucky souls...you've either just stepped off a plane (Welcome to Ethiopia! Lucky you!) and can experiment with your first genuine Ethiopian meals, or you've just arrived from several weeks in Ethiopia's wilds (How amazing was that?! Lucky you!) and can now say goodbye to repetitive *injera* and *wat* (stew) and sloppy pasta. Middle Eastern or Italian? French or Ethiopian? It's all here for you to enjoy.

Many restaurants, particularly the smarter ones, add a 15% tax and 10% service charge to their bills; check before you order.

Many Ethiopian restaurants offer a 'traditional experience': traditional food (called 'national food') in traditional surroundings with traditional music in the evening. You sit in short traditional Ethiopian chairs, eating from a communal plate on a *mesob* (Ethiopian table).

If you feel more adventurous, try the *kitfo bets,* which are typically ignored by tourists. These restaurants usually serve little other than *kitfo* (minced beef or lamb like the French steak tartare, usually served warmed – but not cooked – in butter, *berbere* – red, spicy powder – and sometimes thyme).

If meat isn't your thing, you'll love Wednesday and Friday because fasting food (a variety of vegetarian dishes) is served by all Ethiopian restaurants.

Cafes and pastry shops are omnipresent in Addis, and you'll find them perfect for an afternoon or early-morning pick-me-up. For places that stand out for their drinks, see p53, while those that make the grade in the edible end of the spectrum are found here.

Check out the Ethiopian Cuisine chapter, p259, for more information about Ethiopian cuisine and eating etiquette.

### CENTRE

### Dashen Traditional Restaurant
ETHIOPIAN $$

(Map p38; ☑0115-529746; off Itegue Taitu St; mains Birr100-145; ☺10am-10pm) From the outside, this Ethiopian eatery doesn't look promising. However, if you venture in past the courtyard, you'll find a lovely, low-key dining area, with stone walls, local art and bamboo furniture. The soft lighting and intimate surrounds are perfect for your first awkward attempts at *injera*. Its fasting food is particularly good (it's also available with fish). There's live music Wednesday to Sunday evenings.

### Shaheen
INDIAN $$$

(Map p38; ☑0115-171717; Sheraton Hotel, Itegue Taitu St; mains US$11-35; ☺noon-3pm & 7-11.30pm) Set within the Sheraton's confines, Shaheen is Addis Ababa's most sophisticated Indian restaurant. The decor in the restaurant is grand and the melange of Indian curries and tandooris is vast.

### Stagion
ITALIAN $$$

(Map p38; ☑0115-171717; Sheraton Hotel, Itegue Taitu St; mains US$14-29; ☺noon-3pm & 7-11.30pm) If *vitello caluzza* (sautéed veal scaloppini with diced tomatoes, peas, white wine and garlic served with spaghetti) or *cartuccio di pesce persico del Nilo con patate e pinoli* (fillet of Nile perch with pine nuts and potatoes) makes your stomach quiver with excitement, slide into this great Italian restaurant.

### Cottage Restaurant & Pub
INTERNATIONAL $$

(Map p38; ☑0115-516359; Ras Desta Damtew St; mains Birr70-120; ☺noon-2pm & 6-10pm) This cosy wooden cottage is an expat favourite for a smart lunch. While the menu is varied, ranging from Madras chicken curry to veal medallions in a *morille* (mushroom) sauce, its speciality is the beef fondue (Birr370 for two).

**China Bar & Restaurant** CHINESE $$
(Map p38; Ras Desta Damtew St; mains Birr60-100;
⊘11.30am-10.30pm) If you're craving something sweet or sour, this central Chinese restaurant is the most convenient place – though not everybody rates the food.

### PIAZZA & THE NORTH
**Itegue Taitu Hotel** ETHIOPIAN $
(Map p44; ☑0111-560787; www.taituhotel.com; mains Birr30-40, lunch buffet Birr59) If you've travelled overland to Addis Ababa, and eaten in a succession of cheap local restaurants serving less than inspiring *injera*, then reward yourself with a taste of high-quality and utterly delicious Ethiopian fare served up in the refined and stately atmosphere of this old hotel's renovated dining room. Its bargain-priced lunchtime buffet (also available on Friday evenings) is immensely popular with both foreigners and well-to-do locals.

**Lucy Gazebo & Restaurant** INTERNATIONAL $$
(Map p34; King George VI St; mains Birr70-120; ⊘8.30am-8pm) Next to the National Museum and a favourite haunt of locals, expats and museum-visiting tourists, this bright and airy restaurant with alfresco dining in the garden serves flavourful pastas (some vegetarian options), curries and good Ethiopian fare. However, you do pay for the location.

**Ristorante Castelli** ITALIAN $$$
(Map p44; ☑0111-571757; Mahatma-Gandhi St; mains Birr60-90; ⊘noon-2.30pm & 7-10.30pm Mon-Sat) Very much an Addis institution, this famous Italian restaurant has fed Swedish royalty, Bob Geldof, Brad Pitt, Angelina Jolie and ex-US presidents. The food is of course good (but maybe not as good as the price tag indicates), but sadly the whole experience can be somewhat marred by the attitude of the owner who seems disappointed that all his guests do not fall into the above fame category! Reservations are wise, but not always honoured.

**Serenade** MEDITERRANEAN $$
(Map p44; ☑0911-200072; mains Birr120-170; ⊘7pm-midnight Wed-Sat, 10am-3pm Sun) Just east of Piazza, off Tewodros St and tucked up a dark cobblestone alley, is this mixed-bag Mediterranean eatery. You're unlikely to be disappointed by its creative menu of Beirut-meets-Milan dishes, including such succulent treats as braised lamb with caramelised onions, lentils, lemon and *raison orange* couscous. But on the downside, we've heard some customers say it's not always as good as it should be considering the price.

**STREET NAMES**

Finding a street sign in Addis can be something of an art form and then, when you do find one, it's likely that no local will actually know the street by that name. In fact, aside from a couple of streets (Churchill Ave, Bole Rd, Meskal Sq and a few others) it's highly unlikely that any local will have any idea what the street is called. Most people, taxi drivers included, use landmarks in order to enquire about the location of something. When trying to get to a specific place, asking for the nearest big hotel to it, or shopping centre or well-known restaurant, is more likely to garner a result than merely giving a street name.

We have included the names of the major streets on our maps, but even so it's likely that with many of these locals will have half-a-dozen different names or no name at all for the same road. So, the moral of the story? Get creative when trying to locate something!

**Raizel Café** INTERNATIONAL $
(Map p44; Hailesilase St; mains Birr20-45; ⊘7am-9.30pm) This slick modern cafe speedily serves tasty cheeseburgers, tuna melts, French fries and breakfast omelettes to a fashionable, young crowd. It's one of several similar places around here.

### BOLE ROAD & EAST ADDIS
This area, taking in Bole Rd, Cameroon St and environs, is the undisputed culinary centre of Addis. This is where the well-to-do and expats of Addis like to hang out, so you can expect high-quality and higher than normal prices. Food types from around the world are represented here as well as flash Western-style coffee shops by the dozen.

**TOP CHOICE La Mandoline** FRENCH $$
(Map p46; ☑0116-629482; behind Bole Medanyalem Church, off Cameroon St; mains Birr55-80; ⊘closed Mon) This upper-crust French restaurant serving superb, and authentic, traditional French dishes might well get our vote as the best-value restaurant in the city. How traditional is the food? Try an excellent salad

for a starter, a delicious steak with Roquefort sauce for a main and a crème brûlée for dessert and you won't know you're not in La Belle France. The French owner works in the kitchen and stalks the dining area checking everything is just perfect. And, frankly, it pretty much is.

### TOP CHOICE Avanti Restaurant & Wine Bar
ITALIAN $$

(Map p46; ☎0111-8622632; Ring Rd; mains Birr80-120) From the outside this new place actually looks a bit run-down, but first impressions deceive. Step inside and relish some of the best Italian food in the city all served in a light and airy environment that's smart without being formal. There's an impressive wine list (around Birr420 for the average bottle).

### Jewel of India
INDIAN $

(Map p46; ☎0115-513154; Gabon St; mains Birr50-70; ☺11.30am-3pm & 6.30-11pm) This authentic Indian-run restaurant specialises in tandoori dishes, but whatever you opt for is certain to tickle your taste buds in just the right way. And what a treat it is to taste spicy food with texture and form rather than just heat!

### Antica Restaurant
PIZZERIA $

(Map p46; ☎0911-225019; off Cape Verde St; pizzas Birr60-90, pasta Birr50-60; ☺noon-2.30pm & 6-10pm) Watch chefs manoeuvre airborne dough while you wait for your delectable thin-crust pizza at this upscale Italian option. There are two-dozen pizzas on the menu – toppings range from anchovies and capers to prosciutto and sausage. We reckon it has the capital's best pizzas. They also do the only home-delivery service in Addis. There's also a bar downstairs that comes alive in the evening.

### Habesha Restaurant
ETHIOPIAN $

(Map p46; ☎0115-518358; Bole Rd; mains Birr60-80; ☺noon-3pm & 6pm-2am) For an Ethiopian meal that looks as good as it tastes, come to this Bole eatery where serving seems to be an art form. After a flurry of handwork, our *injera* was beautifully laden with everything from *gored gored* (raw beef cubes with *awazi*, which is a kind of mustard and chilli sauce) to vegetarian fasting food. There's also live music and traditional dancing every night at 8pm. This is the perfect place for your first taste of Ethiopia.

### Shangri-la Restaurant
ETHIOPIAN $

(Map p46; ☎0116-632424; Cape Verde St; mains Birr50-70, 1kg of meat Birr160; ☺noon-2pm & 6pm-midnight) Shangri-la has earned a well-deserved reputation as an atmospheric place for great Ethiopian food, especially *tere sega* (raw meat; available Saturday only). Fasting food is the way to go on Wednesday and Friday. There's an outdoor dining area with an open fire, and a cosy bar serving quality *tej* (honey wine).

### እፎይ (Efoy)
PIZZERIA $

(Map p46; ☎0911-2134811; Mike Leyland St; pizzas 65-85; ☺noon-midnight) If Addis has something that could be described as a 'boutique' pizza place then this would have to be it. It's small, warm and welcoming, with thin-crust pizzas popping out of the pizza oven to satisfy a young and cool local crowd. Upstairs is an equally intimate bar. The sign is written in Amharic only – the rough translation is 'efoy', which is the sort of sighing noise a contented person makes.

### Kuriftu Diplomat Restaurant
INTERNATIONAL $$

(Map p46; ☎0116-184363; Bole Rd; mains Birr115) Feel on top of the world and enjoy the views over the city at this 5th-floor restaurant inside the Boston Day building. The menu, which takes in steaks, Mexican and pastas, spans the world in all its culinary loveliness. Sadly, it also has the world's most uncomfortable chairs!

### Lime Tree
INTERNATIONAL $

(Map p46; Bole Rd; mains Birr50-75; ☺7am-11pm) The evergreen, ever-lime Lime Tree remains one of the hippest places in Addis to have a light lunch. The menu includes such delights as pita stuffed with tabouli or felafel, and chicken coconut curry, and it sells what we are assured is the best carrot cake in Addis. It's an essential on the expat circuit and there's an in-house bookshop and useful noticeboard for those setting up home in Addis.

### Sana'a Restaurant
MIDDLE EASTERN $$

(Map p46; Gabon St; mains Birr70-100; ☺11am-3pm & 6-9pm) For both the local Muslim and Christian communities this busy place is a lunchtime institution – queues can form out the door for a table. The reason they all flock here? Good, honest Yemeni fare, including spicy hot *salta* (a highland stew/soup) and the house special, Yemeni-style chicken and rice.

**Sangam Restaurant** INDIAN **$**
(Map p46; Bole Rd; mains Birr50-70; ☺11.30am-3pm & 6.30-10pm) If you've developed a craving for a cracking curry, try this atmospheric eatery. Here you can wrap your lips around *mughali biryani* (fragrant rice), tandoori dishes or butter chicken masala – absolutely delicious. There are also great lunchtime *thalis* (mixed meals; Birr80) available every day but Sunday.

**Fasika Restaurant** ETHIOPIAN **$**
(Map p46; mains Birr60-85; ☺11.30am-3pm & 6pm-midnight Mon-Sat) Fasika is a classic Ethiopian restaurant with a great atmosphere, good food, an exotic interior and live music most nights from 8pm. It's located 150m up a dirt lane off Bole Rd's north end.

**17 17** ETHIOPIAN **$$**
(Map p46; Cameroon St; kilo of meat Birr145; ☺noon-midnight) Come dinner and lunch, this local option is alive with action. Tables spill from the restaurant's interior out to a large courtyard topped by flowering vegetation. Buy a big hunk of meat from the butcher out front and have it barbequed up and served with spice and *injera* (or you can just eat it raw) and wash it all down with a beer or three.

**Roomi Burger** BURGERS **$**
(Map p46; Cameroon St; burgers Birr55, pizzas Birr65) Supersized burgers are the obvious highlight of this place, which is a cross between a fast-food joint and a pavement cafe, but pizzas and other non-*injera* delights also light up the menu.

**New York, New York** BURGERS **$**
(Map p46; Bole Rd; burgers Birr45) Missing the Big Macs of the Big Apple? Then fill yourself with Big Boy burgers at this evergreen expat fuel stop.

**Addis Sport & le Petit Café** MIDDLE EASTERN **$**
(Map p46; Bole Rd; mains Birr30-50; ☺6am-2pm) Although it's a jack-of-all-trades restaurant, this place is renowned for its superb *ful* (broad bean and butter purée). It's a popular refuel stop for runners after a morning jog. Note that it's only open in the mornings.

**Rico's Restaurant,
Pizzeria & Bar** INTERNATIONAL **$**
(Map p46; ☏0115-539462; Bole Rd; mains Birr20-35; ☺noon-10pm) A stylish, brightly lit place serving everything from Moroccan kebabs to minestrone soup and the oddly named 'farmer's wife' steak.

**Makush Art Gallery & Restaurant** ITALIAN **$**
(Map p46; ☏0115-526848; Bole Rd; mains Birr50-100; ☺noon-2pm & 6-10pm) Surrounded by vivid paintings, woodcarvings, candlelit tables, attentive waiters and elevator music (hey, nothing's perfect!), the ambience of this restaurant definitely outdoes the food, which can only be described as passable Italian. It's in an office tower above Ethio Supermarket.

**SOUTHWEST**

**Backyard** INTERNATIONAL **$**
(Map p46; ☏0114-673501; Meskal Flower Rd; mains Birr45-60; ☺11am-midnight Mon-Fri, 9am-midnight Sat & Sun) Freshly transported from the Mediterranean, this pastel-cool restaurant has a tasty range of light pastas and salads, but it's the drool-inducing steaks that it's most renowned for – heaven indeed during the fasting period. Considering the low prices the food quality is surprisingly high.

**NORTHEAST ADDIS**

**Elsa Restaurant** ETHIOPIAN **$**
(Map p46; Mike Leyland St; mains Birr55-75, kg of meat Birr150; ☺noon-10pm) This simple outdoor restaurant receives high marks from locals, expats and tourists alike for its quality Ethiopian fare. The *yetsom beyaynetu* (variety of fasting foods) is perfect for vegetarians, while *yedoro arosto* (roasted chicken) and *gored gored* or *tere sega* assuage carnivorous cravings. Half the neighbourhood likes to come here for an afternoon drink.

**Restaurante O'Portugues** MEDITERRANEAN **$$**
(Face of Addis; Map p34; ☏0912-610554; mains Birr80-150) With the ingredients brought from far-away Portugal, you really can eat salty Atlantic *bacalhau* (dry, salted cod) or Alentejo pork washed down with Portuguese wines and an extraordinary view over the whole of Addis. Prices are a bit steep, though.

# 🍷 Drinking

You won't go thirsty in Addis Ababa. Sip some of the world's best (and cheapest) coffee, down a healthy juice or simply sway home after swallowing your share of *tej*.

## Cafes

Addis is currently in the grip of a mass spawning of cafes. At the centre of the scene are the Piazza and Bole Rd areas. Many are cookie-cutter rip-offs of Western-style coffee shops, but among the dross are some gems – some recalling bygone days in small-town Italy, others cool and hip hangouts for the city's growing middle class. The following are our favourites, but you can bet your sweet tooth that by the time you get there you'll find a couple of new ones to add to this list.

### Tomoca
CAFE

(Map p44; Wavel St; coffee Birr7) Ahh, if only all cafes were like this one! Coffee is serious business at this great old Italian cafe in Piazza. The beans are roasted on site (you can literally smell them roasting from a block away) and Tomoca serves what's likely the capital's best coffee. If that isn't enough, it's also dripping in 1920s atmosphere. Beans are also sold by the half-kilo (from Birr60).

### La Parisienne
CAFE

(Map p46; Gabon St; pastries Birr10-15; ⊗6am-8pm) If you're staying in the Bole Rd part of town (in fact, even if you're not), then there's only one place for breakfast and that's this megapopular terrace cafe with superb coffee, fair impersonations of croissants and freshly squeezed orange juice. If the waitresses could only develop more of a Gallic 'I can't be bothered to serve you' shrug then you'd think you were on the Champs-Élysées. There are several other branches throughout the city but this one is considered the best.

### Cup Cake Delights Cafe
CAFE

(Map p46; off Bole Rd; cup cakes Birr15) Red Velvet. Caribbean Breeze. Vanilla Fever. Brunette. The bright and bubbly names and flavours of the cup cakes on sale here are highly appropriate for a cafe that is in itself a bright and bubbly place full of the hopeful and young of Addis. However, if we have one criticism it's that they've gone a little overboard with the amount of icing atop each cake. As any good Englishman or woman will tell you, cup cakes are supposed to be subtle!

### Oslo Cafe
CAFE

(Map p44; Dejazmach Jote St; pastries Birr10-15; ⊗6am-9pm) Luscious lip-gloss red and easily the most popular of the numerous bright, modern Western-style coffee shops around the Piazza area.

### National Café
CAFE

(Map p38; Gambia St; coffee Birr5-7) An ever-popular institution that's little more than a dark hole in the wall. For those not afraid of daylight, there's also a few sun-grabbing tables out on the pavement.

### Ras Hotel
CAFE

(Map p38; Gambia St; coffees Birr7-10) This central hotel's terrace is a perfect place for a late-afternoon coffee.

## Juice Bars

Most of Addis Ababa's cafes also serve freshly squeezed juices or slushy blends of everything from strawberries to avocado.

### Prime Juice House
JUICE BAR

(Map p46; off Haile Gebreselassie Rd; juices Birr23-25) Bored of avocado and mango juices? Then you'll think this place, with such exotics as Energiser (banana, strawberry and yogurt), rocks. We'd even go so far as to say it has the best juice in town.

### Lime Tree
JUICE BAR

(Map p46; Bole Rd; juices Birr20-25; ⊗7am-11pm) With luscious lassis and creative juices, Lime Tree is a premier place to indulge in liquid treats of the chilly variety. We downed a lime juice with mint, and it refreshingly pummelled our thirst.

## Pubs & Bars

Addis Ababa's bar scene is becoming ever more cosmopolitan and diverse, though remember this is still no Nairobi when it comes to the quantity and quality of bars – many are hole-in-the-wall dives where all but the most thick-skinned would feel uneasy. However, a growing middle class and increasing numbers of expats have led to some swanky joints, the majority of which are found in and around Bole Rd.

Small local drinking holes charge Birr20 for a bottle of beer, while established bars can charge up to Birr30. Most places are open until 2am during the week, and 5am on the weekend.

### Black Rose
BAR

(Map p46; Bole Rd; ⊗closed Mon) Hiding in a modern building above the Boston Day Spa, this plush bar possesses a cool vibe and a refined clientele – we felt well out of place! Music ranges from Ethiopian to Western and Indian.

### Mask Bar
BAR

(Map p46) This tiny bar is as gaudy as it is cool. Above the glowing green beer bottles that comprise the bar hang masks of all sorts: some historical, some available in any tourist-tat shop. The crowd ranges from expats to well-heeled locals. It's well signposted off Bole Rd.

### La Vue

BAR

(Map p38; Josif Tito St) Possibly the most oddly situated bar in Addis: it sits on the 10th storey of a residential block (which must endear the owners to the neighbours), just east of Menelik II Ave. The walls are covered in art, the views would be great if it weren't dark and the customers young and well to do.

### Beer Garden

BAR

(Map p46; off Bole Rd) If your tipple is beer then at the German-flavoured Beer Garden you can sit on a long bench and get 3L of the golden liquid for Birr128 or a 1L for Birr44. Parents will appreciate the well-maintained children's play park out front.

### Tej Bets

If authentic experiences are what you're after, there's no better place than a *tej bet* to down the famed golden elixir (honey wine). Most are open from 10am to around 10pm, but are busiest in the evening. They're the traditional haunt of men, so women should try to keep a low profile. They never have signs, so you'll have to ask locals to point them out.

### Topia Tej Bet

BAR

(Map p46) Off Haile Gebreselassie Rd, tucked up an alley behind the Axum Hotel, this is Addis' top *tej bet* and the only one to serve pure honey *tej*. A small flask (Birr14) on an empty stomach had our head spinning. Half-litre (Birr34) and litre (Birr64) bottles are also available. It's a congenial place with tables surrounding a tiny garden.

## ☆ Entertainment

Nightlife in Addis Ababa continues to develop at a steady pace; the scene becomes ever more varied and sophisticated and new places open all the time.

The free publication *What's Up!* and the website Addis All Around (www.addisall around.com) highlight upcoming events on Addis Ababa's entertainment scene.

### Jazz Clubs

**TOP CHOICE** Jazzamba Lounge

JAZZ BAR

(Map p44; Itegue Taitu Hotel; admission Birr50-80; ☺8.30pm-1am) Back in the 1960s the jazz scene in Addis was booming. So big was the scene that Ethiopian jazz even had its own style and name: Ethiojazz. Then along came the Derg and away went the fun. Today the scene is making a slow recovery (though a number of jazz bars have closed down in

the last couple of years) and the centre of that recovery is Jazzamba Lounge, located inside the creaky Itegue Taitu Hotel. Every night there's a live jazz session that attracts renowned local and international artists.

### La Gazelle Piano Bar

JAZZ BAR

(Map p46; Bole Rd) This dark and moody bar has live jazz every night.

### Nightclubs

While most nightclubs open at 11pm, there's no point in arriving before midnight. Those open during the week close around 2am; things wrap up nearer to 5am on weekends. Cover charges vary between Birr50 and Birr100 at most venues, depending on the day (but are sometimes free). Expect to drop a minimum of Birr35 for a beer and Birr50 for a cocktail.

### Farenheit

NIGHTCLUB

(Map p46; off Cameroon St) A reliably good club that's been around a while. It plays a wide range of music and mixes it up with DJs and live bands. It's close to the Edna Mall.

### Club Illusion

NIGHTCLUB

(Map p38; cnr Ras Desta Damtew & Itegue Taitu St; ☺Thu-Sat) This is Addis Ababa's most raucous club and you need to be pretty thick-skinned to survive! It's in the basement of the Ambassador Cinema. There's occasional live music.

### Tam-Tam

NIGHTCLUB

(Map p46; Beyene Abasebsib St; ☺Thu-Sat) This nightclub, which lurks beneath the Global Hotel in southwest Addis Ababa, hosts well-known DJs most weekends as well as lots of prostitutes. It can get very lively and might not appeal to all. Music ranges from Ethiopian to African hip-hop.

### Platinum

NIGHTCLUB

(Map p46; off Cameroon St; ☺Thu-Sat) Currently the flavour of the month and packed every weekend with teenagers and 20-somethings. Beers are a hefty Birr70 to Birr80. It's close to the Edna Mall.

### Memo Club

NIGHTCLUB

(Map p38) About 200m west of Bole Rd, this is another of Addis Ababa's hot spots. Cosy seats, red lights and the odd full-length mirror surround the circular dance floor, which usually reverberates with African and Western tunes. Sadly, it's also popular with expats shopping for prostitutes.

**Flirt** NIGHTCLUB

(Map p46; off Bole Rd) A pulsating club playing a little bit of this and little bit of that.

## Traditional Music, Dance & Theatre

Amharic theatre is hard to come by these days, with venues only hosting shows once or twice a week. Traditional music and dance are much more accessible, with many restaurants putting on traditional shows in the evenings. *Azmari bets* are also atmospheric places to catch both. What in the world is an *azmari bet*? It's similar to a minstrel who ad-hocs amusing song and poetry. For more, check out the boxed text on p253.

**National Theatre** THEATRE

(Map p38; ☑0115-158225; Gambia St) This impressive building, with its massive marble and bronze entrance hall (and odd pigeon), hosts theatre most weekends at 5pm.

**City Hall Theatre & Cultural Centre**
THEATRE

(Map p44; ☑0111-550520; Fitawrari Gebeyehu St; tickets Birr40-50) A plush 1000-seat place in the Piazza, which shows productions on Tuesday and Friday. Sometimes there's traditional Ethiopian music on public holidays.

**Hager Fikir Theatre** THEATRE

(Map p44; ☑0111-119820; John Melly St; tickets Birr25) Hager Fikir occasionally stages theatre, musicals and dancing.

**Yewedale** LIVE MUSIC

(Map p38; Zewditu St) Thanks to some of the city's best *azmaris* performing here, it's resoundingly popular and you may have trouble finding a seat. The sign is in Amharic only, but it's opposite the Samsung shop and next to the Canon shop.

**Fendika Azmari Bet** LIVE MUSIC

(Map p38; Zewditu St) This *azmari bet* rivals any in the city. It's littered with Ethiopian cultural items and is always home to a good time.

## Cinema

Cinema is more popular than ever – even pushing theatre out of most theatres. Most films are in English or have English subtitles (some have both!).

TOP CHOICE **Alliance Éthio-Française d'Addis-Abeba** CINEMA

(Map p44; ☑0111-550213; www.allianceaddis.org; Wavel St; admission free-Birr50) As is almost always the case with French cultural centres, this one hosts an exciting and diverse range of art-house films, experimental theatre, gallery exhibitions, opera and world music. There's also a French-language library, French lessons and, for French speakers, Amharic lessons.

**Matti Multiplex** CINEMA

(Map p46; www.ednamall.net; off Cameroon St; admission Birr50) The multiplex cinema inside the Edna Mall shows all the big-ticket Hollywood, Bollywood, Nollywood and local films, including those in 3D.

**National Theatre** CINEMA

(Map p38; ☑0115-158225; Gambia St; tickets Birr20) There is no more atmospheric place in which to catch a film than this imposing old building. Hollywood showings are normally fairly old.

**Ambassador Cinema** CINEMA

(Map p38; Ras Desta Damtew St; admission Birr20) An institution, this central cinema puts on the usual diet of action-packed and slightly passé Hollywood movies. Films are shown daily in three sessions.

# 🔒 Shopping

Spend some spare change or spend your kid's college fund: the spectrum of prices and quality of goods for sale in the capital is that vast. You'll find most of the cheap souvenir stalls along or around Churchill Ave and in Piazza – haggling is always the way of the day!

**Entoto Market** MARKET

(Map p34; Entoto Ave) If you're interested in blankets or traditional clothing like a *shamma* (toga-style dress worn by highlander men), head to this group of stalls lining Entoto Ave, a few hundred metres north of Botswana St and the Spanish embassy. Unlike Churchill Ave or Piazza, this is where locals do their shopping.

**Gallery 21** CRAFTS

(Map p38; Churchill Ave) Of all the shops/stalls north of Haileselassie Alemayehu on Churchill Ave, this has the biggest selection (if you ask to see the back room) and the best-quality pieces, though the prices are higher than most.

**St George Interior Decoration & Art Gallery** CRAFTS

(Map p38; Itegue Taitu St) This is located near the Sheraton for one obvious reason: nobody staying elsewhere can afford to shop here! However, the artwork and traditionally inspired modern furniture are exquisite and it's worth a wander.

**Makush Art Gallery & Restaurant**   CRAFTS
(Map p46; Bole Rd) Has an excellent, carefully selected collection of high-quality furniture and paintings from various Ethiopian artists.

**Alert Handicraft Shop**   CRAFTS
(Map p34; ☎0113 211518; ☺8am-noon & 1-5pm Mon-Fri, 8am-noon Sat) Here the Berhan Taye Leprosy Disabled Persons Work Group produces and sells beautiful handbags, pillow covers and wall hangings, each emblazoned with vibrant embroidery. The items are so Ethiopian, yet they wouldn't feel out of place in a Kathmandu or Bangkok market. The shop is off Ring Rd, southwest of the city centre in the Alert Hospital compound; follow the signs to the canteen.

**Africans Bookshop**   BOOKSHOP
(Map p44; Hailesilase St; ☺9am-1pm & 2.30-7pm Mon-Sat) The best place for second-hand books on Ethiopia, particularly those out of print. Selection is very limited.

**Bookworld**   BOOKSHOP
Friendship City Center (Map p46; Bole Rd; ☺9am-9pm Mon-Sat, 11am-8pm Sun); Haile Gebreselassie Rd (Map p46; Haile Gebreselassie Rd; ☺8am-9pm); Boston Day building (Map p46; Bole Rd; ☺7am-11pm); Piazza (Map p44; Wavel St; ☺8am-8pm Mon-Sat) The best place for books in English (as well as some in French). There's also a small section on Ethiopia and some foreign magazines. Prices are more than you'd pay at home, but much cheaper than the hotels.

# ⓘ Information

## Dangers & Annoyances

Violent crime in Addis Ababa is fortunately rare, particularly where visitors are concerned. However, petty theft and confidence tricks are problematic.

The Merkato has the worst reputation as pickpockets abound – targeting not just *faranjis* (white foreigners) but Ethiopians as well. An old ploy is for someone to step blindly into you, while another gently lifts your belongings in the subsequent confusion. A less subtle tactic now being used involves someone diving at your feet and holding your legs while another pilfers your pockets. You are advised to leave hand luggage and jewellery in your hotel if you plan on visiting the Merkato.

Other spots where you should be vigilant include Piazza, where many foreigners get pickpocketed or mugged; Meskal Sq; minibus stands; outside larger hotels; and Churchill Ave, where adult gangs have been known to hang around the National Theatre. Common gang ploys are to feign a fight or argument and, when one man appeals to you for help, the other helps himself to your pockets.

Another, increasingly popular one involves the delightful technique of someone 'accidently' spitting on you and as they rush forward to clear up the mess, they, or their accomplices, pickpocket you. Don't let any of this scare you, though – Addis is very safe compared with many other African capitals. On a personal note, in all the time this author has spent in Addis he has never once felt even remotely threatened. For more information, see also the boxed text on p49.

## Emergency
**Police** (☎991)
**Red Cross Ambulance service** (☎917)

## Internet Access
Every midrange and top-end hotel and an ever-increasing number of budget hotels in Addis has

---

**DON'T MISS**

## SOLEREBELS FOOTWEAR

Bethlehem Tilahun Alemu set up **soleRebels Footwear** (Map p34; ☎0118-302326; www.solerebelsfootwear.co; 2nd fl, Adams Pavilion, Sar Bet) as a way of helping the unemployed but tremendously talented artisans in her Addis neighbourhood. Just eight years later soleRebels is one of Ethiopia's best-known companies internationally and the world's first shoe company to have been certified by the World Fair Trade Organization. All its shoes are made using locally sourced natural fibres, hand-made fabric and, for soles, old car and truck tyres, and staff are paid up to four times the average wage in Ethiopia.

soleRebels shoes are available in around 55 countries including a flag-ship shop in Addis Ababa.

good wireless internet or a computer or two for guest use. There are also numerous internet cafes, but due to the fact that these places close, reopen and change their name at the speed of a megabyte we have refrained from naming specific cafes here. If you're in a hotel without internet then ask at reception for the nearest internet cafe.

### Medical Services

**Bethzatha Hospital** (Map p38; ☎0115-514470; ☺24hr) This quality private hospital, off Ras Mekonen Ave, is recommended by most embassies.

**Ghion Pharmacy** (Map p38; ☎0115-518606; Ras Desta Damtew St)

**Hayat Hospital** (Map p46; ☎0116-624488; Ring Rd; ☺24hr) A reliable option near the airport.

**St Gabriel Hospital** (Map p46; ☎0116-613622; Djibouti St; ☺24hr) This private hospital has good X-ray, dental, surgery and laboratory facilities.

**Zogdom Pharmacy** (Map p46; Bole Rd)

### Money

You will have no trouble finding a bank to change cash and most Dashen Bank branches have ATMs that accept foreign Visa and Master-Card (but not Plus or Cirrus). An increasing number of other bank ATMs also accept international Visa cards. When withdrawing cash through an ATM with a foreign card you should select the Credit Card option (whether or not you actually have a credit card) otherwise it may not work.

Travellers cheques can be changed at bigger bank branches but with some reluctance. We've denoted those with nonstandard hours (see p277 for standard hours).

**Commercial Bank** Arat Kilo (Map p34; Adwa St; ☺open through lunch); Bole International Airport (Map p34; Bole Rd; ☺24hr); Bole Rd (Map p46; Bole Rd); Churchill Ave (Map p38; Churchill Ave); Josif Tito St (Map p38; Josif Tito St); Lower Piazza (Map p44; General Wingate St; ☺open through lunch); Meskal Sq (Map p38; cnr Menelik II Ave & Meskal Sq); Mexico (Map p38; Ras Abebe Aregay St); Upper Piazza (Map p44; Hailesilase St; ☺open through lunch) All these branches change cash (US dollars and euros).

**Dashen Bank** Bole Rd (Map p46); Sheraton Hotel (Map p38; Itegue Taitu St; ☺7-11am, noon-7pm & 8-11pm) Offers Visa and Master-Card cash advances. Also changes cash. Most have ATMs accepting international cards.

**United Bank** (Map p38; Hilton Hotel, Menelik II Ave; ☺6am-10.30pm)

**Wegagen Bank** Bole Rd (Map p46; Bole Rd); Meskal Sq (Map p38; Meskal Sq)

### Post

**Junior post offices** Meskal Sq (Map p38; cnr Menelik II Ave & Meskal Sq); Mexico (Map p38; Ras Abebe Aregay St); Piazza (Map p44; Cunningham St) Offers postal services for postcards and letters only.

**Main post office** (Map p38; Ras Desta Damtew St) The only post office for international parcel services.

### Tourist Information

The highly useful, monthly magazine *What's Up!* lists restaurants, shopping venues, nightclubs and events. It's available (haphazardly) at large hotels, smart restaurants and art galleries.

**Tourist Information Centre** (Map p38; ☎0115-512310; Meskal Sq; ☺8.30am-12.30pm & 1.30-5.30pm) This helpful office does its best to provide information about the city and itineraries elsewhere. It also has some informative brochures about the rest of Ethiopia.

### Travel Agencies

For information on travel agencies in Addis Ababa, see p295.

### Websites

**Addis All Around** (www.addisallaround.com) This excellent website previews forthcoming cultural events and lists general city information.

##  Getting There & Away
### Air

#### DOMESTIC FLIGHTS

All domestic flights are operated by **Ethiopian Airlines** (www.flyethiopian.com; Bole Rd Map p46; ☎0116-633163; Bole Rd; Gambia St Map p38; ☎0115-517000; off Gambia St; Hilton Hotel Map p38; ☎0115-511540; Menelik II Ave; ☺7am-8.30pm Mon-Sat, 8am-noon Sun; Piazza Map p44; ☎0111-569247; Hailesilase St). These offices are open daily from 8.30am to 5pm, unless stated otherwise. There are several more offices scattered across the city.

Schedules change quite frequently and flight durations vary depending on which stopovers the plane is making en route.

Major tourist flights leaving from Addis Ababa are listed in the following table. Note that this is not a complete list of all flights.

#### INTERNATIONAL FLIGHTS

For information regarding international flights and international airlines serving Addis Ababa, see the Ethiopia Transport chapter, p287.

### Bus

Buses run to Awasa (Birr138, four to five hours), Debre Zeyit (Birr60, 45 minutes), Lake Langano (Birr31, 4½ hours), Nazret (Birr75, two hours)

## MAJOR DOMESTIC FLIGHTS FROM ADDIS ABABA

| DESTINATION | FARE (BIRR) | DURATION (HR) | FREQUENCY |
| --- | --- | --- | --- |
| Aksum | 3597 | 2 | 1 direct daily, several nondirect daily |
| Arba Minch | 2879 | 1½ | Wed, Fri, Sun |
| Bahir Dar | 2816 | 1 | 2-3 daily |
| Dire Dawa | 2861 | 1 | 2 daily |
| Gambela | 3413 | 1½ | Wed, Fri, Sun |
| Gonder | 3100 | 1½ | 2 direct daily, several nondirect daily |
| Jimma | 2622 | 1 | Wed, Fri, Sun |
| Lalibela | from 3413 | 2-2½ | several nondirect daily |
| Mekele | 3376 | 1 | 3 daily |

and Shashemene (Birr138, four to five hours). For both Lake Langano and Ziway, take a bus to Shashemene and jump off at the turn off, but be warned that to continue onward to any of the accommodation around Lake Langano is a real pain and might well involve a long and hot walk (although hitching is possible). All these buses leave from the **short-distance bus station** (Map p38; Ras Mekonen Ave). Awasa and Shashemene are also serviced from the long-distance bus station.

Long-distance buses depart from **Autobus Terra** (Map p34; Central African Republic St), northwest of Merkato. Buses for the destinations listed in the box leave officially at 6am, but you should be at the station by 4.30am if you've any hope for a ticket. Be very wary of pickpockets and bag snatchers here.

There are several services to Shashemene and Awasa after the first 6.30am departure, though they all leave before noon.

A couple of 'luxury buses' now fly down the country's highways and are proving immensely popular with both foreign visitors and locals. These puppies have reclining seats, aircon, on-board toilets and even free snacks and drinks. The best established is **Selam Bus** (Map p38; ☎0115-548800; www.selambus.com), whose station and ticket office is on Meskal Sq. Book tickets up to a week beforehand if possible. It has the following daily services (all departing at 5.30am). On Tuesday there is also a bus to Shire and Aksum (Birr465).

| DESTINATION | FARE (BIRR) |
| --- | --- |
| Bahir Dar | 290 |
| Dessie | 205 |
| Dire Dawa | 265 |
| Gonder | 375 |
| Harar | 270 |
| Jijiga | 303 |

| DESTINATION | FARE (BIRR) |
| --- | --- |
| Jimma | 165 |
| Mekele | 400 |

Possibly even slicker is **Sky Bus** (Map p44; ☎0111-568080; Itegue Taitu Hotel), which also leaves from Meskal Sq, but the ticket office is handily inside the Itegue Taitu Hotel. These buses are air-conditioned and have toilets. Breakfast is included in the ticket price. Book tickets up to a week beforehand if at all possible. Sky Bus runs to the following:

| DESTINATION | FARE (BIRR) | DURATION/ DEPARTURE |
| --- | --- | --- |
| Bahir Dar | 306.90 | 1 day, 5.30am |
| Dessie | 208.80 | 7½hrs, 6am |
| Dire Dawa | 275 | 9½hrs, 6am |
| Gonder | 372.80 | 1 day, 5.30am |
| Harar | 278 | 1 day, 6am |
| Jimma | 199 | 6hrs, 1pm |

### Car & 4WD

Although it's possible to hire a self-drive car, you're usually restricted to the capital. Hiring a chauffeured 4WD, although expensive, removes most limits on where you can travel. Four-wheel drives are rented by almost all of Addis' travel agents (see p295). For more details on hiring, see p293.

### Minibus

With sealed roads now all but connecting Addis Ababa with Bahir Dar and Gonder, private minibus services are starting to crop up. They're very fast (not always a good thing!) and cut journey times down to six or seven hours for Bahir Dar and 10 hours for Gonder. There's no station per se, but

## LONG-DISTANCE BUSES

| DESTINATION | FARE (BIRR) | DURATION |
| --- | --- | --- |
| Aksum | 308 | 2½ days |
| Arba Minch | 148 | 12 hours |
| Awasa | 80 | 6 hours |
| Bahir Dar via Dangla | 165 | 12 hours |
| Bahir Dar via Mota | 165 | 12 hours |
| Dessie | 120 | 9 hours |
| Dire Dawa | 150 | 11 hours |
| Gambela | 238 | 2 days |
| Goba | 140 | 13 hours |
| Gonder | 216 | 2 days |
| Jijiga | 189 | 1½ days |
| Jimma | 108 | 9 hours |
| Jinka | 227 | 2 days |
| Lalibela | 215 | 2 days |
| Matama (Sudan border) | 272 | 2 days |
| Mekele | 230 | 2 days |
| Moyale | 226 | 1½ days |
| Robe | 140 | 12 hours |
| Shashemene | 75 | 5 hours |

commission agents tend to patrol for customers near the Wutma Hotel in Piazza.

##  Getting Around

Though a sprawling city, Addis Ababa is fairly easy to get around.

### To/From the Airport

**Bole International Airport** (Map p34) lies 5km southeast of the city centre; both international and domestic flights depart from here.

Minibuses from Piazza, Mexico Sq and Meskal Sq serve the airport daily from 6am to 8pm (Birr4.70). Some charge an additional Birr2 or Birr3 for excess luggage.

Blue city taxis to the airport for a local should cost around Birr80 to Birr100 from anywhere south of Meskal Sq to around Birr130 to Birr150 if leaving from Piazza; add Birr20 at night or early in the morning. As a foreigner you're likely to pay at least Birr100 more for either route. From the airport, prices are much higher and normally quoted in US dollars (though they accept Birr).

Heading about halfway along Bole Rd will cost around US$20 and to Piazza around US$35. A taxi association has a booth at the airport's exit. Taxi drivers belonging to this association have

yellow taxis and it's probably safer to use these so as to avoid being overcharged by a random taxi in the chaos outside.

### Bus

Buses in Addis Ababa are considered poor man's transport. They're cheap but slow, run less regularly than the minibuses and are notoriously targeted by pickpockets. The minibuses are a much better bet.

### Car

Parking isn't usually too much of a problem in Addis Ababa. Most of the larger hotels and restaurants have guarded parking spaces and don't usually mind you leaving your car there. In other places, it's worth paying for a guard.

Anywhere you park on the street a 'parking warden' (we're not sure how genuine they are) appears and leaves a little note on your windscreen noting the time of arrival and they then charge you based on that (per hour Birr0.50).

### Minibus

Addis Ababa is served by an extensive network of little blue-and-white minibuses, which are fast, efficient, cheap and a great way of getting around.

Minibuses operate from 5.30am to around 9pm (till 8pm Sunday). Journeys cost roughly Birr1.30 (though exact prices depend on the distance).

Minibus stops can be found near almost every major intersection. Major ones include Arat Kilo, De Gaulle Sq in Piazza, Meskal Sq, Ras Mekonen Ave near La Gare and in front of the main post office on Churchill Ave.

To catch the right minibus, listen to the destinations screamed by the *woyala* (attendants) hanging out the windows. 'Bole!', 'Piazza!' and 'Arat Kilo!' are the most useful to travellers. If confused, ask and someone will point you in the right direction.

### Taxi

Most taxis operate from 6am to 11pm. Short journeys (up to 3km) usually cost foreigners Birr40 to Birr50 (more at night). Medium/long journeys cost Birr80/100. If you share a taxi, the normal fare is split between each person.

If you want to visit a lot of places in Addis Ababa, negotiate with a driver for a half- or full-day fare (Birr400 for a full day is pretty reasonable). A 'city tour' lasting a couple of hours should cost around Birr200 to Birr250.

Taxis can be found outside larger hotels, as well as the National Theatre, national stadium and on De Gaulle Sq in the Piazza. At night, many line up outside the nightclubs.

# AROUND ADDIS ABABA

The cacophonous sounds of traffic can chase even the most ardent Addis Ababa adorer into the hills occasionally. Lucky for them, the hills contain some historic churches (one hewn from rock in the 12th century) and some remote wilderness.

As well as the places listed here, sights further afield outside Addis Ababa that can still make good day trips include the crater lakes of Debre Zeyit (p174), Menagesha National Forest (p209), Ambo (p198), Mt Wenchi (p199) and the stelae field at Tiya (p134).

## Entoto Mountains
### የእንጦጦ ተራራ

North of town are the Entoto Mountains, the site of Menelik's former capital. There's a terrific but windy panoramic view of Addis Ababa below. Near the summit is the octagonal **Entoto Maryam Church** (Map p34; ☉Sun), which hosted Menelik's coronation. A small **museum** can also be found here.

To get to Entoto, take a taxi or minibus to the terminus of Entoto Ave from Arat Kilo. From there another minibus will take you to Entoto Maryam Church.

On the way up you will pass by the **Women Fuel Wood Carriers Project**, an organisation set up to protect the rights of women gathering firewood on the mountain. Traditional clothing items, hats and baskets can be purchased.

## Washa Mikael Church
### ዋሻ ሚካኤል ቤተ ክርስቲያን

The **Washa Mikael Church** (Map p34; admission/camera/guide Birr30/60/150; ☉8.30am-5pm) is located a few kilometres east of the town centre. Though local priests date it back to the 3rd century AD, it most probably dates back to the 12th century. If you're mad and not planning to visit the churches at Lalibela or Tigray in the north, it's definitely worth a peek as an example of the extraordinary rock-hewn architecture Ethiopia is so famous for. Unfortunately, from July to October it's usually flooded with rainwater.

The church is tricky to find, so ask locals en route (most know it as Tekle Haymanot). Finally, a word of warning: a number of tourists have been mugged on the road up to the church. Go with a friend or two.

# Northern Ethiopia

## Best of Culture

» Lalibela's rock-hewn churches (p119)

» Gonder's Royal Enclosure (p77)

» rock-hewn churches of Tigray (p108)

» Awra Amba (p72)

## Best of Nature

» Irta'ale Volcano (p117)

» Dallol (p118)

» Simien Mountains National Park (p87)

## Why Go?

For most visitors to Ethiopia, it's all about the north. Unlike anywhere else on Earth, northern Ethiopia has the ability to wow you day after day after day.

Known as the Historical Circuit, there are over two millennia's worth of ancient treasures scattered about, from giant obelisks and hidden tombs at Aksum to a collection of castles in and around Gonder, to unique churches in Lalibela, Tigray, Lake Tana and many other places. Not to be outdone by human mastery, Mother Nature really let her creative juices flow here. The Danakil Depression, an esteemed destination among adventure travellers, features a permanent lava lake and a bright-yellow sulphuric plain, while canyons and peaks wrinkle the land just about everywhere else.

Though you can hit the highlights in a couple of weeks, there is so much to see and do here it takes three or four weeks for proper exploration. No matter how long you stay, the northern circuit is so mesmerising that you'll probably find yourself still wanting a few more days.

## When to Go

### Gonder

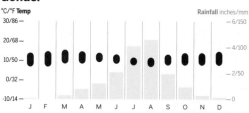

**Jan** Time for Timkat, the festival celebrating Jesus' baptism.

**May–Sep** The rainy season doesn't stop travel, but it makes trekking tough.

**Oct** The best time to travel. The rain's mostly gone, but the land remains green and gorgeous.

# Northern Ethiopia Highlights

**1** Immerse yourself in Christianity in its most raw and powerful form in the mind-blowing rock-hewn churches in **Lalibela** (p119)

**2** Smell the sulphur, see the lava and stare in disbelief at the thermometer in the **Danakil Depression** (p117)

**3** Get far away from urban life and very close to the locals on a **community trek** around Lalibela (p125) or Tigray (p111)

**4** Roam the hallowed halls of the royal retreats in **Gonder** (p77)

**5** Don't lose your balance as you trek along the endless Abyssinian abysses in the **Simien Mountains** (p87)

**6** Explore the magnificent rock-hewn churches of **Tigray** (p108)

**7** See an Ethiopian wolf in pristine habitat at the **Menz-Guassa Community Conservation Area** (p130)

**8** Dream of hidden treasure in the dank gloom of ancient Aksumite tombs beneath the stelae of **Aksum** (p93)

**9** Don't look down while climbing up to **Debre Damo** (p106) monastery

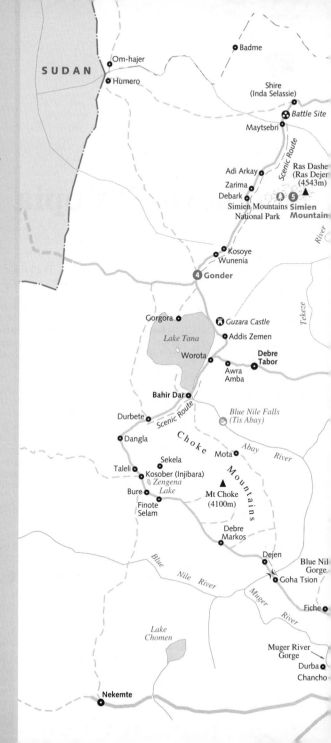

### ⊕ Getting There & Away

**Ethiopian Airlines** (www.flyethiopian.com) connects Addis Ababa with Bahir Dar, Gonder, Lalibela, Aksum and Mekele.

Most people who enter northern Ethiopia overland are travelling by bus from Addis Ababa, which sits conveniently at the bottom of the Historical Circuit. It's also possible to come from the Asaita region in eastern Ethiopia via roads to Woldia and Dessie. A rare few people access the Addis Ababa–Bahir Dar road from the western town of Nekemte. The only open border crossing is from Sudan at Metema (p290).

### ⊕ Getting Around

Ethiopian Airlines has flights connecting Bahir Dar, Gonder, Lalibela and Aksum.

The 2500km circular drive through the north is now nearly all paved (though still expect some rough sections) except between Debark and Shire and even that will be mostly completed early in the lifetime of this edition. The exception is the 45km from Debark to Zarima, which almost certainly will not. This stunning stretch of road, along with a further 30km on to Adi Arkay snakes down the western end of the Simien Mountains and is one of Africa's most beautiful roads. It makes the Blue Nile Gorge seem like just a Sunday drive in comparison.

The only areas in which you'll have trouble finding regular public transport are the Simien Mountains National Park and around the rock-hewn churches of Tigray, though it's possible in both.

To visit the Danakil Depression, you must travel with a tour company.

## ADDIS ABABA TO BAHIR DAR

In a private vehicle you can whip from Addis to Bahir Dar in as little as eight hours. Though there are no must-sees, some historical and natural sights allow you to break up the journey.

### Debre Libanos ደብረ ሊባኖስ

Lying 100km north of Addis Ababa is one of Ethiopia's holiest sites. Debre Libanos monastery (admission Birr100) was founded in the 13th century by Tekla Haimanot, a priest credited not only with the spread of Christianity in the highlands, but also the restoration of the Solomonic line of kings. Today he's one of Ethiopia's most revered saints. Since his time, Debre Libanos has served as the principal monastery of the old

Shoa region, and remains one of Ethiopia's largest and most important. Many Ethiopians make pilgrimages and some seek out its curative holy waters, said to be good for warding off evil spirits and for stomach disorders.

Although no trace of the ancient monastery remains (a casualty of the Muslim–Christian Wars), the site is impressively set beneath a waterfall-rich cliff (many of the monks live in caves up there) on the edge of the large Jemma River Gorge and is a peaceful place to wander.

The present church was built in 1961 by Haile Selassie, against the wishes of the local priests, after hearing a prophesy that a new church would ensure a long reign. It's monumental and pretty awful on the outside, but the stained-glass windows are attractive.

It's got one of the most interesting church museums in Ethiopia. Besides the usual ecclesiastical items there are Italian guns, giant cooking pots, crowns of past emperors and their wives, musical instruments and an old wooden shackle. Fifteen minutes up the hill from the monastery is Tekla Haimanot's cave, where the saint is said to have done all his praying. It's also the source of the holy water. A monument in front of the church memorialises the hundreds of innocent priests, deacons, and worshipers who were massacred here by the Italians following an assassination attempt on the notoriously brutal viceroy Graziani in 1937 (he was later imprisoned by the Italians as a war criminal for crimes against humanity).

Though the local guides insist this small stone-arch Portuguese bridge (Birr22) was erected by the Portuguese in the 16th century, it was actually built at the turn of the 19th century by Ethiopians: though in the old Portuguese style. The narrow span makes a pretty picture and the gushing (in the rainy season) cascade just below it is even more impressive. The 300m access trail running along the edge of the Jemma River Gorge starts at the Ethio-German Park Hotel.

### 🛏 Sleeping & Eating

**Ethio-German Park Hotel**   HOTEL $
(☏0116-563213; d without view Birr200, d/f with view Birr250/400; 🅿) Just past the turnoff to the monastery, this simple lodge, owned by an Ethiopian man who fled the Derg to Germany and his German wife, makes the most of its gorge views and is a popular pit

**LEGLESS IN LIBANOS**

Tekla Haimanot, descendant of Zadok, the priest who anointed King Solomon, is one of the most revered saints in Ethiopia thanks both to his part in restoring the Solomonic dynasty to Ethiopia and for his miracle-working prowess. He started working his magic even before he was born, when his mother was molested by a pagan king, Tekla Haimanot called forth the Archangel Mikhael (hidden inside a thunderstorm) who promptly turned the king mad. While still in his teens he could perform that old biblical favourite of turning water into wine and by the time of his death, he'd performed every miracle in both the Old and New Testaments. But it's for his devotion to prayer that he's best remembered. For 22 years he stood stock still and prayed until eventually his right leg turned rotten and fell off. Unperturbed he carried on for a further seven years, balancing on his remaining leg. Today what people believe is his right leg is kept inside the Debre Libanos monastery. Three times a year it's brought out and pilgrims kiss the box it's kept in to cast out evil spirits.

stop for those driving north, and a weekend getaway for residents of Addis Ababa. The more-basic-than-you'd-expect rooms have solar lights and hot water and those facing the gorge sport little porches.

The menu (mains Birr30 to Birr50) is limited to a handful of pasta and local dishes (fasting food is available daily), but they're both pretty good. A coffee ceremony costs Birr150 per group.

### ⓘ Getting There & Away

The monastery is 4.2km off the Addis–Bahir Dar highway. Usually four minibuses run daily from Addis Ababa to the monastery (Birr76, two hours).

## Blue Nile Gorge አባይ ሸለቆ

Around 200km from Addis Ababa, one of Ethiopia's most dramatic stretches of road begins its serpentine descent to the bottom of the Blue Nile Gorge, 1km below. Here a pair of bridges (photography prohibited), cross the river. A new Japanese suspension bridge handles traffic while the Italian original is now used by shepherds. The gorge is less dramatic than the Grand Canyon, with which it's inevitably compared, but it's still spectacular in places. Unfortunately the beauty on the southern side is frequently marred by cement company quarries.

## North to Bahir Dar

Across the gorge the landscape of rolling hills and long plains doesn't change, but the Oromo people are replaced by the Amhara, who rarely wear shoes and the men rarely go anywhere without their *dula* (wooden staff).

The shortest route to Bahir Dar is via Mota, but nobody uses this road because it's unsealed and in terrible condition.

Although it's not as dramatic as the crater lakes in southern Ethiopia, **Zengena Lake** (Birr20), with its perfectly circular shore, is still beautiful and the 3.4km track around it makes a nice walk or drive. Plenty of birds and vervet monkeys live in the natural forest blanketing the slope. A short trail at the parking area leads down to the shore where a boat makes a good picnic shelter while it waits for permission from the nearby church to begin giving trips on the water. You can camp (Birr25 plus Birr150 for two guards) and a lodge is planned. The lake is signed, just 100m off the highway, 4km before Kosober (Injibara).

After Kosober you'll pass Gish Abay and Bikolo Abay, described on p75.

### 🛏 Sleeping

For anyone who left Addis late or is choosing to mosey rather than motor up north, Debre Markos and Finote Salem are the best spots to split the journey.

**Tilik Hotel**                                      HOTEL **$**
(✆0587-712203; Debre Markos; d/tw/f Birr220/275/330; ℙⓈ) This place paints a far weaker first impression than the FM International in the heart of Debre Markos, but when it comes to the rooms this newish place wins hands down. All have mini-fridges, satellite TVs, little balconies, better maintenance and cleaning, and lower rates.

**Damot Hotel**                                      HOTEL **$**
(✆0587-751111; Finote Salem; d/tw/ste Birr250/350/450; ℙⓈ) For such a small town, Finote

Selam has a pretty good choice of hotels. The chandelier in the lobby of this large and unmissable place sets a pseudo-fancy tone that continues to the in-room furniture. The suites feature steam bath showers and all rooms have satellite TV.

# BAHIR DAR & LAKE TANA

This relaxing town and the scenic lake on which it sits form the first major stop on the Historical Circuit. It's a great place to spend a few days. Besides some minor sights around town, you're on the doorstep of the lake's mystical monasteries.

## Bahir Dar    ባሕር ዳር

POP 170,300 / ELEV 1880M

Some people like to describe Bahir Dar as the Ethiopian Riviera. The moniker sounds strange, but when you pull into town and see the wide streets shaded by palm trees and sweeping views across Lake Tana's shimmering blue waters, you'll understand.

In the 16th and 17th centuries, various temporary Ethiopian capitals were established in the vicinity of Lake Tana. It was here that Jesuits attempted, with disastrous consequences, to impose Catholicism on the Ethiopian people. One moss-covered Jesuit building, which was built by the well-known Spanish missionary Pedro Páez, can still be seen today in the compound of St George's monastery.

## ◉ Sights

For those Lake Tana monasteries you may have heard about, see p72. Information on Blue Nile Falls is found on p76.

**Lake Shore**                                    LAKE

Lounging lakeside is an essential part of the Bahir Dar experience. You'll often glimpse the flimsy, yet unsinkable *tankwa* canoe. Made from woven papyrus, they can take huge loads, including oxen! They're exactly the same as the papyrus boats depicted on the walls of ancient temples in Egypt. They're made in the village of **Weyto**, but the men here will ask for ludicrous fees to watch them. You can also sometimes see them being made at Debre Maryam monastery (p74).

**Main Market**                                   MARKET

If you are allergic to scenic lakesides and love dusty action, visit the large and lively main market. It's busiest on Saturday. Getting lost is half the fun. The delightful *agelgil* (goat-skin lunch boxes) are no longer sold in the market; they're mostly sold by the makers near the tourist office. Some souvenir shops sell them, but they buy from the makers too.

**Fish Market**                                   MARKET

There's a one-table fish market in the mudhut deacon's village behind St George's Church. The catch is brought in by *tankwa* in the morning and pelicans come to feed on the scraps in the afternoon.

**Blue Nile Bridge**                              BRIDGE

You can only reach the famous outlet of the Blue Nile by boat (see p75), but you can get pretty close along the Gonder road, 2km past the post office, where a bridge spans the river. You can see the dam that has ruined Tis Abay Falls (p76) and maybe some hippos and crocodiles. There are many *tankwa* in this area too, though not on the river itself.

**Martyrs Memorial Monument**          MONUMENT

(Map p73; admission Birr15) Just past the bridge is a large Martyrs Memorial Monument dedicated to those who died fighting the Derg (p233). Its fountain cascading down to the Blue Nile is quite the sight, especially if someone is having a wedding here and has paid to turn it on. The museum (◷8.30am-5.30pm) is full of photos, some labelled in English, from the resistance in Amhara Region.

**Palace of Haile Selassie**            VIEWPOINT

(Map p73) Two and a half kilometres south of the memorial is Bezawit Hill. Its summit hosts a former palace of Haile Selassie, which isn't open to visitors and can't be photographed. Viewpoints both in front and behind offer panoramic views over the lake, river and town. They're great at sunset. No public transport comes near here.

## ☞ Tours

The following are noted for arranging boat trips onto Lake Tana.

**Ghion Hotel**                               BOAT TOURS

(☏0582-200111) Best for budget travellers looking to share costs.

**Zelalem Memory**                            BOAT TOURS

(☏0913-122671; zelalemtadele@gmail.com; ◷8.30am-5.30pm Mon-Sat) With notice, this operator can arrange island camping.

# Bahir Dar

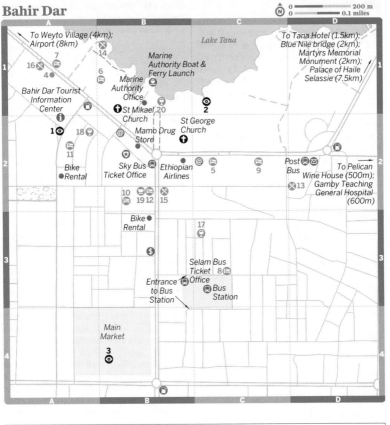

---

## Bahir Dar

### ◎ Sights
1 Craft Kiosks ................................................. A2
2 Fish Market ................................................. C1
3 Main Market ................................................ B4

### ✦ Activities, Courses & Tours
Ghion Hotel ............................................. (see 6)
4 Zelalem Memory ......................................... A1

### 🛏 Sleeping
5 Dib Anbessa Hotel ..................................... C2
6 Ghion Hotel ................................................. B1
7 Kuriftu Resort & Spa .................................. A1
8 Menen Hotel ............................................... C3
9 Summerland Hotel ..................................... C2
10 Tsehay Pension ......................................... B2
11 Walia Hotel ................................................ A2

12 Zimamnesh Guesthouse ......................... B2

### 🍴 Eating
13 Amanuel Restaurant ................................. D2
14 Desset Resort ............................................ B1
Mango Park .............................................. (see 20)
15 Wawi Pizzeria ........................................... B2
16 Wude Coffee .............................................. A1

### 🍷 Drinking
17 Araki Bars ................................................. C3
18 Bahir Dar Hotel ........................................ A2
19 Flavor Juice .............................................. B2
20 Mango Park .............................................. B1

### 🎭 Entertainment
Balageru Cultural Club ........................ (see 13)

## 🛏 Sleeping

**Dib Anbessa Hotel**  HOTEL $
(☎0582-201436; d/tw incl breakfast Birr300/400; 📶@📶) An older hotel with lots of carved wood giving it character. This doesn't extend into the rooms, but overlook the frayed carpets and you'll find that with their soft beds, satellite TV and balconies they offer fair value.

**Menen Hotel**  HOTEL $
(☎0582-263900; d Birr180-250, tw Birr300-400; 📶) A newish place very near the bus station that offers clean rooms, fair value and good service. The lowest priced rooms lack TVs and hot water. Rooms in front can be a bit noisy.

**Ghion Hotel**  HOTEL $
(☎0582-200111; campsites per tent Birr100, s Birr200-300, d Birr250-300; 📶@📶) Although the rooms here are as tired and worn as your favourite pair of travel socks, there's no denying the allure of Ghion's lakeside setting (now marred by the ugly fence) and garden full of flowers and paradise flycatchers. Rooms aren't identical and you need to let them know if you're interested in the cheaper, smellier ones. It's easily the most popular place for backpackers to get their heads down. The hotel offers free airport transfers and generally reliable travel advice, though it doesn't always keep reservations and drink prices aren't fixed.

**Summerland Hotel**  HOTEL $$
(☎0582-206566; www.summerbahirdar.com; s/d/tw incl breakfast Birr550/750/830; 📶@📶) While the brown curtains, brown furniture, brown walls, brown floors and fairly brown atmosphere may not remind you of carefree summer days, this hotel is functional and comfortable. And though the price is rather high, it won't let you down.

**Walia Hotel**  HOTEL $$
(☎0582-200151; d without bathroom Birr400) The tiny but immaculately presented rooms here get fresh coats of paint on a regular basis, which leaves them looking like the smartest boy at the party. Even the communal toilets don't smell! The owner is there daily to keep everything ship shape.

**Tsehay Pension**  HOTEL $
(☎0582-221550; s Birr150, d Birr150-200, s without bathroom Birr100, d Birr100-150) Meticulous housekeepers and fair prices make this city-centre spot popular. All rooms have satellite TV and the private showers have hot water. Unusually for Ethiopia, you don't need to be a couple to share a double room.

**Zimamnesh Guesthouse**  PENSION $
(☎0911-534983; d Birr200) The top pick of several similar spots in this central (and thus noisy) area, this guesthouse has six rooms at the top of the tower. Next to the huge bedrooms, the bathrooms are comically small, but that's the main complaint. There's satellite TV and a minifridge.

**Tana Hotel**  HOTEL $$$
(☎0582-200554; s/d US$38/51; 📶) Known for its sunset views, Tana's top selling point is the forested lakeside setting. Some funky touches, like the goat-skin wall in the restaurant (mains Birr43 to Birr81), brighten up the older building. Though maintenance is not Tana's strongpoint, and the hot water is only turned on mornings and early evenings, overall it's a good choice.

**Kuriftu Resort & Spa**  RESORT $$$
(☎0920-959797; www.kurifturesortspa.com; s with half board US$132-139, d/tw/ste US$167/173/194; 📶❄@📶🏊) There's lots of new luxe lodging going up in Bahir Dar, but this attractive spot will surely remain one of the best. Kuriftu's large, refined stone-and-wood cottages are filled with lovely furnishings and artistic touches. Be sure to request a lakeview room: they don't cost extra. The service is excellent and the shady grounds ooze relaxation. Rates include one massage, manicure or pedicure.

## 🍴 Eating & Drinking

This being Bahir Dar you should have at least one meal lakeside. Desset Resort, which puts you right on the shore, is our favourite lakeside spot, but Mango Park is the most fun and Tana Hotel has the best sunsets.

The Balageru Cultural Club serves food, along with laughs. If you want a drink that will knock you off your feet, visit the hole-in-the-wall *araki* (grain spirit) bars near the bus station.

**TOP CHOICE** **Desset Resort**  EUROPEAN, ETHIOPIAN $
(mains Birr28-85) This popular restaurant really makes the most of its long landscaped shoreline. Both the *habesha* (Ethiopian) and *faranji* (foreigner) dishes (try the roasted lamb) are quite good and the menu is bigger than normal.

**Wawi Pizzeria**  ITALIAN, ETHIOPIAN $
(mains Birr23-54) As long as you're not in a hurry, join the crowd on the 1st-floor balcony for a pretty good pizza. There's also lasagne and chicken *tibs* (pan-fried sliced lamb)

**Wude Coffee**  CAFE $
(mains Birr18-28) For high-class Ethiopian fare in a chic city-style cafe, come munch here; either inside or at an outdoor table.

**Mango Park**  ETHIOPIAN $
(mains Birr13-30) The most central and popular lakeside spot for a chilled-out afternoon drink. It's usually packed with local students and families, though the pelicans that once joined them have fled. A floating barge has a full menu and costs Birr2 entry.

**Amanuel Restaurant**  ETHIOPIAN $
(mains Birr14-40) The menu here may look just like any other, but order the fish in any of its forms to see why Amanuel stands out.

**TOP CHOICE / Pelican Wine House**  WINE BAR
(small/large bottle Birr17/34; ⊙noon-midnight Mon-Fri, 9am-midnight Sat & Sun) A chemistry degree from Bahir Dar University led owner Yordanos into a life of wine and she now makes her own honey, date, mango, apple and grape varieties. You can pair them with burgers and chips from her sister's kitchen. It's easy to find; head past the post office and then south 500m from the university gate.

**Flavor Juice**  JUICE BAR
(juices Birr12) Has the best fruit selection of Bahir Dar's many juice bars.

**Bahir Dar Hotel**  BAR
(beer Birr11; ⊙7.30-10pm) Though it's a popular drinking spot throughout the week, the Friday and Saturday 'campfire nights' really pack the house.

## ☆ Entertainment

**Balageru Cultural Club**  COMEDY $
(admission free; mains Birr17-50, beers Birr20) If you'd like an entertaining cultural experience and a good laugh, visit this place. Various *azmari* (see the boxed text, p253) do their thing nightly (from around 7.30pm to 2am) to the rapturous joy of locals. If you're brave enough to dance, you'll win lots of friends.

## ℹ Information

Women, accompanied by male companions or not, should not walk along the waterfront path behind the Ghion Hotel. There can be serious hassle from men hanging out here. Don't walk anywhere in town after about 8pm.

Tourist hustlers can be a problem. Most 'know' the best place to stay or the 'cheapest' boat operators: thankfully you know better.

**Bahir Dar Tourist Information Center** (☎0582-201686; ⊙8.30am-12.30pm & 1.30-5.30pm Mon-Fri) Although staff are keen to help, it offers little more than brochures on the area.

**Dashen Bank** Has branches with ATMs at both ends of the main street through town.

**Gamby Teaching General Hospital** (☎0918-143195; ⊙24hr) The town's best medical facility.

**Mamo Drug Store** (☎0918-760909; ⊙8am-9pm Mon-Sat, 11am-9pm Sun)

**Memory Internet Café** (per hr Birr15; ⊙8am-9pm) One of several internet points with broadband connections in this block.

**Wegagen Bank** Has a branch along the main road.

## ℹ Getting There & Away

### Air
**Ethiopian Airlines** (☎0582-200020; www.flyethiopian.com) has two (some days three) daily flights to Addis Ababa (US$55, one hour) and a thrice-weekly flight to Lalibela (US$41, 35 minutes).

### Bus
Two ordinary buses make the long trip to/from Addis Ababa (Birr100, 11 to 12 hours, 6am). Sky Bus (Birr307) has an office near the lake and uses Mango Park as its 6am departure point. The Selam (Birr290) ticket office is at the bus station, but the buses park in front of St George's Church and depart at 5.30am. The Post Bus (Birr216) departs at 5.30am from Bahir Dar three days a week. Minibuses travel at night (which makes them dangerous) and can do the trip in as little as seven hours. Your hotel can reserve a seat for you, or ask around for an agent at the north gate of the bus station to avoid the hotel's commission.

Two buses travel to Gonder (Birr55, three hours) at 6am and minibuses (Birr65) go about hourly. For a steep fee, most hotels will call and have the minibus come pick you up so you can avoid the chaotic bus station. Some travellers prefer to band together and hire a private minibus to Gonder, which can cost as little as Birr850.

There's nothing direct to Lalibela, but you can take one of about five morning minibuses (Birr100, three hours) or the 6am bus (Birr97, 3½ hours) to Woldia and get off at Gashena to catch a connection there.

### Ferry
A ferry sails every Sunday at 7am for Gorgora (Birr253, 1½ days), on the northern shore of Lake Tana. It stops for loading at Dek Island (with

enough time to wander around) and overnights in Kunzula (Map p73), where there's food and a couple of grotty hotels. It's far from luxe with a toilet and limited seating in what they call '1st class'. Snacks and drinks are sometimes available, but its best to bring your own. Buy tickets from 2pm to 4pm the day before at the Marine Authority office.

## ❶ Getting Around

Bikes are perfect for Bahir Dar. Ghion Hotel has some for Birr16 per hour. Out on the street, such as at the spots south of Ghion and near Zimamnesh Guesthouse, prices are a bit cheaper.

If you're in a hurry, flag a passing *bajaj* (autorickshaw). A normal trip is Birr2. You can contract one for Birr10 to just about anywhere in the city.

Most of the pricier hotels provide a free ride to the airport. By *bajaj*/taxi the trip will set you back Birr100/200.

For details on getting to the monasteries around Lake Tana, see p75.

---

# Lake Tana & its Monasteries
ጣና ሃይቅና ገዳማት

Lake Tana's beauty can only be truly appreciated when you get out beyond the city and see its azure waters lapping on lush shores, islands dotting its distant horizon and squadrons of pelicans flirting with its surface. There's also some artificial beauty in the form of centuries-old monasteries full of paintings and treasures.

This lake is Ethiopia's largest, covering over 3500 sq km, and its waters are the source of the Blue Nile, which flows 5223km north to the Mediterranean Sea.

## ◉ Sights

While the boat engine's buzz is anything but a throwback to ancient times, your first meetings with the cross-wielding priests after stepping onto the islands just may be. Most monasteries date from the late 13th and 14th centuries, though the current church buildings were erected later. There are no architectural wonders like those at Lalibela and Tigray, but the murals adorning the monasteries' walls are full of all the colour, life, wit and humanity of Ethiopian art at its best and provide a compendium of Ethiopian saints, martyrs and lore. If you want help deciphering them, check out Know Your Ethiopian Saints, p245.

---

## THE PURSUIT OF A PERFECT WORLD: AWRA AMBA

Education is our source of income and helping each other is our culture.

*Awra Amba tour guide.*

Awra Amba village is like no other in Ethiopia. The residents have a utopian world vision of total equality (regardless of gender, age, race, social standing, etc), shared responsibility based on ability, and hard work and education as the best path to a good life. They also reject formal religion, though they do believe in a creator. The village's founder, Zumra Nuru, began imagining this sort of society as a child. Most people in his village thought he was crazy, but over time he met some likeminded people and in 1986, 18 of them joined him in founding this village. It's since grown to 460-plus residents (in over 140 households) and has attracted respect from around the country.

Ninety-minute guided village tours (Birr6) start with the preschool, where ethics and human rights are taught alongside the ABCs, and also visit the village's libraries, retirement home and weaving workshop. There's not enough land to go around so weaving is one of the ways the village stays self-sufficient. Note that there's no weaving every other Saturday. You may also have the chance to speak to the humble founder. Begging is very shameful here so please avoid giving handouts. Some visitors choose to help out by buying the villagers' products or giving some books to the library.

The simple (earthen walls, sheet metal doors and a bathroom out back) **guesthouse** (d/tw without bathroom Birr30/60) has about the cleanest shoestring lodging you'll ever see. The small **restaurant** (mains Birr10-14) has pasta and national dishes.

Awra Amba is 73km from Bahir Dar on the Woldia road, 10km after Worota. Several minibuses (Birr30, one hour) pass the signposted junction from where it's a 2km walk.

# Lake Tana & its Monasteries

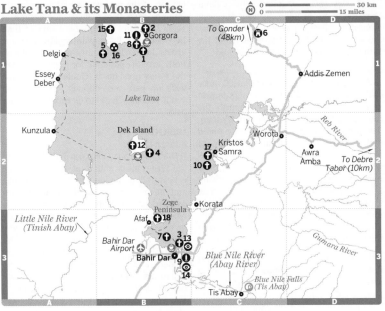

# Lake Tana & its Monasteries

Although it's possible to see all the monasteries over several long days, you'll likely have had your fill after just one day; especially considering that each church charges entry and they don't look all that different from each other. Women can visit all but a few of the monasteries. If visiting those on the Zege Peninsula, you'll be required to take a local guide (Birr90 per group of one to three people, Birr110 per group of four to 10). Generally speaking they're among the most annoying guides in Ethiopia.

All the stated journey times are for a one-way trip from Bahir Dar in a 25HP fibreglass speedboat. Metal boats are cheaper, but slower. See Getting Around (p75) for boat-hire information. The northernmost monasteries at Gorgora are covered later (p85).

## ZEGE PENINSULA

Walking between the monasteries on this forested peninsula, full of birds and vervet monkeys, is an enjoyable way to spend half a day. Better, in our opinion, than spending long hours sitting in a boat visiting distant islands. It's about 40 minutes from Bahir Dar, and most people only visit the four monasteries near the shore. Most paintings are from the 18th century or later; not the 14th like the guides will tell you.

### Ura Kidane Meret
MONASTERY

ኡራ ኪዳነምህረት (admission Birr100, video camera Birr100) The Zege Peninsula's largest and most famous monastery is hardly the most attractive on the outside, but it's maqdas (inner sanctuary) is beautifully painted and it holds an important collection of 14th- to 20th-century crosses and crowns which will soon be displayed in a big new museum. Outside its gate is the private Zeghie Satekela Museum (admission Birr20; ☺8am-5pm) with a collection of household items displayed in a 300-year-old home. The monastery is a 20-minute walk from the landing.

### Bete Maryam
MONASTERY

ቤተ ማርያም (admission Birr100, video camera Birr100) Founded in the 13th century, Bete Maryam, near the tip of the peninsula, is the oldest monastery on Zege and its attractive church has some excellent murals that, unfortunately, suffered water damage. It's a short walk from the landing through lemon and coffee trees. Just uphill from Bete Maryam, Bete Giorgis is being rebuilt from scratch following a fire. Its small museum with an important collection of crowns is still open.

### Azuwa Maryam
MONASTERY

አዙዋ ማርያም (admission Birr100, video camera Birr100) The thatch roof atop the church at Azuwa Maryam helps make it the best looking church on Zege (currently Bete Maryam is the only other church with thatch), though its paintings and small museum are more ordinary. Don't miss the religious school for priests and deacons here. Azuwa Maryam is a two-minute walk from the landing; the same landing used for Ura Kidane Meret.

### Bete Selassie & Tekla Haimanot
MONASTERIES

ቤተ ስላሴ እና ተክለ ሐይማኖት (admission Birr100, video camera Birr100) Two very rarely visited (the deacons and priests probably won't have receipt books) monasteries sit high up in the hills. Bete Selassie (men only) is a 30- to 45-minute walk from the shore. The simple exterior of the church (rebuilt in 1858) gives no clue to the wonderfully vivid paintings (arguably the best on the lake) inside, most of which date from the 1930s.

On top of the peninsula's highest point, 10 minutes from Bete Selassie, the church at Tekla Haimanot is similar but smaller than Bete Selassie's. It has paintings by the same artists but lacks the historic atmosphere. Both have the potential for great views, but the forest prevents it. Guides consider the walk up here very difficult (it's not!) and you'll probably have to negotiate a higher price.

## ISLANDS

### Kebran Gabriel
MONASTERY

ከብራን ገብርኤል (admission Birr100) Though the 17th-century church at Kebran Gabriel is beautiful, it's no longer open to the public and the museums (one each for men and for women) have nothing you won't see elsewhere. It's 20 minutes away by boat directly on the way to Zege Peninsula, which is why guides encourage people to stop here. The small island next door hosts the completely modern and, frankly, uninteresting Entos Eyesu (admission Birr100), which offers the novelty of monks and nuns living together. The tiny treasury has a few old books and pictures.

### Debre Maryam
MONASTERY

ደብረ ማርያም (admission Birr100, video camera Birr100) The original 14th-century (some say 12th-century) church at Debre Maryam was rebuilt by Tewodros in the 19th century. It's unattractive both outside and in and the treasury is meagre. The main reason to visit is that sometimes men make *tankwa* here. Also, it's across from the outlet of the Blue Nile. It's 15 minutes by boat and a short walk through coffee, mango and fig trees. In the dry season you can visit Debre Maryam by *tankwa*. Head north of Bahir Dar to just before the Nile bridge and then walk west about 1km to the lake on the road with the family planning sign. Locals pay Birr1.5 return, but you're unlikely to get it for less than Birr20.

### Narga Selassie
MONASTERY

ናርጋ ስላሴ (admission Birr100, video camera Birr100) Set in the middle of the lake on Dek Island, Narga Selassie is peaceful, atmospheric and little visited. Built in the mid-18th century, it has a Gonderian influence and the fine original paintings include a portrait of Mentewab and there's also a bas-relief of James Bruce (smoking his pipe) at the main entrance. It's three hours by boat and a two-minute walk from the landing.

### Dega Estefanos
MONASTERY
ደጋ እስጢፋኖስ (admission Birr100, video camera Birr100) One of the lake's most sacred monasteries, Dega Estefanos (men only) was rebuilt in the mid-19th century and though the church isn't too interesting it holds a good selection of treasures (including a 16th-century painting of the Madonna) and the mummified remains in glass coffins of five former Ethiopian emperors (13th to 17th centuries). One of the bodies is Zara Yaqob; one of the most important Ethiopian emperors. The founder of this monastery, locals believe, was a saint who sailed to the island in 1268 on a stone boat. The 'boat' is still visible halfway along the trail to the monastery. It's about 2½ hours from Bahir Dar and 45 minutes from Narga Selassie, up a steep half-hour-long trail.

### Tana Cherkos
MONASTERY
ጣና ጨርቆስ (admission Birr150, video camera Birr100) It's said the Ark of the Covenant was hidden at Tana Cherkos for 800 years, which would seem to indicate it's an interesting destination; but the present 19th-century church and its modern paintings are rather modest. Its unique feature is its ancient Judaic sacrificial stones. Tana Cherkos is 2½ hours from Bahir Dar by boat. From the landing it's a 30-minute walk uphill. Because most of the treasures of **Mitsele Fasiladas** (on an island just south of Tana Cherkos and a short walk from the landing) were stolen

in the 1990s, and the church is ordinary, few people visit, though the setting is attractive.

#### OUTLET OF THE BLUE NILE
You don't visit the outlet of the Blue Nile to say hello to the river. You visit to say goodbye to Lake Tana's water and wish it well on its 5223km journey to the Mediterranean. In the morning you'll see lots of birds and maybe a hippo or two. It's only 20 minutes from Bahir Dar.

Many people will tell you Lake Tana isn't really the great river's source, but, since some 60 rivers feed the lake, picking just one is meaningless. However, somehow a spring called **Gish Abay** (the village of Sekela near the spring is 39km east of the Addis Ababa road) has earned the local vote as the 'real' source and it's now a holy site where people come to bathe away their sins, though it's hardly worth the long trip. It feeds the **Bikolo Abay** (Little Abay) river, which the Addis Ababa road crosses on a two-lane bridge 45km southwest of Bahir Dar.

### ℹ Getting Around
There's no shortage of boat operators in Bahir Dar, and shifty commission agents lurk everywhere. People who've been happiest have booked boats through their hotel or the travel agencies listed earlier; also see p82. You could save money organising boats yourself at the landings across

### MARY & ZARA

The Virgin Mary is held in high esteem in Ethiopia. It often seems she's bigger than her son. No other saint has as many saint days and no other brings forth such genuine devotion.

It wasn't always like this though. It was the 15th-century King Zara Yaqob, a fanatical Christian, who elevated her to such heights. Zara Yaqob was a man of determination who rekindled the glory of Aksum, reunited the fractured kingdom and commissioned numerous controversial works of religious literature. He was also a vicious tyrant who executed monks who didn't accept his reforms, beat his own wife to death and had his son tortured and thrown in the slammer. But it was religion and the worship of the Virgin in particular that really got him excited. Paranoid that the world was full of fallen angels determined to bring evil to his court, he had a team of priests pace the corridors of his palace day and night reciting prayers and splashing holy water about. He also ordered all his subjects to affix a crucifix to their processions and have 'I renounce the accursed, I am the slave of Mary, mother of the Creator of the universe' tattooed on their left arm, 'I deny the devil' on their right and a crucifix on their foreheads (the latter is still common practice today).

Despite his more eccentric traits Zara Yaqob is regarded as one of the most important Ethiopian emperors both for holding the nation together and for his elevation of Mary.

from Bahir Dar University along the Gonder road, but few of the pilots speak English.

Prices are always negotiable, but the standard half-day tour to the Zege Peninsula, nearby island monasteries and the outlet of the Blue Nile costs Birr800 for a group of five people in a fibreglass boat with a 25HP engine. A short trip to Debre Maryam and the outlet is just Birr300 while a full-day trip out to distant islands will likely cost Birr2400. Always ask if a guide is included in the cost. Although last-minute arrangements are possible, it's best to arrange things the day before.

Before departing, ensure your boat has life jackets (demand to see them; don't take anyone's word for it) and spare fuel.

A ferry to the Zege Peninsula (Birr54) departs Bahir Dar at 7am (come at 6.30am to buy tickets) arriving at the landing near Ura Kidane Meret monastery around 8am and Afaf village 15 minutes later. It departs Afaf at 4pm. There are also a few minibuses to Afaf (Birr12, 1½ hours), the last returning to Bahir Dar around 4pm.

## Blue Nile Falls (Tis Abay)
### ጢስ አባይ

The Blue Nile looks like a sluggish beast as it meanders out of Lake Tana, but not far out of Bahir Dar you'll see the Nile in a very different mood. The river pours over the side of a sheer 42m-tall chasm and explodes into a melange of mists and rainbows (best at 10am) before continuing on its tumultuous path to Khartoum where it finally gets to kiss the White Nile.

The catch to this impressive scene is that hydroelectric projects upstream have stolen most of the energy from Tis Abay (adult/student/child Birr30/20/free, personal video cameras Birr50, mandatory guide Birr60, over 5 people Birr120; ⊙7am-5.30pm), the 'Nile that Smokes'. Though far smaller than its natural 400m-wide flow, the three-pronged waterfall is still jaw-droppingly huge in August and September. From around January or February until March it's now known as 'Blue Nile Shower' and it's not really worth a visit. The in-between time is still beautiful enough that most people enjoy the trip; though note that one of the hydro plants only operates on standby and if it's turned on during this time the waterfall gets turned off. You may want to ask fellow travellers who've recently been to the falls about the flow, as tourist industry operators won't always give you a straight answer.

The ticket office is at the very end of the road through the town of Tis Abay. The road to the falls starts 50m west of here and it's 1.5km to the start of a rocky footpath that

---

### JAMES BRUCE: IN SEARCH OF THE SOURCE

Half undressed as I was by the loss of my sash, and throwing my shoes off, I ran down the hill towards the little island of green sods, which was about two hundred yards distant...

...It is easier to guess than to describe the situation of my mind at that moment – standing in the spot which had baffled the genius, industry and enquiry of both ancients and moderns, for the course of near three thousand years.

*James Bruce, Travels to Discover the Source of the Nile (1790)*

One of the first European explorers in this part of Africa was a Scot named James Bruce. After serving as consul-general in Algiers, he set off in 1768 in search of the Nile's source: a puzzle that had preoccupied people since the time of the Egyptian pharaohs. After landing in Massawa, Eritrea, he made his way to the powerful and splendid court of Gonder, where he became close friends with Empress Mentewab.

In 1770 he reached the source of the Abay, the main river that empties Lake Tana. There he declared the mystery of the Nile's source solved. He dedicated his discovery to King George III and returned home to national acclaim.

In fact, Bruce had traced only the source of the *Blue* Nile River, the main tributary of the Nile. Not only that, but he'd been beaten to his 'discovery' (as he very well knew) over 150 years earlier by a Spanish Jesuit, Pedro Páez.

Of greater interest was the account of his journey, *Travels to Discover the Source of the Nile,* published in 1790. It remains a useful source of information on Ethiopia's history and customs. His contemporaries considered much of it a gross exaggeration, or even pure fiction. Given his earlier claims, it's no wonder.

leads down to a 17th-century Portuguese bridge (which was the first bridge to span the Blue Nile) along the so-called eastern route. From here the trail climbs up through a small village and a gauntlet of children selling souvenirs to reach the main viewpoints. Some people backtrack from here, but the better option is to take the suspension bridge over the narrow Alata River and walk down to the base of the falls. In the dry season you can swim at the bottom and walk behind the watery curtain. You can complete a circuit by using a path above the falls and crossing the river by motorboat. The **boat service** (one way Birr20) usually operates 7am to 6pm, but when the river runs too fast the boats can't cross. Look for crocs during dry-season mornings. The entire walk is about 5km and takes about 2½ hours with lots of gawping time. As it's not very steep, less energetic or mobile people may want to approach and return from the falls along this western route.

## ⓘ Getting There & Away

The falls are located 28km southeast of Bahir Dar down a bad dirt road. Buses from Bahir Dar leave about hourly for Tis Abay village (Birr13, one hour). The last bus back usually leaves about 4.30pm, but to be safe, plan to return around 3.30pm. You don't need to pay anyone to hold a seat for you. If you miss the bus, hitching back isn't tough, though it will probably be expensive.

The Ghion Hotel in Bahir Dar runs a daily tour at 3pm (and mornings if demand warrants) to the falls for Birr150 per person.

# GONDER & THE SIMIEN MOUNTAINS

The legendary city of Gonder and the nearby Simien Mountains National Park are a perfect marriage of history and beauty. Gonder is a modern town that has managed to grow and thrive without erasing much of its past, while the park's dramatic peaks and vast valleys offer scenery on par with any other place in Africa.

# Gonder ጎንደር

POP 227,100 / ELEV 2300M

It's not what Gonder is, but what Gonder was that's so enthralling. The city lies in a bowl of hills where tall trees shelter tin-roofed stone houses, but rising above these, and standing proud through the centuries, are the walls of castles bathed in blood and painted in the pomp of royalty. Often called the Camelot of Africa, this description does the royal city a disservice: Camelot is legend, whereas Gonder is reality.

Surrounded by fertile land and lying at the crossroads of three major caravan routes, it's easy to understand why Emperor Fasiladas (reigned 1632–67) made Gonder his capital in 1636. To the southwest lay rich sources of gold, civet, ivory and slaves, to the northeast lay Massawa and access to the Red Sea, and to the northwest lay Sudan and Egypt.

At the time of Fasiladas' death, Gonder's population already exceeded 65,000 and its wealth and splendour had become legendary. Drifting through the old palaces, banqueting halls and former gardens, it's not difficult to imagine the courtly pageantry, ceremony and intrigue that went on here.

The city flourished as a capital for well over a century before infighting severely weakened the kingdom (see The Rise and Fall of Gonder, p225). In the 1880s what remained of Gonder was extensively looted by the Sudanese Dervishes. Despite this, and further damage sustained by British bombs during the liberation campaign of 1941, much of Gonder remains intact.

Although Gonder is fairly spread out, it's still a great place to navigate on foot. The Italian-built piazza marks the centre of town and packs in most shops and services travellers need. The Royal Enclosure is just south of the piazza while the road leading north is dotted with restaurants and hotels.

## ⊙ Sights

**Royal Enclosure** PALACE

የፋሲለደስ ግቢ (Map p80; adult/student Birr100/75, personal video cameras Birr75; ☉8.30am-12.30pm & 1.30-6pm) The Gonder of yesteryear was a city of extreme brutality and immense wealth. Today the wealth and brutality are gone, but the memories linger in this amazing World Heritage Site. The entire 70,000-sq-metre compound containing numerous castles and palaces has been restored with the aid of Unesco. Knowledgeable, well-trained guides cost Birr100 and are well worth it.

*Fasiladas' Palace*

By far the most impressive, and also the oldest, building is Fasiladas' Palace, just inside the entrance gate. It stands 32m tall and has a crenulated parapet and four domed **towers**. Made of roughly hewn stones, it's reputedly the work of an Indian architect and shows an unusual synthesis of Indian, Portuguese, Moorish and Aksumite influences. The main floor was used as **dining halls** and a formal **reception area**. Note the wall reliefs, including several Stars of David, which trumpet Fasiladas' link to the Solomonic dynasty. The small room in the northern corner boasts its original beam ceiling and some faint frescoes. On the 1st floor, Fasiladas' **prayer room** has windows in four directions, each

# Gonder

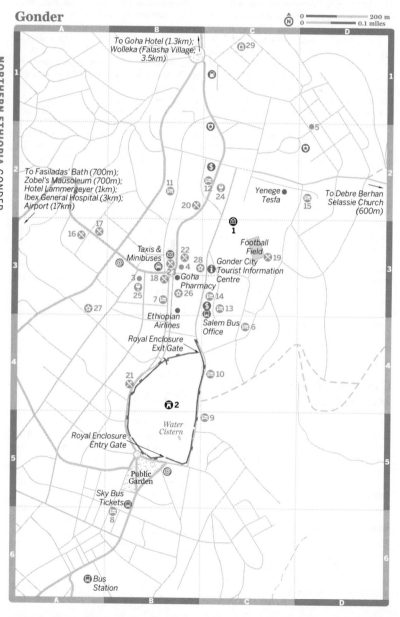

0                 200 m
0                 0.1 miles

overlooking Gonder's important churches. Religious ceremonies were held on the roof, and it was from here that he addressed his people. Above Fasiladas' 2nd-floor **bedroom** was the **watchtower**, from where it's (apparently) possible to see all the way to Lake Tana. Behind the castle are various ruined buildings, including the **kitchen** (domed ceiling), **steambath**, and **water cistern**.

### Palace of Iyasu I

To the palace's northeast is the saddle-shaped Palace of Iyasu I, with its unusual vaulted ceiling. The son of Yohannes I, Iyasu I (r 1682–1706) is considered the greatest ruler of the Gonderine period. The palace used to be sumptuously decorated with gilded Venetian mirrors and chairs, with gold leaf, ivory and beautiful paintings adorning the walls. Visiting travellers described the palace as 'more beautiful than Solomon's house'. Although a 1704 earthquake and British bombing in the 1940s have done away with the interior and most of the roof, its skeletal shell reeks of history.

### Other Southern Buildings

North of Iyasu's palace are the relics of its **banquet hall** and **storage facilities**. To the west is the quadrangular **library** of Fasiladas' son, Yohannes I (r 1667–82), which was plastered over by the Italians in a non-historic renovation. (In fact, all plaster found in the Royal Enclosure compound was added by the Italians.) Once an impressive palace decorated with ivory, only the tower and walls of **Fasiladas' Archive** remain. It sits northwest of the library.

### Northern Buildings

The compound's northern half holds vestiges of **Dawit's Hall**, known as the House of Song, in which many religious and secular ceremonies and lavish entertainments took place. Emperor Dawit (r 1716–21) also built the first of two **Lion Houses** (the second was built by Haile Selassie) where Abyssinian lions were kept until 1990. When Dawit came to a sticky end (he was poisoned in 1721), Emperor Bakaffa (r 1721–30) took up the reins and built his **palace** with a huge **banqueting hall** (the current ceiling was added by the Italians) and the impressive **stables**. Between the stables and Dawit's Hall is the **Turkish bath** *(wesheba)*, built by Iyasu I at the advice of a French physician to deal with his skin conditions. It apparently also worked wonders for those

**NORTHERN ETHIOPIA GONDER**

---

## Gonder

# Royal Enclosure

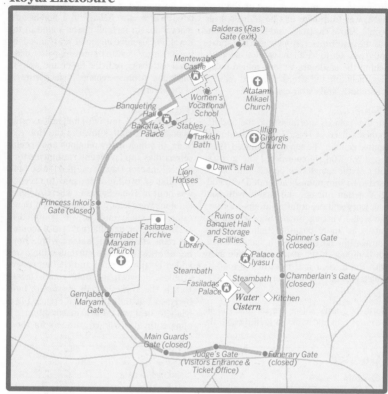

Balderas (Ras')
Gate (exit)

Mentewab's
Castle

Women's
Vocational
School

Atatami
Mikael
Church

Banqueting
Hall

Bakaffa's
Palace

Stables

Ilfign
Giyorgis
Church

Turkish
Bath

Dawit's Hall

Lion
Houses

Princess Inkoi's
Gate (closed)

Fasiladas'
Archive

Ruins of
Banquet Hall
and Storage
Facilities

Spinner's Gate
(closed)

Gemjabet
Maryam
Church

Library

Palace of
Iyasu I

Steambath

Steambath

Chamberlain's Gate
(closed)

Fasiladas
Palace

Water
Cistern

Kitchen

Gemjabet
Maryam
Gate

Main Guards'
Gate (closed)

Judge's Gate
(Visitors Entrance &
Ticket Office)

Funerary Gate
(closed)

suffering from syphilis! At the southern end you'll see the fire pit and the ceiling's steam vents. The Italians added windows and made it a kitchen.

Bakaffa's consort was responsible for the last palace, **Mentewab's Castle**, a two-storey structure that's now the site's office. Note the Gonderian cross being used as a decorative motif. Mentewab (r 1730–55) also built the **women's vocational school** to the front, where classes included facial tattooing and chicken cutting.

### Atatami Mikael Church

Atatami Mikael church, just outside the Royal Enclosure's exit gate, was built by Emperor Dawit III. The church itself is off-limits, but the interesting little **museum** (admission Birr25) has lots of beautiful illustrated manuscripts and a few other items like giant pots for making beer.

**Fasiladas' Bath**   HISTORIC BUILDING

የአጼ ፋሲለደስ መዋኛ (admission incl in Royal Enclosure ticket; ⊙8.30am-6pm) Around 2km northwest of the piazza lies Fasiladas' Bath, which has been attributed to both Fasiladas and Iyasu I. The large rectangular pool is overlooked by a charming building, thought by some to be a vacation home. It's a beautiful and peaceful spot, where snakelike tree roots digest sections of the stone walls.

Although the complex was used for swimming (royalty used to don inflated goat-skin lifejackets for their refreshing dips!), it was likely to have been constructed for religious celebrations, the likes of which still go on today. Once a year, it's filled with water for the **Timkat** (p19) celebration. After the water is blessed by the bishop, the pool becomes a riot of splashing water, shouts and laughter as a crowd of hundreds jumps in. The ceremony replicates Christ's baptism in the Jordan River and is seen as an important renewal of faith.

Just east of the main compound is **Zobel's Mausoleum**. Local legend states it's named after Yohannes I's horse, which ran so fast that he was able to escape some bandits he encountered while out hunting buffalo. Or, another tale says that it heroically brought Iyasu (Yohannes' son) back from Sudan after his father's death. Not only was the horse a good walker, but it could jump 25m in a single leap.

If you don't want to walk, minibuses (Birr2) leaving from near the piazza pass here. A contract *bajaj* is Birr15. You must obtain your ticket at the Royal Enclosure before visiting Fasiladas' Bath.

### Debre Berhan Selassie Church    CHURCH

ደብረ ብርሃን ስላሴ ቤተክርስቲያን (adult/ student Birr50/25, personal video camera Birr75; ⊙8am-12.30pm & 1.30-6pm) If it weren't for a swarm of bees, the beautiful church of Debre Berhan Selassie would have probably been destroyed like most of Gonder's other churches by the marauding Sudanese Dervishes in the 1880s. When the Dervishes showed up outside the gates of the church, a giant swarm of bees surged out of the compound and chased the invaders away. This was a lucky intervention: with its stone walls, arched doors, two-tiered thatch roof and well-preserved paintings, Debre Berhan Selassie is one of the most beautiful churches in Ethiopia.

The roof, with its rows and rows of winged **cherubs**, representing the omnipresence of God, draws most eyes. There's space for 135 cherubs, though 13 have been erased by water damage. Aside from the cherubs the highlights have to be the devilish Bosch-like depiction of hell and the Prophet Mohammed atop a camel being led by a devil. Although local tradition attributes most paintings to the 17th-century artist Haile Meskel, this is unlikely because the building only dates back to the late 18th century. The original circular church, created in the 1690s by Iyasu I, was destroyed by lightening.

A large **stone wall** with 12 rounded towers surrounds the compound and these represent the 12 apostles. The larger 13th tower (entrance gate) symbolises Christ and is shaped to resemble the Lion of Judah. If you have a keen eye, you'll be able to spot the lion's tail above the doorway in the wall west of the church.

Flash photography inside the church is forbidden. Priests offer tours but a small contribution for the church should be left afterwards.

### Empress Mentewab's
### Kuskuam Complex    PALACE

የእቴጌ ምንትዋብ ቁስቋም ደብር (admission Birr50, personal video cameras Birr75; ⊙8am-6pm) It might not be as well-preserved as the Royal Enclosure or as sacred as Debre Berhan Selassie, but what this royal compound, known as Kuskuam, lacks in order and holiness it more than makes up for in melancholy. The complex was built in 1730 for the redoubtable Empress Mentewab, after the death of her husband (Emperor Bakaffa). It's said that she chose to move out here because she was a bit too keen on boys and living out here would keep her out of gossip's way. Gossip and the boys didn't stay away though: according to locals, when James Bruce stayed here with the empress during his explorations of the highlands, he got to discover more than just the source of the Blue Nile.

Like the Royal Enclosure, it's made up of a series of buildings, including a long, castellated **palace** used for state receptions and to house the royal garrison. Its exterior is trimmed with red volcanic tuff; figures include St Samuel, a lion and the same Gonderian crosses on her palace in the Royal Enclosure. Her palace and several nearby buildings were damaged by the British during WWII.

There used to be a fine church here, but that was destroyed by the Dervishes and the rebuilt sanctuary is uninspiring. The star attraction in the adjacent **museum**, under one of the egg-shaped towers, is a small glass-fronted coffin with the remains of the empress, her son Emperor Iyasu II and her grandson Iyo'as, the last emperor of Gonder. Below the complex lies a series of tiny doll-sized mud-and-stick houses that religious students live in while training to become monks or priests.

The complex lies in the hills 4km northwest of town. A one-way *bajaj* from the piazza, taking in the palace and Fasiladas' Bath, should cost about Birr80 return.

### Wolleka (Falasha Village)    VILLAGE

ወለቃ (የፈላሻዎች መንደር) Just 3km north of Gonder, several craft stalls with 'Stars of David' and 'Falasha Village' signs signal what's really the *former* Falasha village of Wolleka. Once the home to a thriving population of Falashas (Ethiopian Jews), most were airlifted to Israel in the 1980s and to-day none remain. There are, however, a few original houses with interesting artwork on their fronts and the small **synagogue**; for Birr10 per person you can look inside, but be prepared for an entourage of persistent sales kids.

After the adoption of Christianity as the state religion, Falashas had their land confiscated for refusing to convert. To survive, many became skilled craftspeople. Research suggests Falashas may have provided the labour for the construction and decoration of Gonder's castles. Sadly, the pottery for which they were once famous has mostly degenerated into half-hearted art, though the figurine trinkets do make cool souvenirs. **Project Ploughshare Women's Crafts Training Center** is helping disadvantaged women rekindle this craft, along with traditional Amhara weaving and basketry. You can watch the women working Monday to Saturday and buy the high-quality pottery every day.

### Saturday Market                                  MARKET
የቅዳሜ ገበያ (◉8.30am-6pm) Originally the city's weekly market, Kidame Gebya is now packed throughout the week, though Saturday remains the biggest day. Sunday is rather quiet. Traditional clothes vendors are right at the top while the vegetable sellers use ancient-looking dirt perches in the back. It's 500m southwest of the bus station.

### Ras Gimb                                         MUSEUM
ራስ ግምብ Though its early history is murky (it was likely built in the 17th century though some say 18th) this attractive palace once served as a retreat for Haile Selassie, a residence for Italian generals and a torture chamber for the Derg. It's now under renovation to serve as a museum of Gonder's history that will include some of Haile Selassie's furniture and objects found at the palace and Portuguese Cathedral at Gorgora.

## ☞ Tours

The guides at the Royal Enclosure can be hired for any other place in town. The prices are fixed and posted at the entrance and you can walk, ride bikes, hop on local minibuses or charter a *bajaj* (around Birr70 an hour).

The following reliable agencies can arrange everything from city tours to Simien Mountains treks. Prices vary and negotiations are always in order. For more Simien Mountains tours and treks, see p89.

**Explore Abyssinia Travel**  WALKING, HORSE RIDING
(☏0581-118965; www.exploreabyssinia.com) This excellent company behind Circle Hotel, which also owns Lodge du Chateau, leads walking and horse-riding trips to the villages around Gonder. It also has a book exchange.

**Explore Simien Tours**                            TOURS
(☏0581-119066; fasilm_675@yahoo.com; Quara Hotel) A do-it-all agency with an excellent reputation.

**Simen Fox Trekking**                          TREKKING
(☏0918-770887; www.simenfoxtrekking.com; Terara Hotel) Trekking specialist.

**Simon Tour**                                       TOURS
(☏0911-733479;    www.simonethiopiatour.com) While the other agencies listed here have been around for a long time, this brand-new company lacks a track record. However, the owner seems to have his act together.

**Trek in Ethiopia Tours**                      TREKKING
(☏0911-904792; www.trekinethiopia.com) Run by former Simien Mountains trekking guide Alebachew Abebe. There is no office; call with questions or to arrange a meeting.

## ✹ Festivals & Events

Gonder is famous for its **Timkat** celebration (see Fasiladas' Bath p80) and **Meskel** is also big here. For more information on these festivals, see p19.

## 🛏 Sleeping

*Faranji* prices (often 100% or more above local prices) are the norm here, so always ask for a discount.

**TOP CHOICE** **Lodge du Chateau**       HOTEL $$$
(☏0918-152001;  www.lodgeduchateau.com;  dm/ s/d/tw incl breakfast US$20/45/50/50; 🅿@🛜) Doing things their own way, this owner-managed spot next to the Royal Enclosure has the friendliest service in town, an attention to detail and a real commitment to community involvement. The rooms are nicely decorated and have good mattresses and the dining room–lounge is perched high to make the best of the valley views.

**TOP CHOICE** **Lodge Fasil**              HOTEL $$
(☏0581-110637; s/d/tw incl breakfast US$30/40/ 40; 🅿🛜) A stone's throw from the Royal Enclosure's exit, this new place features eager staff and spotless rooms set back from traffic

noise among plenty of trees. Those on the upper level have pretty views of the valley below. Overall it has a good vibe.

### L-Shape Hotel
HOTEL $

(☑0918-787634; d Birr150-200, tw Birr300; P🛜) Rooms here are in better shape than the hallways would lead you to believe and the absence of *faranji* prices (though who knows how long this will last) makes it highly recommended, especially if you score a room with a view. The attractive two-level restaurant (serving a good pizza) below is popular with university students for its classy atmosphere.

### Taye Hotel
HOTEL $$$

(☑0581-112180; www.tayebelayhotel.com; s/d/ste incl breakfast US$60/70/85; P@🛜) Gonder's top digs, and thus the choice of most NGO and UN workers, lords over the heart of the city. Some of the front-facing rooms have enormous balconies, others have the tiniest balconies you've ever seen, but all have nice views. All rooms feature full satellite TV and other mod-cons, plus a pool, gym and sauna are in the works.

### Central Gonder Hotel
HOTEL $

(☑0581-117020; d Birr288) Beyond a little wear and tear, the rooms, with satellite TV and some with good people-watching views, can't be faulted and the inflated *faranji* prices are definitely open to negotiation. The food is pretty good too.

### Goha Hotel
HOTEL $$$

(☑0581-110634; www.gohahotel.com; s/d/ste incl breakfast US$59/73/100; P@🛜) Perched on a high natural balcony providing a vantage point that would make a soaring vulture sick with envy, the views are what make this stone-walled hotel a popular choice. The rooms have been gussied up with wool wall hangings and embroidered bedding and are comfortable, but not worth the price. A *bajaj* into town costs Birr70.

### Hotel Lammergeyer
HOTEL $$

(☑0581-122903; belayadu@yahoo.com; s/d/tw incl breakfast US$29/41/41; P🛜) Close to Fasiladas' Bath, this clean and original place, which receives lots of positive feedback, has a warm, family vibe; bright rooms with modern furnishings; and good service. There's a decent cafe-restaurant and a kiddie pool.

### Belegez Pension
PENSION $

(☑0918-772997; d without/with bathroom Birr115/170; P) Formerly wearing the crown of best-

value cheapie in Gonder, the small and simple rooms here are starting to decay. But with limited choices in this price range and a very traveller-aware staff it remains a good option.

### New Day Pension
PENSION $

(☑0924-507265; r without bathroom Birr60) The rooms here, set around a tiny courtyard behind a popular restaurant, are pretty rough, but the price is fair.

### Zozamba Hotel
HOTEL $

(☑0918-700584; d Birr250-300, tw Birr350; P) Between the piazza and Debre Berhan Selassie Church, this quiet new hotel is excellent value...if you're Ethiopian. But, even at *faranji* prices it's worth considering.

### Queen Taytu Pension
PENSION $

(☑0581-122898; d without bathroom Birr120, d/tw Birr200/300) This popular backpacker spot has the same broken doors and toilet seats you expect at cheaper places. It's worth considering, however, if they'll drop the price.

### Hibret Hotel
HOTEL $

(☑0581-120400; s without bathroom Birr160, s/d/tw Birr220/240/280) Near the bus station and a mosque, peace and quiet is not on the amenities list, but the rooms are clean and fairly well maintained.

## 🍴 Eating

TOP CHOICE/ Habesha Kitfo
ETHIOPIAN $

(mains Birr30-65) Traditionally decked out with wooden stools, cowhide chairs, and woven wool rugs (plus pet ducks roaming around), this place drips character and is the ideal spot in which to sample new Ethiopian dishes. *Kitfo* (minced beef or lamb like the French steak tartare) is the house speciality, of course, but this restaurant stands out by having a full vegetarian fasting platter available daily. Don't miss the art gallery downstairs.

TOP CHOICE/ Four Sisters
EUROPEAN, ETHIOPIAN $

(mains Birr50-90) The food here is fine, but it's the ambience, with stone walls and Debre Berhan Selassie–inspired paintings plus nightly traditional music, that sets it apart. Actually owned and operated by four sisters, the service is good too. It's pricier than other options, but makes for a fun evening and even locals come here for a special night out. The road is unlit, so take a torch. Women may want to ask them to call a *bajaj* if leaving late. Special programs, such as learning how to make *tej* (honey wine) and *injera* (Ethiopian pancakes) are available.

### EEPCo Coffee House
CAFE $

(macchiato Birr6) You'd be hard-pressed to find a Gonderian who doesn't consider the brew here the city's best coffee, and we think it serves the best cake.

### Tele Café
ETHIOPIAN $

(mains Birr17-46) Despite *faranji* prices, we rather like this popular breakfast spot. It serves good *ful* (broad bean and butter purée) and samosas and is a great piazza people-watching spot.

### Damera Top Restaurant
ETHIOPIAN $

(mains Birr35-69) The 'top' of the building, where this otherwise ordinary restaurant sits, provides a good view of the Royal Enclosure. It's busiest at lunch, but the photography is better during an early dinner.

### Habesha Coffee
CAFE $

(mains Birr29-92) A stylish cafe with great coffee, good food and terrible service.

### Ethiopia Café
ETHIOPIAN $

(drinks Birr8-15) This classic, though subtle, art-deco Italian cafe in the heart of the piazza is a throwback to the days of yesteryear, except for the modern use of *faranji* pricing.

### Quara Hotel
EUROPEAN, ETHIOPIAN $

(mains Birr25-89) While the menu doesn't break the mould, it does offer a few meals not often available in Ethiopia like curry-spiced noodles. Unfortunately, execution is inconsistent.

### Best Supermarket
SELF-CATERING

(⏰8am-8pm) Definitely earns its name.

The restaurants at **Taye Hotel** (mains Birr44-123) and **L-Shape Hotel** (mains Birr43-69) are expensive, but very good. Both serve above-average pizzas. **Elilta** and **Shewe Beye**, listed under Entertainment, are also good dining options.

##  Drinking

### Goha Hotel
BAR

(beer Birr18; 📶) There's nowhere better in town for a sunset drink than this hotel's lofty garden terrace. Besides the overpriced beers, there's a variety of local and imported wines.

### Golden Gate Bridge
BAR

(beer Birr12) A well-stocked bar in a room over the street that never gets boisterous and attracts those looking for a low-key night.

### Dashen House
BEER GARDEN

(drinks Birr15) The large outdoor terrace here is indisputably the town centre's most popular beer joint.

##  Entertainment

### Elilta
TRADITIONAL MUSIC, DANCE $

(admission free) There's traditional Gonderian music and dance on stage here nightly from 7pm to midnight. There's no English menu (mains Birr23 to Birr58), but pasta and lamb *tibs* are safe bets if nobody around can translate for you.

### Shewe Beye
COMEDY

(admission free; beers Birr15) Gonder produces Ethiopia's best *azmaris* (see Minstrels & Masenkos, p253). While many end up starring in Addis Ababa, there are still some good *azmari bets* (bars) here. This is the most fun and packed. Look for the signs with the lutes.

### Camelot House
CLUB

(admission free; beers Birr15) A dark and cosy modern club where the band plays and the people dance until at least 2am.

## Shopping

### Habesha Kitfo
HANDICRAFTS

This popular restaurant has an interesting gift shop and one of the owners is an artist who sells his paintings in the basement. His cherubic rocks, inspired by Debre Berhan Selassie Church, are a unique keepsake.

### Kindu Trust
HANDICRAFTS

(www.kindutrust.org; ⏰8.30am-noon & 2-5pm) This child-sponsorship charity has a small store selling baskets, banana art and beads made from recycled magazines. If you book in advance, they can also prepare a local lunch during your visit. Some items are also sold at Lodge du Chateau (p82).

## Information

### Dangers & Annoyances

Various 'guides' will seek you out, but they don't have any historical knowledge and they aren't allowed inside the Royal Enclosure. Their favourite scam is a half-day trip to the Simien Mountains, but this is impossible and they'll only take you to Wunenia or Kosoye.

You'll also need to deal with children seeking out tourists with improbable sob stories and apparently some even dress 'homeless' to pique your sympathy.

### Internet Access
**Facebook Internet Café** (per hr Birr15; ⊗8.30am-7.30pm)
**Galaxy Computer** (per hr Birr15; ⊗8am-8pm)

### Medical Services
**Goha Pharmacy** (✆0581-113978; ⊗8.30am-9.30pm) Helpful and well stocked.
**Ibex General Hospital** (✆0581-118273) Gonder's best medical facility has a 24-hour casualty and pharmacy.

### Money
**Dashen Bank** The branch north of the piazza has an ATM, as do some others further out of town.
**Wegagen Bank** Has an ATM inside Taye Hotel.

### Tourist Information
**Gonder City Tourist Information Centre** (✆0581-110022; ⊗8.30am-12.30pm & 1.30-5.30pm Mon-Sat, 8.30am-12.30pm Sun) One of the best tourist offices in Ethiopia, staff here go out of their way for visitors. They don't sell tours, though they often know when companies have clients looking for others to join them to share costs.

### ❶ Getting There & Away
#### Air
**Ethiopian Airlines** (✆0581-117688) flies twice daily to Addis Ababa (US$65, one hour) and once to Lalibela (US$41, two hours) via Aksum (US$45, 40 minutes).

#### Bus
It's a rare traveller who heads direct to or from Addis, but it can be done in 13 to 14 hours with the luxury buses. Sky Bus (Birr373, 5am) departs from the Royal Enclosure entrance gate and the ticket office is nearby in the Genet Café. Selam (Birr375, 5.30am) departs from the Royal Enclosure exit gate and has a ticket office at Taye Hotel. The Post Bus (Birr283, 4.30am) has Monday, Wednesday and Friday Gonder departures and Sunday, Tuesday and Thursday Addis departures. Ordinary Addis buses (Birr250, 5am) require an overnight stop along the way.

Shorter trips to Bahir Dar (Birr55 to Birr65, three hours) and Debark (Birr48, 2½ hours) are easiest by minibus, though there are early-morning buses too. For Aksum, catch a connection in Shire (Birr120, 10 to 11 hours, 5.30am).

There's nothing direct to Lalibela, but you can take the 5.30am bus (Birr85, four to five hours) or one of the minibuses (Birr160, four hours)

headed to Woldia and get off in Gashena where you can easily catch a connection, as long as you don't arrive too late.

For information about reaching Sudan, see p290.

### ❶ Getting Around
A shared taxi from the airport, which is 17km from town, costs Birr50 per person. Many hotels have free airport shuttles.

Chartering a *bajaj*/taxi to see Gonder's sights costs about Birr70/110 per hour, but you'll have to negotiate hard for this. Minibuses charge between Birr1 and Birr1.50 for hops around town. *Bajaj*, taxis and minibuses congregate just west of the piazza.

## Around Gonder
**WUNENIA & KOSOYE** ውንኒያ እና ኮሶዬ
Despite what anyone may tell you, the Simien Mountains are not visible from either of these two ridgetop viewpoints, 22km and 29km northeast of Gonder respectively, but the views are awesome nonetheless. At both, friendly local guides will lead you on walks of about an hour for a small tip. They're not mandatory at Wunenia, but they know the best viewpoints and can help you find gelada monkeys. Longer treks are also possible.

The **Befiker Kossoye Ecology Lodge** (✆0911-250828; www.semienkossoye.com; campsites US$20, s/tw incl breakfast US$65/80; ℗) at Kosoye isn't worth considering at this price, though low-season prices drop by half and the three-course set lunch or dinner (Birr150) in the attractive restaurant is welcome post-walk. Other lodges, including some simple *tukuls* (huts) at Wunenia, are in the pipeline. The tourist office in Gonder will have the latest updates.

Any minibus to Debark can drop you off.

**GORGORA** ጎርጎራ
POP 1500 / ELEV 1830M
The little lakeshore town of Gorgora, 60km southwest of Gonder, has a slow tropical vibe. It provides the chance to see rarely visited monasteries and makes a good excursion for birders. Mostly, it offers an easy, comfortable escape from the ordinary.

### ◉ Sights
With the exception of Debre Sina, you'll need a local guide to find these sights. Guides usually hang out at the Gorgora Port Hotel and charge Birr100 per day for a small group. Andrayano Tesema, who speaks pretty

good English (he's probably the only one), can also do birdwatching trips.

### Mussolini's Stele    MONUMENT

(Map p73) Gorgora was a hard-fought prize during the Italian occupation and on the way into town you'll pass Mussolini's stele, high on a hill, which commemorates the capture. In town, the historic-looking ruins on a much lower hill are nothing more than a recent, never-completed hotel.

### Church of Debre Sina    CHURCH

(Map p73; admission Birr100, personal video cameras Birr100) The most interesting relic of Gorgora's former days as a short-lived capital is the attractive Debre Sina church. Built in 1608 by Emperor Susenyos' son and future founder of Gonder, Fasiladas, on the site of a 14th-century monastery, it's decorated with fading original paintings. These are older and thus less vivid and complex than the paintings in the monasteries on the southern side of the lake and interesting because of the difference. Locals believe the 'Egyptian St Mary' painting (which is supposed to have come from Egypt, but looks no different than the other paintings), has the power to heal. The church's thatch roof and surrounding stone buildings lend this monastery a more ancient feel than most.

### FREE Susenyos' Old Palace    PALACE

(Map p73) Emperor Susenyos (r 1607–32) built his palace (known by locals as Susenyos Ghimb) on a peninsula (called Old Gorgora) 10km west of town, which can be reached in an hour by boat. Compared with Gonder, it's a shambles but historical architecture buffs should make the trip.

### FREE Portuguese Cathedral    CATHEDRAL

(Map p73) Near Susenyos' palace is the Portuguese Cathedral he funded. The decrepit state (due largely to a 1995 earthquake) symbolises his failed attempt to force Catholicism on his people. The Spanish government has funded some restoration and research here. Except in the rainy season, you can drive close to it or walk (three to four hours each way) the whole way from town. The road begins 7.4km north of Gorgora in Abrecha village, the one with the tourism sign at the junction.

### Lake Tana Monasteries    MONASTERIES

Of Tana's four other far northern monasteries, all west of Gorgora, Mandaba Medhane Alem (Map p73; admission Birr100, men only), which hosts ancient biblical manuscripts and some of Ethiopia's most dedicated priests, is the only one that most consider worth a trip; even though its paintings only date to 1991. It takes 30 minutes by boat, 90 minutes by *tankwa* (available at Tim & Kim Village lodge) or two hours walking from town.

If you're a serious monastery lover, or just want to stretch your legs on the way to and from the palace, the other three monasteries are Angara Tekla Haimanot (Map p73; admission by donation, men only) where the current church was built by Haile Selassie; Birgida Maryam (Map p73; admission by donation, men only), the most rewarding of the three, known for its jungle and dedicated monks; and Galila (Map p73; admission by donation, men only), which is the oldest.

## 🛏 Sleeping & Eating

### TOP CHOICE Tim & Kim Village    LODGE $$

(☎0920-336671; www.timkimvillage.com; campsites with own tent Birr90, with hired tent s/d Birr200/250, s/d Birr460/575; P) Just over the hill west of Gorgora, this Dutch-run spot is in an idyllic little lakeside valley. The six solar-powered thatch-and-stone cottages are cosy and the welcome is warm. Tim leads day and overnight canoeing and trekking trips and you can paddle your own *tankwa*. Meals are normally only available for guests, but with notice day guests (Birr25) are usually welcome. Some proceeds go toward community projects.

### Gorgora Port Hotel    HOTEL $

(☎0583-467000; campsites Birr50, s/d/tw without bathroom Birr60/120/205, d/tw 200/325, 3-bedroom cottage Birr450; P) An old, rather than historic, hotel with a range of rooms, but all except Mengistu's old cottage are tired and just waiting to be revived. Electricity and water (cold showers only) are sporadic, but available more often than not. It's the relaxing flowered garden and lakeshore setting that are recommended and many people do enjoy a night here. The restaurant (mains Birr12 to Birr30) has decent food; the catfish cutlet is the speciality of the house.

### Tana Bir Pension    PENSION $

(d without bathroom Birr35-50; P) Gorgora's third and final choice has dark and dirty rooms and appalling toilets. It's the green, unsigned-in-English place just outside the entrance to the Port Hotel.

### ❶ Getting There & Around

A daily bus departs Gonder (Birr26; two to three hours) at 5.30am and another when full, usually around noon. The second bus sometimes takes up to five hours. The buses depart Gorgora at 5.30am and 8am.

The ferry sails to Bahir Dar every Thursday at 6am (Birr253, 1½ days). See p71 for more information. Buy tickets at the Lake Tana Transport Enterprise office (next to Gorgora Port Hotel) up to two days before.

Boats for touring the monasteries out on the lake are available through this same office. Ask your guide or someone at your hotel to call. It's Birr1325 out to the palace and monasteries. Fishermen will charge less, but their boats won't have roofs or life vests.

**GUZARA CASTLE**   የጉዛራ ቤተ-መንግስት

Though there's little solid evidence about its history, this tall castle (Map p73; admission Birr50) peering out over Lake Tana could have been built in the 1580s by Emperor Za-Dengel, founder of the Gonder dynasty, and thus would have been the prototype of Gonderian design. Or, it may have been built later by Emperor Fasiladas. The attractive ruins are fun to explore, but probably not worth a detour unless you have your own transportation. Someone will show up to collect the entry fee and try to charge you Birr100 for guiding services, which isn't necessary. It's 74km south of Gonder and then east up a steep 1.3km 4WD track.

## Simien Mountains National Park
የሲሜን ተራሮች
ብሔራዊ ፓርክ

No matter how you look at them, the Simien Mountains are awesome. This massive plateau, riven with gullies and pinnacles, offers tough but immensely rewarding trekking along the ridge that falls sheer to the plains far below. It's not just the scenery (and altitude) that will leave you speechless, but also the excitement of sitting among a group of gelada monkeys (see the boxed text, p274) or watching magnificent walia ibex joust on rock ledges. Whether you come for a stroll or a two-week trek, the Simiens make a great companion to the Historical Circuit's monument viewing.

Thanks to the combination of scenery and wildlife, the park is a World Heritage Site. However, it's long been on the World Heritage in Danger list due to the large number of people living in the park and the local authorities' lack of serious action on the problem. Despite this, as one of Africa's most beautiful ranges, the Simiens aren't to be missed.

### Geography & Geology

Comprising one of Africa's principal mountain massifs, a number of peaks rise above 4000m, including Ethiopia's highest, 4543m-tall Ras Dashen. (It's actually Ras Dejen, though to avoid confusion we use the common-but-incorrect name.) It's touted by Ethiopian tourism officials as the fourth-highest mountain in Africa; it's actually the 10th.

The Simiens' landscape is incredibly dramatic. It was formed by countless eruptions, some 40 million years ago; layer upon layer of molten lava piled up. The subsequent erosion produced the mountains' jagged and spectacular landscapes. The famous pinnacles that sharply and abruptly rise from the surrounding landscape are volcanic necks, the solidified plumbing of the ancient volcanoes.

### Ecology

The park extends from 1600m to 4543m in elevation and much of its 412 sq km lies within the 'Afro-alpine' zone, above 3200m, but there's also heath forest and high montane landscapes.

The highlands are home to three of Ethiopia's larger endemic mammals: the walia ibex (population estimated around 1100), the gelada monkey (5000) and the elusive Ethiopian wolf (100). While wolves are rarely encountered (Chenek offers the best chance) you're nearly guaranteed to meet hundreds-strong troops of gelada monkeys (those near Sankaber are the most tame) and stand a good chance of seeing the walia ibex (especially around Chenek), which are found only in the Simien Mountains. Other notable mammals are rock hyraxes, jackals, Menelik's bushbucks, klipspringers and leopards.

The often-seen thick-billed raven and the less common black-headed siskin, wattled ibis, spot-breasted plover and Abyssinian woodpecker are some of the 16 Ethiopian–Eritrean endemic birds. Though common, one of the most memorable sights is the low-soaring lammergeyer.

### Planning

Although organising trekking yourself at park headquarters in Debark is straightforward,

# Simien Mountains National Park

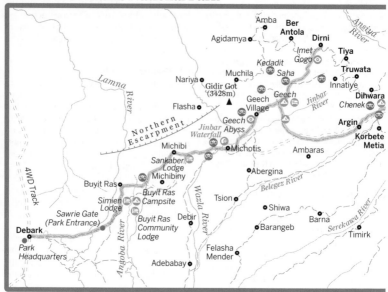

it can take up to two hours. It's best to arrive the afternoon before you plan to trek.

### When to Go

December to March is the driest time. In October, after the rains, the scenery is greenest. During the main rainy season, between June and September, mist often obscures the views and trails can be slippery. However, you'll usually get several hours of clear, dry weather for walking since the rain tends to come in short, sharp downpours. Wildflowers come out in August and last until October, except the ivory-coloured Abyssinian rose, an Ethiopian endemic, which blooms March to May.

Daytime temperatures are consistently between 11.5°C and 18°C, while 3°C is typical at night. Between December and April night-time temperatures often dip below freezing.

### Park Fees

Park fees are payable at the **park headquarters** (☏0918-704211; admission per day Birr90, vehicle Birr20; ◷8.30am-12.30pm & 1.30-5.30pm) in Debark. During the busy season, hours are extended.

Entrance fees won't be refunded once paid. However, if mules, cooks, guides and scouts aren't used (because of bad weather

or acclimatisation difficulties), their fees can be refunded.

### Maps

The most useful trekking map is produced by the Institute of Geography, University of Berne, Switzerland: the *Simen* [sic] *Mountains Trekking Map* (2003; 1:100,000). It's sold all around Gonder, at Debark's Simien Park Hotel and at park headquarters for Birr300.

### Equipment

Mattresses (Birr40 per day), sleeping bags (Birr40 per day), two-person tents (Birr60 per day) and cooking equipment including gas stoves (Birr50 per day for two people) can be hired at park headquarters. Tents should be checked carefully and using two sleeping bags ensures a warm night.

### Supplies

Trekking foods such as biscuits, pasta, tomato sauce, milk powder, packet soups, tinned tuna and Snickers bars are available in Debark, but Gonder is a better place to stock up as Debark's shops sometimes run out. Debark also has a bakery.

Outside Debark, there are no shops, though you can buy eggs, chickens and sheep at villages. If you don't have a cook,

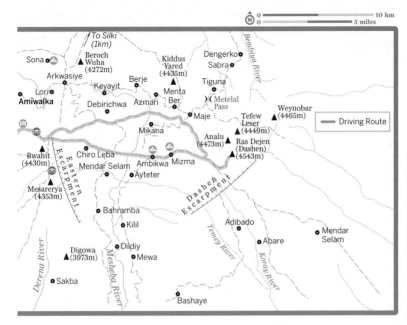

mule handlers will gladly kill, skin and roast a sheep if they can tuck in too. Water is available during the trek, but should be treated.

### Guides, Scouts, Cooks & Mule Men

Cooks, scouts, mules and guides are all organised at park headquarters. 'Scouts' (armed park rangers) are compulsory (Birr75 per day). Guides (Birr200 per day) are only required for people travelling with an agency, but highly recommended for their knowledge of the mountains and command of English. Some trekkers, unable to communicate with the scout, end up regretting not having a guide along. They're trained by the national park on courses established by an Austrian team. In general the guides are excellent. We've heard that some try to rush their clients on the final day to get home sooner, though; should this happen, refuse to play along and report it when you return. The guides work on a rota basis directly with the park, but you can request a particular guide if, for instance, you hear a good report from a fellow traveller.

Cooks cost Birr120 per day (cooking for one to six people), a welcome luxury for some. Porters aren't available, but mules (Birr60 per day) with handlers (Birr70 per day) are. Two handlers can handle three mules and each mule can carry 45kg. If you plan on covering two days' worth of trekking in one, you'll have to pay your team double for the day.

Guides, scouts, cooks and mule handlers should bring their own food and they usually do when the trekkers aren't hiring a cook. Regardless, you should make sure the park official organising your trip and/or your guide ensures the team is not going to look to you for sustenance. Or, just bring extra packets of rice etc and make the team happy.

See p280 for post-trek tipping advice.

### Organised Treks

There are numerous tour operators and travel agencies in Addis Ababa (see p295) and several more in Gonder (p82) that can arrange transport, guides, equipment rental and food. However, they charge you more for exactly the same services that you can easily arrange yourself at park headquarters. On the other hand, they probably have quality camping gear.

Some of the park's top guides, such as Shiferaw Asrat (☏0918-776499; www.simien trek.com), Nurlign Hassen (☏0910-373904; www.simienmountainstour.com) and Birhan Asmamaw (☏0918-731724; www.simientrekguide. com), also organise all-inclusive trips starting in Gonder or Addis, which should be cheaper than going through one of the bigger agencies.

## 🏃 Trekking

The foot that is restless, will tread on a turd.

*Ethiopian proverb*

Once on the mountains you'll mostly be following centuries-old paths that crisscross the slopes and connect villages with pasturelands, but sometimes you'll also use the main park road. On some stretches the walking is fairly level, but there are long, steep climbs and descents in many places.

Be sure to allow time for acclimatisation, particularly if you fly to Gonder right after arriving in Ethiopia. Review the Safety Guidelines for Trekking and Responsible Trekking boxed texts.

### Choosing a Trekking Route

Most people trek for four or five days and begin in Debark. In four you can trek to Geech and back; with an extra day you could get to Chenek, taking in Mt Bwahit. If time is of the essence then in two days you could walk from Debark to Sankaber and back; add a third day and you can get to Geech, which has the most spectacular scenery. With eight days to play with, you could summit Ras Dashen.

Many people maximise their mountain experience by using vehicles to access Sankaber and/or Chenek. A minibus can get you to Sankaber year-round, but you'll need 4WD to reach Chenek during the rainy season. Arranging pick-up or drop-off at Chenek allows a long but satisfying three-day trek to/from Debark.

If you have time, strong legs and a hatred of doubling back, you could finish your trek at Adi Arkay, 75km north of Debark. This allows a mix between highland and lowland scenery and the views up the valleys are just as amazing as the views down into them. Note that since it takes the guides, mules and other members of your team two days to return to Debark from Adi Arkay, you must pay two days' extra fee. For further details see p91.

Though it's rarely done, guides can even take you all the way to Lalibela. You'll need to swim across some rivers, carry food for nearly the entire 15 to 17 days and will probably have to purchase rather than hire the mules.

### DEBARK-TO-CHENEK TREK

The following Debark-to-Chenek trek is the classic five-day route. The times have been estimated in consultation with local guides, but times vary from person to person and also depend on whether exact routes are followed.

#### DEBARK TO BUYIT RAS (10KM; THREE TO FOUR HOURS)

Sankaber can be reached in a single day, but many trekkers prefer to (or, if they arrive from Gonder that day, *must*) break at Buyit Ras, where there's an abundance of gelada monkeys. There's also a community lodge and camping spot with beautiful views or the expensive Simien Lodge. Some people prefer to drive to Buyit Ras, bypassing the heavily populated areas outside the park, and trek to Sankaber (13km; three to four hours) from there.

#### BUYIT RAS TO GEECH CAMP VIA SANKABER (25KM, SEVEN TO EIGHT HOURS)

The road will take you straight to Sankaber, but the scenic route along the escarpment

---

## SAFETY GUIDELINES FOR TREKKING

Before embarking on a trek, consider the following points to ensure a safe and enjoyable experience.

» Pay any fees and possess any permits required by local authorities.

» Be sure you are healthy and feel comfortable walking for a sustained period.

» Obtain reliable information about physical and environmental conditions along your intended route (eg from park authorities).

» Trek only in regions, and on trails, within your realm of experience.

» Be aware that weather conditions and terrain vary significantly from one region, or even from one trail to another. Seasonal changes can significantly alter any trail. These differences influence what you should wear and what equipment you carry.

» Ask officials before you set out about the environmental characteristics that can affect your trek and how you should deal with them if they arise.

## RESPONSIBLE TREKKING

Trekking in Ethiopia has the potential to put great pressure on the environment. You can help preserve the ecology and beauty of the area by taking note of the following information.

» Carry out all your rubbish. Never ever bury it.

» Minimise the waste you must carry out by taking minimal packaging and taking no more food than you'll need.

» Where there's no toilet, at lower elevations bury your faeces in a 15cm-deep hole (consider carrying a lightweight trowel for this purpose). At higher altitudes soil lacks the organisms needed to digest your faeces, so leave your waste in the open where UV rays will break it down – spreading it facilitates the process. Always carry out your toilet paper (zip-lock bags are best). With either option make sure your faeces is at least 50m from any path, 100m from any watercourse and 200m from any building.

» Don't use detergents or toothpaste within 50m of watercourses, even if they're biodegradable.

» Stick to existing tracks and avoid shortcuts that bypass a switchback. If you blaze a new trail straight down a slope, it will erode the hillside with the next heavy rainfall.

» Avoid removing any plant life as they keep topsoils in place.

» Try to cook on lightweight kerosene, alcohol or Shellite (white gas) stoves instead of burning dead erica wood or eucalyptus. Never burn indigenous trees.

» Be aware of local laws, regulations and etiquette about wildlife and the environment.

» Never feed animals, as it messes with their digestive system and leads them to become dependent on hand-outs.

» If camping, try to camp on existing sites. Where none exist, set up away from streams on rock or bare ground, never over vegetation.

isn't to be missed. There are particularly good views between Michibi and Sankaber. From Sankaber to Geech is between four and five hours' walk.

### GEECH CAMP TO CHENEK VIA IMET GOGO (20KM, SEVEN TO NINE HOURS)

Geech to Chenek could take about five to six hours, but you'd be crazy not to take in Imet Gogo, around 5km northeast of Geech. The promontory, at 3926m, affords some of the most spectacular views of the Simien Mountains. It adds about 1½ hours one way. To make a day trip of it, you could also visit the viewpoints at Saha and Kedadit (2.5km, 30 minutes) and then return to Geech Camp.

From Imet Gogo you have two choices: the first is to return to Geech by your outward route, then head directly south and back across the Jinbar River to where you'll meet the dirt road that leads to Chenek. The alternative, which is harder but more scenic, is to follow the escarpment all the way to Chenek.

Chenek is probably the best spot in the Simien Mountains for wildlife. A short walk away often brings you to a herd of walia ibex

and near Chenek is **Korbete Metia**, a stunning spot where lammergeyers are often seen.

### CHENEK TO MT BWAHIT & RETURN (6KM, FIVE TO SIX HOURS)

If you can spare more time, the ever-tempting summit of Mt Bwahit (4430m) lies to the southeast of Chenek camp.

### RETURN ROUTES

For the return journey you can either retrace your footsteps (Sankaber is seven to eight hours away from Chenek), though most people just hike back along the road.

### CLIMBING RAS DASHEN

Ras Dashen, frankly, doesn't offer a great deal beyond the satisfaction of 'bagging it'. And thanks to an odd perspective from its summit, nearby peaks actually look higher. This has led disgruntled trekkers to drag their guides up the other peaks, repeatedly musing the 'one over there' is higher! It's not.

If you want to skip the initial trek, you can drive to Chenek and start the climb there. But, even though this trek only takes three days the park will charge you for six!

### CHENEK TO AMBIKWA (22KM, EIGHT TO NINE HOURS)

Heading on from Chenek, the first day takes you along a track leading eastward and then southeastward up towards a good viewpoint on the eastern escarpment north of Mt Bwahit. To the east, across the vast valley of the Mesheba River, you can see the bulk of Ras Dashen.

### AMBIKWA TO RAS DASHEN & RETURN (17KM, EIGHT TO 10 HOURS)

Most trekkers stay two nights at Ambikwa and go up to the summit of Ras Dashen on the day in between. It's a good idea to start at first light. If you don't have a mule man, it's recommended that you hire another scout here to guard your tent for the day.

At Ras Dashen there are three distinct points, and much discussion about which is the true summit. The total walk from Ambikwa to reach the highest summit is about five to six hours. If you want to knock off the others, add two to three hours for each. Returning by the same route takes about three to four hours. Although there's some scrambling at the very end, overall the trek isn't very difficult.

### RETURN ROUTES

Most trekkers return from Ambikwa to Debark (77km; three days) along the same route to Chenek and then follow the road to Sankaber.

One alternative is to trek from Ambikwa to **Arkwasiye**, northeast of Chenek, taking in the nearby peaks of **Beroch Wuha** (4272m) and **Silki** (4420m). From Arkwasiye to **Adi Arkay** will take two to three days of strenuous walking. The total route from Ambikwa to Adi Arkay is about 65km (three to five days). Note that facilities down here are very basic and you may end up sleeping in villages. From the last campsite it's two hours to Adi Arkay, which lies 75km north of Debark. From there you can continue to Aksum in stages using minibuses or hitchhiking.

### DAY TRIPS

It's only a two-hour dry-season drive to Chenek, which leaves lots of time for strolling, taking photos, and lounging with gelada monkeys at various spots along the way. During the rainy season the narrow **Jinbar Waterfall**, estimated to drop 500m, is an almost mandatory stop. It's unsigned 4km after Sankaber down a short (15-minute) muddy trail.

The six- or seven-hour roundtrip walk from the road near Ambaras to the amazing **Imet Gogo** viewpoint would be a popular day trip if the park authorities didn't insist on charging tourists the price of a two-day trip. (Park guides, knowing this policy is taking away business from them, have protested and it could change.)

Although there'll be precious little time actually in the park, you can drive there and back from Gonder in a day.

## 🛏 Sleeping & Eating

### DEBARK

Hotels in Debark tend to overcharge *faranji;* always request a discount.

**Simien Park Hotel**　　　　　　　HOTEL $
(☏0581-170005; s/d without bathroom Birr80/100, s/d/tw Birr200/250/300; 🅿) About 1km north of park headquarters, this is the most popular hotel and it's often booked solid. It's not the rooms that inspire the loyalty, it's the fact that it has the most reliable hot water (and just plain water) supply. Service is friendly and the food (mains Birr35 to Birr55) is fine too. Debark's only internet cafe is next door.

**Unique Landscape Hotel**　　　　HOTEL $
(☏0581-170152; www.uniquelshotel.com; d/tw/tr Birr250/300/450; 🅿) The rooms here are almost as good as at the neighbouring Simien Park Hotel and the food (mains Birr35 to Birr63) is even better.

**Simien Long View**　　　　　　　HOTEL $
(☏0581-170563; d/tw Birr200/300; 🅿) Not as good as 'Unique', but cheaper.

**Berhane Lewath Hotel**　　　　　HOTEL $
(☏0918-033456; s/d Birr50/100) Behind a busy bar, this was one of the first hotels in Debark, and it shows. You'll be hoping you don't need to use the toilet often. There's no shower, but the owners let *faranji* wash (cold water) in their house out back.

### ON THE MOUNTAINS

Sleeping and eating with locals used to be normal, but it's now actively discouraged by guides because they've dealt with so many trekkers complaining about the basic conditions. Your bed will most likely be the floor and you'll share space with children, chickens, cows and fleas.

**Camping**　　　　　　　　CAMPGROUND $
(per night Birr10) With a few exceptions, you're required to camp at the official sites. The three busy highland camps have showers and all the camps have long-drop loos as well as huts for your guides and scouts.

**Community Lodges**  HOSTEL $
(dm Birr80) Funded by the Austrian government and managed by locals, these simple two-room, four-bed dorms (at Buyit Ras, Geech and Chenek) offer an alternative to camping; though you should still bring a sleeping bag. Guests staying in them must still pay the park camping fee. Local meals (pasta, *tibs*, etc) and drinks are available.

**Sankaber Lodge**  HOSTEL $
(dm Birr80) Similar to the community lodges, but without meals, this park-run lodge has 20 beds.

**Simien Lodge**  LODGE $$$
(☑0582-310741; www.simiens.com; s & tw incl breakfast US$160-170; P) At 3260m this is Africa's highest hotel. The thatch-and-stone *tukuls* are large and comfy and most guests enjoy their stay, but also feel they don't get nearly enough in return for the four-star price. Although the situation has improved, hot water still can't be guaranteed and the featured solar-powered underfloor heating is largely ineffective. Reviews of the food (three-course set meal US$12; Dashen beer Birr40), on the other hand, are mostly positive. The *faranji* owner funds local charity projects. There's a van for picking up guests in Gonder.

### ❶ Getting There & Away

Two morning buses and lots of minibuses run from Debark to Gonder (Birr48, 2½ hours). The only bus to Shire (for Aksum) is the Gonder service that passes through Debark around 8am, but it's often full. If you want to guarantee a seat, the national park office, your guide or hotel will reserve you a place by getting somebody in Gonder to ride in your seat between Gonder and Debark. They charge Birr300 to Birr350 for this service; arrange it a day in advance. Hitching is possible, but you may need more than one day to reach Shire.

### ❶ Getting Around

There's usually a bus at 6am from Debark to Janamora, which can drop trekkers anywhere along the way; you'll probably need to pay Birr100 no matter where you get off. It can't be used on the return trip because there's almost no chance of a free seat. Convincing your guide to let you use the occasional Isuzu supply trucks is likely to be tough since it's illegal, but some trekkers who get to Chenek and find they've had their fill of the mountains manage to do it, albeit at an extortionate rate.

The park gate opens at 6am and driving is not permitted before this or after 6pm. Guides can arrange minibus and 4WD hire, though the latter can be very expensive because it usually comes from Gonder. Minibuses can reach everywhere most of the year, but 4WD is required to go beyond Sankaber between July and September.

# AKSUM & THE FAR NORTH

Despite its captivating mix of influential historical sights and small-town life, Aksum is the place most likely to be skipped on shortened versions of Historical Circuit tours, but if you have the time, don't miss it. From mountaintop monasteries to underground tombs, there's a fantastic mix of history and adventure.

## Shire ሺሬ
POP 57,200 / ELEV 1953M
The sun-blinded and dusty town of Shire, marked on some maps as Inda Selassie, is of interest to travellers only because it provides a link with Aksum, 60km to the east.

If you get stuck in Shire (very possible if you arrive here after 5pm) there are some decent places to sleep. The **Gebar Shire Hotel** (☑0344-443427; www.gebarshirehotel.com; d without bathroom Birr240, d incl breakfast Birr477-720, tw Birr653; P@) is an almost-flash hotel on the main roundabout in the centre of town; the only thing to criticise is the high *faranji* price. The lunch-stop of choice for most tour operators is **Africa Hotel** (☑0344-440101; d without bathroom Birr105, d & tw Birr125-155, mains Birr25-95; P) because the food is decent and it tends to come quickly. The rooms are less popular because they're loud and some have an odour, but they outshine the competition at this price. The **National Hotel** (☑0912-086151; d without bathroom Birr40, d Birr58; P) behind the bus station has ragged cold-shower rooms at a fair price.

There are a few buses and many minibuses (Birr23, 1½ hours) to Aksum and one morning bus to Gonder (Birr120, 10 to 11 hours, 5.30am). Travel times to Gonder will drop considerably as road paving progresses.

## Aksum አክሱም
POP 54,000 / ELEV 2130M
Aksum is a riddle waiting to be solved. Did the queen of Sheba really call the town's dusty streets home? Does the very same Ark of the Covenant that holds Moses' 10

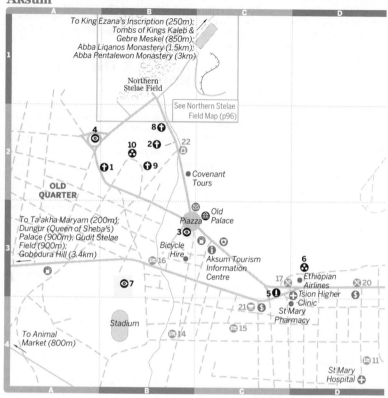

Commandments reside in a small Aksum chapel? Are there still secret hordes of treasure hidden inside undiscovered tombs? And what exactly do those famous stelae signify?

Dr Neville Chittick once described Aksum (often incorrectly spelled Axum) as 'the last of the great civilisations of Antiquity to be revealed to modern knowledge'. Yet even today, despite being one of the most important ancient sites in sub-Saharan Africa, this Unesco World Heritage Site has revealed only a tiny fraction of its secrets, and an exploration of its ruined tombs and palaces is sure to light a spark of excitement.

Aksum is more than just a collection of lifeless ruins, though. Proudly Tigrian, the town remains rural at heart and has a vibrancy, life and continuing national importance very rarely found at ancient sites. Pilgrims still journey here in the thousands to pay homage at its great churches and what they have no doubt is the magical Ark of the Covenant.

## History

The early history of Aksum, like most Ethiopian history, is shrouded in such a fog of legend that the truth remains largely unknown. While debate continues between historians and the majority of Ethiopians about whether or not Aksum really was the Queen of Sheba's capital in the 10th century BC, what's certain is that a high civilisation started to rise here as early as 400 BC.

By the 1st century AD, Greek merchants knew Aksum as a great city and the powerful capital of an extensive empire. For close to 1000 years, Aksum dominated the vital sea-borne trade between Africa and Asia and the kingdom was numbered among the ancient world's greatest states. But then, quite suddenly, the power of Aksum collapsed and the city turned into a forgotten backwater. Only now, a millennium later, are archaeologists starting to take a serious interest in the city. For more informa-

## Aksum

### ◉ Sights
1 Arbatu Ensessa Church .......................B2
2 Ark of the Covenant...........................B2
3 Basket Market....................................B3
4 Da'Ero Ela Fig Tree .............................A2
5 Ezana Park.........................................C3
6 King Bazen's Tomb.............................D3
7 Main Market......................................B3
8 New Church of St Mary of Zion..........B2
9 Old Church of St Mary of Zion............B2
10 Throne Stones...................................B2

### ◉ Activities, Courses & Tours
Abune Yemata Tours & Travel...(see 13)

### ◉ Sleeping
11 Abyssinia Hotel ...................................D4
12 Africa Hotel...........................................F3
13 Ark Hotel...............................................F3
14 Huruy Hotel ..........................................B4
15 Kaleb Hotel...........................................C4
16 Tekla Haimanot Pension......................B3

### ◉ Eating
17 AB Traditional Restaurant...................C3
18 Abinet Hotel..........................................E3
19 Atse Yohanes International
    Restaurant .........................................F3
20 Ezana Café............................................D3

### ◉ Drinking
21 Nati Juice .............................................C4

### ◉ Shopping
22 Abyssinia Handcraft Shop-
    Sunlight Fitsum ..................................B2

---

tion see Kingdom of Aksum (p220) and the boxed text, p97.

## ◉ Sights

One admission ticket (adult/student Birr50/ 25) covers all of Aksum's historical sights, except the St Mary of Zion church compound and the monasteries of Abba Pentalewon and Abba Liqanos. The ticket is good for three days and is sold at the Aksum Tourism Information Centre (p104). All sights are open between 8am and 6pm, though the guards at the minor ones will take off for lunch. Carry a torch for the tombs.

Although you can see the monuments on your own, an official guide (Birr250 per day) adds greatly to the experience. All are trained and many are history students, so you'll get much more out of your visit. The Aksum Guide Association office is next to the Northern Stelae Field entrance. **Rufael**

**Fitsum** (☏0913-125540; rufael12@yahoo.com), **Tedros Girmay** (☏0910-081534) and **Solomon Belay** (☏0914-743768) are all recommended. Rufael can also guide you to the rock-hewn churches of Tigray.

If you can get your hands on Stuart Munro-Hay's *Ethiopia: The Unknown Land* you'll find an excellent compendium to Aksum's history, archaeology and major sites and monuments.

**Aksumite Stelae** MONUMENTS
(Map p96) Ancient Aksum obelisks (stelae) pepper the area, and whether you're looking down on a small specimen or staring up at a grand tower, you'll be duly bowled over. The closer you get the more amazing they are. See the boxed text, p98, for the lowdown.

**Northern Stelae Field Tombs**   HISTORIC SITE
(Map p96) Despite the dizzying grandeur of the numerous rock needles reaching for the stars, it's what's under your feet here that's most important. Amazingly, about 90% of the field hasn't yet been dug, so no matter where you walk, there's a good chance there's an undiscovered tomb with untold treasures under your feet. This is part of Aksum's appeal: the thought that fascinating finds and secrets lurk in the depths.

All of the tombs excavated to date had been pillaged by robbers, so very little is known about Aksumite burial customs or the identities of those buried.

### Tomb of the False Door

In 1972 the unique Tomb of the False Door (known locally, and inaccurately, as the Tomb of King Ramhai) was discovered. It lies in the western extremity of the Northern Stelae Field and is thought to date around the 4th century AD. Complex in structure, its stone blocks are also larger and more finely dressed than those found in some other tombs. Comprising an antechamber and inner chamber, it's surrounded on three sides by a passage.

Above the tomb, at ground level, a rectangular, probably flat-roofed building would once have stood (measuring some 12 sq metres by 2.8m high). Above the stairs descending into the tomb's chamber was a stone slab carved with a false door almost identical to those found on the stelae. Look for the iron clamps fixing blocks of stone together like giant staples.

Judging from the lengths to which the grave robbers went to gain access, it's thought to have contained objects of great value. A single stone base that held the sarcophagus can still be seen.

### Mausoleum

The so-called mausoleum has a monumental portal (hewn from a single slab of granite) marking the tomb's entrance and is carved with the stelae's curious false-door motifs. The portal leads into a passageway with 10 chambers. In total the tomb covers some 240 sq metres. Part of the tomb was disfigured at some unknown date by robbers, who succeeded in digging through 1.5m of solid masonry.

### Tomb of the Brick Arches

Dating from the end of the 3rd century, this tomb is remarkably well preserved and contains four rock-cut chambers, subdivided by a series of brick arches built with lime mortar. These arches are the same as those that

# Northern Stelae Field

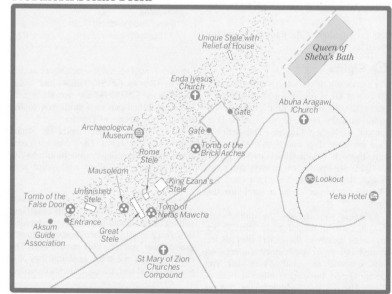

## AKSUM'S FALL

After Aksum lost its grip on the Red Sea trade due to the rise of Islamic Arabs' fortunes, the society quickly imploded and sent Ethiopia into the dark ages for five centuries. Why this happened when it was still rich in natural resources is the subject of many theories.

The environmental argument suggests that Aksum's ever-increasing population led to overcropping of the land, deforestation and eventually soil erosion. The climatic explanation claims that a slight 'global warming' took place, which finished Aksum's agriculture and eventually led to drought and famine. The military argument claims that Aksum was undermined by continual incursions from neighbouring tribes.

According to tradition, Aksumite power was usurped around the 9th century by the dreaded warrior Queen Gudit (or Judit), a pagan or Jew, who killed the ruling king and burnt down the city. This legend seems to be born out by at least two documents written at about this time and may represent a rare case of Ethiopian tradition meshing, at least partly, with reality.

had been in the mausoleum before the grave robbers damaged it.

The tomb was first excavated by archaeologists in 1974, and though tomb robbers had beaten them to it by centuries, they still discovered fragments of gold jewellery, beads, bronze objects, weapons and glass objects. Nobody knows who was buried here, but archaeologists surmise that the tomb contained the bodies of an elderly woman, a man and one other person and that the treasures found within indicate that they were people of high standing.

The tomb remains closed because archaeologists think further excavation is warranted, but you can clearly see one of the arches through the gate.

### Tomb of Nefas Mawcha

The megalithic Tomb of Nefas Mawcha consists of a large rectangular central chamber surrounded on three sides by a passage. The tomb is unusual for its large size, the sophistication of the structure and the size of the stones used for its construction (the stone that roofs the central chamber measures 17.3m by 6.4m and weighs some 360 tonnes!). The force of the Great Stele crashing into its roof caused the tomb's spectacular collapse.

Locals believe that under this tomb is a 'magic machine', the original implement the Aksumites used to melt stone in order to shape the stelae and tombs. The same type of machine was apparently also used to create some of the rock-hewn churches of Tigray.

### Archaeological Museum    MUSEUM

አርኪዮሎጂ ሙዚየም (Map p96) This well-laid-out museum in the Northern Stelae Field contains an interesting variety of objects found in the tombs, ranging from ordinary household objects, such as lamps and incense burners, to quite sophisticated glassware. You'll also see beautiful lion gargoyles, a charming pot shaped like a three-legged bird, well-preserved Sabaean and Ge'ez inscriptions dating back over 2500 years, an amphora from Turkey or Cyprus that provides evidence of ancient trading routes and a particularly nice collection of Aksumite coins. You can take a coffee ceremony outside the exit.

### St Mary of Zion Churches    CHURCHES

ጺዮን ማርያም ቤተክርስቲያን (Map p94; admission Birr200, personal video cameras Birr100; ⓧ7.30am-12.30pm & 2.30-5.30pm Mon-Fri, 9am-noon & 2.30-5.30pm Sat & Sun) Though religions have come and gone, Aksum remains a holy city throughout. Opposite the Northern Stelae Field, in a walled compound, lies the centre of the universe for Christian Ethiopians.

A church of some form or other has stood at this spot since the very earliest days of Ethiopian Christianity and it was God himself who, descending from heaven, indicated that a church should be built here, though the original church is long gone. The rectangular old church (men only) at the southern end of the complex is a remarkable example of traditional architecture built by the Emperor Fasiladas, the founder of Gonder, in 1665. Inside there are fine original murals, including a painting of the Nine Saints (p107). Some say the foundation on which it sits may belong to Africa's first church, supposedly erected by King Ezana in the 4th century and destroyed in the 9th century during Queen Gudit's devastating raid, and then a rebuilt version was destroyed during the incursions of Ahmed Gragn the Left-Handed in 1535. More remains of this church can be seen next to the museum.

The huge **new church** of St Mary of Zion was built in the 1960s so women had a place

## A QUICK GUIDE TO AKSUM'S STELAE

For as long as 5000 years, monoliths have been used in northeast Africa as tombstones and monuments to local rulers. In Aksum, this tradition reached its apogee. Like Egypt's pyramids, Aksum's stelae were like great billboards announcing to the world the authority, power and greatness of the ruling families. Aksum's astonishing stelae are striking for their huge size, their incredible state of preservation, and their curiously modern look. Sculpted from single pieces of granite, the later ones come complete with little windows, doors and even door handles and locks that make them look remarkably like tower blocks.

Despite the stone being famously hard, Aksum's masons worked it superbly, often following an architectural design that mirrored the traditional style seen in Aksumite houses and palaces (for more details on Aksumite architecture, see p257).

Metal plates, perhaps in the form of a crescent moon and disc (pagan symbol of the sun), are thought to have been riveted to the top of the stelae both at the front and back. The crescent is also an ancient pagan symbol, originating from southern Arabia. In 1996 a broken plate that could have matched the rusty rivet holes atop a stele was excavated from the Tomb of Brick Arches. It bore the effigy of a face, perhaps that of the ruler to whom the plate's stele was dedicated. It's on display in the Archaeological Museum. Despite locals having long ago assigned king's names to each stele, nobody knows who they were dedicated to. (Though it *is* certain the kings chosen by locals are incorrect.) For this reason, historians only use numbers to identify each stele.

Ethiopian traditions have it that the Ark of the Covenant's celestial powers were harnessed to transport the mighty monoliths 4km from the quarries, and raise them; the largest weighed no less than 520 tonnes! Archaeologists are confident that the earthly forces of elephants, rollers and winches were responsible.

### Northern Stelae Field የሰሜን የመቃብር ትክል ድንጋዮች መስክ

The Northern Stelae Field is Ethiopia's biggest and most important stelae field. It contains 66 stelae from the 3rd and 4th centuries AD, though the original number was higher; some have been removed, others may lie buried.

The stelae range from 1m to 33m in height and from simple slabs of stone (the majority) to finely dressed rectangular blocks, usually with flat sides and a rounded or conical apex. Though they were undoubtedly connected with the practice of human burial, it's not yet certain if every stele marks a tomb. The three largest and most famous stelae (King Ezana's Stele, Great Stele and Rome Stele) are found here; see Map p96.

#### KING EZANA'S STELE

Although standing slightly off kilter, the magnificent 23m-high, 160-tonne **Stele 3** has done something no other stele of similar stature has done: remained standing (albeit today it's aided by a sling). Henry Salt, the British traveller and first foreigner to describe it in 1805, proclaimed it 'the most admirable and perfect monument of its kind'. The stone platform at its base is believed to have served as an altar. Within the platform are four foot-deep cavities, which probably collected blood during sacrificial offerings. It's the oldest of the three and only has carvings on three sides.

#### GREAT STELE

Lying like a broken soldier, the massive 33m **Stele 1**, also known locally as King Ramhai's Stele, is believed to be the largest single block of stone that humans have ever attempted to erect, and overshadows even the Egyptian obelisks in its conception and ambition.

Scholars theorise that it fell during its erection sometime early in the 4th century. Comparing the unworked 'root' (only 2.7m long) with the sleek, carved base and the intricate

to worship and it displays Haile Selassie's usual hideous taste. Still it does cut a dramatic silhouette on the skyline. Beside it, a disproportionately tall bell tower, inspired by the stelae, sprouts heavenwards.

Nearby is a **museum** (soon to be moved and expanded) containing an impressive haul of treasure, including an unsurpassed collection of former Ethiopian rulers' crowns and a dazzling display of gold and silver

walia ibex carvings near its top gives you a vivid idea of the precision, finesse and technical competence of Aksum's stoneworkers.

As it toppled it collided with the massive 360-tonne stone sheltering the central chamber of Nefas Mawcha's tomb (p97). This shattered the upper portion of the stele and collapsed the tomb's central chamber, scattering the massive roof supports like tooth-picks. Seeing that no other stele was ever raised here, it's obvious the collapse sounded the death knell on the long tradition of obelisk erection in Aksum. Some scholars have even suggested that the disaster may have actually contributed to the people's conversion to Christianity. More controversially, some propose it may have been sabotaged deliberately to feign a sign of God. Whatever the origin of its downfall, the stele remains exactly where it tumbled 1600 years ago, a permanent reminder of the defeat of paganism by Christianity.

### ROME STELE

At 24.6m high and 170 tonnes, **Stele 2** is the second-largest stele ever produced at Aksum. Like the Great Stele, its ornate carvings of multistoreyed windows and doors adorn all four sides. Pillagers raiding the site are believed to have accidentally caused its collapse sometime between the 10th and 16th centuries. It broke into three pieces and the cracks are clearly visible.

In 1937, the stele's remains were shipped to Italy on Mussolini's personal orders. On arrival it was reassembled and raised once more in Rome's Piazza di Porta Capena where it was known as the Aksum Obelisk. It remained in Rome until 2005, when decades of negotiations were finally victorious over diplomatic feet-dragging. It was returned to Aksum that year and Unesco raised it in 2007, just in time for the Ethiopian millennium celebration. It's now the most impressive of all the stelae.

### OTHER STELAE

Lying prone between the Mausoleum and Tomb of the False Door is another important stele, albeit unassuming and unfinished; hence it's known as the **unfinished stele**. The fact it's unfinished is evidence that the final carving of stelae was finished on site and not at the quarries.

Although none still stand, there are several large stelae in the field east of Enda Iyesus church. The most notable boasts decoration near the top, and is sometimes called the **unique stele**. The large relief of a house-like object, formed by a rectangle surmounted by a triangle is claimed by some to be early proof of Aksum's claim to house the Ark of the Covenant.

## Gudit Stelae Field የጉዲት የመቃብር ትክል ድንጋዮች መስክ

Though they're far less arresting than those found in the centre of town, the stelae in the Gudit Stelae Field are still worth a visit.

Named after Queen Gudit (see Aksum's Fall, p97), most stelae in this field are small, undressed and lie on the ground. Locals suggest the largest stele, alongside the road to the east, marks the Queen of Sheba's grave. But, neither of these associations are possible since the stelae date to the 2nd century AD.

Despite excavations in the 1970s and 1990s, little is known about the field. Though some mark graves, neither rock-hewn nor constructed tombs have been found. Finds here did include a set of fine 3rd-century glass goblets, which has led scholars to suggest the area was the burial site of Aksumite society's lesser nobles.

The entire field is cropland so from June into October you can only walk on the footpath through the middle and along the road.

chalices, crosses, jewellery and even drums. It clearly demonstrates the immense wealth of the Church. Museum guides expect a tip.

Also of historical interest, beyond the gate in front of the old church, are the **throne stones** where local nobles were coronated.

Finally, in between the old and new churches, is the real reason for most people's devotion: a tiny, carefully guarded chapel that houses what most Ethiopians believe is the legendary **Ark of the Covenant**. For more on the Ark and the Ethiopian claim to it, see p222. Don't think you can take a peek: just one specially chosen guardian has access to the Ark. Nobody else is allowed in the chapel and foreigners aren't even allowed to approach the fence guarding the chapel grounds because previously some foreigners tried to scale the fence and rush into the chapel! No matter what you think of the legend, there's no denying that to be in this church compound during a major service or festival, when thousands of pilgrims pour into the city, is an experience of pure devotion and faith that that will leave you spellbound.

Note that the building currently has a leaky roof and the ark may be moved, at least temporarily.

### Arabtu Ensessa Church     CHURCH
አርባዕቱ እንስሳ ቤተክርስቲያን (Map p94) The 'Four Beasts' Church, named after the writers of the Biblical Gospels, was rebuilt in the 1950s and is worth a look for the wonderful murals (most modern, but a few old) covering nearly every inch of the interior. The saints and angels on the ceiling are particularly delightful. Though it has its own gate, entry is included with the St Mary of Zion churches ticket.

### Tombs of Kings Kaleb & Gebre Meskel     TOMBS
የንጉስ ካሌብና የንጉስ ገብረ መስቀል መቃብር (off Map p94) Set on a small hill 1.8km northeast of the Northern Stelae Field and offering views of the jagged mountains of Adwa, local tradition attributes these two tombs (now under metal roofs) to the 6th-century King Kaleb (see the boxed text, p101) and his son, King Gebre Meskel.

Although the twin tombs' architecture resembles the Tomb of the False Door, they show more sophistication, using irregular-shaped, self-locking stones that don't require iron clamps. The 19th-century British traveller Theodore Bent exclaimed magnanimous-ly that the tombs were 'built with a regularity which if found in Greece would at once make one assign them to a good period'!

The Gebre Meskel (south) tomb is the most refined. The precision of the joints between its stones is at a level unseen anywhere else in Aksum. The tomb consists of one chamber and five rooms, with one boasting an exceptionally finely carved portal leading into it. Inside that room are three sarcophagi, one adorned with a cross similar to Christian crosses found on Aksumite coins. This points towards an age around the 6th century, which, as seldom happens, corresponds with local tradition. Though the rest of the story has Meskel buried at Debre Damo.

Like Meskel's tomb, King Kaleb's is accessed via a long straight stairway. Inside you'll notice the stones are larger, more angular and less precisely joined. Of those who attribute the making of the tomb to Kaleb, few accept that he was actually buried here. The common theory is that his body lies at Abba Pentalewon Monastery, where he lived after abdicating his throne. The tomb's unfinished state fits with the theory. Local rumour has it that there's a secret tunnel leading from here to the Red Sea.

Above ground, a kind of raised courtyard combines the two tombs. Some scholars have suggested that two parallel churches with a basilica plan lay here, probably post-dating the tombs.

### King Ezana's Inscription     MONUMENT
የንጉስ ኢዛና ፅሁፍ (off Map p94) On the way up to the tombs of Kings Kaleb and Gebre Meskel, you'll pass a little shack containing a remarkable find which three farmers stumbled upon in 1988: an Ethiopian version of the Rosetta Stone. The pillar, inscribed in Sabaean, Ge'ez and Greek, dates from between AD 330 and AD 350 and records the honorary titles and military victories of the king over his 'enemies and rebels'. One section of script thanks the God of War, thus placing the stone's age before Ezana's conversion to Christianity. The guardian who opens the hut expects a small tip.

### Ezana Park     PARK
የኢዛና መናፈሻ (Map p94) A rather ugly tin-roofed hut in this central park holds a stone with identical text to King Ezana's Inscription, but it's in poorer condition and in a less attractive location. The park also contains one tall stele and a few random carvings.

### Queen of Sheba's Bath
HISTORIC SITE

የንግስት ሳባ መዋኛ (Map p96) Despite the colourful legends, this large reservoir wasn't where Sheba played with her rubber duck. It was an important reservoir rather than a swimming pool or gargantuan bath. Nobody is totally sure of its age, but it's certainly been used as a water source for millennia. Its large size (17m deep) is even more impressive considering it's hewn out of solid rock. It's also known as Mai Shum, which translates to 'Chief's Water'.

Sadly, the outer portion of the bowl was coated with concrete in the 1960s, making it look more like a modern trough than an ancient relic. It's used for Timkat celebrations, just like Fasiladas' Bath (p80) in Gonder.

### Abba Pentalewon
MONASTERY

አባ ጸንተለዎን (off Map p94; admission men/women Birr80/60, personal video camera Birr20) High above Aksum, on top of a tall, narrow peak, is Abba Pentalewon Monastery. Tradition states it was built by Abba Pentalewon, one of the Nine Saints (see p107) and a man who is said to have prayed nonstop for 40 years, and that this is where King Kaleb retired to after abdicating his throne. The site of the monastery was sacred to pagans and it's thought the monastery was built here to bolster Christianity and eradicate pagan beliefs.

The original church, whose foundation can still be seen, may date to the 6th century but the attractive 'old' church (men only) is from the 1940s. Some centuries-old paintings hang amidst the new. Women can enter the new church to see similar but only new paintings. There's no museum for the treasures (which include crowns of King Kaleb and Gebre Meskel), but a monk will bring them out to show you; and his show is kind of fun.

The main access path (walking only) is past the tombs of Kings Kaleb and Gebre Meskel. For the return trip you can head downhill to Aksum's main road near the Consular International Hotel.

### Abba Liqanos
MONASTERY

አባ ሊቃኖስ (off Map p94; admission Birr200) On the way to Pentalewon you'll pass Abba Liqanos Monastery (men only), which again was supposedly built by one of the Nine Saints and also boasts excellent views. *But* there's no treasure to see; the modern church (a replacement for the one destroyed by the Derg when the area was occupied by rebels) is uninteresting and there's little return for the admission price.

### King Bazen's Tomb
TOMB

የንጉሱ ባዜን መቃብር (Map p94) Despite being the crudest of tombs, roughly hewn into solid rock instead of constructed with fine masonry, this place has a slightly magical feel about it. A rectangular pit above the tomb contains a row of burial chambers, including a few that appear to be unfinished. Judging from the number of tombs and stelae found nearby, the burial site may once have been quite large and important.

According to local beliefs, King Bazen is thought not just to have reigned at Christ's birth, but to have been Balthazar, (one of the three wise men from the Bible; he brought Frankincense) and it was he who carried news of the birth of Christ to Ethiopia.

### Dungur (Queen of Sheba's) Palace
RUIN

ደንጉር (የንግስት ሳባ) ቤተ-መንግስት (off Map p94) The structure at Dungur is popularly known as Queen of Sheba's Palace, though historians think it's the mansion of a nobleman. It's fully excavated and, though in places rather clumsily restored, you can make out enough of the 44-room layout to make a visit interesting. Nobody is certain of the complex's age, but it probably dates to around the 6th century AD.

It has small undressed stones and walls recessed at intervals and unusually tapering with height. The well-preserved flagstone floor is thought to have belonged to a throne room. The palace also contains hidden treasure rooms, a private bathing area and a

---

### SWAPPING GOLD FOR GOD

King Kaleb was the richest and most powerful ruler the Aksumite empire ever saw. By AD 540 he controlled a vast swathe of land from the mountains of Ethiopia to the deserts of Arabia, and his power was rivalled only by Persia and Byzantium. But despite having everything money could buy and much that it couldn't, one day, after a vicious campaign in Arabia, he let it all go and, abdicating his throne and sending his crown to hang in the Church of the Holy Sepulchre in Jerusalem, he retired to the Abba Pentalewon Monastery where he lived out his life in prayer.

## AKSUMITE COINS

Aksumite coins are valuable not just for their beauty: they also provide a vital source of information on the ancient kingdom. The coins bear the names, effigies and sometimes lineage of 23 different kings providing a rare factual record of who ruled and when. The historians who studied them found something that rocked the foundations of traditional Ethiopian history. Many of the kings of the traditional history failed to appear on the coins while those on the coins failed to appear in the historical lists.

Beautifully struck, the coins depict the royal crowns, clothing and jewellery of the kings (even the large earrings worn by some monarchs) and probably served propagandist purposes. A curiosity still unexplained by historians is the fact that almost all the coins are double-headed: on one side the king is depicted with his crown; on the other he dons a modest head cloth.

Farmers frequently find coins in their fields and because the Ethiopian government lacks the budget to buy them, most are sold illegally to collectors and tourists. Both the sale and purchase is illegal and airport staff are trained to look for them during security searches so you're taking a risk (and harming historical research) if you buy them.

kitchen, where a large brick oven can still be seen. The stairwells suggest the existence of at least one upper storey.

### Ta'akha Maryam                                  RUIN
ተክአ ማርያም (off Map p94) Early excavations revealed that Ta'akha Maryam (enter from the north) was a magnificent palace, probably dating from the 6th century AD or earlier. Covering a vast area of some 120m by 80m, Ta'akha Maryam is bigger than Dungur and would have been far larger than medieval European palaces of the time. Today there's little more than piles of rubble and a couple of dressed stone blocks strewn on either side of the road that the Italians cut straight through, but the families who had built homes here have been relocated and a long-awaited excavation is set to begin. The Archaeological Museum has a model of how it may have looked.

Just to the north is **Enda Semon**, another palace ruin with even less to see. Excavation is also due to begin here.

### Gobodura Hill                                   HILL
ጎቦዱራ ተራራ (off Map p94) A site known as Wuchate Golo is one of the four ancient quarries of Aksum, the birthplace of the famous stelae. Several stelae (all unmarked) were almost completely freed from the rock, but then abandoned. Mystery still surrounds the exact tools that were used by the master craftsmen of Aksum, but here you can see clearly the process by which they cut the hard stone from the rock. After the intended break was mapped out, a row of rectangular sockets was cut. Then, perhaps, dry wooden

wedges were inserted into the sockets and made to expand by the use of water.

Just as interesting is the **Lioness of Gobodura** (የጎዱራዋ እንስት አንበሳ). It was here that the Archangel Mikael fought a tremendous battle with a fierce lioness. The fight ended when the saint hurled the beast into a massive boulder with such force that its outline is still visible today. Or an exceptionally talented artist carved a very lifelike relief. Its age is unknown, but it probably dates back no further than the 3rd century AD since that's when people began adding carvings to the stelae.

The parking area is signed 3km west of Aksum off the Shire road. It's quite a rough walk from the road over boulders and through scrub, and you'll need a guide to help you find anything. It's typically a one-hour circular trip, but it's a beautiful spot for walking and some choose to wander here for hours.

### Basket Market                                   MARKET
(Map p94; ⊗8.30am-2.30pm Sat) Aksum has two interesting markets that burst to life on Saturday; both are best between 10.30am and noon. This one takes place under the massive fig tree shading the heart of the piazza. It's absolutely huge at festival time when visiting Ethiopians stock up on high-quality Tigrayan workmanship.

### Animal Market                                   MARKET
(⊗8.30am-3.30pm Sat) The animal market, south of town and a bit west of the out-of-place high-rise, is one of the biggest in the north. It's ripe with donkeys, goats, sheep and cows but no camels. These are only sold straight from the huge caravans that pass

through the nearby countryside from the Danakil to Sudan.

### Main Market
MARKET

(Map p94; ⏰8am-6pm) The main market, with spices and the like, runs all week, but is busiest on Saturday.

### Old Quarter
NEIGHBOURHOOD

It's worth taking a wander around the old quarter surrounding the Northern Stelae Field and stretching west to Ta'akha Maryam. It's in these dusty streets that it really hits you how Aksum is more than just a collection of dead ruins; rather it's a living, breathing community where the past persists. Camels and donkeys carting heavy loads trudge past homes that feel as ancient as the ruins, and pilgrims in white stream in from the countryside.

## ✦ Festivals & Events

Though smaller than that in Gonder, Aksum's Timkat celebrations, held at Queen of Sheba's Bath, are just as interesting. Hosanna (Palm Sunday) is also a big deal here. For more information on these festivals, see p19.

### Festival of Maryam Zion
RELIGIOUS

This is one of Ethiopia's largest festivals. In the days leading up to the event on 30 November, thousands of pilgrims arrive and sleepy Aksum truly awakens. Celebrations start in front of the Northern Stelae Field, where the monarchs of the Orthodox church line the steps and watch performers in the street below.

For an unforgettable experience make your way to the compound of the St Mary of Zion church between 1am and sunrise on the day of the festival and witness a sea of white-robed pilgrims curled up asleep. Standing among the slowly shifting sea are a few scattered priests reading by candlelight.

### Mehelela
RELIGIOUS

On the first seven days of each month (on the Ethiopian calendar), St Mary of Zion's replica Ark (the original replica) is paraded through the streets surrounding the church compound to request forgiveness from God. The procession starts at 5am and includes a short 'special mass' in front of Da'Ero Ela fig tree (Map p94).

## ☞ Tours

The following specialise in trips to the rock-hewn churches of Tigray (p108), but can take you anywhere.

### Abune Yemata Tours & Travel
TOURS

(Map p94; ☎0911-532526; www.abuneyemata tours.com) At Africa Hotel; it's best for travellers looking to join other travellers to share costs.

### Covenant Tours
TOURS

(Map p94; ☎0347-752642; www.covenantethiopia. com) Reliable, with many years of experience.

## 🛏 Sleeping

Rooms become scarce and prices rise during major festivals. Reservations are essential. Budget hotels are better value here than in any other tourist town in the north, but at top-tier hotels, you should always ask for a discount.

### ⬛ TOP CHOICE Africa Hotel
HOTEL $

(Map p94; ☎0347-753700; www.africahotelaxum. com; s/d/tw/tr Birr175/200/250/300; P@🛜) With an eager (too much sometimes) and engaged owner, this place offers a smooth stay and is easily the most popular budget guesthouse in town, so it's a good place to meet other travellers. The rooms are simple and bright and the bathrooms very clean. There's also a restaurant with mediocre food. Call for a free airport transfer.

### Abyssinia Hotel
HOTEL $

(Map p94; ☎0347-751043; tw without bathroom Birr120, d Birr100) A clean and comfortable hotel that has yet to discover *faranji* pricing. One of the ensuite rooms lacks hot water, as do the common showers, but the owner plans to rectify this. The pretty good pastry and nice views are bonuses.

### Ark Hotel
HOTEL $

(Map p94; ☎0347-752676; s/d/tw Birr200/250/ 300; P) Very near the Africa Hotel, this place has essentially the same quality rooms, but minus the mostly *faranji* clientele.

### Yeha Hotel
HOTEL $$$

(Map p96; ☎0347-752377; www.yehahotelaxum. com; s/tw/ste US$57/76/102; P@) Perched atop a bluff overlooking the stelae and the Mary of Zion churches, this hotel has the most enviable location, and though it's too old to be able to claim the best rooms in town, all things considered it remains the best place to stay. The lobby is full of stone and wood.

### Huruy Hotel
HOTEL $

(Map p94; ☎0347-753540; d without/with bathroom Birr40/60; P) The rooms are clean and the bar in front attracts an older, thus quieter, crowd. While the common facilities reek, you can't hope for more at this price. It's the three-storey yellow building with the St George Beer sign.

### Kaleb Hotel
HOTEL $

(Map p94; ☑0347-752222; d without bathroom, d Birr150-250, tw Birr280; P) With quiet rooms set around a garden courtyard, Kaleb has the nicest budget setting. The rooms are large and decent, but a bit overpriced.

### Consular International Hotel
HOTEL $$$

(off Map p94; ☑0348-750210; d US$55-60, tw US$75; P@) This six-storey tower on the Adwa end of town is served by Aksum's first elevator. The rooms are big and well appointed (some with steam showers) but lack's Yeha Hotel's atmosphere.

### Tekla Haimanot Pension
PENSION $

(Map p94; ☑0346-752240; d/tw Birr120/250; P) Clean, functional rooms on the west side of town, a convenient walking distance to Aksum's main attractions. The double rooms are good value, even with the *faranji* pricing. Look for the green-and-yellow 'clean bed rooms' sign.

## Eating & Drinking

Restaurants tend to wrap things up early in Aksum, with most places not attached to a hotel shutting down by 8pm.

For something entirely different, seek out a *tella bet* (local bar serving home-brewed barley and millet beer; *suwa* in Tigrinya) in the tiny streets around town. They're marked by cups on top of small poles, but you'll need a local to decode the various colours.

### Atse Yohanes International Restaurant
AMERICAN, ETHIOPIAN $

(Map p94; mains Birr45-75) The American half of the Ethio-Virginian couple who owns this pleasant spot has brought cinnamon rolls (high season only) and proper hamburgers to Aksum, but he's otherwise mostly hands off in the kitchen. This is also a great spot for Ethiopian food, and there's a good coffee ceremony, too.

### Ezana Café
ETHIOPIAN $

(Map p94; mains Birr13-25) An awesome breakfast spot with excellent *ful* and 'special *fata*' (bread *firfir* with yoghurt and egg). Complete your meal with a juice from No Name Juice House next door.

### Abinet Hotel
ETHIOPIAN $

(mains Birr35-81) If you ask locals where the best place to eat is, they'll direct you to Yeha or Consular. But if you ask them where they like to eat, there's a good chance they'll answer Abinet.

### Yeha Hotel
EUROPEAN, ETHIOPIAN $

(Map p96; mains Birr51-82, set 3-course lunch Birr108) The food is fair but the view is grand. The menu has a large choice of *faranji* food with many selections rarely encountered outside Addis, such as 'Indian-style' fish and chicken with mushrooms. The lofty terrace of this hotel is the perfect place for a cool beverage, especially during a scenic sunset when kites (the feathered kind) ride the fading thermals and soar low overhead.

### AB Traditional Restaurant
ETHIOPIAN $

(Map p94; mains Birr40-90) Decorated with bamboo and crafts, this restaurant is calm and peaceful and a great spot to dig into *shekla tibs*, with goat fresh from the butchery inside the dining room. But give the pasta and rice dishes a pass: they can take forever to prepare and don't taste very good.

### Natinail Yared Juice House
JUICE BAR

(Map p94; juice Birr15-20) Pineapple, banana, avocado and mango meet lips.

##  Shopping

Aksum has more souvenir shops than any other town in Ethiopia. The road between the piazza and Northern Stelae Field has the most, but there are also many on the main road. Most feature basketry and weavings, but you can also buy silver crosses and old triptych paintings. **Abyssinia Handcraft Shop-Sunlight Fitsum** (Map p94; ☺7am-7.30pm) has a good selection of the latter.

## ℹ Information

**Aksum Tourism Information Centre** (☑0347-753924; www.aksumtourism.com; ☺7am-6pm) One of the country's most helpful offices. Also knows about the rock-hewn churches to the east.

**New Tech Internet Café** (per hr Birr30; ☺8am-9.30pm) Fast connections (sometimes) and fresh juice.

**Sol Business Centre** (per hr Birr24; ☺8am-10pm) Internet access.

**St Mary Hospital** (☑0347-752013; ☺24hr)

**St Mary Pharmacy** (☑0347-752646; ☺8am-noon & 2-10pm Mon-Fri, 8am-10pm Sat & Sun) Helpful and well stocked.

**Tsion Higher Clinic** (📞0347-754455; ⏰4.30-10pm Mon-Fri, 8.30am-noon & 2-10pm Sat, 3-10pm Sun) Helpful clinic and the doctor speaks decent English.

**Wegagen Bank** For the time being, has the only ATM in town.

## ℹ Getting There & Away

**Ethiopian Airlines** (📞0347-752300) flies twice daily to Addis Ababa (US$80, one to three hours), sometimes direct and sometimes via Lalibela (US$46, 45 minutes) and Gonder (US$45, 40 minutes).

For buses to Gonder and Debark (for the Simien Mountains), go to Shire (Birr23, 1½ hours) first. There's only one bus (6am) and few minibuses to Adigrat (Birr44, 3½ hours), but services are more frequent from Adwa (Birr12, 30 minutes). There are two morning buses to Mekele (Birr82, seven hours, 6am), which can drop you in Wukro (Birr65, six hours).

Aksum's travel agencies (see p123) and numerous freelance agents rent vehicles (including driver and guide) for trips to Yeha, Debre Damo and the rock churches of Tigray. Birr1300 (excluding fuel) is a fair price for minibus trips of more than one day, but it may require lengthy negotiations.

## ℹ Getting Around

A taxi to/from the airport, 5.5km from town, costs Birr40 'shared'. Almost all the popular hotels have vans waiting to meet incoming flights, though you may want to call just to be sure yours will be there.

Contract *bajaj* charge foreigners Birr15 to Birr20 from the Africa Hotel area to the Northern Stelae Field. A shared *bajaj* is Birr1.5 to cross town.

Bicycles (Birr10 per hour) can be hired just south of the piazza.

# Adwa                                                     አድዋ

POP 49,000 / ELEV 1907M

Like Aksum, unassuming, urban Adwa belies its status. For Ethiopians, the town holds huge significance. It was in the dramatic mountains surrounding Adwa that the Emperor Menelik II inflicted the biggest defeat ever on a colonial army in Africa, thus saving Ethiopia from colonisation. Later, many key figures in the Ethiopian People's Revolutionary Democratic Front (EPRDF) came from Adwa, including long-time Prime Minister Meles Zenawi.

Today you might wonder if Adwa has in fact just been involved in a new war: a road-widening project has left row after row of half-razed houses and shops. And with little to see, and its proximity to Aksum, Adwa is very missable.

**NORTHERN ETHIOPIA ADWA**

---

## THE BATTLE OF ADWA

In September 1895, as the rains began to dwindle, Emperor Menelik II issued a decree: all the able-bodied men of his empire should gather for a march north, a march for all of Ethiopia. Behind the vast army trundled 40 cannons, hundreds of mules and 100,000 rifles. In the north, the Italians were ready.

Initial skirmishes followed and amazingly the Ethiopians and their sturdy mules captured the Italian strongholds at Amba Alage and Enda Iyesus. Serious shortages of food soon followed, leading both sides to sue for peace, but Italy's continued insistence on their protectorate claim meant an agreement couldn't be reached.

In February 1896 Francesco Crispi, Italy's prime minister, sent his famous telegram to General Baratieri. In it he declared the motherland was 'ready for any sacrifice to save the honour of the army and the prestige of the monarchy'.

In the early morning hours four days later, the Italians made their move. Stumbling over difficult terrain, with inaccurate maps and with no communication between the three offensive brigades, the surprise attack was a disaster. Menelik, whose spies had long before informed him of the forthcoming attack, met the Italians with thundering artillery and fierce fighting on every front.

Nearly half the Italian fighting force was wiped out (over 10,000 soldiers were injured, captured or killed) and of the five Italian field commanders, three were killed, one was wounded and another was captured. Finally, laying down their arms, the Italians ran. Though the Ethiopians had lost almost equal numbers, the day was clearly theirs.

To this day the Battle of Adwa is celebrated annually and, like the Battle of Hastings in Britain or the Declaration of Independence in America, it's the one date (1 March 1895) every Ethiopian child can quote.

## ◉ Sights

On the Aksum side of town is a **monument** to the victims of and victors over the Derg (p233). A museum has been constructed behind it but never opened, and some locals doubt that it ever will.

Up in the mountains about 5km due east of Adwa is the **monastery of Abba Garima** (admission Birr120, men only). Said to have been founded by one of the Nine Saints in the 6th century, it's known for its collection of religious artefacts, including what may be Ethiopia's two oldest manuscripts, perhaps dating to sometime between 330AD and 650AD. They're kept in a proper museum in glass cases along with a few old crosses, crowns, robes, etc. The main church has modern paintings, mostly behind plastic sheeting, but the geometric ceiling paintings are an unusual sight. Head 6km south of Adwa before turning east for the final 2.5km.

## 🛏 Sleeping

Good places to stay are the **Setit Humera Hotel** (☑0914-301627; d Birr350-575, tw/f Birr600/1000; ℗) in the town centre not far from the bus station and the frumpy but clean **Semayata Hotel** (☑0347-712153; d Birr60-120, tw Birr180) on the Askum side of town.

## ❶ Getting There & Away

Numerous minibuses connect Adwa to Aksum (Birr12, 30 minutes). There are 10 buses or minibuses to Adigrat (Birr34, three hours), six for Yeha (Birr13, 50 minutes) and five to Abi Adi (Birr25, two hours).

tion. The 7th-century BC Great Temple's limestone building blocks, measuring up to 3m in length, are perfectly dressed and fitted together without a trace of mortar. The whole temple is a grid of perfect lines and geometry.

Just northeast, behind a little restaurant that has some photos of the site from 1906 on its walls, are the remains of **Grat Be'al Gebri**, a monumental structure with the oldest sections dating to the 8th century BC. It's distinguished for its unusual, square-sectioned, monolithic pillars (which could have been taller than the tallest known in South Arabia at the Temple of the Moon in Ma'rib in Yemen). Important rock-hewn tombs have also been found in the vicinity.

Next to the temple is the new **Church of Abuna Aftse**, which was built in the 1940s over the 6th-century-AD original. Incorporated into its walls are stones removed from the temple and in the west wall there are exceptional reliefs of ibexes, a sacred animal of southern Arabia. Entry is not allowed to tourists. The tiny **museum** (admission incl with ruins) contains a collection of beautifully incised ancient Sabaean inscriptions believed to originate from the temple, as well as some similarly ancient pottery plus the usual church paraphernalia. A proper historical museum is under construction.

## ❶ Getting There & Away

See Adwa's and Aksum's Getting There & Away sections for transport information. The last minibus back to Adwa leaves the village at about 4pm.

## Yeha ␣ የሃ

Yeha is considered the birthplace of Ethiopia's earliest known civilisation nearly three millennia ago. Many features here, such as the immense, windowless, sandstone walls of the so-called **Great Temple** are identical to those found in temples in Saba, Yemen and debate continues among scholars as to whether it was founded by Sabaean settlers from Arabia or by Ethiopians influenced by Sabaean ideas. The current thinking is that it was created by a mix of the two groups.

Yeha's **ruins** (admission Birr100, personal video cameras Birr50), now in the midst of a major restoration, are impressive for their sheer age as well as their stunning construc-

## Debre Damo ␣ ደብረ ዳሞ

It was Abuna Aregawi, one of the most revered of the Nine Saints, who established **Debre Damo** (admission Birr150, men only) monastery atop this sheer-sided *amba* (flat-topped mountain). It may seem like it would have been impossible for the first person to reach this island in the sky, but Abuna Aregawi had God on his side and God, knowing this was a fine place for a saint to find peace, made a giant snake lower its tail down the mountain and allow Aregawi to clamber up it to the summit.

Today, for those without God on their side, there's a thick leather rope to climb and the monks will tie a second line around your torso and help pull you up (Birr50) the

15m cliff. Even so, it takes some nerves and a good head for heights. (If you're short of confidence, don't look at the laces holding the strips of rope together until after you've come down!) Women, some might say luckily for them, aren't allowed up.

Debre Damo is one of the most important monasteries in Ethiopia and is thought to date back to Aksumite times and the 6th-century reign of King Gebre Meskel. The monastery's formidable cliffs also allowed Aksumite monarchs to coop up excess male members of the royal family here, thus removing possible threats to their reign. Today it hosts some 150 monks, who are entirely self-sufficient. They grow their own crops, raise their own livestock (all male) and have water reservoirs hewn deep into the rock.

Its remarkable **Abuna Aregawi church** is likely the oldest standing church in the country (10th or 11th century AD) and possibly all of Africa. Thanks to a major restoration in 1948 it's in excellent condition, but still has a truly ancient feel. It's an almost prototypical example of Aksumite architecture and features the same style of doors and windows found on Aksum's stelae. Notable are the beams and ceiling, famously decorated with carved wooden panels depicting Ethiopian wild animals. Debre Damo has long been used as a safeguard for religious treasures and its collection includes some of Ethiopia's oldest **illuminated manuscripts**.

### ⓘ Getting There & Away

There's no public transport to Debre Damo, although any transport on the Aksum–Adigrat road can drop you at the well-signposted junction. From there it's a toasty 14.5km (around three hours') walk. Catching rides to Adwa, Adigrat or Aksum from the junction is tough in the late afternoon. If there's a group of you, it's easiest to hire a minibus in Aksum or Adigrat. Debre Damo is usually a first-day stop on Tigray rock-hewn church tours out of Aksum.

Passing deep canyons and terraced barley fields, the road running southeast of Debre Damo towards Adigrat is a contender for Ethiopia's most beautiful drive.

## Adigrat አዲግራት

POP 69,700 / ELEV 2475M

Tigray's second-largest town is situated on what was Ethiopia's most important junction with Eritrea before the border was closed. Adigrat's a humdrum place and mostly used as a lunch-stop on the way from Aksum to Hawzien or Mekele. But if you're filling in time, strolling the cobblestone backstreets south of the piazza is very enjoyable; though the scarcity of visitors, plus the fact that many people are paranoid about Eritrean terrorists, means you need to be sensitive about photography.

### ◉ Sights & Activities

Two 20th-century churches are worth a look. The fortress-like **Golgota Medhane Alem** was built in 1978 and **Holy Saviour Catholic Cathedral** went up in 1969. Both feature paintings by the famous artists Tekle Afewerk, but are usually closed. The labyrinth of tin shacks that's now the **market** is 500m east of Golgota Medhane Alem church.

The **original cathedral** is on a hill above town, 5km northeast of the piazza in the Don Bosco compound. Below it is a tidy **Italian war cemetery**. The serrated wall you see behind the 'Welcome' gate of the army camp halfway to Don Bosco is an old **Italian Fortress**, but you're definitely not welcome to visit or photograph it.

You can also do **community trekking** from here; see the Trekking Tigray boxed text on p111.

### 🛏 Sleeping & Eating

**TOP CHOICE Hohoma Hotel** HOTEL $
(☏0344-452469; d/ste Birr150/200) The onsite owner ensures this is one of the cleanest budget hotels in Ethiopia. She's a fine cook too and many locals told us Hohoma is one of the few places in Adigrat that makes a

---

### THE NINE SAINTS

Though it was Abba Salama who first brought the Christian faith to Ethiopia in the year AD 330, he didn't make great inroads into converting the masses. Instead this task was left to a group of wandering holy men who were eventually to become known as the Nine Saints. In the 5th century they arrived in Ethiopia from the Middle East and each chose a mountaintop on which to construct a monastery and preach the new religion. All nine are frequent subjects of church paintings.

good *tihlo* (barley balls dipped in a spicy sauce).

### Eve Hotel
HOTEL **$**

(☏0344-451120; d/tw/ste Birr253/345/460; Ⓟ) This wannabe smart hotel in the centre of town charges around 100% mark-up for *faranji*, but unusually this is more a matter of the *habesha* prices being lower than expected: all things considered the large rooms with satellite TV offer okay value. The restaurant (mains Birr46 to Birr75) is expensive, but they actually know how to cook *faranji* food, which makes it the lunch-stop of choice for nearly every tour company passing through.

### Agoro Lodge
LODGE **$$$**

(☏0348-450202; www.agorolodge.com; tw Birr920-1035; Ⓟ@🛜) Since it's a charitable entity (profits are reinvested into the community) we'll be charitable with our description and simply say the rooms are simple for such a high price. They are, however, comfortable enough. It's 4km south of town.

### Geza Gereslase
### Cultural Restaurant
ETHIOPIAN **$**

(mains Birr52-92) If it's Ethiopian food you're after, the big *tukul* across the street from Eve Hotel housing Geza Gereslase Cultural Restaurant is a better choice. Dashen Bank has an ATM in the same building.

## ❶ Getting There & Away

There are at least 10 daily buses to Mekele (Birr36, 2½ hours) and countless minibuses. Use the latter for Freweyni (Birr12, 45 minutes) and Wukro (Birr22, 1½ hours).

Going west, there are several buses and minibuses to Adwa (Birr34, three hours) and Aksum (Birr44, 3½ hours), but just one bus direct to Shire (Birr67, six hours, 6am).

# ROCK-HEWN CHURCHES OF TIGRAY

The landscapes of northern Tigray are almost fairytale-like. The luminous light bathes scattered sharp peaks that rise high into the sky out of a sandy, rolling semidesert. The stratified plateaus, particularly between Dugem and Megab in the Gheralta region lead to inevitable comparisons with the USA's desert southwest.

And the 120-odd churches are as intriguing as the landscape is beautiful. Very different from the more famous monolithic (carved out of the ground and only left attached to the earth at the base) churches of Lalibela, the Tigrayan churches are generally semimonolithic (only partially separated from the host rock) or built into pre-existing caves. Most sit high atop cliffs and the improbable perches add to their attraction. To approach these hidden galleries after a long sweaty and sometimes slightly scary slog makes for a very rewarding excursion. And beyond a few famous churches, you'll likely get to explore on your own, even in the high season.

### History

Until the mid-1960s, the churches were almost unknown outside Tigray itself and still very little is known about their real history, as opposed to their oral histories. Their remote and precarious positions have led scholars to think they were being hidden from raiding Muslims.

While local tradition attributes most of the churches to 4th-century Aksumite kings Abreha and Atsbeha, as well as to 6th-century rulers, most historians confidently date them between the 9th and 15th centuries. Thus the early churches represent an artistic, cultural and technical link between Aksum and Lalibela.

## ⊙ Sights

Most churches are part of clusters, each described below. Most churches charge Birr150 for admission. For more on money issues see the The Trouble with Tigray boxed text, p110.

Patience and a positive attitude are essential for your enjoyment as it can take up to an hour to locate some priests. Also, remember that when a local person tells you they know where the priest is they only really know where the priest last was or is supposed to be, so if someone takes you up a mountain with a promise that the priest is there but he isn't, the guide was probably not lying. But, always make it clear that payment to a guide is dependent on getting inside the church: no entry, no money.

Good walking shoes are essential. Bring a torch, but don't take it out too fast; letting the priests show you around by candlelight is wonderful. Also, bring lots of small notes (priests never have change) and water.

### GHERALTA CLUSTER

The Gheralta cluster is home to the most famous, most visited and simply the most (about 30) rock-hewn churches. Since it gets by far the most visitors, there are more reports of hassles: see the boxed text, p110. It's the improbably high and remote locations as much as the churches themselves that provide the attraction and visitors must be properly fit to reach many of them. There's no public transport, and little traffic at all, between Wukro and Megab, where most of the churches lie. The exception is on Wednesday, market day, when two buses leave Wukro for Hawzien (Birr21, two hours) in the morning and return (completely full, so you can't rely on them stopping to pick

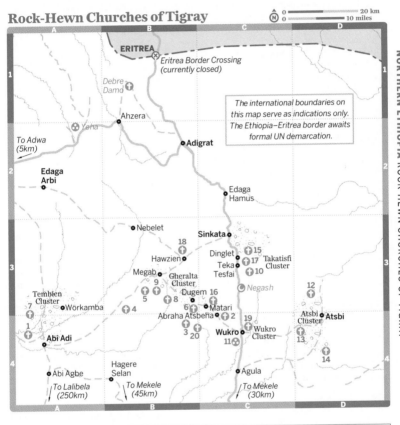

## Rock-Hewn Churches of Tigray

The international boundaries on this map serve as indications only. The Ethiopia–Eritrea border awaits formal UN demarcation.

## Rock-Hewn Churches of Tigray

## THE TROUBLE WITH TIGRAY

The rock-hewn churches of Tigray are spectacular, but visiting them comes with strings attached. Years of tourists handing out coins, pens, sweets, etc around the Gheralta cluster has created a climate of aggressive begging that's now so rotten kids sometimes throw stones at people who don't hand over bounty. All locals we talked to insist the situation is improving, in part because police visit schools to teach kids not to hassle tourists, but the frequency of reports from travellers and tour guides contradict this. Hiring a local Tigrinya-speaking guide is a good, but only partial, defence. Making things more frustrating is the attitude among many locals that if you go alone and have trouble it's your own fault.

But, kids aren't the only problem. Some priests expect, and often demand, extra money. Many visitors balk at tipping priests because the admission fees are so high, but fees go to the church bureaucracy. (Unless a receipt is not issued, in which case it *might* go to the church.) True, with the huge profits being made from tourism the church should compensate the priests for this extra work, but it doesn't. Priests here are not full-time preachers. They have homes, families and farms just like everyone else who lives near the churches, so a tip (Birr10 to Birr20 is usually fine) is entirely justified. (Anyone who goes to find a priest or walks you to a church deserves a small tip too.) But when they won't turn on lights or point anything out unless even more money is donated, the whole experience becomes frustrating. In fact, one of the authors of this book was locked inside a church by a priest who refused to let him go until he handed over more money! On the other hand, it must be said that virtually every priest we met was friendly and helpful.

you up) in the afternoon. Gheralta Lodge hires 4WDs and there are some people with motorcycles in Hawzien and Megab who charge around Birr500 per day to drive you, depending on the distance. Ask for them at your hotel, the bus station or the guide office.

In addition to those below, other churches of note in this cluster include **Giyorgis Debre Mahar** (admission Birr50), **Mikael Minda'e** (admission Birr50) and **Tekla Haimanot Hawzien**. The latter is just on the edge of Hawzien town, but as only the maqdas is hewn into the rock it's not too interesting.

### Abuna Yemata Guh
CHURCH

አቡነ የማታ ጉህ Although less impressive architecturally than most, this church is among the most rewarding. It's spectacularly located within a cliff face, halfway up a sheer rock pinnacle 4km west of Megab. The first 45 minutes of the climb is mildly challenging, with a couple of tricky sheer sections requiring toehold action. The last two minutes require nerves of steel. Even if you can't make the final scramble and precarious ledge walk over a 200m drop, it's still worth getting that far as the views from the baptism chamber are astounding. Inside are beautiful and well-preserved frescoes that adorn two cupolas, while the bones of monks from the open-air tombs lie around.

### Maryam Korkor
CHURCH

ማርያም ቆርቆር Although an unsightly green from the outside, this impressive, cross-shaped church is known for its architectural features (cruciform pillars, arches and cupolas), fine 17th-century frescoes and church treasures. It's also one of the largest churches in the area. The path begins around 1km from the road just southeast of Megab and involves a fairly steep one-hour ascent. Just a couple of minutes' walk from Maryam Korkor is the seldom-used church of **Daniel Korkor**, which is included in the admission fee. It sits atop a paralysing precipice and offers astounding views.

Maryam Korkor is easily combined with nearby Abuna Yemata Guh into an all-day trek from Megab.

### Dugem Selassie
CHURCH

ዱግም ስላሲ (admission Birr50) Built into a small outcrop rather than a big hill, this church feels like a tomb and may have been one before being converted. The 19th-century 'new' church alongside it is partially cut from the rock and topped by plastered stone construction, which is easily distinguished because it's painted white. It's along the road on the eastern edge of the village of Dugem.

### Abuna Abraham    CHURCH

አቡነ አብርሀም Rectangular in shape, with six massive freestanding pillars, this large and impressive 14th-century church (AKA Debre Tsion) is known for its diverse architectural features, including decorated cupolas, bas-reliefs and carved crosses on the walls and ceiling. It also has beautiful, though faded and damaged, 16th-century murals and an unusual, large 15th-century ceremonial fan. It sits like a fortress on a hill about 500m south of Dugem and can be accessed either from this village or the same parking area as Yohannes Maequdi; either way, it's a steep one-hour walk up the back of the mountain.

### Yohannes Maequdi    CHURCH

የሃንስ መቁዲይ High atop the mountain and not visible from the ground below, this rectangular chapel has six freestanding pillars that support a ceiling carved with geometrical designs. While it's best known for well-preserved murals, it's less striking overall than Abuna Abraham and most visitors remember the intense atmosphere rather than the architecture. It's accessed from the village of Matari (park by the school) and is around a one-hour walk via a steep footpath.

### Abuna Gebre Mikael    CHURCH

አቡነ ገብረ ሚካኤል Though not visited very often, this is considered one of Gheralta's finest churches. The cruciform plan is hewn into a domelike rock and it has good unfaded frescoes and carefully carved columns, pillars, cupolas and arches. It's around 15km southwest of Abuna Yemata Guh and requires a steep climb of at least an hour, negotiating a few obstacles on the way.

### WUKRO CLUSTER

Both of these churches are very easy to reach. Also, a planned museum in Wukro town will display finds from the Yeha-era (p106) **Meqaber Ga'ewa** temple archaeological site 6km southwest of town, which is itself being transformed into an open-air museum.

### Wukro Cherkos    CHURCH

ዉቅሮ ጨርቆስ This crooked cruciform sandstone church is semimonolithic and boasts beautiful cruciform pillars (notice the swirling sandstone laminae), cubical capitals, an outstanding Aksumite frieze and a barrel-vaulted ceiling. In 1958 Haile Selassie himself, apparently, ordered the angular roof squared with concrete for either aesthetic reasons or to protect the church from water seepage (which has severely damaged the geometric ceiling designs), depending on who you ask. It's on the northern edge of Wukro, making it the most easily accessible church.

### Abraha We Atsbeha    CHURCH

አብርሃ ወ አጽበሃ Architecturally speaking, this 10th-century church is one of Tigray's finest. It's large and cruciform in shape, with cruciform pillars and well-preserved 17th- and 18th-century murals. The obtrusive portico was an attempt by Italians to win over locals by proving they weren't Muslims. Some of the church treasures, including what's believed to be King Atsbeha's golden shoes (though not the crucifix said to belong to Abba Salama, the first Christian in Ethiopia), are properly displayed in glass cases in a new **museum** (admission Birr50). It's 15km west of Wukro.

### TAKATISFI CLUSTER

With four churches in easy walking distance from each other just 2km off the highway, Takatisfi is the perfect cluster for independent travellers. As an added bonus, the priests are easily found. The best approach is from the village of Dinglet (a minibus from Wukro is Birr10, 30 minutes), which

## TREKKING TIGRAY

Because most of the Tigray churches are in remote places, short treks are required to reach them. Until recently there were no organised overnight treks; luckily, for adventurous travellers, this has changed.

Although the locally inspired architecture is different, the set up of the new trekking program is otherwise nearly identical to the excellent one around Lalibela. There are currently four community-run camps (at altitudes between 2200m and 3000m) spread out in the remote mountains southwest of Adigrat. Most people begin trekking near Hawzien, but the guides can also meet you at Adigrat or Aksum and start closer to these towns. Treks run year-round and booking is handled by **Tesfa Tours** (☎0923-490495; www.tesfatours.com) in Addis Ababa.

is just 2.2km from Petros We Paulos. From there, head south to the other two churches and then take the southwest-running road back to the highway south of Teka Tesfai, 5km south of Dinglet. If you're travelling by vehicle, it needs to be 4WD. You can drive to within a 10-minute-or-less walk of all the churches. Mikael Meka'e is a minor, rarely visited church 15 minutes' walk north of Petros We Paulos.

### Petros We Paulos                          CHURCH

ጴጥሮስ እና ጳውሎስ (admission Birr50) Only partly hewn, this wood, stone and mortar church, now out of service, is built on a steep ledge and is more interesting from the outside than in, though the old, rapidly deteriorating murals of saints and angels are delightfully unsophisticated. Behind the church the skulls of some former monks are lying around enjoying the view. It's a five-minute climb up a rickety wooden ladder, much like those used at Ethiopian construction sites. The new Petros We Paulos, carved into the rock after God told a local man to do it, is down below. Note that the priest's home is closer to the highway than the church. He usually sends one of his children to open the doors.

### Mikael Milhaizengi                        CHURCH

ሚካኤል ምልሃዘንጊ This tiny church, with its stooped doorway, is hewn into the top of a small bleached hill and is thought to date from the 8th century. It's known for its 3m-high carved dome ceiling that resembles a *himbasha* (a favourite round bread of Tigrayans) and it's believed by locals to be the stamp of God. It's about 30 minutes' walk from Medhane Alem Kesho and 15 minutes from Petros We Paulos.

### Medhane Alem Kesho                        CHURCH

መድኃኔዓለም ከሾ Also known as Adi Kesho, after its location, this church is one of Tigray's oldest (perhaps *the* oldest), tallest and finest rock-hewn churches. Its exterior and interior walls are roughly hewn, which only makes the elaborately carved coffered ceiling that much more special. Ask to watch them unlock the door from the inside: rather ingenious indeed! From the end of the 4WD track, it's a steep-but-easy 10-minute climb up to the church. From the highway, you can walk there in about an hour.

### ATSBI CLUSTER

A seldom-visited but very rewarding cluster with plenty of public transport between Wukro and Atsbi (Birr11, one hour) town. Minor churches in the Atsbi cluster include Cherkos Agebo and Zarema Giyorgis. Market day is Saturday.

### Mikael Barka                              CHURCH

ሚካኤል ባርካ (admission Birr50) Atop a small but panoramic hill and behind an ugly 1960s facade sits this better-than-average rock-hewn church. It has thick cruciform pillars, small carved ceiling domes, a few paintings so faded you wouldn't even see them if the priest didn't point them out, and a solitary carving of a foot. Be sure to pop into the nunnery next door. It's 18km from Wukro and you'll instinctively know which hill it is when you round the bend and see it. Reaching it involves a 10-minute climb. Buses and minibuses between Wukro and Atsbi pass by, but when they head back to Wukro, they're usually full so you may have to wait a while; it could be quicker to continue to Atsbi and return from there.

### Mikael Debre Selam                        CHURCH

ሚካኤል ደብረ ሰላም This church or 'church within a church' has an exceptional brown-and-white, Aksumite-style facade fronting its inner rock-hewn section. The bright, modern paintings at the front and its beautiful carved arch add an odd but interesting contrast. The setting is lovely and it's one of our favourites.

The 45-minute climb is strenuous but otherwise not difficult. The church is clearly visible in the distance, so you could walk there on your own, but finding a direct path would be tough, so hiring a guide is recommended. The walk usually begins 8km northwest of Atsbi. Stay left at the first junction and then turn west at the sign (6km north of Atsbi) until you hit the river; in the growing season you'll have to stop at the school, 1km before the river. The four daily minibuses from Atsbi to Dera can drop you at the signed junction (Birr10, 10 minutes), but you'll almost certainly have to walk back to town.

### Mikael Imba                              CHURCH

ሚካኤል እምባ Of all Tigray's rock-hewn churches, Mikael Imba, possibly dating from the 11th century, most resembles those seen at Lalibela. A three-quarter monolith, the interior is huge (16.6m wide and 9m deep) with 25 pillars (nine freestanding) holding up the 6m-high ceiling. The view from here is great. It's 9km south of Atsbi and has an easy 20-minute ascent, which is finished with a short ladder. There's no public transport here.

### TEMBIEN CLUSTER
Isolated from the other clusters, Tembien receives so few visitors that on our last visit no children asked us for anything; not even 'highland'. Abi Adi, the nearest town, sits gorgeously in a half-ring of mountains. It's best approached from Adwa or Mekele. The direct road from Hawzien is often impassable requiring a 135km drive through Nebelet. Market day is Saturday.

#### Abba Yohanni                    CHURCH
አባ የሃኒ Impressively located halfway up a 300m-high sheer cliff face, this church is reached by a 15-minute climb using steps, tunnels and little bridges. The crooked carving and large cracks make the three-aisled, four-bayed interior as fascinating as the facade and the bright afternoon light makes it easy to photograph. As a bonus, it's an active monastery, so the key is never far away. On the downside, it means women are prohibited. Architecturally it can't compete with many others, but all things combined, it's one of the best. It sits 13.5km from Abi Adi on the back of the mountain. The last 7.5km is on a 4WD-only road that gets very little traffic, except on market day.

If the church has captured your imagination, you'll be pleased to know that another 42 churches founded by Yohannes are in the vicinity. The only problem is that not only are they all invisible, some are also guarded by a sword-yielding Yohannes.

#### Gebriel Wukien                    CHURCH
ገብርኤል ውቁን In a grove of trees on the other side of the same mountain as Abba Yohanni, this architecturally interesting 15th-century church, entered through a rock-hewn trench, has three aisles and four bays with well-carved details; six massive, finely hewn freestanding pillars; and three cupolas. Unfortunately, the priest lives an hour away, meaning unless you're lucky and he's at the church when you come, you need to plan on up to a two-hour wait to get inside. It's 14km northwest of Abi Adi, just 1km off the main road (plenty of public transport passes the junction), and involves a not-too-tough 10-minute climb.

## 🛏 Sleeping & Eating

There's accommodation in many towns around the churches, but only Wukro, Abi Adi and Hawzien provide a level of comfort and cleanliness that most people expect.

### HAWZIEN
This is the base for most tour companies. If you're there on a Wednesday, take time for a stroll through the market. It's one of Tigray's most important and between mid-October and May it even receives camel caravans bringing salt from the Danakil. You may also want to look at the patch of ruined houses and bomb craters on the west end of town that remain from an attack by the Derg in 1988 that killed 2500 people.

#### 🟦TOP CHOICE Gheralta Lodge                    LODGE $$$
(☑0346-670344, Addis office 0116-632893; www.gheraltalodgetigrai.com; incl breakfast from s/d/tw/tr Birr600/1200/1200/1400; 🅿) In a word: fantastic. This lovely Italian-owned, African-themed lodge has great facilities and service and many guests declare it the best night of their trip to Ethiopia. Big low-season discounts are available. Don't miss eating at the restaurant, which provides a set Italian-inspired menu (Birr120 to Birr140) that may be some of the finest food you eat in Ethiopia. Book as far ahead as possible.

#### Tourist Hotel                    HOTEL $
(☑0346-670238; tw without bathroom Birr150, s/d Birr173/230; 🅿) Rooms at this decent, family-run hotel look and feel almost brand new, though they aren't. Even the toilet seats remain attached.

#### Laliyibela Pension                    PENSION $
(☑0346-670011; d without bathroom Birr60; 🅿) Spiffy little rooms around a cheery concrete courtyard.

### WUKRO
Wukro is by far the biggest town in the rock-hewn church zone and has the most services, including several small supermarkets, but at its heart it's still just an oversized village. Water shortages are endemic here and while you can rely on running water every day at the big hotels, you can't expect it all day.

Most accommodation is on the southern side of town. The under-construction Wukro Lodge to the north promises (though we won't guarantee it will deliver) a higher standard than anything currently available.

#### Hewan Pension                    PENSION $
(☑0344-430483; d/tw without bathroom Birr60/120, d Birr120) You don't expect much from

the stark exterior, but the small rooms are very clean and even the shared toilets are odour-free.

### Fisseha Hotel
HOTEL $

(☑0914-730898; d without bathroom Birr100, d Birr180-300, tw Birr320; P@) Though it's the newest and cleanest hotel in town, with good mattresses, the lighting is the dim, orange variety found in many super cheapies; that's inexcusable at these high *faranji* prices.

### Lwam Hotel
HOTEL $

(☑0348-430042; www.lwamhotel.com; d/tw without bathroom Birr121/73, d Birr200; P) Once a very nice place to stay, Lwam is slipping fast and many of the ensuite rooms stink; take a sniff before accepting one. However, the *faranji* food (mains Birr30 to Birr60) here is the best in town by a long shot.

### Zemenawi Snack
HOTEL $

(☑0914-784238; r Birr35) Simple but clean rooms with a price that even the most tightly sealed of wallets can't fault.

#### ATSBI

### Salem House
HOTEL $

(☑0914-63582; d without bathroom Birr30) This yellow-red-black-pink spot on the south side of town is your best bet; the toilets smelled less here than at any other place we saw.

#### DUGEM

### Abrahatesfe Restaurant
HOTEL $

(☑0914-412198; d without bathroom Birr50) Has three ultra-basic rooms, bucket showers, a friendly owner and too-high-for-the-quality-offered *faranji* prices.

#### MEGAB

### Werkanesh Hotel
HOTEL $

(d without bathroom Birr100) This is the better of Megab's two woeful hotels, though just barely. Even if, as promised, it builds a shower, the price is a rip-off. Some negotiation is possible, but nothing will get you even close to the Birr20 *habesha* price.

#### ABI ADI

Like Wukro, Abi Adi suffers regular water shortages.

### Mylomine Botanical
### Garden Lodge
LODGE $$

(☑0344-460754; d/tw incl breakfast Birr480/580; P) An unexpectedly relaxing spot, Mylomine has five too-expensive but otherwise decent Sidamo-style (the owner is from Awash) bamboo huts in a quiet garden.

There's pleasant dining (meals Birr23 to Birr30) on the large veranda. It's signposted above town on the Adwa Rd.

### Ras Alula Hotel
HOTEL $

(☑0344-460621; d Birr100; P) This green tower near Mylomine is fairly dreary, but it's fair for the price.

### Gide Araya Pension
PENSION $

(☑0344-460251; d without/with bathroom Birr55/75; P) Rooms are spartan, but bright and breezy. All toilets are the squat variety.

## ① Information

The helpful staff at the Tigray Tourism Commission offices in **Wukro** (☑0344-430340; ⊙8am-noon & 1.30-5pm), Aksum and Mekele advise on itineraries and provide brochures. The staff in Wukro can act as guides if they're not busy. Official guides from the **Gheralta Local Guide Association** (☑0914-616851; 1-3 people per day Birr250, 4-6 people Birr350) are mandatory for Abuna Yemata Guh and Maryam Korkor (where going alone is potentially dangerous; see The Trouble with Tigray, p110), but they can be hired for other places too. Their office is at the main junction in Megab. You can also hire 'scouts' to carry bags and chase away children.

If you're really keen, search for Ivy Pearce, David R Buxton or Ruth Plant's research on Tigray before leaving home.

## ① Getting There & Around

Quite good gravel roads now connect the villages with the trailheads to most churches, but a few are down bad roads that require a 4WD. These can be hired in Aksum, Mekele and Gheralta Lodge (p113). Contract minibuses are available in Hawzien, Wukro and Abi Adi.

If you're patient, exploration by public transport is possible. There are many minibuses from Adigrat (Birr22, 1½ hours) to Wukro and also from Mekele to Wukro (Birr15, one hour) and Hawzien (Birr33, 2½ hours) via Freweyni. Further public transport information is given in the coverage of each clusters and some of the individual churches. There's always much more traffic on market days.

There are also organised treks in the region; see Trekking Tigray, p111.

# MEKELE & THE DANAKIL

A lava lake, a yellow desert, camel caravans, vicious heat and the legendary Afar warriors put the Danakil Depression on the must-see lists of serious travellers. Most visits begin and end in the pleasant city of Mekele.

# Mekele መቀሌ

POP 261,200 / ELEV 2062M

The relaxing and rapidly expanding university city of Mekele, Tigray's capital, owes its importance to Emperor Yohannes IV, who made it his capital in the late 19th century. Though hardly anyone comes to see the town itself, most travellers enjoy killing time waiting for their Danakil tour to depart.

## ◉ Sights

**Yohannes IV Museum** MUSEUM

ዮሐንስ አራተኛ ሙዚየም (admission Birr24; ◉8am-5pm) The Italian-designed stone palace built for Emperor Yohannes IV (r 1872–89) is now an interesting museum. Although the palace itself is undergoing a thorough restoration, the three-part collection (royal regalia, religious paraphernalia and Tigrayan artesania) is on display in another building.

**Martyrs' Memorial** MEMORIAL

የሰማዕታት መታሰቢያ ሐውልት (admission Birr10; ◉6am-6pm) From a distance, this memorial to the victims of the Derg could be mistaken for the world's biggest golf ball and tee. From up close it's another story, with larger-than-life statues flanking the tower that illustrate the true cost of war. The domed building just to the north is a museum (admission incl with memorial; ◉8am-noon & 1.30-5.30pm) that exalts the successes and sacrifices made by the Tigrayan People's Liberation Front (TPLF) during the 1970s and '80s.

**Markets** MARKETS

Seemingly half-full of traditional clothes, Mekele's Adi Hake Market is far more worthy of a stroll than the modern new market. Camel caravans still arrive from the Danakil on Monday mornings, but they no longer come inside the city and the bars of salt are brought to market by truck. All markets are at their busiest on Mondays, and that's usually the only day you'll find camels and donkeys for sale in the Livestock Market.

There are several churches, both old and new, dotting the city and their towers are visible throughout. Southwest of the 'bazaar', the intriguing monument in the roundabout is a memorial to the victims of the Derg bombing in Hawzien.

## ☞ Tours

The following run trips to Danakil and the rock-hewn churches of Tigray. The two locally based outfits aren't the most organised companies you'll encounter on your travels, plus promises to provide air-conditioned vehicles and sleeping bags sometimes prove empty. On the other hand, their drivers are outstanding.

**Danakil Tours** (☑0344-407414)

**Ethio Travel & Tours** (☑0923-228181; www.ethiotravelandtours.com) The local branch of the Addis-based company, it's alongside Milano Hotel.

**GK Ahadu** (☑0344-406467; www.ethiopia-tour-travel-ahadu.com; Axum Hotel)

## ⌷ Sleeping

**Hatsey Yohannes Hotel** HOTEL $

(☑0344-406762; d Birr180-300, ste Birr380; P@) This is a sweet choice; it's well run, clean and has carpeted rooms, though the satellite TV has more static than TV. The frilly bedspreads are a highlight, if you like that kind of thing.

**Atse Kaleb Hotel** HOTEL $

(☑0344-415255; d without bathroom Birr60, d Birr100-120, tw Birr140; P) Simple but clean and even most of the toilet seats remain firmly attached. It's quieter than the nearby and otherwise mostly similar Merkeb Hotel.

**Yordanos Hotel** HOTEL $$$

(☑0344-413722; s incl breakfast US$40, d US$50-65, tw US$65, ste US$74-85; P@) You'll find unexpected style at this pricey, central hotel that features some clever Tigrinyan decoration. All rooms have desks, fridges, satellite TV and large beds and the suites even have hot tubs with room for two.

**Hilltop Hotel** HOTEL $

(☑0344-405683; d Birr250-301, tw/ste Birr350/500; P) A bit out of town, the hilltop perch brings limited views. The bungalows out the back are large with satellite TV and mini-fridges and though the cheapest are a bit tired, all offer good value. The restaurant (mains Birr28 to Birr63) is not bad either.

**Abreha Castel Hotel** HOTEL $$

(☑0344-406555; s/tw without bathroom US$18/23, s US$16-30, tw/ste US$27/44; P☎) Though the rooms are rather dowdy, this would be a nice place to stay if it weren't for the elevated *faranji* prices. It warrants a mention, however, because it's in an actual historic nobleman's palace, albeit one far more humble than Yohannes' palace. Also bear in mind that just eight rooms (five with common shower) are inside the castle itself, the rest are down below.

# ✗ Eating

**Karibu Kitchen & Bar**  EUROPEAN, ETHIOPIAN $
(mains Birr25-90) This garden restaurant is
the first choice for *faranji* food. The wood-
fired pizza is the star of the show.

**Geza Gerlase**  ETHIOPIAN $$
(Guna St; mains Birr60-100) This cultural res-
taurant within a traditional *tukul* is a great
place to enjoy excellent Ethiopian dishes.
Specialities include *zilzil tibs* (strips of
lamb, fried and served slightly crunchy with

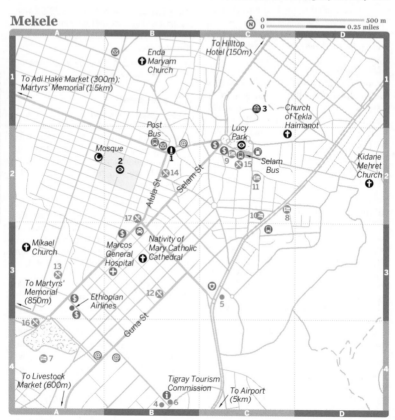

**Mekele**

## Mekele

### ⊙ Sights

### ⊕ Activities, Courses & Tours

### ⬚ Sleeping

### ✗ Eating

mustard-and-chilli *awazi* sauce) and *kitfo*. Vegetarians steer clear. There's a cultural dance show on Thursday, Saturday and Sunday nights.

**Hatsey Yohannes Hotel**   EUROPEAN, ETHIOPIAN $
(mains Birr38-82) The 1st-floor balcony is an ideal people-watching perch and both the national and *faranji* dishes are pretty good.

**Yordanos Restaurant**   EUROPEAN, ETHIOPIAN $
(mains Birr38-74) Part of the stylish hotel of the same name, this place is a wonderful spot for Western dishes, including a good fried chicken and okay pastas. There are two other branches in town, one of which, Yordanos I, serves decent thin-based pizzas (Birr73 to Birr80).

**Nur Supermarket** is Mekele's best stocked grocery. **Seti Supermarket** is also good.

## ⓘ Information

There are five ATMs in Mekele, all shown on the map.
**Marcos General Hospital** (☏0344-409220) A reliable clinic with a diagnostic laboratory.
**Tigray Tourism Commission** (☏0914-721280; Axum Hotel; ☉8.30am-noon & 2-6pm) Helpful office that can advise on Danakil and rock-hewn church visits.
**Ubuntu Internet Café** (Guna St; per hr Birr10; ☉8am-9.30pm) One of many internet cafes in this part of town.

## ⓘ Getting There & Away

**Ethiopian Airlines** (☏0344-400055) flies three times daily to Addis Ababa (Birr1327, 1 to 1½ hours).

Numerous minibuses run to Adigrat (Birr36, 2½ hours), while one bus runs to Aksum (Birr82, seven hours, 6am). For the Tigray churches, vehicles leave from the bus station daily for Abi Adi (Birr35, 3½ hours), Wukro (Birr15, one hour) and Hawzien (Birr33, 2½ hours) via Sinkata.

There's no direct transportation to Lalibela so you must transit through Woldia. With a bit of luck, it's usually possible to make it in one day. To get to Woldia either take an Addis Ababa–bound bus (Birr140, six hours) or take a minibus to Alamata (Birr45, four hours) and continue to Woldia (Birr30, 1½ hours) from there. Vehicle hire can be arranged through travel agencies or the tourist office from Birr2000/2500 for a minibus/4WD.

To Addis Ababa, you have the choice of normal service (Birr230, two days, 5am daily), deluxe Selam Buses (Birr340, 1½ days, 6am daily) or Post Bus (Birr300, 1½ days, 6am thrice weekly).

# Danakil Depression
## የደንከል በረሃ

Bubbling volcanoes light up the night sky, sulphurous mounds of yellow contort into otherworldly shapes, and mirages of camels cross lakes of salt. Lying 100m and more below sea level, the Danakil Depression is about the hottest and most inhospitable place on Earth. In fact it's so surreal that it doesn't feel like part of Earth at all. If you want genuine, raw adventure, then few corners of the globe can match this overwhelming wilderness. But come prepared because with temperatures frequently saying hello to 50°C and appalling 'roads', visiting this region is more an expedition than a tour.

Trips here can be organised through tour operators in Addis Ababa (p295) or Mekele (p123). The Mekele companies are in the habit of joining travellers together into large groups and you can usually just show up and find a trip departing in a day or two. The going rate in Mekele is US$500 per day with a big enough group, but all prices are negotiable. Four-day tours visiting Irta'ale, Dallol and Lake Asale are the norm. You can also add one day and add Lake Afdera to the itinerary or do only Dallol in two days or just Irta'ale in three. Some companies will take you year-round, but between July and early October there's a good chance of flooding and you may not be able to make it to Irta'ale or Lake Afdera.

The main base is the half-village, half-tourist camp of Hamedela where you'll sleep outdoors or inside simple shelters against the wind, if necessary. Tours starting in Addis usually enter or exit from the south via Serdo, with formalities handled in Semera, p179. From the Mekele side, registration and hiring of security is done in Berhale. Private travel is no longer allowed.

This is a largely lawless area and there have been killings and kidnappings in recent years, so do check the situation carefully before going. But the climate is a more serious concern: people with heart conditions shouldn't visit and everyone should heed signs of heat exhaustion (p345).

### IRTA'ALE VOLCANO

The Danakil's most amazing site is Irta'ale Volcano (613m), which has been in a state of continuous eruption since 1967. Its small southerly crater is one of the only permanent lava lakes on the planet. The climb is

## SALT FOR GOLD

Since earliest times and right up to the present day, salt, a precious commodity for people and their animals, has been used as a kind of currency in Ethiopia. According to Kosmos, a 6th-century Egyptian writing in Greek, the kings of Aksum sent expeditions west to barter salt, among other things, for hunks of gold.

Mined in the Danakil Depression, the mineral was transported hundreds of kilometres west across the country to the Ethiopian court in Shoa. Later, the salt was cut into small, rectangular blocks, which came to be known as *amole;* their value grew with every kilometre that they travelled further from the mine.

To this day, Afar nomads and their camels continue to follow this ancient salt route. Cutting the bars by hand from the salt lakes in eastern Ethiopia, they spend weeks travelling by caravan to market, where the bars will be bartered.

Though nowadays the people of the Danakil Depression mine salt in order to earn gold in the highland markets, once upon a time it was the other way around. Long ago, so long that nobody really remembers, the salt of the Danakil was all gold – endless thousands of tonnes of pure gold. People say that Danakil had more gold than anywhere else on earth and its people lived like royalty. Wealth made them greedy, lazy and forgetful of God. In order to punish them, God turned all the gold to salt. But one day, so the locals say, when the people are no longer greedy, God will turn it all back into gold again and then the people of Danakil will once more be able to swap gold for salt.

long (15km; three to four hours) but not steep; the heat and darkness (you climb after dinner) create the difficulty. Camels will transport the gear for the night and riding one is an option. You'll need a torch and it can get cool enough at the summit that you may want a light jacket or sleeping bag.

### DALLOL

The Danakil's other must-see is Dallol (-125m at its base), about 20km north of Hamedela, where great warts of twisted sulphur and iron oxide paint a yellow and orange landscape that looks more like a coral reef than anything you've ever seen above the waterline. The base of the hill is the lowest place in Ethiopia and the hottest place on Earth with a year-round average temperature of 34.4°C. The dry, cracked lakebed of **Lake Asale** alongside Dallol is where the Afar people hack blocks of salt out of the ground. The famous camel caravans load up here and you can stop to watch.

### LAKE AFDERA

Seldom visited (usually only by tours starting in Addis) is Lake Afdera (-102m), sometimes called Afrera, which is 60km (up to six hours by 4WD!) south of Irta'ale. Salt is extracted from its green waters and you can swim in it or the nearby hot springs.

# LALIBELA & AROUND

If you're only going to see one thing in Ethiopia, this should be it. The rock-hewn churches are magical and the religious passion of Orthodox Ethiopians remains mystical. Many people consider their days here as the highlight of their Ethiopian adventure.

## Lalibela                ላሊበላ
POP 19,100 / ELEV 2630M

> I am weary of writing more about these buildings, because it seems to me that I shall not be believed if I write more...but swear I by God in Whose power I am, that all that is written is the truth, and there is much more than what I have written, and I have left it that they may not tax me with its being falsehood.
>
> *Francisco Alvares (early 16th-century Portuguese writer) from* Ho Preste Joam das Indias: Verdadera informa-cam das terras do Preste Joam *(1540)*

Lalibela is history and mystery frozen in stone, its soul alive with the rites and awe of Christianity at its most ancient and unbending. No matter what you've heard about Lalibela, no matter how many pictures you've seen of its breathtaking rock-hewn churches, nothing can prepare you for the reality of seeing it for yourself. It's not only a World Heritage Site, but truly a world wonder. Spending a night vigil here during one of the big religious festivals, when white-robed pilgrims in their hundreds crowd the courtyards of the churches, is to witness Christianity in its most raw and powerful form. Unfortunately, for both independent travellers and the locals who benefit from tourism, the new Birr1000 (tripled from the previous Birr350) entry fee means that some people now choose not to come here.

With its cobblestone streets, distant views, good food and lack of cars, the town itself is a pleasant surprise.

### History

Lalibela, initially known as Roha, was the Zagwe dynasty's capital in the 12th and 13th centuries. In a rare consensus, scholars and local tradition both claim that the churches date from around the time of King Lalibela (r 1181–1221). But, the consensus is thrown out the window for everything else.

True believers say all work was completed in 23 years and this was possible because every night the earthly workforce was replaced by a celestial one. However, regardless of angelic masonry skills, the buildings are so different from each other in style, artisanship and state of preservation that they surely span a far longer period than even Lalibela's reign. It's also unlikely they were all originally churches.

Long a victim of the usual 'it can't be African' chauvinism, a few people now insist that the Knights of Templar were the real builders, but there's no evidence to suggest this. In fact, exceptional masonry skills had been refined during the days of Aksum, and indeed most of the churches show clear Aksumite characteristics; in particular, the doors and windows.

One of the many local legends about the site's origin states that the king wanted to make a new Jerusalem so pilgrims didn't have to make the long, dangerous journey to the real one. Another claims that Lalibela was poisoned by his brother (or half-brother, or half-sister) and while in a coma he went on a journey to heaven where God commanded him to return to Ethiopia and re-create the holy city of Jerusalem there. A multitude of sites, from Calvary to the Jordan River, have taken names from the Holy Land and local tradition also has decided that the northwestern group represents the real Jerusalem while the southeastern group is the 'heavenly' Jerusalem.

## ◉ Sights

### Rock-Hewn Churches

Lalibela's **rock-hewn churches** (admission for 5 days Birr1000, personal video cameras Birr300; ⊗6am-noon & 2-6pm), all built below ground level, aren't just carved into the rock but freed from it. And the carving, both inside and out, is exceptionally refined. Although time has treated most with gentle gloves, Unesco has built protective roofing. Fortunately, despite the intrusive design, this won't detract much from your enjoyment.

The **ticket office** (⊗8am-noon & 2-5pm) lies at the northwestern group (which makes the southeastern group less busy in the morning) and an uninspired **museum** (⊗8am-noon & 2-5pm) down below displays the usual church items. Local licensed guides can be arranged at the ticket office. The fee is Birr350 per site. Lalibela town is considered one site, but if you go to several of the churches outside Lalibela the guides will be expecting a big payday. Realistically, prices are all negotiable. Although visiting without a guide is possible (getting lost in the warren of tunnels and trenches is quite memorable), you'll miss out on many of the amazing subtleties each church has to offer. The guides also know many good photo viewpoints.

Some people rush through in a half-day, but this simply isn't enough time. A second day allows proper appreciation. A 6am visit to see the locals in private worship can be enchanting. Many of the priests are more than happy to show off their church's treasures and pose obligingly beside them for photos. Since they get a cut of the entry fee, it's not necessary to tip for this. Note that camera flashes inside churches cause great damage to the paintings, so please resist using one.

Lastly, don't forget to bring your torch for the tunnel between Bet Gabriel-Rufael and Bet Merkorios, or in case there's a power cut.

**Bet Giyorgis**                                    CHURCH
ቤተ  ጊዮርጊስ Resting off on its own, St George's Church is Lalibela's masterpiece. Representing the apogee of the rock-hewn tradition, the Bet Giyorgis is the most visually perfect church of all, a 15m-high three-tiered plinth in the shape of a Greek cross; a shape that required no internal pillars. Due to its exceptional preservation, it also lacks the obtrusive roofing seen over the other churches.

# Lalibela

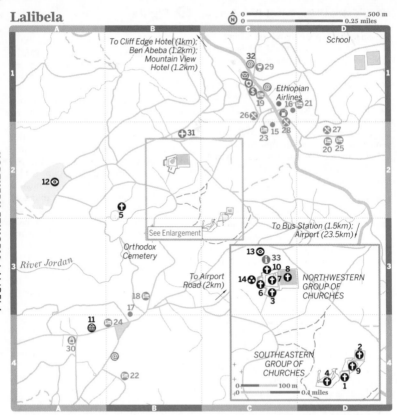

Inside, light flows in from the windows and illuminates the ceiling's large crosses: beauty in simplicity. Peer over the curtain to see the maqdas' beautiful dome. There are also two 800-year-old olive-wood boxes (one with opposing corkscrew keys) that locals believe were carved by King Lalibela himself and now hold the church's treasures. Some of the cavities in the walls surrounding the church hold mummified corpses.

### NORTHWESTERN GROUP OF CHURCHES

This group contains seven of Lalibela's 13 churches. From a size perspective, as well as the quality of the interior art, this group is easily the most impressive.

### Bet Medhane Alem    CHURCH

ቤተ መድኃኔዓለም Resembling a massive Greek temple more than a traditional Ethiopian church, Bet Medhane Alem (House of the Saviour of the World) is impressive for its size and majesty. Said to be the largest

rock-hewn church in the world, it measures 33.5m by 23.5m and is over 11.5m high. Some scholars have suggested it may have been a copy in rock of the original St Mary of Zion church in Aksum.

The building is surrounded by 34 large, rectangular columns (many are replicas of the originals). The three jointed at each corner are thought to represent the Holy Trinity. The interior consists of a barrel-vaulted nave and four aisles with 38 columns supporting the gabled roof. The three empty graves in one corner are said to have been prepared symbolically for Abraham, Isaac and Jacob. On Sundays, worshippers come hoping to be blessed or healed by the famous 7kg gold Lalibela Cross.

### Bet Maryam    CHURCH

ቤተ ማርያም Connected to Bet Medhane Alem by a tunnel is a large courtyard containing three churches. The first, Bet Maryam, is small, yet designed and decorated to

# Lalibela

an exceptionally high standard. It's the only church with porches extending off it. Dedicated to the Virgin, who's particularly venerated in Ethiopia, this is the most popular church among pilgrims. Some believe it may have been the first built by Lalibela.

On its eastern wall you'll see two sets of three windows. The upper set is thought to represent the Holy Trinity, while the lower three, set below a small cross-shaped window, are believed to represent the crucifixion of Jesus and the two sinners. The lower right window has a small opening above it, a signal that this sinner was accepted to heaven after repenting his sins and asking for Jesus' help. The lower left window, which represents the criminal who went to hell, has the small opening below it.

Above the western porch and squeezed beneath the roof is a rare and beautifully carved bas-relief of St George fighting the dragon.

Inside, the ceilings and upper walls are painted with very early frescoes, and the columns, capital and arches are covered in beautifully carved details including a curious two-headed eagle and two fighting bulls,

one white, one black (thought to represent good and evil). At the eastern end of the tall nave, surrounded by seven galleries, is a holy column with inscriptions in Ge'ez, Hebrew and Greek kept permanently wrapped in cloth.

**Bet Meskel**                                        CHAPEL
ቤተ መስቀል Carved into the courtyard's northern wall at Bet Maryam is the tiny semi-chapel of Bet Meskel. Four pillars divide the gallery into two aisles spanned by arcades.

**Bet Danaghel**                                        CHAPEL
ቤተ ደናግል To the south of the Bet Maryam courtyard is the chapel of Bet Danaghel (House of Virgins), said to have been constructed in memory of the maiden nuns martyred on the orders of the 4th-century Roman emperor Julian in Edessa (modern-day Turkey).

**Bet Golgotha & Bet Mikael**              CHURCHES
ቤተ ጎልጎታ እና ቤተ ሚካኤል A trench at the southern end of the Bet Maryam courtyard connects it to the twin churches of Bet Golgotha and Bet Mikael (also known

as Bet Debre Sina). The pair have the only cruciform pillars of Lalibela's churches. The entrance leads first to Bet Mikael and then to Bet Golgotha, which women can't enter.

Bet Golgotha is known for containing some of the best early examples of Ethiopian Christian art including some amazing life-size depictions of the 12 Apostles carved into the walls' niches. Four are visible with the other eight behind the curtains in the off-limits **Selassie Chapel**, one of Lalibela's holiest sanctuaries and home to more fantastic art and also the reputed tomb of King Lalibela himself.

### Bet Uraiel
CHURCH

ቤተ ኡራኤል In the trench fronting the western facade of Bet Golgotha, past the symbolic Tomb of Adam (a giant, hollowed-out block of stone), Bet Uraiel opened as a church in 1998 in what may have been a storeroom. Its rough-hewn rooms are rarely visited by worshippers or tourists.

#### SOUTHEASTERN GROUP OF CHURCHES
Although smaller in size than the northwestern group, the southeastern cluster offers Lalibela's most finely carved exteriors.

### Bet Gabriel-Rufael
CHURCH

ቤተ ገብርኤል እና ቤተ ሩፋኤል Its entrance flanked to the west by a sloping sliver of hewn rock known as the 'Way to Heaven', this imposing twin-church marks the main entrance to the southeastern group. Unlike most Lalibela churches its entrance is at the top and it's accessed by a small walkway, high over the moat-like trench below. This, along with its curious, irregular floor plan and non-east-west orientation, has led scholars to propose that Bet Gabriel-Rufael may have been a fortified palace for Aksumite royalty as early as the 7th century.

The entrance takes you into Bet Gabriel and then another doorway accesses Bet Rufael. Although the section of Bet Rufael's roof that collapsed has been rebuilt, services only take place in Bet Gabriel. Once inside the surprisingly small complex you'll realise its monumental facade was its most interesting feature.

### Bet Merkorios
CHURCH

ቤተ መርቆርዮስ Reached via a series of trenches and tunnels (one is long, narrow and pitch-black) that starts from Bet Gabriel-Rufael, this church may have started as something altogether different. The discovery of ankle shackles among other objects has led scholars to believe it may have served as the town's prison, or house of justice.

Due to a large section of it collapsing, the interior is a fraction of its former size and the brick walls are an unfortunate necessity. Don't miss the beautiful fresco (maybe 15th century) sometimes said to represent the Three Wise Men; but since they're holding crosses, this can't be correct. With their little flipper hands and eyes that look askance, they're delightful. The 12 Apostles are represented below in a less attractive and probably later fresco. The Passion of the Christ painting on cotton fabric next to the frescoes probably dates from the 16th century. Formerly, such paintings were plastered to the church walls with a mixture of straw, ox blood and mud.

### Bet Amanuel
CHURCH

ቤተ አማኑኤል Freestanding and monolithic, Bet Amanuel is Lalibela's most finely carved church. Some have suggested it was the royal family's private chapel. It perfectly replicates the style of Aksumite buildings, with its projecting and recessed walls mimicking alternating layers of wood and stone seen at places like Yemrehanna Kristos and Debre Damo.

The most striking feature of the interior is the double Aksumite frieze atop the nave. Although not accessible, there's a staircase to an upper gallery. In the southwest corner, a hole in the floor leads to a subterranean tunnel that connects the church to Bet Merkorios. The chambers in the walls are the graves of pilgrims who requested to be buried here.

### Bet Abba Libanos
CHURCH

ቤተ አባ ሊባኖስ Bet Abba Libanos is hewn into a rock face and is unique among Lalibela's churches in that it's a hypogeous church. In English, that means only the roof and floor remain attached to the strata. Like Bet Amanuel, many of its architectural features, such as the friezes, are Aksumite. Curiously, although it looks large from the outside, the interior is actually very small. The carved corners of its cubic capitals are unique; some guides say they may represent angel eyes. Legend says it was constructed in a single night by Lalibela's wife, Meskel Kebra, with a little help from angels.

## Other Sights
Lalibela's **Saturday Market** (⊘9.30am-4pm) is quite large.

**FREE** Lalibela World
**Cultural Centre**                                    MUSEUM
(☉8am-noon & 1.30-5pm) The new and still
mostly empty Lalibela World Cultural Centre has permanent and sometimes temporary displays about Lalibela's history, both
past and present.

## 🍴 Courses

**Lalibela Cooking School**                    COOKING
(☎0333-360380; per person US$40) The short
classes at Lalibela Cooking School at the
Blue Lal Hotel are an expensive option. A
better alternative, both cheaper and long
enough to start with a trip to the market to
buy ingredients, is rumoured to be coming
to Unique Restaurant.

## ☞ Tours

For information on agencies offering treks of
the villages, churches and monasteries surrounding Lalibela, see p125.

## ✦✦ Festivals

The most exciting time to visit is during a
major festival, when thousands of pilgrims
crowd in. **Timkat** and **Leddet** are the biggest, but Lalibela draws masses for all the
major ones. See p19 for dates and details.
Outside these periods, try to attend at least
one church's monthly saint day.

## 🛏 Sleeping

Discounts, often very large ones, are negotiable in most hotels from April through
August. Vacancies are almost nonexistent
during the festival period and European
Christmas, so reservations are wise. However, prices for reserved rooms during these
times can quintuple or more. If you arrive
during a festival without reservations, look
for brokers who work the centre of town hiring out rooms in people's homes.

Lalibela no longer suffers from water shortages, but electrical cuts are still
possible.

**TOP CHOICE** Cliff Edge Hotel                    HOTEL $$
(☎0333-360606; www.cliffedgehotel-lalibela.com;
d/tw incl breakfast; US$45/55; **P**🛜) Both the
rooms and the views from the balconies are
just as good as its pricier neighbour Moun-
tain View. They seem quick to discount, so
always ask. A restaurant is planned.

**TOP CHOICE** Asheton Hotel                        HOTEL $
(☎0333-360030; d/tw Birr150/250; **P**) This
classic budget-traveller haunt offers older
whitewashed rooms with a touch of local art
to brighten them up. The service is pleas-
ant and the garden courtyard a quiet spot
to relax.

**Alef Paradise Hotel**                            HOTEL $$
(☎0333-360023; alparahotel@yahoo.com; old
block d/tw US$10/15, new block d/tw US$25/35;
**P**) Alef's pleasant new rooms are bright,
tiled and clean with bathtubs and views. The
older rooms, though dark and uninspiring,
are still decent value. The restaurant makes
a good choice for this part of town.

**Mountain View Hotel**                            HOTEL $$$
(☎0333-360804; www.mountainsviewhotel.com;
s incl breakfast US$66-77 d/tr US$77/100; **P**🛜)
Built by two former tour guides who re-
ceived a miraculous business loan from a
generous tourist, this comfortable hotel
has an enviable perch with great views and
a lovely stone-and-glass design. Rooms, all
with balconies, are rather ordinary, but offer
nothing to complain about.

**Lalibela Hudad**                                 HOTEL $$$
(☎9110-29052; www.lalibelahudad.com; campsites
incl breakfast US$35; s/d/tr without bathroom incl
breakfast US$62/76/86; ☉Sep–mid-Jul; @) This
peaceful new (and still developing) eco-
lodge in the hills above Lalibela (two hours
by foot: many people use mules) has stone-
and-thatch *tukuls*, incredible views and
resident gelada monkeys. Despite the high
price, the *tukuls* are very simple (shared
drop toilets) though hot showers and decent
food (lunch and dinner cost Birr100) are
available. Of course there's good walking in
the area: the summit of Abuna Yosef is about
four hours away.

**Selam Guest House**                              PENSION $
(☎0333-600374; d/tw Birr150/200) This very
friendly four-room guesthouse has been
around awhile, but the on-site owner makes
sure it still has that new out-of-the-wrapper
look. The rooms are plain and simple, but
the calm friendly vibe makes the price fair
for Lalibela.

**Aman Hotel**                                     HOTEL $$
(☎0333-360076; s/tw US$25/35; **P**@) Bland
but overall decent newish rooms smack in
the heart of town; those in the back are qui-
eter and have good views.

### Seven Olives Hotel
HOTEL $$

(☎0333-360020; www.sevenoliveshotel.com; campsites per tent US$15, d/tw/tr US$34/42/52; P@) The oldest hotel in Lalibela, now owned by the church, is set in a bird-filled garden. The asking price is way too high for the tired rooms, but if you can get a big discount, or it follows through with the promised renovation, it's an okay choice.

### Tukol Village
LODGE $$

(☎0333-360564; www.tukulvillage.com; d/tw incl breakfast US$49/67; P@🖾) Although the large rooms outshine the Mountain View Hotel, this Ethio-Dutch–owned place lags far behind its competitor in the scenery and culinary departments. Three-course set lunches and dinners cost Birr145.

### Unique Pension
PENSION $

(☎0333-360125; d without bathroom Birr50) Four simple rooms with clean cold-water showers (hot water coming soon) and squat toilets. Inquire at Unique Restaurant.

### Jordan Guesthouse
PENSION $

(d Birr100) Quite a dump, really, but it fills a budget bracket right in the centre of town and the views are nice.

## ✕ Eating & Drinking

### TOP CHOICE Ben Abeba
EUROPEAN, ETHIOPIAN $

(mains Birr35-69) Hands down the coolest restaurant in Ethiopia, this Ethio-Scottish–owned, Dali-esque jumble of walkways, platforms and fire pits is perched on the edge of the ridge for 360-degree views. And while it would be expected to jack up the *faranji* prices, it doesn't. The only improvement would be a bigger menu, but what it does, it does well. Stop by at 11am to see the *injera* being made.

### TOP CHOICE Mountain View Hotel
EUROPEAN, ETHIOPIAN $$

(mains Birr85-109; 🖾) As much as we love Ben Abeba, when it comes down to the food itself, Mountain View isn't just tops in Lalibela, it's one of the best restaurants in Ethiopia. The diverse menu offers some Indian- and Jamaican-inspired dishes.

### TOP CHOICE Unique Restaurant
EUROPEAN, ETHIOPIAN $

(mains Birr35-58) This understated but cosy little restaurant ('bad house, good food' is what charming owner Sisco tells people who hesitate outside her door) serves the usual mix of national and *faranji* dishes (the fasting pizza is unexpectedly good). It receives regular positive reviews from happy punters and stays open until 10pm; later than most Lalibela restaurants.

### Zewditu Bar & Restaurant
EUROPEAN, ETHIOPIAN $

(mains Birr27-60) The partners behind this restaurant used to work in other restaurants before striking out on their own. Both the pastas and the *tibs* are delicious and the cute traditional dining room is very inviting.

### Seven Olives Hotel
EUROPEAN, ETHIOPIAN $$

(mains Birr32-121) This old-timer features half-decent *faranji* fare, but most people come because the leafy, bird-filled terrace makes it the most pleasant spot in the town centre; and this is why they can get away with prices like Birr32 for a juice.

### John Café
ETHIOPIAN $

(mains Birr20-35) A great little local breakfast spot in the town centre.

### Torpido Tej House
BAR, COMEDY

(flask of tej Birr30) Also known as Askelech, it serves *tej* (honey wine) along with traditional *azmari* (see the boxed text, p253) song and dance after 8pm. Everyone is expected to dance. Yes, it's a tad touristy (not surprisingly, *faranji* prices are double), but it's really fun. And unlike the more earthly *tej* houses, you are ensured good quality wine.

## 🛍 Shopping

### Fine Art Gallery
GALLERY

(☉2-6pm) The one shop that stands out from Lalibela's throng of souvenir shacks. Inside are beautiful watercolour and sepia paintings created by local artist Tegegne Yirdaw. He's often around outside normal shop hours.

## ℹ Information

Almost anyone who starts a conversation with you on the street or in a restaurant is going to eventually ask you to hire them as a guide or buy them an exercise book for school. And, if you should be so foolish as to do the latter, they'll promptly return it to the store and keep the cash.

**Dashen Bank** Has Lalibela's only ATM.

**Lalibela Health Center** (☎0333-360416; ☉24hr)

**Smart Business Center** (per hr Birr24; ☉7.30am-noon & 2-9pm) Of the few internet cafes in town, this is the biggest and best.

**Tourism Information Center** (☻8.30am-12.30pm & 1.30-5.30pm Mon-Fri) Unsigned behind the church ticket office.

## ℹ Getting There & Away

**Ethiopian Airlines** (☑0333-360046) flies twice daily to Addis Ababa (US$65, 45 minutes) and once daily to Gonder (US$41, two hours) and Aksum (US$46, 45 minutes). It's not currently possible to fly from Lalibela to Bahir Dar, though you can do it in the opposite direction thrice weekly.

Overland, the best approach using public transport is via Gashena. There are two morning buses (Birr57, four hours) and usually four minibuses (Birr72) to/from Woldia, the last leaving about 2pm. You can also take a more frequent minibus to Gashena (Birr40, 2½ hours) and try to hitch from there, though there's little traffic in the afternoon and passing vehicles ask high prices from *faranji*. Gashena can also be reached from Bahir Dar and Gonder by taking a Woldia-bound bus. With your own vehicle (or oodles of patience; there are buses from Sekota to Lalibela, but not daily), it's a rewarding journey to arrive from the north via Abi Adi and Sekota. On that note, there's now a proper petrol station in Lalibela.

A bus departs daily for Addis Ababa (Birr225, two days, 6am), overnighting in Dessie (Birr97, eight to nine hours). The other option is the brokers (ask around for them in the town centre, or have your guide or hotel call) who arrange rides in minibuses (Birr300) or people's personal vehicles (Birr350 to Birr500) which can make the trip in 13 to 14 hours.

## ℹ Getting Around

Minibuses (starting at Birr70) meet every flight at the airport, which is 23km south of town, and trips to the airport can be booked at all hotels.

The bus station is an inconvenient couple of kilometres out of town. Sometimes buses will continue into the centre and some hotels will come pick you up if you have a reservation, otherwise you can take a contract minibus (Birr100) or make the long, hot walk, which can be reduced a bit by shortcut foot trails. When leaving Lalibela, you can also arrange to have the minibus pick you up at your hotel; for a price, of course.

Ask your hotel or, for better prices usually, your guide, about arranging 4WD hire. If you think Landrovers are crude brutes, you can hire a mule for treks at the church ticket office. A full day will set you back Birr300 per mule with handlers to the more distant churches.

# Around Lalibela

Many other fascinating churches and monasteries lie in the stunning countryside with-in a day's striking distance of Lalibela, and a journey to them, whether by foot, mule or 4WD, is rewarding. Overnight treks, whether visiting churches along the way or not, are rightfully popular.

## 🏃 Trekking

Though it's less of a wilderness experience than the Simien and Bale Mountains, trekking through the villages and valleys surrounding Lalibela is a wonderful experience that mixes astounding scenery, historical riches and a fascinating insight into the life of Ethiopian highlanders. You'll likely meet gelada monkeys and there's a small chance of Ethiopian wolves in the highest reaches. Plus there's a good variety of bird life, from lammergeyers to bee-eaters. The treks were originally set up by a now-defunct NGO called TESFA and many people refer to trekking here as 'tesfa trekking'.

Treks are typically three to five days long and routes can be designed based on time, fitness, churches, chances of animal encounters or whatever you want. The Lasha area northwest of Lalibela, home to Abuna Yosef, Ethiopia's third-highest peak (4300m), and the part of the Meket Plateau to the southeast, offer rugged treks with some heavy-duty climbs. Further away, the part of the Meket Plateau west of Gashena, has low gradients and the walking is fairly easy.

There are 11 community-run lodges (and an additional seven lunch stops) near villages, each consisting of traditional yet comfortable mud-and-stone *tukuls* and loos with views. Most have showers.

### INFORMATION & BOOKING

Bookings are managed by Addis Ababa–based **Tesfa Tours** (☑0923-490495; www.tesfatours.com), under an agreement with the local communities. It's best to book as far in advance as possible, especially at peak seasons: October, December and early January. At other times of the year you can usually just show up and head out the next day, but maybe not on the route you had in mind. Make arrangements locally with the guides in Lalibela through the **Lasta Lalibela Community Tourism Guiding Enterprise** (LLCTGE; ☑0913-244479; www.lalibelactge.com).

The treks, including guides, pack mules, accommodation, meals, tea and coffee (beer, soft drinks and water are sold at each lodge), cost Birr978 per person per 24 hours. Any transportation, if necessary, to and from trailheads costs extra. Solo trekkers pay an additional Birr250 per night and there's a Birr50 fee per group per night if booking less than three days in advance. There are discounts for children.

Though a few of the community lodges are open year-round, during the heaviest rains from mid-July to late-September most are closed and you won't likely have much fun anyway. During this time, it would be better to head to the drier Tigray region.

A new Lalibela-based company, Highland Trekking (☎0912-130831; www.highlandtrekking. com), and some of the licensed church guides, such as Girma Derbie (☎0913-513763; girmaderbie123@yahoo.com), can also lead trekking trips at slightly lower prices because they have their guests sleep in villages (it's not as romantic as it sounds and many people don't enjoy the rough, hectic conditions; others love it, though) or use tents instead of the community lodges. This may be your only option if you book late during the high season.

## Churches & Monasteries

The churches around Lalibela vary greatly in style, design and age and offer a different experience from the churches in Lalibela. Tucked away and still absent from most modern maps, many require a guide to find them. Also, the already too-high entry fees may rise.

See Lalibela's Getting Around section for transport details.

### Yemrehanna Kristos CHURCH

ይመርሃነ ክርስቶስ (admission Birr150, personal video cameras Birr50) Despite Yemrehanna Kristos being one of Ethiopia's best-preserved late-Aksumite buildings, few people reward themselves with a visit. And a reward it is.

The church is different because it's built rather than excavated. Seeing the stepped exterior facade, created from alternating wood and stone layers, you'll understand why so many of Lalibela's rock-hewn churches look like they do. And knowing that Yemrehanna Kristos may predate Lalibela's churches by up to 80 years, you have before you a virtual blueprint of greatness.

Incredibly, the whole church sits on a foundation of carefully laid olive-wood panels, which 'float' it perfectly above the marshy ground below. The carving and decoration are exceptional, especially the cruciform windows and the elaborate nave ceiling. Behind the church lies a pile of mummified bodies: some are those of

pilgrims who've come here to die over the centuries; others are said to be those of the workmen.

This entirely inspiring and slightly spooky complex sits within a cave roofed by basalt lava flows. The ugly brick wall at the front was built in 1985 to improve the church's security.

The church is about 1½ hours (45km) north of Lalibela by 4WD. It can easily be visited along with Arbatu Ensessa, Bilbila Giyorgis and Bilbila Chirkos; 4WD hire should be about Birr1500. It's also possible to get here by foot or mule. Both options take about five hours to cover the shorter 20km distance.

### Arbatu Ensessa CHURCH

አርባቱ እንስሳ (admission Birr100) On the way to Yemrehanna Kristos, around 35km from Lalibela, is this three-quarter monolith church in a wild, overgrown but rather beautiful setting. It's thought to have been built by King Kaleb in AD 518. *Arbatu ensessa* means 'the four beasts' after the four Evangelists, Matthew, Mark, Luke and John. It's five minutes' walk from the road.

### Bilbila Giyorgis CHURCH

ቢልቢላ ጊዮርጊስ (admission Birr100) Lying west of Arbatu Ensessa, around 32km from Lalibela, Bilbila Giyorgis is also attributed to King Kaleb. It resembles Bet Abba Libanos in design. According to tradition, five swarms of bees took up residence shortly after the church was completed. They still reside here and their sacred honey is said to have curative properties, particularly for psychological disorders and skin problems. The priest will let you taste it. It's 20 to 30 minutes' walk up the hill from the road.

### Bilbila Chirkos CHURCH

ቢልቢላ ጨርቆስ (admission Birr100) Also near Arbatu Ensessa, some 5km off the main road, this is an interesting three-quarter monolith known particularly for its ancient frescoes. Also attributed to King Kaleb, it's thought to date from AD 523. It's a three-minute walk from the road.

### Ashetan Maryam MONASTERY

አሽተን ማርያም (admission Birr50) Set at 3150m, atop Abune Yosef mountain, the local priests believe they're 'closer to heaven and God' here, and it's easy to see why. The monastery's construction is believed to span Lalibela's and Na'akuto La'ab's reign; some even claim King Na'akuto La'ab lies buried

## PRESTER JOHN OF THE INDIES

I, Prester John, who reign supreme, exceed in riches, virtue and power all creatures who dwell under Heaven...In our territories are found elephants, dromedaries and camels and almost every kind of beast. Honey flows in our land, and milk abounds...No poison can do harm here and no noisy frogs croak, no scorpions are there, and no serpents creep through the grass. No venomous reptiles can exist or use their deadly power.

*Prester John*

The letter the mysterious Christian ruler Prester John wrote to the Byzantine Emperor Manuel Comnenus I in 1165 went on to inform of how his kingdom contained 'Centaurs, Amazons and shrinking giants'. There was a river that flowed from Paradise 'and in it are found emeralds, sapphires and many other precious stones'. His palace, so he said, was a 'palace of crystal with a roof of ebony and everyday 30,000 sit down to eat at tables of gold supported by columns of amethyst'. The great ruler himself wore robes spun from gold by salamanders that lived on a mountain of fire.

It was impressive stuff, but what really grabbed the attention of medieval Europe was Prester John's promise that he would ride forth from his kingdom with 10,000 cavalry and 100,000 foot soldiers and, alongside the armies of Western Europe, they would retake the Holy Lands from the Muslims.

The Christian Crusaders had lost much of the Holy Land and were on the verge of losing Jerusalem itself. News of Prester John's letter spread like wildfire throughout Christian Europe. It was partially in order to find Prester John's kingdom that the Portuguese launched the age of European exploration that changed the world forever.

Having first looked unsuccessfully in Asia, the focus turned to Ethiopia. When the Portuguese finally reached Gonder, they found a Christian kingdom that was a far cry from the glorious legend and certainly in no position to aid the reconquest of Jerusalem.

And of Prester John? It turned out that one of the most intriguing figures of medieval Europe was nothing more than collective imagination, and the letter that started it all was a fake created by a German monk.

in the chapel. Church treasures include parchment and some icons. Although the architecture here compares pretty poorly with Lalibela, it's the stunning mountain scenery you really come for. The two-hour climb (one way) is quite steep. Many travellers ride mules (Birr200), though you'll still need to walk in places.

### Na'akuto La 'ab CHURCH
ናአኩቶ ለአብ (admission Birr150) Lying 7km from Lalibela, just off the airport road, this is a simple but attractive church (apart from the outer security wall). It's attributed to King Lalibela's successor and is built under a natural cave. It was almost certainly the site of a much older shrine. Empress Zewditu built the inner red-brick building. Some very old stone receptacles collect the precious holy water as it drips from the cave roof. The church boasts various treasures said to have belonged to its founder, including crosses, crowns, gold-painted drums and an illuminated Bible.

### Geneta Maryam CHURCH
ገነተ ማርያም (admission Birr150) Geneta Maryam is thought to have been built around 1270 by Yekuno Amlak, who restored the Solomonic line. With its rectangular shape and 20 massive rectangular pillars that support it, Geneta Maryam resembles Lalibela's Bet Medhane Alem. It's also known for its remarkable 13th-century paintings, though most are very faded. There's a moon-shaped face of Christ on the western wall. Whoever built the hideous protective roof over it should be ashamed. It's about five hours by foot from Lalibela, or 1½ hours by vehicle.

### Mekina Medane Alem CHURCH
መኪና መድኀኔዓለም (admission Birr100) Two to three hours' walk from Geneta Maryam and six hours' walk from Lalibela, this remote church was, according to Ethiopian tradition, constructed by three virgins during the reign of King Gebre Meskel in AD 537. The church is constructed under an overhanging rock in a natural cave. It rather resembles Yemrehanna Kristos in design

and many features are Aksumite, but its beautiful frescoes, some of hunting scenes with one-eyed lions, are the main attraction. There are also many bricked-up tombs in the church.

# WOLDIA TO ADDIS ABABA

It's possible to finish the home-stretch of the Historical Circuit in one *long* day, but most people prefer two, overnighting in Dessie or Kombolcha.

# Woldia            ወልዲያ
POP 50,400 / ELEV 2112M

Woldia used to be a necessary overnight stop for public-transit travellers to Lalibela. Better roads and more frequent departures mean most people now arrive early enough to catch a connection that same day, but an unlucky few still get stuck here. For a transit town, it has a surprisingly pitiful selection of hotels and water shortages are common. There are many internet cafes and the Dashen Bank in the old town above the bus station promises an ATM soon.

## 🛏 Sleeping & Eating

**Lal Hotel**                              HOTEL $
(☏0333-310367, www.lalhotelsandtours.com; s Birr267, d & tw Birr356-445; ℗) This is the best available hotel. Turn into the entrance and it looks inviting, but enter and you'll find deferred maintenance and a lack of hot water in many of the rooms. Neither acceptable at these prices. The restaurant, however, has Woldia's broadest menu (Birr40 to Birr110) and best food, including a decent pizza.

**Yordanos Hotel**                         HOTEL $
(☏0333-311357; d without bathroom Birr50, d & tw Birr70-120; ℗) A scruffy place, it has satellite TV in the rooms and offers a fair price, and the lines of vines over the courtyard are a nice touch.

## ❶ Getting There & Away

Two buses to Lalibela (Birr57, four hours) generally leave around 6am and 9am. Tickets aren't sold the day before. The last Lalibela-bound minibus (Birr72) departs between 1pm and 3pm. Two buses leave for Addis Ababa (Birr150, 12 hours) at 5.30am. There are also minibuses to the capital, but since they're illegal they mostly travel at night, which isn't safe. Vehicles are pretty frequent for Dessie (Birr45, 2½ hours) and Alamata (Birr30, 1½ hours), where you can get a connecting minibus to Mekele (Birr45, four hours). The bus station is about 1km uphill from the town centre. A *bajaj* ride costs Birr1.

# Hayk            ሃይቅ
POP 14,319 / ELEV 2030M

Lying 26km north of Dessie, the little town of Hayk is known for its monastery and eponymous lake.

The museum at **Hayk Estifanos Monastery** (admission Birr60), on a long peninsula 4km northeast of town, dates from the mid-13th century and was founded by Abba Iyasus Moa. Between the 13th and 15th centuries it was among Ethiopia's most important monasteries. Today the museum holds the oldest-known manuscript to record its own date (the book of the four gospels produced for the monastery between 1280 and 1281) and other items like Moa's stone cross and various cooking utensils. It's open to men only, and the church building is modern and ordinary, so overall it's really only worth a visit if you have a serious interest in Ethiopian churches.

For most people the lovely lake, surrounded by tall hills, is a bigger draw; especially if you've got an eye for birds. Signed as 'Erkum' the lakeside **Rikum Lodge** (☏0911-877780; d/tw Birr170/280; ℗), has basic bamboo huts and a garden restaurant (mains Birr19 to Birr66), perfect for a lingering lunch.

Many minibuses run to/from Dessie (Birr8, 30 minutes).

# Dessie            ደሴ
POP 131,600 / ELEV 2470M

Dessie's tall and solid downtown, surrounded by a vast city of rusted roofs, appears to offer the promise of something interesting; but it doesn't. On the other hand, the presence of the **Dessie Museum** (admission Birr20; ⊙8.30am-noon & 2-7pm Mon-Fri), where old weapons form the core of the varied collection, does put it ahead of the curve in the attractions department over most Ethiopian towns.

## 🛏 Sleeping & Eating

Rooms can be in short supply, so it's best to call ahead.

**Tossa Pension**                          PENSION $
(☏0331-119225; d without bathroom Birr50, d/tw Birr149/172; ℗) Not only the best rooms in

Dessie, but with satellite TV and good mattresses, it's also the best value. Even the common facilities are very clean. It's on the far north end of town, a longish walk from any restaurants.

### Qualiber Hotel
HOTEL $

(☎0331-111548; d/tw Birr230/276; 🅿) Exceptionally clean and well cared for, Qualiber defies the norm for older hotels. We can't quite call it cosy, but this whitewashed spot on a quiet secondary street above the city centre does have character.

### Kokeb Pension
PENSION $

(☎0331-116366; r without bathroom Birr40) A simple setup around a tiled courtyard with clean, newly painted rooms, it's leagues better than most hotels in its class across Ethiopia, as long as you don't mind squat toilets. It's in a yellow building with a faded sign about 200m north of the bus station.

### Ayetegeb Café
EUROPEAN, ETHIOPIAN $

(mains Birr18-70) Formal in an Ethiopian kind of way, this hard-to-miss place on the main drag in the heart of town has a large crowd-pleasing menu of European and national dishes plus offers half-pizza for solo travellers. There's a bakery in front.

## ❶ Information

There are many internet cafes (Birr21 per hour), pharmacies, banks and small supermarkets along the main drag. The Dashen Bank in the unmissable Hajji Mohammed Yassin tower at the southern roundabout has an ATM.

## ❶ Getting There & Away

The bus station is located smack in the city centre. Normal buses leave for Addis Ababa (Birr118, nine hours, 10 daily) or you can treat your battered bottom to Selam (Birr175, eight hours, 5.30am) and Sky Bus (Birr209, eight hours, 6am), whose ticket offices are near the bus station. There's one daily bus to Lalibela (Birr97, eight to nine hours, 6am) and Mekele (Birr112, eight hours, 7am) and frequent buses and minibuses to Woldia (Birr45, 2½ hours) and Kombolcha (Birr8, 30 minutes).

If you're going to stop anywhere before Addis you'll either need to pay the full Addis fare or travel slowly in stages using multiple minibuses.

---

# Kombolcha
ኮምበልቻ

POP 64,200 / ELEV 1850M

The dramatic and curvaceous descent from Dessie to Kombolcha outdoes anything the twin towns have to offer. Kombolcha is less of a transportation hub than Dessie, but it's less dirty and noisy, which makes it a more pleasant option to break your journey.

## 🛏 Sleeping

### Sunny Side Hotel
HOTEL $$

(☎0335-512869; www.sunnyside-hotel.com; s/d/tw/ste incl breakfast Birr600/750/850/1000; 🅿@🛜) What do you do when stylish furniture and satellite TV make you the best hotel around, but faulty doors, broken lamps, plugged drains and other age-decay piles up? At Sunny Side, you jack up the already too-high *faranji* prices by up to 23%. Since it plays posh better than any other hotel in Kombolcha or Dessie, tour companies continue to fill the rooms. Anyone who cares about value should look elsewhere.

### Hikma Pension
HOTEL $

(☎0335-510015; d/tw Birr172/250) This very clean spot on the main traffic circle has colourful carpeted rooms with faux-flowers and better mattresses than Sunny Side. Despite limited choice, the terrace restaurant (mains Birr25 to Birr30) is popular.

## ❶ Getting There & Away

Frequent minibuses serve Dessie (Birr8, 30 minutes). Two buses leave daily for Addis Ababa (Birr110, seven hours, 6am).

---

# Bati
ባቲ

POP 18,400 / ELEV 1502M

The little town of Bati, 39km east of Kombolcha, is renowned for its massive **Monday market** (⊗9am-3pm), which attracts up to 10,000 Afar, Oromo and Amhara, and even some traders from Djibouti. It's Ethiopia's largest after Addis Ababa's Merkato, but it far eclipses the capital's for interest and exotica. Within the market is an old **gallows** (dating from the emperor's day) and on the other side of town are the livestock and chat markets. The town has some extremely obnoxious guides (one tried very persistently to charge us Birr600 to look at the gallows on a Sunday) and while they're not mandatory now, they might be in the future.

If you want an early start, **Vasco Tourist Hotel** (☎0335-530548; d Birr100) is the pick of the bunch.

Two buses and many minibuses serve Kombolcha daily (Birr17, one hour) and five buses head to Logiya (Birr70, four hours).

## Menz-Guassa Community Conservation Area

የመንዝ-ጓሳ ማህበረሰብ የእካባቢ ጥበቃ

Truly off the beaten track, the 98-sq-km Guassa Plateau has one of the smallest but best protected Afro-alpine habitats in Ethiopia. In fact, it's been a locally managed natural resource management area since the 17th century. The most notable wildlife are the three dozen Ethiopian wolf (best seen 6am to 7am and 4pm to 7pm) and the many gelada monkeys (see the boxed text, p274). There are also some leopards, spotted hyenas, servals, klipspringers and honey badgers. The locally common Auger buzzard (one of many raptors) and endangered Ankober serin are two of 114 bird species.

### 🏃 Trekking

A community-run trekking (☎0116-851326; www.guassaarea.org; per person per 24hr Birr100, guide per group Birr120) program initiated by the Frankfurt Zoological Society has made tourism in the area much easier – reservations are required. There are currently two basic campsites (Birr100) out in the wild with no facilities or you can do day treks using the lodge as a base. Mules for riding or carrying gear are available for Birr50 per day, plus a muleteer (who can handle two mules) costs another Birr50 per day. Note that as elsewhere in the north, July and August are the rainiest months, but here October is third rainiest. In the cold season temperatures can drop to -10°C.

### 🛏 Sleeping & Eating

**Guassa Community Lodge**              LODGE $
(campsites Birr100, dm Birr250; P) This place has four simple but almost cosy upper-floor bedrooms plus a lounge with fireplace and a kitchen (Birr100 per group). It's still quite rustic, but small improvements (such as hot showers, solar electricity and meals) are planned and the view over the plain is superb. For now, you must bring all your own food. Reservations required.

### ❶ Getting There & Away

From Tarmaber, 45km east of Debre Berhan, a rocky, seldom-travelled road begins south and takes you over the highway tunnel. It passes huge valleys for 80km (at least two hours' driving) to the headquarters.

Buses from Addis Ababa (Birr100, seven hours, 6am) and Debre Berhan (Birr60, four hours) to Mehal Meda pass the lodge/headquarters.

# Southern Ethiopia

## Why Go?

Southern Ethiopia is a canvas ripped in two. Its landscape is being torn apart by the Great Rift Valley, leaving a trail of lakes where you can go see crocodiles, hippos and birds – or just drink in the scenery from you hotel.

Move east and the Bale Mountains offer rewarding treks across a plateau amid Afro-alpine plants and rare wildlife. It's here you'll encounter the world's rarest canid, the Ethiopian wolf, hunting giant molerats.

But it's the seemingly timeless tribes of the Lower Omo Valley, such as the lip-stretching Mursi and body-painting Karo, that leave the deepest impression on visitors. To meet them 20 years ago was nearly unheard of. To travel there today is very easy, but still a privilege. Not that it always seems so. Frustration, born of the vast (but narrowing) cultural chasm, is almost inevitable. But while the irritation quickly fades, the memories never will.

## Best of Culture

» Lower Omo Valley (p161)

» Machekie (p160)

» Dorze (p158)

» Awasa's Fish Market (p140)

» El Sod (p151)

## Best of Nature

» Ethiopian wolves (p146)

» Sanetti Plateau (p145)

» Crocodile Market (p156)

» Senkelle Swayne's Hartebeest Sanctuary (p140)

## When to Go

### Arba Minch

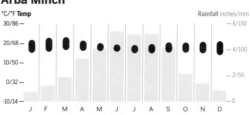

| **Jan–Apr** Prime months for Jumping of the Bulls ceremonies. | **Apr–May & Oct** The rainy season around the Lower Omo Valley; travel to some villages is impossible. | **Aug–Oct** The wettest months in the Bale Mountains; trekking can be difficult. |

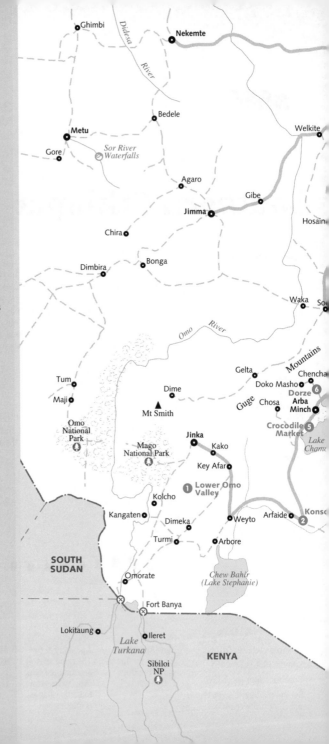

# Southern Ethiopia Highlights

**1** Barter for an inscribed calabash at a tribal market in the **Lower Omo Valley** (p161)

**2** Get lost in labyrinthine **Konso villages** (p160)

**3** Stand still so you don't frighten away an Ethiopian wolf in **Bale Mountains National Park** (p144)

**4** Imagine yourself in a fairytale forest while horse trekking from **Dodola** (p143)

**5** Don't rock the boat as you approach the reptilian residents of Lake Chamo's **crocodile market** (p156)

**6** See how the people of **Dorze** (p158) weave their houses

**7** Marvel at the strength of the men who work the black ooze in the **House of Salt** (p151)

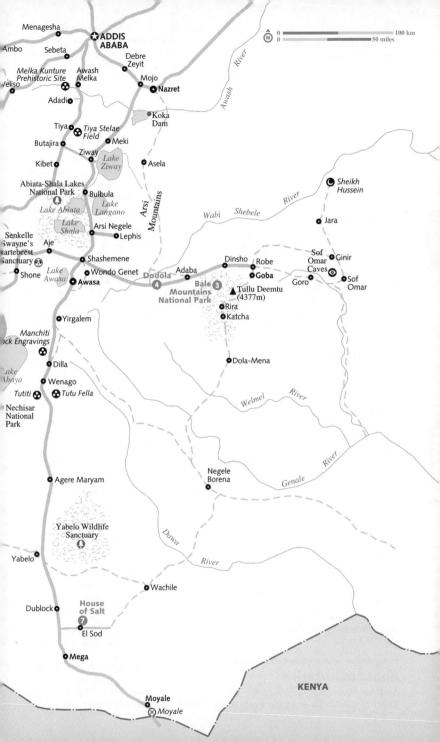

## ❶ Getting There & Away

**Ethiopian Airlines** (www.flyethiopian.com) connects Addis Ababa with Arba Minch.

Overland, there are three routes from Addis Ababa into southern Ethiopia. The Hosaina Road, the shortest route to the Lower Omo Valley; the Shashemene Road, which follows the Rift Valley for its first half; and the newly paved Asela Road which takes you direct to the Bale Mountains.

There are also direct links from the western towns of Jimma (to Sodo) and Welkite (to Hosaina; another road to Butajira is under construction) and from Kenya via Moyale and Omorate. There's public transport available along all routes except through Omorate.

## ❶ Getting Around

All three routes into the south are almost completely paved (the pavement ends in Jinka) and in generally good condition, as are the Butajira–Ziway, Shashemene–Sodo, and Sashemene–Goba roads. Most other roads are seriously rough and can be problematic during rain.

Daily buses and minibuses cover virtually all the routes in this chapter including most in the Lower Omo Valley. Jinka to Turmi, served only on market days, is the notable exception, though trucks fill the gap. Most people visiting isolated areas hire 4WDs from tour operators in Addis Ababa (see p295), although they can also be rented in Arba Minch, Jinka, Awash and sometimes Turmi.

# HOSAINA ROAD

The Hosaina Rd is the most direct way to Arba Minch and the Lower Omo Valley. Only paved relatively recently, it still feels remote and facilities are fewer and further between (and more basic) than along the long-standing Rift Valley route. The two routes merge at Sodo. Though still rough over long stretches, the whole road should be paved soon after the publication of this book.

A straight run can get you from Addis Ababa to Arba Minch in about eight hours. Although public transport is less frequent than on the Rift Valley route, some long-distance buses run this road and plenty of minibuses make short hops.

If driving, using this route to Lake Ziway (p135) rather than the Rift Valley route adds about 20km, but saves an hour.

## South to Butajira

An hour from Addis, just over the Awash River, is the **Melka Kunture Prehistoric**
**Site** (admission Birr30; ⊘8.30am-12.30pm & 1.30-4.30pm), where many stone tools and fossils, dating back 1.8 million years, have been found. Examples are displayed in four *tukuls* (huts), including tools used by the *Homo erectus* who once inhabited the area, and there's also an open excavation site down a sometimes muddy path. It's modest but interesting.

Around 4km south of Melka Kunture, there's a signposted turn-off to Ethiopia's southernmost rock-hewn church, **Adadi Maryam** (admission Birr50, camera/video Birr10/100). Believed to date from the 12th or 13th century, Adadi Maryam is fairly crude in comparison with its counterparts in Lalibela, but if you won't be travelling north, don't miss it. It sits on the far side of Adadi village, 12km west of the turn-off. Public transport runs to and from Awash Melka (Birr10, 45 minutes) throughout the day.

The World Heritage–listed **Tiya Stelae Field** (admission Birr50; ⊘8am-noon & 1-5pm) is the most important of the hundreds of stelae clusters dotting the countryside from here all the way down to Dilla (p151). Tiya contains 41 stelae up to 5m in height (including the buried portions), engraved with enigmatic symbols including swords. They mark graves of individuals aged between 18 and 30 who died around 700 years ago and were buried in the foetal position, though little is known about the culture that carved them. The site is about 35km after the turn-off to Adadi, at the south end of Tiya village. The **NOK Hotel** (☎0911-038578; r Birr100), hidden behind its namesake petrol station, is unexpectedly decent.

## Butajira     በቱጃራ

Located about 40km from Tiya is the town of Butajira. It comes too early to be a convenient overnight stop for most people journeying south, but if you're one of the exceptions, the older, but well-maintained **Fikado Asore Hotel** (☎0461-150443; d/tw Birr190/225; ℗) is a popular pick from a surprisingly good selection of hotels. Minibuses run frequently to/from Ziway (Birr15, one hour).

**Lake Hare Sheitan** (Devil's Lake), marked by a green sign 9km south of Butajira (turn east and look for the *tukul* on its rim 1km from the highway), is an incredible circular crater lake with the rim soaring perhaps 150m above the deep-green waters. About 500m beyond the lake, in a smaller, dry crater, is **Aynage Cave**. A friendly family moved in after they lost their land and they enjoy visitors – for a small donation, of course. We were even invited to spend the night. The vivid green hill across from the cave is Agode Lobrera and it has a small lake at the top. The roadside sign also indicates **Asano Stelae**, but it's really 11km south at **Asano village** and is hardly worth a stop.

## Hosaina                                     ሆሳዕና

After the lake, the Hosaina road passes numerous nondescript small towns and then climbs to Hosaina, which feels like it was thrown together overnight. Travellers rarely stop here. Currently the best, though not quietest, lodging is **Lemma International Hotel** (☎0465-554453; d Birr150-210, tw Birr260; **P**@) alongside the bus station. It has billiards tables, a sauna (per hour Birr70), a good restaurant and scenic views from front-facing rooms. The nearby Dashen Bank has an ATM.

The road drops out of Hosaina past a noticeably large number of **Protestant churches**: evangelical missionaries have been very successful here over the past decade. Eventually the road climbs to Sodo.

## Sodo                                       ሶዶ

The hillside capital of Wolaita Zone, Sodo is as forgettable as Hosaina, but it's a better overnight stop. If you're not in a rush, visit **Sodo Museum** (admission Birr50; ⊙8.30am-12.30pm & 1.30-5pm Mon-Fri). It has various objects on display in the big round hall – the metal and brick exterior covers a traditional-style king's palace – including 2m-long musical horns, elephant-skin shields and a typical family's home. It's just past the southern roundabout on the new road. Someone from the Tourism Bureau (the building by the painted trees) will open the door, turn on the lights and spray air freshener for you.

Newish and overpriced, **Fanta Vision Hotel** (☎0465-514747; s/tw from Birr250/350; **P**) is the best of a very uninspiring selection of hotels, though new places are supposedly on the way. It's on the new road, north of the traffic circle. With few exceptions, the lunch stop of choice for tours passing through is **Day Star Restaurant** (mains Birr23-92), 3km south of the hilltop on the Arba Minch road.

The Dashen Bank on the Arba Minch road has an ATM. There are frequent buses to Arba Minch (Birr49, 3½ hours) and Awasa (Birr46, 2½ hours), plus two morning departures to Addis Ababa (Birr115, six or seven hours). See p208 for travel details to Jimma.

## South of Sodo

Eighteen kilometres out of Sodo is the large Thursday **cattle market** (⊙10am-6pm) in little **Humbo**. Continuing on, you can see Lake Abaya (p153) in the distance as the road drops slowly into the Rift Valley. Thirty-eight kilometres out of Sodo you'll cross a bridge and see a tall two-tiered **waterfall** on your right, unless it's the dry season, when it disappears. From there, the road runs between the lake and the forest-clad Guge Mountains all the way to Arba Minch (see p153), tossing out some stunning scenery in the early stages. About 10km before Arba Minch is the turn-off for Dorze (p158).

# RIFT VALLEY LAKES

The traditional route to southern Ethiopia heads southeast out of Addis and departs the Harar road 70km later at Mojo. The many shade houses you'll pass supply the European market with flowers and vegetables. Also keep an eye out for colourful **Oromo tombs** that dot the countryside, particularly after Lake Ziway.

The route follows one of our planet's grandest geographical features: the massive Great Rift Valley. A 4000km scar that stretches from the Red Sea to Mozambique, it's a work in progress, and millions of years from now the rifting process will have split Africa in two. The most visible manifestation of the subterranean forces in this area is a string of five lakes along the road.

## Lake Ziway                     ዝዋይ ሐይቅ

Surrounded by volcanic hills and covering a massive 425 sq km, Lake Ziway is the largest of the northern group of Rift Valley lakes.

### ⊙ Sights & Activities

Typically the lake earned just a quick hit on a southern sojourn, for a look at the many white pelicans, hamerkops, sacred ibises, African fishing eagles, marabou storks and other **birds** that hang around the busy earthen **jetty** (per person Birr10, per vehicle

Birr10) waiting to feed on fishermen's cast-offs. But the formalised organisation of boat trips to the islands should lead more people to extend their stay.

**Visitor Information Centre**  BOAT TOUR
(📞0927-340309; ziwayboatservice@gmail.com; ⊙8am-5pm) Boat trips are booked here near the jetty, 1km east of Bekele Mola Hotel. The most popular outing is the half-day Short Boat Tour (one to four people Birr620), which visits the historic monastery on **Debre Sina island**, takes a close look at the residents of **Bird Island**, finds the **hippo pods** (which can sometimes be seen from the jetty), and stops to climb up to a viewpoint.

Another half-day trip (Birr1300) goes out to the largest island, **Tullu Gudo**, to visit the Zay village and the legendary **Maryam Tsion** (Birr50) monastery. According to tradition, it housed the Ark of the Covenant for 70 years when priests, fleeing the destruction of the city of Aksum at the hands of Queen Gudit in the 9th century, brought it here. Interestingly, the oldest written documents about Aksum were discovered here. A full-day Tullu Gudo trip (Birr1500) provides enough additional time to climb up to the **ruins** of the original monastery. A small community-run restaurant on Tulu Gudo serves fresh tilapia.

You can also hire guides at the Visitor Information Centre for birdwatching or cultural tours.

## 🛏 Sleeping & Eating

Camping is permitted on Ziway's islands and there's talk of a lodge opening on Tullu Gudo.

**Bethlehem Hotel**  HOTEL $
(📞0464-414104; d Birr288, bungalow Birr460; 🅿) This new option on the road to the jetty is now the top digs in the Ziway area. Rooms are clean and quiet and they don't follow a cookie cutter design.

**Bekele Mola Hotel**  HOTEL $
(📞0464-412077; d Birr110-220; 🅿) Behind the OiLibya station, Bekele Mola's aged but clean rooms surround a courtyard that's full to the brim with birds. The 'new' rooms are really quite good. Only some of the old rooms have hot water.

**Ziway Tourist Hotel**  HOTEL $
(📞0464-413993; d without bathroom Birr90, d Birr150-400; 🅿) It can't beat its rival, Bekele Mola, in the lodging department since it charges less and delivers less, but it's an acceptable back-up if needed. However, it

has become the lunch stop of choice (mains Birr20 to Birr100) for those on their way to, or back from, the south.

## ℹ Information

Ziway town hugs the Addis–Shashemene Rd. There's an internet cafe (Birr15 per hour) just north of Bekele Mola Hotel and another just north of the telecommunications office. There's also a Dashen Bank with an ATM near the latter.

## ℹ Getting There & Around

Transport runs regularly to Shashemene (Birr28, 1½ hours), Butajira (Birr15, one hour) and Addis Ababa (Birr46, three hours). For Lake Langano you may have to pay the full Shashemene fare, even in a minibus. For Nazret, take a minibus to Mojo (Birr27, one hour) first.

Shared *bajaj* (auto-rickshaws) run up and down the highway, but to the jetty you'll have to charter for Birr10.

If you make arrangements the day before, you may be able to ride the early morning boat that takes locals to Tullu Gudo, but for sure you won't pay the local price.

# Lake Langano
ላንጋኖ ሐይቅ

Lake Langano resembles a giant puddle of milky English tea set against the blue curtain of the Arsi Mountains. The water may be brown and unappealing, but it's one of the few Ethiopian lakes to be declared bilharzia-free and thus safe for **swimming**. And, like all the Rift Valley lakes, the **birdwatching** is good.

Our best advice: avoid the weekends, when every man and his ghetto blaster make the 180km trip from Addis Ababa.

## 🛏 Sleeping & Eating

Accommodation and dining options around Lake Langano are limited to large, expensive lodges. The following rates are for weekdays (Sunday through Thursday); weekend prices are up to 30% higher.

A new place is set to replace the old Bekele Mola Hotel, which had a great setting near the entrance to Abiata-Shala Lakes National Park, but nobody there could give us any details.

**TOP** CHOICE **Sabana Beach Resort**  LODGE $$$
(Map p137; 📞0461-191180; www.sabanalangano.com; s/d incl breakfast US$59/71; 🅿) Occupying an elevated position with impressive views

over the lake, Sabana sets the standard for Langano. Unlike most places in Ethiopia, the quality of the workmanship shows and the 25 cottages are as good as they are lovely. The pavilion-like restaurant has picture windows and the landscaped gardens may provide the best birding on the western shore. Sabana doesn't do boat trips, but it has canoes and massage service. It's 2.8km from the highway.

**Bishangari Lodge**          LODGE $$$
(☎0461-191276; www.bishangari.com; tukuls s/ tw US$41/73, s/tw bungalow incl breakfast from US$78/137; Ⓟ) Hyped as Ethiopia's first ecolodge when it opened in 1997, Bishangari is ideal for those wanting a natural getaway. Nine beautiful *godjos* (bungalows) are nestled privately along the lake's southeastern shore, 18km (one hour) from the highway along a corrugated road. Each is decorated with woven ceilings, local artwork and natural woods. There are also basic *tukuls* with shared facilities that sit unappealingly outside the forest next to the car park. The Tree Bar, wrapped around a giant fig tree that attracts troops of monkeys, is particularly evocative and the forest is full of birdlife. Boat trips, horse riding, mountain biking and nature walks to see hippos are sometimes possible.

**Wenney Eco-Lodge**          LODGE $$$
(☎0911-430835; www.wenneyecolodge.com; campsites Birr55, d/tw US$66/78; Ⓟ) Near Bishangari, the key word here is 'less'. The accommodation is less refined (including no hot water) than Bishangari's bungalows and there's less forest, less wildlife and less peace and quiet. On the other hand, it costs less. Its best feature is the open-air dining hall, beautifully decorated with funky furniture, and it offers many of the same activities as Bishangari.

**Borati Resort**          LODGE $$
(Map p137; ☎0942-647979; d Birr760, f Birr1870-2800; Ⓟ) It's easy to criticise this new place on the northwest end of the lake since there's much half-finished construction and the only restaurant is down near the beach, far from the clifftop cottages. Despite this, the rooms are comfortable and tasteful, and the views are excellent, and in all regards it's *way* better than Langano's other lower-priced options. It's 3.6km from the highway.

### ⓘ Getting There & Away

To get to/from Lake Langano, take any bus or minibus plying the Addis Ababa–Shashemene road, and ask to be dropped off/picked up at the turn-off to your hotel. For a bus, you'll likely have to pay full fare to either Shashemene or Ziway.

## Abiata-Shala Lakes National Park
### አባያታ ሻላ ሐይቅ ብሔራዊ ፓርክ

West of Lake Langano lie the **twin lakes of Abiata and Shala**, which form part of the 887-sq-km **national park** (admission per person per day Birr90, vehicle Birr20, mandatory scout Birr70). Identical twins these lakes are not: Shala's 410-sq-km surface sits within a collapsed volcanic caldera and depths exceed 260m in some areas, making it the deepest lake in Ethiopia, while Abiata's highly alkaline waters rest in a shallow pan no more than 14m in depth. And Abiata is shrinking dramatically as water is diverted to irrigation projects and a soda-ash factory. The increased salinity has killed off the fish and forced most birds to go elsewhere to feed.

The land has suffered along with the lake and this is now a national park in name and decree only. Illegal settlers have invaded nearly its entirety, turning the thick woodland into charcoal and replacing much of

## Abiata-Shala Lakes National Park

it with villages and farm fields. Despite the destruction, a short visit remains enjoyable.

A typical visit lasts about two hours and starts with a walk through the fenced land around the headquarters where semi-tame ostrich, gazelle and warthogs (almost certainly the only nonwinged **wildlife** you'll encounter) live. Then you drive (or walk) 5km to an **overlook** of the two lakes, followed 3.5km later by a spread of gurgling sulphurous **hot springs** on the northeast shore of Shala where locals wash clothes and bathe. Another 7km takes you to the shrunken shore of Abiata to look for **flamingos**, which have increased dramatically since the fish die-off (because they feed on algae) and can be seen in flocks of thousands, especially from October to February.

At Shala's southwestern shore there's a second hot spring and a stunning, pint-sized crater lake. Looking 80m down from the rim to **Lake Chitu** and spotting its 2000 or so semiresident flamingos is a sight worth the effort. The south shore is accessed via **Aware** or **Aje**, but admission can only be paid at the main park entrance and at Horakelo.

**Camping** (per tent Birr40) is permitted anywhere in the park, though there are no facilities and you must have the scout with you. Don't leave your camp unattended.

### ❶ Getting There & Around

The main park entrance, where the headquarters is, lies right along the highway. Buses doing the Addis Ababa–Shashemene run can drop you off, as can many minibuses.

For driving inside the park, a 4WD is essential.

## Shashemene ሻሸመኔ

POP 118,900 / ELEV 1700M

Shashemene is a grubby crossroads town and most travellers prefer nearby Awasa. Shashemene does have one trick up its sleeve, however: it's the Rastafari capital of Africa and if this interests you, you're going to love it.

When Ras Tafari was crowned Emperor Haile Selassie in 1930, he gained subjects far beyond his own kingdom. In Jamaica, Marcus Garvey's 'return to Africa' movement saw the emperor's coronation as fulfilment of the ancient biblical prophesy that 'Kings will come out of Africa'. Identifying themselves passionately with Ethiopia's monarch, as well as with Ethiopia's status as an independent nation, Garvey's followers created a new religion. In it, the emperor was accorded divinity (the Messiah of African Redemption) and the new faith given his pre-coronation name. What did the Emperor think of all this? Well, it was said that he was rather embarrassed. That is until 1963, when he overcame his bashfulness and granted the Rastafarians land in Shashemene.

Although nothing came of it in the end, much to the thanks of the entire population of Jamaica, Shashemene was briefly in the

---

### LEPHIS

Up against the Duro Mountains north of Shashemene is the lovely and relatively pristine Lephis Forest, home to Menelik's bushbuck, mountain nyala, leopard, spotted hyena, warthog, black-and-white colobus and olive baboon. The rich birdlife includes the beautiful white-cheeked turaco and Abyssinian oriole. As an incentive to protect the remaining forest from the axe, the **Lephis Ecotourism Cooperative** (🖉0928-828530), based in Lephis village, has begun **trekking** trips, either on horseback (must book in advance) or foot. The project is new – this author was their first walk-in customer – and has some things to work out still, but everything seems promising.

The two- to three-hour waterfall trail (per group Birr250, horse per person Birr100) climbs to the lovely, 45m-tall Lephis Waterfall, passing several smaller falls as it loops back on the other side of the Lephis River. Treks on the Dungago Trail (per group Birr400, horse per person Birr200) can last a full day and it's the trail of choice for **birdwatchers**.

A **campsite** (2 people Birr200, each additional person Birr50) 6km up the Dungago Trail allows early morning and late afternoon wildlife watching. The price includes use of its camping gear.

The 'welcome *tukul*' is 17.5km east of Arsi Negele (Birr7, 45 minutes) and buses run about hourly.

news when Bob Marley's wife announced that she was going to have his remains moved here.

## ◉ Sights

### Rastafarian Community NEIGHBOURHOOD
Shashemene's Rastafarian community, known locally as Jamaica, straddles the main road just north of town. It's readily distinguished by its tri-coloured buildings, dread-locked inhabitants and rounded vowels of Caribbean English. A shared *bajaj* from the bus station costs Birr2, or if you're arriving from the north, just hop off when you pass it.

Various local teenagers (none of them real Rastas) serve as unofficial, and often unwelcome, guides. They'll take you to see some churches and the defunct Black Lion Museum, which is just a family's home with paintings of the Emperor on the walls, but their real aim is to sell you *ganja* (marijuana), which is held sacrosanct in Rastafarianism but is illegal in Ethiopia. You've been warned.

If you want to really meet and learn about the 'Jamaicans', the Zion Train Lodge and **Banana Art Gallery** (admission Birr15; ⊘hours vary) are two good places to start. The latter is the home-cum-workshop-cum-museum of Haile Selassie medals and memorabilia of Ras Hailu Tefari (Bandy), originally from St Vincent in the Caribbean. His extraordinary 'paintings' use only material from banana plants without even additional colouring. It's 500m down the dirt road opposite the Black Lion.

### Wondo Genet SPRING
The name of this hot springs resort 16km southeast of Shashemene translates as 'Green Heaven', which was more applicable before the hills were cleared of most of their forest. The only lodging is the **Wabe Shebelle Hotel** (☎0461-190705, r/ste incl breakfast Birr740/2000; ℗), which sits in flowering gardens, but its run-down rooms make it a contender for most overpriced lodging in Ethiopia. (The suite was originally built for Haile Selassie, so it's got that going for it.) The cement **hot springs pools** (admission Birr25; ⊘6am-10pm) have more the feel of a water treatment plant than a resort; they should pay you to use the toilets.

The well-trained **Wondo Genet Ecotourism Guide Association** (☎0928-768347) offers a variety of one-hour to one-day walks in the area. Its office is by the resort gate.

Minibuses run regularly (until 5pm) from Shashemene to Wondo Wosha (Birr6, 40 minutes) village, 2.5km from the springs. From there, walk up the hill or take a *bajaj* (Birr4).

## ⌂ Sleeping & Eating

### TOP CHOICE / Zion Train Lodge GUESTHOUSE $$
(☎0911-887680; www.ziontrainlodge.com; campsites Birr20, d with/without bathroom Birr450/250; ℗) This surprising oasis, run by a French Rastafarian family, features large Sidamo-style huts and also some shared bathrooms, all attractive and comfortable. The restaurant (mains Birr20 to Birr48) does healthy cooking using some organic ingredients. It's signposted 1km from Jamaica.

### Shashemene Rift Valley Tourist Hotel HOTEL $
(☎0461-105710; d Birr193-385, tw Birr495-550; ℗⊛) There are three levels of rooms in an old and new building. They're a bit overpriced, but you pay a premium for the multi-level garden full of trees and art, which takes you a world away from the rest of the town. The restaurant (mains Birr35 to Birr53) has a larger than normal roster of local and international fare. A swimming pool is promised.

### Barentuma Pension PENSION $
(☎0461-102165; d with/without bathroom Birr120/70; ℗) New, reasonably priced and right by the bus station. Go out the south exit and turn right. There's an internet cafe and grocery next door.

### Bekele Mola HOTEL $
(☎0461-103344; d Birr165; ℗) If you need to stay in the centre, these weathered but well-scrubbed rooms, each with a verandah facing the green courtyard, are a good choice.

### Spicy Caribbean Delight CARIBBEAN $
(plate of the day Birr25; ⊘Mon-Sat) The daily menus feature Trinidadian and some Jamaican dishes like curried goat, while a few options, like the tasty lentil burger, are always available. It's next to the Banana Art Gallery and closes at 7pm.

## ❶ Information

There's a post office and many internet cafes and banks stretched along the main drag. Dashen Bank has an ATM. Several small groceries both downtown and by the bus station have better selections than any in the gateway towns for Bale Mountains trekking.

### ⓘ Getting There & Away

Shashemene is the principal transport hub of the south, and the huge bus station is located along the new bypass, northeast of the city centre. Buses run frequently to Sodo (Birr40, three hours), Addis Ababa (Birr90, four hours) via Ziway (Birr28, 1½ hours) and Goba (Birr59, three hours) via Dodola (Birr24, one hour). There's also one early morning bus direct to Moyale (Birr100, 11 to 12 hours) via Dilla (Birr30, three hours) and two to Negele Borena (Birr116, 10 to 11 hours). Minibuses to Awasa (Birr8, 30 minutes) depart nearly constantly.

## Senkelle Swayne's Hartebeest Sanctuary

ሰንቀሌ የስዋይን ቆርኪዎች መጠለያ

**Senkelle** (admission per person per day Birr90, vehicle Birr20, park guide Birr100) was established to protect Ethiopia's endemic Swayne's hartebeest, and though the population of around 700 is a far cry from the huge herds of the past, it's large enough to make a visit enjoyable.

A typical visit, whether driving or walking, goes through the savannah, where Swayne's and oribi antelope are sure to be seen, and then up to Borena Hill, 6km from the headquarters, for views of Lake Awasa and likely **wildlife encounters** with warthogs, olive baboons, vervet monkeys and bushbuck. Don't count on seeing any of the few remaining leopards, cheetahs, spotted hyenas or caracals. The globally threatened greater spotted eagle is one of 191 **bird species** documented, and swallow-tailed kites are often seen.

Going deeper into the 57-sq-km park, there are **lakes** and **hot springs**. Wherever you go, a park guide is mandatory.

Camping is permitted, though there are no facilities or food. The town of Aje provides the closest lodging, but nothing's clean enough to be recommendable over any other.

### ⓘ Getting There & Away

The road towards the park lies 2km west of Aje and then the turn-off is after 10.3km at Debu, from where you follow the signs 4.6km to the headquarters. Public transport runs frequently from Shashemene (Birr10, 30 minutes) and Sodo (Birr60, two hours) to Aje, and from Aje a few minibuses pass Debu (Birr10, 30 minutes); from Debu you need to walk.

## Awasa                           አዋሳ

POP 200,400 / ELEV 1708M

Perfectly poised at Lake Awasa's edge, the capital of the Southern Nations, Nationalities and People's Region (SNNPR) is large, modern and a bit of a shock to the system for those who've been slogging it through the south for a long time. While Awasa (officially Hawassa, but this new name hasn't completely caught on yet) has no major sights, the lake and its surrounds offer a relaxing respite from the rigours of southern travel.

### ◎ Sights & Activities

**Lake Awasa**                          LAKE

With its mountainous backdrop, Lake Awasa is a lovely sight. You could easily spend a few pleasant hours strolling the lakeshore trail at the end of town, watching men fishing from papyrus rafts, seeing the various shorebirds feeding in the reeds, and stopping for fried tilapia and a coffee ceremony at one of the many rustic restaurants.

To gain a pelican's perspective of Awasa's shimmering waters, clamber into a **boat** (1hr motorboat hire or 3hr rowboat hire Birr450) at the base of the main drag. The boatmen will take you anywhere you request, but most people choose **Tikur Wuha** (Black Water) to see the hippos.

**Fish Market**                        MARKET

(admission Birr20, mandatory guide per group Birr50; ◷7-10am) Lake Awasa's fishermen head out in their little wooden boats in the afternoon and return the next morning laden with tilapia and catfish. The men are amazingly deft at gutting, scaling, skinning and flicking the eyes out of their catches. Massive marabou storks do janitorial duty while vervet monkeys beg around the nearby bar. Behind the fish market it's possible to hike up to the views atop steep and stubby **Tabour Hill**.

[FREE] **Sidamo Zone Ethnographic Museum**                    MUSEUM

(◷8.30am-12.30pm & 1.30-5.30pm) The small, neglected collection here isn't really worth your time; the man with the key is probably on a five-hour lunchbreak anyway. But a large new regional museum that, we were told, will cover the region's 56 ethnic groups, should be worth a visit when it opens.

# Awasa

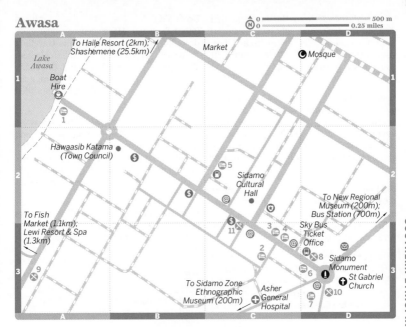

## 🛏 Sleeping

**Time Café**                                 HOTEL **$**

(☎0462-206331; d Birr230; P) The new rooms in back of this good restaurant score on all accounts: clean, comfy, good location and good value. Be sure to ask for a room away from the noisy kitchen.

**Haile Resort**                              HOTEL **$$$**

(☎0462-208444; www.haileresort.com.et; s/d/tw incl breakfast US$89/101/126; P@🖥🏊) A project of famed distance runner Haile Gebrselassie, this lakeside place on the Addis-side of town is a tasteful, art-filled international-standard hotel. There are plenty of extras, like tennis courts, sauna, putt-putt golf and mountain bikes, plus top-notch dining. Paying extra for a lake view is worth it.

**Hotel Pinna 1**                             HOTEL **$**

(☎0462-210335; d/tw Birr280/395; P🖥) An older property that, unusual for Ethiopia, is well maintained and up to date with wi-fi and satellite TV. Very good value.

**Hotel Pinna 2**                             HOTEL **$$**

(☎0462-210336; d Birr355-465, tw Birr465; P🖥) Next door to its older sister, this place is younger and smarter, though beyond the funky furniture in the lobby, just as plain. The higher price also gets you a few more

gadgets such as a minifridge and nifty showers that convert into steam baths.

**Lewi Resort & Spa**                         RESORT **$$$**

(☎0462-214143; www.lewihotelandresort.com; s/tw incl breakfast US$49/103, d incl breakfast US$69-119; P@🖥🏊) Not to be confused with any of the other Lewis in town, this expensive lakeside place serves four-star luxury in a completely Ethiopian way. There's a large variety of rooms, from the basic 'garden view' to the tacky and ugly (cue '70s porn music) bungalows. The 'deluxe' rooms have large private balconies. There's putt-putt golf and a playground for the little kids and a gym and mountain bikes for the big kids.

**Lewi Piazza** HOTEL $$
(☏0462-201654; www.lewihotelandresort.com; d/tw incl breakfast Birr525/750; P@☎) Fairly swish by Ethiopian standards, it's got the most mod cons (including in-room safes, massage showers and an elevator) available in this price range.

**TM Pension** PENSION $
(☏0462-204447; d/tw without bathroom Birr50/80, d Birr70; P) The rooms here are small and functional and offer excellent value. The Amharic name is 'Tami'.

**Circle of Life Hotel** HOTEL $
(☏0462-207800; d/tw without bathroom Birr57/87, d Birr150; P) Though the rooms are dark and a tad rank, it deserves consideration for being so near the lake and having such a vivid garden.

**Hotel Kasech Pension** PENSION $
(☏0462-214593; d Birr160; P) A superclean older place with in-room TVs.

**Lakeside Motel** HOTEL $$
(☏0462-210337; d Birr400-470; P) A demerit for false advertising (it's nearly 1km to the lake) but kudos for the rooms that, though overpriced, are solid. It's behind Dolce Vita restaurant.

## ✖ Eating

For self-caterers, Abazir Supermarket and Hawassa Supermarket are Awasa's best-stocked groceries.

**Time Café** ETHIOPIAN-EUROPEAN $
(mains Birr20-65) A stylish cafe popular with young Awasians. Coy couples come here to giggle under the patio umbrellas and share ice-cream sundaes and plates of fries. It also has good burgers and pizzas.

**Pinna Hotel** ETHIOPIAN-EUROPEAN $
(mains Birr40-110; ☎) If the cakes in the ground-floor pastry shop don't sidetrack you, head upstairs to a very *faranji* (foreigner)-friendly menu. Specialities include ravioli with spinach, stir-fried chicken and fish with pineapple. The lightning fast wi-fi should divert your attention from the glacial service.

**Dolce Vita** ITALIAN $
(mains Birr46-92) Many people, apparently decompressing after a long time travelling in the south, rave about this Italian kitchen. We enjoyed the food here (and the shady terrace), which is clearly above average for Ethiopia, but don't quite share the unbridled enthusiasm.

**Lewi Resort** ETHIOPIAN-EUROPEAN $
(mains Birr55-114) Not to dismiss the food (everything from pizza to pepper pot soup), but it's the shady stone terrace along the lake that really pleases the throngs. With a lengthy drinks list it's also a perfect sundowner spot.

**Luwa Bar & Restaurant** ETHIOPIAN $
(mains Birr20-50) Sit under the woven bamboo parasols and enjoy top-notch national food.

## ❶ Information

The banks, a host of internet cafes (per hour Birr15) and nearly everything a traveller needs can be found between the Sidamo Monument and the lake.

**Asher General Hospital** (☏0462-206153; ☺24hr) Awasa's best medical facility. Includes a pharmacy.

**Commercial Bank** Has an ATM.

**Dashen Bank** Has an ATM at its downtown branch, and another across from the bus station.

**Wagagen Bank** Has an ATM at its downtown branch, and another at Lewi Resort.

## ❶ Getting There & Around

The **bus station** lies about 1km northeast of the centre. A shared/contract *bajaj* to the centre costs Birr1.50/30.

Around 10 buses daily run to Addis Ababa (Birr85, four to five hours) and Sodo (Birr46, 2½ hours), plus two to Arba Minch (Birr83, six hours). There are many buses and minibuses to Dilla (Birr27, 2½ hours) and nearly constant minibus departures to Shashemene (Birr8, 30 minutes). For Moyale, go to Shashemene or Dilla and get a bus direct from there. The deluxe **Sky Bus** (Birr138) departs to Addis from in front of the bus station at 6am. The ticket office is in the Alliance Marketing Centre building downtown.

# BALE MOUNTAINS

Once one of the country's worst roads, the fresh pavement on the mountain-tracing highway east of Shashemene has opened up the Bale Mountains, though visitors have yet to descend in any great numbers. But surely they will. This unique region offers great trekking amid rare wildlife; a surreal underground river; and a fertile countryside lorded over by rugged horsemen.

# Dodola & Around

Resting between Shashemene and Bale Mountains National Park, the diminutive town of Dodola is the base for some lauded horse treks. Initially set up by the German aid organisation GTZ to conserve the environment by offering local people an alternative income to felling the local forests, it's now self-sufficient and locally run.

## 🏃 Trekking

Due to the high altitudes and steep gradients, most people **trek on horseback**, but this isn't mandatory. The trekking territory lies adjacent to Bale Mountains National Park (p144) and many people choose to trek at both. The national park offers significantly better wildlife watching, but most people find the scenery here superior and enjoy the cultural exchange with villagers along the way. The ecosystem and climate are essentially the same, so see that section for additional background information.

Also see the Safety Guidelines for Trekking (p90) and Responsible Trekking (p91) boxed texts before embarking.

### Planning

Thanks to five cosy lodges built along the route, trekking here is perfect for those without camping gear; however, bringing your own sleeping bag is recommended. Typical camping food (pasta, lentils, biscuits, tomato paste etc) can be purchased in Dodola and bread, porridge, sheep and goats can be obtained en route. Stoves, cooking utensils, beer and soft drinks are all found within the lodges. Optional cooks cost Birr150 per day.

The Commercial Bank in Dodola changes money.

### Guides, Horses & Handlers

Located in a gated compound on the west side of town but hoping to relocate, the **Dodola-Adama Tour Guide Association** (📞0226-660700; www.baletrek.com; ⏱8.30am-12.30pm & 1.30-5.30pm) organises horses (per day Birr50), horse handlers (one per two horses, per day Birr50) and mandatory guides (per day Birr187). Visitors must also pay Birr40 entry.

### Treks

Treks typically start from Dodola and follow a dirt road to the tented camp at **Changiti**

## Dodola Trekking

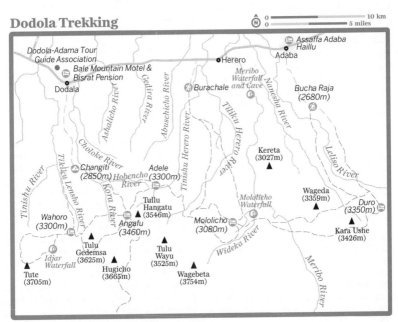

(2850m, 11km, 2½ hours), but if you start by 9am you can ride straight to the first lodge, **Wahoro** (18km, five to six hours), either following the thick, fairytale forest along the Tikiku Lensho River or taking a higher route with good views. From here you work your way eastward to the lodge **Angafu** (3460m, 10km, three to four hours); typically it's a short trip, but there's the option to trek (sans horse) the long way via the Wagabeta Ridge, which has much wildlife including Ethiopian wolves. The ridge could also be visited the next day before the easy ride to **Adele** (3300m, 5km, 1½ to two hours). Then it's a long, lovely ride to **Mololicho** (3080m, 18km, five to six hours) and finally the last lodge at **Duro** (3350m, 20km, six to seven hours), which most agree has the best vistas. From here it's a 20km (five- to six-hour) descent to the town of **Adaba**, 22km east of Dodola.

To complete the full circuit, stopping one night at each lodge, takes seven days, but many people skip Changiti and Adele and do it in five. Shorter rides are also possible or you can extend the journey into the Sanetti Plateau in Bale Mountains National Park; your Dodola guides will hand you over to a new guide and horse at the border. In the rainy season, when rivers flow fast and high, Duro may be blocked and you'll need to descend from Mololicho to Herero (20km, four to five hours).

## 🛌 Sleeping & Eating

**Mountain Lodges**                LODGE, TENTED CAMP **$**
(campsites/dm Birr45/65) Each of the five lodges has two sleeping rooms (eight beds total) complete with mattresses and bedding and a fully equipped kitchen. Hot showers cost Birr5. Changiti is a more basic permanent tented camp.

**Bisrat Pension**                          PENSION **$**
(☏0912-944942; Dodola; d with/without bathroom Birr120/90; ℗) Near the guide office, it lacks the garden of its competitor, but the rooms at this family-owned place are about as spotless as a budget hotel can be. A restaurant is planned.

**Bale Mountain Motel**                     HOTEL **$**
(☏0226-660016; Dodola; campsites Birr40, s/d/tw Birr100/150/200; ℗) Also near the guide office but set in a quiet garden with many birds, this long-running place has been spruced up a bit, but the simple rooms remain dreary. The shared toilets are nothing to sing about,

but thankfully they're nothing to scream about either. Meals cost Birr18 to Birr40.

**Asseffa Hailu Hotel**                     HOTEL **$**
(☏0226-630002; Adaba; old bldg s/d without bathroom Birr100/150, s/d Birr150/200, new bldg s/d 200/250; ℗) Adaba's original (now second) high-rise is friendly and well-maintained with good mattresses and a 4th-floor restaurant (mains Birr35 to Birr80; we figure the 'Gordon Brown' is really cordon bleu), though the owner has heartily embraced the *faranji* tax so it's poor value. The blue rooms in the old building across the street provide even less bang for your birr.

## ℹ Getting There & Away

Public transport is frequent along the main road and you won't have to wait long for Adaba (Birr8, 20 minutes), Dinsho (Birr20, one hour) or Robe (Birr35, two hours).

To/from Addis Ababa (Birr104, five hours) you can ride the Robe or Goba buses, since no buses to Addis start here. They'll be full when they arrive so either go to Shashemene (Birr24, one hour) and catch a connection there or ask your guide to call Robe and have the conductor hold a seat for you.

Nazret must be done in stages. There are Dodola–Asela (Birr42, two hours) buses in the morning, and sometimes a minibus after lunch. Transport runs all day on the Asela–Nazret (Birr24, one hour) leg.

# Bale Mountains National Park

የባሌ ተራሮች
ብሔራዊ ፓርክ

More than any other park in Ethiopia, this soon-to-be World Heritage site is known for its wildlife, but it's a very beautiful place, too. As you approach from Dodola, ridges to the east are punctuated with fortress-like escarpments, standing out from the gentler, rounded rock pinnacles to the north, and the great wildlife watching commences right from the start when the road cuts through the Gaysay Grassland in the valley between them, which is home to the densest concentration of large mammals in Ethiopia.

Up in the hills, accessible by footpath and road, are deep gorges, alpine lakes, rushing streams, several waterfalls, lava flows and views that go on almost forever. If it weren't located in such a remote corner of the country it would probably be as popular as the Simien Mountains.

## Climate & Geography

Bale can be rewarding at any time. Although the nights are cold, November to March is dry and visibility is at its best, thus it's the ideal time to trek. August to October is the wettest time and wildflowers are most abundant. Though the rain usually comes only in the afternoon the fog can last for days. Negative temperatures are normal at night on the Sanetti Plateau, whose name means 'Where strong winds blow' in Oromo.

The park stretches over 2400sq km and ranges in altitude from 1500m to 4377m. It covers the largest area above 3000m in Africa. The Harenna Escarpment splits the park in two, running fracture-like from east to west. North of the escarpment lies the high-altitude plateau known as the **Sanetti Plateau** (4000m), which is dotted with several peaks, including Tullu Deemtu (4377m), the second highest in Ethiopia. To the south, the land falls away from the plateau, and a

thick heather belt gives way to the 4000-sq-km Harenna Forest.

## Ecology

The park can be divided into three main ecological zones. The northernmost area, the Gaysay Grassland, near the park headquarters at Dinsho, consists of grassy, riverine plains and bushland. From 2500m to 3300m, woodland of mainly *Hagenia abyssinica* and *Juniperus procera* is found. The abundant wildflowers in the area include geranium, lobelia and alchemilla. Higher up, montane grassland gives way to heather, which here rarely grows tall.

The second zone, the Sanetti Plateau, is home to the continent's largest swathe of Afro-alpine plants, some of which have adapted to the extreme conditions by either remaining very small or becoming very large. The best known is the curious-looking giant lobelia *(Lobelia rhynchopetalum),* which can soar to 9m in height. The silver

SOUTHERN ETHIOPIA BALE MOUNTAINS NATIONAL PARK

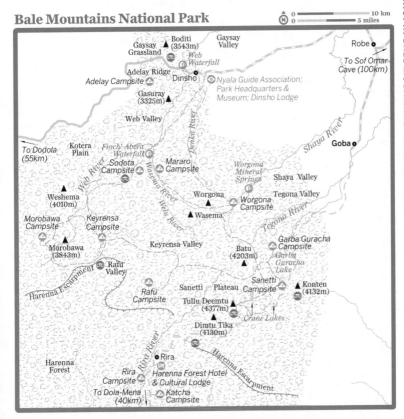

Bale Mountains National Park

*Helichrysum* ('everlasting' flowers) are the dominant wildflowers. Keep an eye out for the indigenous Abyssinian rose.

The third habitat, the moist, tropical Harenna Forest, is the second-largest remaining forest in Ethiopia, and its only cloud forest. It's little explored and scientists are still revealing new species. It's home to some enormous podocarpus and fig trees and wild coffee still grows in their shadows. At its highest reaches, around the Harenna Escarpment, the giant heather stands, with twisted trunks draped in 'old man's beard' lichens and thick moss, and with cloud swirling around, the forest is straight out of a Grimm brothers fairytale.

### Wildlife

Seventy-eight mammal species reside here, but none excites like the Ethiopian wolf; sightings are almost guaranteed on the Sanetti Plateau. The rare mountain nyala is also likely to be seen. Other common sightings include Menelik's bushbucks, Bohor reedbucks, grey duikers, spotted hyenas, warthogs and black-and-white colobus. The area around the park headquarters and the nearby Gaysay Grassland are two of the best places to see many of the larger mammals.

The Bale Mountains are a hot spot for endemic wildlife and there are more endemic mammals (including giant molerats and the bamboo-eating Bale monkey) in this spot than in any other area of equal size in the world. There are also many endemic amphibians.

In the Harenna Forest reside giant forest hogs, black-and-white colobus, leopards, lions and African hunting dogs. The latter three are rarely seen.

The Bale Mountains' bird list is 280 species strong, but, again, it's the nine Ethiopian-Eritrean endemics (including the locally endemic Bale parisoma) that set Bale apart. On the plateau, sightings of the blue-winged goose, wattled ibis, thick-billed raven, black-headed siskin, spot-breasted plover and Rouget's rail are almost guaranteed. The birdlife in the juniper forests around the park headquarters is outstanding, too, where Abyssinian catbirds and Abyssinian longclaw are two top ticks. See p269 for more on Ethiopia's endemic birdlife.

## ◉ Sights & Activities

### Dola-Mena Road                    SCENIC DRIVE

There's no need to trek at Bale. Awesome scenery and abundant wildlife can be seen along the highest all-weather road in Africa. It takes you right through the park, up over the Sanetti Plateau and down into the Harenna Forest while a 4km side road brings you to Tullu Deemtu's summit.

Whether you're driving or riding the bus, it's best to leave early; pay park fees in Dinsho the day before. The long climb takes about 30 minutes from Goba and if you reach the plateau by 7am, you're almost guaranteed to see Ethiopian wolves while they are out searching for food. They're also usually visible from 3pm to 5pm.

Guides aren't needed here, unless you plan to get out and walk, but they're good at spotting wolves so you may want to bring one anyway.

### Trekking

Most trekking is fairly gentle and undemanding, following well-trodden paths. But don't forget to factor in the altitude, and

---

### THE ETHIOPIAN WOLF

The Ethiopian wolf (*Canis simensis*) is the rarest canid (dog-family member) in the world. Found only in the Ethiopian highlands, it's teetering on the verge of extinction with only about 500 believed remaining. The Bale Mountains are home to the largest population, with approximately 350.

In Amharic, the wolf is known as a *key kebero* (red jackal), and indeed it does outwardly resemble one. Living in family groups of around 13 adults, the wolves are highly territorial and family oriented. When the dominant female in the pack gives birth to her annual litter of between two and six pups, all members chip in to rear the young. When it comes to hunting, however, the wolves forage alone, favouring giant molerats and other rodents.

The main threat to the wolves is rabies, caught from the domestic dog population. These days wolves and dogs are vaccinated. Lack of genetic diversity is also a problem.

Visit the Ethiopian Wolf Conservation Programme (www.ethiopianwolf.org) to learn more.

review the Safety Guidelines for Trekking (p90) and Responsible Trekking (p91) boxed texts before lacing up. The routes included here are just recommendations. Your guide can put together a trek of any length to any place.

### PLANNING

Entry fees must be paid and treks arranged at **park headquarters** (☎0221-190758; www. balemountains.org; admission Birr90, vehicles Birr20; ☺8.30am-5.30pm), which sits 1km from Dinsho village. All fees are good only for a single day (not the normal 24 hours) and include entry to the small **museum** (☺8.30am-5.30pm Mon-Fri). A new trekking map and the dated *Bale Mountains: A Guidebook* are available at the museum or from your guide. There are banks in all three gateway towns, but no ATMs.

A few stores in Dinsho and Robe sell the basics (instant noodles, pasta, rice, tomato paste, canned sardines, jam, biscuits etc), so if you're planning elaborate menus stock up in Awasa or Addis Ababa. Guides supply their own food (as do the horse handlers), but they'll often agree to be your cook if you feed them. Professional cooks can be hired for Birr150 per day. Water is available in various places on the mountain, but it should be treated.

Some guides hire out tents, sleeping bags and camping stoves, but there aren't many to go around so it's best to bring your own. They can also fix you up with rods for trout fishing.

### GUIDES, HORSES & HANDLERS

Organising the 'team' (guide, horse and horse handler) is done through the **Nyala Guide Association** (☺8.30am-6.30pm) at park headquarters and should be arranged the day before you plan to start. Guides for anything other than a stroll around the headquarters are compulsory and cost Birr250 per day. They have a good reputation.

Porters aren't available, but horses (per day Birr60) and horse handlers (per day Birr100) can be hired. You must take a minimum of two horse handlers, even if you're trekking alone.

If you are using horses, the trek needs to start at Dinsho (or you have to pay to get the horses to your trailhead of choice), though if you are schlepping your own bags you can begin anywhere.

See the boxed text on p280 for post-trek tipping advice.

## DAY TREKS

Each of the destinations comprising the three-day Quick Trip trek can be done individually as day treks. You can also use the Dola-Mena Rd to access the Sanetti Plateau and Harenna Forest and walk there.

### TREKS

**Quick Trip** THREE DAYS

Bale's most popular route covers diverse landscapes in a short time and is even better for wildlife watching than treks concentrating on higher altitudes.

**Day one** (4–6 hours) Walk southwest from Dinsho up the lovely Web Valley, usually following a dirt road, to Finch' Abera Waterfall and on to the Sodota campsite.

**Day two** (4–5 hours) Head to the Kotera Plain, a good wolf habitat, and loop back past Gasuray Peak (3325m) to Adelay campsite. The good visibility here makes this the best birdwatching spot in the north of the park.

**Day three** (6–8 hours) Descend to the flat Gaysay Grassland for excellent wildlife viewing and the small Web Waterfall before returning to Dinsho.

**Mountains & Lakes** SEVEN DAYS

This trek, usually done in a week, focuses on the desolate highlands, and your challenge won't be spying wolves, it'll be keeping count of how many you've seen. There's the option of adding a night or two in the Harenna Forest after day five, either by walking or hitchhiking along the Dola-Mena road. You could also cut the trek short and hitch out of the park.

**Day one** (4–6 hours) Dinsho–Sodota, as described above.

**Day two** (5–6 hours) Continue southwest up the Web Valley to Keyrensa campsite, in an area home to many klipspringers and rock hyraxes.

**Day three** (4–5 hours) Head east past many viewpoints to the Rafu campsite, surrounded by rock pillars caused by a lava flow.

**Day four** (5–6 hours) Under the shadow of Tullu Deemtu (Bale's highest mountain), head across the Sanetti Plateau to Garba Guracha camp with its picture perfect view of its namesake Lake.

SOUTHERN ETHIOPIA BALE MOUNTAINS NATIONAL PARK

**Day five** (6–7 hours) Trek over to the seasonal Crane Lakes, which attract thousands of birds from July to October, and up to the summit of scree-covered Tullu Deemtu. Return to Garba Garucha.

**Day six** (4–5 hours) Head north across Shaya Valley, bagging Mt Batu (4203m) if you wish, before arriving at Worgona camp.

**Day seven** (5–6 hours) Follow the Denka River back to Dinsho.

## 🛏 Sleeping & Eating

The park headquarters is near Dinsho, but accommodation there is too basic for some people. Those who need a little more comfort will find it in Robe and Goba, 30km and 42km east of Dinsho respectively. These towns are also the best base for those heading up to the Sanetti Plateau or Harenna Forest early in the morning. If you'll be using the bus to reach them, then Goba is your only option.

The newly paved road has made Robe, the capital of Bale Zone, a boom town, with some boosters fancifully predicting a city rivalling Awasa in the not-distant future. Pipedreams aside, some new, quality hotels are supposedly in the works so have a look around when you arrive.

### ON THE MOUNTAINS

**Camping**                                    CAMPGROUND $
(per tent Birr40) Campsites are spread throughout the park, and a few can be reached by road. There are also three (with more on the way) mountain huts with roofed campsites, kitchens, solar lights, toilets and hot showers. You should bring your own gear, but some of the guides hire out tents, sleeping bags and cooking gear. If you're driving, **Katcha campsite** in the Harenna Forest is a great destination and you'll see and hear lots of wildlife.

**Harenna Forest Hotel &**
**Cultural Lodge**                          GUESTHOUSE $
(☏0912-740350, per person Birr100; ℗) In the village of Rira, just north of the Harenna Forest, this family-run spot has really cool woven bamboo huts. There's little English and no electricity, but the welcome is warm. Someone will cook meals if you ask.

### DINSHO

**Dinsho Lodge**                               LODGE $
(campsites Birr40, dm Birr70, bungalow Birr400; ℗) Located above park headquarters (park

fee applicable), a stay here would be a no-brainer if it didn't resemble an abandoned ski chalet. Some call it rustic; some call it decrepit. When you factor in the abundant wildlife in the surrounding forest, we lean towards the former. It's due to be privatised, which should change the equation. There's a lounge with a smoky fireplace and a sauna.

**Rift Valley Safari Lodge**                      HOTEL
(☏0115-152462; ℗) Though construction was still ongoing during our visit to Dodola, this place will without a doubt be leagues better than the other two hotels in town.

### ROBE

**Abadma Hotel**                              HOTEL $
(☏0226-652381; d/tw Birr100/150; ℗) This new Muslim-owned spot (no alcohol allowed) on the Goba road 500m south of the bus station has the best rooms available in the area: as long as you won't miss the two channels of satellite TV available at Wabe Shebelle in Goba. There's no English menu in the decent restaurant (mains Birr12 to Birr25), but you'll be able to decipher some of the Oromo words.

**Peacock Hotel**                             HOTEL $
(☏0911-908924; d Birr60; ℗) Fairly basic, but priced fairly. It's on the Dinsho side of town.

### GOBA

**Wabe Shebelle Hotel**                       HOTEL $$
(☏0226-610041; d/tw incl breakfast Birr404/454; ℗@) Long the top dog in these parts, this one-time classy place isn't bad, but it simply charges way too much for its tired and sometimes water-challenged rooms. Its best features are the quiet setting away from the road, and the area's best restaurant (mains Birr45 to Birr89).

**Orion Hotel**                               HOTEL $
(☏0226-612076; d Birr150; ℗@) The *faranji* price is a bit over the top, but this salmon and green high-rise on the north end of town has pretty good rooms and an internet cafe downstairs.

**Baltena Hotel**                             HOTEL $
(☏0226-611189; d without bathroom Birr40; ℗) Down a dirt road west of the bus station's north end, across the road from its namesake restaurant, this ordinary place has wooden floors and cleaner than average common facilities (which feature hot water for Birr5).

## ❶ Getting There & Around

If coming from Addis Ababa, catch an early-morning bus to Robe or Goba and leap off in Dinsho (Birr145, nine hours). The return buses will surely be full when passing Dinsho so either have your guide reserve you a seat the day before or head to Shashemene (Birr59, three hours) and continue from there.

Minibuses run roughly every 15 minutes between Robe and Goba (Birr6, 20 minutes) and less frequently from Robe to Dinsho (Birr10, 40 minutes).

The Nyala Guide Association can arrange 4WD hire.

## Sof Omar Cave
### የሶፍ አማር ዋሻ

One hundred kilometres east of Robe, the fast-flowing Web River runs through a deep gorge and then cuts straight through a long limestone hill. Though the river is only underground for 1.5km, the aeons of erosion have carved 15km of passages. Proposed for World Heritage listing, the vaulted chambers, flying buttresses, massive pillars and fluted archway sometimes resemble an Antonio Gaudí cathedral.

If you walk through you'll cross the river seven times, either wading or swimming. It takes about two hours. You can also ride a four-passenger boat. Some Sof Omar villagers (none of whom speak English) act as guides and, though prices aren't fixed, you can expect to pay Birr150 to walk through and Birr50 just to look around the entrance. They have torches, but for safe spelunking one is never enough; bring your own. From August to October the water is usually too high to get through, though the beautiful rock formations near its mouth can be seen anytime. The guides at Bale Mountains National Park know about the cave's water levels and if you want someone who speaks English, you can hire one to come with you.

The cave is venerated by area Muslims due to Sheikh Sof Omar Ahmed reputedly taking refuge here in the 11th century. There's a pilgrimage every November.

## ❶ Getting There & Away

From the village of Goro, 60km east of Robe, buses leave for Sof Omar (Birr23, two hours) on market days (Thursday, Friday and Saturday) at 6am and return about 4pm. Other days you'll have to rely on sporadic pick-up trucks. A few daily buses connect Goro to Robe (Birr28, two hours).

## Dola-Mena     ዶላ መና

Dola-Mena's intense heat and the striking Somali herdsmen bringing camels to market on Wednesday and Saturday are novelties after the Bale Mountains.

Few visitors sleep here, but if you're travelling without your own wheels and are planning to carry on to the wilds further south, you'll likely need to wait until the morning to find transportation. With not-too-smelly tin-shack toilets and the only 'tourist food' (mains Birr10 to Birr25) in town, unsigned **Bire's Hotel** (d without bathroom Birr40; Ⓟ) near the bus station is probably the best bet. **Makuriya Mengistu Hotel** (✆0226-680163; d without bathroom Birr40; Ⓟ) northwest of the bus station is similar.

## ❶ Getting There & Away

There are usually three buses to Goba (Birr45, four hours), the last out the gate about 1pm. If you're not going to backtrack, there are buses to Negele Borena (Birr70, six hours) on Thursday and Sunday (Dola-Mena's market days), arriving from Negele Borena the day before. Trucks travel most days: try to strike a deal for a front seat with the driver the day before. From Negele Borena, there are daily buses to Mega (Birr75, six to eight hours) and to Shashemene (Birr116, 10 to 11 hours) via Awasa, plus daily trucks to Yabelo.

# SOUTH TO KENYA

The northern half of this route takes you through verdant *enset* ('false-banana' trees), maize and coffee fields and past two minor archaeological sites. Minutes after Hayere Maryam, there's a rapid change from lush, fertile farms to the dusty, sparsely populated cattle country of the Borena people, where you can witness singing wells and salt-filled craters before wiping sweat from your brow as you enter the baking plains and desolate glory that continues into northern Kenya.

## Dilla     ዲላ

POP 75,400 / ELEV 1570M

From a traveller's perspective the only noteworthy thing about the capital of Gedeo Zone is that within its sphere of influence lie two of southern Ethiopia's most important **stelae fields**. And those who've been in the south for some time may relish the chance

**WORTH A TRIP**

## AREGASH LODGE

The only thing of interest in Yirgalem (ይርጋኣፐም), Aregash Lodge (✆0462-251136; www. aregashlodge.com; incl breakfast s & d US$60, tr & q US$90; P@) is one of Ethiopia's most lauded lodges. The Sidamo-inspired thatched huts are rustically plush with bamboo furniture and lots of space while the grounds are home to 100-plus species of bird and black-and-white colobus. Hyenas come to feed during the evening coffee ceremony. The excellent buffet meals cost Birr150 to Birr170 and use vegies from the garden. Walks to local villages are available and so is horse riding if you book in advance.

to check their email and raid the Dashen Bank's ATM.

### 🛌 Sleeping & Eating

**Lalibela Pension** PENSION $
(✆0463-312300; d with/without bathroom Birr200/100; P) Though it's an older property, the quiet Lalibela is well cared for and even at these higher *faranji* prices offers fair value. It's signposted off the main street west of Rendezvous Restaurant.

**Afomiya Pension** PENSION $$
(✆0463-314444; s/d/tw Birr400/500/600; P) At least until the Rendezvous Hotel opens in the city centre, Dilla's best hotels are on the western edge of town. And because Afomiya's bar (there's no restaurant) is for hotel guests only, it's quieter than the competition.

**FS Pension** PENSION $
(d with/without bathroom Birr80/50) Directly across from the bus station, this place has been under slow-motion construction for over a year but is a solid choice at these prices.

**Rendezvous Restaurant** EUROPEAN-ETHIOPIAN $
(mains Birr16-39) Popular with locals and visitors, it offers the usual dishes plus bakery items, juices and internet.

### ❶ Getting There & Away

A 6am bus departs for Yabelo (Birr65, six hours) and Moyale (Birr120, nine to 10 hours) and at least one goes to Addis (Birr108, 10 hours). You can also go south by minibus in stages. Minibuses are the best option for Shashemene (Birr30, three hours) and Awasa (Birr27, 2½ hours).

## Yabelo የቤሎ

POP 20,700 / ELEV 1857M

The Borena town of Yabelo is a base for visiting Yabelo Wildlife Sanctuary and also offers road access to the Omo Valley via Konso. No

traveller comes for the town itself, though it's not an unpleasant place.

### 🛌 Sleeping & Eating

Almost everyone stays at the Yabelo/ Moyale–Shashemene road junction, 5km east of town.

**Hawi Hotel** HOTEL $
(✆0464-461114; d Birr200-400, tw Birr500; P) Actually providing decent value, this unpretentious place provides a clean room (and pretty clean bathroom) with good mattresses and one-channel TV. The newer upstairs rooms are better and have satellite TV.

**Borana Lodge** LODGE $$$
(✆0913-306105; www.yabeloboranalodge.com; s/d incl breakfast US$88/96; P☀) A newish place popular with birdwatchers due to its 50-hectare grounds, 7km southwest of town. The widely spaced rooms have the feel of a college dorm more than a luxury lodge and don't warrant the high prices, but you're paying for the overall experience. The swimming pool often sits empty.

**Kelaa Green Pension** PENSION $
(✆0911-765784; d without bathroom Birr80; P) The cheeriest of several cheapies by the junction, rooms are good and have little verandahs out the front while the shared squat toilets are about what you'd expect. There's also a little grocery.

**Yabelo Motel** HOTEL $$
(✆0464-460795; www.mazethiopia.com.et; d with/ without bathroom US$40/20, tw US$65; P@) It's got good clean rooms, some with satellite TV, and a leafy garden, but the *faranji* prices are beyond ridiculous. Yabelo's best restaurant (mains Birr35 to Birr80) is here and it's also overpriced, but less so.

**Green Hotel** HOTEL $
(d with/without bathroom Birr80/60; P) The best place near the bus station has dark rooms

and a noisy bar at night (as do all the others around here) but it's clean enough.

## ℹ Getting There & Around

All buses (including those starting elsewhere and passing through) use the bus park in town, while the more frequent minibuses leave from the Total station out at the junction. There are many minibuses throughout the day and one 6am bus to Moyale (Birr65, four hours). The bus to Shashemene (Birr101, seven hours) departs every other day at 6am. Legally, minibuses can't travel all the way to Shashemene or Awasa (though many do) so you may have to do it in stages, changing at Hagere Maryam and Dilla. Buses to Konso (Birr50, three hours) leave about 7am and 1pm.

Locals pay Birr3 for a *bajaj* between the town and the junction.

## Yabelo Wildlife Sanctuary
የቢሎ የዱር አራዊት ፓርክ

Covering an area of 2496 sq km, the **Yabelo Wildlife Sanctuary** (per person Birr90, vehicle per day Birr20) was originally created to protect Ethiopia's endemic Swayne's hartebeest. Hartebeests have since been poached out of the preserve, along with most other wildlife (cows are now the only large mammal in abundance, though visitors will also probably see some zebra). These days **birdwatchers** are pretty much the only visitors, here to add the locally endemic Ethiopian bush crow and white-tailed swallow to their life lists.

Visitors must hire a scout (per day Birr100) from the **headquarters** (☎0464-460087; ☒8.30am-12.30pm & 1.30-5.30pm Mon-Fri) in the town of **Yabelo**. Walking is allowed and the staff can explain how to

get near the entrance by public transport. **Camping** (per tent Birr45) is allowed.

## Yabelo to Mega

The 100km between Yabelo and Mega offers up some interesting cultural and physical phenomena.

Delve into Borena territory near **Dublock**, about 70km south of Yabelo, where there's a big Friday **market** and some of the famous *ela*, or **'singing wells'** (p152). They're only genuinely worked during the dry season (December through May), but the men are glad to demonstrate at other times, for a hefty fee: tour companies usually pay Birr150 per person and another Birr150 for the guide to arrange it.

The village of **El Sod** ('Chew Bet' in Amharic), 35km south of Dublock, lies beside a bizarre crater lake known as the **House of Salt** (admission per person Birr50, per vehicle Birr50, compulsory guide Birr150). It's about 800m across and 600m below the crater rim and is so dark in colour that it looks like an oil slick amid the ruddy rocks. Valuable and muddy, black salt has been extracted from the lake for centuries, carried up on the backs of donkeys. It's a half-hour, knee-trembling walk down and a full-hour, thigh-burning slog back up. It's best to visit during the morning's cooler temperatures when the salt gatherers are actually working. Don't expect to learn much about this fascinating endeavour from the guides; their English is very limited. There's also a 'singing well' here.

Just before you arrive in Mega you'll see the ruins of an Italian **fort**.

---

### THE STELAE FIELDS AROUND DILLA

This region around Dilla is the southern end of a string of ancient burial sites marked by mysterious stelae that stretch all the way north to Tiya (p134). The two most interesting sites at this end of the chain lie near the highway and are easy to reach.

The nearly 1500 tapered stones at **Tutiti** (admission Birr50) are up to 7.5m tall, though few remain standing. The Tutiti field rests on a hill in **Dichika village**, 3.4km west of the highway; the turn is signposted 5.4km south of the Tutu Fella turn-off. Due to their smaller size, the 267 (or so they say) densely packed stelae at **Tutu Fella** (admission Birr50) are less impressive, but they are variously carved with facial features, ribs and breasts. It's accessed from a turn-off 2.5km south of Wenago. Head 2km east and then uphill at the Protestant church behind the big fence for another 1km.

Both sites have caretakers, but they're neither knowledgeable nor able to speak English. Minibuses from Dilla (Birr10) can drop you at either turn-off.

Many buses and even more minibuses ply the Yabelo and Moyale road and can drop you off at the various turn-offs. From the turn-off for El Sod, you'll need to hitch the 14km to the village.

# Moyale ሞ ያሌ

POP 32,900 / ELEV 1090M

There's only one truly compelling reason to visit Moyale: Kenya.

A porous border cuts the one-street town in two and the difference between the sides is immediately palpable. The Kenyan half, with dust-swept dirt streets, exudes a true wild-frontier atmosphere while the Ethiopian side is more of a proper town with better everything, except banking facilities.

## 🛏 Sleeping & Eating

### ETHIOPIA

**Koket Borena Hotel** HOTEL $$
(📞0913-487500; campsites with own/hired tent Birr60/80, s Birr360-405, d & tw Birr520; P@) With some simple but cute bamboo *tukuls* (plus ordinary concrete rooms) and friendly staff, this place up the hill is the best lodging on either side of the border.

**Tourist Hotel** HOTEL $
(📞0464-440513; s/d without bathroom Birr60/70; P) Sheltered behind its cool Rasta-inspired bar, this little sleeping option has colourful rooms that include private showers. While we've seen better shared toilets, we've certainly seen much worse.

**Fekadu Hotel** HOTEL $
(📞0464-440049; d/tw Birr100/150; P) Simple and somewhat overpriced self-contained rooms set around an excellent courtyard restaurant and a decent bar.

### KENYA

Prices are quoted in Kenya shillings; the exchange rate is around US$1 to KSh86. (For current exchange rates see www.xe.com.)

**Al-Yusra Hotel** HOTEL $$
(📞0722-257028; r from KSh2500) The tallest building in Moyale is its only good hotel. It's hardly fantastic, but it does have running water that's sometimes even hot, and no strange creatures sharing your bed.

**Sherif Guest House** HOTEL $
(d without bathroom KSh300) Sitting above the bank, this place has vaguely clean rooms, though the communal toilet is memorable for all the wrong reasons.

**Prison Canteen** KENYAN $
(mains Ksh150-200) It says a lot about the quality of life up here when the best place to eat, drink and party is inside the town jail. It provides a great atmosphere and an excellent *nyama choma* (barbecued meat). Open for lunch and dinner.

## ℹ Information

The border is open from 6am to 6pm daily. Three-month Kenyan tourist visas are available at the border for most Western nationalities for US$50. You *cannot* get an Ethiopian visa at the border.

There are banks on both sides of the border, but the only ATM is at the Commercial Bank in Kenya. If you need to change between shillings and birr, ask at your hotel.

## ℹ Getting There & Away

A bus leaves Ethiopian Moyale for Addis Ababa (Birr250) each morning around 5am. The two-day journey is broken with a night's sleep at Awasa. Many minibuses go to Yabelo (Birr65, four hours).

---

## THE SINGING WELLS OF THE BORENA

The Borena are seminomadic pastoralists who occupy lands that stretch from northern Kenya to the dry, hot plains around Yabelo. Their lives revolve entirely around their cattle and during the dry season it's a constant struggle to keep their vast herds alive. To combat the problem, the Borena developed a unique system of deep wells. A long channel drops about 10m below the ground and funnels the cattle to troughs dug close to each well's mouth. When it's time to water the cattle, the men create a human chain down the well (which can be 30m deep), tossing buckets of water between one another from the bottom up to the top, where the troughs are gradually filled. The men often sing to keep rhythm as they pass up the buckets, hence the name. Several hundred or even thousand cattle come to drink at a time. For travellers, it's certainly a memorable and unique sight, though new pumps are slowly ending the tradition.

For those heading south into Kenya, get ready for some teeth-rattling rides: see p289 for details.

For those driving, petrol is cheaper and more reliable on the Ethiopian side.

# ARBA MINCH & AROUND

Bordered by verdant mountains and home to two of Ethiopia's largest Rift Valley lakes, this region is more than a convenient overnight stop on the southern circuit. With Nechisar National Park and the highland Dorze villages on its doorstep, it deserves to be a destination on its own.

## Arba Minch    አርባ ምንጭ

POP 95,500 / ELEV 1285M

Arba Minch is two cities in one. Its dual settlements of Shecha and Sikela, separated by 3km of virtual no-man's land, have distinct personalities. Larger Sikela is more commercial and chaotic than her ever-so-slightly more refined sibling up the hill. Shecha also offers fantastic views over the lakes.

### ⊙ Sights & Activities

A modern, multipurpose **cultural centre** is currently under construction on the cliff next to Bekele Mola Hotel. It will include a museum about the five tribes of Goma-Gofa Zone.

**Lakes Abaya & Chamo**                    LAKES
Divided by the lyrical 'Bridge of God', Lakes Abaya and Chamo are both beautiful. Measuring 1160 sq km, Lake Abaya is Ethiopia's second-largest lake. Its peculiar reddish-brown waters are a result of elevated natural concentrations of suspended sediments. While the more conventionally coloured Lake Chamo supports a much larger population of crocodiles, Abaya's are more aggressive against people and animals because the lake has few fish, their preferred food.

**Arba Minch Crocodile Ranch**  CROCODILE FARM
(admission US$10; ⊙8.30am-noon & 1.30-5.30pm) Walking between the masses of crocs in their concrete tanks at this government-run facility is more humdrum than it sounds, except during feeding, which usually happens Monday and Thursday between 3pm and 5pm. And even then, it's hardly worth the price. The crocodiles are either hatched from eggs collected in the lakes or pulled out as youngsters and reared on the farm. Most of the hapless crocs are killed at about 2m length (five years old) when their skin is the best quality, and will end up as handbags or belts in European stores – Italy and Greece, mostly. It's signposted almost 6km from Sikela. There's no public transport. The local boat association, 800m after the ranch, can take you for a ride on Lake Abaya.

### ☞ Tours

**See Us Tour Guide Association**       TOURS
(☏0468-810117; ⊙7am-6pm) A guide will cost you Birr300 a day.

### 🛏 Sleeping

Overall, Shecha's accommodation and restaurant options outgun Sikela's. It's significantly cooler in the hot season, too. We weren't allowed to poke around, but the new lodge going up next to Soma looks promising.

#### SHECHA
**Swayne's Hotel**                     LODGE $$$
(☏0468-811895; campsites per tent Birr250, s/d/ tw incl breakfast US$67/73/90; 🅿) Though not without its faults, Swayne's is a good choice. The bungalows, with their colourful local artwork and hand-carved wooden furniture, give this place a quirky yet traditional feel. Eighteen of the 72 rooms are along the clifftop, but be warned: many of their porches have very obstructed views.

**Soma Lodge**                          LODGE $$
(☏0911-737712, tw Birr600; 🅿) Like giant, upturned onions, the beautifully crafted Sidamo huts here each have a small lounge, two bedrooms (with two beds and en suite in each) and fantastic views over Nechisar National Park. It's too rustic for some, but if you're in a group of four, or can convince them to rent you just one room for half the price, it's a nice choice.

**Zeweda Hotel**                        HOTEL $
(☏0468-810364; d Birr60; 🅿) Simple and spartan (there are squat toilets and cold-water showers) but lacking mildewy odours, this small family-run spot is the first choice of many tour drivers. Even if they discover *faranji* pricing, it will probably still be worth considering.

# Arba Minch

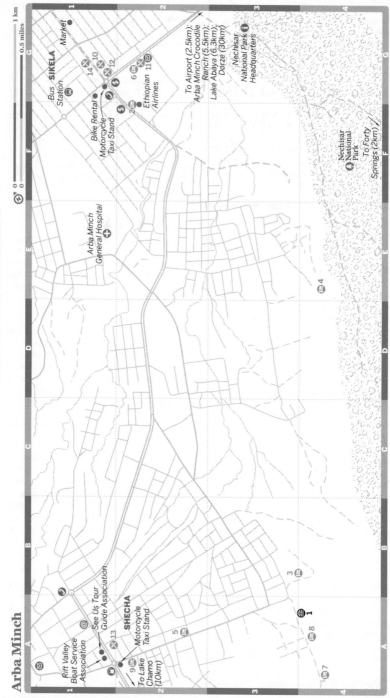

1 km
0.5 miles

To Airport (2.5km);
Arba Minch Crocodile
Ranch (5.5km);
Lake Abaya (6.3km);
Dorze (30km)

Nechisar
National Park
Headquarters

Nechisar
National
Park

To Forty
Springs (2km)

**SIKELA**

Market

Bus
Station

Bike Rental

Motorcycle
Taxi Stand

Ethiopian
Airlines

Arba Minch
General Hospital

Rift Valley
Boat Service
Association

See Us Tour
Guide Association

**SHECHA**

Motorcycle
Taxi Stand

To Lake
Chamo (10km)

# Arba Minch

**Bekele Mola Hotel**                    HOTEL **$$**

(☎0468-810046; camping Birr100, r Birr440; **P**) Although the lake views are excellent, this places feels more like a 1970s workers' compound than a hotel and the prices are way too high.

**Rift Valley Pension**                    PENSION **$**

(☎0468-812531; d/tw Birr130/130; **P**) Yet another place with too-high *faranji* prices, the rooms here feel older than they really are, but are clean, quiet and satellite TV–equipped.

**Arba Minch Hotel**                    HOTEL **$**

(☎0468-810206; r Birr100; **P**) If Zeweda is full, as it often is, this similar place makes a reasonable backup, though it's not as good.

### SIKELA

**TOP CHOICE** **Paradise Lodge**                    LODGE **$$$**

(☎0468-812914; www.paradiselodgeethiopia.com; campsites with own/hired tent US$15/20, d/tw incl breakfast US$59/85; **P**🛜) This upmarket lodge staring straight at the national park's 'Bridge of God' features comfortable Konso-inspired huts, all but a few with views, built from stone and wood. The staff is on the ball and massages and steam baths are available. A swimming pool is planned. It's perched between the two towns up a very rough 1.9km road.

**Sikela Pension**                    PENSION **$**

(☎0912-894662; d Birr100) In a noisy, nondescript office block on the way into town; rooms are basic but bright and clean.

**Arba Minch Tourist Hotel**                    HOTEL **$$**

(☎0468-812171; s/d/tw Birr350/400/440; **P**🛜) With dowdy, overpriced rooms, and early morning church noise, we assume the only reason it's popular with *faranji* is the wi-fi.

## 🍴 Eating

Fish has long been a staple in the diet here, though overfishing means it's a lot more expensive these days. Unlike with lodging, Sikela holds its own against Shecha in the dining department.

### SHECHA

**Swayne's Hotel**                    EUROPEAN-ETHIOPIAN **$**

(mains Birr30-100) This hotel restaurant has what some consider the best Western fare in town. Soak up the views from inside, behind the floor-to-ceiling windows, or outside along the clifftop.

**Soma Restaurant**                    EUROPEAN-ETHIOPIAN **$**

(mains Birr40-120) This unassuming restaurant (now charging much higher *faranji* prices) has made quite a name for itself with its mouth-watering grilled fish dishes, most of which are big enough to share. Much of the same is available at Soma Lodge.

### SIKELA

**Paradise Lodge**                    EUROPEAN **$**

(mains Birr45-100; 🛜) Predictably pricey, the lovely ridgetop dining room, together with menu choices like ginger garlic fish, makes this the most impressive restaurant and best sundower spot in Arba Minch.

**Arba Minch Tourist Hotel**   EUROPEAN-ETHIOPIAN **$**

(mains Birr22-60) Though the wait staff can be a touch clueless at times, this leafy compound with resident dik-dik roaming around looking for handouts is a great place to dine, and the food is quite good. Western dishes are popular, but the large menu makes this a good place to try some new Ethiopian foods.

**Fiory Pizza & Burger**   EUROPEAN-ETHIOPIAN **$**

(mains Birr25-70) A simple place aimed at university students, both of its namesake dishes are pretty good. The friendly owner also serves pasta and local dishes and does coffee ceremony.

**Zebib Café & Snack**   EUROPEAN-ETHIOPIAN $
(mains Birr20-30) Fast food (*ful*, pasta, etc) served in a pleasant garden out the back.

**Abi Restaurant**   ETHIOPIAN $
(mains Birr15-50) Known for *shekla tibs* made with goat from its on-site butchery.

**Fruit Supermarket**   SELF-CATERING $
Small, but it's the best-stocked grocery in town and has a few exotic items like peanut butter and imitation Cocoa Puffs.

## ❶ Information

The telecommunications offices in both Shecha and Sikela still handle international calls. The internet cafes (per hour Birr30) with the most reliable connections are those in front of the Tourist Hotel in Sikela.

**Arba Minch General Hospital** (☑0468-810839; ☺24hr) The region's best hospital.

**Commercial Bank** Still changes Amex travellers cheques.

**Dashen Bank** Hosts Arba Minch's sole ATM.

## ❶ Getting There & Away

**Ethiopian Airlines** (☑0468-810649) flies between Addis Ababa and Arba Minch (US$57, one hour) three times a week.

At least three buses leave Sikela's **bus station** for Addis Ababa (Birr147, nine hours) and there's at least one daily to Jinka (Birr101, six hours) and Awasa (Birr83, six hours). All depart at 6am. Many minibuses serve Konso (Birr32, two hours).

Though most people contract with a tour agency in Addis Ababa, it's possible to begin Lower Omo Valley tours in Arba Minch. The See Us Tour Guide Association and some hotels, including Paradise Lodge and Dorze's Mekonen Lodge (p158), hire out 4WDs for US$150 to US$160 per day, including fuel and driver. One local guide with several solid recommendations is **Tuti Mesfin** (☑0911-805971; tutiman_utd@yahoo.com), who offers both 4WD and cheaper minibuses, which can get to most Omo destinations. With notice he can also arrange fully supported boat trips on the Omo River.

## ❶ Getting Around

Frequent minibuses connect Sikela and Shecha (Birr2.50) from around 5am (for getting to the bus station) to 9pm. For a motorcycle taxi/*bajaj* between the two, try to bargain for Birr15 to Birr20. To reach the airport, hire a minibus (Birr100) or *bajaj* (Birr70).

Bikes can be hired near Sikela's roundabout for Birr8/40 per hour/day.

# Nechisar National Park
ነጭ ሳር ብሔራዊ ፓርክ

Spanning the narrow yet mountainous 'Bridge of God' that separates Lakes Chamo and Abaya, Nechisar National Park ranks among the most scenic national parks in East Africa.

Although only 514 sq km, the park contains diverse habitats ranging from wide-open savannah and acacia woodland to thick bush and sections of riparian forest. The bleached savannah grasses actually spawned the park's name, which means 'white grass' in Amharic. It's the scenery that makes Nechisar special, but there's still wildlife left, despite the government's refusal to tackle the rampant land encroachment and poaching.

On the Nechisar Plain (where animals are most easily seen), the Burchell's zebra is the most conspicuous, sometimes gathered in herds of 100-plus animals. Visitors usually also see Swayne's hartebeest, greater kudu and Grant's gazelle. A small population of lions still roams the park, too, but don't expect to meet them. Olive baboons, black-and-white colobus and Guenther's dik-dik can often be seen between the headquarters and Forty Springs. The birdlife is more diverse: 351 species have been counted and there isn't a birder alive who doesn't want to see the Nechisar nightjar (see the sidebar on p269), but you'll probably have to settle for Abyssinian ground hornbills and Kori bustards.

Whether entering by land or water, you must pay park fees at the **park headquarters** (admission US$10, vehicle US$2; ☺6.30am-5.30pm). **Armed scouts** (up to 12hr US$6, up to 24hr US$10) are mandatory for everywhere except the Crocodile Market.

## ◉ Sights & Activities

**Crocodile Market**   WILDLIFE ENCOUNTER
Where the Kulfo River empties into Lake Chamo you'll find oodles of crocodiles sunning themselves. Both the size of the congregation and the size of the crocs (6m is common) makes this one of Africa's best crocodile displays. There are also plenty of hippos, fish eagles and shore birds.

# Nechisar National Park

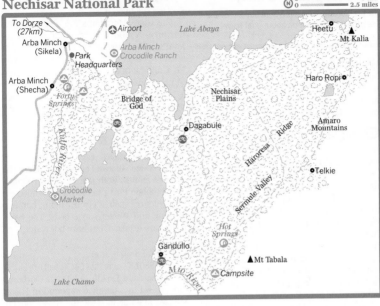

The **Rift Valley Boat Service Association** (Map p154; ☎0468-814080; ⊙7am-5.30pm), whose office is in Shecha, holds a monopoly on the trips, which is why prices are so high. The cost of the boat (which has a roof) for a group of up to six people is Birr770 and hiring the mandatory guide from the **See Us Tour Guide Association** (p153) costs Birr120. You also have to transport the guide and boat driver to the launching point, 11km from Shecha. If you don't have your own wheels, hiring a minibus costs up to Birr400, round trip.

While it's only a 20- to 30-minute boat ride to the crocs (there's actually not a single spot – their preferred perch changes with the seasons), allow two hours for the trip. It's best to visit mid-afternoon or early morning.

### Nechisar Plain          WILDLIFE ENCOUNTER

The main wildlife-watching circuit crosses the Bridge of God to the park's namesake savannah, but the road is so atrocious that many tour companies prefer not to come here; nobody will attempt it when it's wet. It takes about three hours to reach the plains so there's no chance of wildlife watching during the morning hours unless you camp.

Another option is to boat across and then walk, though because of past armed robberies the park turns permission for this on and

off with some regularity. You'll need to bring an armed scout from the park headquarters. A boat from the association (see above) costs Birr1760 for up to six people and can cross in about 90 minutes.

### Forty Springs          SPRING

Arba Minch, which is Amharic for 'Forty Springs', is named after the innumerable little **springs** (⊙8am-6pm) that bubble up right at the base of the ridge below the town. All the development (the city pumps its water from here) and the fact that it's not especially scenic to begin with makes it worth visiting only if you've already paid park fees. The 3km road there from the headquarters, however, *is* beautiful and makes a good, easy walk.

## 🛏 Sleeping

### Campsites          CAMPGROUND $

(per tent US$4, tent hire 1-3 person US$10, 4+ person US$12) The park has three official campsites: one on the road to Forty Springs, another nearby along the Kulfo River and one at the back of the park in the Sermule Valley. There are no facilities and the latter lacks a water source in the dry season. Consider them mere recommendations since camping is actually allowed anywhere.

## ⓘ Getting There & Away

The park headquarters is 800m beyond Sikela. See p156 for information about boat travel.

---

# Dorze &.C.1b

High up in the Guge Mountains, northwest of Arba Minch, is cold and cloudy Dorze territory. Dorze people are famous for their towering homes and fine cotton weaving.

## ◎ Sights & Activities

### Hayzo VILLAGE

(admission Birr50) This is one of the few Southern Nations' villages that has succeeded in turning the influx of tourists into a positive experience for all concerned. You can see the traditional way of life with few hassles from begging kids and no need to pay for photos. Guides are mandatory and can be found at the newly organised Besa Gamo Chencha Local Guide Association (☑0916-345341; per day Birr150; ⊙8am-5pm) near the office, though most people hire a guide (same price) from Mekonen Lodge further up the hill.

The standard short tour usually kicks off with a look inside one of the famed Dorze huts (see p158), followed by visits to the weaving cooperative (women spin the thread and men work the looms) and pottery workshop. You'll probably also get to bake and eat *kocho,* a delicious, fermented, unleavened bread made from *enset* (see the boxed text, p259). It's eaten with honey or *data* (a delicious hot sauce). With more time you can see and do pretty much anything else, like visiting coffee plantations, fruit farms and local hooch stills. A dance demonstration (per person Birr100, minimum Birr300) can also be arranged.

Colourful markets can be found at Hayzo on Monday and Thursday and at Chencha, 8km further up the road, on Tuesday and Saturday. The Monday and Saturday markets are the biggest.

The Guge Mountains are also trekking territory. A 30m-tall waterfall is just an hour's walk away and others are further afield. A longer option is the five-day trip up Mt Guge (4200m) and then down to Arba Minch. A guide for overnight trips is Birr300 a day and Mekonen Lodge charges Birr300 per day for tent and sleeping bag hire. Pack horses are also available.

## 🛏 Sleeping & Eating

Dorze's two lodges each call themselves 'Dorze Lodge': to avoid confusion we use the owners' names. Both feature similar Dorze-style bamboo huts fitted with a few modern conveniences such as electric lights, bamboo flooring and Western-style beds. The bathrooms are external, but have hot water.

**TOP CHOICE** **Mekonen Lodge** GUESTHOUSE $

(☑0913-880720; campsites Birr30, tent hire Birr50, dm incl breakfast Birr100; ℗) Dorze's original lodge is set in a family compound in Hayzo village, making it ideal for those looking for cultural immersion. The 15 huts are arranged around a central courtyard that doubles as the restaurant (dinner buffet Birr50). Mekonen offers 4WD hire (per day including fuel US$150).

**TOP CHOICE** **Tsehay Lodge** LODGE $

(☑0916-825205; campsites Birr50, s/tw without bathroom Birr200/300; ℗) Perched on the edge of a cliff peacefully away from any village, this lodge has views that are, without a hint of hyperbole, amazing. Its village tours usually go to seldom-visited Amara. Meals (order well in advance) cost Birr80. The 1km-long, 4WD-only access road is signposted 2km before Hayzo.

---

## DORZE HUTS

Standing 12m high when first built, Dorze homes are essentially massive upturned baskets. Woven from bamboo and thatched with *enset* leaves, they don't use a central pillar for support and can be picked up and moved to a new location. On the inside a partitioned area is reserved for livestock (which provide heat), while the section that juts out at the entrance serves as a small reception room. If you imagine this as the trunk and the upper vents as eyes, the homes resemble massive elephant heads.

Though fragile-looking, the huts can last 60 to 80 years. Smoke from the central fire helps keep the homes dry (preventing rot) and largely termite free, though termites do slowly eat the homes from the base up. As they do, the lower portion is sliced off, resulting in a progressively shorter home.

## ❶ Getting There & Away

A series of switchbacks affords some spectacular views over Lake Abaya. Although, be warned; when it rains, the road is slippery.

Buses (Birr20, one hour) leave Arba Minch's Sikela bus station about hourly. They return when full with the last departing about 6pm, but aim to leave by 5pm to be sure.

# Konso                              ኮንሶ

POP 4593 / ELEV 1650M

While the gateway town for the Lower Omo Valley is unequivocally unattractive, the Konso people and their architecturally inspiring villages around the town make it a must-stop. The stone walls, terraced fields and ceremonial structures comprise such a unique lifestyle that the whole Konso Cultural Landscape was declared a Unesco World Heritage Site.

## ◉ Sights

**Konso Museum**                        MUSEUM
(admission Birr20, per group tour agency fee Birr50; ☺8am-noon & 1-5pm) High above the town, across from Kanta Lodge, this new centre provides a very brief introduction to Konso culture, but it's the excellent collection of totemistic *waga* that makes it a must-see. These carved wooden sculptures are raised in honour of Konso warriors after their death and not only depict the 'hero' but also his family, and the enemies and dangerous animals he has killed. This collection is so important because most *waga* have been stolen for sale in Addis Ababa, and erection of new *waga* is dying out due to the influence of missionaries who oppose ancestor worship. You must pay at the tourist office (p160).

**Konso Cultural Centre**       CULTURAL BUILDING
(☺8.30am-12.30pm & 1.30-5.30pm Mon-Sat) Though more a local resource centre than tourist attraction, there's a pottery display (ask staff to unlock the rooms) and sometimes special exhibitions. It's 500m before the roundabout.

**Dokatu Market**                        MARKET
(☺10am-4pm Mon & Thu) Perched on a ridge 2km west of town, this market proffers grand views over the Rift Valley. For sale, you'll find women's traditional skirts, cassava, *cheka* (home-brewed sorghum beer) and *etan* (the incense used in coffee ceremonies).

**Komaya Heart of Konso Cultural Handicraft Market**        MARKET
This beautiful hilltop spot is a developing project (it's supposed to open during the lifetime of this book) to provide an income for local craftspeople. There's a weaving workshop and other craft demonstrations, a cafe and, of course, a shop. The turn-off is across from the Dokatu Market, from where it's another 1km.

## 🍴 Sleeping & Eating

Konso's electricity is often offline and hotels only run the generators from 6pm to 10pm. Strawberry Fields' solar cells, however, generally provide power 24/7.

**Strawberry Fields Eco Lodge**       LODGE $
(☏0468-840755; www.permalodge.org; campsites Birr60, s/d/tw without bathroom Birr200/350/380; 🅿) Very simple mud-and-straw-walled, grass-roofed huts are surrounded by the lodge's permaculture garden, which supplies the limited selection of organic meals. It's 'too hippy' for some and a serene heaven for others, some of whom stay for weeks to study farming. What both camps can agree on is that, considering the rudimentary facilities and muddy walk to the huts, the prices make absolutely no sense. It's just over 1km from the traffic towards Arba Minch.

**Kanta Lodge**                        LODGE $$
(☏0467-730403; campsites Birr200, d/tw incl breakfast US$46/58, d/tw cottage incl breakfast US$58/78; 🅿) Though it doesn't live up to its price, Kanta Lodge is a friendly, comfortable place with lovely views. The tightly packed *tukuls* are simple and plain and the standard rooms are simply spartan. There's no ablutions block for campers, but if a room is free you can use it. Kanta is also the top spot to dine (mains Birr35 to Birr90), though that's only because there's no real competition. Perhaps the under-construction Korebta Lodge even higher up the hill will force Kanta's prices down to something reasonable.

**St Mary Hotel**                        HOTEL $
(☏0911-547112; tw without bathroom Birr80, d/tw from Birr100/150; 🅿) Set on the town's only roundabout, there are 46 cold-water rooms of varying age and quality set around a large, busy (ie noisy) compound used by many truck and bus drivers. The newest rooms are simple, but surprisingly nice for the price. They usually run the generator until 11pm.

### Green Hotel
HOTEL **$**

(☎0467-730151; d/tw from Birr150/200; **P**) Rooms at this budget hotel on the way into town from Arba Minch aren't quite as good as those at St Mary, but are usually quieter.

### Edget Hotel
ETHIOPIAN **$**

(mains Birr25-50) Opposite St Mary Hotel, Edget is the top dining spot inside the city. Not because of any culinary skills, but because the owner keeps the generator running all day long, ensuring the Cokes and St Georges are cold.

## ❶ Information

The Konso Cultural Centre charges Birr60 per minute for internet and there's also an internet cafe at the roundabout. The tourist information centre also plans to open an internet cafe. The Commercial Bank, by the cultural centre, exchanges cash.

**Konso Tourist Information Centre** (☎0467-730395; www.konsotourism.gov.et; Jinka Rd; ⊗8.30am-5.30pm) Stop here before visiting the museum or villages. It can also arrange trekking trips (Birr200 per day).

## ❶ Getting There & Away

A daily bus runs in each direction between Arba Minch (Birr32, two hours) and Jinka (Birr70, 3½ hours), picking up passengers here en route. Minibuses to both destinations start in Konso. There are also two buses to/from Yabelo (Birr50, three hours).

# Around Konso

Walking through the narrow maze of paths inside the defensive walls of Konso *kantas* ('villages'; see Map p161) feels like entering another world. The twisting stone-walled walkways connect family and clan compounds, each with a clutch of thatched-roof homes, communal *mora* (where young men sleep at night to serve as watchmen and community servants for the village) and public squares where generation poles (one pole is raised every 18 years) and sometimes battle stones (commemorating victories over and defeats by enemy tribes) stand tall. These squares traditionally also contain the famous Konso *wagas* (see Konso Museum, p159). Any *wagas* found inside a family compound were carved only to earn birr from snap-happy tourists.

The most visited village, simply because it's the easiest to reach, is Gamole, 6km west of Konso town. Just as interesting architecturally, and better overall because of the much lower number of visitors, is Machekie, 14km southwest of Konso. It still has three original sets of weathered *wagas* and also a rare newly erected set. Near Machekie, the village of Gesergio itself gets few visitors, but the oddly eroded valley alongside it does. Thanks to the towering pinnacles that someone decided resemble skyscrapers, it's now commonly known as 'New York'. One local legend explaining the landscape states that it's the result of a magic spell cast by village elders to reveal the location of a chief's stolen sacred drums. Fasha, between Gesergio and the turn-off to Machekie, hosts the biggest market (⊗11am-6pm Sat) in Konso-land; Tuesday is a smaller affair. The road to Machekie and Gesergio passes the home of Chief Kalla Gezahegn (admission Birr50), one of the nine Konso clan chiefs. A former civil engineer in Addis Ababa, he speaks fluent English and welcomes (paying) visitors.

Though seldom visited because it requires walking or riding a motorcycle 4km, Busso (5km southwest of Konso) is perhaps the loveliest village because it surrounds a rocky point. It's also home to some original *wagas*. Dekatu, about 1km off the main road near the Dokatu Market, is the nearest traditional village to Konso town and also very interesting. It's best accessed by foot because the road is so bad. Usually a stop on the way to the Lower Omo Valley, Arfaide (per person Birr50), 20km out of town along the Jinka road, has a large collection of old *waga* that were recovered after being stolen.

Gersale is the one village of note along the Arba Minch Road. It's just north of town and is visited for a new tree-planting program (plant a tree for US$20), where a small plaque with your name is placed in front of your tree, and for the half-hour traditional dance performances rather than its architecture. Inquire at the tourist office or Kanta Lodge.

Before visiting any of these villages (except Arfaide) you must pay fees (village fee per day Birr50, vehicle Birr10, group tour agency fee Birr 50) and hire a guide (per group Birr150) at the Konso Tourist Information Centre (p160). You'll likely be charged an additional Birr20 to enter individual compounds and Birr1 or Birr2 per picture of people. Your guide can go to town with you to hire a minibus or motorcycle if you're travelling without your own wheels.

Camping is allowed at the villages for Birr20 per person.

The children's *faranji* frenzy (a result of previous visitors handing out sweets, pens, etc) gets irritating at times, but it's only truly aggressive at Gesergio. If you want to give something, ask your guide to take you to the local school.

# THE LOWER OMO VALLEY

The villages of the Lower Omo Valley are home to some of Africa's most fascinating ethnic groups and a trip here represents a unique chance for people to encounter a culture markedly different from their own. Whether it's wandering through traditional Daasanach villages, watching Hamer people performing a Jumping of the Bulls ceremony or seeing the Mursi's mind-blowing lip plates, your visit here will stick with you for a lifetime. This is quite a beautiful region, too. The landscape is diverse, ranging from dry, open savannah plains to forests in the high hills and along the Omo and Mago Rivers. The former meanders for nearly 800km, from southwest of Addis Ababa all the way to Lake Turkana on the Kenyan border.

South Omo, as it's also known, is not a land frozen in time as many visitors with visions of *National Geographic* articles imagine it, though ancient traditions still form the backbone of daily life. But perhaps not for much longer. Outside factors such as huge hydroelectric dams, sugarcane and palm oil plantations, road construction, oil exploration and laws aiming to 'civilise' the people (like outlawing stick fighting) are forcing rapid change. Tourism, though not without its problems, is about the last stabilising influence on the tribal culture because tourists are generally interested in and respectful of it.

## Planning

Decent roads allow visits all year, though note that even just one day of rain (April, May and October are the wettest months) can render some roads south of the main Konso–Jinka route temporarily impassable due to both mud and lack of bridges. Most of the park is below 500m elevation, so temperatures can soar over 40°C, but some nights get cool enough to necessitate a light jacket. For a cultural insight into the region, the best time to visit is January to April when many celebrations take place, including marriages and initiation ceremonies. The driest period (January and February)

## Lower Omo Valley & its Tribes

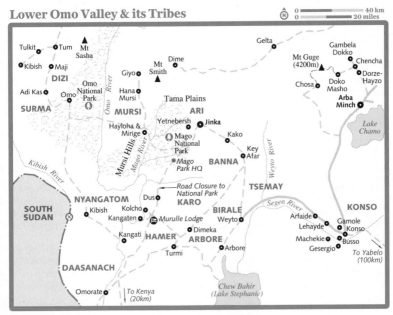

increases the odds of animal sightings in Mago National Park.

The towns featured here are completely ordinary, with modern buildings that look no different from elsewhere in the country because they were built and populated mostly by Ethiopians from elsewhere in the country. Tribal peoples generally only visit on market days (see p168) and you should try to coincide with as many markets as you can. Likewise, the surrounding villages have few people on the market days, at least until late afternoon when they return home.

Accommodation is mostly rough and ridiculously overpriced. Even the 'luxury' places in Turmi and Jinka are prone to electricity (and sometimes water) failures.

## PEOPLES OF THE LOWER OMO VALLEY

The Lower Omo Valley is unique in that it's home to so many peoples in such a small area. And despite the close confines, many of the 16 ethnic groups are dramatically different from their neighbours. Historians believe that this region served for millennia as a kind of cultural crossroads, where Cushitic, Nilotic, Omotic and Semitic peoples met as they migrated from the north, west, south and east.

Described here are some of the Lower Omo Valley's most notable peoples.

### The Ari አሪ

By far South Omo's largest tribe, almost 290,000 Ari live around Jinka. Most are farmers (sorghum and coffee) but cattle-raising remains important and all villages have full-time blacksmiths and potters. They also produce large amounts of honey from beehives made with bark and dung, often for trade. The women wear skirts made from the *enset* ('false-banana' tree), but now only on special occasions.

### The Banna በና

Numbering around 27,000, the Banna inhabit the higher ground around Key Afar. Most practise agriculture, though their diet is supplemented by hunting. Culturally, they're closely related to the Hamer, and they dress quite similarly. The easiest way to tell them apart (though this isn't foolproof) is that the Banna wear beads that include the colour blue, while the Hamer don't. After killing a buffalo, they decorate themselves with clay for a special celebration and feast for the whole village.

### The Daasanach ዳሰነች

Roughly 48,000 Daasanach people live along both sides of the Omo River between Omorate and Lake Turkana. They're closely related to the Arbore and the languages are mutually intelligible. Originally purely pastoralists, the villages now all raise maize, sorghum and tobacco, and some have adopted fishing, though cows are still the mainstay of life. They are one of the poorest peoples of the valley.

Like their enemies, the Nyangatom, women make beads from scraps of plastic, but Daasanach women wear fewer necklaces.

### The Hamer ሃመር

The Hamer, who number around 46,500, are subsistence agropastoralists. They cultivate sorghum, vegetables, millet, tobacco and cotton, as well as rear cattle and goats. Honey is also an important part of their diet.

The people are particularly known for their remarkable hairstyles. The women mix together ochre, water and a binding resin before rubbing it into their hair. They then twist strands again and again to create coppery-coloured tresses known as *goscha*. These are a sign of health and welfare.

Traditionally if they've recently killed an enemy or dangerous animal, men are permitted to don clay hair buns that sometimes support magnificent ostrich feathers. With the help of *borkotos* (special headrests) for sleeping, the buns last from three to six months, and can be 'redone' for up to one year. These days they're done for decoration.

Generators usually only run from 6pm to 10pm. Reservations in Jinka and Turmi are recommended for January to February and September to December.

ⓘ **Getting Around**

Currently Konso is the only gateway, though a new road from Sodo to Jinka will change things. As long as you're not in a hurry or in need of comfort, it's now quite easy to visit independently. Buses run daily from Konso and Arba Minch to Jinka, and on market days from Jinka to Turmi and Omorate. The bus prices we've given are for locals: you'll almost surely pay much more. On days when there's no bus, the local guide associations can easily arrange rides in private cars and trucks for a small fee. It's illegal (for everybody, though only enforced with *faranji*)

The Hamer are also considered masters of body decoration, much of it improvised: nails, mobile phone cards and wristwatch bands are all incorporated into jewellery. The women wear iron coils around their arms, and bead necklaces. The *ensente* (iron torques) worn around the necks of married and engaged women indicate the wealth and prestige of their husband. Unmarried girls wear a metal plate in their hair that looks a bit like a platypus bill.

The iron bracelets and armlets are an indication of the wealth and social standing of the young girl's family. When she gets married, she must remove the jewellery; it's the first gift she makes to her new family.

Hamer territory is concentrated around Turmi and Dimeka.

### The Karo ካሮ

With a population of about 1500 people, the Karo are one of the Omo Valley's smallest groups. Inhabiting the Omo's eastern bank northwest of Turmi, some of these traditional pastoralists turned to agriculture (growing sorghum and maize) after disease wiped out their cattle.

In appearance, language and tradition, they somewhat resemble the Hamer, to whom they're related. The Karo are considered masters of body painting, using white and sometimes coloured chalk to create bold patterns.

### The Mursi ሙርሲ

The 7500 or so Mursi are mainly pastoralists who have been relocated out of Mago National Park to the drier hills west of it. Traditionally the Mursi would move during the wet and dry seasons and practise flood retreat cultivation along the Omo River, though raising cattle is the most important part of their life.

The most famous Mursi traditions include the fierce stick-fighting between the men (now illegal and so never done for tourists), and the lip-plates worn by the women. Made of clay and up to 12cm in diameter, the plates are inserted into a slit separating their lower lip and jaw. Due to the obvious discomfort, women only wear the lip-plates occasionally, leaving their distended lips swaying below their jaw. The hole is cut around age 15 and stretched over many months. At this time the women also have their four lower front teeth pulled out, while men remove only the lower two. The origin of the practice is no longer known, but it probably began as a purely aesthetic practice done to mark entry into adulthood. Women's large ear holes are cut at about age five.

### The Nyangatom ያንጋቶም

Inhabiting the land west of the Omo River all the way to South Sudan (but sometimes bringing their cows to the Omo's east bank to graze) are around 25,000 Nyangatom. Related to the Turkana in Kenya, the Nyangatom are agropastoralists, growing sorghum and maize as well as rearing cattle and goats. They also hunt, and those along the river smoke bees out of their hives for honey. Known as great warmongers, they used to be the enemies of just about everybody, but today only have significant cattle-raid conflicts with the Daasanach.

Nyangatom women are best known for their distinctly thick pile of necklaces. In the past the beads were made of ostrich egg (still used to decorate their goat-skin skirts) but these days they mould round beads from melted scraps of plastic such as broken jerry cans.

to ride in the Isuzu cargo trucks. Note that the government has closed the direct Jinka–Omorate road south of Mago National Park because of the oil exploration taking place.

Most people visit with a tour agency from Addis Ababa, though you can also book fully outfitted tours in Arba Minch and Jinka. If you want to join with others to reduce costs, Addis is best. Most companies will try to do this for you and you may also have success finding other travellers on Lonely Planet's Thorn Tree online forum. You could also try posting on the message board at the Itegue Taitu Hotel in Addis Ababa.

Jinka and Konso have petrol stations, but they're often dry. Do as all tour companies do; fill your tank and jerry cans in Arba Minch.

### Dangers & Annoyances

Because there are many tourists, '*faranji* frenzy' (p281) is as bad here as it is in northern Ethiopia. Just keep smiling and remember that the stress will pass.

Photography can also be stressful. Locals love having their photo taken – because they charge you for the privilege. Posing for photos is the best and sometimes only source of cash the villagers have. (Keep in mind that, generally speaking, women are more likely to spend the money on useful things like plastic buckets or flashlights; men mostly buy *areke*, homemade liquor.) They'll often aggressively approach you, demanding that you start snapping. In fact, most of the face and body painting and elaborate headgear were once worn only for battle or special occasions, but it's now done daily to prompt

---

### TRAVEL THE OMO RIVER

It's now possible to avoid the growing masses of tourist 4WDs crowding into the Omo Valley and visit villages by boat instead. From September to February, fully outfitted three- to five-day trips head down the Omo River from near the Karo village of Dus. It's still a new venture, but holds a lot of promise. Contact **Tuti Mesfin** (✆0911-805971; tutiman_utd@yahoo.com) in Arba Minch or **Pamela Robbie** (✆0912-637056; destinationethipiatours@gmail.com) in Addis Ababa for more information.

The Omorate Local Guide Association (p170) plans to offer simpler, overnight trips out of Omorate.

---

tourists to snap photos. The clothing (or lack of it in the case of the Mursi), however, is genuine. The price is always negotiable but Birr2 for a quick pose or Birr10 for a longer one is normal. The days of your model counting camera clicks is mostly over. During village-wide celebrations your guide will negotiate a flat fee for photography, but this is very rarely acceptable during normal village visits because when the money is paid to the chief, he will generally keep it all.

In an attempt to get you to stop and take their picture, many kids have taken to dancing, selling whistles and doing acrobatics alongside the road, which is dangerous enough. Some even do their shtick in the middle of the road to force you to slow down. In either case, please don't promote this behaviour (which also encourages them to skip school) by giving them anything.

For many ethnic groups, raiding is a part of life. Camps should never be left unattended.

---

## Jinka                          ጂንካ

POP 25,800 / ELEV 1500M

Set in the hills above Mago National Park, fast-growing Jinka is the biggest town in this region, although its facilities and services remain limited. Because it's the only practical base for visiting the Mursi, it's often bursting at the seams with tour groups.

### ◎ Sights

**Market**                                    MARKET
Jinka's famous Saturday market, the largest in the region, sits 300m northwest of the roundabout. It attracts a variety of ethnic groups including Ari, Banna, Mursi and sometimes Bashada. Though smaller and significantly less colourful the rest of the week, when it's mostly just the local Ari people trading, it's still worth a long wander.

**South-Omo Museum &**
**Research Centre**                          MUSEUM
(✆0467-750332; www.southomoresearch.org; admission Birr50; ◎8am-6pm) Perched on a hill northeast of town (look for the green roof), the museum is good but also disappointing. There are several interesting exhibitions, particularly the Q&A with women from across the region, but there's really very little background information on the groups, and not all are represented. There's also a collection of ethnographic DVDs to view.

## 👉 Tours

The two rival guide associations – **New Vision Local Guide Association** (☏0916-712096; localtour.organizer@gmail.com; ⊙8am-7.30pm) and **Pioneers Local Guide Association** (☏0467-751728; ⊙6.30am-6.30pm) – work alternate days of the week and you have no choice of which to use to hire the mandatory guide for day visits to Mursi villages. For longer trips, like multiday treks between Ari or Mursi villages, you can contract with the group of your choice. Both have some good guides, but also some who are completely unqualified and many tourists complain about their guide's lack of knowledge or lack of English. Their offices are next to the airstrip at the roundabout.

## 🛏 Sleeping

Even in the rainy season, Jinka can run out of water.

**Goh Hotel** HOTEL $
(☏0467-750033; d without bathroom Birr81, d/tw Birr287/310; P) The Goh is cheaper than its inferior neighbour, Orit Hotel, and attracts a wide cross-section of travellers. The rooms are slightly aged and worn but relatively bright and clean while the bathroom-less ones out the back aren't quite as good as those at Tesfa Pension. The quality restaurant is a good incentive to stay.

**Eco-Omo** LODGE $$$
(☏0959-200706; www.eco-omo.com; camping per tent US$16.50, s/d incl breakfast US$58/92; P🛜) Jinka's fanciest (though least friendly) address is 4km out of town on the road to Mago. Simple safari tents on thatched-roof platforms are in a large patch of green sloping down to the Neri River. Hot water is available mornings and evenings only, but unlike at hotels in town you can count on it being available. A pool and spa are planned.

**John Lucy Campsite** CAMPGROUND $
(campsites per tent Birr50; P) For now it's just a peaceful patch of green grass filled with birdsong. But the friendly owner is in the process of landscaping and says he will build a restaurant and lounge areas. It's west of the airstrip.

**Red Cross Pension** PENSION $
(d Birr100; P) Ordinary rooms in the centre of town.

**Tesfa Pension** PENSION $
(☏0467-750306; d without bathroom Birr70; P) Rooms are brighter and toilets less aromatic than most of Jinka's many other shared-bath cheapies.

## 🍴 Eating

**Central Bar & Restaurant** ETHIOPIAN $
(mains Birr9-22) This is the pick of the local eateries because the food is good, there's an English menu and there's no *faranji* tax. Despite its name, it's not very central: walk 400m out of town from the Goh Hotel, past the road to Key Afar.

**Goh Hotel** EUROPEAN-ETHIOPIAN $
(mains Birr20-70) A sound choice with salads, soup, rice and spaghetti. The Ethiopian food is good, too.

**Eco-Omo** ITALIAN $
(mains Birr35-100) If the novelty of *injera* and oily spaghetti gravy has worn thin, head out to this Italian-owned lodge's Italian restaurant.

## ℹ Information

**Dashen Bank** Has Omo's only ATM.
**Commercial Bank** Will cash travellers cheques.
**Jinka Zonal Hospital** (☏0467-750046; ⊙24hr)
**Pioneers Local Guide Association** (☏0467-751728; ⊙6.30am-6.30pm) Has an internet cafe in the front charging Birr1 per two minutes, and a very public campground.

## ℹ Getting There & Away

It's expected that a new airport will be built and Ethiopian Airlines will resume flights.

There's a daily bus to Arba Minch (Birr101, six hours) leaving at 6am, several daily minibuses to Konso (Birr70, 3½ hours) and one bus to Omorate (Birr100, 3½ hours) via Turmi (Birr70, 2½ hours) on Tuesday, Thursday and Saturday, returning the next day.

The guide associations rent out 4WDs with drivers and fuel for an outlandish US$185 a day (definitely bargain) and also have motorcycles available for tours. For anything more than a day, it's better to deal directly with **Bereket Tadesse** (☏0928-310295, meetthetribes@gmail.com), who is half-Mursi, and **Lalo Dessa** (☏0913-363077; www.lalo-tours.com), two Jinka-based guides who can organise total Omo packages starting in Addis or anywhere else for reasonable prices.

SOUTHERN ETHIOPIA JINKA

# Around Jinka

## MURSI VILLAGES  የሙርሲ መንደር

For almost all visitors, the Mursi is the most anticipated Lower Omo tribe. The unique chance to meet half-naked women with giant lip and ear plates and ritually scarred bodies simply proves irresistible. But visiting comes with a catch. Even though things have improved in recent years, the Mursi are the most aggressive tribe in their interaction with tourists and you can expect to have your arm, clothes, camera bag and maybe even hair pulled. Things are worse in the afternoon, after lots of alcohol has been consumed.

There are five Mursi villages. The most visited is Hayloha. It's the biggest and even has a few 'modern' buildings. Smaller and purely traditional, Mirige tends to come with fewer hassles. The other three villages are down horrible roads and rarely visited. All charge Birr100 per person entrance.

Guides (per day Birr200: includes visiting an Ari village if you want) must be hired in Jinka through the local guide associations (p165) which can also arrange transport by 4WD and motorcycle. And, since the villages are just west of Mago National Park, you must also pay all park fees (p167) just to drive there. Visitors can sleep in any of the villages for Birr100 per person.

### ⓘ Getting There & Away

Supposedly the road to the villages will be paved during the lifetime of this book, but in the meantime it takes about two hours to drive there. It's passable even when it rains, though the Yilima River has no bridge and can occasionally run so high it strands 4WDs for days at a time.

A possible, albeit extremely impractical option, if you plan to spend the night, is to use the new bus service between Jinka and Hana Mursi, which passes within walking distance of the villages. It leaves Jinka on Tuesday, Thursday and Saturday at about 4pm and returns the next morning when full.

---

**LOCAL KNOWLEDGE**

## JOEY L'S TIPS FOR PHOTOGRAPHY IN THE OMO VALLEY

Joey L (www.joeyl.com) is a renowned Canadian photographer and filmmaker. He's spent extended periods of time working in the Omo Valley. We met him in the Surmi area of Southwest Omo and asked for tips on photographing the peoples of the Omo Valley.

**You need a good guide:** When I travel, I need a guide to help bridge me between my culture and the one I am visiting. This is someone who will show me around, translate for me...a sort of co-pilot. Your guide should be used to working with photographers. Other things to consider are their language skills; how flexible they are in unpredictable situations; whether they can help you find unique perspectives that help tell the story of the place and its people, rather than taking you to the typical tourist spots; and whether they are physically able to help you carry some of your gear if necessary.

I've lucked out and had a couple of great guides on my trips to the Omo Valley. I've made a great friend, Anteneh Endale Mamo (☎0911-536954; anteneh.endale34@gmail.com). Anteneh is from the south of Ethiopia and knows the area well, having grown up among the various ethnic groups living here. The people respect him, and by association, they respected me too, and that made things a lot easier. He's often on the road and out of contact, though.

**Hard drives:** When I travel for photography, I know that the most valuable things I have are not my cameras or equipment, but the images I am creating. I have a very simple formula: I travel with a laptop, and dump my images to two different hard drives. I always keep those two hard drives in separate places. For example, one is in my pocket at all times and the other is left at the guesthouse. With this system, it's hard for both drives to go missing.

**Charging batteries:** Hotels and guesthouses in the Omo Valley are run on gas generators. The manager will only turn them on for a short time at night. If you need to charge something during the day, bring extra gasoline in a jerry can and offer it to the manager. Gasoline is hard to come by in such a remote area, so this goes a long way and becomes a great bartering tool for keeping your stuff charged.

**This is not a safari or zoo:** You are in another person's backyard. This is someone's home. If you want to take photographs, ask permission first.

## MAKE IT MEANINGFUL

Far too often, people treat their visits to Omo Valley villages like human safaris. The villagers line up, the tourists pick some out, cameras click, birr flies, and the tourists jump back into their Land Cruiser to rush off to the next stop. It doesn't have to be this way, but to avoid it you'll probably need to take the initiative because most guides do little more than negotiate the photography fees.

Village visits are so much better when there's genuine interaction. Start by *not* starting with the photos. Stroll through the village first. Visit some houses and ask questions. (Have your guide translate your questions to the villagers rather than answer himself.) The answers will often surprise you, and you'll not only learn interesting things about their lives, you might gain new perspectives on your own.

### MAGO NATIONAL PARK
*የማጎ ብሔራዊ ፓርክ*

Although by Ethiopian standards wildlife is fairly abundant in this dramatically beautiful 2162-sq-km park (admission per person US$10, vehicle US$2, mandatory scout up to 12hr US$6, up to 24hr US$10), there's no chance of an East African safari–style experience. Poaching remains a problem and the thick acacia woodland dominating the plains makes seeing what wildlife remains quite tough. About the only animals you can expect to see along the northern road during most of the day are dik-diks, baboons and guinea fowl. Wildlife watching is much better along the road to the headquarters and at the abandoned airstrip 5km further on where you can expect to spot buffalo, Burchell's zebras, lesser kudus, defassa waterbucks, gerenuks, black-and-white colobus, and (with some luck) one of the 300 elephants. Lions, leopards, cheetahs and giraffes are rarely encountered. If you make arrangements with your guide the day before you can leave Jinka very early and spend several hours in the park before visiting the Mursi.

If you're serious about searching out wildlife, you'll need to overnight at the campsite (per tent US$4, tent hire 1-3 person US$10, 4+ person US$12) near the headquarters and Neri River. (There are no crocodiles, so bathing is safe.) There's a water pump and pit toilets, and drinks can be bought at the headquarters. Tsetse flies are problematic: avoid wearing blue or black, which seems to attract them.

### ❶ Getting There & Around

Even though buses now pass through the park, they're of no use to visitors. The northern road is graded, but a 4WD is needed for the really rough 12km drive to the headquarters and campsite. Walking in the park is allowed and recommended. The ranger station at the entrance to the park is usually closed in the morning, but it's routine to pay when leaving.

### ARI VILLAGES
*የአሪ መንደር*

The Ari is the most 'modern' of the region's ethnic groups. They dress no differently than city dwellers these days, but village life remains interesting. In almost all villages you'll meet potters, blacksmiths and women grinding grain to make the Ari version of *injera*, which uses maize or sorghum instead of tef and has *dagussa* ('finger millet') mixed into it. If you're lucky someone may invite you to try *bunaketele*, a delicious drink made from coffee leaves, chillies and several spices including lemongrass. Guides most often take people to Yetnebersh (per person Birr50), 7km west of Jinka, which is as good as any around.

### KEY AFAR
*ቀይ አፋር*

A rather large modern town, what Key Afar lacks in atmosphere for six days out of the week it more than makes up for on Thursday with one of the best markets around. Thousands of Banna, Hamer and Tsemay descend on the town, along with every tourist in the vicinity.

All visitors must hire a guide from the Anomba Local Tour Guide Association (☑0920-282170; guide per group Birr150; ☺8am-5pm) across from the Nasa Hotel. On nonmarket days they can take you to visit surrounding Banna villages (each with a Birr100 per person entrance fee), some of which are within easy walking distance. Jumping of the Bulls ceremonies (see p169) and *evangadi* (Hamer night dances; Birr200 per person) take place in these villages. The guide fee doubles if they take you to see the bulls.

Nasa Hotel (☑0462-710021; d with/without bathroom Birr150/100; ℗), on the road that leads to Weyto, and the squat-toilet-only

## MARKET DAY IN THE OMO VALLEY

Since most people have long journeys to and from the towns, markets are best visited between 10.30am and 3pm. Notable markets include the following:

| TOWN | DAY | TRIBE |
|---|---|---|
| Arbore | Mon | Arbore & Tsemay |
| Dimeka | Tue & Sat | Banna, Bashada, Hamer, Karo & Tsemay |
| Jinka | Tue & Sat | Ari, Banna, Bashada & Mursi |
| Giyo | Thu | Ari, Bacha, Dime, Mursi & Surma |
| Hana Mursi | Sun | Ari, Bacha, Dime, Mursi & Surma |
| Kako | Mon | Ari & Banna |
| Kangaten | Tue & Sat | Nyangatom & Karo |
| Key Afar | Thu | Banna, Hamer & Tsemay |
| Omorate | Tue & Sat | Daasanach |
| Turmi | Mon & Thu | Bashada & Hamer |
| Weyto | Sat | Tsemay |

The markets at Dimeka (Saturday), Key Afar and Turmi (Monday) are among the biggest and best, but also full of tourists. Market days do change, so it's wise to inquire before making your schedule.

Zarsi Hotel (☏0911-608751; d Birr150; P) on the way to Jinka are acceptably clean, except for the toe-curling common toilets at the former, which will make you want to upgrade. Both serve local food.

### ❶ Getting There & Away

The frequent buses and minibuses between Jinka (Birr20, 45 minutes) and Konso (Birr50, two hours) can drop you here, but there are rarely empty seats when you want to get on. Buses go to Turmi (Birr45, two hours) via Dimeka on Tuesday, Thursday and Saturday afternoons.

## Turmi & Around

While Jinka and most of the rest of the northern half of the region sit at elevation and are relatively cool, these towns in the south serve up the burning hot days you were expecting.

### TURMI                        ቱርሚ

Despite being an important transit and tourist hub, Turmi is just a speck of a town. It's surrounded by Hamer villages and on Monday the villagers, along with nearly every tourist in the valley, descend on the large market. The smaller Thursday market is almost tourist-free.

No guide is required for the market (this may change), but you do need one to visit villages, several of which are in walking distance. Try the Evangadi Local Guide Association (☏0916-825037; guide per group Birr200), which can also do multiday trekking trips and sometimes arrange 4WD hire. They can also take you to see a Jumping of the Bulls ceremony (see p169) or an *evangadi*. While the bull jumping is never done specially for tourists, the *evangadi* (minimum Birr1000 for a group) usually is. It's still fun, though.

### 🛏 Sleeping & Eating

During the high season, reservations are wise.

TOP CHOICE Buska Lodge                    LODGE $$$
(☏0111-567837; www.buskalodge.com; campsites own tent s/d US$8/13, tent with bed s/d US$35/50, bungalows incl breakfast & dinner s/d/tr US$75/100/150; P🛜) By far the best place to stay in the valley, Buska has nice green *tukuls* and rooms amid plenty of trees and flowers. The campsite has 'islands' with concrete pads and thatched roofs and there are good facilities. The restaurant (mains Birr44 to Birr86) stretches beyond the ordinary with dishes like Hungarian goulash and a big wine list. Staff pack a variety of lunch

boxes, too. Massage is available. It's east of town, 1km off the Weyto road.

### Kaske Campsite
CAMPGROUND **$**

(☏0928-162836; campsites per tent Birr85, tent hire Birr100, r Birr250; **P**) Thanks to a canopy of lush mango trees, there's plenty of shade at this campsite next to the Kaske River. The stark concrete rooms (only one with its own bath) are better than the cheapies in town, as are the rudimentary but clean shared facilities. It's 4km east of Turmi, a long hot walk to town for meals, or a short walk to Buska Lodge.

### Turmi Lodge
LODGE **$$$**

(☏0116-631481, www.turmilodge.com; campsites s/d US$15/21, s/d incl breakfast US$65/75; **P**) A less-attractive alternative to Buska Lodge, the ugly pink-tin-roofed rooms are plain but maintained and the service is good. The nearby church means there's an early weekend and Orthodox holiday wake-up call. The good restaurant is a long walk from the rooms and the menu (mains Birr37 to Birr81) has pizza; sometimes the kitchen does, too. Massage is available. It's 1km north of town.

### Tourist Hotel
HOTEL **$**

(☏0911-190209; d with/without shower Birr200/70; **P**) Popular with travellers for its overall cleanliness and friendliness, this simple place on the road to Weyto is well run, though unreasonably priced. The common toilets are cleaner than average, though the shower shack is less than private. The restaurant (mains Birr30 to Birr60) serves the best food within the town.

### Arba Minch Hotel
HOTEL **$**

(d/tw without bathroom Birr80/140; **P**) Conveniently right at the market, the rooms aren't too grubby, but we can't say the same about the facilities.

### ❶ Getting There & Away

The Tuesday, Thursday and Saturday buses between Jinka (Birr80, three hours) and Omorate (Birr30, one hour) stop in Turmi. On other days it's easy to find a truck to both towns.

The direct route to Weyto sees little traffic other than tour company 4WDs. Those driving themselves should inquire about the road before heading out because when it rains in the highlands, some of the dry riverbeds can fill up and become too high to cross.

## DIMEKA
ዲመካ

Dimeka, 28km north of Turmi, is the biggest town in Hamer territory and we think its Saturday **market** (Tuesday is smaller) is the best of the big ones. The **Dimeka Negaya Local Guides Association** (⊙8.30am-12.30pm & 1.30-4pm) charges Birr150 per group for the mandatory guide through the market and another Birr200 to take you to surrounding villages, including the Bashada (Hamer who make pottery, to oversimplify things) village of **Argude** 5km away. They can also take you trekking overnight up Mt Busca, the area's highest peak, if you have your own camping gear.

Few *faranji* sleep here, and when you see the state of the three pensions (each with grubby common toilets, lack of showers and Birr200 initial asking prices) you'll probably want to join the masses and head to Turmi.

SOUTHERN ETHIOPIA TURMI & AROUND

---

DON'T MISS

## BULL JUMPING

Whipping, teasing, screaming, horn-blowing and leaping are part of the Jumping of the Bulls ceremony. It's a rite of passage into manhood for all Hamer and Banna boys and is truly a sight to behold. After 15 to 30 bulls have been lined up side by side, each naked boy taking part must cross the line of bulls, jumping on the beasts from back to back. If they fall, they're whipped and teased by women. If they succeed, they must turn around and complete the task three more times!

Before the bulls, young female relatives of the boys beg to be whipped with sticks; the deeper their scars, the more love they show for their boy. It's as disturbing as it is intriguing.

January to April is the peak season, but the ceremonies can happen any time. The whole event lasts more than a day, but the main activities happen between 2pm and 6pm. You must, of course, go with a guide, from either Turmi or Dimeka. Prices are up to the chief and so you may not know the cost until you get to the village, but it's not going to be less than Birr300 per person.

The market day buses between Jinka (Birr50, three hours) and Turmi (Birr20, 30 minutes) pass through. At other times, it's usually not tough to hitch a ride.

## KANGATEN & KOLCHO ካንጋተን እና ቆላቾ

This pair of Omo River–side destinations makes an excellent day trip out of Turmi, though most people only visit Kolcho. Both are largely hassle-free, though it's best to visit in the Nyangatom villages in the morning because many men are quite drunk by the afternoon. This way you also avoid the morning caravan of 4WDs occupying Kolcho.

The Nyangatom, whose women wear massive stacks of beaded necklaces, only inhabit lands west of the Omo River and many villages lie within a few kilometres' walk from the regional town of Kangaten. Park at the secure compound across the river called 'The Store'. Here you'll lighten your wallet of a Birr100 parking fee, Birr150 per group subdistrict fee, Birr50 per person village fee, Birr200 per group guide fee and Birr60 per person round-trip boat fare.

Only a few kilometres northeast of Kangaten, but an hour by car, the clifftop village of Kolcho is the smallest of three Karo villages. And with its lofty views over a U-bend in the Omo River, it's one of the most beautifully set in all of Ethiopia. The village remains very traditional, and Hamer women routinely come daily to trade milk for sorghum or *cheka* (local beer). Guides charge Birr100 per group and Birr350 per vehicle. Dance demonstrations (at least Birr1500 per group) can be arranged.

### 🛏 Sleeping & Eating

Kolcho has no lodging, but camping (Birr50) on the clifftop is magical. A small kitchen is available, but bring food and water, or trudge down to the river like the villagers do. A small shop sells drinks.

Mahailet Hotel (d Birr50) is marginally the pick of Kangaten's two rough hotels, both of which are attached to busy bars.

### ℹ Getting There & Away

Each of the villages is about 65km from Turmi and can be reached in less than two hours, unless there's heavy rain. A high-clearance vehicle is a must. You'll need to come with someone who knows the way since there are no signs and the roads to these villages pass through something of a no-man's land so there's no chance to ask directions. Also note that heavy rains in the highlands can fill the normally dry Kizo River, temporary blocking access.

A bus runs from Jinka to Kangaten (Birr80, six hours) on Monday and Saturday (leaving around lunchtime) and departs Kangaten on Sunday and Tuesday as early as 10am.

Truck traffic is so scarce that hitching to either village is simply not a realistic option.

## OMORATE ኦሞራቴ

The region's hottest and dustiest town hugs the eastern bank of the Omo River, 72km southwest of Turmi. Omorate is visited almost exclusively as a morning trip out of Turmi. For now the only attraction is the Daasanach villages (village fee per person Birr100, guide per group Birr100), but the Omorate Local Guide Association is planning to begin overnight boat trips on the river. For now they have no office, but guides will find you when you arrive.

Most people visit villages across the river, since it's fun to ride the dugout canoes (per person Birr50) or the more reassuring motorboat (per person Birr60), but the villages on the east are just as traditional. The Daasanach are the only people willing to consider flat-fee photography, either for a single family or the whole village, so discuss this with your guide and they'll take you to the market to buy something to give in exchange (paying cash is not popular since the chief keeps the money) for unlimited photo access.

Omorate's Tuesday and Saturday markets aren't very big, but differ from others in that there are many products, like bed sheets and beads, imported from Kenya. As this is considered a border area, travellers need to register their passport at Immigration upon arrival.

There's hardly a difference between the three hotels in town and the supposedly better (but still with external facilities) hotel just out of town had been appropriated for oil workers.

### ℹ Getting There & Away

One bus connects Omorate to Jinka (Birr100, 3½ hours) via Turmi (Birr30, one hour) heading south on Tuesday, Thursday and Saturday and back north the following days.

The road north to Jinka through Mago National Park has been closed, and likely won't reopen any time soon. For details about crossing into Kenya, see p289.

## ARBORE ኤርቦሬ

Arbore rests 50km south of Weyto on the Turmi road and remains a traditional village with only a few scattered modern buildings. The Arbore people are a mixed bunch, with ancestry linking back to both the Omo Valley and Konso highlands. With their beads and aluminium jewellery, they almost resemble the Borena people. Locals outside the village know it as 'mosquito town'. To escape the notorious pests many Arbore sleep on platforms high in their houses rather than on the ground.

The **Arbore Grevy's Zebra Local Guide Association** (✆0926-163015) charges some of the highest fees (Birr250 per vehicle and Birr150 per person) in the valley even though visits are usually less than an hour. Additionally, visitors are hassled quite a bit so many people skip Arbore.

The Arbore Tourist Camping Site is set to open just outside the village. The price will be Birr100 per person and some food will be available. It looks like it will be a decent place.

There's no public transport along this road, and not much traffic at all since it's actually faster to drive the long way between Konso and Turmi via Key Afer. Additionally, there are some dry riverbeds that can fill and block the route when it rains.

**WEYTO**                                    ወይጦ

The first town you encounter coming from Konso is in the territory of the Tsemay (part farmers, part pastoralists who dress similarly to the Banna, but are culturally differ-

---

---

ent). No guide is needed to visit the market, which is a very laid-back experience. Now that the road is paved, hardly any tourists or truck drivers stop here anymore, but if you get hungry or sleepy **Meheret Hotel** (✆0916-547506; campsites Birr50, d with/without bathroom Birr100/70; 🅿) has some acceptable rooms and local food (mains Birr30 to Birr50). You can bus to/from Jinka (Birr50, two hours) and Konso (Birr45, 1½ hours) but there's no public transport to Turmi, just the occasional truck.

# Eastern Ethiopia

## Best of Culture

» Harar's old walled city (p185)

» Harar's cultural guest-houses (p190)

» Koremi (p193)

» Dire Dawa's markets (p189)

## Best of Nature

» Babille Elephant Sanctuary (p193)

» Hyena Feeding (p189)

» Fantale Crater (p176)

» Valley of Marvels (p194)

## Why Go?

Most of Eastern Ethiopia is a stark landscape of dust-stained acacia scrub and forgettable towns. But scattered around this cloak of the commonplace are gems of genuine adventure. Undoubtedly, the east's pièce de résistance is the walled city of Harar. There's still a patina of myth about this ancient town, handed down from the days when its markets served as the Horn's commercial hub and attracted powerful merchants, artisans and Islamic scholars. The colonial-rural melange that is the modern city of Dire Dawa delights in its own odd way, while nature lovers can get their kicks at Babille Elephant Sanctuary and Awash National Park, where the volcanic landscape takes top billing over the wildlife. The truly intrepid can follow the seemingly endless ribbon of asphalt north to the desolate southern Danakil Desert; the territory remains virtually unexplored since legendary adventurer Wilfred Thesiger first thrilled the world with tales of the proud Afar.

## When to Go
### Harar

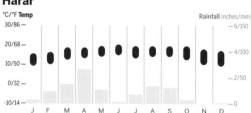

**May-Sep** Rainy and hot season sends lowland temperatures up to 45°C.

**Sep** The seemingly barren Asaita road is painted yellow by the Meskel flower.

**Nov-Jan** Driest months; best to see elephants at Babille and the lakes near Asaita.

## ⓘ Getting There & Away

**Ethiopian Airlines** (www.flyethiopian.com) flies from Addis Ababa to Dire Dawa and Jijiga, and also between Dire Dawa and Djibouti. You can enter eastern Ethiopia overland from Djibouti City by bus and, assuming passenger service resumes as promised, by train to Dire Dawa; by bus-minibus combination from Djibouti City to Logiya; and by connecting minibuses from Hargeisa (Somaliland) to Jijiga. For more information see p288.

## ⓘ Getting Around

Decent sealed roads connect all main cities, including remote Asaita. Public transport is available on all routes.

# ADDIS ABABA TO AWASH

The long stretch of road dropping from Addis Ababa down to Awash offers little to tempt tourists to stop. Debre Zeyit, near the start, has lakeview lodging, and Awash

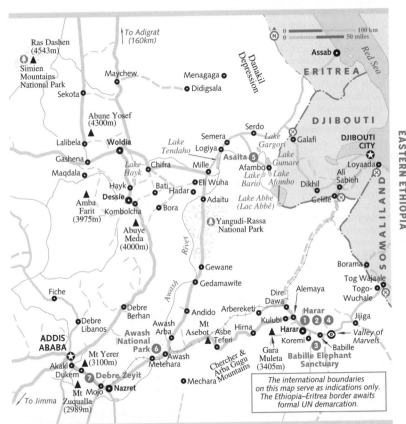

**EASTERN ETHIOPIA**

The international boundaries on this map serve as indications only. The Ethiopia–Eritrea border awaits formal UN demarcation.

## Eastern Ethiopia Highlights

❶ Explore the warren of alleyways in Harar's **old walled city** (p185)

❷ Bite down on a stick wrapped with meat as **hyenas** (p189) pull it from your mouth in Harar

❸ Get out of the car and track elephants on foot at **Babille Elephant Sanctuary** (p193)

❹ Bed down in a piece of living history in an **Adare guesthouse** (p190) in Old Harar

❺ Follow in the footsteps of Wilfred Thesiger around the lakes near **Asaita** (p180)

❻ Take a geological safari at **Awash National Park** (p176)

❼ Decompress at a lakeside resort in **Debre Zeyit** (p174)

National Park at the end offers some modest wildlife watching and interesting geology, though, truthfully, both are missable.

Your trip will begin in a traffic jam that can last all the way until Mojo, although a new road will improve things eventually. The third-biggest town in Ethiopia, Nazret (its name derived from the Christian town in Israel), 100km from Addis, served briefly as the capital of Oromia region and you'll pass the large government complex as you enter town. It's modern, clean and orderly but has nothing to offer tourists other than ATMs and an abundance of good hotels. Not long after Nazret you'll enter a region pocked with cinder cones, calderas and other volcanic scars. It's the home of the Kereyu, who are often in conflict with the Afar. They're mostly pastoralists, but along this highway many families have switched to field crops due to the availability of irrigation.

## Debre Zeyit ደብረ ዘይት

POP 118,300 / ELEV 1920M

There's no love at first sight with Debre Zeyit, known in the Oromo language as Bishoftu. But turn off the highway and you'll find a dishevelled necklace of maars (flat-bottomed, steep-sided volcanic crater lakes) strung around the town, and these make it a favourite playground for those escaping the capital for a weekend.

They're certainly beautiful, though with a recent spurt of new hotels around them has largely ruined the mood. And, for that matter, the lakes of southern Ethiopia (p135), with their crocodiles, hippos, fishermen, and flamingos, have more straight-up tourist appeal. Rather than being a link in your Ethiopian itinerary, Debre Zeyit is best as a final-night alternative to Addis Ababa.

### ◉ Sights & Activities

#### Lake Bishoftu                                         LAKE

ቢሾፍቱ ሐይቅ The best way to appreciate this lake is from the crater rim at Dreamland Garden Restaurant, drink in hand. The view is superb. To get up close and personal with this body of water, scramble down one of the cattle trails and join the children for a swim. But take care: according to local lore, this, the second-deepest lake in Ethiopia, is home to a sleeping devil. From time to time his evil gases kill the fish and send them bobbing to the surface to be scooped up by delighted waterbirds.

#### Lake Hora                                             LAKE

ሆራ ሐይቅ Less developed than Lake Bishoftu, though probably not for much longer, Lake Hora lies just north of the town centre and has some outstanding birdlife. The Hora Recreation Centre (admission Birr4; ⊗6am-7.30pm) can get a bit noisy at weekends, but it's easy enough to escape the crowds: just follow the footpath around the lake as it winds through the forested slopes of the crater. A circumnavigation of the lake takes around 1½ hours. Theft is a real concern, so take a guide (price negotiable) from the restaurant (mains Birr20-35). Or, savour the scenery from a rowboat.

On the first Sunday following Meskel, the Oromo people celebrate Irecha here. Thanks are given to Waka (One God) and good fortune sought for the upcoming planting season. Devotees gather around an ancient fig tree to smear perfume, butter and katickala (a distilled alcohol) on the trunk and share ceremonial meals.

#### Other Lakes                                           LAKE

If you feel lake-addicted after Bishoftu and Hora, follow the road to the north past the Defence Engineering College and Agriculture Research Centre until you reach a fork marked by a painted 'Galilee Center' sign. Continue straight to Lake Babogaya (formerly named Bishoftu Guda), with its beautiful backdrop of volcanic Mt Yerer, or turn right to little Lake Kuriftu.

Shallow Lake Chelekleka, 2km west of the roundabout, is not a crater lake and lacks the dramatic scenery of the others. But it's a birdwatcher favourite and lesser flamingos are sometimes seen.

### 🛏 Sleeping

#### TOP CHOICE Viewpoint Lodge                            LODGE $$

(☑0911-465693; lakebabogaya@live.com; s/d incl breakfast Birr700/900; ℗@) If you're looking for a casual place to kick back and unwind, then look no further. Refreshingly out of the ordinary, the rooms have a semi-traditional theme and the grounds are mowed by giant tortoises. The stilted rooms below the rim have the best views, though their bathrooms are up above, and there's also a 'treehouse' for those not afraid of heights. There are canoes and a water bike to use on Lake Babogaya and binoculars for the birds. Meals (lunch/dinner Birr80/150) must be ordered well in advance. It's just 50m past the Galilee junction.

**Dreamland Hotel & Resort**     HOTEL $$

(☑0114-371520; www.ethiodreamland.com; d/ tw incl breakfast Birr664/727; P☎) Once the town's flashiest digs, Dreamland is now middle of the road, but provides the best Bishoftu views. All rooms have satellite TV, richly polished furniture, and private balconies facing the lake.

**Asham Africa**     HOTEL $$$

(☑0114-370021; www.ashamafrica.com; r incl breakfast Birr1425; P) This new hotel at Lake Bishoftu defines itself with stylish, oversized rooms and a pan-African theme for its plentiful art and its menu.

**Bishoftu Afaf Hotel**     HOTEL $

(☑0114-338299; r Birr150; P) The rooms are ordinary, but a steal at this price considering it's perched on Lake Bishoftu's crater rim. Unfortunately, the terrace restaurant overlooking the lake is enclosed by dirty glass windows.

**Kuriftu Resort & Spa**     RESORT $$$

(☑0114-336860; www.kurifturesortsspa.com; d/tw incl breakfast & foot massage from US$180/193; P☎@≋) Popular with Addis Ababa's elite this is a massive but attractive resort, the only one on Lake Kuriftu. There's a wide variety of rooms, all with nice little touches such as mosaics around the sinks. The great location affords the stone and timber restaurant (mains Birr76 to Birr114) great views. Prices are sky high, but they often offer discounts.

## ✗ Eating

**Dreamland Garden Restaurant**     EUROPEAN, ETHIOPIAN $

(mains Birr32-95) Its lofty perch on Bishoftu's crater rim and a serenade of birdsong makes this *the* place to dine; and makes the high prices excusable. The menu is the same as every other hotel restaurant in Ethiopia.

**Asham Africa**     EUROPEAN, ETHIOPIAN $$

(mains Birr75-130) There was just an ordinary expensive hotel menu when we visited, but there's a plan to go pan-African by adding dishes like *jollof* rice and *ugali*.

**Farmer's House**     ETHIOPIAN $

(mains Birr22-76) If you're in an *injera* mood you can't do better than this spot on the main road, though the menu is only partially in English. They also have salads and less-greasy-than-usual pasta sauces.

**Debre Zeyit**    ◉   0 —— 400 m / 0 —— 0.2 miles

## ❶ Information

The only ATM (Dashen Bank didn't have one when we visited, but should have by the time this book hits the shelves) and internet cafe are in the 'new' town near the bus station.

EASTERN ETHIOPIA DEBRE ZEYIT

## ℹ Getting There & Around

Buses and minibuses leave roughly every 20 minutes for Addis Ababa (Birr10, 1½ hours) and Nazret (Birr16, 40 minutes).

From the bus station to the turn-offs for the Lake Bishoftu hotels, a shared/contract *bajaj* costs Birr2/10; to Lake Babogaya is Birr4/40.

---

# Awash National Park
## እዋሽ ብሔራዊ ፓርክ

Easily accessible from Addis Ababa, 756-sq-km **Awash National Park** (per person per day Birr90, vehicle Birr20; ⊙6am-7pm) is one of Ethiopia's most visited parks. However, if you're here for the thrill of staring slack-jawed at lions crunching through bones, you'll be seriously disappointed. It's much lower-key and ongoing incursions by Kereyu pastoralists have done little to help wildlife numbers. Nevertheless, it's a must for birders and the volcanic landscape of blister cones and fissures is interesting and beautiful. If the latter interests you, try to find a copy of Frances Williams' excellent self-published booklet *Awash National Park, Ethiopia: Geology and Scenery in a Unique Environment* in Addis or at Awash Falls Lodge.

### Wildlife

The park lies on an important migratory route between the north and the south, bestowing an astonishing amount of birdlife. More than 460 species have been recorded, among them the extremely rare yellow-throated seedeater and somber rock chat, both found only in and near Awash.

Two especially good spots to observe birds are around Filwoha Hot Springs and around the Awash River campsites, where francolin, barbets and hoopoes are all seen. On the plains, kori bustards are quite easily spotted, and sometimes secretary birds. An ostrich reintroduction program has recently begun. Among the many raptors are fish eagles, lammergeyer and pygmy falcons.

In the south of the park, the grassy Illala Sala Plains is the one place devoid of the dominant thick acacia scrub that makes wildlife spotting tough. The beautiful beisa oryx and Soemmering's gazelles are easily seen here. Also present are salt's dik-dik, greater and lesser kudus (particularly in the area called Kudu Valley), defassa waterbucks, warthogs and black-and-white colobus, which prefer the riverine forest. Lions, leopards, cheetahs, black-backed jackals, caracals, servals, wild-

cats and aardwolves are also found in the park, but thank your lucky stars if you manage to spot one of them: they're rarely seen.

### Dangers & Annoyances

Armed scouts (Birr100) are compulsory. There are carnivores, but in reality the greatest risk is from local tribespeople. If you plan to camp, you'll need two scouts.

Malaria is rife here and watch out for the baboons; they're adept camp-pillagers.

## ◉ Sights & Activities

### Game Drive                              WILDLIFE ENCOUNTER

Perhaps better called the oryx and gazelle drive, because these are the only sure sightings. The 30km loop that starts at the main gate cuts across the Illala Sala Plains and passes Awash Falls.

### Awash Falls                                      WATERFALL

**እዋሽ ፏፏቴ** Just past the headquarters there are viewpoints above and below this mighty waterfall, which tumbles into the magnificent **Awash Gorge** along the park's southern boundary. Awash Lodge has a brochure for a short self-guided hike in the gorge below the falls. Park staff tell us you can swim here because the large crocodiles don't attack people; it's up to you whether or not you trust them. Nearby is a small **museum** (⊙6am-6pm) filled with dusty skins, skulls and stuffed animals, plus good written information about the wildlife.

The gorge is 150m deep and at its most beautiful by the abandoned Kereyou Lodge, a short detour off the game drive. You can also spy a wide stretch of the gorge in Awash town: head 500m down the dirt road next to Park Hotel and continue on the main footpath across the train tracks.

### Fantale Crater                                    VOLCANO

**ፈንታሌ** Towards the west end of the park, 600m above the plains (it would have been twice as tall before it collapsed) lies Fantale Crater (2007m). With its terrific vistas, total quiet and cool air, this dormant volcano makes a great trek. At the top (a two- to three-hour walk; the 4WD track is no longer driveable) the 360-degree view is phenomenal and the elliptical caldera, which measures an enormous 3.5km in diameter, is quite an eerie sight in the morning when the steam vents can be seen.

### Filwoha Hot Springs                               SPRING

**ፍልውሃ** At Filwoha Hot Springs in the far north of the park, around 30km from the

# Awash National Park

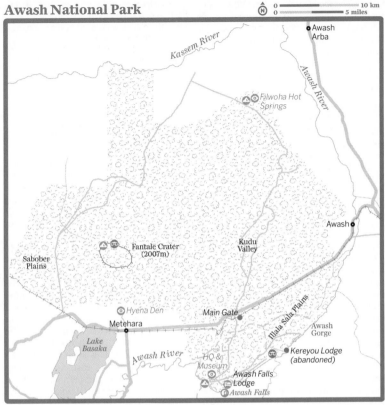

N

0 — 10 km
0 — 5 miles

Awash Arba

Kassem River

Awash River

Filwoha Hot Springs

Awash

Fantale Crater (2007m)

Kudu Valley

Sabober Plains

Hyena Den

Metahara

Main Gate

Lake Basaka

Awash River

Illala Sala Plains

Awash Gorge

HQ & Museum

Kereyou Lodge (abandoned)

Awash Falls Lodge

Awash Falls

highway, you can swim in the turquoise-blue pools but they're not as refreshing as they look: temperatures touch 45°C and crocodiles lurk in the cooler areas.

The beauty is boosted around the springs by the doum palms, used by the local people to make mats. After 5pm, the area comes alive with birds, and lions can sometimes be heard at night.

### Hyena Den                    WILDLIFE ENCOUNTER

የጅብ ጎራ Below Fantale, a few kilometres north of Metahara, you can routinely see dozens of spotted hyenas exit their dens around dusk. A fee of Birr200 is paid to the community and your park scout gets an extra Birr100 for going with you.

## 🛏 Sleeping & Eating

Most visitors who don't stay in the park stay in **Awash**. Coming from Addis, **Metahara** is a more convenient base, but it's a grubby

truckstop town without very good services and is famous among Ethiopians for being hot. Most people are happy to drive straight through.

### Camping                    CAMPGROUND $

(per tent Birr40) The shady sites along the Awash River in the area known as 'Gotu', just above Awash Falls, are muddy but attractive. Two of the four, Gumare (hippo) and Azo (Crocodile), have a rudimentary kitchen.

Two other camping options are located near Filweha Hot Springs and on Fantale's crater rim.

### Awash Falls Lodge                    LODGE $$$

(☎0221-191182; www.awashfallslodge.com; camping own/hired tent US$12/20, s/tw incl breakfast US$70/100, d US$80-100; ℗) This attractive place right above the falls has comfortable traditional-style *tukuls* and a restaurant with great views. There's 24-hour power, but not all the *tukuls* had hot water when we visited. The food (Birr57 to Birr120) is good, though *very* pricey, and there's even a small selection of South African and Ethiopian wines. The owner is serious about conservation, and guides lead a variety of wildlife and village walks (including camel trekking), and cultural shows can be arranged at the lodge. There are low-season discounts.

**Genet Hotel**                          HOTEL **$$**
(☑0222-240040; Awash; d in old bldg Birr120, d/tw with fan 345/402, with air-con Birr402/465; ℗) A solid though overpriced (discounts seem to be easy to come by) tower on the park end of Awash town near the bus station. Rooms in the new building have satellite TV, though make sure the air-con works before you pay. The older, cheaper rooms are quite scruffy. There's a decent restaurant (mains Birr35 to Birr92) here.

**Buffet d'Aouache**                     HOTEL **$**
(☑0222-240008; Awash; r without bathroom Birr71, d Birr150-172; ℗) Originally built by the French to service the Djibouti railway and now run by a Greek family, there's no more atmospheric place around. If all you require is a clean bed, mosquito net and a cold shower you'll like this potted-plant-filled place. The common facilities are very clean and there are two rooms with their own bathrooms, though they lack fans. Rooms back across the railway tracks in a newer building feature fans and plumper beds but less atmosphere. If you have lots of spare time, decent meals (Birr22 to Birr65) can be had.

**Hiwot Hotel**                          HOTEL **$**
(☑0222-260015; Metahara; d without bathroom Birr70, d Birr100-150; ℗) If you do stay in Metahara, the Hiwot is the best of a sorry bunch. Rooms in the main building have a fan and all have very necessary mosquito nets. It's on the west side of town.

### ❶ Getting There & Around

The park gate is 14km before Awash and the headquarters and waterfall lie 10km south of the gate. There are no Awash buses from Addis (four hours); you'll either need to pay the full Dire Dawa fare (Birr151 to Birr275) or use two vehicles, changing in Nazret (Birr39, 2½ hours). For Harar and Dire Dawa, head to Asbe Teferi (Birr40, 1½ hours) and catch a connection there. Waiting for a bus to Harar or Dire Dawa that started in Addis and has a free seat is likely to prove futile, but if you want to try, wait along the main road in front of the bus station.

Except for climbing the volcano, strolling along the river or short jaunts from your vehicle to get better photos, walking is not allowed in the park, nor are bikes and motorcycles. Contract minibuses (around Birr1200 per half-day) can be hired in Awash and Metahara and unless it has recently rained these can get you around the game drive circuit. A 4WD is necessary everywhere else.

## AWASH TO ASAITA

The lonely road north to Asaita crosses a hauntingly bleak landscape of parched plains, ferocious sun and barren scenery. Besides some occasionally beautiful vistas and a rifle-toting Afar tribesman or two picking their way through acacia scrub, there's little to stop the perpetually curious spiralling into a freefall of boredom.

The Djibouti road as it's now known (it used to be the Assab road) branches north just after Awash (officially Awash Sabat: 'Awash Seven') and crosses **Awash Arba** (Awash 'Forty') 10km to the north. After another 37km you'll hit **Andido** where you can detour to a pair of wanna-be upscale lodges. It's then 70km to the featureless town of **Gewane**, which doesn't warrant a full stop, just a slow-down to admire Mt Ayele looming to the east. After Gewane, the country begins to resemble Djibouti more and more: arid and desolate. The road passes through **Yangudi-Rassa National Park** but, frankly, don't expect much wildlife other than ostrich and gazelle; there's probably less here than in any national park in Ethiopia.

One hundred and twelve kilometres north of Gewane is **Adaitu**. Built mostly of sticks and sheet metal, it's one of three Issa (a tribe often in deadly conflict with the dominant Afar) towns along the road. Both peoples are traditionally pastoralists and live in domed thatch huts which are light and easy to transport. As you'll see, plastic sheeting is now part of the standard design. Just after town, the road crosses the Awash River. **Mille**, 30km after Adaitu, is spread between an upper and lower town on opposite sides of its eponymous river. Lower Mille has internet and a Commercial Bank.

Southwest of Mille is **Hadar**, the famous archaeological site where the fossilised remains of the hominid Lucy (see p218) were discovered. It's a long way to go just to see a memorial plaque, but if you want to, head west 40km to Eli Wuha and then 25km south to Hadar town where you can get an Afar guide to lead you the final 9km drive and 3km walk to the top of the hill. You'll need a 4WD for the very rough road and if it rains you probably can't reach it. You'll first need to pick up a permit in Semera. There's talk of a museum at Eli Wuha, but don't count on it.

The second half of the 48km stretch of road north of Mille takes you through a virtually lifeless expanse of rust-coloured volcanic boulders and, just after the Lake Tendaho, whose impoundment feeds sugar-cane fields, the road deposits you in **Logiya**, the most developed town along the highway. There's a reasonably well-stocked supermarket on the south end, a telecommunications centre on the north, business centres with internet at both ends and a Commercial Bank in the centre. But don't expect airs and graces: it has the same surfeit of seedy bars and brothels as all the other towns.

Atop the plateau 6km north of Logiya, it's a shock to come suddenly upon **Semera**, the Afar region capital. With its soulless mix of workers barracks, administrative buildings, sheet-metal shacks and petrol stations, it looks like a crummy little desert version of Brasília, and about the only people who live here are government workers and university students. Permission papers (Birr100 per person per place) to visit Hadar archaeological site, the lakes around Asaita (see p180) and to enter the Danakil Depression (p117) are handed out at the **Culture & Tourism Bureau** (☎0336-660488; ⊘7am-noon & 3-6pm Mon-Fri) in the regional office on the way into town. The office is in the building out the back that was supposed to be the 'Lucy Museum'.

Eight kilometres past Semera, the easy-to-miss asphalt road to Asaita (look for the Commercial Bank sign) branches off to the right.

## 🛏 Sleeping & Eating

If you need to break your journey, the choice of reliable accommodation is very limited. Most hotels are scruffy and spartan and cater primarily to Ethiopian truck drivers on their way to and from Djibouti port.

The following options are listed as encountered from south to north, and in all cases are indisputably the best in town. The resorts should be booked in advance. For lodging in Awash, see p177.

### Bilen Lodge                          LODGE $$$
(☎0111-508869; www.village-ethiopia.net; Andido; s/d tukul incl breakfast US$60/80, s/d full board US$115/184; P) This hideaway, a favourite with birdwatchers, has 16 traditional-style reed huts with concrete floors perched on a ridge overlooking the reedy expanse of the Bilen hot springs. The huts are small and simple and the showers are cold, making them overpriced (the meals are very overpriced), but it all adds up to a relaxing escape and the lodge's guides can take you to visit nearby Afar villages. It's poorly signed, 10.5km from the highway; look for the water tower.

### Animalia Lodge                       LODGE $$$
(☎0115-509364; libahsafari_dimitri@yahoo.com; Andido; cottage d/tw US$50/70; P) Inferior to Bilen Lodge in every way except price (the savings coming mostly in meal costs), this utilitarian hunting lodge lacks atmosphere but is nevertheless an OK choice. It's perched on a ridge though some cottages sit far away from it. It's 8.5km from the highway.

### Endegena Motel                       HOTEL $
(☎0221-170016; Gewane; d with/without bath Birr40/30, P) If you play loose with the definition, you can call this vast bucket-shower place clean. It's next to the Kobil petrol station. Check in at the green and yellow restaurant.

### Tareke Hotel                         HOTEL $
(☎0332-230119; Mille; d without bathroom Birr70; P) Clean and generally decent, the rooms in the green and yellow sections have fans; rooms in the blue section don't. It's in Upper Mille across from the tall brown minaret.

### Nazret Hotel                         HOTEL $
(☎0332-500222; Logiya; r without bathroom Birr70-250; P❄) The rooms at this well-managed place are in three compounds. The one next to the restaurant is the newest and has some air-con rooms, but even these share a bathroom. Nazret serves good food (Birr20 to Birr100) too, though there's no menu. The new, two-storey Nazret #2, promising self-contained, air-conditioned rooms for Birr300, was under construction on the Mille end of town.

### Erta-Ale Motel                       HOTEL $$$
(☎0912-213532; Semera; s/d US$42/54; P❄) The rooms are ordinary and with these prices (local prices are less outlandish, but still too high) it's not surprising that it's usually empty.

## ❶ Getting There & Away

This is not the road less travelled: countless Ethiopian trucks ply this route to and from Djibouti, and because it is such an important corridor the road is in excellent condition. It's possible to hitch a lift with one of these trucks; however, the drivers ask high prices.

Public transport is more frequent than it used to be and though you'll need to travel in stages it's usually possible to get from Awash to Asaita in a day. From Awash's bus station one morning bus goes to Logiya (Birr127, six to seven hours) while most minibuses to Gewane (Birr53, 3½ hours) leave from in front of rather than inside the station. Minibuses from Gewane to Logiya (Birr110, three hours) are infrequent; they drive the main road looking for passengers.

Logiya is the region's main transport hub and minibuses go at least hourly to Semera (Birr2, 10 minutes) and Asaita (Birr26, one hour). A contract *bajaj* to Semera can cost Birr50. There are usually four buses to Dessie (Birr85, seven hours) via Woldia (Birr60, 5½ hours) where you can continue to Addis Ababa and Lalibela respectively. These buses pass through Mille, but there's virtually no chance of them having an empty seat when they do. See p288 for details on transport to Djibouti.

## Asaita                         አሳይታ

POP 20,900 / ELEV 300M

Asaita is a cul-de-sac at the end of the world and the paved road taking you there is buried in sand, which appropriately sets the mood. This is the starting point from which to explore the salt lakes in the area and the surrounding Danakil Desert, but Asaita itself has a look and feel all its own, so it's worth a visit even if you aren't planning to be a modern day Wilfred Thesiger. No matter what your reason for coming be prepared: the heat is unbearable for most of the year and the swarms of flies are bigger than even those in the towns you passed earlier on your way here.

Tuesday is market day – a must if you're in town.

## ◉ Sights & Activities

The little-explored territory and the **salt lakes** scattered around Asaita are something of a holy grail for serious adventurers, but an exploration here shouldn't be undertaken lightly. This area remains one of the most inhospitable corners of the Horn, appearing much the same as when explorer Wilfred Thesiger laid eyes upon it in the 1930s. The scenery is as stark, desolate and surreally beautiful as it is foreboding.

To explore this region independently you'll need stamina and patience. Start by obtaining permission papers from the tourist office in Semera (p179), which is easy enough. Then you'll have to arrange armed Afar escorts (who almost certainly won't speak English) in either Asaita (at the Tourism Bureau across from Asaita Hospital) or the village of Afambo near the lakes. You'll be asked high prices for the privilege and there'll be other monetary demands at the start and along the way, including a neces-

---

### THE AFAR

'The Danakil invariably castrated any man or boy whom they killed or wounded, removing both the penis and the scrotum. An obvious trophy, it afforded irrefutable proof that the victim was male...'

Sir Wilfred Thesiger, *The Life of My Choice* (1987)

Fuelled by early accounts from European travellers and explorers, the Afar have gained an almost legendary reputation for ferocity. And, as they are one of the few tribes capable of surviving the harsh conditions of northeastern Ethiopia, perhaps that aura of myth is deserved.

On your journey north, look out for Afar men striding along in simple cotton *shirits* (sarongs), with their famous *jile* (curved knives), water-filled gourds hanging at their side and a rifle slung casually across a shoulder. Even today many Afars still lead a nomadic existence and when the herds are moved in search of new pasture, the huts in which the Afars live are simply packed onto the backs of camels and carted away. In the relatively fertile plains around the Awash River, some Afars have turned to cultivation, growing cotton and maize. Inter-clan rivalry is still alive and conflicts occasionally break out.

sary boat crossing on a reed raft. Buy everything you'll need in Asaita, or better still in Addis, as there are no real shops after this, and bring camping gear as there's no lodging. The Afar will know where to find water along the way.

The easiest way to do things is as a day trip from Asaita to Lakes Afambo and Gumare using your own vehicle or the government-workers bus from Asaita to Afambo (Birr20, one hour) that leaves at 8am and returns at 4pm. It's not possible to drive beyond Afambo, so you'll have to go on foot or camelback. The legendary **Lake Abbe**, the ultimate destination of the Awash River's waters, is at least a three-day trip. Called Lac Abbé in French-speaking Djibouti, it can be approached much more easily from that side (see p309).

### 🛏 Sleeping & Eating

**Basha Amare Hotel**                    HOTEL $
(☏0336-550119; bed in courtyard Birr50, d/tw without bathroom Birr80/160) The best option by far is this friendly hotel on the cliff above the Awash River, where you might see crocodiles in the day and hear hippos at night. It has small rooms and better than average shared facilities. If the slow-mo fans can't cool you off, use the natural air-con and sleep in the courtyard. Omelettes, rice, *tibs* (sliced lamb) and fresh yoghurt are available in the restaurant (mains Birr25 to Birr35) out front.

**Lem Hotel**                    HOTEL $
(☏0336-550050; r without bathroom Birr30, r without toilet Birr40) If Basha is full, this place makes an acceptable plan B. The rooms with showers have a small odour, but the common facilities are some of the cleanest we've seen.

### ℹ Information

**Commercial Bank** (⏱7-11.30am & 3-5pm Mon-Fri, 7-11.30am Sat) Next to Basha Hotel, changes cash (US dollars, euro and pounds).
**Community IC Center** (⏱8am-noon, 4-6pm & 7.30-9pm; per hour Birr20) About 500m off the main square. Connections are nearly impossible at night.

### ℹ Getting There & Away

Leaving from the main square, near the lighthouse-like minaret, buses and minibuses go about hourly to Logiya (Birr26, one hour). There's one bus to Dessie (Birr98, 10 hours). For Djibouti, you'll have to go back to Logiya; trucks won't pick up hitchhikers along the highway.

# DIRE DAWA, HARAR & AROUND

These two cities are another world from the rest of the country and few other Ethiopian towns reward random wandering as richly as they do; especially historic Harar. Despite the excellent offerings, this region remains far from the tourist trail.

This is the reputed origin of the addictive stimulant *chat* (p260) and it's not only a major export commodity replacing coffee on many farms (look for the slender trees with shiny, dark-green leaves planted in neat rows), a huge percentage of the population spends most afternoons lying on the ground is a drunken-like stupor.

During the celebrations in Kulubi (p184), hotels in Harar and Dire Dawa are booked out months in advance and prices can triple.

## Dire Dawa     ድሬ ዳዋ
POP 256,800 / ELEV 1200M
The fourth-most populous city in Ethiopia, Dire Dawa usually elicits strong reactions. We think its colourful storefront, tree-lined streets, neat squares, and foreign influence (look for Arab, French, Italian and Greek styles in some of the architecture and design) are a refreshing change from the filthy disorder and lack of character in most Ethiopian towns. Others just consider it a more vibrant version of tedium.

Dire Dawa is made up of two distinct settlements, divided by the trash-strewn Dechatu Wadi (seasonal river). Lying to the north and west is the European-influenced 'new town' known as Kezira. To the east is the more colourful 'old town', known as Megala, which has a distinctly Muslim (and, coincidently, a slightly Mexican) feel.

### History
The great Addis Ababa–Djibouti railway was supposed to pass through the old commercial town of Harar, but with ever-burgeoning costs, the project was falling into difficulties. Then a momentous decision was taken: to bypass the Chercher Mountains and keep to the lowlands and build a new city to service it. In 1902 Dire Dawa was born. Today, along with Addis Ababa, it's one of Ethiopia's two autonomous cities.

## ◎ Sights

Dire Dawa's main highlights are its thriving markets.

### Kafira Market                    MARKET

With its Babel-like ambience, the enormous Kafira Market, sprawling way beyond its Moorish-style arches, is the most striking. Delving into the organised chaos of its narrow lanes is an assault on the senses. This market attracts people from miles around, including Afar and Somali herders, Oromo farmers and Amhara merchants. Charcoal and firewood is brought in from the hinterlands by camel; look for them in the wadi.

### Dire Dawa Market                    MARKET

Also known as 'Taiwan', this is a modern, orderly covered market mostly full of clothing and fabric, though some of the cheap electronic goods that used to dominate this space remain.

### Ashawa Market                    MARKET

The similarly stocked Ashawa Market is less orderly and more interesting than Dire Dawa Market, especially the sheet-metal shacks in the back.

### Chattara Market                    MARKET

*Chat* (see the boxed text, p260) is sold all over town, but the trade at the Chattara Market is so frenetic it deserves a look.

### Camel Market                    MARKET

This morning market is in the wadi behind Ashawa.

### Ethiopia-Djibouti Railway Line
### Rehabilitation Project Office          RAILYARD

(⏰7am-noon & 3-5.30pm Mon-Fri, 7am-noon Sat) Rail fans can clamber through what remains of the once great Imperial Railway Company of Ethiopia. Ask in room three of the project office and you'll be rewarded with an ID badge and a guided tour (tip expected) of rusty carcasses of disused engines, the still-

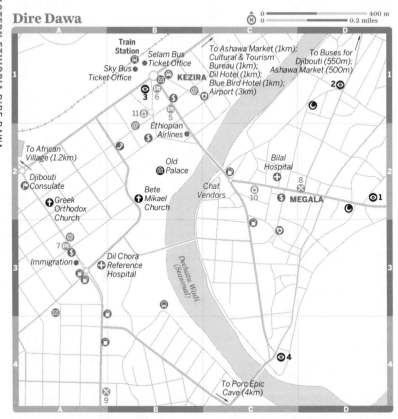

# Dire Dawa

operational roundhouse and Haile Selassie's private carriage.

##  Tours

### Yige Tour
DRIVING TOUR
(☑0915-732313; yigeremut@yahoo.com) Yigeremu Tadess is the man behind the business, and he charges Birr400 a day for trips around Dire Dawa and more beyond the region. Just be sure you know what kind of vehicle you're getting; 4WDs are hard to come by out here.

## Sleeping

### Samrat Hotel
HOTEL $$
(☑0251-130600; samrat@ethionet.et; d Birr643-750, tw Birr822; P❄@☎☲) The dour exterior of Dire Dawa's best lodging hides a classy lobby. The rooms themselves are in-between, but lean more towards the latter than the former and are well appointed (though not all have air-con), with the stiff mattresses being the biggest knock. There's a good nightclub and restaurant.

### African Village
HOTEL $
(☑0251-126006; www.african-village.net; s incl breakfast Birr173-253, d incl breakfast Birr253-288; P☎) An attractive mesh of traditional and modern, the comfortable rooms with satellite TV surround a communal courtyard and excellent restaurant. The only real knocks are the squat toilets in the cheapest rooms and the lack of air-conditioning

in the pricier rooms, though the traditional construction does help cool the rooms. The Swiss owner prohibits alcohol. It's west of the centre, signposted down a side street.

### Blue Bird Hotel
HOTEL $$
(☑0251-130219; s incl breakfast Birr300-350, d incl breakfast Birr400-450; P❄☎) Formerly Salem Hotel, this blue-glass spot northeast of the centre along the road to the airport was once the smartest in town and now offers the best value. All rooms are good, but the suites, with ornately carved beds and wardrobes, are a steal at this price. Its nightclub is popular.

### Continental Hotel
HOTEL $
(☑0251-111546; d without bathroom Birr45, tw Birr90) A bit noisy because of the popular restaurant-bar, but rooms at this old-timer are clean enough and offer fair value.

### Mekonnen Hotel
HOTEL $
(☑0251-113348; d without bathroom Birr70) Housed in an old Italian colonial building facing the train station, the rooms and hallways are quite clean, but no amount of scrubbing can bring the common bathrooms up to the same level.

## Eating & Drinking

### Samrat Hotel
INDIAN, EUROPEAN $
(mains Birr28-120; ☎) Besides the usual European dishes and some token Ethiopian ones, this Indian-owned hotel brings the flavours of the subcontinent to weary taste buds. It's also home to Dire Dawa's top nightclub.

### African Village
EUROPEAN, ETHIOPIAN $
(mains Birr18-85; ☎) Whether you're still a newbie to Ethiopian food or you'd like to explore beyond the ordinary, the clear explanations on the menu here will guide you along. There are also burgers, pastas and pizzas.

### Paradiso Restaurant
ITALIAN, ETHIOPIAN $
(mains Birr35-75; ☉lunch & dinner) A slice of Rome it ain't, but the menu at this 'old time' Italian mansion has arguably Dire Dawa's best Italian (though don't get too excited), as well as more traditional *kitfo* (raw meat) and *tibs*.

### Al-Hashimi Sweets
SWEETS $
Battle through the throngs to get some baklava so sweet that it frightens dentists.

### Mekonnen Hotel
ETHIOPIAN
Cheap beers and great people-watching. From around 6pm the sidewalk tables are

**EASTERN ETHIOPIA DIRE DAWA**

packed with men talking politics and sipping coffee and beer.

##  Shopping

You can buy fresh, export-quality Ethiopian coffee at **Green Gold** (⊘8am-noon & 3-5.30pm) near the train station and **Bashanfer** (⊘8am-noon & 3-6pm Mon-Fri, 8am-noon Sat) across the bridge.

##  Information

**Bilal Hospital** (☏0251-113636) Dire Dawa's best medical facility. Has a pharmacy.

**Dashen Bank** Has ATMs in Kezira near the train station and in the heart of Megala.

**Dire Dawa Telecentre** (⊘6am-5.30pm) You can make international calls here.

**Djibouti Consulate** (⊘8am-noon & 3.30-5.30pm Mon-Thu, 8am-noon Fri) One-month visas cost Birr1200 and require two photos.

**Immigration** (⊘8am-noon & 2-5.30pm Mon-Fri) You can renew your visa here, saving the long trip back to Addis Ababa. Dollars only.

**Wegagen Bank** Has an ATM near Samrat Hotel.

##  Getting There & Away

### Air

There are two daily **Ethiopian Airlines** (☏0251-113069; www.flyethiopian.com; ⊘7.30-noon & 3-5.45pm) flights between Addis Ababa and Dire Dawa (US$57, one hour), one continuing to Jijiga (US$33, 25 minutes) and the other to Djibouti (US$448, 50 minutes).

### Bus

A few regular buses depart daily to Addis Ababa (Birr151, 10 hours) between 4.30am and 5.30am. For better comfort, use the daily Sky Bus (Birr275) and Selam (Birr235 to Birr265) or the thrice-weekly Post Bus (Birr198), all with 5am departures and ticket offices in front of the train station. Stopping anywhere along the way requires paying the full Addis fare.

Minibuses run every 10 minutes or so to Harar (Birr21, one hour).

See p288 for details on the daily buses to Djibouti.

### Train

Trains should resume to Djibouti City early in the life of this book.

##  Getting Around

A contract taxi to or from the airport should set you back around Birr80. A typical trip in a shared *bajaj* costs Birr2.

# Around Dire Dawa

## HARLA ሀርላ

The former capital of Harla Kingdom was a 13th-century walled city that excavations have shown did much trade with the Middle East. A few minor remnants of its glory days are still around but it's the future that makes Harla, perhaps, of interest to travellers. Addis Ababa's **Zoma Contemporary Art Center** (☏0911-249374; www.zcac.net) has built a branch of its artist-in-residence centre here and visitors are welcome to stop by to see what's going on. For the time being, that's likely to be nothing, but eventually it should become more active. It's 15km out of Dire Dawa. Catch a minibus (Birr10, 20 minutes) from in front of the NOC petrol station instead of the bus station.

## KULUBI ቁልቢ

Twice a year, tens of thousands of pilgrims converge on the little town of Kulubi and its hilltop cathedral, **Kulubi Gabriel**, built by Ras Mekonen to thank St Gabriel for the victory over the Italians at Adwa (see p105). Many people come to express thanks for fulfilment of a wish, and babies feature prominently: up to 1000 infants may be christened during celebrations. If you're in the area around 26 July and 28 December, it's an amazing experience.

# Harar ሐረር

POP 108,200 / ELEV 1850M

World Heritage–listed Harar is a place apart. With its 368 alleyways squeezed into just 1 sq km, it's more reminiscent of Fez in Morocco than any other city in the Horn. Its countless mosques and shrines, animated markets, crumbling walls and charming people will make you feel as if you've floated right out of the 21st century. It's the east's most memorable sight and shouldn't be missed. And, as if that wasn't enough, there are many chances to get up-close and personal with wild hyenas. It's a rare traveller who doesn't enjoy themselves here.

### History

Harar is steeped in history, though its origin is unknown. Evidence suggests it was founded by Arabian immigrants, including Sheikh Abadir (see Shrines & Tombs, p188) in the 10th century, though local legend declares the Sheikh arrived in the 13th century. Other sources date the first settlement all the way

## CAVE ART AROUND DIRE DAWA

Dire Dawa is known for its many prehistoric cave paintings. Dating back an estimated 5000 years, the crude red, white and black figures depict humans and animals. They're important to archaeologists, though lay visitors may end up disappointed.

You'll need to find the man with the key, who'll take you to the caves. The price for this service is not fixed, but Birr100 to Birr150 should do it. The guards at the gate will also expect a tip and others may have their hands out along the way. Going with a guide from town smoothes things considerably. If you're going without a guide from Dire Dawa, you first need to go to the Tourism Development and Promotion Core Process office at the **Cultural & Tourism Bureau** (Dire Dawa Administration Council Bldg, 1st fl, ⊗7.30am-noon, 2-5.30pm Mon-Fri) next to Blue Bird (previously Salem) Hotel and get a permission paper for Birr50 per cave.

### Lega-Oda ለጋ-ኦዳ

By far the best cave art site around Dire Dawa, this 70m-long rock shelter holds some 600 paintings. The figures clearly show humans, antelope, anteaters, camels, and groups of lines and dots. The cave is 38km (one hour's drive) southwest of Dire Dawa, an easy 20-minute walk from the road. You'll find the man with the key in **Wuchale** village, about 1km from the trailhead. One minibus from Dire Dawa passes Wuchale (Birr20, three hours) each morning, but you'd be reliant on hitching back.

### Goda-Ajawa ጎዳ-አጃዋ

Though the paintings in this lofty cave are good, including some palm prints, they're fewer and less varied than at Lega-Oda, and graffiti around the paintings mars the site. It's 28km (about one hour) southeast of Dire Dawa on a much rougher road than to Lega-Oda. The man with the key is usually in **Awale**, but he could be off in one of several other villages that you'll pass as you drive there. The long, uphill-almost-the-whole-way walk takes about an hour (less if you come with a 4WD and can park closer). There are a few minibuses to Awale (Birr15, two hours) which leaves you with about a two-hour walk to the cave.

### Porc-Epic ፖርርፒክ እፒክ

The best-known and easiest-to-reach cave has a few rock formations, making it the most geologically interesting of the three, but the paintings are largely obscured by soot. It's 4km past the bus station to a wadi, the last 2km on a very rough road, and then a 30-minute climb takes you 140m up to the cave. The man with the key will likely be out shepherding his goats and will find you after you arrive.

back to the 7th century. Regardless, it grew into a crossroads for commerce between Africa, India and the Middle East and a place where great dynasties of rich and powerful merchants grew and the arts flourished. European merchants eventually joined the mix and though it did decline in importance over the years, it was still significant enough that the Egyptians came and conquered it in 1875 and held on for 10 years.

In the 17th and 18th centuries, Harar became known as an important centre of Islamic scholarship and spearheaded Islam's penetration into the Horn. There's an oft-repeated myth that Harar is the fourth holiest city in Islam (after Mecca, Medina and Jerusalem), but this is purely a local invention.

In 1854 British explorer Richard Burton, disguised as an Arab merchant, was the first non-Muslim to penetrate the city. French poet Arthur Rimbaud (see p190) later spent many years here. In 1887 the city surrendered to Emperor Menelik, who sought to expand and unify his empire, but the Hararis still retain their own ethnic identity, language and culture to this day.

## ⦿ Sights

### Old Town

Harar's old walled town (known as Jugal) is a fascinating place that begs exploration.

# Harar

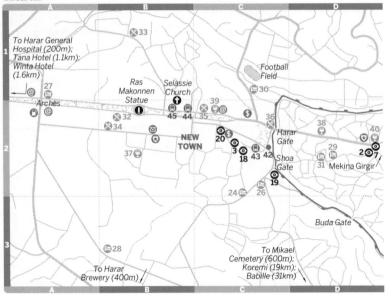

EASTERN ETHIOPIA HARAR

The thick, 5m-high walls running 3.5km around town were erected in the 16th century in defensive response to the migrations northwards of the Oromo, and little development occurred outside them until the early 20th century. Within the walls the city is a maze of narrow, twisting alleys replete with historic buildings, including 82 mostly tiny mosques (two dating back to the 10th century), over 100 shrines and tombs, and about 2000 traditional Harari houses.

But what breathes life into these landmarks is the community that still lives within the city walls. Prepare to encounter the magnificent Adare (Harari) women, known for their colourful dress, and the sweat-soaked blacksmiths near Buda Gate who still labour over open fires.

### City Gates                                    GATES
There are six gates: five 16th-century originals and the car-friendly **Harar Gate**, also known as Duke's Gate after Ras Makonnen, the first Duke of Harar, who added it in 1889. The photograph on this gate is Emir Abdullahi, the last of Harar's 72 Emirs and the city's last Muslim leader. The nearby **Shoa Gate** (Asmaddin Bari) and the **Buda Gate** (Bedri Bari) are also attractive, though they no longer have their wooden doors. **Erer Gate** (Argob Bari), the one Richard Burton entered

through, and the little-used **Sanga Gate** (Suqutat Bari) lie to the east. To the north is busy **Fallana Gate** (Assum Bari).

### Traditional Adare Houses              HOUSE
Visiting a traditional Adare house is a must. The best way is to stay at one of the guesthouses (see p190). Even if you aren't sleeping in one, guides usually take people to see them as part of their standard tour; a Birr20 tip will be expected. Also, some families have opened souvenir shops in their courtyards, but you shouldn't have to tip to visit one of these.

If you don't have the chance to visit a lived-in house, don't worry: the **Harari Cultural Centre** (admission Birr16; ⊗8am-noon & 2-5pm Mon-Thu & Sat, 8-11.30am & 2-5pm Fri, 8am-noon Sun), an old house converted into a museum, is almost as good as the real thing.

### Feres Magala                              SQUARE
ፈረስ መጋላ The main square is a bustling place with several minor points of interest. Most conspicuous is the monument to those who died fighting against Menelik's conquest of Harar. It shows the five original gates. To the north, the Egyptian-built building that's now Wesen Seged Hotel was once a store house (and perhaps also an office) used by Arthur Rimbaud, as was the white

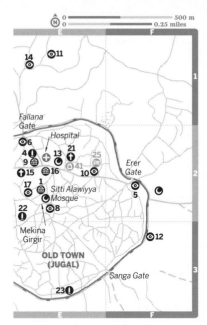

building with the balcony across the road. Across the square is a **chat market**, one of many in the city. To the east is the rather unimpressive **Medhane Alem Cathedral**, built by Ras Makonnen on the site of an Egyptian mosque.

**Arthur Rimbaud Center** MUSEUM
የራምቦ ቤት (admission Birr20; ☻8am-noon & 2-5pm Mon-Sat, 8am-noon Sun) Near the middle of the walled city, and often mistakenly called Rimbaud's House, is this museum dedicated to the poet Arthur Rimbaud with a series of illustrated wall panels (mainly in French) about his life. It's in an attractive Indian merchant house built on the site of an earlier house where it's said Rimbaud lived.

There's an excellent photographic exhibition of turn-of-the-20th-century Harar – with several of the photos taken by Rimbaud – that show some similarities to the city of today but also many significant differences. In front is a women's association where you can sometimes see basket weaving.

**Ras Tafari's House** HOUSE
የራስ ተፈሪ ቤት Within pouncing distance of Rimbaud's House is the conspicuous Ras Tafari's House. The house was built by an Indian trader and many of its features, such as the Ganesh carving above the door, are

Eastern in origin. Haile Selassie spent his honeymoon here: hence the house bears his pre-coronation name. It's now the home of the **Sherif Harar City Museum** (Birr30; ☻8.30am-noon & 2-5pm). The museum houses a private collection of weaponry, coins, jewellery, household tools and cultural dress. The owner will probably offer to show you his book-restoration workshop upstairs.

**Mekina Girgir** STREET
መኪና ጊርጊር Leading southeast from Feres Magala, this narrow, atmospheric street is jam-packed with tailors' workshops, which is how it came to be called 'Sewing Machine Sound Street'.

**Gidir Magala** MARKET
ጊደር መጋላ At the end of Mekina Girgir you'll stumble upon the arcades of the Gidir Magala, the main market (previously known as the Muslim market) and the city's biggest butchery. Watch how the locals hide their meat purchases from the black kites that fearlessly swoop down trying to steal it.

**Ras Makonnen's Palace** PALACE
የራስ መኮንን ቤተ መንግስት Don't expect a fairy-tale castle. This late-19th-century 'palace' is a sharp-edged, charmless building currently under renovation. During construction, and surely after it as well, you can climb to the top floor and soak up the views. What is called **Queen Taitu's Palace** next door is also undergoing restoration, and when finished a handicraft centre where the craft makers will work on-site is supposed to open.

**Harar National Museum** MUSEUM
የሐረር ብሔራዊ ሙዚየም (admission Birr20; ☻8am-noon & 2-5pm Mon-Fri, 8am-noon Sat & Sun) This modest museum used to be housed in Ras Makonnen's Palace, and may again after

---

ⓘ **OLD TOWN ALLEYS**

Fear not: you can't get lost in the Old Town for too long. Harar's walled Old Town is so compact that no matter how deep you get into the maze of alleyways you'll eventually come to a wall or a larger street that will lead you either to the bustling central square, Feres Magala ('Horse Market'), or Andegna Menged ('Main St') between Feres Magala and Harar Gate.

# Harar

restoration work is finished. Much of the collection is stuff you've already seen inside a traditional Harari home, but the jewellery, clothing and weapons make it worth a stop.

**St Mary Catholic Church** CHURCH
ቅድስት ማርያም ካቶሊክ ቤተክርስቲያን
One of just two churches in Old Harar, St Mary Catholic Church is a haven of peace and a good spot if you need to unwind. It's a French Catholic mission dating from 1889. The carved wooden door is particularly attractive.

**Jamia Mosque** MOSQUE
ጃሚያ መስጊድ Harar's great mosque is the only one inside the wall big enough to host both men and women. The mosque was built in the 16th century, though according to local tradition, a mosque has stood on the site since the 12th century. While not architecturally distinct, its white-tile mina-rets can be seen from all over the city. It's off-limits to non-Muslims.

**SHRINES & TOMBS**
Some of the shrines devoted to local religious leaders are peaceful, interesting and well-kept places. But they're unsigned and so hard to find. Most are under large trees. The caretaker will expect a Birr10 tip for unlocking the door.

**Emir Nur's Tomb** resembles a spiky green beehive. It's devoted to the ruler who built the city's walls, and his wife is buried inside too. You enter the tomb normally, but when leaving, you should back out.

Another tomb that can easily be visited is the **Tomb of Said Ali Hamdogn**, an important 12th-century religious leader. The tomb looks a little like a miniature mosque without the minaret.

The most important is the **Tomb of Sheikh Abadir**, Harar's legendary founder and second emir. His tomb still attracts worshippers seeking solutions to daily struggles, and if their prayers are answered devotees return to make gifts of rugs, incense or expensive sandalwood. Non-Muslims are usually refused entry, but might be allowed in during the Thursday night gatherings (around midnight) when devotees come to play drums, read the Quran and pay respect.

### New Town

Everything outside the walls counts as New Town; most of it sits alongside the boulevard heading west from Harar Gate.

**Hyena Feeding Sites**          WILDLIFE ENCOUNTER

As night falls (beginning around 7pm), two sets of 'hyena men' set themselves up just outside the city walls: one at the shrine of Sheikh Aw Anser along the eastern wall and the other north of Fallana Gate by the Christian slaughterhouse.

The first sight of Africa's second-largest predator is usually of vague shadows and luminous green eyes as they skulk in and out of the shadows. As the pack grows more confident, they dart forward with their peculiar gait until all reservations are lost and they approach the hyena men to be fed, literally climbing on top of them to make a show of it. Watching costs Birr50 and if you're game you can feed them yourself, holding the meat stick in your hands or mouth. Most people go with a guide, but it's not required. Taxis (Birr100 round trip) cost more than *bajaj* (Birr50) but it's worth it because they have brighter headlights.

**Mikael Cemetery**          CEMETERY

ሚካኤል መካነ-መቃብር You don't come to this place below Mikael Church for the graves, but the excellent views of the old town from the road below them. Photography is best in the afternoon. A contract *bajaj* should cost Birr10. If the driver doesn't know it, tell him Deker Condominium.

**Harar Brewery**          BREWERY

ሐረር ቢራ ፋብሪካ Built by the Czechs in 1984 and purchased by Heineken in 2011, this is a very modern brewery. Half-hour tours take you through pretty much the whole facility and at the end you can even drink unpasteurised beer direct from the bottling line. They might give you a free shirt and hat too. Tours are always available on Fridays, but local Harar guides can usually arrange them on other weekdays. Morning (8am to 11am) is best because in the afternoon, it can take some time to find the person in charge.

### Markets

No visit to Harar would be complete without wading through its shambolic markets. They're packed with Oromo people from the surrounding countryside coming to town to sell their goods (mostly firewood) and then spend their earnings on food and household goods. All the fresh markets are busiest after 3pm and are pretty quiet on Sundays.

Elbow your way through the **Shoa Gate Market** (also known as the Christian Market) to find *etan* (incense) from the Jijiga area; it's used in the famous coffee ceremonies (see p263). This odoriferous market also has spices and bark, roots and twigs used in the preparation of traditional medicine plus heaps of vegetables.

Behind the Shoa Gate Market's burnt-out half is the **Recycling Market** where men repair metal materials and beat scrap into useful utensils. This alleyway transforms into a second-hand and custom-made clothing market, called **Cigaratera** ('Cigarette Row') after it's former incarnation, which is at the backside of the **Smugglers' Market**, chockfull of counterfeit clothing and electronics (some real stuff too) from China; most of it is smuggled in from Somaliland either by

EASTERN ETHIOPIA HARAR

> ### HYENA FEEDING
>
> The practice of feeding scraps of meat to hyenas began in the 1950s. The original hyena man (his family is the one living and working by the shrine today) started doing it to acquire good luck, but when some tourists started showing up he realised he could make money too. The inspiration is an older tradition in which hyenas were given porridge to discourage them from attacking livestock during a drought. Following that an annual feeding began during a festival called Ashura, in which hyenas are fed porridge as a foretelling of the city's fortune for the upcoming year.
>
> Many hyenas roam Harar's streets at night and if you go for an after-hours stroll, especially in Old Harar, you might just meet them. It's a frightening experience, but we've been assured multiple times that they pose no risk.

night caravans of camel and donkey across the remote desert frontiers or cleverly concealed in trucks.

Across the Old Town, straddling the city wall, are the Erer Gate Market (Oromo Market) and the Fallana Gate Market, both of which are smaller, meatless versions of Gidir Magala (p187). North of Fallana Gate is the weekday Livestock Market with cows, goats and sheep, but no camels: these are sold at Babille (p193).

## Tours

Good city maps are sold at most of Harar's museums, but for your first foray it's quite a good idea to hire a guide. Guides know the location of less-visited corners and the best Harari houses and arts and crafts shops. They can also arrange vehicles for out-of-town excursions, but note that hire costs are high here and 4WDs are rare.

Although there are official guides (ask to see their ID), there's no official price. Birr300 a day is standard for a small group. Most people arrange a guide through their hotel and most hotels only work with good guides. Three guides that come particularly recommended are Biniyam Woldesemayat (☎0913-448811; biniym.weld@yahoo.comYes), Hailu Gashaw (☎0913-072931; hailu_harar@yahoo.com) and Abdul Ahemed (☎0915-740864), one of the longest-serving guides in Harar.

## Sleeping

Even if you normally don't do shared bathrooms, consider staying in one of the Adare homes now functioning as a guesthouse. It's a wonderful experience. Reservations are advised, though English is limited. Many people have their guide reserve for them.

### Old Harar

**Rewda Cultural Guesthouse**  TOP CHOICE  GUESTHOUSE $
(☎0256-662211; d/tw without bathroom incl breakfast Birr350/700) This genuine Adare house percolates tradition and history into a comfy brew of warm welcome amid exotic decorations. Set in the heart of the old town down a nondescript side street (it's best approached from Shoa Gate; people will point you the right way), these four spotless bedrooms share two bathrooms. Note that the

---

## ARTHUR RIMBAUD: A POET ADRIFT

In 1875 one of France's finest poets turned his back on his poetry, his country, his wild living and his lover to reverse his fortunes and see the world. He was just 21 years old, broke and bitter.

By 1880 Arthur Rimbaud had travelled to Germany, Italy, Cyprus, and Java (with the Dutch Colonial Army from which he later deserted) and, in the service of a coffee trader in Aden (Yemen), became the first white man to travel into the Ogaden region of southeastern Ethiopia and finally lived like a local in a small house in Harar. His interest in culture, languages and people made him popular and his plain speaking and integrity won him the trust of the chiefs and Ras Makonnen, the governor of Harar. His commercial dealings were equally as colourful and included coffee trading and running guns to King Menelik of Shoa.

In 1891 Rimbaud developed a tumour on his right knee. Leaving Harar in early April, he endured the week's journey to the coast on a stretcher. Treatment at Aden was not a success and Rimbaud continued onto Marseilles, where his right leg was amputated. By this time the cancer had spread and he died later that year at the age of 37.

During his self-imposed exile to Ethiopia, Rimbaud's poetry had become increasingly known in France for its daring imagery and beautiful and evocative language. Sadly this belated recognition brought him little satisfaction and he remained indifferent to his fame until his dying day.

'I drifted on a river, I could not control

No longer guided by a bargemen's ropes

...

When my bargemen could no longer haul me

I forgot about everything and drifted on.'

*Extracts from Rimbaud's* The Drunken Boat *(1871)*

## ADARE HOUSES

A distinct architectural feature in Harar, the *gegar* (traditional Adare house) is a rectangular, two-storey structure with a flat roof. The house is carefully constructed to remain cool whatever the outside temperature: clay reinforced with wooden beams that is then whitewashed. Sometimes bright colours adorn the facades, but the old style of uncovered stone remains common. A small courtyard, usually facing east, is often shared by several families.

The upstairs room used to serve as a food storeroom; today it acts as a bedroom. The main living room consists of five raised platforms of different levels, which are covered in rugs and cushions. Guests and members of the household sit on the platform befitting their status. These platforms are usually painted bright red to symbolise the blood that every Harari was prepared to shed during the resistance against Menelik.

Hung on the walls are colourful baskets and black wooden bowls. Eleven niches are built into the wall for cups, pots, plates, Qurans, and these days sometimes expensive electronics. One shelf always holds four *aflala* (tall clay containers) that are used to store money, gold, medicine and seeds. Every house also a rack for spears.

A rolled carpet on the rack above the front door indicates an eligible daughter resides within. After marriage, newlyweds retire to a tiny room that lies to the left of the living quarters. They remain there for one whole week, during which time they are passed food and water through a hatch.

'honeymoon suite' (See p191 for an explanation) has no door separating it from the common lounge.

(See p191 for an explanation)

#### TOP CHOICE Zubeyda Cultural Guesthouse
GUESTHOUSE **$**

(☑0256-664692; d/tw without bathroom incl breakfast Birr350/700) Zubeyda is Rewda's sister and this operation is less friendly but virtually the same. The biggest difference is that the courtyard here is shared by another family, which makes the experience more authentic but slightly less cosy.

#### Amir Cultural Guesthouse
GUESTHOUSE **$$**

(☑0912-601956; azokutinta@yahoo.com; d/tw without bathroom incl breakfast Birr450/900) Definitely second-tier compared to the other two despite the higher price. It's also an old Adare home but it's far less attractive, is a guesthouse only (the owner lives nearby) and you can't rely on reservations being honoured.

### New Town

#### Tana Hotel
HOTEL **$**

(☑0256-668482; d/tw Birr105/135; P) This large outfit up the hill on the Dire Dawa road is a solid budget choice. The odd cockroach or two aside, the rooms are cleaner, the staff friendlier and the water more reliable than others in this price range. The rooms come with a tiny TV and hot water, plus there's a bar and restaurant specialising in Ethiopian dishes out front.

#### Winta Hotel
HOTEL **$$**

(☑0256-64267; d Birr500-700; P ☎) Currently Harar's best hotel by a big margin, rooms at Winta are comfortable, with satellite TV and minifridge. Since it has only eight rooms, reservations are wise. It's near the top of the hill in New Town, 100m north of Aretenya Mosque. The food (mains Birr20 to Birr60) isn't half bad.

#### Belayneh Hotel
HOTEL **$**

(☑0256-662030; s/d Birr175/225) The big drawcards here are the balcony views over the Shoa Gate Market and the hotel's proximity to the bus station and Old Town. The rooms themselves are noisy and bland but fine with several satellite TV channels, and the water shortages appear to be a thing of the past. Give the bathrooms a smell test before choosing a room; some won't pass. If you're not sleeping here, the same views are available from the undistinguished top-floor restaurant (mains Birr30 to Birr50).

#### Abay Minch Hotel
HOTEL **$**

(☑0256-661098; d with/without bathroom Birr69/57) Scruffy, but brighter and airier than others in this price range, it's worth considering but check if the water is working.

#### Heritage Plaza Hotel
HOTEL **$$**

(☑0256-6665137; www.plazahotelharar.com; s/d/tw Birr607/810/901; P @) Despite unattractive rooms that don't come anywhere near the quality they should for the price and lots of

EASTERN ETHIOPIA HARAR

road noise, the 'Plaza' is popular with tour companies. Consider it a backup if you need a certain level of comfort and Winta is full.

### Tewodros Hotel
HOTEL $

(☏0256-660217; d with/without bathroom Birr160/75; P) Not many places pride themselves on their view of the local garbage pile, but guests in some of the east-facing rooms might see hyenas in the early morning light, and they'll surely hear them at night. For a sure sighting, walk over to the football field after about 9pm. The hyenas, however, are the only thing recommendable. Both the rooms and the service are simply bad (though house guide Girma gets good reviews), making the prices a complete rip-off, plus odds are against having running water.

### Harargey International Hotel
HOTEL

Work was underway on this new hotel when we passed through Harar. The sign promising a 'Five Star Hotel Coming Soon' is bollocks, but if it's even half as good as the pictures it will be the new best in Harar.

## ✖ Eating

### Hirut Restaurant
EUROPEAN, ETHIOPIAN $

(mains Birr35-70) Decorated with traditional woven baskets and specialising in authentic local cuisine, this is the most atmospheric place in Harar to sink your teeth into a super-filling *kwanta firfir* (dried strips of beef rubbed in chilli, butter, salt and *berbere*) or swill a glass of Gouder wine. The European food is good too. The choice between the cosy lounge and the well-shaded garden is a difficult one. It doesn't serve breakfast.

### Fresh Touch
EUROPEAN, ETHIOPIAN $

(mains Birr35-121) We won't rave about this below-street-level place the way some visitors to Harar do, but the *faranji* food (including pizzas and stir-fries) is definitely better than average for Ethiopia and that's made this a long-term favourite for locals and visitors alike. The prices are reasonable and the national dishes are good too.

### Mizrak Hotel
ETHIOPIAN $

(mains Birr25-60) It's the hyenas, not the food, that makes this a recommended night-time dining option. They usually arrive around 8.30pm to scavenge the nearby dumpsters, but if you have some flesh to offer them (hang it on a stick rather than use your hand, of course), they'll come dine at your sidewalk table.

### Sherif Hotel
ETHIOPIAN $

(mains Birr19-77) The speciality of this Muslim restaurant is *hanid* (goat; you pick which part – the feet, ribs and head are the most popular) served on rice pilaf.

### Weyzro ('Miss') Zewde
SAMOSAS $

(samosa Birr1.5; ⊙5-10pm Mon-Fri) This woman makes what are probably the best samosas (*sambusa* in Amharic) in Harar. Find her and her deep-fryer sitting street-side across from Harar Gate.

## 🍺 Drinking

If you're pining for a beer try a locally brewed Harar brand, a light-bodied lager, or Hakim stout. Non-alcoholic Sofi is designed for Harar's Muslims. And of course, you'll want to try Harari coffee: it's hailed as one of the best in the world.

### Tesh Fresh Juice
JUICE BAR

(juice Birr14-16) Delicious fresh juice and cakes. If you're lucky they'll have banana, orange, pineapple, custard apple or something else not found in most shops; but usually it's just papaya and avocado.

### Wesen Seged
BAR

On Feres Magala, this is a good place to mull over a cheap coffee, Coke or beer from your front-porch bar stool and watch life rush by.

### Samson Hotel
CLUB

This Old Town place gets going early. Music kicks off around 8pm and dancing soon follows. It's done by midnight, when most revellers head to National Hotel.

### National Hotel
CLUB

Hallelujah! Live music is on from Wednesday to Sunday, from around 9.30pm to 2am. The music is a mixture of Ethiopian pop and reggae, with some traditional tunes thrown in. There's no cover, but a bottle of beer costs Birr15. If you don't like the band, head across the street to see what the DJ is spinning at the Tourist Hotel.

## 🔒 Shopping

In some old town houses, enterprising Adares have set up souvenir shops displaying beautifully made silver and (usually fake) amber jewellery and baskets. None have signs and only a few are outside the compounds (ie, visible when you walk by), but the guides know them all. If you're lucky, some of the women will be weaving when you drop by.

**Nure Roasted Harar Coffee**    COFFEE
(⊘8am-6pm Mon-Sat) One step inside and the swoon-inducing scents will have you hooked. It sells 1kg and 500g packets of excellent whole and ground beans, and you can watch the sorting, roasting and grinding.

## ❶ Information

Water shortages remain a problem in Harar and can last for days. Good hotels have water tanks, but even these may not outlast the outages. Power cuts still happen, but they're no longer very common.

**Dashen Bank** Has the only ATM near the city centre.

**Harar General Hospital** (☎0256-664766; ⊘24hr) Harar's top medical facility. Has a pharmacy.

**Kosmo Fast Internet** (per hr Birr35; ⊘7.30am-noon & 2-7pm) Often delivers what the name promises and English-speaking owner Mark is friendly and helpful.

**SAM Fast Internet** (per hr Birr30; ⊘8am-7pm Mon-Sat, 8am-noon Sun)

**Tourist office** (⊘8am-12.30pm & 2-5.30pm Mon-Thu, 8-11.30am & 2-5pm Fri) In Ras Ma-konnen's Palace, it's somewhat helpful.

## ❶ Getting There & Around

The bus station is near Harar Gate. Minibuses run frequently to Dire Dawa (Birr21, one hour) and Jijiga (Birr40, 1½ hours).

For Addis Ababa (nine to 10 hours), three normal buses (Birr180) leave around 6am from the bus station while Sky Bus (Birr275) and Selam (Birr270) depart at 5.30am from their ticket offices on opposite sides of Selassie Church. The minibuses that do the capital-run are less comfortable and more dangerous than the buses, but they do travel faster and they'll pick you up at your hotel. There's a choice of the 'night van' (Birr200, 6pm to 7pm) and the safer (relatively) 'early trip' (Birr220, 3am to 4am). Pretty much any business with a sign depicting a minibus sells tickets. You can also buy tickets from your hotel, but you'll pay a commission. Book tickets departing from Addis with **Adil Transport** (☎0911-955521).

A short hop in a shared taxi or *bajaj* costs Birr1 to Birr2. Hiring a *bajaj* for one hour costs Birr70.

## Around Harar

With your own transport, these four spots can be combined into one great day trip.

**KOREMI**    ኮረሚ
The clifftop village of Koremi, 19km south-east of Harar above the Erer Valley, is the largest of several villages of the Argoba, a deeply traditional people whose ancestors arrived in these parts in the 12th century. Unlike most of the Adare homes of Harar, the old **stone houses** here are unpainted and unplastered. Though the large number of sheet-metal roofs detracts from the ambience a bit, this shows what Harar looked like before modernisation.

There's no scheduled transport to or any tourist facilities in any of these villages.

**BABILLE ELEPHANT
SANCTUARY**    ባቢሌ የዝሆኖች መጠለያ
Despite considerable tree-cutting, livestock grazing, and land encroachment, judged by notoriously low Ethiopian environmental standards **Babille** (admission Birr90, vehicle Birr20, mandatory scout Birr150) is better protected than many of Ethiopia's national parks, and the population of elephants (which some authorities identify as a unique subspecies, *Loxodonta africana orleansi*) has risen to around 400. Also resident, though unlikely to be seen, are lions (notable for their black manes), leopards, cheetahs, Menelik's bushbuck, Soemmerring's Gazelle, and greater and lesser kudu. The bird list is at least 227 species strong.

The best way to see the elephants is driving through the Erer Valley, which comprises the majority of the 6982-sq-km sanctuary, to near where they were last spotted and then get out and walk. With enough patience and perseverance you stand a good chance of finding them. They prefer the thick brush so are difficult to see clearly (climbing trees provides the best vantage), but you can often get quite close. Wear long trousers; there are many thorn trees and cacti.

The signed turn-off is 20km from Harar on the Jijiga Road at Kile, and then it's another 12km to the office. Except during heavy rain, a taxi or minibus can handle the road through the reserve.

**Camping** (per tent Birr20) is allowed anywhere, but there are no facilities.

**BABILLE**    ባቢሌ
If you're travelling on a Monday or Thursday, don't pass this otherwise unremarkable village without taking a look at the **livestock market**, one of Ethiopia's biggest, which attracts buyers of camels, cows and goats from as far as Djibouti and Somaliland. The market runs from about 10am to 2pm but because sales go fast it's best to visit early. Buses from Harar (Birr11, 45 minutes) are frequent.

EASTERN ETHIOPIA AROUND HARAR

## VALLEY OF MARVELS     ጸሕታ

The drive from Harar to Jijiga is quite beauti-ful. The best stretch begins about 4km past Babille where the road enters the Dakhata Valley, better known as the Valley of Mar-vels. Here, tall rocks have been sculpted into strange, often phallic shapes by the elements. The name oversells things, but the Valley of the Pretty Cool doesn't have the same ring. Most people just see it from the road, but a half-day ramble is the better choice.

## Jijiga     ጅጅጋ

POP 142,500 / ELEV 1696M

There's little to see and less to do in Jijiga. Its size provides the only clue to its status as capital of the Somali region. Some people come hoping to get a taste of Somalia, but it's better to just get on the next minibus to the border and experience the real thing.

If you've got time to kill, explore the large **market** where most things, except for the fresh food, are smuggled in from Somali-land. The **livestock market** (⊙8am-2pm Sat-Thu), about 3km south of the bus station, is also big. Go early if you want to see camels since they tend to sell out fast.

## ⊨ Sleeping

**Africa Hotel**     HOTEL **$**

(d Birr100) A reliable pick in the town centre (just south of the big roundabout), conven-ient to Selam bus. Simple, clean rooms at a good price.

**Hamba Hotel**     HOTEL **$**

(☑0257-754678; d/tw without bathroom Birr184/276, d/tw Birr253/368; ℗) The best in town, and thus often full of UN and NGO workers, the rooms are big and clean and all come with satellite TV and hot-water showers. The en-suite rooms also have a minifridge. There's a water tank and generator as de-fence against Jijiga's frequent utility out-ages. It's on the Harar side of town.

## ❶ Getting There & Away

### Air

**Ethiopian Airlines** (☑0257-752030) flies daily to Addis Ababa (US$66, two hours) via Dire Dawa (US$33, 25 minutes). The airport is 14km out of town, Birr150 in a *bajaj*.

### Bus

The bus station is about 3km east of town. Minibuses and a few buses leave frequently throughout the day for Harar (Birr40, 1½ hours) and Togo-Wuchale (Wajaale on the Somaliland side; Birr30, one hour), on the Somaliland bor-der. See p290 for details of entering Somaliland.

There's one regular bus to Addis Ababa (Birr200, 15 hours) at around 2pm. More com-fortable Selam (Birr320) buses to Addis depart 5am daily from their office located in the town centre.

# Western Ethiopia

## Best of Culture

» Kibish (p205)
» Itang (p213)
» Gambela (p209)
» St Maryam Church (p198)
» Jimma (p205)

## Best of Nature

» Gambela National Park (p212)
» Omo National Park (p205)
» Mt Wenchi (p199)
» Menagesha National Forest (p209)
» Gibe Sheleko National Park (p209)

## Why Go?

Western Ethiopia is undisturbed and seldom visited, yet it's one of the most beautiful regions in Ethiopia. Rain forests, coffee plantations and muddy agricultural towns share the landscape with savannah grasslands, wildlife-infested swamps and high plateaus carpeted in fields of tef (an indigenous grass cultivated as a cereal).

As impressive as the scenery is, it's the ethnic diversity that is the real attraction: white-robed highlanders flock to churches; Surmi women with giant lip plates and men painted white like spirits of the night patrol the lowlands; and, on the South Sudan border, ritually scarred Nuer peoples stride across the grasslands with their long-horned cattle. The Anuak peoples of the Gambela region believe that to continue travelling west is to fall off the edge of the world. The Anuak are wrong on this score: the world doesn't end in western Ethiopia, it just feels that way.

## When to Go

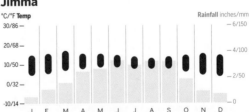

**Jimma**

**Jan–Mar** Huge numbers of antelope move through Gambela National Park.

**Oct–Nov** Meskel flowers bloom: the countryside glows green and yellow.

**Dec–Mar** The dry season is the easiest time to get to southwest Omo Valley.

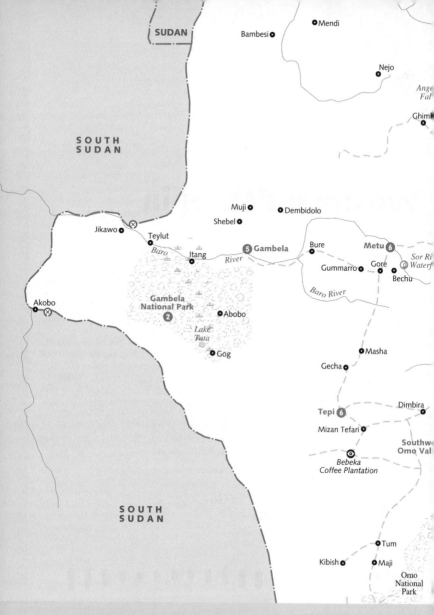

# Western Ethiopia Highlights

❶ Experience African tribal life at its most raw and wild in the endlessly fascinating **southwest Omo Valley** (p204)

❷ Be among the first to witness one of the greatest migrations of large mammals anywhere on Earth in **Gambela National Park** (p212)

❸ Wrap your legs around a scrawny horse for a scenic descent into the lake-filled crater of **Mt Wenchi** (p199)

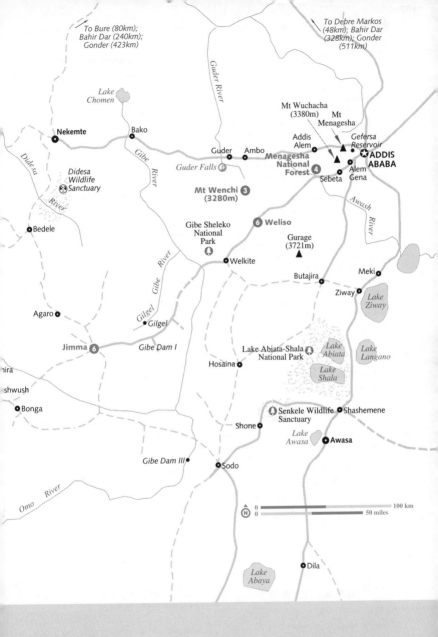

To Bure (80km);
Bahir Dar (240km);
Gonder (423km)

To Debre Markos
(48km); Bahir Dar
(328km); Gonder
(511km)

*Guder River*

**Nekemte**

Bako

*Lake
Chomen*

Mt Wuchacha
(3380m)

Mt
Menagesha

**Addis
Alem**

*Gefersa
Reservoir*

☆ **ADDIS
ABABA**

Guder  Ambo

**Menagesha
National
Forest** ④

Alem
Gena

*Didesa
River*

*Gibe
River*

*Didesa
Wildlife
Sanctuary* ⊛

*Guder Falls* ⑦

Sebeta

*Awash
River*

**Bedele**

**Mt Wenchi** ③
(3280m)

Gibe Sheleko
National
Park ⑥ **Weliso**

Gurage
(3721m) ▲

Meki

**Welkite**

Butajira

*Gibe
River*

Ziway

*Lake
Ziway*

**Agaro**

*Gilgel
River*

• *Gilgel*

**Jimma** ⑥

Gibe Dam I

Lake Abiata-Shala
National Park ⊕

*Lake
Abiata*

*Lake
Langano*

Hosaina

*Lake
Shala*

…ira

…shwush

**Bonga**

Senkele Wildlife ❶
Sanctuary

**Shashemene**

Shone

*Lake
Awasa*

**Awasa**

Gibe Dam III

Sodo

*Omo River*

Dila

*Lake
Abaya*

Ⓝ  0 ————— 100 km
   0 ————— 50 miles

④ Search for birds, colobus
monkeys and Menelik's
bushbuck while meandering
on the slopes of Mt Wuchacha
in the **Menagesha National
Forest** (p209)

⑤ Wonder if you're still in
Ethiopia while making friends
with the Nuer and Anuak
peoples of **Gambela** (p209)

⑥ Stare steadily at the
striking scenery moving past
your window while driving
from **Jimma** to **Weliso** (p208)
and from **Metu** to **Tepi** (p203),
the birthplace of coffee

## ❶ Getting There & Around

**Ethiopian Airlines** (www.flyethiopian.com) connects Addis Ababa with both Gambela and Jimma three times a week.

Most people who enter western Ethiopia overland are travelling by bus from Addis Ababa, which provides access to the southwest via Jimma and to the northwest via Nekemte. On the southern route the road is sealed from Addis to Jimma, after which it continues as a dirt road of varying quality as far as Metu. The northern road is sealed as far as Ambo. Afterwards it's a mixture of dirt roads and patches of sealed tarmac as far as Metu. The road from Metu to Gambela and onward to the South Sudan border is excellent. Like elsewhere in Ethiopia, Chinese-led construction crews are in the process of upgrading many roads within this area.

It's possible to reach Jimma from Sodo in the south and to reach Nekemte from the Addis Ababa–Bahir Dar road in the north by public transport, thus allowing you to connect western Ethiopia with both southern and northern Ethiopia without backtracking to Addis.

With the exception of the remote southwest Omo region, most areas are covered by regular bus services. However, during the wet season, roads and schedules can run equally amok.

# THE WESTERN HIGHLANDS

Carpeted in lush forests, dense patchworks of cultivation, shady coffee plantations and deep river valleys, the western highlands seem like an Ethiopian Arcadia.

## Gefersa Reservoir የገፈርሳ ግድብ

If you're into **birdwatching**, a stop at the Gefersa Reservoir may be warranted. Wattled ibis, endemic blue-wing geese and, occasionally, pelicans peruse its sparsely vegetated

### WALK THIS WAY

There is something peculiar afoot in Ambo. If you look carefully you'll notice that locals use one side of the street for walking east and the other side for walking west. This way, they say, they can easily spot out-of-towners who insist on battling the tide of human traffic.

shores. The reservoir lies 18km west of Addis Ababa and supplies the capital with its water.

## Addis Alem አዲስ አለም

POP 13,424 / ELEV 2360M

This unremarkable agricultural town 55km west of Addis Ababa was to be the site of Emperor Menelik II's future capital – Addis Alem literally means 'New World' in Amharic. The emperor had sent engineers and builders to start construction here when Addis Ababa was crippled by late-19th-century firewood shortages. The introduction of eucalyptus trees ended up saving the new flower (Addis Ababa) and killed the new world.

Of the remaining buildings, **St Maryam Church** (admission Birr100) is the most interesting. It stands out for its lavish decoration: the basilica's exterior, as well as the *maqdas* (inner sanctuary), is entirely covered with murals. The adjacent **museum** (admission Birr50; ⊙9am-noon & 1-3pm) displays crowns and clothing belonging to Menelik and Haile Selassie, as well as relics from the Battle of Adwa and a gold inland box that local legend says once contained the Ark of the Covenant. The site sits atop a rocky hill 600m south of the main road.

Numerous buses pass heading east to Addis Ababa (Birr15, 1½ hours) and west to Ambo (Birr25, two hours).

## Ambo አምቦ

POP 49,500 / ELEV 2101M

Mineral water is Ambo's claim to fame; it's bottled here and sold throughout Ethiopia. The water is so fizzy that it continues to sparkle even in a glass left overnight! Although you can't visit the factory, you can take a dip in the famous **thermal pool** (admission Mon-Thu Birr11, Fri-Sun Birr17; ⊙6am-6pm) run by Ambo Ethiopia Hotel. Despite the murky green colour, the pool is cleaned weekly.

The town also offers an interesting Saturday **market** where you can find brightly coloured Ambo baskets.

You'll find a Dashen bank with an ATM accepting Visa cards on the main drag, as well as an internet cafe or two.

### 🛏 Sleeping & Eating

**Ambo Ethiopia Hotel**          RESORT **$**
(☑0112-362002; per tent Birr100, s/d Birr142/203) Set around flowering gardens, this old colo-

nial place has bundles of old-world charm. Though it shows its age in places, it's still quite comfortable and some rooms have satellite TV. The classic dining hall (mains Birr50 to Birr75), which alone makes a stay worthwhile, serves Western and Ethiopian selections. Guests have free use of the town's mineral pool. It's located 150m west of the bus station.

**Abebech Metaferia Hotel**  HOTEL $
(☑0112-362365; tw Birr155-265, d/ste Birr255/ 350) This modern (and rather ugly) tower, just east of the bus station, houses what are feted as Ambo's smartest rooms. This might well be true, but sadly there's zero character and lots of road noise.

**Hoteela Jibaatifi Maccaa**  HOTEL $
(☑0112-362253; d Birr104-150; P) Set in a large compound, this place has cheap old rooms that the cheerful and commendably honest owner described as 'bad', or rooms in a new block that have cold showers but are otherwise clean and very good value. It is located next to the turn-off for Mt Wenchi.

### ❶ Getting There & Away

A dozen daily minibuses serve Addis Ababa (Birr33 to Birr37, three hours). Price depends on vehicle type. One daily bus serves Nekemte (Birr66, five hours). For Guder (Birr4, 15 minutes), minibuses run approximately every 30 minutes.

## Mt Wenchi ወንጪ ተራራ

ELEV 3280M
Resting within the beautiful collapsed caldera of Mt Wenchi, 31km south of Ambo, is **Lake Wenchi**, an **island monastery** and several **hot springs**. The scenery, a patchwork of cultivation run through with the occasional stand of natural forest, is a tonic for any city-weary soul. If you want a quick taste of the highlands within easy reach of Addis this is absolutely the place to come.

Visiting Lake Wenchi is a refreshingly well-organised experience. The **Wenchi Eco Tourism Association** (☑0113-560009, 0912-968516; ⊙8am-5pm), the office of which is located a kilometre or so before the parking area on the Ambo side of the crater, provides the compulsory guide (Birr150 for up to five people) and optional horses (Birr100 per horse). This is also where you pay your entry fee (Birr30), boat transfers to the island monastery (Birr25 return) and hot springs (Birr50 return via the monastery), and car parking (Birr20).

Without a horse, it takes about 45 minutes to walk the 4km down to the lake and just over an hour for the hot slog back up. Horses can do it in half this time. If you have a 4WD it is also possible to drive.

Once at the lake's edge, little wooden boats ferry visitors across to the tiny island monastery of **Cherkos**. Other than a small church, there isn't much here but you can ask to see the large 'Gonder bell', which once belonged (according to tradition) to Emperor Fasiladas.

From Cherkos the boats continue to the far side of the lake, where you begin a stunning walk (four to five hours in total) through a countryside of grazing horses, babbling brooks (not so good in the wet season) and water-powered mills to the **hot springs**. The springs are said to have magical curative properties and the caves in the surrounding area house pilgrims, here to treat their afflictions.

For accommodation, the most enjoyable option is to bring your own tent, food and plenty of warm clothes and camp near the springs. Otherwise there's the open one minute, closed the next **Wenchi Lodge** (☑0113-560122; s/d Birr100/200). It occupies a commanding hilltop position and, should it be open, rooms are in circular concrete huts with thatched roofs.

### ❶ Getting There & Away

For those with vehicles, Mt Wenchi makes for a wonderful day trip from Addis Ababa. For everyone else, Mt Wenchi is best visited on Friday and Sunday from Ambo in the north or Weliso to the south when one or two buses (Birr25, 1½ hours from either town) head to the market at the village of Haro Wenchi, which is where the Eco Tourism Association office is. Buses from either Ambo or Weliso leave between 7am and 8.30am. They usually return sometime between 4pm and 5pm.

A minibus with driver can be hired in Ambo. A return trip costs a very negotiable Birr1000. Ask at the bus station.

## Guder & Around

The journey towards Nekemte soon takes you through **Guder**, 11km west of Ambo. About 1km from Guder, after crossing the river, you'll see a gate for **Guder Falls** (admission Birr30; ⊙7am-6pm). It isn't spectacular, but is worth a peek in the wet season. The ubiquitous Ethiopian red wine, Gouder, was ostensibly named after the river, and a few vineyards can still be seen covering the surrounding area. If you want to stay, the **Guder Falls Recreation Area Hotel** (✆0911-896012; cottages Birr55) is a peaceful place set above the falls in beautifully tended gardens. Sadly the same love hasn't been extended to the cottages themselves.

As you climb from Guder the views open up and you'll see endless fields of quilted yellows, reds and greens. Although the views down are great, don't forget to look up, too – there are some impressive columnar basalt flows along the road cut above Guder.

About 65km from Ambo you'll reach an escarpment offering westward vistas over distant volcanic landscapes. Heading further west, things become less cultivated. This area is part of the historical Wolega province and is home to gold reserves and precious frankincense. Both still fetch high prices in Middle Eastern and Egyptian markets.

# Nekemte   ነቀምት

POP 103,623 / ELEV 2101M

Nekemte, 203km west of Ambo, is the sprawling commercial and administrative centre for the Oromia region's East Wolega zone. Although there's few sights besides a well-put-together museum, Nekemte has decent facilities and makes an obvious spot to break your westward journey.

## ◉ Sights

Worth a wander is Nekemte's **market**, which bustles most on Wednesday, Thursday and Saturday. Although the **Church of St Gabriel** casts a nice silhouette from

town, it can be classed as good from afar, but far from good.

**Wolega Museum**   MUSEUM
(admission Birr25; ◷9am-12.30pm & 2.30-5.40pm Tue-Sun) The remains of an Italian military plane shot down by the Black Lion Patriots in 1935 proudly sits in front of the Wolega Museum. Inside, displays give a good insight into the Wolega Oromo life and culture. It contains traditional musical instruments, as well as displays of the local spinning, carving and basket-weaving industries. Admission includes a guided tour.

**Kumsa Moroda Palace**   HISTORIC BUILDING
(admission Birr25; ◷9am-noon & 1.30-5pm Tue-Sun) Built by the King of Wolega in the 1870s, the Kumsa Moroda Palace has only recently been opened to the public after long years of neglect. It sits 1km north of the museum and served as residence to the prominent Worra Bekere family until they were hauled off to Addis Ababa during the Derg. The compound consists of around 10 buildings, and admission includes a guide who can explain what each building was used for (although ours couldn't really speak English but waved his arms with enthusiasm). Outside are a number of places to get a traditional Ethiopian coffee in a park-like setting. Note that opening hours of the palace are a little flexible and on Sunday morning everyone is likely to be at church.

## ⊨ Sleeping & Eating

**Farm Land Hotel**   HOTEL $
(✆0576-615150; d/tw Birr250/300; ☞) It's not the most exciting hotel we've ever seen,

# Nekemte

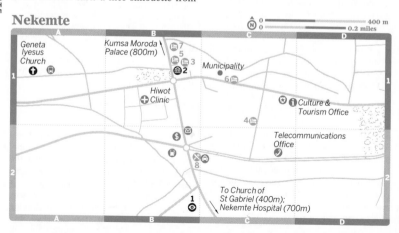

but because it was brand new at the time of research it was still shiny and lovely and thus the town's top choice. The large rooms have flat-screen TVs and bathrooms you'll be happy to hang about in. At the time of research there was no sign, but being so big and glossy you can hardly miss it.

**Benori Pension**  HOTEL $
(☎0576-614096; d Birr300; 🛜) Sitting on a quiet side street, this modern multistorey hotel has very small, but otherwise exceedingly comfortable, rooms with double-glazed windows, satellite TV and good mattresses on the beds. However, compared to similar competition in town it's a smidgen overpriced.

**Adugna Geleta Hotel**  HOTEL $
(☎0576-618225; s/d/tw Birr165/190/220; 🛜) Vast rooms with parquet flooring, well-equipped bathrooms and teeny balconies sitting atop a busy bar and cafe make this a good value place to bed down for the night.

**Kebede Hotel**  HOTEL $
(☎0576-612394; d Birr92-115) The rooms in this multistorey job are spotless and light with large windows and clean bathrooms, though only in the more expensive rooms does hot water spurt forth from the taps.

**Dhalas Cafe & Bed**  HOTEL $
(d Birr62-92) For the price you can't really fault this place; rooms are clean and host beds with comfortable foam mattresses. Only the more expensive rooms have hot water.

**Classic Internet Cafe**  INTERNATIONAL $
(mains Birr30-40) This popular snack bar and internet cafe serves a variety of sandwiches, pizzas and burgers, and some token Ethiopian dishes.

## Nekemte

## ⓘ Information

Besides the services listed below, Nekemte also has a post office, Commercial Bank and a telecommunications office.

**Culture & Tourism Office** (☎0576-611315; ⊙8am-12.30pm & 1.30-5.30pm Mon-Fri) Friendly although under-resourced.

**Hiwot Clinic** (☎0576-612036; ⊙7am-12.30pm & 2-5.30pm) A better bet than the local hospital.

**Classic Internet Cafe** (per hr Birr18; ⊙8am-9pm) Not just internet, but also a proper cafe.

## ⓘ Getting There & Away

Half a dozen daily buses serve Addis Ababa (Birr90 to Birr97 depending on bus quality, eight to 10 hours). Other services include Ambo (Birr58 to Birr65, five hours) and Bedele (Birr40, four hours), Dembidolo (Birr113, nine to 10 hours) and one bus a day to Jimma (Birr98, seven to eight hours) at 6am.

## Nekemte to Bedele

The road from Nekemte to Bedele is as smooth as silk – well at least for the first 3km; the other 102km are well-graded gravel, but work was being done on it when we last passed by. Roughly halfway between Nekemte and Bedele is the 1300-sq-km **Didesa Wildlife Sanctuary**. Although there's currently no access, you'll have a glimpse of its beauty when crossing the Didesa River Bridge. Animals do live here, but the only larger mammals you are really likely to see are baboons on the side of the road.

## Bedele  በደለ

POP 19.517 / ELEV 2162M

Scrappy Bedele lies 105km south of Nekemte and sits at an important crossroads linking Metu, Jimma and Nekemte. Besides a tour of the celebrated **Bedele beer factory** (☎0474-450134; admission free; ⊙8am-4pm Mon-Fri) or a tasting session, there's little reason to stop.

If you're stuck here, try **Peensiyoonii Weqinesh** (d with cold/hot shower Birr80/90), which has very cramped rooms that are basically as messy as the town itself. It's above the Oromia International Bank in a pink and green building near the main roundabout.

Between 6am and noon several buses pass heading for Jimma (bus/minibus Birr45/50, three hours). Going in the other direction buses head to Metu (Birr44, three

## KING SOLOMON'S GOLD

The Old Testament describes King Solomon's famous temple in Jerusalem as being overlaid with the purest of gold brought from the mines of Ophir. Just where this mysterious Ophir was located has long baffled historians and archaeologists and over the centuries provided grist to the mill of thousands of dreamers, writers and explorers.

The candidates for the title of the Biblical Ophir have ranged from India to Haiti and China to Zimbabwe. But others claim that the real location of the gold mines of Ophir is close to modern day Nejo in western Ethiopia. Certainly, there is some evidence to indicate that this might just be true. The Ancient Egyptians are known to have mined gold in Nubia close to the border of western Ethiopia and we know that Ethiopia also has reserves of gold that have been mined for a very long time. And the oldest of all these ancient mines are thought to be the open quarries close to the small town of Nejo, northwest of Nekemte, where locals still sometimes dig up ancient shards of pottery.

For a rollicking adventure story on this fascinating topic get hold of a copy of Tahir Shah's book *In Search of King Solomon's Mines*.

hours). There's a couple of buses to Nekemte (Birr40, four hours) and, at 6am, a single bus each to Addis Ababa (Birr147, 10 hours) via Jimma and to Gambela (Birr100, eight hours).

## Metu       መጡ

POP 28,782 / ELEV 1600M

Spreading over the slope of a small hill 115km west of Bedele is Metu, the capital of the old Ilubador province. For travellers, Metu acts as the primary gateway to the western lowlands, as well as a springboard for trips south through some of the west's most wild and beautiful scenery to Tepi and Mizan Tefari. If you're going to choose between getting stuck for the night in Bedele or here then don't hesitate to choose Metu. It's not great but it's a lot better than Bedele!

### ⊙ Sights

**Sor River Waterfalls**     WATERFALL

ሶር ወንዝ ፏፏቴ A worthwhile excursion from Metu is to the Sor River Waterfalls, one of the most beautiful falls in Ethiopia. It lies close to the village of Bechu, 13km southeast of Metu. The last 15 minutes of the one-hour walk (5km) from Bechu takes you through dense forest teeming with birds and monkeys. If it has been raining the mud will be deep enough to suck the shoes off your feet. At the falls, Sor River suddenly drops 20m over the lip of a wide chasm into a fern-lined amphitheatre. You can take a dip in the pool below.

A daily minibus leaves Metu for Bechu (Birr10, one hour) around 7am. It returns as soon as it's full, which means you may have to walk back to Metu or battle a night of fleas in Bechu. To find the falls, enlist the help of a Bechu villager (tip expected) or ask one of the children who invariably tag along. With a 4WD you could make the return trip from Metu in less than four hours.

### 🛌 Sleeping & Eating

**Hoteela Antanah**     HOTEL $

(☑0474-411002; d Birr100-120) Only 50m from the bus station, this is the town's best place to rest weary heads. Its *faranji*-priced upstairs options are large and bright. The downstairs Birr100 rooms are still clean but lack the finer touches (like light bulbs and toilet seats).

**Sena Hotel**     HOTEL $

(d with/without bathroom Birr92/40) is more noteworthy for its restaurant-cum-bar (mains Birr15-25) than for its simple rooms, even though its selection of dishes is limited and vegies are few and far between . It's near the Commercial Bank, 1.4km east of the bus station.

### ℹ Getting There & Away

Buses depart for Gambela (bus/minibus Birr64/80, three hours, several daily), Bedele (Birr44, three hours, five daily) and Addis Ababa (Birr182, 1½ to two days, 6am) via Jimma (Birr82, eight hours).

To reach Tepi take a minibus to Gore (Birr7, around 35 minutes) and then catch a bus to Masha (Birr20 to Birr27, three hours) and go from there. If you start early enough, you can reach Tepi or Mizan Tefari in a day.

# Metu to Tepi

Twenty-five kilometres south of Metu is the inconsequential junction town of Gore, from where the road strikes south for Tepi and west to Gambela.

Heading south, the road snakes along a ridge and offers sublime vistas over a lush, green quilt of small fields pockmarked with thatched-roof huts, and patches of dense forest ringing with the sound of birds and monkeys. Some of the larger trees, shrouded in vegetation, seem to have ecosystems of their own. You may spot a colobus monkey or two peering from vine-draped trees.

North of muddy Masha you'll pass through rolling hills carpeted in neat tea plantations, before entering thick sections of forest and the occasional stand of bamboo south of town.

After Gecha, the road winds through *enset* ('false-banana' tree) plantations, traditional villages and yet more jungle. As you near Tepi, you'll start to see coffee drying outside homes along the roadside.

All up we rate it as one of the most scenic drives in Ethiopia.

In a private vehicle the journey takes between 5½ and seven hours, depending on the season. It's also possible in a day by riding local minibuses, though you'll likely have to change minibuses at Gore and Masha.

## Tepi                                  ·ʈ·ʈ.

POP 19,231 / ELEV 1238M

Tepi is famous for its state-owned coffee plantation. It's Ethiopia's second-largest, and stretches over 6290 hectares. Just over 2000 hectares lies around Tepi while the remainder, including Beshanwaka (a beautiful crater lake), is in the Gambela region about 30km away. The state-run plantation produces about 25,000kg of raw arabica coffee each year.

It should be possible to arrange a tour of the plantation by requesting through the Coffee Plantation Development Enterprise (☑0118-962395/4) in Addis Ababa or at the plantation (manager's office ☑0475-5560007/5561117) itself, close to the Coffee Plantation Guesthouse. Unfortunately, it's not possible to buy coffee here.

### 🛏 Sleeping & Eating

All of the places to stay only have cold-water bathrooms.

**Coffee Plantation Guesthouse**          HOTEL $

(☑0475-560062; d Birr200) The semidetached concrete bungalows vaunt bright-green laminate floors, frilly bedspreads, small verandahs and clean washrooms with, as the person showing us around so proudly pointed out, 'showers'. Unfortunately, when he turned on the showers to show us how amazing they were, nothing happened... If you order ahead, the 'workhouse club' can prepare meals and if not the cockroaches racing across the ancient coffee machine can at least be considered a form of entertainment.

**Genet Guest House**                      HOTEL $

(☑0475-5562145; d with/without bathroom Birr115/80) Four-hundred metres past the main roundabout along the road to Jimma, this fairly new place has clean rooms with tiny bathrooms built around a courtyard bar and garden with parking.

### ❶ Getting There & Away

Three buses run daily to Masha (Birr39, three hours) and onward to Gore and occasionally Gambela. From Gore there are frequent minibuses to Metu (Birr7, 35 minutes). One, sometimes two, buses serve Jimma (Birr98, seven hours). For Mizan Tefari (Birr22, 1½ hours), seven buses run daily.

## Mizan Tefari        ʻ7.ʍ3  ʈ·ፊ.ፊ

POP 19,300 / ELEV 1451M

The stunningly sited small town of Mizan Tefari, the old capital of the Bench people, serves as a base for a visit to the 9337-hectare Bebeka Coffee Plantation (☑0471-118621). The plantation is 28km southwest of Mizan Tefari (an hour's drive) and is Ethiopia's largest and oldest coffee farm.

As with Tepi, there are no longer any official tours, but you may be able to wrangle a letter of introduction by calling the Coffee Plantation Development Enterprise (☑0118-962395/4) in Addis Ababa and pleading your case. Armed with such a letter and your own 4WD (the plantation is far too big to take in on foot), the manager will usually provide a guide.

### 🛏 Sleeping & Eating

As impressive as the town's setting is, lolling across luminous green hills, the town itself is a bit of a dump and certainly the most unappetising town on the whole western Ethiopia tourist circuit. Unfortunately, though,

## BEAN ALL OVER THE WORLD

At some point between the 5th and 10th centuries, in the Ethiopian kingdom of Kafa, an astute herder named Kaldi noticed that his goats were behaving rather excitedly each time they ate a certain plant's berries. Trying it himself, he discovered that after a few chews and a couple of swallows, he was one hyper herder! When he told the local monastery they reprimanded him for 'partaking in the Devil's fruit' and flung the berries on the fire. They soon changed their minds, however, when they smelt the aroma emanating from the roasting beans.

Soon the monks were drying the berries for transport and shipping them to Ethiopian monasteries far and wide. There, priests would rehydrate them in water, eat the fruit and drink the fluids to keep themselves awake for nocturnal prayers.

Soon Arabs began importing the bean, and in the 15th century the Turks brewed the roasted beans into the drink we know today. From Turkey, coffee spread to Europe via Italy and then to Indonesia and the Americas.

Today an estimated four out of five Americans drink coffee at least once a day, and America (Seattle, to be precise) is the home of Starbucks – a coffee empire that encompasses over 16,000 stores in 49 countries.

But the bean didn't stop there. Coffee is now the top agricultural export for 12 countries, with the livelihood of over 100 million people depending on its production, and has become the world's second-most-valuable commodity after petroleum!

unless you have private transport to get you to the Bebeka Coffee Plantation Guesthouses, you'll probably have no choice but to spend a night here. It's unlikely to be fun.

**TOP CHOICE** Bebeka Coffee
**Plantation Guesthouses**　　　GUESTHOUSE $
(☏0913-761742; campsites Birr75, d/tw Birr200/400, cottages Birr500-700) Set in the thick of the coffee plantation and surrounded by birdlife, there's little doubt that this is the best place to stay in the vicinity of Mizan Tefari. It's simply the very definition of tranquillity. Rooms are impressively clean and have high ceilings, giving them a colonial feel, but they're also fairly simple and on the downside have cold-water bathrooms. Superb Ethiopian meals (mains Birr20 to Birr30) are available in the on-site restaurant.

**Hotel Salayish**　　　HOTEL $$
(☏0473-330542; d without bathroom Birr500) This 26-room hotel is widely considered the town's top choice, and while that might well be true it's hardly a ringing endorsement. Rooms are bright and sort of clean – well, OK, they're not as dirty as other places – usually. Like the hotel, the downstairs restaurant (mains Birr25 to Birr35) is regarded by locals as the best place in town to eat.

### ❶ Getting There & Away

Buses run to Tepi (Birr22, two hours, seven daily) and Jimma (Birr72 to Birr75, 7½ hours, one daily).

Since you require your own 4WD for a tour of Bebeka Coffee Plantation, there is little point arriving here on foot.

## Southwest Omo Valley

Prepare to be amazed! The Omo Valley and its fascinating ethnic peoples is nowadays one of the biggest tourist attractions in Ethiopia. The vast majority of visitors to this region focus on the easier to reach, safer and ethnically more diverse eastern side of the valley (see p161), but for those with a streak of adventure a mile wide, there is another side to the Omo Valley and it's one filled with the spirit of pure, raw Africa.

This near roadless wilderness is the home of the Surmi – a people adorned with lip plates and spirit-like white paint, whose cattle-herding lifestyle remains, for the moment at least, fairly untouched by outside influences. To spend time with these people, experiencing a genuine slice of tribal African life, is an honour and a privilege, but it is not one that comes easily.

Visiting this western half of the valley is a very different kettle of fish to the eastern side. Great patience and understanding is required, as is a fair amount of money. Getting here is a serious undertaking. There is no public transport (a few goods lorries do travel down here but you will not be allowed to go with them) so you will need to hire a jeep through a tour company in Addis. The road system is almost nonexistent and even in the dry season getting here and around can be very hard going. After rain most of the few tracks become completely impassable. There are almost no tourist facilities here. Unless you are prepared to put up with one of the exceedingly rough local 'hotels' (think barn) in Kibish village then you will need to bring camping gear, food, water and everything else you need with you.

All up, unless you are prepared for real adventure, some discomfort and a certain amount of danger, then stick to the easier eastern side of the valley. If, however, none of the above puts you off then welcome to a place you'll never forget.

### KIBISH & AROUND

The main settlement in this area is the colourful village of **Kibish** (village fee per day Birr50, government fee per day Birr100, guide fee per group per day Birr250, compulsory armed guard per day Birr200). Set in a bowl in the forested hills, it is a fascinating place populated by the striking Surmi people. Photographing the Surmi attracts a fee of Birr5 per photo of an adult and Birr2 per photo of a child. Photographers likely to take a lot of photos will be better off negotiating a fee for unlimited photos over a set period of time (Birr30 for 10 minutes per person is fair).

Days spent in Kibish will be filled with visits to small surrounding villages (extra village entry fees apply), and evenings bathing in the river. It might not sound like much, but trust us. It is.

There are few facilities: no mains electricity or water and just a handful of poorly stocked shops. Most people pitch a tent in the **campsite** (per tent Birr30, guardian fee Birr100) on the southern edge of the village. There's a hut with a fire pit in which to cook, but no other facilities whatsoever. However, camping under the African stars makes up for a lot!

### OMO NATIONAL PARK

Omo National Park is arguably the most remote park in Ethiopia and travelling here can be incredibly tough – but never less than fascinating. Because there is virtually no tourist infrastructure within the park, you will need to be totally self-sufficient with your own food, camping gear and vehicle.

Like other parks in Ethiopia, wildlife here has come into conflict with the indigenous tribes who live here, but despite this you do stand a pretty good chance of seeing various

## WARNING

The southwest Omo Valley is an area with a highly volatile security situation. Cattle rustling and tribal fighting are very common and can lead to significant loss of life (indeed, a week or so before our last visit around 200 people were rumoured to have been shot in the market place of Kibish village). There is also a not-insignificant risk of banditry. This is a particular problem along the Mizan Tefari to Kibish route where a sparsely inhabited 50km stretch has seen a number of attacks on passing vehicles.

Be aware that the situation changes very fast here. It's rare for foreign embassies to have much in the way of solid information on the current security situation and Addis-based tour companies often have only fairly old news. Having said that they should be your first port of call for the latest, but do be prepared for plans to change at the last second in this region due to the fluid security situation.

antelope species and there's some fantastic **birding**.

With the bridge down, no roads connect Omo National Park with the neighbouring Mago National Park (see p167) on the opposite side of the Omo River, but it's possible to cross between the two by boat and have a vehicle meet you on the other side.

## Jimma                             ጅማ

POP 123,000 / ELEV 1678M

Western Ethiopia's largest city, and a major university town, Jimma is a raucous place with wide (and, thanks to a major refurbishment program currently taking place, very dusty) streets, lots of honking horns and a massive coffee pot rising from its main roundabout. The town has a fairly substantial expat community (most of whom are involved with NGOs), but for a tourist there's little real reason to linger here other than to get to an ATM and break up a long journey.

For centuries, a powerful Oromo monarchy ruled the surrounding fertile highlands from its capital at Jiren (now a suburb of present-day Jimma). The region owed its wealth to its situation at the crux of

## THE SURMI

Formerly nomadic pastoralists, the Surmi (sometimes wrongly called the Surma) now largely depend on the subsistence cultivation of sorghum and maize. The Surmi have a fearsome reputation as warriors, in part inspired by their continual search for grazing lands. Fights against the Bumi, their sworn enemies, still occur.

It's believed that the Surmi once dominated the area, but their territory has been reduced to the western parts of the Omo National Park and surrounding areas. The population of 45,000 is split into three subgroups: the Chai, Tirma and Bale. Like the related Mursi, the Surmi men stick fight and the women don distending lip plates. However, stick fighting is now technically illegal – and, as in the main Omo Valley area, you should not put pressure on a guide or driver to take you to one of the illegal flights. Also, lip plates are dying out among the young generation.

The Surmi are also known for their white, almost ghost-like body painting. White chalk is mixed with water to create a kind of wash. The painting is traditionally much less ornamental than that found in other tribes (although tourism is starting to change this and children in Kibish and other popular tourist villages now routinely paint themselves up like prancing peacocks in order to gain camera attention) and is intended to intimidate enemies in battle. Sometimes snake and wave-like patterns are painted across the torso and thighs.

several major trade routes and to its abundant crops. At its height, the kingdom stretched over 13,000 sq km. When Menelik came to power in the late 1800s, he required the region to pay high tribute.

When the Italians entered the picture in the 1930s, they had grand plans to create a modern city in the heart of Ethiopia's breadbasket and Jimma was subsequently born from Jiren.

### ◉ Sights

If you're a connoisseur of Italian Fascist architecture, take a peek at the cinema, post office, municipal buildings and some of the old hotels.

**Jimma Museum**  MUSEUM
ጅማ ሙዚየም (☏0471-115881; admission Birr25; ⊘9am-noon & 2-5pm) Admission price to the Muuziyemii Jimmaa includes a guided tour in English of the seven small rooms that make up the museum. We don't want to steal the guide's thunder (such as it is), but our favourite pieces include a ceremonial throne that cost Birr146,000 to build but was only used by Haile Selassie for 20 minutes, and a royal portable toilet that looks like a frying pan with a hole in it. Other oddities include a poster with the entire Koran written on it in a script of almost microscopic proportions, and an Italian-made walking stick–cum-gun.

At the time of research a new home for the museum was under construction immediately behind the current building.

**Palace of Abba Jiffar**  PALACE
የአባ ጆፋር ቤተ መንግስት (admission Birr25; ⊘9am-noon & 2-5pm Wed-Thu & Sat-Mon) Looking more out of America's Wild West than the Kafa kingdom, the increasingly fragile Palace of Abba Jiffar looks as if a strong wind could blow it away. It sits atop a hill 7km northeast of the town centre, near the village of Jiren, and has views back down over Jimma that are worth the price of admission alone.

King Jiffar (1852–1933), who was one of the most important Kafa kingdom rulers, held power at the end of the 19th century. The palace contains a private family mosque (which is still in use) and rooms that used to serve as a library, throne room, reception chamber, king's guard room, sentry tower, courthouse and guesthouse. Almost 1.6km back down the hill lies the tomb of the king.

To get here either take a minibus (Birr5) from the marketplace in town or contract a taxi (Birr120, including waiting time).

**Boye Dam**  BIRDWATCHING
የቦዬ ግድብ (admission Birr20, vehicle Birr100) Located 5km east of town off the road to Addis, the dam has some good birdwatching opportunities, but take the locals' claims of hippos with a hippo-sized pinch of salt. There are also caves and hot springs in the vicinity.

### 🛏 Sleeping

Jimma hotels have openly embraced the *faranji* price scheme – the one where you pay double! Prices listed here are *faranji* rates.

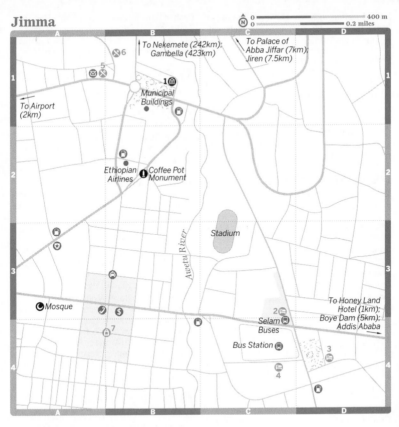

## Jimma

**Central Jimma Hotel** HOTEL **$**

(☎0471-118283; d without bathroom Birr72, d with bathroom Birr84-169, tw Birr121-217; @⊠) The courtyard and garden bar-and-pool complex at this old-timer are abuzz with the constant activity of people coming and going (Sunday lunchtime it's simply the place to be). The rooms are unfussy, clean and a good size and come in a bigger array of styles and prices than a zebra has stripes. Room rates include the use of the pool (which is otherwise Birr25/50 on weekdays/weekends).

**Honey Land Hotel** HOTEL **$$**

(☎0471-111515; d Birr426-651; P☎) Way out on the eastern fringes of town on the road to Addis, this place touts itself as the best hotel in town and with undeniably comfortable rooms that might well be true. What is also hard to deny is that compared to other options in town it seems overpriced.

**Temky Pension** HOTEL **$**

(☎0471-112565; d with/without bathroom Birr95/75, tw Birr175) The large lawn, garden tables and cleanish rooms make this the best budget option in town. However, the music in the lively garden courtyard can be irritating for those needing an early night.

### Wolde Aregaw & Family Hotel HOTEL $
(☏0471-112731; d with bathroom Birr150-340, tw Birr400; 🖥) If you can cope with the noise of all the early departing buses in the neighbouring bus station blurting on their horns at 6am, then this place offers really quite decent value. The cheaper rooms are better value, although hotel staff only reluctantly rent these to 'rich *faranji*'.

### ✖ Eating & Drinking

Try tasting the local *besso* drink, made from ground barley.

### Central Jimma Hotel INTERNATIONAL $
(mains Birr35-60) For a fine view of the bus station, a cold beer and some cheap eats, stick to the roadside cafe. For shish kebab, chicken Maryland and grilled fish, head to the more upmarket poolside Sennait Restaurant. For locals this is THE place to eat at weekends.

### Jimma Degitu Hotel INTERNATIONAL $
(mains Birr45-74) The *faranji* food here is quite good (if you remember you're in Ethiopia) and more varied than elsewhere. We happily wolfed down a cheeseburger and some cold French fries. The pizzas are also worthy of mention.

### Wolde Aregaw &
### Family Hotel INTERNATIONAL $
(mains Birr35-60) The wood panelling and calf-skin decor give this a lived-in vibe, and if you're at a loose end you can watch the satellite TV in the bar while munching on a steak sandwich. Next door, the restaurant serves meals such as *doro arrosto* (roast chicken) and spaghetti.

### Café Variety CAFE $
(light meals Birr17) Its shaded terrace vaunts the best selection of cakes and fruit juices in town. It's popular with students, who flock here for the juice and coffee. There are a couple of similar places nearby.

### 🛍 Shopping

Thursday is the main **market** day; seek out Jimma's famous three-legged stools, quality basketware and locally renowned honey.

### ℹ Information

There are plenty of hole-in-the-wall internet cafes throughout the town centre.

**Dashen Bank** (🕗8am-noon & 1-5pm Mon-Fri, 8am-noon Sat) Currency-exchange services and an ATM that accepts Visa. There's another Dashen ATM outside the Honey Land Hotel.

### ℹ Getting There & Away

**Ethiopian Airlines** (☏0471-110030; www.flyethiopian.com) flies Wednesday, Friday and Sunday to Addis Ababa (Birr2622, one hour to 2½ hours depending on route).

**Selam Buses** (☏0115-544831; www.selambus.com) has a daily bus to Addis Ababa (Birr165, six to seven hours) at 6am.

There are numerous buses throughout the day for Addis Ababa (Birr92 to Birr102, seven hours). The gates to the bus compound usually open around 6am. Get your elbows ready and be prepared for a mad scramble.

Amid the early morning free-for-all you'll find buses for Tepi (Birr 98, eight hours), Mizan Tefari (Birr75, 7½ hours), Metu (Birr82, eight hours), Bedele (Birr50, 4½ hours) and Nekemte (Birr98, nine hours). There are up to six minibuses to Welkite (Birr70, 5½ hours).

It's possible to travel by public transport from Jimma down to southern Ethiopia without transiting through Addis Ababa as a road now connects Jimma with Sodo, from where you can continue onward to Awasa or Arba Minch. The journey must be done in stages by first taking a bus to Chida (Birr50, 2½ to three hours) and changing there for Sodo.

### ℹ Getting Around

*Bajajs* (auto-rickshaws) cost around Birr5 for hops around town, depending on distance. No buses or minibuses go to the airport, but a taxi will charge around Birr50.

## Jimma to Weliso

After Jimma, the road begins to wind back in a northeastern direction towards Addis Ababa. Approximately 57km out of town, the road detours around Gilgel's **Gibe Dam** I. Further south, work on the controversial Gibe III dam is well underway. For more on this project see p273.

Much further west you'll see several impressive bulbous **rock pinnacles** rising from the seemingly subdued plateau in the distance. Once you pass the major outcrop, the road serpentines down into the gaping **Gibe River Valley**.

Around the 115km-from-Addis mark is the small town of **Weliso**, which makes a great base for exploring the crater lake in the middle of Mt Wenchi (see p199).

## 🛏 Sleeping & Eating

**Negash Lodge**                    LODGE $$
(✓ in Weliso 0113-410002, in Addis Ababa 0115-511417; www.negashlodge.com; incl breakfast d Birr759-885, tw Birr759-1012; P@☎⛱) At the end of a long day's hiking return to Weliso and luxuriate in Negash Lodge, which is not just by far the best hotel in western Ethiopia, but one of the best value places to stay in all of Ethiopia. It's centred on a swimming pool complex fed by a hot spring (during quiet times they might empty the pool) and surrounded by lush gardens that are home to all manner of birds (including lots of prehistoric-looking ravens), monkeys, tree hyraxes and dik-dik. Accommodation comes in a range of styles, from tribally decorated rondavels to stylish rooms in the 'Addis Ababa' block. The service is excellent, there's a decent **restaurant** (mains Birr120-160) serving European and Ethiopian dishes (and they'll prepare a picnic for you to take to Wenchi) and there's a cool bar situated halfway up a graceful old tree.

## Menagesha National Forest

Still closer to Addis is this **national forest** (admission Birr50). Almost a dozen trails (up to 9km in length) meander through the forest, with one even heading above the treeline to Mt Wuchacha's 3380m summit. On the crater's western slopes some of the giant juniper and *wanza* (Podocarpus) trees are said to be over 400 years old.

The forest is accessed via the small town of **Sebeta** roughly 30km from Addis. Just before arriving in Sebeta (if travelling east toward Addis) turn left at the green sign reading 'Dhaabbata Bosona Finfinetti' and 'Finfine Forest Enterprise' and it's a 17km drive to the park headquarters where the well-signed **walking trails** begin.

There's also a **Mt Menagesha** in the vicinity. This is not the same place. According to local tradition, this Menagesha is where many Ethiopian kings' coronations were held. It's best accessed from the Ambo road.

# THE WESTERN LOWLANDS

The Gambela federal region is somewhat of an oddity within Ethiopia – its swampy lowlands stand in stark contrast to the lush landscapes seen in the western highlands. Many of its people have stronger cultural ties with neighbouring South Sudan than they do with the rest of Ethiopia.

## Gambela                    ጋምቤላ

POP 31,282 / ELEV 526M
Set on the banks of the sluggish, chocolate-brown Baro River, at a lowly altitude of 526m, Gambela, the capital of the 25,274-sq-km Gambela federal region, is

---

WORTH A TRIP

### GIBE SHELEKO NATIONAL PARK

Gazetted in 2011, the **Gibe Sheleko National Park** (Gibe Valley National Park; ✓0462 208490/210480; www.southtourism.gov.et; admission Birr150, walking guide per day Birr70, campsites Birr40) covers 360 sq km of upland plateau, parts of the Gibe River gorge area and patches of endemic forest. The diverse, but rather elusive, **wildlife** includes 17 mammal species, such as Greater Kudu and, in the river valley, a few hippos. The **birdwatching** is also good with over 200 species recorded including red-winged phtyilia and white-winged cliff chat.

Although the wildlife might be shy, the views, off the plateau and down to the Wabe Plains, are anything but. To make the most of the scenery get out there on foot; guides are available from the park office and they can take you on day long or multiday hikes. There are two basic campsites, or a range of accommodation is available in the nearby town of **Welkite**.

The park is brand new and hasn't yet received many visitors so it's possible there will be a few hiccups along the way while staff get to grips with dealing with tourists (though, saying that, we were very impressed by the organisation of the place).

The park headquarters is signed 178km west of Addis just beyond the town of Welkite.

# Gambela

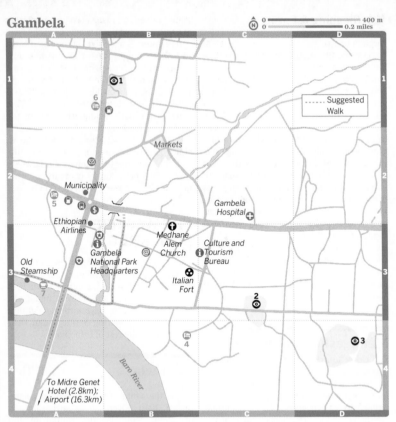

## Gambela

### ◉ Sights
| | |
|---|---|
| **1** Anuak Market | B1 |
| **2** New Land (Nuer Villages) | C3 |
| **3** New Land (Nuer Villages) | D4 |

### 🛏 Sleeping
| | |
|---|---|
| **4** Baro Gambella Hotel | B4 |
| **5** Green Hotel | A2 |
| **6** Tadessech Hotel | A1 |

### 🍷 Drinking
| | |
|---|---|
| **7** Coffee & Tea Stalls | A3 |

muggy, swampy and sweaty. It's a place that's utterly removed from everything else you'll have come to associate with Ethiopia. Long-horned cattle, trailing clouds of dust and led by tall, elegant Nuer and Anuak tribesmen, sweep through the wildlife-haunted savan-nahs that surround Gambela, while in the town itself people loll riverside under the spreading branches of giant trees. All up it's one of the more exotic corners of Ethiopia.

Although the terrible ethnic and political violence that has occurred sporadically over the past decade may seem to say otherwise, most people here seem to get along just fine nowadays. Although initially appearing reti-cent and deeply suspicious, the people here are actually incredibly hospitable. Using *daricho* (the Anuak greeting), or *male* (the Nuer greeting), helps break the ice.

### History
Thanks to the Baro River being the only truly navigable watercourse in Ethiopia, its strategic and commercial significance has long dictated the fortunes of Gambela's tur-bulent past.

Prior to the 19th century the Baro River was principally used by raiding slave parties to transport captured men. Later, at the end of the 19th century, Menelik II dreamed of linking Ethiopia with Egypt and Sudan via the White Nile. To help create the great inland shipping service, the emperor agreed to grant the British, who were already in control of Sudan, an enclave on the Baro River. In 1907 the site was chosen and Gambela was formally inaugurated as a port and customs station.

Soon steamers were chugging up and down the wide river, laden with valuables ranging from coffee to cotton. Commerce flourished and Gambela boomed.

The Italians briefly captured Gambela in 1936, and vestiges of their fort are still visible. The British won back the river port in 1941 and amazingly made it part of Sudan 10 years later. When Sudan gained its independence in 1956, the protectorate was given back to Ethiopia. It was around this time that the old shipping service formally ceased and Gambela began to sink slowly back into the mud from which it had sprung.

Interethnic tensions have plagued the region for decades. These culminated in a massacre of Anuak communities in Gambela township in 2003, resulting in the displacement of tens of thousands of people. In 2006 the Anuak attacked the Gambela police station and prison and killed several officers, including the state police commissioner, and freed an unknown number of prisoners. More recently in 2012 a public bus was attacked just outside Gambela town by unknown assailants. The allocations of vast areas of land for agricultural investments has further exacerbated tensions between ethnic groups, as has the arrival of large numbers of highlanders looking for new opportunities.

### Dangers & Annoyances
The good news is that the recent tension between the Anuak and the Nuer peoples seems to have dissipated and, at least for the time being, peace prevails. Nonetheless, as a precaution we strongly suggest that you keep your eye on developments around Gambela before visiting the western lowlands.

## PEOPLES OF THE WESTERN LOWLANDS

The Nuer and the Anuak are the two main ethnic groups within the Gambela region and form the vast majority of the population.

### The Nuer

The Nuer people, who are relatively recent arrivals to the region, originated in the Nilotic-speaking regions of Sudan and now form the largest ethnic group in Gambela. They're largely cattle herders and much of Nuer oral literature, including traditional songs and poetry, celebrates their beasts.

Unlike the Anuak, the Nuer like to live together in large villages. Very tall and dark, the Nuer women are fond of ornamentation, including bright bead necklaces, heavy bangles of ivory or bone and, around Gambela at least, increasingly rarely, a spike of brass or ivory that pierces the lower lip and extends over the chin. Cicatrising (considered sensual) is also widely practised: the skin is raised in patterns and decorates the face, chest and stomach; rows of dots are often traced on the forehead.

### The Anuak

The Anuak's language closely resembles that of the Luo tribes in Kenya. Fishing is their main means of survival, though some grow sorghum. Outside Gambela most live in extended family groups, rather than villages, composed of a cluster of huts in a small compound.

Anuak huts are characterised by low doorways and thickly thatched roofs. The eaves, which stretch almost to the ground, keep out both the torrential rain and baking sun.

A common practice among many Nilotic peoples of Ethiopia and Sudan, including the Anuak, is extraction of the front six teeth of the lower jaw at around the age of 12. This is said to have served originally as a precaution against the effects of tetanus or lockjaw.

### The Majang

The Majang, also known as Majangir, are the third major group living in and around Gambela (as well as up towards Metu and Tepi). The last census recorded only around 15,000 of them and many claim to feel persecuted by national and local governments and other tribal groups. They speak a Nilo-Saharan language of the Surmic cluster.

Security issues aside, your biggest concern should be reserved for some of Gambela's smaller residents – mosquitoes. Malaria continues to kill an extraordinarily high percentage of the population here, and adequate precautions are essential (see p342). Giardia is also common.

Photographers should know that taking photos of, or from, the bridge is strictly forbidden. The Anuak and Nuer people are also notoriously camera-shy. Always ask permission before taking photos – if you don't, warm hospitality may turn to aggression.

## ◉ Sights & Activities

A pleasant **walk** around Gambela includes the riverside where you'll find an old boat or two and a pier (visible from the riverbank), the bridge and the markets. This walk is marked on the Gambela map.

At sunset, locals gather at the river beneath the bridge to bathe, walk or catch up on gossip. Once every few years (usually during the wet season), a villager is taken by a crocodile.

**WORTH A TRIP**

## GAMBELA NATIONAL PARK

ጋምቤላ ብሔራዊ ፓርክ Less than 50 years ago, Gambela National Park, spreading over 5061 sq km and abutting the even larger Boma National Park of South Sudan, was considered one of Ethiopia's richest places for large mammals. Elephants, lions, leopards, giraffes, buffaloes, topis, tiangs, roan antelopes, hartebeests, white-eared kob, Nile lechwe and waterbucks were found here in huge numbers.

Then to both Ethiopia and neighbouring Sudan (now South Sudan) came decades of war, civil unrest and refugees. And with these Gambela National Park became largely forgotten and abandoned. War and wildlife generally don't mix well and experts quite logically assumed that the wildlife of both Gambela and Boma National Parks would have been decimated. But then in 2007, when peace started to return to the wider region, conservationists from the New York–based **World Conservation Society** (www.wcs.org) embarked on aerial surveys of South Sudan's Boma National Park and were shocked to find that not just had the wildlife merely survived the dark years of violence but that it was flourishing. In fact, what they discovered were herds of migrating white-eared kob and Nile lechwe over a million strong. In addition they found thousands of elephants and buffalo and healthy populations of predators.

Between 2007 and 2012 all the focus was on Boma park, but logic always said that it was likely the wildlife would be following the rains and grazing over the border and into Gambela National Park. Today surveys are also taking place here, and the first indications are that Gambela park is also home to huge numbers of animals.

### Planning

Just because Gambela National Park might have wildlife populations to rival the famous reserves of Kenya and Tanzania that doesn't mean you'll actually see much wildlife. This is a very remote and swampy park with absolutely nothing in the way of an infrastructure (although there are plans afoot to build a road system within the park as well as establish designated camping areas and even a lodge). To make matters more complicated the animals are thought to be concentrated in the southwestern parts of the park – the swampiest, and hardest to reach area. Anyone visiting this park must be totally self-sufficient and have a LOT of time at their disposal. From August to October the park is largely flooded and impossible to visit. The best time to visit is between January and early April, with January to March being the peak for the antelope migration. The **Gambela National Park Headquarters** (☏0475 510912; omotagwa@yahoo.com; admission per 24hr Birr200; ☺7am-noon & 3-5.30pm Mon-Fri) in Gambela organises the compulsory guides (Birr200 per day) and is where you pay your entrance fees and can offer sound advice.

If a mission into the park is too ambitious for you then an alternative is to visit the area around the small town of **Abobo**, 40km south of Gambela along a decent road. There's a pool and dam here that attracts some wildlife.

For any trips within the park, you'll really need to come with your own sturdy 4WD, but one can sometimes be rented from the park offices (per day Birr2000 excluding fuel).

In the north of the town is the **Anuak market**. Vendors sit in the shade of the trees selling cereals, firewood, large Nile perch and tobacco. To pass the time, many indulge in *akowyo* (water pipe) smoking. You can taste the *borde* (traditional 'beer'), served to thirsty marketgoers from metal buckets.

It's possible to visit both Nuer and Anuak villages. The Nuer villages on the outskirts of town, known as **New Land**, are the easiest to get to, but for those with their own wheels a better excursion is to the large village of **Itang** and its satellite hamlets some 51km west of Gambela along the excellent road leading to the South Sudan border. Itang, like Gambela itself, is home to both Nuer and Anuak peoples, and most residents live in traditional thatch-and-wattle huts of extraordinary complexity. The Nuer villages on the northern side of Itang tend to be the most receptive to visitors, but wherever you go you can expect to be the subject of extreme curiosity – foreign visitors are very rare indeed around here.

Whichever village you choose to visit, a local guide (Birr300 per group) is not just essential, but compulsory, as is a letter granting permission to enter a village (Birr100). Both guide and letter are provided by Gambela's Culture and Tourism Bureau (see p213) and take about 15 minutes to sort out. You'll also have to pay a little extra for any photos you take. Note that the Culture and Tourism Bureau is closed at weekends and on holidays so try to time your stay to coincide with weekdays. If you do arrive at the weekend try calling **Aychlum** (☑0917-804646), who works at the tourist office and will hopefully come and sort everything out for you.

## 🛏 Sleeping & Eating

Decent hotels and restaurants are not Gambela's forte. Having said that, at the time of research a couple of 'glossy' new hotels were under construction on the road into town – well, the architect's plans showed glossy hotels, but let's wait and see... All accommodation has cold-water showers only.

**Baro Gambella Hotel**     LODGE **$**
(☑0475-510044; s/tw Birr205/267) Locals might tell you that some of the town's newer hotels are better but, frankly, we beg to disagree. Yes, OK, the rooms might be worn and tired, but the birdsong-filled gardens and helpful management give this place real character. Add in a restaurant (mains Birr45 to Birr65) serving Western and Ethiopian dishes that

---

### THE ETHIOPIAN SLAVE TRADE

Ethiopia's slave trade was a lucrative one. From the 16th century right up to the 19th century, the country's main source of foreign revenue was from slaves. At the height of the trade, it's estimated that 25,000 Ethiopian slaves were sold every year to markets around the globe.

---

is hands down the best in town and all up you get a good place to stay. Room 11 has the hotel's only air-conditioner, although it's hard to know which is worse – putting up with the heat or the noise of the air-con. It was due for major renovation at the time of research so expect big changes in the future.

**Mider Genet Hotel**     HOTEL **$**
(☑0475-512212; d Birr150) This sky-blue new place, out along the road to the airport, offers good-value, large, clean rooms with comfy beds. There's a simple bar-restaurant out the front. Its biggest drawback is its distance from town, meaning only those with their own wheels are likely to want to stay here.

**Tadessech Hotel**     HOTEL **$**
(☑0475-510559; d/tw Birr300) This new, and modern, block on the main road into town has very ordinary rooms that are overpriced. However, it's an awful lot more enticing than some of the competition in town.

**Green Hotel**     HOTEL **$**
(d Birr100-200) A stone's throw from the bus station, the rooms here are simple, sparse and essentially clean. The difference between the room prices comes down to size and the addition of a TV.

## 🍷 Drinking

There is a string of **coffee and tea stalls** strung along the road following the Baro River. Perched on a log, coffee balanced precariously on one knee and surrounded by Nuer tribesman, this is travel at its rawest.

## ℹ Information

The electricity supply can only be described as erratic, and usually cuts out halfway through composing an email. If you get sick, head to Metu – Gambela's hospital is grim.

WESTERN ETHIOPIA GAMBELA

**Commercial Bank** (⊙7.30am-11.30am & 3-5.30pm Mon-Fri, 7.30-11.30am Sat) No ATM but it will reluctantly exchange US dollars and euros.

**Culture and Tourism Bureau** (✆0475-512351/512529; ⊙7am-12.30pm & 3-5pm Mon-Fri) If you're planning on visiting outlying villages or the national park make sure you don't arrive over a weekend because getting your permits sorted might be tricky.

**Gambela National Park Headquarters** (✆0475-510912/510918; ⊙7am-noon & 3-5.30pm Mon-Fri) Unusually useful and helpful when it comes to planning a trip to the national park.

**Kal Telecenter** (per min Birr0.30) The town's only internet cafe.

##  Getting There & Away

**Ethiopian Airlines** (✆0475-510099; www.flyethiopian.com) flies to and from Addis Ababa (Birr3413, 1¼ hours) on Wednesday, Friday and Sunday. Flights are frequently cancelled during the rainy season.

One bus leaves daily at 6am for Addis Ababa (Birr240, two days) overnighting en route. Another bus goes to Bedele (Birr100, nine hours, 6am departure) and several go to Metu (bus/minibus Birr64/80, three hours). An early-morning bus occasionally leaves for Tepi (Birr150, 12 hours), although it may be easier to go to Gore first and change there.

The border to South Sudan is firmly closed to foreigners (but locals can cross). However, there's local talk of this changing so it's worth enquiring. If it opens then buses go to the border town of Jikawo (Birr70, 4½ hours) daily at 6am.

##  Getting Around

A short hop in a shared *bajaj* around town costs Birr3, but they can be contracted for Birr15. The only option besides walking is cycling.

Ethiopian Airlines provides transport to and from the airport, which is 16.5km south of town. Passengers meet at the airline office first and, if the flight hasn't been cancelled, proceed to the airport together.

Both the Gambela National Park Headquarters and the Culture and Tourism Bureau claimed they could organise a 4WD (Birr2000 per day including driver but excluding fuel), but when push came to shove, it turned out both cars were inoperable. If you manage to hire the park's car then park entry and guide fees are waived.

# Understand
# Ethiopia

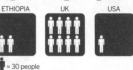

**population per sq km**

ETHIOPIA    UK    USA

≈ 30 people

# Ethiopia Today

» Area:
1,104,300
sq km

» Population:
91 million

» Life expect-
ancy: 56.56
years

» GDP per cap-
ita: US$1100

» Literacy rate:
42.7%

» Fertility rate:
5.39 per woman

» Highest point:
Ras Dajen
(4533m)

» Lowest Point:
Danakil Depres-
sion (-125m)

## Political Change

The year 2012 will go down in modern Ethiopian history as a year of great change. On 20 August of that year it was announced that Meles Zenawi, the man who had led the country since the overthrow of the Derg regime in 1991, had died. Zenawi had made economic growth and development his number-one priority and during his 21-year rule the country changed for the better, beyond all recognition of the Ethiopia Zenawi had inherited. Today, a new man, Hailemariam Desalegn, stands at the helm as acting prime minister (the next elections are scheduled for 2015). Though the governing Ethiopian People's Revolutionary Democratic Front (EPRDF) is solidly behind him, many observers wonder if he has the political clout to hold together such a diverse country and one that, despite its progress, remains blighted with problems and surrounded by such unstable neighbours as Eritrea, Somalia, Sudan and South Sudan.

## Religious Change

The year 2012 wasn't just a year of political change for Ethiopia: it was also a year of religious change. Just four days before the death of Meles Zenawi, the Patriarch of the Ethiopian Orthodox Church, Abune Paulos, died unexpectedly. Paulos had brought change to the Ethiopian Church and was largely credited with modernising it. Ethiopia had never before lost its political and spiritual leadership in such a short space of time. Paulos' successor, chosen in 2013, will face the challenge of retaining the traditional power of the Church while adapting to a country that, with a new political leader, may well change in unexpected ways.

## On Screen

» *In Search of Myths and Heros* The first in Michael Wood's sumptuously filmed series seeks the truth behind the Sheba legend.

» *Lost Kingdoms of Africa* Dr Gus Casely-Hayford explores ancient Ethiopian cultures and legends.

» *The Great Rift: Africa's Wild Heart* A finely crafted portrait of the Rift Valley and its wildlife.

» *Origins of Us* Exploring who we are and where we came from, this BBC series starts where it all began – Ethiopia.

## Ethiopian Icons

» Haile Gebrselassie: the world's most famous long-distance runner?

» Mohammed Hussein Al Amoudi: Ethiopia's richest man.

» Teddy Afro: Ethiopian singer.

» Liya Kebede: Ethiopian supermodel.

## belief systems
(% of population)

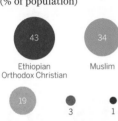

| | |
|---|---|
| 43 | 34 |
| Ethiopian Orthodox Christian | Muslim |

19   3   1

Protestant   Traditional   Other

## if Ethiopia were 100 people

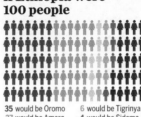

**35** would be Oromo   6 would be Tigrinya
27 would be Amara   4 would be Sidama
6 would be Somali   **22** would be other

## Progress

Ethiopia has been developing at an astonishing rate. In the nine years leading up to 2013, economic growth has, thanks to a huge investment in agriculture (particularly the flower-export market), been at record highs, sometimes reaching the giddy heights of 11%. Foreign investment has been tumbling into the country and the nation's infrastructure given a much needed overhaul. This is most notable in the transport system, which has been undergoing a major makeover, with Chinese road construction crews turning what have long been pot-hole-infested tracks into supersmooth highways. But this has not come without a price. The Gibe III dam (see p273) being only the most controversial. Elsewhere local farmers have complained of being forcibly removed from their land in order to make way for huge foreign-owned farming projects, and the government have been accused of cracking down on media freedom and political dissent.

Though a trend of urbanisation is starting to emerge, 83% of the people still live in rural areas.

## Foreign Relations

That Ethiopia is now a regional powerhouse is beyond doubt. The country is increasingly flexing its military and diplomatic muscles, whether this be in Somalia where the Ethiopian military is once again tackling Islamic militants or in UN-sponsored peace-keeping missions on the disputed Sudan–South Sudan border. One problem that never seems to get solved, though, is the ongoing border dispute with arch-enemy Eritrea. The two nations fought a bitter war between 1998 and 2000 and have come close to war since. For the moment a wary calm prevails, but everyone knows that the merest spark could re-ignite a war that neither country can afford.

## Dos & Don'ts

» Do take the time to talk with older Ethiopians – it's amazing how far Ethiopia has come in so short a time.

» Do learn a few words of Amharic – Ethiopians will open their hearts to you if you do.

» Do come with an open mind regarding Ethiopian history, legends and culture.

» Don't eat with your left hand.

» Don't attempt to enter a monastery if you're female unless specifically told it's OK.

## Conversations

» Football: after 31 years Ethiopia qualified for the 2013 Africa Cup. They'll be talking about this for years.

» Gibe III Dam: it'll change south Ethiopia, but for better or worse?

» Cost of living: it's going up and everyone has an opinion.

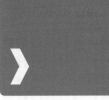

# Ethiopia's History

From the ancient Aksumite civilisation's obelisks to the fascinating architectural wonders of medieval Lalibela to the castles of Gonder to the communist monuments of the Derg, Ethiopia wears its history on its sleeve. And what a history it is.

## Cradle of Humanity?

In palaeoanthropology, where years are measured in tenths of millions, 40 years is less than a blink of an eye. However, 40 years worth of palaeoanthropological study can rock the very foundations of human history.

After Richard Leakey's discovery of skull 1470 near Kenya's Lake Turkana in 1972, which proved *Homo habilis* (the direct ancestor of *Homo sapiens*) had lived alongside *Australopithecus africanus* and therefore couldn't have evolved from them, the search was on for a new species that had branched into the genera *Homo* and *Australopithecus,* a species that would likely be Darwin's 'missing link'.

On 30 November 1974 Lucy was discovered in a dried-up lake near Hadar in Ethiopia's northeast. She was a new species, *A. afarensis,* and she miraculously walked on two legs 3.2 million years ago. Lucy's bipedal (upright walking) anatomy also shattered previous theories that hypothesised our ancestors only started walking upright after evolving larger brains. Lucy, the oldest and most complete hominid ever found, was famous and Ethiopia was tipped to claim the prize as the cradle of humanity.

After further finds in Ethiopia, including the 1992 discovery of the 4.4-million-year-old *A. ramidus,* whose foot bones hinted at bipedism, the ink on Ethiopia's claim was almost dry. However, recent computed-tomography (CT) scans on a six-million-year-old hominid skeleton *(Orrorin tugenensis)* found in Kenya in 2001, and computer-aided reconstruction of a six- to seven-million-year-old skull *(Sahelanthropus tchadensis)* in Chad seem to suggest that Lucy and *A. ramidus* may not be part of the direct line of human evolution, but rather a lateral branch of it.

Lucy was named after the Beatles' song 'Lucy in the Sky with Diamonds'. It was playing in the archaeologists' camp when she was discovered.

| TIMELINE | c 3.2 million BC | 3500–2000 BC | 2000–1500 BC |
|---|---|---|---|
| | Lucy collapses and awaits discovery and fame 3.2 million years down the line. Ethiopia uses her as the basis of its claim to be the birthplace of humankind. | The Ancient Egyptians trade with the Land of Punt, which many people consider to be somewhere on the Eritrean or Somalian coast. | Ge'ez, the precursor to the Amharic and Arabic languages, is developed somewhere in the vicinity of northern Ethiopia. Amazingly it is still spoken by priests in Ethiopia and Eritrea today. |

## WHICH HISTORY?

This chapter contains the factual 'real' history that historians like to use, but it's important to remember that for the majority of Ethiopians this isn't the history they believe in. In Ethiopia, like in much of Africa, legends concerning magical deeds, ghostly creatures and possibly nonexistent folk heroes are not just legends, but are taken as solid fact, and who cares if the historians say the dates and places don't add up! History is what you make of it and how you translate it, so just because there is no historical evidence proving that the Queen of Sheba existed, the people believe she did and recount it as their history, so in Ethiopia that makes her real. It is important to keep this in mind when travelling through Ethiopia. You will find this 'people's history' recounted throughout this book.

## Land of Punt

Though this period is shrouded in darkness, Ethiopia (and Eritrea) are believed to have formed part of the ancient Land of Punt, an area that attracted the trading ships of the Egyptian Pharaohs for millennia.

Many valuable commodities such as gold, myrrh, ivory and slaves were issued from the interior of the region and were exported from the coast.

It's thought the northern coastal region saw much migration from surrounding areas, and by 2000 BC it had established strong contacts with the inhabitants of southern Arabia.

## Pre-Aksumite Civilisation

The cultural significance of the southern Arabian and the East African cultures mixing was enormous. One consequence was the emergence of a number of Afro-Asiatic languages, including Ge'ez which laid the foundation for modern Amharic. Amazingly, Ge'ez script is still read by many Christian priests in Ethiopia.

Most significant was the rise of a remarkable civilisation in Africa's Horn in 1500 BC. The fact that the influence of southern Arabia was so clear (in the Sabaean script and in the worship of Sabaean gods), that the civilisation appeared to mushroom overnight and was very localised, and that it benefited from specialist crafts, skills and technologies previously unknown in the area, led many scholars throughout history to believe that the civilisation was actually spawned by Arabian settlers, and not Africans.

However, scholars of late argue with great conviction that this civilisation was indeed African and while undoubtedly influenced by Sabaean ideas, it developed from within from local effort and initiative.

**Top Sites for Ancient History**

» Aksum (p93)
» Yeha (p106)
» National Museum, Addis Ababa (p33)
» Melka Kunture Prehistoric Site & Tiya (p134)
» Dilla (p149)
» Lega-Oda (p185)

| 1500–400 BC | 955–587 BC | 400 BC–AD 200 | 200–500 |
|---|---|---|---|
| An Arabian-influenced civilisation rises in northern Ethiopia; the country's first capital, Yeha, is founded, but by whom? Historians remain uncertain whether Yeha and Africa ruled Arabia or Arabia ruled Yeha. | The Ark of the Covenant, the sacred chest built by Moses containing the Ten Commandments, vanishes from Jerusalem at some point in this period. | The great Aksumite kingdom is formed and thrives on Red Sea trade and rich natural resources. It is first mentioned in the 1st-century-AD book *Periplus of the Erythraean Sea*. | The Aksumite kingdom reaches its apogee. At its height the kingdom controls lands from the Nile to Arabia and is counted among the most powerful kingdoms of the ancient world. |

Whatever the origin, the civilisation was a very important one. The most famous relic of the times is the extraordinary stone 'temple' of Yeha.

# Kingdom of Aksum

The Aksumite kingdom, which grew to rank among the most powerful kingdoms of the ancient world, was the next civilisation to rise in present-day Ethiopia. The first written evidence of its existence (*Periplus of the Erythraean Sea,* written by a Greek-speaking Egyptian sailor) was from the 1st century AD, but by this point its realm of influence was wide, suggesting it rose to prominence much earlier. New archaeological evidence hints it may have emerged as early as 400 BC.

Aksum, its capital, is thought to have owed its importance to its position, situated at an important commercial crossroads. To the northwest lay Egypt, and to the west, near the present-day Sudanese border, were the rich, gold-producing lowlands. To the northeast, in present-day Eritrea, was the Aksumite port of Adulis, positioned at the crux of an extensive trading route. Exports included frankincense, grain, animal skins, rhino horn, apes and, particularly, ivory (tens of thousands of elephants were reported to roam the region). Imports of dyed cloaks, cheap unlined coats, glassware, and iron for making spears, swords and axes flowed in from Egypt, Arabia and India. Syrian and Italian wine and olive oil were also imported, as was much gold and silver plate for the king. The flourishing trade allowed the Aksumite kingdom to thrive.

Aksum also benefited from its well-watered agricultural lands, which were further exploited by the use of dams, wells and reservoirs.

Ethiopia was named by the Greeks, who saw the country as a far-off realm, populated by remarkable people and extraordinary animals. It means 'Land of the Burnt Faces'.

According to the Greek poet Homer (800 BC), the Greek gods, including Zeus himself, visited Ethiopia. Homer refers to the people as 'blameless Ethiopians'.

## THE DAYS BEFORE SHEBA

Historians might like to insist that little is known about the founding of the Aksumite Kingdom, but ask the average Ethiopian and they'll tell you something very different. Aksum, they will say, was founded by none other than the Great-Grandson of Noah, Aksumawi. His new kingdom flourished for a while, but one day Wainaba, a giant snake, 170 cubits long, attacked the city, killed the king and then ruled for 400 dark years. The snake was a foul-tempered and dangerous creature and in order to placate him the people of Aksum fed him a diet of milk and virgins. Eventually salvation came in the form of a man named Angabo who, crossing the Red Sea from the land of the Sabeans, offered to kill the serpent in exchange for the throne. The people of Aksum agreed, but rather than fighting the serpent as the Aksumites expected, Angabo proved himself wise and fed the serpent a goat laced in poison.

The kingdom quickly recovered, Angabo married and had a daughter. That daughter was named Makeda and on her father's death she became the woman we today know as the Queen of Sheba.

During its heyday between the 3rd and 6th centuries, the Aksumite kingdom stretched into large parts of southern Arabia, and west into the Sudanese Nile Valley. Aksumite society was rich, well organised, and technically and artistically advanced. During this era, an unparalleled coinage in bronze, silver and gold was produced and extraordinary monuments were built, all of which are visible in Aksum today. The kingdom also exerted the greatest influence of all on the future of Ethiopia: it introduced Christianity.

## The Coming of Christianity

The Ethiopian church claims that Christianity first reached Aksum at the time of the Apostles. According to the Byzantine ecclesiastical historian Rufinus, it arrived on Ethiopian shores by accident rather than by design, when two young Christian boys from the Levant were given to the King (for the full story on this see p246).

Whatever the truth of the matter, what's certain is that Christianity didn't become the state religion until around the beginning of the 4th century. King Ezana's stone inscription (p100) makes reference to Christ, and his famous coins bear the Christian cross – the world's first to do so.

The end of the 5th century AD brought the famous Nine Saints, a group of Greek-speaking missionaries from the Levant who established well-known monasteries in the north of the country, including Debre Damo (see p107). At this time, the Bible was first translated from Greek into Ge'ez.

Christianity shaped not just Ethiopia's spiritual and intellectual life, but also its cultural and social life, including its art and literature. Today almost half of Ethiopia's population is Orthodox Christian.

## The Coming of Islam & the Demise of Aksum

According to Muslim tradition, the Prophet Mohammed was nursed by an Ethiopian woman. Later, the Muslim Hadith (collection of traditions about Mohammed's life) recounts that Mohammed sent his daughter (and successor) along with some of his followers to Negash in AD 615, to avoid persecution in Arabia.

When things calmed in Arabia, most refugees returned home. However, Negash continues to be a crucial pilgrimage point for Ethiopia's Muslims.

Good relations between the two religions continued until at least King Armah's death. Thereafter, as the Arabs and Islam rose to prominence on the opposite side of the Red Sea, trade slowly shifted away from Christian Aksum and it eventually became isolated.

The ox and plough is thought to have been in use in Ethiopia for at least 3000 years. This same technology didn't appear in much of the rest of sub-Saharan Africa until early colonial times.

Those intrigued by the ancient civilisation of Aksum should pick up Professor David W Phillipson's *Ancient Ethiopia*. It's excellent and is an easy read.

King Ezana is thought to be the man behind the first church in Ethiopia. Built in the 4th century its remains can still be seen next door to the St Mary of Zion church in Aksum.

ETHIOPIA'S HISTORY THE COMING OF CHRISTIANITY

### 1137–1270

The Zagwe dynasty rises from Ethiopia's 'dark ages' and produces, with a little helping hand from a gang of angels, the astounding rock-hewn churches of Lalibela.

» Bet Abba Libanos (p122), Lalibela

### 1165–1600

Rumours about Prester John, a powerful Christian king based in Ethiopia, spread throughout Europe. Excitement mounts that he will help Christian Europe gain control of the Holy Lands.

## THE ARK OF THE COVENANT

'Mounted on his stead and dressed in robes of mysterious colour and wearing vestments that his forefather King David had worn when he led the Ark of Zion into Jerusalem, King Iyasu rode past the priests and deacons who had lined the road to greet him and entered the sanctuary of the Ark. Here he requested that the Priests bring forth the Ark of Zion. When it's carried to him the Ark is locked in a chest with seven seals, each of which has its own key and own technique for opening. The first six seals are opened but when the priests get to the seventh seal it will not open. But then, when the King himself stands before the Ark, the seventh seal miraculously springs open and the King speaks to the Ark and it replies and advises him on how to rule wisely.'

*From the Royal Chronicles of King Iyasu, 1691.*

Few other objects in history match the enduring legend of the Ark of the Covenant. But what is this Ark and is it really sitting inside a small Aksum chapel? The Old Testament says that the Ark was constructed on Mt Sinai by Moses, and that it houses the two stone tablets on which were inscribed the Ten Commandments. It is also said to contain the Rod of Aaron (Moses' brother) and a jar of manna (an edible substance that, according to Abrahamic doctrine, God provided for the Israelites during their travels in the desert). Other more recent descriptions of its contents include that of 17th-century Ethiopian Emperor Susenyos who said that it contained the 'figure of a woman with very large breasts'. Such a figure was common in ancient fertility beliefs.

In Old Testament days the Ark was housed in King Solomon's Great Temple in Jerusalem and was used by the Israelites as an oracle. It was also carried into battle. After the sacking of the Great Temple in 587 BC, the Bible falls silent as to the Ark's whereabouts – some say it was buried in a secret chamber under the Temple Mount in Jerusalem, and others say it was destroyed. But according to Ethiopian tradition, the Ark of the Covenant was carried

After Aksum's decline around AD 700, Ethiopia endured what is commonly known as its 'dark age'.

## Lalibela & the Zagwe Dynasty

The 12th century witnessed a new capital (Adafa) rise in the mountains of Lasta, not far from present-day Lalibela. It was established under a new power: the Zagwe dynasty.

Although the Zagwe dynasty reigned from around AD 1137 to 1270, and left the rock-hewn churches of Lalibela, this period is shrouded in mystery. Seemingly, no stones were inscribed, no chronicles written, no coins minted, and no accounts of the dynasty by foreign travellers have survived.

It's not certain what brought the Zagwe dynasty to an end; it was likely a combination of infighting within the ruling dynasty and local op-

Check out J Spencer Trimingham's *Islam in Ethiopia* for an insight into Ethiopia's second-most popular religion.

| 1270 | 1400 | 1400–1600 | 1490–1529 |
|---|---|---|---|
| Yekuno Amlak establishes the 'Solomonic dynasty' and Ethiopia enters its well-documented Middle Ages. | French aristocrat Duc de Berry sends the first European ambassador to Ethiopia. In turn, Ethiopians journey to Europe where many join churches, particularly in Rome. | The *Kebra Negast*, Ethiopia's national epic, is written. There remains much debate about the exact date it was written. | Mahfuz declares jihad on Christian Ethiopia and starts the bloody Muslim–Christian wars, the most costly in the country's history. His successor, Ahmed Gragn the Left-Handed, eventually defeats the emperor. |

off from Jerusalem and brought to Ethiopia in the 1st millennium BC by Menelik, the son of Solomon and Sheba (see p240). It's now believed to sit in Aksum's St Mary of Zion church compound (p97).

Today, every other Ethiopian church has a replica of the Ark (or more precisely the Tablets of Law that are housed in the Ark) known as the *tabot*. Kept safe in the *maqdas* (Holy of Holies or inner sanctuary), it's the church's single most important element, and gives the building its sanctity.

During important religious festivals, the *tabot* is carried in solemn processions, accompanied by singing, dancing, the beating of staffs or prayer sticks, the rattling of the sistrum (a sophisticated rattle, thought to be directly descended from an ancient Egyptian instrument used to worship Isis) and the beating of drums.

'They carried the Ark of God on a new cart...David and all the house of Israel were dancing before the Lord with all their might, with songs and lyres and harps and tambourines and castanets and cymbals.'

*2 Samuel 6:3–5*

That the chapel at Aksum contains something of great spiritual significance is undoubted, but is it the real Ark of the Covenant? The simple answer is that nobody actually knows. The biggest problem with Ethiopia's claim for the Ark is that if it was brought to the country by Menelik I, then why is its presence not widely mentioned in written documents until the 14th century? At the end of the day though, does it really matter what exactly is inside that Aksum chapel? The very fact that many people believe that this chapel contains the word of God should be enough to make it real.

position from the clergy. In 1270 the dynasty was overthrown by Yekuno Amlak; political power shifted south to the historical province of Shoa.

## The Ethiopian Middle Ages

Yekuno Amlak, claiming to be a descendant of King Solomon and Queen Sheba (see the boxed text, p240), established the 'Solomonic dynasty', which would reign for the next 500 years. His rule would also ring in the start of what's known as the Ethiopian Middle Ages, a period that, up until the modern age, was more documented than any other in the nation's past.

With its all-powerful monarchy and influential clergy, the Middle Ages were a continuation of the past. However, unlike the past, the kingdom's capitals were itinerant and were little more than vast, moving military

| 1529–42 | 1543–59 | 1550 | 1582 |
|---|---|---|---|
| Ahmed Gragn the Left-Handed expands his kingdom and by 1532 has taken most of eastern and southern Ethiopia. In 1542 he defeats a Portuguese/Ethiopian army near Lake Tana. | Emperor Galawdewos, with help from Portugal, finally defeats and kills Muslim raider Ahmed Gragn. Intermittent fighting continues for many years until Galawdewos is killed in an attack on Harar. | The Oromo people move north from Kenya and plunge the country into 200 more years of intermittent armed conflict. It's during this period that the walls of Harar are built. | Much of the Christian world adopts the revised Gregorian calendar, but Ethiopia stays with the Julian calendar – staying seven years behind the rest of us. |

## ITINERANT COURTS

During the Ethiopian Middle Ages, the business of most monarchs consisted of waging wars, collecting taxes and inspecting the royal domains.

Obliged to travel continuously throughout their far-flung empire, the kings led a perpetually nomadic existence. And with the rulers went their armies, courtiers and servants; the judges, prison officers and priests; the merchants; the prostitutes; and a whole entourage of artisans. The camps could spread over 20km; for transportation up to 100,000 mules were required.

The retinue was so vast that it rapidly exhausted the resources of the location. Four months was usually the maximum possible length of stay, and 10 years had to pass before the spot could be revisited.

The peasantry were said to dread the royal visits as they dreaded the swarms of locusts. In both cases, everything that lay in the path of the intruders was consumed.

camps. There was no longer minted coins, and trade was conducted by barter with pieces of iron, cloth or salt.

Culturally, the period was important for the significant output of Ge'ez literature, including the nation's epic *Kebra Negast* (p255). It was also at this time that contacts with European Christendom began to increase. With the rising threat of well-equipped Muslim armies in the East, Europe was seen as a Christian superpower.

Europe, for its part, dreamed of winning back Jerusalem from the 'Saracens', and realised the important strategic position occupied by Ethiopia. At the time, it was almost the only Christian kingdom outside Europe.

In the early 15th century, the first European embassy arrived in Ethiopia, sent by the famous French aristocrat Duc de Berry. Ethiopians in their turn began to travel to Europe, particularly to Rome, where many joined churches already established there.

Mahfuz timed his annual raids to take advantage of Christian Ethiopia's weakened state during their 55-day fast before Fasika (Orthodox Easter).

## The Muslim–Christian Wars

The first decades of the 16th century were plagued by some of the most costly, bloody and wasteful fighting in Ethiopian history, in which the entire empire and its culture came close to being wiped out.

From the 13th century, relations between Christian Ethiopia and the Muslim Ethiopian emirates of Ifat and Adal were showing signs of strain.

In the 1490s animosities came to a head. After establishing himself at the port of Zeila in present-day Somalia, a skilled and charismatic Muslim named Mahfuz declared a jihad against Christian Ethiopia. Emperor Lebna Dengel finally halted Mahfuz's incursions, but not before he had carried off huge numbers of Ethiopian slaves and cattle.

| 1629 | 1636 | 1706–21 | 1755–1855 |
|---|---|---|---|
| Emperor Susenyos converts to Catholicism and tries to force his people to do likewise. His subjects are not happy and in the civil war that follows an estimated 32,000 die. | Emperor Fasiladas founds Gonder, the first permanent capital since Lalibela; he also expels all foreigners from the empire. The new capital flourishes and Ethiopia enters another golden age. | The court in Gonder is thrown into turmoil as coups, assassination and court rumour become a virtual hobby for the people of the royal city. | Emperor Iyasu II dies and the central government in Gonder quickly collapses. Ethiopia slips back into the dark ages and a century of endless civil war and skirmishes follows. |

An even more legendary figure was Ahmed Ibn Ibrahim al Ghazi, nicknamed 'Ahmed Gragn the Left-Handed'. After overthrowing Sultan Abu Bakr of Harar, Ahmed declared his intention to continue the jihad of Mahfuz. Carrying out several raids into Ethiopian territory, he managed in March 1529 to defeat Emperor Lebna Dengel.

Ahmed then embarked on the conquest of all of Christian Ethiopia. Well supplied with firearms from Ottoman Zeila and southern Arabia, the Muslim leader had, by 1532, overrun almost all of eastern and southern Ethiopia.

In 1535 the Emperor Lebna Dengel appealed in desperation to the Portuguese, who were already active in the region. In 1542 an army of 400 well-armed musketeers arrived in Massawa (in present-day Eritrea), led by Dom Christovão da Gama, son of the famous mariner Vasco da Gama. They met Ahmed near Lake Tana, where he quickly routed them before lopping off the young and foolhardy head of Dom Christovão.

In 1543 the new Ethiopian emperor, Galawdewos, joined ranks with the surviving Portuguese force and met Ahmed at Wayna Daga in the west. This time, the Christians' huge numbers proved too powerful and Ahmed was killed.

## Oromo Migrations & the Jesuits

A new threat to the Ethiopian empire arose in the mid-16th century. The nomadic pastoralists and warrior horsemen of the Oromos began a great migration northwards from what's now Kenya.

For the next 200 years intermittent armed conflict raged between the empire and the Oromos.

Early in the 17th century the Oromo threat led several Ethiopian emperors to seek an alliance with the Portuguese-backed Jesuits. Two emperors, Za-Dengel and Susenyos, even went as far as conversion to Catholicism. However, imposing Catholicism on their population provoked widespread rebellion. Za-Dengel was overthrown and, in 1629, Susenyos' draconian measures to convert his people incited civil war.

Eventually Susenyos backed down and the Orthodox faith was reestablished. Susenyos' son and successor, Fasiladas, expelled the meddling Jesuits and forbade all foreigners from setting foot in his empire.

Recounting events over the past half a century across Africa, Martin Meredith's *The State of Africa* includes a couple of chapters on Ethiopia and is by far the best history of modern Africa currently available.

## The Rise & Fall of Gonder

In 1636, following the old tradition of his forefathers, Emperor Fasiladas decided to found a new capital. However, Gonder was different from its predecessors: it was to be the first permanent capital since Lalibela.

By the 17th century's close, Gonder boasted magnificent palaces, beautiful gardens and extensive plantations. It was also the site of sumptuous feasts and extravagant court pageantry, attracting visitors from around the world.

| 1855 | 1855–72 | 1872–76 | 1875–76 |
|---|---|---|---|
| Kassa Haylu outsteals, outwits and outmanoeuvres his rivals to become Emperor Tewodros; he unites a feuding Ethiopia and embarks on ambitious modernisation programs. | Tewodros builds numerous roads, establishes an army and promotes Amharic over Ge'ez as the language of everyday use. He also makes the mistake of imprisoning a group of Britons attending his court. | After helping the British dispose of Tewodros, Kassa Mercha wins the battle of succession with Emperor Tekla Giorgis and rises as Emperor Yohannes. | Egyptian forces attempt to invade the country, but Emperor Yohannes puts up a good fight and ends their ambitions. |

## FATHER OF MODERN ETHIOPIA

Considered the father of modern Ethiopia, Amda Seyon (also known as Gebre Meskel) ruled from 1314 to 1344. Known as a military mastermind, he vastly expanded the size of the Christian Empire through the use of force, and his rule is considered something of a golden age for Ethiopia. Military mastermind he may have been, but man of morals he wasn't. He was accused of sleeping with at least one of his sisters and marrying his father's concubine!

Under the ample patronage of Church and state, the arts and crafts flourished. Impressive churches were built, among them the famous De-bre Berhan Selassie, which can be seen to this day (p81). Outside Gonder, building projects included some remarkable churches at Lake Tana's historic monasteries (p72).

But not all was sweet in Gonder's court, and between 1706 and 1721 everyone from royal bodyguards, the clergy and nobles to ordinary citizens tried their hand at conspiracy. Assassination, plotting and intrigue became the order of the day, and the ensuing chaos reads like something out of Shakespeare's *Macbeth*. No fewer than three monarchs held power during this turbulent period, with at least one meeting a sticky, poisonous end. Emperor Bakaffa's reign (1721–30) briefly restored stability, during which time new palaces and churches were built, and literature and the arts once again thrived.

> It's hard to find but if Prester John's your man then sci-fi writer Robert Silverberg turns his hand to historical detective in the excellent book *The Realm of Prester John*.

However, by the time of Iyasu II's death in 1755, the Gonder kingdom was back in turmoil and the provinces started to rebel.

Between 1784 and 1855 the emperors were little more than puppets in the hands of rival feudal lords and their powerful provincial armies. The country disintegrated and civil war became the norm.

## Emperor Tewodros

After the fallout of Gonder, Ethiopia existed only as a cluster of separate and feuding fiefdoms. That was until the mid-19th century, when a unique man dreamt of unity.

Kassa Haylu, raised in a monastery and the son of a western chief, had first been a *shifta* (bandit) after his claim to his deceased father's fief was denied. However, he eventually became a Robin Hood figure, looting the rich to give to the poor. This gained him large numbers of followers and he began to defeat the rival princes, one after another, until in 1855 he had himself crowned Emperor Tewodros.

The new monarch soon began to show himself not just as a capable leader and strong ruler but as a unifier, innovator and reformer as

| 1888 | 1889 | 1889 | 1896 |
|---|---|---|---|
| Cattle imported by the Italians introduces a rinderpest epidemic. In combination with a severe drought and an increase in the locust population, a famine develops that was to last four years. | Yohannes' successor, Emperor Menelik, signs a friendship treaty with Italy and grants the region that is now Eritrea to Italy. | Addis Ababa, the New Flower, is founded and made capital of Ethiopia. | Emperor Menelik stuns the world by thrashing the Italian army in the Battle of Adwa. The 1889 Friendship Treaty is annulled and Italy recognises Ethiopian independence but hangs onto Eritrea. |

well. He chose Maqdala, a natural fortress south of Lalibela, as his base and there he began to formulate mighty plans. He established a national army, an arms factory and a great road network, as well as implementing a major program of land reform, promoting Amharic (the vernacular) in place of the classical written language, Ge'ez, and even attempting to abolish the slave trade.

But these reforms met with deep resentment and opposition from the land-holding clergy, the rival lords and even the common faithful. Tewodros' response, however, was ruthless and sometimes brutal. Like a tragic Shakespearean hero, the emperor suffered from an intense pride, a fanatical belief in his cause and an inflated sense of destiny. This would eventually be his downfall.

Frustrated by failed attempts to enlist European, and particularly British, support for his modernising programs, Tewodros impetuously imprisoned some Britons attending his court. Initially successful in extracting concessions, Tewodros overplayed his hand, and it badly miscarried. In 1868 large, heavily armed British forces, backed by rival Ethiopian lords, inflicted appalling casualties on Tewodros' men, many of them armed with little more than shields and spears.

Refusing to surrender, Tewodros played the tragic hero to the last and penned a final dramatic and bitter avowal before biting down on a pistol and pulling the trigger.

## Emperor Yohannes

In the aftermath of Tewodros' death, there arose another battle for succession. Using his weaponry gained from the British in exchange for his support of their Maqdala expedition, Kassa Mercha of Tigray rose to the fore. In 1871, at the battle of Assam, he defeated the newly crowned Emperor Tekla Giorgis.

After proclaiming himself Emperor Yohannes the following year, Kassa reigned for the next 17 years. In contrast to Tewodros, Yohannes staunchly supported the Church and recognised the independence of local lords.

Yohannes also proved himself a skilful soldier. In 1875, after the Egyptians had advanced into Ethiopia from the coastal area, Yohannes drew them into battle and resoundingly routed them at Gundat and then again at Gura in 1876.

But soon another power threatened: the Italians. The opening of the Suez Canal in 1869 greatly increased the strategic value of the Red Sea, which again became a passageway to the East and beyond.

In 1885 the Italians arrived in Massawa (in present-day Eritrea), and soon blockaded arms to Yohannes. The failure of the British to impede the arrival of the Italians made Yohannes furious. He accused them of contravening the 1884 Hewett Treaty. Though protesting otherwise, Britain

EMPEROR TEWODROS II

ETHIOPIA'S HISTORY EMPEROR YOHANNES

Philip Marsden tells the ultimately tragic tale of Emperor Tewodros II in his beautifully executed book on Ethiopia, *The Barefoot Emperor*.

| 1913–16 | 1915 | 1930 | 1931 |
|---|---|---|---|
| Emperor Menelik dies and Lij Iyasu takes over the reins of power before being deposed and succeeded by Menelik's daughter, Zewditu, who rules through a regent, Ras Tafari Makonnen. | Thanks to the shoe-making skills of two engineers the Djibouti–Addis Ababa rail line is completed, expanding Ethiopian trade and ushering in the rapid development of Addis Ababa. | After the death of Zewditu and years of careful posturing, Ras Tafari is crowned as Emperor Haile Selassie and dubbed the Chosen One of God. | Ethiopia gets its first written constitution, which grants Emperor Haile Selassie almost total power; his body is even declared sacred. |

privately welcomed the Italians, both to counter French influence on the Somali coast (in present-day Djibouti), and to deter Turkish ambitions.

Meanwhile, the Mahadists (or Dervishes) were raising their heads in the West. Dislodging the Egyptians and British, they overran Sudan before arriving in Ethiopia and eventually sacking Gonder in 1888.

Yohannes rushed to meet the Dervishes at Qallabat in 1889 but, at the close of yet another victory, he fell, mortally wounded by a sniper's bullet.

## Emperor Menelik

Menelik, King of Shoa since 1865, had long aspired to the imperial throne. Confined at Maqdala for 10 years by Tewodros, he was yet reportedly much influenced by his captor, and also dreamt of Ethiopia's unification and modernisation.

After his escape from Maqdala and his ascendancy in Shoa, Menelik concentrated on consolidating his own power, and embarked on an aggressive, ruthless and sometimes brutal campaign of expansion.

Relations with the Italians were at first good; Menelik had been seen as a potential ally against Yohannes. On Yohannes' death, the Italians recognised Menelik's claim to the throne and, in 1889, the Treaty of Wechale was signed. In exchange for granting Italy the region that was later to become Eritrea, the Italians recognised Menelik's sovereignty and gave him the right to import arms freely through Ethiopian ports.

However, a dispute over a discrepancy in the purportedly identical Amharic and Italian texts – the infamous Article 17 – led to disagreement. According to the Italian version, Ethiopia was obliged to approach other foreign powers through Italy, which essentially reduced Ethiopia to a lowly Italian protectorate. The Amharic version differed in its wording.

In the meantime, the Italians continued their expansion in their newly created colony of Eritrea. Soon, they were spilling into territory well beyond the confines agreed to in both treaties.

Despite the Italians' attempts to court Tigray's local chiefs, the latter chose to assist Menelik. Nevertheless, the Italians managed to defeat Ras Mangasha and his Tigrayan forces and occupied Mekele in 1895.

Provoked at last into marching north with his forces, Menelik shocked the international world by resoundingly defeating the Italians at Adwa (see The Battle of Adwa, p105). This battle numbered among the very few occasions when a colonial power was defeated by a native force in Africa. Ethiopia stood out as the only independent nation left in Africa.

Menelik then set his sights on modernisation. He abandoned the Shoan capital of Ankober and soon founded the new capital, Addis Ababa. During his reign, electricity and telephones were introduced; bridges, roads, schools and hospitals were built; and banks and industrial enterprises were established.

Donald N Levine's imaginative *Wax & Gold* provides outstanding insight into Amharic culture, though chapter six is rather far-fetched!

| 1935 | 1936 | 1936 | 1937 |
|---|---|---|---|
| Italy invades Ethiopia; illegal use of mustard gas and repeated bombing of civilian targets, including Red Cross hospitals, kills 275,000 Ethiopians; Italy loses 4350 men. | In 1936 the Italians capture Addis and Selassie flees the country. Mussolini triumphantly declares: 'Ethiopia is Italian'. The King of Italy is made Emperor of Ethiopia. | In June Haile Selassie makes a plea to the League of Nations asking for help, but the league lifts sanctions against Italy. | The 1700-year-old Aksum Obelisk is dismantled and removed from Ethiopia by the Italians. In 1998 Italy agrees to return it, but the Ethiopia–Eritrea war prevents it being returned until 2003. |

# Iyasu

Menelik died a natural death in 1913. Iyasu, his raffish young grandson and nominated heir, proved to be very much a product of the 20th century. Continuing with Menelik's reforms, he also showed a 'modern' secularist, nonsectarian attitude.

The young prince built mosques as well as churches, took several Muslim as well as Christian wives, and supported the empire's peripheral populations, which had for years suffered at the oppressive hands of Amharic settlers and governors.

Iyasu and his councillors pushed through a few reforms, including improving the system of land tenure and taxation, but they faced ever-deepening opposition from the church and nobility.

Finally, after also upsetting the allied powers with his dealings with the Weimar Republic (Germany), Austria and the Ottoman Empire, a pretext for his removal was found. Accused by the nobles of 'abjuring the Christian faith', the prince was deposed in 1921.

Zewditu, Menelik's daughter, was proclaimed empress. Things were not plain sailing for her, though. Zewditu had a rival to the throne, Ras Tafari (the son of Ras Makonnen, Menelik's cousin, and grandson of an earlier Showan monarch). The conservative Ethiopian aristocracy largely supported Zewditu, but they had severe misgivings about other members of her family. In the end a kind of 'power sharing' agreement was reached with Zewditu being empress and Ras Tafari proclaimed the prince regent.

# Ras Tafari

Prince Ras Tafari boasted more experience and greater maturity than Iyasu, particularly in the field of foreign affairs.

In 1923 Tafari pulled off a major diplomatic coup by securing Ethiopia entry into the League of Nations. Membership firmly placed Ethiopia on the international political map, and also gave it some recourse against the grasping designs of its European, colonial neighbours.

Continuing the tradition begun by Menelik, Tafari was an advocate of reform. A modern printing press was established as well as several secondary schools and an air force. In the meantime, Tafari was steadily outmanoeuvring his rivals. In 1930 the last rebellious noble was defeated and killed in battle. A few days later the sick empress also died. Ras Tafari assumed the throne.

# Emperor Haile Selassie

On 2 November 1930 Tafari was crowned Emperor Haile Selassie. The extravagant spectacle was attended by representatives from across the

*The Emperor* by Ryszard Kapuscinski offers bizarre insights into Haile Selassie's imperial court through interviews with servants and close associates of the emperor. Some historians question its authenticity though.

» Obelisks (p95), Aksum

**1940–50**

Ethiopia establishes its first national bank, a new national currency, its first university and its first (and only) airline – Ethiopian Airlines.

**1941–42**

British Commonwealth and Ethiopian forces liberate Ethiopia from Italian occupation; Haile Selassie reclaims his throne and Ethiopia its independence. In the following years the country modernises rapidly.

globe and proved a terrific public-relations exercise. It even led indirectly to the establishment of a new faith, Rastafarianism (see p138).

The following year, Ethiopia's first written constitution was introduced. It granted the emperor virtually absolute power. The two-house parliament consisted of a senate, which was nominated by the emperor from among his nobles; and a chamber of deputies, which was elected from the landholders. It was thus little more than a chamber for self-interested debate.

Ever since the day of his regency, the emperor had been bringing the country under centralised rule. For the first time, the Ethiopian state was unambiguously unified.

## Italian Occupation

By the early 20th century Ethiopia was the only state in Africa to have survived European colonisation. However, Ethiopia's position between the two Italian colonies of Eritrea and Somalia made it an enticing morsel.

From 1933, in an effort to undermine the Ethiopian state, Italian agents, well heeled with funds, were dispatched to subvert the local chiefs, as well as to stir up ethnic tensions. Britain and France, nervous of pushing Mussolini further into Hitler's camp, refrained from protests and turned a blind eye.

In 1934 a minor skirmish known as the Wal Wal incident took place between Italian and Ethiopian forces. Italy had found its pretext.

On 3 October 1935 Italians, overwhelmingly superior in both ground and air forces, invaded Ethiopia from Eritrea. First the northern town of Aksum fell, then Mekele.

The League of Nations issued sanctions against Italy, but their enforcement by various European nations was lacklustre and had little impact.

### Campaigning

Terrified that the international community would impose more serious embargoes, and keen to keep Italian morale high, Il Duce pressed for a swift campaign.

Impatient with progress made, he soon replaced De Bono, his first general. Pietro Badoglio, his replacement, was authorised 'to use all means of war – I say all – both from the air and from the ground'. Implicit in the instructions was the use of mustard gas, which contravened the 1926 Geneva Convention.

Despite overwhelming odds, the Ethiopians succeeded in launching a major counterattack, known as the Christmas Offensive, at the Italian position at Mekele at the end of 1935. However, the Italians were

The second edition of Bahru Zewde's widely acclaimed *A History of Modern Ethiopia 1855–1991* contains two particularly readable sections: Harold G Marcus' *Ethiopia* and Richard Pankhurst's *The Ethiopians.*

| 1960 | 1962 | 1962 | 1972–74 |
|---|---|---|---|
| In response to growing discontent over the emperor's autocratic rule, the imperial bodyguard stage a coup d'etat, which is defeated by the army and air force. | Addis Ababa is made the headquarters of the Organisation of African Unity. | Haile Selassie unilaterally annexes Eritrea; separatist Eritreans launch a bitter guerrilla war. | A dreadful famine strikes and around 200,000 people die. This further increases resentment towards the emperor, and students start protesting. |

soon on the offensive again. Backed by hundreds of planes, cannons and weapons of every type, the Italian armies swept across the country.

Meanwhile, Emperor Haile Selassie had fled Ethiopia (some Ethiopians never forgave him for it) to present Ethiopia's cause to the world. On 30 June 1936 he made his famous speech to the League of Nations in Geneva. However the league lifted the sanctions later that year against Italy – only the USSR, the USA, Haiti, Mexico and New Zealand refused to recognise Italy's conquest.

## THE BEST ETHIOPIAN BOOKS

With a country as endlessly fascinating as Ethiopia it's little surprise that a small library of books has been written documenting Ethiopia's wonders. The following are our favourites:

» *The Chains of Heaven,* by Philip Marsden. If you're going to read one book on Ethiopia make it this one. The author walks across the north Ethiopian plateau and in the process reveals much about Ethiopian culture and history.

» *Sheba: Through the Desert in Search of the Legendry Queen,* by Nicholas Clapp. Successfully blending personal travel accounts through Ethiopia, Yemen and elsewhere with thorough academic research to shed light on one of history's most famous characters.

» *Eating the Flowers of Paradise,* by Kevin Rushby. The author travels the old trade route from Ethiopia to Yemen. Chewing *chat* leaves with everyone he meets, Rushby reveals much about the culture surrounding this drug.

» *The Prester Quest,* by Nicholas Jubber. An entertaining voyage from Venice to Ethiopia tracing the story behind Prester John.

» *The Sign and the Seal,* by Graham Hancock. Hancock attempts to solve the mystery of the 'disappearance' of the Ark of the Covenant. Though his research and conclusions raised an eyebrow or two among historians, this detective story is very readable – however tenuous the facts may be!

» *In Search of King Solomon's Mines,* by Tahir Shah. A riveting quest to find the mythical gold mines of King Solomon. In typical Shah fashion it's full of magic and bizarre encounters.

» *The Mountains of Rasselas,* by Thomas Pakenham. The authors fascination with the historical anecdotes revolving around Ethiopia's *ambas* (flat-topped mountains) is the basis of this engaging and nicely illustrated coffee-table book.

» *Remote People,* by Evelyn Waugh. Although very dated, this book includes some wry impressions of Ethiopia in the 1930s.

» *Les Afars d'Éthiopie,* by Jean-Baptiste Jeangène Vilmer and Franck Gouéry (in French). Beautiful images of the Danakil, and descriptions of the Afar and other peoples who make their lives in this harshest of climates.

| **1974** | **1975** | **1975** | **1976–90** |
|---|---|---|---|
| After years of growing discontent and increasing street protests, Haile Selassie is unceremoniously deposed as emperor on 12 September. The Derg declare a socialist state on 20 December. | The last emperor of Ethiopia, Haile Selassie, dies while in custody. The cause of death is unknown but many believe he was smothered with a pillow by Mengistu. | The Tigrayan People's Liberation Front is founded. Its first attacks are a raid on a jail and a bank robbery in Aksum in 1975. It goes on to launch a war for autonomy. | Collectivisation of agriculture begins and forced resettlement and villageisation takes place. One of the stated goals is to help reduce famine. Most experts believe it had the opposite effect. |

## Occupation & Resistance

Soon Ethiopia, Eritrea and Somalia were merged to become the colonial territory of 'Africa Orientale Italiana' (Italian East Africa).

Hoping to create an important economic base, Italy invested heavily in its new colony. From 1936 as many as 60,000 Italian workers poured in to work on Ethiopia's infrastructure.

Ethiopia kept up a spirited resistance to Italian rule throughout its brief duration. Italy's response was famously brutal. Mussolini personally ordered all rebels to be shot, and insurgencies were put down using large-scale bombing, poison gas and machine-gunning from the air.

Ethiopian resistance reached a peak in February 1937 with an assassination attempt on the much-hated Italian viceroy, Rodolfo Graziani. In reprisal, the Italians spent three days shooting, beheading or disembowelling several thousand people in the capital.

The 'patriot's movement' (the resistance fighters) was mainly based in the historical provinces of Shoa, Gonder and Gojam, but drew support from all parts of the country; many fighters were women.

Graziani's response was simple: 'Eliminate them, eliminate them, eliminate them'. But Ethiopian resolve stiffened and resistance grew. Although in control of major towns, Italy never conquered the entire country.

The outbreak of WWII, particularly Italy's declaration of war against Britain in 1940, dramatically changed the course of events. Britain at last reversed its policy of tacit support of Italy's East African expansion and initially offered Ethiopia assistance on the Sudan–Ethiopia border. Later, in early 1941, Britain launched three major attacks.

Though not then widely recognised, the Ethiopian patriots played a major role before, during and after the liberation campaign, which ended on 5 May 1941 when the emperor and his men entered Addis Ababa.

The ultimate guide to the historical treasures of the north is Stuart Munro-Hay's *Ethiopia: The Unknown Land: A Cultural and Historical Guide*.

## Postliberation Ethiopia

The British, who'd entered Ethiopia as liberators, initially seemed to have simply replaced Italy as occupiers. However, Anglo-Ethiopian treaties in 1942 and 1944 eventually marked Ethiopia's resumption of independence.

The 1940s and '50s saw much postwar reconstruction, including (with US assistance) the establishment of a new government bank, a national currency, and the country's first national airline, Ethiopian Airlines.

In 1955 the Revised Ethiopian Constitution was introduced. Although for the first time the legislature included an elected chamber of deputies, the government remained autocratic and the emperor continued to hold all power.

In 1962 Addis Ababa became the headquarters of the Organisation of African Unity (OAU) and, in 1958, of the UN Economic Commission for Africa (ECA).

| 1977 | 1977–78 | 1977–78 | 1984 |
|---|---|---|---|
| Colonel Mengistu Haile Mariam emerges as leader of the Derg. He appeals to the Soviet Union and Cuba among others for aid. | Somalia invades the Ogaden region of Ethiopia. Somali forces are eventually defeated in 1978, but only with massive help from Cuban and Soviet forces. | The Derg launch a violent crackdown on opponents; thousands die in what becomes known as the Red Terror campaign. | Israel launches 'Operation Moses', a six-week operation to secretly airlift 8000 Ethiopian Jews to Israel. |

# Discontent

Despite modernisation, the pace of development was slow, and dissatisfaction with it, and with the emperor's autocratic rule, began to grow. Finally, taking advantage of a state visit to Brazil in December 1960, the emperor's imperial bodyguard staged a coup d'etat. Though put down by the army and air force, it signalled the beginning of the end of imperial rule in Ethiopia.

Discontent simmered among the students too, who protested in particular against land tenure, corruption and the appalling famine of 1972–74 in which an estimated 200,000 died.

Meanwhile, international relations had also been deteriorating. In 1962 Ethiopia abrogated the UN-sponsored federation with Eritrea and unilaterally annexed the Eritrean state.

Then war broke out in 1964 with Somalia over joint claims to Ethiopia's Somali-inhabited region of the Ogaden Desert.

## The 1974 Revolution & the Emperor's Fall

By 1973 an increasingly powerful and radical military group had emerged. Known as the Derg (Committee), they used the media with consummate skill to undermine the authority of the emperor himself. They famously flashed striking footage of starvation from Jonathan Dimbleby's well-known BBC TV report on the Wolo famine in between clips of sumptuous palace banquets.

The result was an unprecedented wave of teacher, student and taxi strikes in Addis Ababa. Even army mutinies began to be reported. At crisis point, the prime minister and his cabinet resigned and a new one was appointed with the mandate to carry out far-reaching constitutional reforms. But it was too late.

On 12 September 1974 Emperor Haile Selassie was deposed, unceremoniously bundled into the back of a Volkswagen and driven away to prison. Ministers, nobles and close confidants of the emperor were also arrested by the Derg. The absolute power of the emperor and the divine right of rule of the century-old imperial dynasty were finished.

The Derg soon dissolved parliament and established the Provisional Military Administrative Council (PMAC) to rule the country.

Emerging as the leader of the Derg was Colonel Mengistu Haile Mariam who rode the wave of popular opposition to Selassie's regime, as well as the Marxist-Leninist ideology of left-wing students.

And what happened to the emperor? The official line at the time was that he died of 'respiratory failure' in August 1975 following complications from a prostate operation. However, many people believe he was murdered by Mengistu himself. In 1992, after the fall of the Derg, Selassie's

Aidan Hartley's *The Zanzibar Chest* recalls his days as a foreign correspondent throughout Africa and includes chapters on the last days of the Derg. It's one of the most powerful and wonderfully crafted books you could hope to read.

**ETHIOPIA'S HISTORY** DISCONTENT

| 1984–85 | 1991–93 | 1992 | 1993 |
|---|---|---|---|
| Famine haunts much of highland Ethiopia and up to a million people die. The reasons for the famine are climatic and political. A huge relief operation spearheaded by Bob Geldof is launched. | The Derg are defeated by the rebel EPRDF; Ethiopia's experiment with communism ends, and Mengistu scuttles off to Robert Mugabe's Zimbabwe where he remains to this day. | Haile Selassie's remains are found buried under a toilet in the royal palace. He is finally reburied eight years later in the Holy Trinity Cathedral. Turn out is much lower than funeral organisers predicted. | Following a referendum Eritrea finally gets its long-sought independence. Relations between the two new neighbours are excellent. |

FAMINE

bones were discovered buried under a concrete slab in the grounds of the palace in Addis.

## The Socialist Experiment

On 20 December 1974 a socialist state was declared. Under the adage *Ityopya Tikdem* or 'Ethiopia First', banks, businesses and factories were nationalised as was the rural and urban land. However, few of the projects launched by the Derg proved to be successful and agricultural output stagnated.

In the meantime, the external threats posed by Somalia and secessionist Eritrea were increasing. The Derg responded to these threats with a wave of mass arrests and executions. In July 1977 Somalia invaded Ethiopia. Thanks to the intervention of the Soviet Union, which flooded socialist Ethiopia with Soviet state-of-the-art weaponry, Somalia was beaten back. In Eritrea, however, the secessionists continued to thwart Ethiopian offensives.

Meanwhile internal political debate also degenerated into violence. The leadership of the Derg split into two groups, with one, the Ethiopian People's Revolutionary Party (EPRP) proclaiming that the Derg had 'betrayed the revolution'. Verbal violence between the two groups quickly turned to physical violence and the then Vice-Chairman of the Derg, Mengistu, used the unstable political situation to justify a purge of the upper echelons of the Derg. The result was the execution of a number of party leaders and the promotion of himself to undisputed leader of the Derg.

### Red Terror

Shortly afterwards, in an effort to suppress all political opponents, Mengistu launched the Red Terror campaign with an infamous speech in Addis Ababa that involved him smashing three bottles filled with what appeared to be blood on the ground and proclaiming 'Death to counter revolutionaries! Death to the EPRP!'. The Red Terror turned out to be a highly appropriate name as, at a very conservative estimate, 100,000 people were killed (Amnesty International estimates the number may have been as high as 500,000) and thousands more fled the country.

Families of victims of the Red Terror were ordered to pay for the cost of the bullet that killed their relatives before the victim's body was returned. Anyone who was suspected of being opposed to the Derg was liable to arrest or execution. At the height of the Red Terror, the general secretary of Save The Children stated: '1000 children have been killed and their bodies are left in the street and are being eaten by wild hyenas.

In the past, the causes of famine have had less to do with environmental factors – Ethiopia has abundant natural resources – and more to do with economic mismanagement and inequitable and oppressive governments.

| 1995 | 1996 | 1997 | 1998–2000 |
|---|---|---|---|
| The Federal Democratic Republic of Ethiopia is proclaimed and elections are held. Former guerrilla leader Meles Zenawi is proclaimed prime minister. | The Italian Ministry of Defence finally admits to the use of mustard gas in the Abyssinian campaign. | Eritrea drops the birr as its national currency and introduces the nakfa. This leads to a souring of the relationship between the two neighbours. | Ethiopia and Eritrea's leaders go to war over a sliver of barren wasteland. By the close of hostilities 70,000 have died and tens of thousands are internally displaced. |

You can see the heaped-up bodies of murdered children, most of them aged 11 to 13, lying in the gutter, as you drive out of Addis Ababa'.

## The Demise of the Derg

Red Terror only cemented the stance of those opposing the Derg. Numerous armed liberation movements arose, including those of the Afar, Oromo, Somali and particularly Tigrayan peoples. For years, with limited weaponry, they fought the military might of the Soviet-backed Derg, which had the second-largest army in sub-Saharan Africa.

The various opposition groups eventually united to form the Ethiopian People's Revolutionary Democratic Front (EPRDF), which in 1989 began its historic military campaign towards Addis Ababa.

The Derg was doubly confronted by the EPRDF in Ethiopia and the Eritrean People's Liberation Front (EPLF) in Eritrea. With the fall of his allies in Eastern Europe, and with his state in financial ruin as well as his own military authority in doubt, Mengistu's time was up and he fled the country on 21 May 1991. Seven days later, the EPRDF entered Addis Ababa and the Derg was done.

When the EPRDF rolled into Addis Ababa it was navigating with photocopies of the Addis Ababa map found in Lonely Planet's *Africa on a Shoestring*.

### FAMINE IN ETHIOPIA

If there's one word everyone associates with Ethiopia it's 'famine'. The country has regularly been plagued by drought, food shortages and famine. The famine of 1972–74 in Wolo and other northern provinces, and the governments mishandling of it, added greatly to the general dissatisfaction with the government, and this contributed to the fall of Selassie and the Imperial government.

The most infamous famine of all was that of 1984–86, in which between 400,000 and a million people died. Though the conditions that led to famine are widely blamed on drought, it's been shown that widespread drought conditions actually occurred only some months after the famine was underway and that for many areas the harvest of 1982 delivered something of a bumper crop. Instead, the major cause was the civil unrest and rebellions taking place in many parts of the country, the failed government resettlement campaigns, communal farms and 'villageisation' programs – all of which aggravated the disaster in many areas. In addition Derg leader Mengistu's disinclination to help the province of Tigray – the worst affected region and home to the powerful Tigrayan People's Liberation Front (TPLF) – caused thousands more to die.

Drought continues to haunt the Horn of Africa today. A severe drought, said by many to be the worst in 60 years, affected (and at the time of writing continues to affect) a large part of eastern Africa. However, with a much more organised national and international response the death toll has been far lower and famine was declared only in parts of war-torn Somalia.

| 2000–01 | 2001 | 2005 | 2006 |
|---|---|---|---|
| A formal peace agreement is signed by Ethiopia and Eritrea and a demilitarised zone is established along the border under the supervision of the UN Mission in Ethiopia & Eritrea (UNMEE). | Two Ethiopian scientists discover possible human fossils dating back some 5.8 to 5.2 million years. They are tentatively named as a subspecies of *Ardipithecus ramidus kadabba*. | After 15 May elections, mass protests turn deadly when government troops fire on unarmed demonstrators. Thousands of people, including opposition politicians, journalists and newspaper editors are detained by police. | Construction begins on the controversial Gibe III dam, the biggest dam project in Africa. Debate rages over whether the dam will bring advantages or disadvantages. |

Mengistu received asylum in Zimbabwe, where he remains to this day, despite being tried in absentia in Ethiopia and sentenced to death.

## The Road to Democracy (1991–95)

After the war of liberation Ethiopia showed zeal and determination to rebuild the country.

In July 1991 a transitional charter was endorsed, which gave the EPRDF-dominated legislature a four-year, interim rule under the executive of the TPLF leader, Meles Zenawi. First and foremost, Mengistu's failed socialist policies were abandoned, and de facto independence was granted to Eritrea.

In August 1995 the Federal Democratic Republic of Ethiopia was proclaimed, a series of elections followed, and the constitution of the second republic was inaugurated. Meles Zenawi formed a new government.

## Ethiopia–Eritrea War

Despite being friends and having fought against the Derg side by side for more than a decade, Meles Zenawi and Eritrea's president, Isaias Afewerki, soon clashed. The cause? Eritrea's introduction of the nakfa currency to replace the Ethiopian birr in November 1997.

In early May 1998 a number of Eritrean officials were killed near the border. On 12 May Eritrea upped the stakes by occupying the border town of Badme. Over the next month there was intense fighting between the two sides. In early June the Ethiopians launched air raids on the airport in Asmara to which the Eritreans retaliated by bombing Mekele airport. In both cases civilians were killed.

In February 1999 a full-scale military conflict broke out that left tens of thousands dead on both sides before it finally ceased for good in mid-2000. During this time there were mass exportations of Eritreans from Ethiopia and Ethiopians from Eritrea.

Although Ethiopia had agreed to peace earlier, it wasn't until Ethiopia recaptured all territory and went on to occupy parts of central and western Eritrea that Eritrea finally agreed to a ceasefire.

In December 2000 a formal peace settlement was signed in Algiers. In April 2001 a 25km-wide demilitarised strip, which ran the length of the internationally recognised border on the Eritrean side, was set up under supervision of the UN Mission in Ethiopia and Eritrea (UNMEE).

In late 2005 a commission at the Permanent Court of Arbitration in the Hague ruled that Eritrea broke international law when it attacked Ethiopia in 1998 and triggered the war.

Since the guns fell silent there have been periods of extreme tension between the two nations that have seen forces massed on both sides of

Although only published locally, *Eritrea's War* by Paul Henze delves into the 1998–2000 Ethiopia–Eritrea War.

| 2006–09 | 2006–09 | 2007 | 2008 |
|---|---|---|---|
| Ethiopia invades Somalia in order to dislodge the Islamic Courts Union. It becomes embroiled in a guerrilla war and finally pulls out in early 2009. | Tensions between Ethiopia and Eritrea come close to boiling over and both sides begin massive troop build-ups in the border region. Fortunately tensions subside and war is averted. | In September Ethiopia celebrates the new millennium. Why is it seven years 'late'? It uses a different calendar to Western countries. | The UNMEE mandate expires after 'crippling restrictions' from Eritrea, and UN troops withdraw from the border region, leaving the two nations eyeing each other nervously. |

the border, and today the two armies continue to eye each other suspiciously over the desert.

## Protests & Invasions

The 15 May 2005 elections returned the EPRDF and Zenawi to power, but while the election run-up and the voting polls were witness to few irregularities, there were numerous reports by EU observers about questionable vote counting at the constituency level and the announcing of the results by state-run media.

In the years leading up to the elections, discontent with the government had been growing and then, during the election campaigning, opposition parties alleged cases of intimidation and arrests of their supporters. On the morning of 15 May, when the first results were first announced, it appeared that the opposition parties had made sweeping gains, but then later that afternoon the EPRDF announced that, aside from in Addis itself, it had in fact won a majority of seats. Straight away opposition parties and supporters cried foul play and mass protests broke out in Addis. Government troops arrested thousands of opposition-party members and killed 22 unarmed civilians. Similar protests and mass strikes occurred in early November, which resulted in troops killing 46 civilians and arresting thousands more. Leaders of political party Coalition for Unity and Democracy, as well as owners of private newspapers, were also arrested and charged with inciting the riots. The government's actions were condemned by the EU and many Western governments, but the election result stood.

In 2006 Ethiopia launched an invasion of Somalia in order to dislodge the Islamic Courts Union (ICU), which had gained control of much of the country (and ironically brought the first semblance of peace Somalia had seen in years). By the end of the year Ethiopian troops had pushed the ICU back to the far south of Somalia, but they soon found themselves tangled up in a messy guerrilla war, with the ICU slowly beginning to win back lost ground. Many observers suspected that Eritrea was secretly arming and aiding the ICU in its war with Ethiopia. Unwilling to get bogged down in a long and bloody battle in Somalia, Ethiopia called for an African Union (AU) force to take its place and the Ethiopians began to withdraw in early 2009.

Despite the official withdrawal, the Ethiopian military made repeated incursions over the border to fight al-Shabaab (the Islamic militant group who rapidly replaced the ICU after their demise, and quickly came to control much of southern Somalia) throughout the remainder of 2009 and up to 2011. Many of these incursions were denied by the Ethiopian government. In late 2011 the Ethiopian military, working with the

**Best Historical Museums**

» Ethnological Museum, Addis Ababa (p32)
» National Museum, Addis Ababa (p33)
» Archaeological Museum, Aksum (p97)
» St George Cathedral & Museum, Addis Ababa (p36)
» 'Red Terror' Martyrs Memorial Museum, Addis Ababa (p36)
» Sherif Harar City Museum, Harar (p187)
» Wolega Museum, Nekemte (p200)

| 2010 | 2011 | 2012 | 2012 |
|---|---|---|---|
| Colonel Mengistu Haile Mariam announces he is writing his memoirs. In 2012 a leaked version, entitled *Tiglatchn*, appears on the internet. | In late 2011 Ethiopian forces, in an effort to support the government of Somalia in their battle against al-Shabaab militants, re-enter Somalia alongside a coalition of African Union and Kenyan troops. | Ethiopia jails prominent journalist Eskinder Nega for 18 years for violating the country's anti-terrorism legislation after he wrote an article questioning arrests under that very same act. | Ethiopia's most acclaimed modern artist, Afewerk Tekle, dies. |

## THE DEATH OF A PATRIARCH

In 2012 Ethiopia didn't just mourn for Zenawi, but also for Abune Paulos, the patriarch of the Ethiopian Orthodox Church who died suddenly at the age of 76 just four days before the death of the prime minister.

Jailed by Mengistu in the 1970s he later fled to the US and remained there in exile until the overthrow of the Derg. He became head of the Church in 1992 and has been credited for modernising it.

An election to decide the next patriarch is due to be held as this book goes to print.

transitional government, AU forces and the Kenyan military, officially re-entered Somalia as part of a concerted drive to destroy al-Shabaab.

Despite a slightly condescending view of the 'primitive negroes' Alan Moorehead's *The Blue Nile*, which depicts the history of the river, land and those who sought its source, remains a classic of the genre.

## The End of an Era

The elections of 2010 saw Zenawi and the EPRDF returned to power. This time there was none of the violence that marked the 2005 election but international observers criticised the elections saying they fell short of international standards. Human Rights Watch claimed the government had a strategy of systematically closing down space for political dissent and independent criticism.

In July 2012 rumours began to circulate that Zenawi, who hadn't been seen in public for some weeks, had died. The government denied these rumours but admitted that Zenawi had been hospitalised, but that his condition was not serious. On 20 August 2012 it was announced that after 21 years of leading Ethiopia, Zenawi had died of an infection contracted after an operation to remove a brain tumour.

**2012**

The Patriarch of the Ethiopian Coptic Church, Abune Paulos, dies unexpectedly.

**2012**

On 20 August it is announced that Meles Zenawi, the man who has dominated the Ethiopian and regional political scene for 21 years has died.

**2012**

The government announces that Hailemariam Desalegn, from southern Ethiopia, is to be the acting prime minister until elections in 2015. The transition of power runs smoother than many dared hope.

**2012**

The Ethiopian national football team qualifies for the 2013 Africa Cup, the first time it has managed this in 31 years. Ethiopians celebrate as if they've already won the cup!

# Ethiopian Culture

Encompassed on all sides by the enemies of their religion, the Aethiopians slept near a thousand years, forgetful of the world, by whom they were forgotten.
Edward Gibbon, *The History of the Decline and Fall of the Roman Empire, 1776–88*

## Who Are the Ethiopians?

The Ethiopians are nothing if not proud, and for good reason. To them, Ethiopia has stood out from all African nations and proved itself to be a unique world of its own – home to its own culture, language, script, calendar and history. Ethiopian Orthodox Christians and Muslims alike revel in the fact that Ethiopia was the only nation on the continent to successfully fight off colonisation. So strong is this sense of being unique that it's not unusual to here Ethiopians refer to people from other parts of Africa as 'Africans', as if they themselves were nothing to do with the rest of the continent!

But with their pride comes other traits. The Ethiopians can be a stubborn, violent and xenophobic people; but on the flipside they can be incredibly gregarious, warm, welcoming and kind and will often go miles out of their way to help a stranger. Proud though they are, it wasn't long ago that many Ethiopians seemed desperate to be somebody else. Many of the younger generations, brought up on hand-outs by aid agencies, were anything but proud of Ethiopia and sometimes it felt as if every other young Ethiopian you met, at least in urban areas, wanted to run away to America. Fortunately, over the last couple of years, as Ethiopia increasingly takes its place on the regional and world stage, that attitude seems to be becoming rarer. In fact, nowadays there's an undeniable sense of optimism among most Ethiopians.

The highlands have been dominated by a distinctive form of Christianity since the 4th century. Although undeniably devout and keen to dispense centuries' worth of Orthodox legends and tales dating back to Aksum and the Ark of the Covenant, Christians, like all Ethiopians, nonetheless still cling to a surprising amount of magic and superstition.

Belief in *zar* (spirits or genies) and *buda* (the evil eye with the power to turn people into mischievous hyenas by night) is rife and as such even Christians adorn their children, from baptism, with charms or talismans around their necks to deter such spirits and terrible diseases.

Yet this apparent religious contradiction is quite natural to Ethiopians. In a historically isolated area where rhetoric and reasoning have become highly valued and practised, where eloquent communication and sophisticated wordplay are considered an art form and where the ability to argue a case in point while effectively sitting on the fence is now aspired to, ambiguity and complexity are as much a part of the Ethiopian psyche as it is a part of their religion.

Want to woo the locals and have some serious fun streetside? Hone your table-tennis and table-football skills before arriving!

## The People of Ethiopia

Ethiopia's population has squeezed past the 91-million mark, an astounding figure considering the population was just 15 million in 1935. Ethiopia has one of the fastest growing populations in the world. This population explosion is arguably the biggest problem facing Ethiopia today. In 2012 its population growth rate was estimated at a worryingly high 2.9%; which, if growth rates continue at around that level, will leave

### WHO DOES SHE THINK SHE IS?

The most beautiful and alluring woman ever to live had hairy legs and the cloven foot of the devil. Her fame has lasted 3000 years, yet nobody remembers her name. She's a player in the ancient legends of Judaism, Christianity and Islam, yet no one knows where she lived. She's the mother of the throne of Ethiopia, the most famous daughter of Yemen and the original Jerusalem pilgrim. Even today she remains a household name, and any girl seen to be getting above herself can expect to be compared with her. She is, of course, the Queen of Sheba, but she may never even have existed.

Though she appears in the writings of all three monotheistic religions, it's the Ethiopian story (in which she is known as *Makeda*) of her life that is most famous in the West, while for Christian Ethiopians the story is virtually the very cornerstone of their culture, history and lifestyle.

According to the Kebra Negast (Ethiopia's national epic), the Queen of Sheba's first public appearance was when she paid a visit to the court of King Solomon in Jerusalem in the 10th century BC. The reasons and results of her visit vary and though many people say that King Solomon was the wisest person in the world and that the queen travelled to Jerusalem in order to test his wisdom with 'difficult questions and riddles', it seems more likely that trade was the real reason for the meeting.

The Ethiopian legend reveals how after her arrival Solomon became enraptured with her beauty and devised a plan to have his wicked way with her. He agreed to let her stay in his palace only on the condition that she touched nothing of his. Shocked that Solomon should consider her capable of such a thing, she agreed. That evening Solomon laid on a feast of spicy and salty foods. After the meal, Sheba and Solomon retired to separate beds in his sleeping quarters. During the night Sheba awoke, thirsty from all the salty food she had consumed, and reached across for a glass of water. The moment she put the glass to her lips Solomon awoke and triumphantly claimed that she had broken her vow. 'But it's only water', she cried, to which Solomon replied, 'And nothing on earth is more precious than water'.

Ethiopian tradition holds that the child that resulted from the deceitful night of passion that followed was to become Menelik I, from whom the entire royal line of Ethiopia claims direct descent (in truth the line, if it ever existed, has been broken a number of times).

But there's more to this tale than just the birth of the Ethiopian royal line. This is also the story of the arrival of the Ark of the Covenant in Ethiopia and the conversion of its people to Judaism. It's said that the centrepiece of Solomon's famous temple was the Ark of the Covenant, and that as long as the Jews had the Ark nothing bad could come of them. However, when Menelik travelled to Jerusalem to meet his father, his luggage was a little heavier on his return trip. Secreted away among his dirty laundry was the Ark of the Covenant.

Finding out whether Sheba existed and where her capital was located has not proved easy. The strongest claims have come from both Ethiopia, which claims that Aksum was her capital, and Yemen, which says it was Ma'rib. Both cities were important trade and cultural centres and it's quite likely that both were, if not ruled by the same monarch, then certainly closely tied through trade. However, so far neither has yielded any evidence to suggest that the Queen of Sheba ever existed. Whatever the truth, the legend persists, and every Ethiopian will swear to you that Aksum was the home of the most beautiful cloven-footed woman to ever live.

## ETHIOPIA'S STREET KIDS

Throughout Ethiopia there are a range of charities working to help the country's many street children. In many cases working with these charities involves a considerable commitment of time as well as having a certain skill to offer. In these cases it's usually easiest for a short-term visitor to just donate money to their chosen charity after they've returned home.

A more hands-on approach is the distribution of meal tickets. Some local centres sell booklets of meal tickets that are then distributed to needy children. Each day hundreds of children redeem the tickets for a meal at the centre.

Addis Ababa–based **Hope Enterprises** (Map p38; ☎0111-560345; Churchill Ave; ⏰8am-noon & 1-5pm Mon-Sat) sells booklets of eight meal tickets (Birr8).

In Gonder, local NGO **Yenege Tesfa** (Map p78; www.yenegetesfa.org) runs an orphanage and provides educational and medical programs. Tourists are encouraged to visit some of its project sites. It sells 'bread coupons' that children can exchange for a loaf of bread. A booklet of 10 tickets is Birr20.

Ethiopia bursting at the seams with almost 120 million people in 2025. However, AIDS, which affects 2.1% of the population, will inevitably slow future growth.

Although 84 languages and 200 dialects are spoken in Ethiopia, the population can be broken down into eight broad groups, which are detailed in the following pages. For information about the Lower Omo Valley's unique peoples, see p162, and for more on the peoples of the western lowlands, see p211.

## The Oromo

Although traditionally most of the Oromo were nomadic pastoralists, it was the skilled Oromo warrior horsemen who put fear into Ethiopians when they migrated north from present-day Kenya in the mid-16th century. It was the Oromo who inspired Harar's leaders to build a wall around the city and even led Ethiopian emperors to (briefly and much to the disgust of the general population) accept Catholicism in order to gain Portugal's military support.

Today, most Oromo are settled, making a living as farmers or cattle breeders. They are Muslim, Christian and animist in religion, and are known for their egalitarian society, which is based on the *gada* (age-group system). A man's life is divided into age-sets of eight years. In the fourth set (between the ages of 24 and 32), men assume the right to govern their people.

They are the largest ethnic group in the country, making up 34.5% of its population. Over 85% of the massive 350,000-sq-km Oromia region's population are Oromo. Many Oromo resent the Tigray-led national government, and the Oromo Liberation Front (OLF) continues to lobby for separation from Ethiopia.

## The Amharas

As great warriors, skilful governors and astute administrators, the Amhara have dominated the country's history, politics and society since 1270, and have imposed their own language and culture on the country. In the past this was much resented by other tribal groups, who saw it as little more than a kind of colonialism.

Amhara tend to be devoutly Christian, although there are some Muslim Amhara. They're also fanatical about their land and 90% of them are traditional tillers of the soil: they produce some of the nation's best *tef* (endemic cereal grain used for *the* national staple, *injera*).

According to Homer the ancient Greek Gods often travelled to the edges of the Hellenic world to enjoy the company of a people who, unlike Mediterranean man and his gods, were renowned for their grace and virtue: the blameless Ethiopians.

A staggering 13% of Ethiopian children are missing one or both parents. Nearly a quarter of these parents have been lost through AIDS.

Making up 26.9% of Ethiopia's population, they're the second-largest ethnic group. Over 90% of the Amharaland region's people are Amhara.

## The Tigrayans

Much like the Amharas, the Tigrayans are fiercely independent and zealously attached to their land. They disdain all manual labour with the single exception of agriculture.

Most live in the Tigray region, where both Christianity and Islam were introduced to Ethiopia. Ninety-five per cent of Tigrayans are Orthodox Christian, and most devoutly so. Tigrayans are Ethiopia's third-largest ethnic group, comprising around 6.1% of the population.

As a result of the Tigrayan People's Liberation Front (TPLF) playing the major role in the bringing down of the Derg (see p235), many Tigrayans feature in Ethiopia's government. This has caused resentment among other groups.

## The Somali

The arid lowlands of the southeast dictate a nomadic or seminomadic existence for the Somali. Somali society is 99% Muslim, strongly hierarchical, tightly knit and based on the clan system, which requires intense loyalty from its members. In the harsh environment in which they live, ferocious competition for the scant resources leads to frequent and sometimes violent disputes (thanks to an abundant supply of AK-47s) over grazing grounds and sources of water.

The Somali make up 95% of the Somali region's people, and 6.2% of Ethiopia's population.

## The Sidama

The Sidama, a heterogeneous people, originate from the southwest and can be divided into five different groups: the Sidama proper, the Derasa, Hadiya, Kambata and Alaba. Most Sidama are farmers who cultivate cereals, tobacco, *enset* (false-banana tree found in much of southern Ethiopia) and coffee. The majority are animists and many ancient beliefs persist, including a belief in the reverence of spirits. Pythons are believed to be reincarnations of ancestors and are sometimes kept as house pets. The Sidama social organisation, like the Oromo's *gada* system, is based on an age-group system.

The Sidama comprise about 4% of Ethiopia's population and most live in the Southern Nations, Nationalities and People's region.

## The Gurage

Semitic in origin, the Gurage practise herding or farming, and the *enset* plant is their favoured crop. They are known as great workers, clever improvisers and skilled craftspeople. Many work as seasonal labourers for the highlanders. Their faith is Christian, Muslim or animist, depending on the area from which they originate.

*Every Ethiopian emperor (bar one) since Yekuno Amlak established the Solomonic dynasty in 1270 has been Amhara. Yohannes (r 1872–89), who was Tigrayan, is the only exception.*

*EMPERORS*

---

### ETHIOPIAN HAIRSTYLES

Hairstyles in all societies form an important part of tribal identification. Reflecting the large number of ethnic groups, Ethiopian hairstyles are particularly diverse and colourful. Hair is cut, shaved, trimmed, plaited, braided, sculpted with clay, rubbed with mud, put in buns and tied in countless different fashions. In the Omo Valley, hairstyles are sometimes so elaborate and valued that special wooden headrests are used as pillows to preserve them.

In rural areas, the heads of children are often shaved to discourage lice. Sometimes a single topknot or tail plait is left so that 'God should have a handle with which to lift them unto Heaven', should he decide to call them.

They comprise only 2% of Ethiopia's population, but make up more than 10% of the population in the Southern Nations, Nationalities and People's region.

## The Afar

The Afar, formerly also known as the Danakils, inhabit the famous region of Dankalia, which stretches across Ethiopia's east, Djibouti's west and into Eritrea's southeast. It's considered one of Earth's most inhospitable environments. Rightly or wrongly, they've proudly latched onto early-20th-century adventurer Wilfred Thesiger's portrayal of them as famously belligerent and proud. Thesiger wrote of the Afar winning social prestige in the past for murdering and castrating members of an opposing tribe. Fortunately for male travellers this is somewhat rarer today!

The Afar comprise 1.7% of Ethiopia's population.

## The Harari

Like the Gurage, the Harari people (sometimes known as Adare) are also Semitic in origin. They have long inhabited the walled Muslim city of Harar. The people are particularly known for their distinct two-storey houses, known as *gegar* (see the boxed text, p191), and for the very colourful traditional costumes still worn by many Harari women today. In the past, the Harari were known as great craftspeople for their weavings, baskets and bookbinding. They're also renowned Islamic scholars.

## The Falashas

Falashas (Ethiopian Jews) have inhabited Ethiopia since pre-Christian times. Despite actively engaging in wars over the years to defend their independence and freedom, few now remain: war, some persecution (though much less than seen elsewhere) and emigration in the latter part of the 20th century have greatly reduced their numbers.

In 1984 around 8000 Falashas fled Ethiopia and walked on foot to Sudan, where the Israeli and US secret services surreptitiously airlifted them to Israel. A further operation took place in 1991, when 34 Israeli aircraft secretly transported some 14,325 Jews to Israel over a 36-hour period (by the time the planes had landed, there were actually two extra passengers as two women gave birth during their flights!).

Tiny populations of Falashas remain north of Lake Tana in the northwest of Ethiopia; their beliefs combine a fascinating mixture of Judaism, indigenous beliefs and Christianity.

For a fascinating look at the cultural clash that occurs when photo-hungry tourists and lip-plate wearing Mursi meet watch *Framing the Other* (www.framing-the-other.com).

## The Ethiopian Way of Life

Other than religion, which undoubtedly plays a huge role in almost all Ethiopians' daily life, it's agriculture and pastoralism that fill the days of well over 80% of the country's population. Everyone is involved, right down to stick-and-stone-wielding four-year-old children who are handed the incredible responsibility of tending and herding the family's livestock.

With almost everyone toiling out in the fields, it's not surprising that only 42.7% (CIA figures; note that other sources give lower, or higher, figures) of the population is literate. Since young children are needed to help with the family plots and animals, only 82% (Unicef figures) of children attend primary school. Older children are in even more demand in the workforce; between 2005 and 2010 only 30% of boys and 23% of girls attended secondary education (Unicef 2012 figures). If all children under 16 were forced to attend school, Ethiopia's workforce would be ravaged and almost half of the country's entire population would be attending classes.

Ethiopian families are incredibly close and most people live with their parents until marriage. After marriage, the couple usually joins the household of the husband's family. After a couple of years, they will request a plot of land from the village, on which to build their own house.

Divorce is relatively easy in Ethiopia and marriage can be dissolved at the request of either party (adultery is usually given as justification). In theory, each partner retains the property he or she brought into the marriage, though sometimes allowances are made for the 'wronged' partner.

Although women continue to lag behind men economically, they are highly respected in Ethiopian society. The same can't be said for gays and lesbians. Homosexuality is severely condemned – traditionally, religiously and legally – and remains a topic of absolute taboo.

The 1984 evacuation of Ethiopian Jews to Israel was captured in an Israeli-French film, Live and Become (2005).

## Women in Ethiopia

Legally, women in Ethiopia enjoy a relatively equitable position compared with some African countries. They can own property, vote and are represented in government, though there are still some cases in which women's rights are impeded.

Life for many women is extremely hard; to make ends meet many have to resort to extreme actions. Many foreigners are shocked to see just how many prostitutes there are in Ethiopia and just how openly it's practised. Put simply, prostitution doesn't have the same social stigma as it does in the West. Often prostitutes are just students trying to get by. Others are widows, divorcees or refugees, all with little or no hope of finding other forms of employment. With no social security system, it's often their only means of survival. Though not exactly a respected profession, prostitution is considered a perfectly viable means of making a living. HIV-AIDS levels among prostitutes is thought to be close to 50% in Addis Ababa (although no official figures exist). Outside the city, men should be warned that almost all women in bars are prostitutes.

Many Ethiopian women also have to endure the practice of female genital mutilation (genital cutting). The UN has stated that 74.3% of Ethiopian women between the ages of 15 and 49 have undergone some form of female genital mutilation; in the Somali regions of Ethiopia this figure rises significantly. One bit of good news though is that among younger women the rate is lower and continuing to decline year on year.

Reasons given in the Horn for genital mutilation vary from hygiene and aesthetics to superstitions that uncut women can't conceive. Others believe that the strict following of traditional beliefs is crucial to maintaining social cohesion and a sense of belonging, much like male circumcision is to Jews. Some also say that it prevents female promiscuity.

### THE ETHIOPIAN 'HANDSHAKE'

Greeting one another in Ethiopia can be a complicated business. Do you just say hello? Do you offer a hand? Do you kiss the other person on the cheek? Or do you go for the 'fighters salute'? Commonly, as Ethiopians shake hands they also gently knock their shoulders together. This is known as the 'fighters salute' and traditionally was used as a greeting between those who fought the Derg. Today, it's used by almost everyone – male and female – but only in informal situations between friends. You would not use this form of 'handshake' at a business meeting!

There are plenty of other ways to greet people in Ethiopia. Multiple kissing on the cheek is also very common among friends and relatives of either sex. It's also considered polite to kiss babies or young children, even if you've just met them.

And if you do just stick with a boring old handshake then deference can be shown by supporting the right arm (near the elbow) with the left hand during shaking. When Ethiopians enter a room they try and shake hands with everyone (including children). If hands are dirty or wet, limp wrists are offered.

# Multiculturalism

Ethiopia's mix of cultures has been pretty stable over the past few centuries, with only the expulsion of Eritrean citizens after the recent Ethiopia–Eritrea War, and influxes of Sudanese refugees into the western lowlands shifting the status quo.

Despite the nation's regions being divided along ethnic lines in 1995, there's still some resentment, particularly among the Oromo, that has led to violence over the fact that the minority Tigrayan and Amhara people largely maintain control of the national government (although the interim prime minister is not from either of these groups).

Many travellers also notice that some Ethiopian highlanders, regardless of their ethnic background, seem to show a slight disdain for Ethiopians from the lowlands.

# Religion in Ethiopia

Faith is an extremely important part of an Ethiopian's life. Orthodox Christians bring religion into everyday conversation just as much as their Muslim counterparts. Although Orthodox believers only slightly outnumber Muslims (43.5% to 33.9%), Christianity has traditionally dominated the country's past. The vast majority of highlanders are Orthodox and the religion continues to heavily influence the highlands' political, social and cultural scene. Most Muslims inhabit the eastern, southern and western lowlands, but there are also significant populations in the country's predominantly Christian towns, including Addis Ababa.

Thanks to the Orthodox calendar, Ethiopia is a full seven to eight years (depending on the exact date) behind the Western calendar. There are also 13 months in a year.

## Ethiopian Orthodox Christianity

As the official religion of the imperial court right up until Emperor Haile Selassie was deposed in 1974, the Orthodox church continues to carry great clout among the Ethiopian people and is regarded as the great guardian and repository of ancient Ethiopian traditions, directly inherited from Aksum (p220).

Ethiopia was the second country (after Armenia) to adopt Christianity as its state religion and it's been a truly unifying factor over the centuries. By the same measure, it's also legitimised the oppression of the people by its rulers.

Ethiopian Orthodox Christianity is thought to have its roots in Judaism – some even say that this is the home of the Lost Tribes of Israel. This Jewish connection explains the food restrictions, including the way animals are slaughtered. Even the traditional round church layout is considered Hebrew in origin. Ancient Semitic and pagan elements also persist.

Circumcision is generally practised on boys, marriage is celebrated in the presence of a priest, and confession is usually only made during a grave illness.

The world's oldest Christian manuscript is thought to be the Garima Gospels, which recent radiocarbon dating suggests dates back to sometime between 330AD and 650AD. It is kept in the Abba Garima monastery near Adwa.

### Know Your Ethiopian Saints

In Ethiopia the air seems to be saturated with the stories of saints, magic, ghosts and monsters. For the majority of Ethiopians (of all faiths) these tales are not wild legends, but solid fact. Don't be surprised if, on asking about the history of a church, you end up listening, spellbound, to a story so unlikely that you assume it's nothing but an ancient legend, only for the storyteller to turn around and announce that the events recounted happened just a year or so ago.

As a traveller, it's important that you don't dismiss these stories out of hand. Ethiopians, like many Africans, live a life very different from those in the West. It's a life lived close to the rhythm of nature, in which the dead are never far away. Every Ethiopian has their favourite saint, and there's hardly an Ethiopian church not adorned with colourful, vibrant

## THE BIRTH OF CHRISTIAN ETHIOPIA

Sometimes finding out what happened in Ethiopia just last week can be tough, so when it comes to finding out what happened nearly 2000 years ago it goes without saying that fact, fiction and an utter disregard of scientific logic are part of the parcel. The story of how Christianity first arrived in Ethiopia is no exception to this rule.

The man credited with bringing Christianity to Ethiopia is a certain St Frumentius, better known in Ethiopia today as Abuna Selama. Born a Christian in early-4th-century Lebanon, legend has it that when still young Abuna and his brother Edesius travelled by boat down the Red Sea to Ethiopia. By all accounts the shores of the Red Sea at that time were filled with people up to no good. As if to prove this point, when the boat they were travelling on stopped at a harbour the locals massacred all aboard except the two boys, who were taken as slaves to the king of Aksum. Quickly gaining the trust of the king they were eventually given their freedom, but when the king died the queen begged the brothers to stay and help bring up her son, and future king, Ezana. Abuna Selama in particular used his position to influence the young Ezana and convert him to Christianity. When Ezana was old enough to become king, Selama travelled to Alexandria in Egypt where he requested the patriarch to send a bishop to Ethiopia. Instead, the patriarch consecrated Selama and sent him back to Aksum, where he baptized Ezana, built a number of churches and set about converting the masses.

Abuna Selama may have brought Christianity to Ethiopia (actually there were already Christian traders living in Ethiopia before Selama's time), but he didn't make much headway converting the rural masses. It wasn't until the 5th century when a group of wandering monks known as the Nine Saints arrived from the Levant and, using a potent mixture of magic, giant snakes and other show-stopping stunts, impressed the locals to such an extent that they quickly converted to Christianity.

murals. In most cases the paintings follow a set pattern, depicting the important personalities of Ethiopia's peculiar pantheon of saints often alongside a bevy of strange creatures. Some of the best-known saints are listed below. Here's a quick key:

**Abuna Aregawi** One day while wandering at the foot of a cliff, Abuna Aregawi spotted a plateau high above him. Deciding it was the ideal spot for a nice, quiet hermit's life, he prayed to God for assistance. Immediately, a large python stretched down from above and lifted him onto the plateau. The famous monastery of Debre Damo was then founded. The saint is usually depicted riding up the snake. He's one of the Nine Saints.

**Abuna Samuel** He lived near the Takezze River, where he preached and performed many miracles, accompanied by a devoted lion. He is usually depicted astride his lion.

**Belai the Cannibal** Although not a saint, he's a favourite theme in religious art. Devouring anyone who approached him, including his own family, Belai yet took pity one day on a leper begging for water in the Virgin's name. After Belai died – some 72 human meals later – Satan claimed his soul. St Mikael, the judge, balanced Belai's victims on one side, the water on the other. However, the Virgin cast her shadow on the side of the scales containing the water, and caused them to tip. Belai's soul was saved.

**Equestrian Saints** They are usually depicted on the north wall of the Holy of Holies and may include Fasiladas, Claudius, Mercurius, Menas, Theodorus and George.

**Mary** Little known outside Ethiopia are the charming legends and miracles concerning Mary, the childhood of Jesus and the flight to Egypt. A tree is often depicted hiding the holy family – and the donkey – from Herod's soldiers during the flight to Egypt; the soldiers are confused by the sound of the donkey braying. Sometimes a furious Mary is shown scolding Jesus, who's managed to break a clay water jug.

*Continued on page 251*

# Legendary Ethiopia

Remember when you were a child tucked in bed and your parents, opening a book, read aloud the words 'Once upon a time'? Within moments you were transported to a magical world where castles were made of crystal, monks from Syria climbed serpents tails to build invisible monasteries, emperors turned solid rock into beautiful churches, a queen known only as Sheba was seduced by a king named Solomon and the words of God were hidden in a secret ark for the world to ponder. Today you are about to venture to Ethiopia. It is your wildest fairy tale brought to life.

Bet Giyorgis (p119), Lalibela

JON BRATT/GETTY IMAGES ©

## Ark of the Covenant

Carried by the Israelites during their 40 years wandering in the desert, and a prized possession of King David and centrepiece of King Solomon's temple, the Ark of the Covenant is now the cornerstone of Ethiopian culture and history, but is it in Aksum?

## The Queen of Sheba

When King Solomon first laid eyes on the Queen of Sheba, ruler of ancient Aksum, he was enraptured with her beauty. According to Ethiopian tradition every emperor up to Haile Selassie was a direct descendant of Menelik I, the son that resulted from that fateful meeting 3000 years ago.

## King of Kings

A biblical prophecy proclaimed that 'Kings would come out of Africa' and for the people of Jamaica that prophecy came true with the 1930 coronation of Haile Selassie. The emperor found himself becoming not just King of Kings to millions of Ethiopians, but also the Messiah of a new religion: Rastafarianism.

## A New Jerusalem

Nearly a thousand years ago a poisoned king was taken by angels to Heaven. Here he was shown a city of rock-hewn churches. Then God himself commanded him to return to Earth and, re-creating what he had seen, build a New Jerusalem. Today it's named after that king: Lalibela.

**Clockwise from top left**

1 Artwork showing the Ark of the Covenant being brought to Aksum, St Mary of Zion's new church (p97) 2 Detail from Piero della Francesca's *Legend of the True Cross*, showing the meeting of the Queen of Sheba and King Solomon 3 Portrait of Haile Selassie

## Mystical Monasteries

The mountains of northern Ethiopia are home to hundreds of ancient monasteries. Some require scrambles up sheer rock faces to reach, some are invisible and guarded by sword-wielding ghosts, some contain the bones of former monks, and one could only be built with the help of a giant snake.

## Prester John

The legendary Christian king, Prester John, was said to be a descendant of one of the Three Magi. His kingdom contained the Fountain of Youth and the Gates of Alexander. And right up until the first Europeans arrived in Gonder it was widely believed that his kingdom was in Ethiopia.

**From top**

1 Debre Damo monastery (p106) 2 Fasiladas' Palace (p77), Gonder

*Continued from page 246*

**St Eostateos** Also known as St Thaddeus, he's said to have arrived in Ethiopia borne up the Nile from Egypt on three large stones. Apparently water continued to obey him: whenever the saint chose to cross a river or a lake, the waters parted conveniently before him.

**St Gabriel** God's messenger is usually represented cooling the flames of a fiery furnace or cauldron containing three youths condemned by Nebuchadnezzar: Meshach, Shadrach and Abednego.

**St Gebre Kristos** This Ethiopian prince sacrificed all his belongings to lead a life of chastity, and ended up a leprous beggar. He's usually depicted outside his palace, where only his dogs now recognise him.

**St Gebre Manfus Kiddus** While preaching peace to the animals in the desert, this saint came across a bird dying of thirst. Lifting it, he allowed the bird to drink the water from his eye. He's usually depicted clad in furs and girded with a hempen rope and surrounded by animals.

**St George** The patron saint of Ethiopia features in almost every church. He's depicted either as the king of saints, with St Bula – who at first refused to recognise his kingship – looking on petulantly in the background, or as the great dragon slayer on his horse.

**St Mikael** The judge of souls and the leader of the celestial army, St Mikael evicted Lucifer from heaven. In most churches, the portals to the Holy of Holies are guarded by a glowering Mikael, accompanied by Gabriel and Raphael.

**St Raphael** He rescued an Egyptian church from the tail of a thrashing beached whale and is usually depicted killing the whale with his spear.

**St Tekla Haimanot** The saint stood bolt upright and prayed nonstop for 22 years until his right leg turned rotten and fell off. Nonplussed he continued praying for a further seven years standing on just one leg, until that one also withered and fell off! Throughout, a bird brought him just one seed a year for sustenance. For his devotion, God awarded him no fewer than three sets of wings. The saint is normally depicted in his bishop's attire, surrounded by bells.

**St Yared** Ethiopia's patron saint of music is sometimes shown standing before his king with an orchestra of monks along with their sistra (sophisticated rattles), drums and prayer sticks. In the background, little birds in trees learn the magic of music.

And finally, no list of Ethiopian saints would be complete without mentioning the names of the Nine Saints who famously brought Christianity to Ethiopia: Abuna i, Abuna Tsama, Abuna Aftse, Abuna Gerima, Abuna Liqanos, Abuna Guba, Abuna Panteleon and Abuna Yemata (the ninth one is Abuna Aregawi; mentioned above) See also p107.

## Islam

Ethiopia's connection with Islam is as distinguished as its connection with Christianity. Though bloody religious wars were fought in Ethiopia in the past, Ethiopia's Christian and Muslim inhabitants generally coexist in harmony. Fundamentalism is rare in Ethiopia, and it's uncommon to see women wearing the *hijab* (veil), though the majority wear either headscarves or *shalmas* (a gauze-thin length of fabric draped around the head, shoulders and torso).

Negash, in Tigray, where Islam was introduced in 615 AD and the shrine of Sheikh Hussein in the Bale region are both greatly venerated and attract national and international pilgrims.

The famous walled city of Harar is also an important Islamic centre in its own right and is home to an astonishing number of shrines and mosques. In the past, it was renowned as a centre of learning.

## Traditional African Beliefs

Traditional African beliefs are still practised either totally or in part, by an estimated 11% of Ethiopia's population, particularly in the lowland

Brush up on the history, culture and latest happenings of the Ethiopian Orthodox Church on www.ethiopian orthodox.org, the Church's official website.

## THE SECRET NAME OF GOD

Belief in talismans and charms is common among all communities in Ethiopia, whether they be Christian, Muslim or animist. Maybe the most intriguing of these is belief in *asmat*, or the secret names of God in which reside his power. God has many *asmat* and these, if invoked by a person, can protect against misfortune or illness. Because of this many Ethiopians wear a talisman around their neck containing a small piece of parchment on which are written *asmat*. When a Christian Ethiopian dies his or her body is wrapped in a shroud containing a thin, body-length strip of linen on which are written the *asmat*. This ensures a safe passage through the underworld and across a river of fire to the gates of Heaven.

areas of the west and south. These range from the Konso's totemism to animism (associated with trees, springs, mountains and stones), in which animals are ritually slaughtered and then consumed by the people. Elements of ancestor worship are still found among the Afar people.

The Oromo traditionally believe in a supreme celestial deity known as Wak, whose eye is the sun.

## Media

In many ways Ethiopia is heading squarely in the right direction, but one sphere where things are taking a decided turn for the worse is in the freedom of media.

When the Ethiopian People's Revolutionary Democratic Front (EPRDF) first came to power the severe restrictions placed on the media by the Derg regime, and before that the imperial regime, were largely lifted and the press given more freedom than it had ever really had before. However, this change of fortunes was not to last.

After the May 2005 elections, the EU had harsh criticism of the state-owned media for regularly releasing unofficial results that highlighted the government's victories and virtually ignoring the victories of opposition parties. They blasted state-owned Radio Ethiopia and Ethiopian TV for 'completely ignoring' the press conferences and important statements given by opposition parties, information that CNN and the BBC thought newsworthy.

Since 1992, when the Press Law came into effect, numerous journalists have been arrested without trial for publishing critical articles of the government. The editor of *Agere* died untried in prison in 1998. Several owners of private media were arrested and their newspapers shut down during the post-electoral violence in 2005.

More recently the situation for journalists has gotten worse. An anti-terrorism law, introduced in 2009, has been used to harass and jail journalists and editors who have published antigovernment articles. According to Journalists Without Borders, in 2011 four journalists, including two Swedes, were given lengthy prison terms for 'terrorist activities'. Under pressure the Swedes were released in 2012. In mid-2012 award-winning Ethiopian journalist Eskinder Nega was imprisoned for 18 years after writing a column questioning the arrest of journalists.

The censorship and repression doesn't stop with print media. Opposition websites and websites criticising the government are frequently blocked, and in early 2012 the government even went as far as making the use of Skype and other VoIP software illegal on 'national security grounds' with possible prison sentences of up to 15 years. Such an uproar followed that the government later backed down on this.

# Arts

The church, traditionally enjoying almost as much authority as the state, is responsible for both inspiring Ethiopia's art forms and stifling them with its great conservatism and rigorous adherence to convention.

Long neglected and ignored, the cultural contributions of Ethiopia's minority ethnic groups are only now receiving due credit and attention.

## Music

Whether it's the solemn sounds of drums resonating from a church, the hilarious ad-libbing of an *azmari* (see the boxed text, p253) or Ethiopian pop blaring in a bus, Ethiopian music is as interesting as it's unavoidable.

Ethiopian music CDs are available throughout the country. Music stalls are everywhere – keep an ear out.

### Church Music

Yared the Deacon is traditionally credited with inventing church music, with the introduction in the 6th century of a system of musical notation.

*Aquaquam* (church music) uses resonating drums – the *kabaro* and the *tsinatseil* (sistrum; a sophisticated rattle, thought to be directly descended from an ancient Egyptian instrument used to worship Isis). Percussion instruments are primarily used since their function is to mark the beat for chanting and dancing. The *maquamia* (prayer stick) also plays an essential role in church ceremonies and, with hand-clapping, is used to mark time. Very occasionally a *meleket* (trumpet) is used, such as to lead processions.

### Secular Music

Strongly influenced by church music, secular music usually combines song and dance, emphasises rhythm, and often blends both African and Asian elements. The Amharas' and Tigrayans' highland music, as well as that of the peoples living near the Sudanese border, is much influenced by Arab music, and is very strident and emotive.

Wind and percussion instruments are used. The *begenna* is a type of harp similar to that played by the ancient Greeks and Romans. The most popular instrument in Ethiopia is the *krar*, a five- or six-stringed lyre, which is often heard at weddings or used to attract customers to traditional pubs or bars.

In the highlands, particularly the Simien and Bale Mountains, shepherd boys can be found with reed flutes. The *washint* is about 50cm

---

### MINSTRELS & MASENKOS

An ancient entertainment that continues to this day is that provided by the singing *azmari* (wandering minstrel) and his *masenko* (single-stringed fiddle). In the past, *azmaris* accompanied caravans of highland traders to make the journey more amusing.

At court, resident *azmaris*, like European jesters, were permitted great freedom of expression as long as their verses were witty, eloquent and clever.

Today, *azmaris* can be found at weddings and special occasions furnishing eulogies or poetic ballads in honour of their hosts.

In certain *azmari bets* (azmari bars) in the larger towns, some *azmaris* have become celebrities in their own right. They prance around grass-covered floors and sing about everything from history to sex, to your funny haircut. Although you won't understand a word (it's all in Amharic), you'll end up laughing; the locals' laughter is simply that contagious. And remember these two things: it's all done in good fun, and really your haircut isn't that bad!

## TEDDY YO'S TOP FIVE MODERN ETHIOPIAN ALBUMS

Addis-born hip-hop star Teddy Yo (real name Tewodros Assefa) is the face of young cosmopolitan Ethiopia. He started rapping at the age of 14, but didn't turn heads until he took traditional Gurage music and combined it with contemporary hip-hop beats and lyrics to create his own musical style, Guragetone (which is also the name of his most famous song). Today he is Ethiopia's best known hip-hop performer. His latest album is 2012's *Zeraf*.

We asked him to give us his essential list of modern Ethiopian music.

**Yachi Neger** by Ja Lude; this is real reggae and the music is full of messages.

**Kulfun Sechin** by Joni Ragga; another great reggae album.

**Ende Kal** by Eyob; the lyrics are powerful and are full of messages for the young.

**Zeritu** by Zeritu Kebede; she introduced modern rock to Ethiopia.

**Tizeta** by Mehamoud Ahemed; he has the voice.

long, with four holes, and makes a bubbling sound that is said to imitate running water. It's supposed to keep the herds close by and calm the animals.

### Modern Music

Ethiopian modern music is diverse and affected by outside influences, and ranges from classical Amharic to jazz and pop. Modern classical singers and musicians include the late Assefa Abate, Kassa Tessema and the late female vocalist Asnakech Worku. The composer Mulatu Astatike is well known for his Ethiojazz.

Amharic popular music boasts a great following with the young. Unlike many other African countries, it's generally much preferred to Western music, and can be heard in all the larger towns' bars and discos.

Among the best known is Tewodros Kassahun ('Teddy Afro') whose political album *Yaasteseryal,* which was released in 2005 during a time of heightened political tension following disputed elections, got him on the wrong side of the government, but sent his popularity sky-rocketing. Four songs from the album were eventually banned by the government. His latest album is *Tikur Sew.*

For a full translation of the Kebra Negast, check out www.sacred-texts.com/chr/kn/.

Ethiopian rap is massively popular among the young in all the big Ethiopian towns. Like many forms of artistic expression in Ethiopia most performers use a certain amount of self-censorship when it comes to rapping about domestic politics, and in general Ethiopian rap seems fairly nonpolitical when compared to some Western rap artists. Current leaders of the Ethiopian rap race are Teddy Yo and the upcoming Yoni Yoyi, whose best-known song is the brilliantly catchy 'Gondergna'.

Female artists more than hold their own. Gonder-born, American-based Aster Aweke has produced 20 albums since the late 1970s. She's popularly known as Africa's Aretha Franklin. Her latest release is 2010's *Checheho.* Hot on Aster's tail for international fame is Ejigaheyehu Shibabaw (known as 'Gigi'), who rose to prominence after her 1997 album *Tsehay.* Her singing was heard in the Hollywood movie *Beyond Borders.* Her latest album is *Mesgana Ethiopia.* One of the biggest female stars at the moment is Zeritu Kebede (also known as 'Baby').

Francis Falceto, an Ethiopian music expert, compiles popular Ethiopian contemporary music into great CDs known as 'Ethiopiques'. Twenty-seven volumes have been produced to date; pick them up from www.budamusique.com.

# Dance

Dance forms an extremely important part of the lives of most Ethiopians, and almost every ethnic group has its own distinct variety. Although the *iskista* – in which the shoulders are juddered up and down and backwards and forwards, in a careful rhythm, while the hips and legs stay motionless – is the best known, there are myriad others.

Dances in praise of nature, such as after a good harvest or when new sources of water are discovered, are still found in rural areas, and dances that allow the young 'warriors' to show off their agility and athleticism. Look out for the *fukara* (boasting dance), which is often performed at public festivals. A leftover from less peaceful times, it involves a man holding a spear, stick or rifle horizontally above his shoulders at the same time as moving his head from side to side and shouting defiantly at the 'enemy'.

Among the tribes of the Omo Valley in the south, many dances incorporate jumping and leaping up and down, a little like the dances of Kenya's Maasai.

# Literature

Literature has a long and illustrious history in Ethiopia. Inscriptions in Ge'ez, a South Semitic language, have been found to date as far back as 2500 years; though it wasn't until Aksumite times that it became widely used as a language of literature. It was during this early period that the Bible was translated from Greek into Ge'ez.

Even though Ge'ez had long since died as a spoken language, the 13th and 14th centuries are considered to mark the golden age of Ge'ez literature, in which many works were translated from Arabic, as well as much original writing produced. It's thought that in the early 14th century the Kebra Negast (p255) was written.

During the 16th-century Muslim–Christian Wars, book production ground to a halt and copious amounts of literature were destroyed. By the 17th century, Ge'ez was in decline as a literary language, but that didn't mean the value of books had been lost. It's around this time that rumours spread of a vast library hidden on the mysterious flat-topped mountain of Amba Gishen. Inside the library's endless halls could be found every kind of book, including the works of Job and Abraham and the lost Book of Enoch. What makes this tale so extraordinary is that in 1773 a Ge'ez version of the lost Book of Enoch was discovered in Ethiopia (to this day it remains the only complete copy ever found).

Amharic, now Ethiopia's official language, was the Amharas' language. It was Emperor Tewodros who encouraged the local language

There is much debate as to the origin and date of the Kebra Negast. Some say it was originally written in Coptic then translated into Arabic and finally into Ge'ez. Some say there was never a Coptic version. Some insist it dates back to the 1300s; others that it was written as late as the 16th century.

## KEBRA NEGAST

Written during the 14th century by author(s) unknown, the Kebra Negast (Glory of Kings) is considered Ethiopia's great national epic. Like the Quran to Muslims or the Torah to Jews, it's a repository of Ethiopian national, religious and cultural sentiment.

It's notoriously shrouded in mystery, perhaps deliberately so. Some controversially suggest it may even represent a massive propaganda stunt to legitimise the rule of the so-called 'Solomonic kings', who came to power in the 13th century and who, the book claims, were direct descendants of the kings of Israel.

Its most important legend is that of Solomon and Sheba (see the boxed text, p240) and it's in the Kebra Negast that (aside from one or two slightly earlier and rather hazy references) we first really hear mention of the Ark of the Covenant being in Ethiopia. This last part is interesting because if Menelik I really had brought the Ark from Jerusalem some 2000 years before it seems strange that it wasn't mentioned before.

## ILLUMINATED MANUSCRIPTS

Without doubt, illuminated manuscripts represent one of Ethiopia's greatest artistic achievements. The best-quality manuscripts were created by monks and priests in the 14th and 15th centuries. The kings, the court and the largest and wealthiest churches and monasteries were the main patrons. The manuscripts were characterised by beautifully shaped letters, attention to minute detail and elaborate ornamentation. Pictures included in the text brought it to life and made it more comprehensible for the uneducated or illiterate.

Bindings consisted of thick wooden boards often covered with tooled leather. The volume was then placed into a case with straps made of rough hides so that it could be slung over a shoulder.

On the blank pages at the beginning or at the end of the volume, look out for the formulae *fatina bere* (literally 'trial of the pen') or *bere' sanay* (literally 'a fine pen'), as the scribes tried out their reeds. Some are also dated and contain a short blessing for the owner, as well as the scribe.

Sadly, due to the Muslim and the Dervish raids of the early 16th and late 19th centuries respectively, few manuscripts date earlier than the 14th century. Modern times have seen huge numbers being pillaged by soldiers, travellers and explorers.

in an attempt to promote national unity. In a continuation of the trend begun in the 14th century, Tewodros and other emperors right up to Haile Selassie funded writers whose compositions and poetic laudatory songs were written to praise the ruler's qualities and munificence.

Under the Derg, both writing and writers were suppressed. Be'alu Girma is a well-known example of one of the many artists who disappeared during their reign.

### Poetry

Written in Amharic as well as other Ethiopian languages, poetry, along with dance and music, is used on many religious and social occasions, such as weddings or funerals. Rhymed verse is almost always chanted or sung in consonance with the rhythm of music.

Poetry places great stress on meaning, metaphor and allusion. In Ge'ez poetry, the religious allusions demand an in-depth knowledge of Ethiopian religious legends and the Bible.

### Folk Literature

Perhaps the source of the greatest originality and creativity is the vast folk literature of Ethiopia, most of it in oral form and existing in all languages and dialects. It encompasses everything from proverbs, tales and riddles to magic spells and prophetic statements. For a country in which most of the population have always been (and continue to be) illiterate, folk literature has been the method by which the nation's history has been passed down from one generation to the next. As a local expression goes, 'Every time an old person passes away, it's as if a whole library were lost'.

The Zagwe dynasty responsible for the Lalibela churches may have built them in order to legitimise their rule to the general population.

## Painting

Traditionally, Ethiopian painting is largely limited to religious subjects, particularly the life of Christ and the saints. Every church in Ethiopia is decorated with abundant and colourful murals, frescos or paintings.

Much Ethiopian painting is characterised by a naive realism. Everything is expressed with vigour and directness using bold colour, strong line and stylised proportions and perspective. Like the stained-glass windows in European Gothic churches, the paintings served a very important purpose: to instruct, inspire and instil awe in the illiterate and uneducated.

Though some modern artists (particularly painters of religious and some secular work) continue in the old tradition (or incorporate ancient motifs such as that of the Aksumite stelae), many artists have developed their own style. Borrowing freely from the past, but no longer constrained by it, modern Ethiopian painting shows greater originality of expression and is now a flourishing medium.

# Architecture

Ethiopia boasts some remarkable historical architecture. Though some monuments, such as the castles of Gonder, show foreign influence, earlier building styles, such as those developed during the Aksumite period, are believed to be wholly indigenous and are of a high technical standard.

More recently, the Italians left behind a few impressive bits of fascist architecture (Gonder has a couple of memorable buildings as does Dire Dawa) and the Derg left behind some Soviet-style works (check out the Derg monument in Addis).

## Aksumite Architecture

The 'Aksumite style' of stone masonry is Ethiopia's most famous building style. Walls were constructed with field stones set in mortar, along with sometimes finely dressed cornerstones. In between came alternating layers of stone and timber, and protruding ends of round timber beams, known as 'monkey heads'. The latter are even symbolically carved into Aksum's great obelisks (see p98), which may just be the nation's greatest architectural achievements. The Aksumites were undoubtedly master masons.

The best examples of Aksumite buildings are seen at Debre Damo and the church of Yemrehanna Kristos (p126).

The Aksumite style is additionally seen in Lalibela's rock-hewn churches, particularly in the shape of the windows, as well as in modern design today. Keep an eye out for the ancient motifs in new hotel and restaurant designs.

## Rock-Hewn Architecture

Ethiopia's rock-hewing tradition probably predates Christianity and has resulted in nearly 400 churches across the country. The art form reached its apogee in the 12th and 13th centuries in Lalibela, where the Zagwe dynasty produced 11 churches that continue to astound. They're considered among the world's finest early Christian architecture.

The churches are unique in that many stand completely free from the rock, unlike similar structures in Jordan and Egypt. The buildings show extraordinary technical skill in the use of line, proportion and decoration, and in the remarkable variety of styles.

The rock-hewn churches of the Tigray region, though less famous and spectacular, are no less remarkable.

## Gonder Architecture

The town of Gonder and its imperial enclosure represent another peak in Ethiopian architectural achievement. Although Portuguese, Moorish and Indian influences are all evident, the castles are nevertheless a peculiarly Ethiopian synthesis. Some have windows decorated with red volcanic tuff, and barrel- or egg-shaped domes.

## Ethiopian Houses

Ethiopian houses are famously diverse; each ethnic group has developed its own design according to its own lifestyle and resources. In general, the round *tukul* (hut) forms the basis of most designs. Circular structures and

Emperor Haile Selassie had a fairly unique taste in architecture. The Church of St Mary of Zion in Aksum and the church at Debre Libanos are exceptional examples of his unusual 'vision'.

Recent evidence from French archaeologists working in Lalibela suggests that the churches of Lalibela were not built in a very short time period as has long been thought but rather over a period of several hundred years.

## HOOFPRINTS & SAINTLY REMINDERS

Few would doubt that the churches of Lalibela are one of the architectural highlights of the early Middle Ages. And of all the churches none are as exquisite as the cruciform Bet Giyorgis. So perfectly composed is this church you could be forgiven for thinking that it could not possibly be the design of mere men. And according to Ethiopian tradition you'd be right.

Just as King Lalibela was finishing off his series of churches, he was suddenly paid an unexpected visit. Astride a white horse and decked out in full armour came Ethiopia's patron saint, George. However, the saint turned out to be severely piqued: not one of the churches had been dedicated to him.

Profusely apologetic, Lalibela promised to make amends immediately by building him the most beautiful church of all.

Today, the priests of Bet Giyorgis (meaning 'Place of George') point out the hoofprints left behind by the saint's horse, permanently imprinted in stone on the side of the trench.

conical thatched roofs better resist the wind and heavy rain. Windows and chimneys are usually absent. The smoke, which escapes through the thatch, fumigates the building, protecting it against insect infestations such as termites.

Sometimes the huts are shared: the right side for the family, the left for the animals. Livestock are not only protected from predators, but in some regions they also provide central heating!

# Ethiopian Cuisine

By now you've read enough of this book to know one thing: Ethiopia is unique. It has a culture that stands apart from all the nations around it; its religious practices are different to all neighbouring nations and its climate is the polar opposite to the searing deserts that hem it in. So, we doubt you'd be surprised to learn that Ethiopian food, and the myriad ways in which it's prepared, is not only some of the most diverse on the continent, but also totally different to any other cuisine you may have encountered.

Plates, bowls and even utensils are replaced by *injera,* a one-of-a-kind pancake of countrywide proportions. Atop its rubbery confines sit delicious multicoloured mounds of spicy meat stews, tasty vegetable curries and even cubes of raw beef.

Whether it's the spices joyfully bringing a tear to your eye or the slightly tart taste of the spongy *injera* sending your tongue into convulsions, one thing's for sure, Ethiopian fare provokes a strong reaction in all and though you might not always enjoy it, you'll never forget it.

## An Ethiopian Meal

Popular breakfast dishes include *enkulal fir fir* (scrambled eggs made with a combination of green and red peppers, tomatoes and sometimes onions, served with bread), the omelette version is known as *enkulal tibs*, *ful* (broad beans and butter purée) and *injera fir fir* (torn-up *injera* mixed with butter and *berbere*, a red powder containing 16 spices or more).

At lunch and dinner the much-heralded Ethiopian staples of *wat* (stew), *kitfo* (mince meat) and *tere sega* (raw meat) come out to play with the ever-present *injera*.

---

### TASTY TRAVEL

With raw meat being a staple in Ethiopia, what dishes could possibly constitute a radical departure for those wishing to truly travel their tastebuds?

High on the exotic factor would have to be *trippa wat* (tripe stew), which still curls our toes and shakes our stomachs. And if unleavened bread that's been buried in an underground pit and allowed to ferment for up to six months suits your fancy, order some *kotcho* with your *kitfo*. *Kotcho* comes from the false-banana plant (known in Ethiopia as *enset*) and closely resembles a fibrous carpet liner.

Fermentation of an entirely different sort can lead you down a very different path. If you're not catching an early bus the next morning, try the local *araki*, a grain spirit that will make you positively gasp (some travellers liken it to a stronger version of Greek ouzo). The Ethiopians believe it's good for high blood pressure! *Dagem araki* is twice-filtered and is finer. It's usually found in local hole-in-the-wall bars.

For something a little stronger, how about knocking back a shot of the holy water used at the Debre Libanos Monastery to wash the 1500-year-old leg of Saint Tekla Haimanot? See the boxed text on p67 for more.

# Injera

Just like your first kiss, your first taste of *injera* is an experience you'll never forget.

It's the national staple and the base of almost every meal. It is spread out like a large, thin pancake, and food is simply heaped on top of it. An American tourist is said to have once mistaken it for the tablecloth. Occasionally, *injera* is served rolled up beside the food or on a separate plate, looking much like a hot towel on an aeroplane.

And just like your first kiss, most first impressions of *injera* are not too positive! The overwhelmingly tangy taste can be enough to make some people retch (though we hope you didn't do that on your first kiss!), but give it another few mouthfuls and it'll start to grow on you. The bitter, slightly sour, taste contrasts beautifully with the fiery sauces it normally accompanies. Like bread, it's filling; like a pancake, it's good for wrapping around small pieces of food and mopping up juices. It's also much easier to manipulate on the plate than rice and it doesn't fall apart like bread – all up *injera* is quite a clever invention, really.

Although *injera* may look like an old grey kitchen flannel, grades and nuances do exist. With a bit of time and perseverance, you may even become a connoisseur.

Low-quality *injera* is traditionally dark, coarse and sometimes very thick, and is made from a very dark *tef* (the indigenous Ethiopian cereal). In some areas millet or even sorghum act as a substitute for *tef*, though it's very unlikely that as a tourist you'd encounter *injera* made of either of these. Good-quality *injera* is pale (the paler the better), regular in thickness, smooth (free of husks) and *always* made from a white *tef*. Because *tef* grows only in the highlands, the best *injera* is traditionally found there, and highlanders tend to be rather snooty about lesser lowland versions.

Kevin Rushby's brilliant book *Eating the Flowers of Paradise* is an entertaining and adventurous story of his journey through Ethiopia, Djibouti and Yemen in search of the perfect *chat* session.

## Know Your Injera

With large Ethiopian populations living in Western countries many people will have tried Ethiopian food in their home cities, but take note that

## EATING THE FLOWERS OF PARADISE

Head to eastern Ethiopia and you don't have to be there long to notice the bulging cheeks of the *chat* chewer. *Chat*, *khat*, *qat* or *miraa* are the leaves of the shrub *Catha edulis*. Originating in the hills of eastern Ethiopia the *chat* plant has spread across parts of East Africa and into southern Arabia, and for many of the inhabitants of this broad swath of land the afternoon *chat*-chewing session has become almost a pivotal point of life.

The effects of *chat* have long been debated – most users will insist that it gives an unbeatable high, makes you more talkative (at least until the come down when the chewer becomes withdrawn and quiet), suppresses hunger, prevents tiredness and increases sexual performance. Others will tell you that it gives no noticeable high, makes you lethargic, slightly depressed, constipated and reduces sex drive! Most Western visitors who try it report no major effects aside from a possible light buzz and an unpleasant aftertaste.

If you're going to chew *chat* then you need to make sure the setting is perfect in order to enjoy the experience. Ask for the sweetest *chat* you can get (most Ethiopians regard this as poor quality *chat*, but first-time chewers find even this very bitter) and get a good group of people together to chew with, because *chat* is, above all else, a social drug. Take yourself off to a quiet and comfortable room – ideally one with a view, sit back, relax and enjoy the conversation while popping leaves individually into your mouth where you literally just store them in one cheek, gently chewing them. All going well you'll be a *chat* 'addict' by the end of the day.

what often passes for *injera* there is not real *injera* at all. Although you *can* get real *injera* outside the Horn of Africa, most of the time you will instead be served something made from a *tef* substitute. *Injera* made like this lacks the slightly fermented, tangy taste and the rubbery feel of real *injera*.

When in Ethiopia, many foreigners quickly find themselves getting fed up with an endless diet of *injera* (and that's without taking into account the sometimes undesired 'side-effects' on your stomach that eating a semifermented bread for days on end can cause some visitors!); this is especially true of those eating only in cheap, local restaurants where *injera* might not be of the highest quality. In fact, when we spoke to tour guides about this most of them thought that around 80–90% of foreign visitors try to avoid eating *injera* again after a week in Ethiopia!

But let's not be too hard on *injera*. Some travellers adore the stuff and happily munch it down for week after week and, being full of proteins and nutrients, it can actually help to keep you healthy on the road.

If *injera* fatigue kicks in for you, then you'll probably find it worth splashing out on an Ethiopian 'banquet' at a more expensive tourist-class restaurant in Addis or any of the big tourist towns. Generally the *injera* at these places is of a very high quality and much less sour. After a couple of meals like this you'll probably be ready to hit the cheap stuff again. And if not, well you can always ask to have your *wat* served with bread instead of *injera*, or even just resort to the (generally pretty disgusting) sloppy pasta and dubious sauce that's sold everywhere!

## Wat

The ubiquitous companion of *injera*, *wat* is Ethiopia's version of curry and can be very spicy – fortunately the *injera* helps to temper the heat.

In the highlands, *beg* (sheep) is the most common constituent of *wat*. *Bere* (beef) is encountered in the large towns, and *fiyel* (goat) most often in the arid lowlands. Chicken is the king of the *wat* and *doro wat* is practically the national dish. Ethiopian Christians as well as Muslims avoid pork. On the fasting days (see p264) of Wednesdays and Fridays, throughout Lent and prior to Christmas, as well as a further couple of occasions, meat and dairy dishes are avoided and various vegetarian versions of *wat* are available. Most foreigners become firm fans of fasting food.

*Kai wat* is a stew of meat boiled in a spicy (thanks to oodles of *berbere*) red sauce. *Kai* sauce is also used for *minchet abesh*, which is a thick minced-meat stew topped with a hard-boiled egg – it's one of our favourites, particularly with *aib* (like dry cottage cheese).

Most Ethiopians seem to be under the impression that all foreigners are terrified of spicy food and so, unless you specifically ask for *kai wat*, you'll often be served the yellow-coloured *alicha wat*, a much milder, and really rather dull-tasting *wat*.

## Kitfo

*Kitfo* is a big treat for the ordinary Ethiopian. The leanest meat is reserved for this dish, which is then minced and warmed in a pan with a little butter, *mitmita* (a stronger version of *berbere*) and sometimes *tosin* (thyme). It can be bland and disgusting, or tasty and divine. If you're ravenous after a hard day's travelling, it's just the ticket, as it's very filling.

Traditionally, it's served just *leb leb* (warmed not cooked), though you can ask for it to be *betam leb leb* (literally 'very warmed', ie cooked!). A *kitfo* special is served with *aib* and *gomen* (minced spinach).

In the Gurage region (where it's something of a speciality) it's often served with *kotcho* (*enset*; false-banana 'bread'). *Kitfo bets* (restaurants specialising in *kitfo*) are found in the larger towns.

ETHIOPIAN CUISINE AN ETHIOPIAN MEAL

If you want to save yourself some embarrassment (unlike us), never inhale as you're placing *injera* laden with *berbere* into your mouth.

If you become a massive fan of *kitfo* or *tere sega*, best get tested for tape worms (see p344) when you get home. Hopefully there'll be no pain to go with your tasty gain.

Another favourite meat dish of ours is *siga tibs*, which consists of small strips of fried meat served with onions, garlic and spices. It's most commonly served *derek* (dry), but you can also find a *merek yalew* version, which comes in a liquid sauce.

## Tere Sega

Considered something of a luxury in Ethiopia, *tere sega* (raw meat) is traditionally served by the wealthy at weddings and other special occasions.

Some restaurants also specialise in it. Not unlike butcher shops in appearance, these places feature carcasses hanging near the entrance and men in bloodied overalls brandishing carving knives. The restaurants aren't as gruesome as they sound: the carcass is to demonstrate that the meat is fresh, and the men in overalls to guarantee you get the piece you fancy – two assurances you don't always get in the West.

A plate and a sharp knife serve as utensils, and *awazi* (a kind of mustard and chilli sauce) and *mitmita* as accompaniments. Served with some local red wine, and enjoyed with Ethiopian friends, it's a ritual not to be missed – at least not for red-blooded meat eaters. It's sometimes called *gored gored*.

## Drinks

Ethiopia has a well-founded claim to be the original home of coffee, and coffee continues to be ubiquitous across the country. As a result of Italian influence, *macchiato* (espresso with a dash of milk), cappuccino and a kind of cafe latte known as a *buna bewetet* (coffee with milk) are also available in many of the towns. Sometimes the herb rue (known locally as *t'ena adam,* or health of Adam) is served with coffee, as is butter. In

---

### DOS & DON'TS

#### Do

» Bring a small gift if you've been invited to someone's home for a meal. Pastries or flowers are good choices in urban areas, while sugar, coffee and fruit are perfect in rural areas.

» Use just your right hand for eating. The left (as in Muslim countries) is reserved for personal hygiene only. Keep it firmly tucked under the table.

» Take from your side of the tray only; reaching is considered impolite.

» Leave some leftovers on the plate after a meal. Failing to do so is sometimes seen as inviting famine.

» Feel free to pick your teeth after a meal. Toothpicks are usually supplied in restaurants.

#### Don't

» Be embarrassed or alarmed at the tradition of *gursha,* when someone (usually the host) picks the tastiest morsel and feeds it directly into your mouth. The trick is to take it without letting your mouth come into contact with the person's fingers, or allowing the food to fall. It's a mark of great friendship or affection, and is usually given at least twice (once is considered unlucky). Refusing to take *gursha* is a terrible slight to the person offering it!

» Put food back onto the food plate – even by the side. It's better to discard it onto the table or floor, or keep it in your napkin.

» Touch your mouth or lick your fingers.

» Fill your mouth too full. It's considered impolite.

## THE COFFEE CEREMONY

The coffee ceremony typifies Ethiopian hospitality. An invitation to attend a ceremony is a mark of friendship or respect, though it's not an event for those in a hurry.

When you're replete after a meal, the ceremony begins. Freshly cut grass is scattered on the ground 'to bring in the freshness and fragrance of nature'. Nearby, there's an incense burner smoking with *etan* (gum). The 'host' sits on a stool before a tiny charcoal stove.

First of all coffee beans are roasted in a pan. As the smoke rises, it's considered polite to draw it towards you, inhale it deeply and express great pleasure at the delicious aroma by saying *betam tiru no* (lovely!). Next the beans are ground up with a pestle and mortar before being brewed up.

When it's finally ready, the coffee is served in tiny china cups with at least three spoonfuls of sugar. At least three cups must be accepted. The third in particular is considered to bestow a blessing – it's the *berekha* (blessing) cup. Sometimes popcorn is passed around.

Enjoy!

the western highlands, a layered drink of coffee and tea is also popular. If you want milk with coffee, ask for *betinnish wetet* (with a little milk).

In lowland Muslim areas, *shai* (tea) is preferred to coffee, and is offered black, sometimes spiced with cloves or ginger.

Most cafes also dabble in fresh juice, though it's usually dosed with sugar. If you don't want sugar in your juice or in your tea or coffee, make it clear when you order. Ask for the drink *yale sukkar* (without sugar). Bottled water is always available, as is the local favourite Ambo, a natural sparkling mineral water from western Ethiopia.

One drink not to be missed is *tej,* a delicious – and sometimes pretty powerful – local 'wine' or mead made from honey, and fermented using a local shrub known as *gesho. Tej* used to be reserved only for Ethiopian kings and their courts and comes in many varieties. It's served in little flasks known as *birille.*

> If looking for quality *tej,* ask a local. They'll know who makes it with pure honey and who cheats by adding sugar.

There are several breweries in Ethiopia that pump out decent beers, including St George, Harar, Bati, Meta, Bedele, Dashen and Castel. Everyone has a different favourite, so explore at will.

Though no cause for huge celebration, local wine isn't at all bad, particularly the red Gouder. Of the whites, the dry Awash Crystal is about the best bet. Unless you're an aficionado of sweet red, avoid Axumite. Outside Addis Ababa, wine is usually only served in the restaurants of midrange hotels.

It doesn't seem to matter how remote you are, all the standard international soft drinks are available everywhere.

In the Somali regions in the east, camel milk is a speciality. Locals claim that it gives most foreigners the shits, but we can happily report that our stomachs are stronger than that!

Finally, in the Omo valley region of southern Ethiopia many tribal people start the day with a calabash of fresh, warm blood straight from the neck of a favourite cow. It sounds disgusting but fans will tell you that not only is it full of goodness but it also makes you very strong. In fact, the male members of many Omo tribes frequently gorge on it in the build-up to a stick fight in order to make themselves as strong as possible. And no harm is done to the cow: they use a miniature bow and arrow to pierce a vein in the neck and the cow appears to suffer no permanent damage.

## Celebrations

Food plays a major role in religious festivals of both Muslims and Ethiopian Orthodox Christians. During the month of Ramadan, Muslims fast between sunrise and sunset, while Ethiopian Orthodox Christians abstain from eating any animal products in the 55 days leading up to Ethiopian Easter.

Orthodox Ethiopians also abstain from animal products each Wednesday and Friday. There are a very large number of Orthodox feast days, of which 33 honour the Virgin Mary alone.

## Where to Eat & Drink

Contrary to the myth started by 18th-century Scottish explorer James Bruce, Ethiopians don't carve meat from living animals. Whether it occurred in ancient times, remains uncertain.

Outside Addis Ababa and major towns, there isn't a plethora of eating options. You're usually constrained to small local restaurants (which in Ethiopia, as in much of East Africa, are often known as hotels or some variation of the word) that serve one pasta dish and a limited selection of Ethiopian food. In larger towns, local restaurants and hotels both offer numerous Ethiopian meals. The hotels' menus also throw some, normally very forgettable, Western meals into the mix.

*Kitfo bets* are specialist restaurants in larger towns that primarily serve *kitfo*. Similarly *tej bets* are bars that focus on serving *tej*.

Unlike Addis Ababa, where restaurant hours vary widely, most restaurants elsewhere are open daily from around 7.30am to 10pm. *Tej bets* tend to open later (around 10am), but also close about 10pm.

## Vegetarians & Vegans

On Wednesday, Friday and throughout the build up to Fasika (Lent), vegetarians breathe easy as these are the traditional fasting days, when no animal products should be eaten. Ethiopian fasting food most commonly includes *messer* (lentil curry), *gomen* (collard greens) and *kai ser* (beetroot). *Ful* is another saviour for vegetarians although this is normally only served at breakfast time.

Apart from fasting days, Ethiopians are rapacious carnivores and vegetables are often conspicuous by their complete absence. If you're vegetarian or vegan, the best plan is to order alternative dishes in advance. If not, some dishes such as *shiro* (chickpea purée) are quite quickly prepared. Note that fancier hotels tend to offer fasting food seven days a week.

If you're really concerned about the availability of vegetarian food the best bet is to come during the 55 days preceding Fasika (p19). It's also a good idea to keep a small stack of vegetarian snacks on hand.

## Habits & Customs

Eating from individual plates strikes most Ethiopians as hilarious, as well as rather bizarre and wasteful. In Ethiopia, food is always shared from a single plate without the use of cutlery.

In many cases, with a simple *Enebla!* (Please join us!), people invite those around them (even strangers) to join them at their restaurant table. For those invited, it's polite to accept a morsel of the food to show appreciation.

### PRICE RANGES

The following price ranges used in this book refer to an average main course.

**$** less than US$5

**$$** US$5–10

**$$$** more than US$10

   In households and many restaurants, a jug of water and basin are brought out to wash the guests' outstretched hands before the meal.

   When eating with locals, try not to guzzle. Greed is considered rather uncivilised. The tastiest morsels will often be laid in front of you; it's polite to accept them or, equally, to divide them among your fellow diners. The meat dishes such as *doro wat* are usually the last thing locals eat off the *injera,* so don't hone in on it immediately!

# Food Glossary

Most of the following are served with *injera*.

## Nonvegetarian

| | |
|---|---|
| **alicha wat** | mild stew (meat and vegetarian options) |
| **asa wat** | freshwater fish served as a hot stew |
| **bege** | lamb |
| **bere** | beef |
| **beyainatu** | literally 'of every type' – a small portion of all dishes on the menu; also known by its Italian name *secondo misto* |
| **bistecca ai ferri** | grilled steak |
| **derek tibs** | meat (usually lamb) fried and served *derek* ('dry' – without sauce) |
| **doro** | chicken |
| **doro wat** | chicken drumstick or wing accompanied by a hard-boiled egg served in a hot sauce of butter, onion, chilli, cardamom and *berbere* |
| **dulet** | minced tripe, liver and lean beef fried in butter, onions, chilli, cardamom and pepper (often eaten for breakfast) |
| **fatira** | savoury pastries |
| **fiyel** | goat |
| **kai wat** | lamb, goat or beef cooked in a hot *berbere* sauce |
| **kekel** | boiled meat |
| **kitfo** | minced beef or lamb like the French steak tartare, usually served warmed (but not cooked) in butter, *mitmita* and sometimes thyme |
| **kwalima** | sausage served on ceremonial occasions |
| **kwanta fir fir** | strips of beef rubbed in chilli, butter, salt and *berbere* then usually hung up and dried; served with torn-up *injera* |
| **mahabaroui** | a mixture of dishes including half a roast chicken |
| **melasena senber tibs** | beef tongue and tripe fried with *berbere* and onion |
| **minchet abesh** | minced beef or lamb in a hot *berbere* sauce |
| **scaloppina** | escalope |
| **tere sega** | raw meat served with a couple of spicy accompaniments (occasionally called *gored gored*) |
| **tibs** | sliced lamb, pan fried in butter, garlic, onion and sometimes tomato |
| **tibs sheukla** | *tibs* served sizzling in a clay pot above hot coals |
| **trippa** | tripe |
| **wat** | stew |
| **zilzil tibs** | strips of beef, fried and served slightly crunchy with *awazi* sauce |

If you already know your *kekel* from your *kai wat* and want to learn more Amharic, pick up Lonely Planet's *Amharic Phrasebook*.

## Vegetarian

| | |
|---|---|
| **aib** | like dry cottage cheese |
| **atkilt-b-dabbo** | vegetables with bread |
| **awazi** | a kind of mustard and chilli sauce |
| **berbere** | as many as 16 spices or more go into making the famous red powder that is responsible for giving much Ethiopian food its kick; most women prepare their own special recipe, often passed down from mother to daughter over generations, and proudly adhered to |
| **dabbo fir fir** | torn-up bits of bread mixed with butter and *berbere* |
| **enkulal tibs** | literally 'egg *tibs*', a kind of Ethiopian scrambled eggs made with a combination of green and red peppers, tomatoes and sometimes onions, served with *dabbo* (bread) – great for breakfast |
| **fendisha** | popcorn |
| **ful** | broadbean and butter purée eaten for breakfast |
| **genfo** | barley or wheat porridge served with butter and *berbere* |
| **gomen** | minced spinach |
| **injera** | large Ethiopian version of a pancake/plate |
| **injera fir fir** | torn-up bits of *injera* mixed with butter and *berbere* |
| **kai ser** | beetroot |
| **kolo** | roasted barley |
| **kotcho** | false-banana 'bread'; a staple food |
| **messer** | a kind of lentil curry made with onions, chillies and various spices |
| **shiro** | chickpea or bean purée lightly spiced, served on fasting days |
| **sils** | hot tomato and onion sauce eaten for breakfast |
| **tihlo** | an eastern Tigray speciality consisting of barley balls dipped in a spicy sauce |
| **ye tsom megeb** | a selection of different vegetable dishes, served on fasting days |

# Ethiopia's Environment

The farmer who eats his chickens as well as all their eggs will have a bleak future.
*Tigrayan proverb*

Some of the earliest humans chose to make Ethiopia their home, and who can blame them? This is a land of extraordinary diversity: where cold evening winds whip across high moorland plateaus and powerful rivers tumble through deep gorges; where elegantly dressed colobus monkeys swing through dense forests, savannah grasslands shimmer in the sun and camel caravans traverse some of the most inhospitable territory on Earth.

For a visitor obsessed with seeing Ethiopia's cultural highlights, the stirring landscapes and eye-catching wildlife often comes as an unexpected, and very welcome, surprise.

## The Land

With a land area of 1,098,000 sq km, Ethiopia is five times the size of Britain and twice the size of Texas. Its topography is remarkably diverse, ranging from 20 peaks higher than 4000m to one of the lowest, hottest, driest and most inhospitable points on the Earths surface: the infamous Danakil Depression, which in parts lies almost 125m below sea level and sprawls into neighbouring Eritrea and Djibouti.

Two principal geographical zones can be found in the country: cool highlands and their surrounding hot lowlands.

Ethiopia's main topographical feature is the vast central plateau (the Ethiopian highlands) with an average elevation between 1800m and 2400m. It's here that the country's major peaks are found, including Ras Dashen (more correctly, but less commonly, known as Ras Dejen) at 4543m, Ethiopia's highest mountain and Africa's 10th highest.

The mountains are also the source of four major river systems, the most famous of which is the Blue Nile. Starting from Lake Tana and joined later by the White Nile in Sudan, it nurtures Egypt's fertile Nile Valley. The other principal rivers are the Awash, the Omo and the Wabe Shebele.

Southern Ethiopia is bisected diagonally by the Rift Valley. Averaging around 50km wide, it runs all the way south to Mozambique. The valley floor is home to many of Ethiopia's most important lakes, including a well-known chain south of Addis Ababa.

The northern end of the Rift Valley opens into the Danakil Depression, a low-lying area that extends through northern Ethiopia to the coast (where the ever-widening Rift Valley will be flooded by sea water

The Danakil Depression has the highest average temperature of anywhere on Earth.

The Earth's crust is rifting apart at the rate of 1cm to 2cm a year in the Danakil Depression and there has been a near continuous sequence of earthquakes here.

## FUNNY FROGS

During a scientific expedition to the Harenna Forest in the Bale Mountains a few years ago, biologists discovered four entirely new frog species in the space of just three weeks. Many of the frogs appear to have made peculiar adaptations to their environment. One species swallows snails whole, another has forgotten how to hop and a third has lost its ears.

sometime in the next couple of million years as East Africa gradually splits off from the rest of Africa).

## Wildlife

Ethiopia's ecosystems are diverse, from high Afro-alpine vegetation to desert and semidesert scrubland. Rounding out the roster of habitats are six more unique ecosystems: dry evergreen montane forests and grassland; small-leaved deciduous forests; broad-leaved deciduous forests; moist evergreen forests; lowland semi-evergreen forests; and wetlands.

The massive Ethiopian central plateau is home to several of these ecosystems, as well as a distinctive assemblage of plants and animals. Isolated for millions of years within this 'fortress environment', and unable to cross the inhospitable terrain surrounding the plateau, many highland plants and animals evolved their own unique adaptations.

Birdwatchers will be thrilled by the newest guide to this region's unique birdlife, *Birds of the Horn of Africa: Ethiopia, Eritrea, Djibouti, Somalia, and Socotra* by Nigel Redman, Terry Stevenson and John Fanshawe.

## Animals

Simply because it lacks large crowds of cavorting elephants, giraffes and rhinos, Ethiopia is mistakenly written off by many Westerners as simply an historical destination. What they don't know is that Ethiopia hosts 279 mammal species, 201 reptile species, 150 fish species and 63 amphibian species. And that doesn't even include the birds!

To date, more than 860 species of birds have been recorded (compared with just 250 in the UK). Of Africa's 10 endemic mainland bird families, eight are represented in Ethiopia; only rockfowls and sugarbirds are absent. Families that are particularly well represented are falcons, francolins, bustards and larks.

More noteworthy is the fact that of all the species in Ethiopia, 31 mammals, 21 birds, nine reptiles, four fish and 24 amphibians are endemic (found only in Ethiopia). The biggest thrill of all is the realisation that you have a pretty good chance of spotting some of the rarest species, including the Ethiopian wolf, which is the planet's rarest canid (dog-family member).

*Endemic Mammals of Ethiopia*, by Jill Last and published by the defunct Ethiopian Tourism Commission, gives decent descriptions of the appearance and behaviour of Ethiopia's mammals. It's usually available in Addis Ababa.

### Animals by Habitat

#### AFRO-ALPINE

The Afro-alpine habitat, within the Bale and Simien Mountains National Parks, boasts the largest number of endemic mammals and hosts mountain nyalas, walia ibexes, Ethiopian wolves, gelada baboons, Menelik's bushbuck and giant molerats. In addition, 16 of Ethiopia's endemic birds are also found in these lofty confines.

#### DESERT & SEMIDESERT SCRUBLAND

At the opposite end of the elevation spectrum, the sprawling deserts and semidesert scrublands of Ethiopia and Djibouti host the endangered African wild asses and Grevy's zebras, as well as the Soemmering's gazelles and beisa oryx. Birds include ostriches; secretary birds; Arabian, Kori and Heuglin's bustards; Abyssinian rollers; red-cheeked cordon bleus; and crested francolins.

## DECIDUOUS FOREST

Widespread but discontinuous deciduous forests are home to greater and lesser kudus, hartebeest, gazelles, De Brazza's monkeys and small populations of elands, buffaloes and elephants. Limited numbers of Grevy's zebras and beisa oryx also inhabit these areas. Birdlife includes the white-bellied go-away bird, superb starling, red-billed quelea, helmeted guinea fowl, secretary bird, Ruppell's long-tailed starling, gambaga flycatcher, red-cheeked cordon bleu, bush petronia and black-faced firefinch.

## EVERGREEN FOREST

Wandering the evergreen forests in the southwestern and western parts of the country are bushpigs, forest hogs, Menelik's bushbucks and more De Brazza's monkeys. Around Gambela, in the lowland semi-evergreen forest, are rare populations of elephants, giraffes, lions and, if rumours are to be believed, massive herds of white-eared kob, a beautiful golden antelope found in larger numbers in southern Sudan. The colourful birdlife includes Abyssinian black-headed orioles, Abyssinian hill babblers, white-cheeked turacos, scaly-throated honeyguides, scaly francolins, emerald cuckoos and yellow-billed coucals.

## DRY EVERGREEN MONTANE FOREST & GRASSLAND

The odd leopard, gazelle, jackal and hyena still roam the dry evergreen montane forest and grassland found in Ethiopia's north, northwest and central and southern highlands. Birds of note include black-winged lovebirds, half-collared kingfishers and several endemic species.

## WETLANDS

Hippos and crocodiles are found around Gambela in the wetlands along the Baro River. They also populate some of the Rift Valley lakes in the south – Lake Chamo is famous for its massive crocodiles. Rouget's rails and white-winged flufftails are found in the wetland swamps, while Senegal thick-knees and red-throated bee-eaters live in riverbank habitats.

# Endangered Species

The International Union for the Conservation of Nature and Natural Resources (IUCN) lists seven species in Ethiopia as critically endangered; one is Ethiopia's endemic walia ibex. Amazingly, you have a pretty good chance of spotting this rare animal in the Simien Mountains National Park.

A further 19 species in Ethiopia are listed as endangered by IUCN. These include the endemic mountain nyala and Ethiopian wolf, both easily viewed in Bale Mountains National Park (and the wolf also in the

The Nechisar nightjar (*Caprimulgus solala*) was long known from a single wing found squashed on the road near Nechisar National Park in 1990. In 2009, after nearly 20 years' wait, the first living birds were claimed to have been seen by a group of respected ornithologists.

## ETHIOPIA'S ENDEMIC BIRDS

There's no denying that the diversity and beauty of Ethiopia's astounding 862 recorded bird species could convert even the most die-hard nonbirder into a habitual and excited twitcher. It's the endemic bird species that really set Ethiopia apart.

An amazing 16 species are found nowhere else in the world. Thirteen more are semi-endemic, shared only with Eritrea.

The best time to visit Ethiopia for birding is between November and February, when some 200 species of Palaearctic migrants from Europe and Asia join the already abundant African resident and intra-African migrant populations. The most likely time to spot birds is from dawn to 11am and from 5pm to dusk, although birds can be seen throughout the day.

newly created Guassa Community Conservation Area). Nechisar National Park formerly hosted the endangered African hunting dog and what is likely Ethiopia's rarest endemic bird, the Nechisar nightjar. Vulnerable bird species are Prince Ruspoli's turaco, Salvadori's serin, Stresemann's bush crow, the Sidamo long-clawed lark, the Degodi lark, the Ankober serin and the white-tailed swallow.

## Plants

Ethiopia's flora is as exceptional as almost everything else about this country. Ethiopia was classed as one of the world's 12 most important hot spots for crop plant diversity by the famous Russian geneticist Nikolai Vavilov, and is thought to possess extremely valuable pools of crop plant genes. Between 600 and 1400 plant species are thought to be endemic; a whopping 10% to 20% of its flora.

The small-leaved deciduous forests can be found all over the country apart from the western regions, at an altitude of between 900m and 1900m. Vegetation consists of drought-tolerant shrubs and trees with either leathery persistent leaves or small, deciduous ones. Trees include various types of acacia. Herbs include *Acalypha* and *Aerva*.

*Where to Watch Birds in Ethiopia,* by Claire Spottiswoode et al and published by Christopher Helm Publishers, is a new guide to the 50 best bird-watching sites in Ethiopia.

The western and northwestern areas of Ethiopia host broad-leaved deciduous forests, while tall and medium-sized trees and understorey shrubs of the moist evergreen forests also occupy the west, as well as the nation's southwest. Even further west are the lowland semi-evergreen forests around Gambela. Vegetation there consists of semi-evergreen trees and shrub species, as well as grasses.

Covering much of the highlands and the north, northwest, central and southern parts of the country, is the dry evergreen montane forest and grassland. This habitat is home to a large number of endemic plants. Tree species include various types of acacia, olive and euphorbia. Africa's only rose, the *Rosa abyssinica,* is here.

Within the Afro-alpine vegetation habitat, you'll see the endemic giant lobelia *(Lobelia rhynchopetalum),* an endemic species of globe thistle, as well as the so-called 'soft thistle'. On the high plateaus at around 4000m are many varieties of gentian.

Look out for fig and tamarind trees along the Baro River in the west, as well as along river banks or *wadis* (seasonal rivers) in the highlands and the northwest.

The Dankalia region, Omo delta and Ogaden Desert contain drought-resistant plants such as small trees, shrubs and grasses, including acacia. Succulent species include euphorbia and aloe. The region is classified as desert and semidesert scrubland.

### SPOT THE ENDEMIC FLORA

Ethiopia has more unique species of flora than any other country in Africa. This fact is becoming abundantly clear thanks to the ongoing Flora of Somalia project, which has documented more than 400 new species of flowering plants in Ethiopia, including a newly discovered acacia tree that grows by the millions over 8000 sq km.

In September and October, look out particularly for Ethiopia's national flower, the famous yellow daisy known as the Meskel flower, which carpets the highlands; it belongs to the sunflower family, six members of which are endemic.

In towns and villages, the endemic yellow-flowered *Solanecio gigas* is commonly employed as a hedge. Around Addis Ababa, the tall endemic *Erythrina brucei* tree can be seen. In the highlands, such as in the Bale Mountain and Simien Mountain National Parks, the indigenous Abyssinian rose is quite commonly found. Also in the Bale Mountains, look out for the endemic species of globe thistle *(Echinops longisetus).*

# National Parks & Wildlife Sanctuaries

In the last few years the Ethiopian government has created a flurry of new national parks and other protected areas. Currently there are 21 national parks, five wildlife sanctuaries and reserves and six community conservation areas in Ethiopia. The most famed of these is the Simien Mountains National Park, a Unesco World Heritage site. Many of the other protected areas actually receive very little protection at all (the government itself has allowed the establishment of sugarcane plantations in Omo and Mago National Parks).

## TOP PARKS & SANCTUARIES

| PARK | FEATURES | ACTIVITIES | BEST TIME TO VISIT |
|---|---|---|---|
| **Northern Ethiopia** | | | |
| Simien Mountains National Park (p87) | Dramatic volcanic escarpments and plateaus; walia ibexes, gelada baboons, Simien wolves, lammergeyers | Trekking, birdwatching, wildlife viewing | Oct-Jan |
| **Southern Ethiopia** | | | |
| Bale Mountains National Park (p144) | Steep ridges, alpine plateaus; Ethiopian wolves, mountain nyala and 16 endemic birds | Trekking, birdwatching | Oct-Jan |
| Abiata-Shala Lakes National Park (p137) | Crater lakes, hot springs; red-billed hornbills, Didric's cuckoos, Abyssinian rollers, superb starlings | Birdwatching, walking | Nov-Dec |
| Mago National Park (p167) | Savannah, open woodland; elephants, hartebeest, buffaloes, many birds | Visiting Mursi people, wildlife drives | Jun-Sep & Jan-Feb |
| Nechisar National Park (p156) | Savannah, acacia woodland; Burchell's zebras, Swayne's hartebeest, crocodiles, greater kudu, 320 bird species | Wildlife drives, boat trips | Nov-Feb |
| Omo National Park (p205) | Savannah, open woodland; elephants, buffaloes, lions | Visiting Mursi, Dizi and Surma groups | Jun-Sep & Jan-Feb |
| Senkelle Swayne's Hartebeest Sanctuary (p140) | Open acacia woodland; Swayne's hartebeest, Bohor reedbucks, spotted hyenas, greater spotted eagles | Wildlife drives | Nov-Feb |
| Yabelo Wildlife Sanctuary (p151) | Acacia woodland, savannah grasses; Stresemann's bush crows, white-tailed swallows, Swayne's hartebeest, gerenuks | Wildlife drives, birdwatching | year-round |
| **Eastern Ethiopia** | | | |
| Awash National Park (p176) | Semiarid woodland; beisa oryxes, Soemmering's gazelles, kudu, six endemic bird species | Birdwatching, wildlife viewing | Oct-Feb |
| **Western Ethiopia** | | | |
| Gambela National Park (p212) | Semiarid woodland, deciduous forests; savannah Nile lechwe, white-eared kobs, elephants | Rugged wildlife drives, trekking | Dec-Mar |

## THE STRANGE CASE OF THE VANISHING TURACO

In a remote patch in the deep south of Ethiopia lives one of the country's rarest, most beautiful and most enigmatic birds – the Prince Ruspoli's turaco, first introduced to the world in the early 1890s. It was 'collected' by an Italian prince (who gave his name to the bird) as he explored the dense juniper forests of southern Ethiopia.

Unfortunately, the intrepid prince failed to make a record of his find, and when he was killed shortly afterwards near Lake Abaya following 'an encounter with an elephant', all hope of locating the species seemed to die with him.

The turaco finally reappeared in the 1940s. Just three specimens were obtained, then the turaco disappeared again. It wasn't until the early 1970s that the bird was rediscovered.

Today, recent sightings in the Arero forest, east of Yabelo, around the Genale River off the Dola-Mena–Negele Borena road, suggest that the bird may not, after all, be as elusive as it would have us believe. You may find your own turaco in acacia or conifer woodlands in the southwestern corner of Ethiopia.

Park borders continue to overlap with local communities, and conflicts over conservation continue, despite wildlife authorities trying to encourage locals' participation in the conservation of wildlife.

One unexpected bit of good news comes from Gambela National Park on the border of South Sudan in the far west of the country. Once known to harbour huge herds of antelope as well as elephants, lions, buffalo and other big mammals, it had long been assumed that conflict in South Sudan and that part of Ethiopia coupled with an influx of refugees into the park would have devastated wildlife populations. But with the results of the first surveys in decades starting to trickle in it seems that we were all wrong and that Gambela is still home to significant populations of animals. See Gambela National Park, p212 for more.

The ox and plough has been in use in Ethiopia for more than 3000 years. It didn't reach much of the rest of sub-Saharan Africa until colonial times.

## Environmental Issues

Despite civil wars taking their toll on the environment, Ethiopia's demographic pressures have been the main culprit. About 95% of Ethiopia's original forest is believed to have been lost to agriculture and human settlement.

Ethiopia's population has almost quintupled in the last 75 years and continues to grow at 2.9%; the pressures for living space, firewood, building materials, agricultural land, livestock grazing and food will only further reduce natural resources and wipe out larger areas of wildlife habitat.

The deforestation has resulted in soil erosion, an extremely serious threat in Ethiopia because it exacerbates the risk of famine. Although hunting and poaching over the centuries have decimated the country's once-large herds of elephants and rhinos, deforestation has also played a role.

Wildlife and forests were both victims of the most recent civil war, where whole forests were torched by the Derg to smoke out rebel forces. Additionally, large armies, hungry and with inadequate provisions, turned their sights on the land's natural resources and much wildlife was wiped out.

Up until recently, armed conflict between ethnic groups in the Omo and Mago National Parks continued to impede wildlife conservation efforts.

Today, things are more under control. Hunting is managed by the government and may even provide the most realistic and pragmatic means of ensuring the future survival of Ethiopia's large mammals. Poaching, however, continues to pose a serious threat to some animals.

In late 2005 a new conservation action plan was put in place which crafted stricter environmental regulations, designed to unite previously scattered wildlife and environmental activities under the umbrella of a radically restructured Ethiopian Wildlife Conservation Authority. This action has started to pay off with new national parks, a little more money pumped into existing protected areas and environmental issues being discussed at higher levels of government.

For more on wildlife conservation, contact the **Ethiopian Wildlife Conservation Authority** (www.ewca.gov.et; PO Box 386, Addis Ababa).

## Gibe III Dam

Essential to the development of Ethiopia or an environmental and social disaster in the making? No conversation about environmental policies in Ethiopia is complete without talk of the huge new Gibe III dam.

The pet project of the late prime minister, Meles Zenawi, the Gibe III dam is part of a huge hydroelectric project being constructed on the Omo river. The Gibe dams I and II have already been completed and eventually five dams will be constructed along the Omo river. The project has several stated goals. Firstly, only around 2% of rural Ethiopians have mains electricity and it's hoped that this project will bring much more of the rural population onto the mains electricity grid. The government also hopes to sell about 50% of the electricity produced to neighbouring countries (though none of them have actually signed an agreement with Ethiopia to do so; Kenya has signed a Memorandum of Understanding).

It is also hoped that the construction of the Gibe III dam (which when completed will be the biggest dam in Africa) and its brothers will help reduce instances of drought and flooding as well as allowing the establishment of large scale sugarcane plantations in the Lower Omo Valley.

Well this all sounds very worthy; so what's the problem? According to the environmental and social impact assessment commissioned by the Ethiopian government (and released two years after construction of the dam began) the dam will cause minimal problems. However, almost every other independent environmental and social body disagrees. The African Resources Working Group has stated that 'Data collected in virtually all major sections of the [government environmental impact] report were clearly selected for the consistence with predetermined objective of validating the completion of the Gibe III hydro-dam'.

And how will it all affect people downriver? This is where things get really heated. In a BBC interview Meles Zenawi said: 'The overall environmental impact of the project is highly beneficial. It increases the amount of water in the river system, it completely regulates flooding which was a major problem, it improves the livelihood of people downstream because they will have irrigation projects, and it does not in any way negatively affect the Turkana Lake'. Environmentalists and social-rights bodies say that thousands of people who live downstream of the Gibe III dam, and are reliant on the annual flooding to fertilise and water their crops, will be adversely affected by its construction.

There are also widespread claims of forced resettlements in order to make room for the sugarcane plantations and repeated reports of human-rights violations by the Ethiopian army against locals who oppose the establishment of these farms.

International Rivers calls Gibe III 'the most destructive dam under construction in Africa' and Survival International claims that it will be a 'disaster of cataclysmic proportions for the tribes of the Omo valley'. The problems are not just limited to Ethiopia. Over the border in Kenya, Lake Turkana lies in an area of extreme aridity and thousands of Kenyans

UK-based Naturetrek (www.naturetrek.co.uk) runs a range of varied wildlife and ornithological tours to Ethiopia.

Want to know more about the Gibe III dam? Check out the project's official site www.gibe3.com.et and International Rivers Gibe III–related pages at www.internationalrivers.org/campaigns/gibe-iii-dam-ethiopia.

ETHIOPIA'S ENVIRONMENT ENVIRONMENTAL ISSUES

## THE BLEEDING HEART BABOON

The gelada baboon (Theropithecus gelada), is one of Ethiopia's most fascinating endemic mammals. In fact not a baboon at all, it makes up its own genus of monkey and so more correctly should be called the gelada monkey.

Of all the nonhuman primates, it's by far the most dexterous. It also lives in the largest social groups (up to 800 have been recorded), and is the only primate that feeds on grass and has its 'mating skin' on its chest and not on its bottom – a convenient adaptation, given that it spends most of its time sitting!

The gelada also has the most complex system of communication of any nonhuman primate and the most sophisticated social system: the females decide who's boss, the young males form bachelor groups, and the older males perform a kind of grandfather role looking after the young.

Although the males sport magnificent leonine manes, their most striking physical feature is the bare patch of skin on their chest. This has given rise to their other popular name: the 'bleeding heart baboon'. The colour of the patch indicates the sexual condition of not just the male (his virility), but also his female harem (their fertility).

Although its population is shrinking, the gelada monkey population is the healthiest of Ethiopia's endemic mammals. Its current population is thought to number between 40,000 and 50,000.

Resented for its alleged damage to crops and pasture, it has become the scapegoat for more sinister goings-on, too. According to local police reports, gelada monkeys are responsible for local thefts, burglaries, rapes and even murders – in one case bursting into a house to drag an adult man 1.5km before shoving him off a cliff face. If in doubt, it seems, blame the bleeding heart baboon.

living in the vicinity of the lake are reliant on the lake for their crops, to water their livestock and generally to maintain their tribal lifestyles. Opponents of the dam say that water levels in the lake will drop by between 2m and 10m and that salinity will increase to such an extent that the waters will become undrinkable for people and livestock.

# Survival Guide

# Ethiopia Directory A–Z

For Djibouti and Somaliland Directory information, see p314 and p335, respectively.

## Accommodation

Anyone who visited Ethiopia 15 to 20 years ago will recall joyous nights sleeping in rural hotels that may as well have been stables for animals, and urban hotels that were essentially brothels. No matter where you stayed, fleas were a constant companion. Fortunately, Ethiopian accommodation has come on in leaps and bounds. Fleas and sheep mostly stay elsewhere now and hotels functioning as brothels are the exception rather than the rule.

### Camping

Tents are useful in Ethiopia for trekking and the exploration of remote regions. If you're just planning a short trek, tents can be hired from Addis Ababa's tour operators (p295) or from businesses in Lalibela, Gonder and Debark.

Campsites have been set up in some of the national parks and in the Omo Valley, but most lack facilities and consist of little more than a clearing beside a river. It's always essential to treat drinking water at the sites.

A fair few upmarket hotels allow camping on their grounds, though prices are close to what you'd pay for nice budget accommodation.

All camping fees in this book are per person unless stated otherwise.

### Hotels

In Ethiopia, hotels will generally play home to everyone who's not camping. There are very few hostels and homestays available to travellers.

Pricing invariably leads to resentment from many travellers as countless hotels charge substantially higher rates (many openly) for *faranjis* (foreigners, especially Western ones). Although you may take offence to a hotel owner calling you a rich *faranji*, remember that you'll always be given priority, as well as the best rooms, facilities and service.

Charging same-sex couples more for rooms than mixed couples is also pervasive but less justifiable.

In Ethiopia, a room with a double bed is called a 'single', and a room with twin beds a 'double'. Single travellers are often forced to pay the same as a couple. In our reviews we've used the Western interpretation of singles, doubles and twins, although singles are listed only where the room price is different from that for a couple.

Reservations are wise in Gonder, Aksum and Lalibela during the major festivals.

While there are no left-luggage facilities in Addis Ababa, most hotels will hold your belongings for no extra charge.

### BUDGET

There are still countless dives, but the number of clean and comfortable budget options continues to rise, especially in the north. Maintenance doesn't seem to be a high priority, so the best budget hotels are often those that have just opened. If you hear of a new hotel in town, it may be the best place to head.

In budget hotels expect the following:

» In smaller, out-of-the-way towns, hotels may double as drinking dens and brothels – bring earplugs

» Many lack glass windows, only having a shutter to let air and light in

### MIDRANGE

Although very comfortable compared with Ethiopian budget options, most midrange hotels here would be

## PRICE RANGES

The following price ranges refer to a double room with private bathroom. Some hotels (particularly government-owned ones) charge a 10% service charge and 15% tax on top of room prices; we've incorporated these extra charges into the room prices listed. More expensive hotels sometimes quote their rates in US dollars, but all accept payment in birr. We have quoted prices in the currency the hotel uses.

**$** Less than US$20

**$$** US$20 to US$50

**$$$** More than US$50

## Electricity

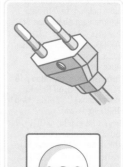

220V/50Hz

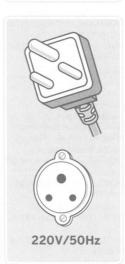

220V/50Hz

scraping by as bare-bones budget options in the Western world. Any that are more than three or four years old typically look tired and run-down, and very rarely offer good value for money.

Midrange hotels typically include the following:

» Private bathroom with hot water

» Satellite TV

» Wi-fi (often doesn't work)

» Restaurant (adequate rather than fine dining)

» Secure parking and sometimes a garden

### TOP END

There are plenty of top-end options in Addis Ababa, and an ever increasing number in popular tourist towns in both the north and south. In the east and certainly in the west there is very little that really qualifies as true top end.

True top-end hotels typically include everything found in the midrange hotels as well as the following:

» Gym and/or swimming pool

» Garden

» Internet and in-room wi-fi (normally works)

» Good-quality restaurant

» Travel services

## Business Hours

Reviews in this book only list opening hours that vary from the standard given here.

**Banks** 8.30am to 11am and 1.30pm to 3.30pm Monday to Friday, 8.30am to 11am Saturday

**Cafes** 6am to 9pm

**Government offices** 8.30am to 11am and 1.30pm to 3.30pm Monday to Friday, 8.30am to 11am Saturday

**Internet cafes** 8am to 8pm Monday to Saturday, limited hours Sunday

**Post offices** 8.30am to 11am and 1.30pm to 3.30pm Monday to Friday, 8.30am to 11am Saturday

**Restaurants** 7am or 8am to 9pm or 10pm; upmarket restaurants in Addis and other big towns generally open from midday to 3pm and 6pm to 10.30pm daily

**Shops** 8am to 1pm and 2pm to 5.30pm Monday to Saturday

**Telecommunications office** 8.30am to 11am and 1.30pm to 3.30pm Monday to Friday, 8.30am to 11am Saturday

## Customs Regulations

There's no limit to the amount of currency that can be brought in, but no more than Birr100 can be exported and imported. You may import 2L of spirits and 200 cigarettes or 100 cigars duty-free.

## Embassies & Consulates

The following list isn't exhaustive (almost every African nation has representation in Addis Ababa), but it covers the embassies that are most likely to be needed.

**Australia** See Canada.

**Belgium** (Map p34; ☎0116-623420; http://diplomatie.belgium.be/ethiopia; Fikremaryam Abatechan St)

**Canada** (Map p34; ☎0113-170000; addis@international.gc.ca; Seychelles St) Also represents Australia.

**Djibouti** Embassy (Map p46; ☎0116 613200; off Bole Rd, Addis Ababa) Consulate (Map p182; Dire Dawa)

**Egypt** (Map p34; ☎0111-550021; egyptian.emb@ethionet.et; Madagascar St)

**France** (Map p34; ☎0111-400000; www.ambafrance-et.org)

**Germany** (Map p34; ☎0111 235139; www.addis-abeba.diplo.de)

**Italy** (Map p34; ☎0111 235717; ambasciata.addis abeba@esteri.it)

**Kenya** (Map p34; ☎0116-610033; kenigad@telecom.net.et; Fikremaryam Abatechan St)

**Netherlands** (☎0113-711100; ethiopia.nlembassy.org)

**Somaliland** (Map p46; ☎0116 635921; off Bole Rd)

**Spain** (Map p34; ☎0111 222544; Botswana St)

**Sudan** (Map p34; ☎0115 516477; sudan.embassy@ethionet.et; Ras Lulseged St)

**South Sudan** (Map p46; ☎0116 620245; off Cameroon St)

**Sweden** (Map p38; ☎0115-180000; www.swedenabroad.com; Yared St)

**Switzerland** (Map p34; ☎0113 711107; www.eda.adm.ch; Ring Rd)

**UK** (Map p34; ☎0116-612354; http://ukinethiopia.fco.gov.uk; Fikremaryam Abatechan St)

**USA** (Map p34; ☎0111 306000; http://ethiopia.usembassy.gov; Entoto Ave)

## Gay & Lesbian Travellers

In Ethiopia and the rest of the Horn, homosexuality is severely condemned – traditionally, religiously and legally – and remains a topic of absolute taboo. Don't underestimate the strength of feeling. Reports of gays being beaten up or worse aren't uncommon.

In Amharic, the word *bushti* (homosexual) is a very offensive insult, implying immorality and depravity. One traveller wrote to us to report expulsion from a hotel and serious threats just for coming under suspicion. If a hotel only offers double beds, rather than twins, you and your companion will pay more or may even be refused occupancy.

Women may have an easier time: even the idea of a lesbian relationship is beyond the permitted imaginings of many Ethiopians! Behave discreetly, and you will be assumed to be just friends.

Note that the Ethiopian penal code officially prohibits homosexual acts, with penalties of between 10 days' and 10 years' imprisonment for various 'crimes'. Although gay locals obviously exist, they behave with extreme discretion and caution. Gay travellers are advised to do likewise.

Information on homosexuality in the Horn is hard to come by, even in the well-known gay publications. Try the **International Lesbian & Gay Association** (ILGA; www.ilga.org) for more information.

## Insurance

» A travel-insurance policy for all medical problems is essential for travel in Ethiopia, while one to cover theft and loss really is helpful but not vital.

» Many insurance companies will not cover you for countries, or parts of a country, that your home government has issued a travel warning for. In Ethiopia the Danakil area, the Eritrea border region and parts of the south can often fall under this category – check before travelling.

» Vehicle insurance is discussed on p294.

» Worldwide travel insurance is available at www.lonelyplanet.com/travel_services. You can buy, extend and claim online anytime – even if you're already on the road.

## Internet Access

» Internet cafes are everywhere in Addis Ababa and other major towns and fairly easy to come by in smaller places that see few tourists. Most are open 8am to 8pm Monday to Saturday; many open with limited hours on Sunday.

» In larger towns in-room wi-fi is increasingly common in many midrange and top-end hotels (and budget hotels popular with foreign tourists).

» In general internet connections in Ethiopia are among the worst on the continent. Connections in internet cafes in most towns are generally reasonable but don't expect much joy with wireless internet as the band width is often insufficient and connections rarely seem to work all that well outside Addis (even in Addis wireless internet can be decidedly hit and miss).

» Internet dongles are available but expensive and almost certainly won't work outside of Addis. Our experience of foreign smart phones in Ethiopia is no better either – web pages never work and emails only seem to download in the evenings and only in Addis. You'll have more luck with a locally purchased SIM card, but not much more!

» It should be remembered that the Ethiopian government is highly suspicious of the internet. Opposition websites and others critical of the government are frequently blocked. In early 2012 it even went as far as banning Skype and similar programs; though after an uproar from locals it reversed its decision.

## Legal Matters

Remember that when in Ethiopia, you're subject to Ethiopian laws. If you're arrested, you must (in theory) be brought to court within 48 hours. You have the right to talk to someone from your embassy, as well as a lawyer. For the most part, police in Ethiopia will show you as much respect as you show them. If confronted by the police, always maintain your cool, smile and be polite. Compared with some other African nations, police here rarely, if ever, ask for bribes (we're yet to experience it).

### Alcohol

Alcohol cannot be served to anyone under 18 years of age in Ethiopia. Disturbance caused by those under the influence of alcohol is punishable by three months' to one year's imprisonment. Driving while under the influence is also illegal and attracts a fine.

## Drugs

Penalties for possession, use or trafficking of illegal drugs (including hashish) are strictly enforced in Ethiopia. Convicted offenders can expect both fines and long jail sentences.

Consumption of the mildly stimulating leaf *chat* (see the boxed text, p260) is permitted in Ethiopia.

## Maps

For simply travelling around the country on public transport, the maps in this guidebook should suffice. For those venturing off into the nether regions with 4WDs, a more detailed map is essential. Since trekking without a guide is illegal in the Simien and Bale Mountains, additional maps aren't necessary, though topographic maps (see the parks' relevant sections for details) can help you plan your routes with more precision.

» In Ethiopia, the map produced by the defunct Ethiopian Tourism Commission (1987; 1:2,000,000) isn't

bad and can be picked up in some Addis Ababa hotels. However the road system is now very outdated.

» A more accurate map (although it lacks distance labels between cities) of the same scale is available from the **Ethiopia Mapping Authority** (Map p38; ☎0115-518445; Menelik II Ave; ⊙8.30am-12.30pm & 1.30-5pm Mon-Thu, 8.30-11.30am & 1.30-4.30pm Fri) in Addis Ababa.

» Of the maps currently available outside the country, the best by far is the new Gizi Ethiopia map (1:2,000,000). It's much more up to date than any other map and includes elevations, but some of the place names are very different to how you'll see them written elsewhere. Currently hard to find in Ethiopia, it was, at the time of research, only available through Abeba Tours Ethiopia (p295) in Addis.

## Money

Ethiopia's currency is the birr. It's divided into 100 cents in one, five, 10, 25 and 50 cent coins as well as a one birr coin, and there are one, five, 10, 50 and 100 birr notes. Despite a weekly auction determining exchange rates, the birr is one of Africa's most stable currencies.

According to National Bank of Ethiopia regulations, all bills in Ethiopia must be paid in birr. But this isn't enforced and Ethiopian Airlines, most major hotels and most travel agencies accept (and sometimes demand) US currency.

One regulation that's strictly enforced is the conversion of birr to US dollars or euros; this transaction can only be done for people holding onward air tickets from Ethiopia. This means people leaving overland must budget accordingly. There are black-market traders around the borders, but rates are poor and it's risky.

---

### PRACTICALITIES

» The best-known English-language daily newspapers are the government-owned *Ethiopian Herald* and the privately owned *Monitor.* Other weekly private newspapers include the *Fortune,* the *Reporter, Sub-Saharan Informer* and the *Capital.* Only the *Ethiopian Herald* is available outside Addis Ababa. The weekly *Press Digest* gives useful summaries of the most important stories from the week's Amharic and English press.

» Radio Ethiopia broadcasts in English from 3pm to 4pm and 7pm to 8pm weekdays. The BBC World Service can be received on radios with short-wave reception, though frequencies vary according to the time of day (try 9630, 11940 and 17640 MHz).

» Ethiopia's ETV1 channel broadcasts in English from 11am to 12pm Monday to Friday and 11pm to midnight daily. ETV2 broadcasts in English daily from 8pm to 9pm. Many hotels and restaurants have satellite dishes that receive BBC or CNN.

» Ethiopia uses the metric system for weights and measures.

## ATMs

Bigger branches of the Dashen Bank in all major towns now have ATMs that accept international Visa cards and an increasing number also accept MasterCard. Many other banks also have ATMs that claim to take international Visa cards though more often than not they don't. Note that foreign Solo, Cirrus or Plus cards do not work in any ATM.

## Black Market

Unlike 10 to 15 years ago when almost all currency exchanges were conducted on a fairly open black market that gave significantly higher rates than the banks, things have now tightened up drastically. The black market still exists, and most hotels will exchange US$ cash or euros for you, but the rates are often worse than those offered by the banks.

The black market is illegal; penalties range from hefty fines to imprisonment.

## Cash

As with many African countries the US dollar is the preferred foreign currency in Ethiopia although the euro is also very easy to exchange. You'll have no trouble exchanging US cash wherever there are Forex facilities.

## Credit Cards

Credit cards (Visa and MasterCard) are increasingly useful in Addis Ababa but remain almost completely useless outside it, with the exception of some Ethiopian Airlines offices and top-class hotels. The travel agencies, airline offices and major hotels that do accept cards typically ding you 2% to 3% extra for the privilege of plastic.

Cash advances are possible at branches of the Dashen Bank in the capital and in larger Historical Circuit cities. Only Addis Ababa's Sheraton can give you US dollars instead of birr.

## Tipping

Tips (*gursha* in Amharic) are considered a part of everyday life in Ethiopia, and help supplement often very low wages. The maxim 'little but often' is a good one, and even very small tips are greatly appreciated.

If a professional person helps you, it's probably better to show your appreciation in other ways: shaking hands, exchanging names, or an invitation to have a coffee and pastry are all local ways of expressing gratitude.

Furnishing yourself with a good wad of small notes – Birr1 and Birr5 – is a very good idea. You'll need these for tips, taking photographs etc.

## Travellers Cheques

Like in many countries travellers cheques are increasingly hard to cash – often impossible. You're much better off relying on plastic and a bit of cash. If you do choose to use cheques then bring US-dollar ones and ask at larger Commercial Bank of Ethiopia branches. Note that most banks ask to see your passport and the cheque's proof-of-purchase receipt (which most travellers-cheque companies advise you to leave at home!).

---

### TIPS FOR TIPPING

Tipping can be a constant source of worry, hassle or stress for travellers. This guide has been compiled with the help of Ethiopians.

» In the smaller restaurants in the towns, service is included, and Ethiopians don't tip unless the service has been exceptional (up to 10%).

» In bars and cafes, sometimes loose coins are left. However, in the larger restaurants accustomed to tourists, 10% will be expected.

» In Addis Ababa's midrange and top-end hotels, staff will expect a minimum Birr20 per service.

» Outside Addis Ababa, midrange and top-end hotels' luggage handlers will expect a tip of around Birr2 to Birr5 per bag, and people acting as impromptu guides around Birr10.

» For the assistance of a child, Birr1 or Birr2 is plenty.

» At traditional music and dance shows in bars, restaurants and hotels, an audience shows its appreciation by placing money (around Birr10) on the dancers' foreheads or in their belts.

» Car 'guards' (often self-appointed) expect Birr2 to Birr3.

» If the service has been good at the end of the trek, a rule of thumb for tipping guides/scouts/mule handlers might be an extra day's pay for every three days' work.

» A good tip for professional English-/German-/Italian-speaking guides and drivers hired from Addis Ababa travel agencies for multiday 4WD tours is around US$10 per day from each person if you're a group of two or three. Less per person per day for a larger group.

---

## Photography & Video

» In general most Ethiopians love having their photos taken, though in remote areas people are still suspicious of cameras and many feel seriously threatened or compromised, especially women. Be sensitive. Always ask permission, even if it is only using basic sign language. Best of all, use a local as an interpreter or go-between. Never take a photo if permission is declined.

» In other areas, where people are starting to depend on tourists for income, the opposite is true. In the Lower Omo Valley, you'll be chased by people demanding their photo be taken! However, their eagerness has to do with the fee they'll claim for each snap of the shutter (around Birr2 to Birr5 per person per picture). Always agree to an amount first. The whole mercenary and almost voyeuristic affair can be rather off-putting for many travellers, but the reality is that for these people modelling is a business and they certainly don't regard it as either wrong or 'corrupting of their culture' as some travellers do.

## Post

» Ethiopia's postal system is reliable and reasonably efficient and the prices are low. Letters should take between five and eight days to arrive in Europe; eight to 15 days for the USA or Australia.

» International parcels can only be sent from the main post office in Addis Ababa. All parcels are subject to a customs inspection, so leave them open until you've had their contents inspected at the counter.

## Public Holidays

Ethiopia's public holidays can be divided into three categories: national secular holidays, Christian Orthodox festivals and Islamic holidays. During the Christian Orthodox festivals, accommodation is hard to come by in Gonder, Aksum and Lalibela, as are open seats on internal flights. While prices rise for rooms during these times, transportation costs remain the same. It's best to book flights as far in advance as possible to avoid problems. See the relevant towns' sections for more details.

National holidays include the following:

**Victory of Adwa Commemoration Day** 2 March
**International Labour Day** 1 May
**Ethiopian Patriots' Victory Day** (also known as Liberation Day) 5 May
**Downfall of the Derg** 28 May

## Safe Travel

Compared with many African countries, Ethiopia is remarkably safe. Serious or violent crime is rare; against travellers it's extremely rare. Outside the capital, the risk of petty crime drops still further.

A simple traveller's tip? Always look as if you know where you're going. Thieves and con artists get wind of an uncertain newcomer in a minute.

Though the following list may be off-putting and alarming, it's very unlikely you'll encounter any serious difficulties – and even less likely if you're prepared for them.

### Civil Disturbances

Most of Ethiopia is fairly trouble free but there are a couple of areas where trouble does flare with worrying frequency. These include the Ogaden region, and parts of the south (at the time of research the Moyale and Surma regions were both experiencing problems) and the Danakil region. It's generally a mixture of rebel activity and ethnic violence. Though you're highly unlikely to get caught up in it, do keep your ear to the ground for developments.

If you're concerned, check your government's latest security reports on countries (such as those published by the British Foreign Office). Don't let these scare you away as they do tend to err on the side of caution (though if they warn you not to venture to a specific area then your travel insurance might be invalid).

### Mobbing & Faranji Frenzy

The infamous 'faranji frenzy', when shouts of 'You, you,

### MAJOR ISLAMIC HOLIDAYS

| ISLAMIC YEAR | NEW YEAR | PROPHET'S BIRTHDAY | END OF RAMADAN | FESTIVAL OF SACRIFICE |
|---|---|---|---|---|
| 1434 | 13 Nov 2013 | 23 Jan 2013 | 9 Aug 2013 | 17 Oct 2013 |
| 1435 | 24 Oct 2014 | 14 Jan 2014 | 30 Jul 2014 | 6 Oct 2014 |
| 1436 | 13 Oct 2015 | 3 Jan 2015 | 19 Jul 2015 | 25 Sep 2015 |
| 1437 | 1 Oct 2016 | 23 Dec 2016 | 8 Jul 2016 | 14 Sep 2016 |
| 1438 | 20 Sep 2017 | 12 Dec 2017 | 27 Jun 2017 | 3 Sept 2017 |

you, you, YOU!' greeted you at every turn is thankfully becoming rarer and rarer – at least in touristy parts of the country. Off the beaten track you can still expect it to be a musical accompaniment to your travels.

If it does start to get to you then just ignoring it or, even better, treating it with humour is probably the best answer in how to deal with it. Anger only provokes children more (there can be few things more tempting than a grumpy *faranji!*). An Amharic '*hid!*' ('clear off!') for a boy, '*hiji!*' for a girl or '*hidu!*' for a group is the Ethiopian response and sends children scuttling; however, it can have the reverse effect and is considered rather harsh from a foreigner.

On a less-friendly note, several travellers have reported stone-throwing children in various parts of the country.

## Scams

Compared with other African countries, Ethiopia has few scams and rip-offs. Those that do exist, like the siren scam in Addis Ababa (see p49) and the notebook scam (where kids beg for notebooks and pens for school, which, if you buy them one, are taken straight back to the shop to exchange for money), are pretty transparent and rather easily avoided.

You'll also hear many 'hard luck' stories, or those soliciting sponsorship for travel or education in Ethiopia or abroad. Although most are

not genuine, some stories are sadly true, so don't be rude.

Also look out for fake antiques in shops.

## Self-Appointed Guides

High unemployment has spawned many self-appointed and unofficial guides. You will be approached, accompanied for a while, given unasked-for information and then charged. Be wary of anyone who approaches you unasked, particularly at the exit of bus stations etc. Unfortunately, there's almost always an ulterior motive. Be polite but firm and try not to get paranoid!

## Shiftas

In some of the more remote areas, such as the southeast's Ogaden Desert, near the Kenyan border, along the Awash–Mille road at night, in the far west and, most commonly, in the Danakil region, *shiftas* (bandits) are sometimes reported. Tourists are very rarely targeted, but it does happen and in early 2012 five foreign tourists were killed and four people kidnapped close to the Erte Ale volcano in the Danakil Depression. The government has blamed Eritrea for the attacks. Nobody has ever been brought to justice.

Check government travel-advice warnings to keep up to date with any recent trouble spots. Tour companies are also a good source of information; though remember that some less than reputable ones (none of which we include in this book) might

tell you a place is safe when it isn't just in order to get your custom and money.

## Theft

Pickpocketing is the biggest concern, but is a problem mainly in Addis Ababa and other large towns, in particular Shashemene, Nazret and Dessie.

Keep an eye on your belongings at bus stations and be wary of people offering to put your bags on the bus roof. Be aware that professional thieves sometimes operate at major festivals and markets, targeting Ethiopians as well as foreigners.

# Telephone

Ethiopia's telecommunications industry is entirely government-run – and it shows. Just like with the internet (run by the same company), Ethiopian telecommunications is years behind most of its neighbours and the industry is in desperate need of an upgrade. Fortunately there are rumours that the industry will soon be privatised and this will probably lead to an increase in the quality of the service.

» Countless shops operate as 'telecentres' and can normally/sometimes/once in a while connect you to the big wide world for Birr15 to Birr25 per minute. Some hotels offer phone services, but they are usually at least 20% more expensive.

» Cheap local calls can also be made from telecommunications offices, telecentres and public phone boxes. Most boxes take both coins and cards (sold at the telecommunications offices in denominations of Birr25, Birr50 and Birr100).

## Mobile Phones

As with everywhere in Africa, mobile phones are ubiquitous. However, like all other aspects of Ethiopian telecommunications, the service can hardly be described

---

## GOVERNMENT TRAVEL ADVICE

The following government websites offer travel advisories and information on current hot spots.

» **Australian Department of Foreign Affairs** (www.smarttraveller.gov.au)

» **British Foreign Office** (www.fco.gov.uk)

» **Canadian Department of Foreign Affairs** (http://travel.gc.ca)

» **US State Department** (http://travel.state.gov)

as reliable. Whether you're using your home phone on a roaming plan or a locally bought phone and SIM card, expect hours, or sometimes days, to go by when, despite having a reception, it's impossible to actually make a call or send a text message.

Internet-enabled smart phones are also unreliable.

### Phone Numbers & Codes

All Ethiopian numbers have 10 digits. The international country code for Ethiopia is ⏚251 and you need to drop the first zero from the number when calling from abroad. Other important telephone numbers are listed in the Need to Know chapter, p14.

## Time

Ethiopia is three hours ahead of GMT/UTC.

» Time is expressed so sanely in Ethiopia that it blows most travellers' minds! At sunrise it's 12 o'clock (6am our time) and after one hour of sunshine it's one o'clock. After two hours of sunshine? Yes, two o'clock. The sun sets at 12 o'clock (6pm our time) and after one hour of darkness it's...one o'clock! Instead of using 'am' or 'pm', Ethiopians use 'in the morning', 'in the evening' and 'at night' to indicate the period of day.

» The system is used widely, though the 24-hour clock is used occasionally in business. Be careful to ask if a time quoted is according to the Ethiopian or 'European' clock (*Be habesha/faranji akotater no?* – Is that Ethiopian/foreigner's time?). For the purposes of this book, all times quoted are by the European clock.

## Toilets

Both sit-down and squat toilets are found in Ethiopia, reflecting European and Arab

---

### OH, TO BE YOUNG AGAIN

In addition to the Ethiopian clock system, another Ethiopian time-keeping idiosyncrasy that confounds many a traveller is the calendar. It's based on the old Coptic calendar, which has its roots in ancient Egypt. Although it has 12 months of 30 days each and a 13th month of five or six days, like the ancient Coptic calendar, it follows the Julian system of adding a leap day every four years without exception (which is the sixth day of the short 13th month). If you're travelling during a leap year and want to attend a specific festival check you've got the dates right – we have heard plenty of stories of people missing Christmas celebrations by a day and that includes people on an organised tour!

What makes the Ethiopian calendar even more unique is that it wasn't tweaked by numerous popes to align with their versions of Christianity, like the Gregorian calendar (introduced by Pope Gregory XIII in 1582) that Westerners have grown up on.

What does this all mean? It means the Ethiopian calendar is 7½ years 'behind' the Gregorian calendar, and you're seven years younger!

---

influences, respectively. In most midrange and all top-end hotels as well as budget hotels catering to foreign tourists, Western style 'sit-down' toilets are the norm. Elsewhere it's squat toilets only.

Public toilets are found in almost all hotels and restaurants, but may not form your fondest memories of Ethiopia. In small towns and rural areas, the most common arrangement is a smelly old shack, with two planks, a hole in the ground and all the flies you can fit in between. You may suddenly find that you can survive the next 1000km after all.

Toilet paper is very rare in any toilet outside a more expensive hotel; you're best advised to carry your own.

---

## Tourist Information

### Local Tourist Offices

In 2005 the Ethiopian government unceremoniously sacked the heads of the Ethiopian Tourism Commis-

sion (ETC) and created the new Ministry of Culture and Tourism. Thankfully, this ministry kept open the ETC's ever-helpful Tourist Information Centre in Addis Ababa's Meskal Sq.

Other especially useful offices can be found in Aksum, Mekele, Konso, Lalibela, Gambela and Wukro.

While in Addis Ababa, the most accurate information on travel outside the capital region is available through tour operators (see p295), though naturally they will expect to sell you something. Outside Addis Ababa, local guide associations and the traveller grapevine are your best sources for up-to-date information. Managers of hotels popular with budget travellers can be fairly clued up as well.

### Tourist Offices Abroad

No national tourist office exists abroad. The Ethiopian embassies and consulates try to fill the gap, but they generally just hand out the usual tourist brochures.

## ROOTS OF ETHIOPIA

**Roots of Ethiopia** (Ethiopia Community Tourism; www.rootsofethiopia.com) is an excellent website listing community-run activities across Ethiopia. It could go a long way towards making your trip a little more sustainable, but do note that not all the projects are actually up and running yet.

An active, nonpolitical organisation in the UK is the **Anglo-Ethiopian Society** (www.anglo-ethiopian.org), which aims 'to foster a knowledge and understanding of Ethiopia and its people'. Membership costs from UK£15 annually. The society holds regular gatherings, including talks on Ethiopia. A well-stocked library on Ethiopia is open to members. There's a tri-annual Newsfile.

## Travellers with Disabilities

There's no reason why intrepid travellers with disabilities shouldn't visit Ethiopia.

» For those with restricted mobility, all the sites on the Historical Route are easily reached by internal flights. Passengers in wheelchairs can be accommodated. Car rental with a driver is easily organised. Some rough roads can be hard on the back.

» Taxis are widely available in the large towns and are good for getting around; none have wheelchair access, though. In Addis Ababa a few hotels have lifts; at least two (the Sheraton and Hilton hotels) have facilities for wheelchair-users. Kerb ramps on streets are nonexistent, and potholes and uneven streets are a hazard.

» Outside the capital, facilities are lacking, but many hotels are bungalow affairs, so at least steps or climbs are fairly minimal.

» For those restricted in other ways, such as visually or aurally, you'll get plenty of offers of help. Unlike in many Western countries, Ethiopians are not shy about coming forward to offer assistance.

» A valuable source of general information is the **Access-Able Travel Source** (www.access-able.com), which has useful links.

» Before leaving home, visitors can get in touch with their national support organisation. Ask for the 'travel officer', who may have a list of travel agents that specialise in tours for people with disabilities.

## Visas & Documents

Be aware that visa regulations can change. The Ethiopian embassy in your home country is the best source of up-to-date information.

» Currently, all visitors except Kenyan and Djiboutian nationals need visas to visit Ethiopia.

» Nationals of most Western countries can obtain tourist visas on arrival at Bole International Airport. Aside from some queuing, the process upon arrival is painless and a tourist visa costs only US$20 or €17. Normally immigration staff automatically grant a one-month visa, but if you request it, three months doesn't seem to be an issue. Immigration officials in Addis Ababa told us that they don't require onward air tickets, though some people have been asked for them.

» Three- and six-month multiple entry visas are also possible.

» Note that visas are NOT available at any land border.

» Ethiopian embassies abroad may (or equally may not; it varies from embassy to embassy) require some or all of the following to accompany visa applications: an onward air ticket (or airline itinerary), a visa for the next country you're planning to visit, a yellow-fever vaccination certificate and proof of sufficient funds (officially a minimum of US$50 per day).

» If your citizenship isn't one that can acquire a visa at Bole and there's also no Ethiopian diplomatic representation in your country, you may be able to ask Ethiopian Airlines or a tour operator to order you a visa before your arrival; otherwise contact the Department of Immigration in Addis in advance. Visas cannot be obtained on arrival without prior arrangement at immigration.

» Travellers of all nationalities can obtain transit visas on arrival or at the embassies abroad; these are valid for up to seven days.

» The **Department of Immigration** (Map p38; off Zambia St, Addis Ababa; ☺8.30am-12.30pm & 1.30-5.30pm Mon-Fri) is very unlikely to grant visa extensions to those travelling on tourist visas. One of the authors of this book was unable to extend his visa in Addis and ended up flying to Nairobi and then straight back again where he was issued with another one-month tourist visa without fuss! Business travellers can get visa extensions but you will need a letter from your employer.

### Other Documents

In theory a yellow-fever vaccination certificate is mandatory, as is a vaccination against cholera if you've transited through a cholera-infected area within six days prior to your arrival in Ethiopia. These are rarely checked (although we have been asked to show it before, but maybe we just look dirty and disease riddled?), but you probably wouldn't want to risk it.

Documentation needed to bring a vehicle into Ethiopia is covered on p293.

All important documents (passport data page and visa page, credit cards, travel insurance policy, air/bus/train tickets, driving licence etc) should be photocopied. Leave one copy with someone at home and keep another with you, separate from the originals.

## Visas for Onward Travel

### Djibouti
Bring US$125 (48-hour service) or US$135 (24-hour service), a hotel reservation, a plane or bus ticket out of the country, and one passport photo to the **Djibouti Embassy** (Map p46; ☎0116-613200; off Bole Rd; ☺9-11am & 2.30-4.30pm Mon-Fri) early in the morning and you'll usually have it by the next day. Visas can also be obtained on arrival at the airport in Djibouti.

### Kenya
The **Kenyan Embassy** (Map p34; ☎0116-610033; keni gad@ethionet.et; Fikremaryam Abatechan St; ☺9am-1pm & 2-5pm Mon-Fri) charges US$50 for three-month tourist visas. One passport photo

is required. Applications are taken in the morning only, with visas ready the following afternoon. Visas are also easily obtained at the Moyale border and at Jomo Kenyatta International Airport in Nairobi.

### Somaliland
The **Somaliland office** (Map p46; ☎0116 635921; off Bole Rd; ☺8.30am-12.30pm & 2-3.30pm Mon-Fri) produces one-month tourist visas for US$40. It requires one passport photo and it's issued while you wait.

### Sudan
Unless you're using the services of a registered Sudanese tour company, then obtaining a tourist visa at the **Sudanese Embassy** (Map p34; ☎0115 516477; Ras Lulseged St; ☺8.30am-12.30pm Mon, Wed & Fri for visa service only) is a mission impossible if ever there was one. Prepare for a lot of sweat, tears, headaches and then a big, fat 'No'. All applications are sent to Khartoum for approval, so the process of being told you can't have one can take over a month to complete. However, don't go changing those plans just yet as there is one way in. Transit visas, allowing up to a fortnight in Sudan, are issued fairly easily. For this you

require an onward visa for Egypt, a photo and, for most nationalities, US$100 cash. Americans, you get to pay US$200. It normally takes a day to issue.

### South Sudan
South Sudan is a new country. It's not used to tourists, and, boy, can you tell that when you go to its **embassy** (Map p46; ☎0116 620245; off Cameroon St; ☺8.30am-12pm & 2-5pm Mon-Thu). When we passed by nobody really appeared to know exactly what was required in order to get a tourist visa. But from what we could decipher the essentials were proof of sufficient funds, a letter stating the purpose of your visit, a photo and US$100. In addition you may be required to supply a letter from your home employer and they may ask you to attend an interview. Once you've done all that one-month visas are issued in 72 hours.

# Women Travellers

Compared with many African countries, Ethiopia is pretty easygoing for women travellers. The risk of rape or other serious offences is likely lower than in many Western countries. The best advice is to simply be aware of the signals your clothing or behaviour may be giving off and remember these unspoken codes of etiquette.

» Drinking alcohol, smoking, and wearing excessive make-up and revealing clothes are indications to the male population of 'availability', as this is also the way local prostitutes behave. Apart from the young of the wealthier classes in Addis Ababa, no 'proper' woman would be seen in a bar.

» Many cheap hotels in Ethiopia double as brothels. Ethiopian men may naturally wonder about your motives for staying here, particularly if you're alone. While there's no cause for alarm, it's best

---

**COMING FROM KENYA**

At the time of writing the Ethiopian embassy in Nairobi was only issuing visas to Kenyan citizens or residents. Not a major problem if flying from Nairobi to Addis where most people can get one on arrival, but a real pain for overland travellers. If coming overland, plan accordingly and get one elsewhere in Africa. Note also that visas are not available at the Moyale border crossing.

If travelling north to south across Africa then the good news is that visas were being issued without much fuss in Khartoum.

The above information is likely to change through the life of this book so double check in advance. **Lonely Planet's Thorn Tree forum** (www.lonelyplanet.com/thorntree) is a great place for up-to-date information.

## FEMALE PHOBIA

In some of the monasteries and holy sites of Ethiopia, an ancient prohibition forbids women from setting foot in the holy confines. But the holy fathers go strictly by the book: the prohibition extends not just to women but to all female creatures, even she donkeys, hens and nanny goats.

to keep a low profile and behave very conservatively – keep out of the hotel bar, for example, and try to meet up with other travellers if you want to go out.

» Accepting an invitation to an unmarried man's house, under any pretext, is considered a latent acceptance of things to come. Dinner invitations often amount to 'foreplay' before you're expected to head off to some seedy hotel. Even a seemingly innocent invitation to the cinema can turn out to be little more than an invitation to a good snog in the back row.

» Be aware that 'respectable' Ethiopian women (even when they're willing) are expected to put up a show of coyness and modesty. Traditionally, this formed part of the wedding-night ritual of every Amhara bride: a fierce struggle with the groom was expected of them. Consequently, some Ethiopian men may mistake your rebuttals for encouragement. The concept even has a name in Amharic: *maqderder* (and applies equally to feigned reluctance for other things such as food). If you mean no, make it very clear from the start.

» If there aren't any other travellers around, here's a quick trick: pick a male Ethiopian companion, bemoan the problems you've been having with his compatriots and appeal to his sense of pride, patriotism and gallantry. Usually any ulterior plans he might have been harbouring himself are soon converted into sympathy or shame and a personal crusade to protect you!

» Adultery is quite common among many of Ethiopia's urban population, for men as well as women. For this reason, a wedding ring on a woman traveller (bogus or not) has absolutely no deterrent value. In fact, quite the reverse.

» The one advantage of Ethiopia being a relatively permissive society is that Western women (in particular, white women) aren't necessarily seen as easier than local women, something that's common in many developing countries due to Hollywood cinematic 'glamour'.

# Ethiopia Transport

## GETTING THERE & AWAY

The vast majority of travellers arrive in Ethiopia by air at Addis Ababa, but for those with time and a spirit of adventure it's possible to enter Ethiopia overland via Sudan, Kenya, Djibouti and even Somaliland. There are no land or air links between Ethiopia and Eritrea. Borders with South Sudan and the rest of Somalia are either closed and/or dangerous.

Flights, tours and rail tickets can be booked at www.lonelyplanet.com/bookings.

## Entering Ethiopia

Entering Ethiopia by air is painless, even if you have to pick up your visa upon arrival at Bole International Airport. Visa and document information is found on p284.

Ethiopian border officials at land crossings are more strict. You *must* have a valid visa to enter overland as none are available at borders. Those entering with vehicles should have all the necessary paperwork (see the box, p289) and expect a lengthier process.

## Air

### Airports & Airlines

Addis Ababa's Bole International Airport is the only international airport in Ethiopia. Although modern, upon arrival there's little more than a 24-hour bank, a restaurant and a few cafes; baggage carts are free. When departing, there's an internet lounge, a bar and duty-free shops.

Ethiopia's only international and national carrier, **Ethiopian Airlines** (airline code ET; www.flyethiopian. com), is rated as one of the best airlines in Africa and has a good safety record. Ethiopian Airlines is also one of the largest African carriers, with a modern fleet of 737s, 757s, 767s and four 787 Dreamliners (with eight more on order). There are 50 or so offices worldwide, which sell both international and domestic tickets directly. Alternatively the website is safe and reliable for online bookings.

If you want to fly with a European airline such as Luthansa or KLM, double-check that you will actually be on one of their planes and not on an Ethiopian Airlines plane. They route share and commonly bundle their passengers onto Ethiopian Airlines and then kindly charge you more than you'd have paid if you'd bought directly with Ethiopian Airlines.

### AIRLINES FLYING TO/ FROM ETHIOPIA

**EgyptAir** (airline code MS; ☑0111 564493; www.egyptair. com; Churchill Ave, Addis Ababa)

**Emirates** (airline code EK; ☑0115 181818; www.emirates. com; Dembel City Centre, Addis Ababa)

**Kenya Airways** (airline code KQ; ☑0115 525548;

## CLIMATE CHANGE & TRAVEL

Every form of transport that relies on carbon-based fuel generates $CO_2$, the main cause of human-induced climate change. Modern travel is dependent on aeroplanes, which might use less fuel per kilometre per person than most cars but travel much greater distances. The altitude at which aircraft emit gases (including $CO_2$) and particles also contributes to their climate change impact. Many websites offer 'carbon calculators' that allow people to estimate the carbon emissions generated by their journey and, for those who wish to do so, to offset the impact of the greenhouse gases emitted with contributions to portfolios of climate-friendly initiatives throughout the world. Lonely Planet offsets the carbon footprint of all staff and author travel.

www.kenya-airways.com; Hilton Hotel, Menelik II Ave, Addis Ababa)

**KLM** (airline code KL; ☎0115 525495; www.klm.com; Hilton Hotel, Menelik II Ave, Addis Ababa)

**Lufthansa** (airline code LH; ☎0111 551666; www.lufthansa. com; Axum Hotel, Cameroon St, Addis Ababa)

**Saudi Arabian Airlines** (airline code SV; ☎0115 614327; www.saudiairlines.com; Ras Desta Damtew St, Addis Ababa)

**Sudan Airways** (airline code SD; ☎0115 504724; www.sudan air.com; Ras Desta Damtew St, Addis Ababa)

**Turkish Airlines** (airline code TK; ☎0116 627781; www. turkishairlines.com; Zimbabwe St, Addis Ababa)

**Yemenia** (airline code IY; ☎0115 526440; www.yemenia. com; Ras Desta Damtew St, Addis Ababa)

## Tickets

For Ethiopia, flights during the month of August, over Easter, Christmas and New Year should be booked well in advance. Ethiopians living abroad tend to visit their families during this time, and tour groups often try to coincide with the major festivals. Ticket prices are highest during this period.

## Land

Travelling to Ethiopia by land is an adventure you'll never forget, no matter where you come from or how you do it.

## Djibouti

Border formalities are usually pretty painless crossing between Djibouti and Ethiopia, but you *must* have your visa prior to arriving as none are issued at the land border (see Visas for Onward Travel, p285).

### ROAD

There are two current road routes linking Djibouti and Ethiopia: one via Dire Dawa and Gelille, and one via Awash and Galafi.

» The Gelille route is best for those without vehicles as daily buses link Djibouti City and Dire Dawa. The journey takes 10 to 12 hours, though it involves changing buses at the border. In Djibouti City, **Société Bus Assajog** (☎77846670) buses depart at dawn from Ave Gamel Abdel Nasser; tickets cost DFr3000 and should be purchased at least a day in advance to be sure of getting a seat. In Dire Dawa, buy your ticket the day of travel at the **Tibuuti Ee City** (☎0915-763203) office north of the 'old town' of Megala by Ashawa Market. Tickets cost Birr230 and buses depart around midnight from a spot north of this office.

» Although longer, the Galafi route is best for those driving as it's sealed the entire way. For those coming from northern Ethiopia, this route can be accessed via a paved shortcut at Woldia.

» Those without vehicles can also travel via Galafi, although it's not straightforward. In Djibouti City, you'll have to take a minibus to Galafi, 5km from the border. From Galafi, you must rely on the single daily minibus to Logiya (Birr100, three hours) or hitch a lift with one of the

many trucks heading into Ethiopia. Those using this route to leave Ethiopia can ride trucks directly to Djibouti City. We were quoted prices of Birr400 to Birr500 for the six-hour journey from Logiya, but there are many drivers and few passengers so negotiation is in order. (See our notes about hitching, p294.)

### TRAIN

Trains are not currently running between Ethiopia and Djibouti, but reconstruction work was taking place and it's thought that trains will start puffing down the line between Dire Dawa and Djibouti again within the lifetime of this book.

## Eritrea

There are three traditional entry points from Eritrea into Ethiopia: Asmara to Adwa and Aksum via Adi Quala; Asmara to Adigrat via Senafe; and Assab to Addis Ababa via Serdo and Dessie. However, all these border crossings have been indefinitely closed since the 1998 war.

With relations on their current path, it seems sadly unlikely that the borders will be reopened during the lifetime of this book.

Currently, the only feasible way of crossing from

---

## THE EMPEROR'S NEW SHOES

Building a railway across the Horn of Africa was never going to be easy. So when two European engineers arrived in Addis Ababa in 1894 to propose such a scheme to Emperor Menelik II, they would have been prepared for the challenges of hacking a rail line through the mountains, but they probably never expected that their first challenge would involve shoes. Menelik was intrigued by the idea of a railway line, but he wanted proof that these two men knew their stuff. In order to test them, Menelik placed the men in a room under armed guard, gave them a length of twine and a sheet of leather, and ordered them to make him some shoes by dawn. Unstitching their own shoes, the engineers used these as patterns and by first light the Emperor had a fine pair of new shoes – and some years later a railway line!

Ethiopia to Eritrea is by plane, travelling via a third country. Travelling via San'a in Yemen is the most obvious and cheapest way. A much more roundabout route is via Cairo in Egypt.

## ENTERING ETHIOPIA OVERLAND

The overland route from South Africa through southern Africa and East Africa to Ethiopia is quite well trodden, and should present few problems, though the last section through northern Kenya is the toughest and still suffers from sporadic banditry. Be aware, though, that Ethiopian visas are only being issued in Nairobi for Kenyan citizens and residents (see the boxed text, p285). If you're heading on to Cairo and the end of Africa, things start to get more complicated after Ethiopia – the main complication goes by the name of Sudan. Tourist visas are notoriously hard to obtain (unless you employ the services of a Sudanese tour company), but transit visas, allowing a generous two weeks in Sudan, are pretty simple to get in Addis.

For important visa and documentation information see p284. For details on travelling with a vehicle see p293.

### Kenya

There are usually few problems crossing between Ethiopia and Kenya (though see the Coming From Kenya box, p285). The only feasible crossing is at Moyale, 772km south of Addis Ababa by road. Moyale has two incarnations, one on either side of the border.

» The northern, Ethiopian, version of Moyale is well connected to the north and Addis Ababa by bus, along a pretty good, but often potholed, section of sealed road (transport details are found on p152). Though security is normally not a problem along the main north–south route and in and around Moyale, there had, at the time of writing, been some serious tribal fighting in the area and tensions were running high.

» Getting solid info on what the situation is like at the moment you want to cross can be a little tricky. Tour companies and government travel-advice websites will know when there has been serious and sustained fighting in the area (which is rare; although at the time of writing that was indeed the case), but for the everyday sort of clashes probably the best source of information is other travellers as well as Lonely Planet's online Thorn Tree forum, which generally has very up-to-date info on this crossing.

» The southern, Kenyan, side of Moyale is truly in the middle of nowhere: some 400km north of the nearest sealed road (although Chinese road crews are busy reducing this distance) and around 800km north of Nairobi. That said, a daily bus connects Moyale with Marsabit (KSh1000, 8½ hours) from where transport is available onto Isiolo and then onward to Nairobi. Trucks servicing the same destinations pick up passengers near the main intersection.

» For those of you in your own vehicles, the road between Moyale and Marsabit is long and hard (on you and your 4WD – bring at least two spare tyres). Thankfully the banditry problems of the past seem to be largely under control, although outbreaks of tribal fighting and banditry do still occur. While this normally takes place well away from the main Marsabit–Moyale road, throughout late 2011 and on into 2012 serious tribal fighting occurred almost to the gates of Moyale, and at one point fighting took place within the town itself. Armed convoys are sometimes used along this route; although only in times of extreme tension. The Wajir route south is still not considered safe. Either way, be sure to check the security section before setting out from Moyale. Also make sure you fill up before leaving Ethiopia as the petrol is half the price.

» The Ethiopian and Kenyan borders at Moyale are open daily. Kenyan three-month visas are painlessly produced at **Kenyan immigration** (⏲6.30am-6pm) for the grand sum of US$50. It's payable in US dollars (some have managed to pay in euros), but not Ethiopian birr. Transit visas cost US$20 (valid for seven days). **Ethiopian immigration** (⏲8am-noon & 2-6pm Mon-Fri, 9-11am & 3-5pm Sat & Sun) cannot issue Ethiopian visas; these must be obtained at an Ethiopian embassy prior to arrival at the border.

» If you're heading south and have a serious 4WD, it's possible to cross the border near Omorate alongside Lake Turkana. Currently the main (a relative term since it's rarely travelled) route for overlanders is a vague sandy track branching off the Turmi road about 15km outside of Omorate. Drivers must come fully prepared for a tough trip with few facilities and most people recommend taking a guide. It's about two days' travel time to Loyangalani. Rainy-season travel is not possible. On the remote chance the long-promised bridge is finally finished (there's also a very expensive ferry – Birr1000 per tonne – but it's often out of commission) the crossing west of the Omo River at Namoruputh is easier because the road is better. Kenyan immigration

## BORDER-CROSSING INFORMATION

| TO/FROM | FROM/TO | BORDER CROSSING NOTES |
|---------|---------|----------------------|
| Ethiopia | Djibouti | Border crossings at Gelille and Galafi |
| Ethiopia | Somaliland | Border crossing at Togo-Wuchale/Wajaale |
| Somaliland | Djibouti | Border crossing at Loyaada |

Note that no visas are obtainable at borders. See the country Directory A–Z for visa information.

is in Todonyang, 7km after the border. Tribal conflicts remain common in this area, so check on the situation before trying either of these routes.

» There's an **Ethiopian immigration post** (☉7.30am-5pm) in Omorate that can stamp you out; there's still no Kenyan post to issue you a visa, so you must obtain one from the Kenyan embassy in Addis Ababa beforehand. Once you reach Nairobi you'll have to get it stamped; immigration officials are used to this. Bring lots of fuel and a big sense of adventure!

### Somaliland

You might brace yourself for adventure, but getting to Hargeisa, Somaliland's capital, is very easy.

» Many buses and minibuses run along the good, paved road between Jijiga and the border town of Togo-Wuchale (Birr30, one to 1½ hours). Get stamped out at Ethiopian immigration (it's the white building with a flag and satellite dish) before walking 100m over the causeway in no-man's-land to the brightly signed Somaliland immigration office in the twin village of Wajaale. The visa must have been acquired or arranged prior to your arrival by a hotel or an agent in Hargeisa – see Visas for Onward Travel on p285 for details.

» Taxis run frequently from a muddy park next to immigration to Hargeisa (Birr120/US$7, two hours), about

90km to the southeast. The drivers will try to get you to pay extra for your bags, but you don't need to.

### Sudan

The main border-crossing point with Sudan is the Metema crossing, 180km west of Gonder. The road between Gonder and Khartoum is now paved all the way. It's imperative that you've obtained your Sudan visa in Addis Ababa (not an easy task; see p285) before heading this way.

» In Gonder minibuses leave daily for Metema (Birr71, three hours). There is also a direct bus from Addis (Birr272, two days).

» After reaching Metema walk across the border into the Sudanese town of Gallabat. From Gallabat, transport can be found to Gedaref (three hours) and onward to Khartoum. If you set off very early and everything goes your way then you might make it from Gonder to Khartoum in a single day. If you get stuck en route then try to stay overnight in Gedaref (better than Gallabat).

### South Sudan

» At the time of research the border between Ethiopia and South Sudan at Jikawo was closed. There was some talk of the border reopening and if this happens buses will go from Gambela to the border town of Jikawo (Birr70, five hours). From there take a shared taxi to Adora (South Sudan).

» Another option, and one that locals in Gambela were currently using, is to hang around the river in Gambela in the hope of securing passage on one of the small boats that occasionally travel to Akobe via the Baro River. We've never heard of any travellers doing this, but if you get the nod from immigration officials then it's certainly going to be an interesting way to cross between Ethiopia and South Sudan.

» Whichever way you try to go check the security situation in South Sudan thoroughly beforehand as at the time if research there had been a lot of fighting in southeast South Sudan.

# GETTING AROUND

## Air

### Airlines in Ethiopia

The national carrier, **Ethiopian Airlines** (www.flyethiopian.com), is the only domestic carrier, with a comprehensive domestic route service and a solid safety record.

It's well worth considering a domestic flight or two, even if you're travelling on a budget. While prices cannot be described as cheap (Addis to Bahir Dar is around US$150 one way if bought outside Ethiopia; around US$59 if bought in country) it does eliminate long, bumpy bus rides. With the lower-altitude flying of the domestic planes and the usually clear Ethiopian skies, you'll still see some stunning landscapes, too. If you want a window seat, check in early.

» Standard security procedures apply at all airports, though there'll be more polite groping during screening at the remote ones. The baggage limit is 20kg on domestic flights. Don't bring bulky hand luggage as the interiors are quite small.

» Most flights leave from Addis Ababa, but not all are nonstop, which means you can also jump from one town to another. For instance, most of the daily Addis Ababa–Aksum flights stop at either Bahir Dar, Gonder or Lalibela en route.

» Buying domestic tickets from an agency on arrival in Ethiopia is always cheaper than buying them online from outside the country.

» Booking early to ensure a seat is particularly important on the Historical Circuit and during major festivals.

» Technically you should reconfirm all domestic flights 72 hours in advance. This is of course a very good idea, though we've never done this and have never had any problems. Still, we've heard stories from travellers who've got stuck after not reconfirming.

» Beware that schedules are occasionally forced to change due to weather or mechanical difficulties, so try not to plan an itinerary that's so tight that it doesn't make allowances for these changes.

## Bicycle

Cycling in Ethiopia is a fabulously rewarding way to explore the country. If you want to cycle across the country, come well prepared with a sturdy bike, plenty of spare parts, a good repair kit and the capacity to carry sufficient amounts of water. Cycles new and second-hand can be bought in Addis Ababa, but they are not generally the type of bike you'd wish to conquer the Historical Circuit with!

In the past, irregular terrain and brutal roads have scared off most adventure addicts and their bicycles, but with today's greatly improving road network it may just be the right time for you to give it a try. For general road conditions, see p294.

» Cyclists should show the usual caution when travelling around the country: never travel after dark, be wary of thieves and keep the bicycle well maintained. Brakes need to be in good working order for the mountainous highland roads.

» Be particularly wary of dogs; sometimes it's best to dismount and walk slowly away. Cycling in the rainy season can be very hard going.

» Punctures are easily repaired: just head for any *gommista* (tyre repairer) or garage. Many mechanics are also more than happy to help with cycle problems, and often turn out to be ingenious improvisers.

» Note the customs regulation regarding the

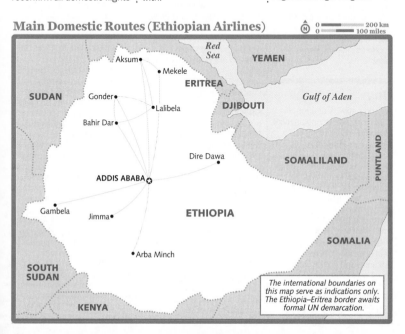

## Main Domestic Routes (Ethiopian Airlines)

0 ——— 200 km
0 ——— 100 miles

*The international boundaries on this map serve as indications only. The Ethiopia–Eritrea border awaits formal UN demarcation.*

## TRAVELLERS' LORE

Once there was a dog, a goat and a donkey. They wanted to go on a journey together, and decided to take a bus. The donkey paid and got out, the dog paid, got out but never got his change, and the goat got out but never paid.

To this day, and whenever a vehicle passes, the dog still chases his change, the goat still scatters at the first approach, and the donkey just plods tranquilly on.

Ethiopian folk tale

importation of a bicycle. A deposit must usually be left (amounting to the cycle's worth) at customs at the port of entry on arrival. When you leave, this will be returned. This is to deter black-market trading.

» Cycles are accepted aboard Ethiopian Airlines international flights. On domestic flights you'll need to check first in advance as it depends on what type of plane is covering the route on that given day.

» Finally, a few tips from a seasoned African cyclist: check and tighten screws and nuts regularly; take a spare chain; take a front as well as rear pannier rack; and pack a water filter in case you get stuck somewhere remote.

## Bus

A good network of long-distance buses connects most major towns of Ethiopia.

» One government bus association and around a dozen private ones operate, though you'll rarely be able to tell the difference between any of them. The biggest differentiating trait between government and private buses is the predeparture rituals.

» Government buses sell seat-specific tickets in advance and passengers must wait in line while the bus is loaded. After that's completed, the queue is paraded around the bus before tickets are checked

and the boarding barrage occurs. Private buses simply open the doors and start selling tickets to the flood of passengers as they cram in. Needless to say, private buses are usually the first to leave. They also tend to be slightly more comfortable than government ones.

» Unlike most African countries, standing in the aisles of long-distance buses is illegal in Ethiopia, making them more comfortable (note that we've said 'more comfortable', which is a far cry from saying comfortable!) and safer. On the longer journeys, there are usually scheduled 20-minute stops for meals.

» Recently a new breed of bus has taken to the roads of Ethiopia and these ones actually are pretty plush (air-con, reclining seats, on-board toilets, TVs and even free snacks). The biggest company is **Selam Buses** (☑0115 548800; www.selambus.com), but **Sky Buses** (☑0111 568080; www.skybusethiopia. com) is fancier and the one to opt for if possible. These bus services are mentioned under the relevant towns.

» In most cases when you arrive at the bus station there'll only be one bus heading in your direction, so any thoughts about it being private or government are a waste of time – get on and get going!

» Once on the road, you'll realise that all buses are slow. On sealed roads you can expect to cover around 50km/h, but on dirt roads

30km/h or less. In the rainy season, journeys can be severely disrupted. Thankfully, new roads are spreading rapidly across the land and turning many troublesome dirt sections into slick sections of sealed road. Unfortunately this has seen an increase in road accidents due to speed (though the rate is still low by African standards).

» Although most long-distance buses are scheduled to 'leave' at 6am or earlier, they don't typically set out before 7am as most are demand-driven and won't leave until full. To be safe you should make an appearance at the prescribed departure time. Remember that the Ethiopian clock is used locally (see p283), though Western time is used when quoting bus times in this book.

» In remote areas long waits for buses to fill is normal – some may not leave at all. In general, the earlier you get to the bus station, the better chance you have of catching the first bus out of town.

» The major drawback with bus travel is the size of the country. For the Historical Circuit alone, you'll spend a total of at least 10 days sitting on a bus to cover the 2500km.

» On those journeys quoted in this book with durations longer than one day, there are overnight stops en route (Ethiopian law stipulates that all long-distances buses must be off the road by 6pm). In many cases you won't be allowed to remove luggage from the roof, so you should pack toiletries and other overnight items to take with you in a small bag on the bus.

» Smaller and more remote towns are usually served by minibuses or Isuzu trucks.

## Costs

Buses are very cheap in Ethiopia. Both government-run and private buses work out at around US$1.50 per 100km.

## Reservations

» Tickets for most long-distance journeys (over 250km) can usually be bought in advance. If you can, do: it guarantees a seat (though not a specific seat number on private buses) and cuts out the touts who sometimes snap up the remaining tickets to resell for double the price to late-comers. Most government ticket offices are open daily from 5.30am to 5.30pm. For short distances (less than 250km), tickets can usually only be bought on the day. For Sky and Selam buses, tickets should be booked as far ahead as possible (a week is a good idea).

» If you would like a whiff of fresh air on your journey, get a seat behind the driver as he tends to buck the Ethiopian trend of keeping windows firmly closed and keeps his window cracked open. Though on the flip side, if there's an accident these are often the worst seats to be in!

## Car & Motorcycle

### Bringing Your Own Vehicle

If you're bringing your own 4WD or motorcycle, you'll need a *carnet de passage* (a guarantee issued by your own national motoring association that you won't sell your vehicle in the country you are travelling), the vehicle's registration papers and proof of third-party insurance that covers Ethiopia.

### Driving Licence

Tourists are allowed three months of using their inter-national driving licence, after which you need an Ethiopian one.

This is rarely enforced and most overlanders we met hadn't bothered with the convoluted process of obtaining an Ethiopian licence and had yet to encounter any

problems – roll the dice if you so please.

## Fuel & Spare Parts

» Fuel (both petrol and diesel) is quite widely available, apart from the more remote regions such as the southwest. Unleaded petrol is not available. Diesel costs from around Birr16.91 per litre, while petrol (called Benzene in Ethiopia) costs around Birr18.78 per litre. These are Addis prices, so expect to pay a little more in more remote areas. Note that your vehicle's fuel consumption will be 25% higher in highland Ethiopia than at sea level because of the increased altitudes.

» While there are helpful garages throughout the country (ask your hotel to recommend one), spare parts are not abundant outside Addis Ababa. It's wise to take stock while in Addis and acquire all that you may need for the journey ahead. Thanks to Toyota Land Cruisers being the choice of most tour operators, their parts are more plentiful and less expensive than those for Landrovers.

## Hire

Most people hire a 4WD. Recent road improvements mean this isn't always necessary, but since all tour companies only offer 4WD it's something of an academic point!

» Despite competition between the numerous tour agents in Addis Ababa that hire 4WDs, prices are steep and range from US$160 per day for older vehicles to US$180 for luxurious newer models. Most companies include unlimited kilometres, a driver, driver allowance (for their food and accommodation), fuel, third-party insurance, a collision damage waiver and government taxes in their rates; check all these details, and ask if service charges will be added afterwards and if there are set driver's hours. Some

companies allow you to pay for fuel separately. This is almost always cheaper than paying an all-inclusive rate.

» Know that prices are always negotiable and vary greatly depending on the period of rental and the season. Despite the hassle, you'll always pay much less organising things yourself in Ethiopia rather than hiring an agency at home to arrange it.

» Drivers are mandatory – currently no agency offers self-drive 4WD outside Addis. These drivers can be very useful as guides-cum-interpreters-cum-mechanics. Although tips are expected afterwards (see the boxed text on p280 for tipping guidelines), a nice gesture during the trip is to share food together (which costs very little).

» Though expensive, the chief advantage of 4WD hire over bus travel is the time that can be saved. Trip durations are at least halved and there's no waiting around in remote regions for infrequent and erratic buses. Note also that some national parks can only be entered with a 4WD.

» Some Addis Ababa–based agencies have branch offices in towns on the Historical Route and can rent 4WDs, but only by prearrangement. Increasingly, private individuals rent to tourists. Be aware of the risks, particularly regarding insurance and the condition of the car.

» Self-drive cars are only hired for use in and around Addis. If you're still interested in hiring one to toot around the capital (and it's hard to see what you'd gain from doing this rather than just taking a taxi), you must have a valid international driver's licence and be between 25 and 70 years old. Vehicles cost from US$120 per day with 50km to 70km free kilometres.

» Motorcycles are not currently rented.

## Insurance

Third-party vehicle insurance is required by law.

» Thankfully, unlike some other African countries, which demand that vehicles are covered by an insurance company based in that country, Ethiopia only requires your insurance from elsewhere is also valid in Ethiopia.

» Although not mandatory, we'd also recommend comprehensive coverage.

» If you don't have either, the numerous offices of **Ethiopian Insurance Corporation** (www.eic.com.et) sell third-party and comprehensive insurance.

## Road Conditions

Ethiopian roads continue to improve at a rapid rate, but even so plenty remain unpaved.

» Roads in the south have generally improved hugely in recent years and many parts of the Omo Valley are now accessible year-round even without a 4WD. However, there are still plenty of patches where potholes add a little bounce to your journey.

» Sealed roads head west from Addis Ababa, reaching Ambo and Jimma. The lowland roads can be diabolical in the rains (though the road from Metu to Gambela is excellent). The rest of the western highlands were undergoing extensive road-upgrading programs at the time of research, though this in itself was causing considerable delays in journeys.

» Decent sealed roads all but link Addis Ababa with most of the main towns on the northern circuit, but there are still some potholed sections.

» Harar and Dire Dawa, both 525km east of Addis Ababa, are connected to the capital with good sealed roads.

## Road Hazards

» On the outskirts of the towns or villages, look out for people, particularly children playing on the road or kerbside. Unmarked speed bumps can also be an unpleasant surprise.

» Night driving is not recommended. *Shiftas* (bandits) still operate in the more remote areas. Additionally, some trucks park overnight in the middle of the road – without lights.

» In the country, livestock is the main hazard; camels wandering onto the road can cause major accidents in the lowlands. Many animals, including donkeys, are unaccustomed to vehicles and are very car-shy, so always approach slowly and with caution.

» During the rainy season, a few roads, particularly in the west and southwest, become impassable. Check road conditions with the local authorities before setting out.

## Road Rules

Driving is on the right-hand side of the road. The speed limit for cars and motorcycles is 60km/h in the towns and villages and 100km/h outside the towns. The standard of driving is generally not high; devices such as mirrors or indicators are more decorative than functional. On highland roads, drive defensively and beware of trucks coming fast the other way. Also keep a sharp eye out for a row of stones or pebbles across the road: it marks roadworks or an accident. Seatbelts are compulsory for the driver (but nobody else), but many vehicles don't have seatbelts!

## Hitching

In the past, if someone asked for a ride in Ethiopia, it was usually assumed that it was because they couldn't afford a bus fare and little sympathy was spared for them. Many Ethiopians also suspected hitchers of hidden motives such as robbery.

However, for some towns not readily served by buses or light vehicles, hitching is now quite normal, and you will be expected to pay a 'fare'. Negotiate this in advance. The best place to look for lifts is at the hotels, bars and cafes in the centre of town.

» Be aware that the density of vehicles on many roads is still very low in Ethiopia; on the remote roads, you'll be lucky to see any.

» Know that hitching is never entirely safe, and it's not recommended. Travellers who decide to hitch should understand that they are taking a small but potentially serious risk. Hitching is safer in pairs. Additionally, try to let someone know where you're planning to go. Women should never hitch alone.

## Local Transport

» In many of the larger towns, a minibus service provides a quick, convenient and cheap way of hopping about town (from around Birr1 for short journeys). 'Conductors' generally shout out the destination of the bus; if in doubt, ask.

» Taxis operate in many of the larger towns, including Addis Ababa. Prices are reasonable, but foreigners as well as well-heeled Ethiopians are always charged more for 'contract services'. Ask your hotel for a fare estimate.

» *Bajajs* (motorised rickshaws) are common in many towns; a seat in a shared *bajaj* across town shouldn't cost more than Birr2. Hiring the vehicle for you alone will cost about Birr10 for the same trip.

» *Garis* (horse-drawn carts) are more often used for transporting goods than people nowadays.

## Minibuses & Isuzu Trucks

» Minibuses are commonly used between towns connected by sealed roads or to cover short distances. Legally they are not allowed to operate over a distance greater than 150km but plenty of drivers flout this rule. Some of these travel at night to reduce the chances of a brush with the police – or, during daylight hours, the driver merely swaps his papers halfway through the journey so as to confuse the police. Minibuses cost slightly more than buses, but they leave more often and cover the distances more quickly. A ride in one is also more likely to kill you! Avoid those travelling at night. You'll usually find them at bus stations.

» Some foreigners used to travel around remote regions in the back of goods trucks. The Lower Omo Valley was a popular place to do this. It's now illegal and, contrary to travellers' rumours that it's in order to make tourists pay for organised tours, it's actually for safety reasons – though yes, the rule only seems to be enforced on foreigners!

## Tours

For the independent traveller, incorporating an organised tour into your travels in Ethiopia is useful for four things: specialised activities such as safaris; access to remote regions with limited public transport such as the Lower Omo Valley or the Danakil Depression; 'themed trips' (such as birdwatching) with expert guides; and to help those with limited time who are keen to see as much as possible.

» If you're interested in taking a tour, contact the agencies in advance and compare itineraries and prices.

» To reduce the cost of tours (few are cheap), hook up with a group of other travellers, or contact the agency far in advance to see if there are pre-arranged tours that you can tag onto. You'll need to be flexible with your dates. The Thorn Tree forum on the Lonely Planet website is an ideal place to hook up with other travellers.

» Agencies offer all or some of the following: guides, 4WD hire, camping-equipment hire, Historical Route tours, birdwatching and wildlife viewing, Omo Valley tours, photo safaris, Simien and Bale Mountain trekking, Rift Valley Lake trips, and Danakil and Afar excursions. Some have branches in towns outside Addis Ababa, from where (if prebooked) you can hire a 4WD or guide or take a tour.

» Though prices are officially fixed, most are very open to negotiation, particularly during the low season. Many agencies now accept credit cards (with a 2% to 3% commission).

The following list is far from exhaustive, but it includes those recommended by travellers and Ethiopians in the tourism industry.

**Abeba Tours Ethiopia** (Map p38; ☑0115 159530; www. abebatoursethiopia.com; Ras Hotel, Gambia St, Addis Ababa) Friendly and very professional, this operator seems to go the extra mile for its customers. It organises general tours throughout the country. The drivers they use are about the best in the business. If travelling by jeep is just too rough for you then they can also organise helicopter tours!

**Ethiopian Quadrants** (Map p34; ☑0115 157990; www. ethiopianquadrants.com; near Adwa Bridge, Addis Ababa) Respected and very well-managed tour company run by knowledgeable staff. All the standard tours as well as birdwatching, butterfly, flower and coffee tours.

**Four Seasons Travel & Tours** (Map p46; ☑0116 613121; www.fstatours.com; Bole Rd, Addis Ababa) A reasonable outfit offering all the standard tours. Reader recommended.

**Galaxy Express Services** (Map p38; ☑0115-510355; www.galaxyexpress-ethiopia. com; Gambia St, Addis Ababa) This long-established agency offers various Ethiopia tour packages. Travel is in new Land Cruisers. It's also an Avis agent and rents self-drive cars for use in and around Addis Ababa.

**Green Land Tours & Travels** (Map p46; ☑0116 299252; www.greenlandethio pia.com; Cameroon St, Addis Ababa) Green Land is one of the biggest agencies, with various hotels and camps set up throughout Ethiopia and some pioneering tours to the remotest corners of the country.

---

## TAXI TERMINOLOGY

In the towns, villages and countryside of Ethiopia taxis offer two kinds of service: 'contract taxis' and 'share-taxis'. Share-taxis ply fixed routes, stop and pick people up when hailed and generally operate like little buses. They become 'contract taxis' when they are flagged down (or 'contracted') by an individual or a group for a private journey. The fare is then split between all the passengers in the taxi.

Though not really 'taxis' at all, minibuses, trucks, 4WDs and various other kinds of cars can all be contracted in the same way as contract taxis. Contracting a large minibus for yourself is seen as perfectly normal.

Before hiring a contract taxi, always negotiate the fare before you get in, or you may be asked to pay far above the going rate at the end of the journey.

**Red Jackal Tour Operator** (Map p44; ☑0111 559915; www.redjackal.net; Itegue Taitu Hotel, Piazza, Addis Ababa) Good-value tours of all the main tourist sites. Used to dealing with backpackers and might be able to help you get a group of other travellers together to reduce costs.

**Travel Ethiopia** (Map p38; ☑0111 508870; www.travel ethiopia.com; National Hotel, Menelik II Ave, Addis Ababa) A self-professed 'ecominded' tour company with multilin-gual guides (English, French, Italian and German).

**T-Tam Travel & Tour** (Map p46; ☑0115 514055; www.ttamtour.com; Bole Rd, Addis Ababa) This is a well-established agency and an International Air Transport Association (IATA) ticketing agent.

**Village Ethiopia** (Map p38; ☑0115 523497; www.village-ethiopia.net; National Hotel, Menelik II Ave, Addis Ababa) This agency offers everything from birdwatch-ing and ethnic tours in the south, to rock climbing in Tigray. It also specialises in the Danakil Depression and has a lodge near its toasty confines.

## Train

The Addis Ababa–Dire Dawa train is indefinitely out of action. (The Dire Dawa–Djibouti section of the line is likely to reopen during the life of this book, followed at some undetermined point in the future by the Addis–Dire Dawa section.)

# Djibouti

## Includes »

## Best of Culture

» European Quarter, Djibouti City (p300)

» Abourma Rock Art Site (p310)

» Bankoualé (p310)

» Obock (p312)

## Best of Nature

» Forêt du Day (p310)

» Lac Abbé (p309)

» Lac Assal (p309)

» Grand Barra (p309)

## Why Go?

This tiny speck of a country packs a big punch. What it lacks in size, it more than makes up for in beauty, especially if you're a fan of geological oddities. Few countries in the world, with the possible exception of Iceland, offer such weird landscapes – think salt lakes, extinct volcanoes, sunken plains, limestone chimneys belching out puffs of steam, basaltic plateaus and majestic canyons. Outdoor adventure comes in many forms with superb hiking, diving and kitesurfing – not to mention snorkelling alongside whale sharks in the Gulf of Tadjoura.

Barring Djibouti City, the country is refreshingly devoid of large-scale development. It's all about ecotravel, with some great sustainable stays in the hinterland that provide a fascinating glimpse into the life of nomadic tribes.

Travelling independently around Djibouti may not come cheap, but despite the high cost of living, you'll surely leave this little corner of Africa with new experiences and wonderful memories.

## When to Go
### Djibouti City

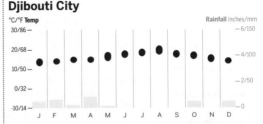

| May–Sep Some like it hot...some like it *hot*. | Oct & Feb–Apr Shoulder seasons are not a bad time to visit. Calm waters for diving. | Nov–Jan Coolest months; perfect for outdoor activities. Whale sharks make annual visit. |

## AT A GLANCE

» **Currency** Djibouti Franc (DFr)

» **Language** Somali, Afar, French

» **Money** ATMs in Djibouti City (most Visa only); credit cards not widely accepted for payment.

» **Visas** Single-entry tourist visas obtainable at the airport for most Western nationals; see p317.

## Fast Facts

» **Area** 23,000 sq km

» **Capital** Djibouti City

» **Country Code** ☑253

» **Emergency** ☑119

» **Population** 906,000

## Exchange Rates

| Australia | A$1 | DFr184 |
|---|---|---|
| Canada | C$1 | DFr176 |
| Euro zone | €1 | DFr233 |
| Japan | ¥100 | DFr194 |
| New Zealand | NZ$1 | DFr146 |
| UK | UK£1 | DFr277 |
| USA | US$1 | DFr174 |

For current exchange rates see www.xe.com.

## Set Your Budget

» **Budget hotel room** DFr7000-10,000

» **Two-course dinner** DFr3000

» **Day trip to Lac Assal** DFr17,000

» **Whale-shark-spotting excursion** DFr14,000

# Entering Djibouti

Most visitors fly into Djibouti's only international airport, which is located near Djibouti City. There are regular flights to/from Sana'a (Yemen), Hargeisa (Somaliland), Addis Ababa (Ethiopia), Dubai (United Arab Emirates), Istanbul (Turkey), Nairobi (Kenya) and Paris. The border with Eritrea is closed; land borders with Ethiopia (Galafi and Gelille) and Somaliland (Loyaada) are open.

## ITINERARIES

### Three Days

First, shed a tear that you only have three days to explore this incredible country. Base yourself in Djibouti City and contact a tour operator to arrange a trip to Lac Abbé and Lac Assal. Make sure you spend a night at Lac Abbé to enjoy the fabulous sunset and sunrise.

### Ten Days

A more realistic timeframe, which allows you to take in the above activities plus a couple of days chilling out on scenic Moucha Island or Plage des Sables Blancs. Then devote at least two days to the Goda Mountains. A hike to the Abourma rock art site could even be on the cards. Afterwards check out Tadjoura and Obock. Back in the capital, sample the country's finest food and take a tour to Decan, a small wildlife refuge. Be sure to take a whale-shark-spotting tour or a diving (or snorkelling) trip to the Gulf of Tadjoura. Spend your last night in the bars and clubs.

Alternatively, if you're a hiking fiend, you could save a week for a trek along an ancient salt route.

# Safe Travel

Djibouti is one of the safest destinations in Africa, partly because of the large Western military presence. Serious crime or hostility aimed specifically at travellers is very rare, and there's no more to worry about here than in most other countries. Apart from the odd street hustler in the centre, Djibouti City is very safe as far as Africa's capitals go. Take care in the crowded areas and markets, as pickpockets may operate there, and avoid walking on your own in the Quartier 1, immediately south of Les Caisses market. The risk of theft and pickpocketing diminishes considerably outside the capital.

Note that Djibouti's security services are sensitive and active. Remain polite and calm if questioned by police officers.

# DJIBOUTI CITY

POP 600,000

Djibouti City is evolving at a fast pace, and there's a palpable sense of change in the air. Today's city is vastly different from the battered French outpost to which it was reduced in the 1980s and 1990s. Thanks to its geostrategic importance and its busy port,

Djibouti City has been transformed from a sleepy capital to a thriving place. In recent years, increasing waves of foreign investment have sparked a number of building projects. Yet under its veneer of urban bustle, the city remains a down-to-earth place, with jarring cultural and social combinations. Traditionally robed Afar tribesmen, stalwart GIs, sensuous Somali ladies and frazzled

## Djibouti Highlights

❶ Catch local vibes while wandering through the animated streets of **Djibouti City**

❷ Dive the wreck of **Le Faon** (p307) in the Gulf of Tadjoura

❸ Sight and swim with **whale sharks** (p301) from November to January

❹ Explore the great salt lake and black volcanic landscape of **Lac Assal** (p309), the lowest point on the African continent

❺ Immerse yourself in the Martian landscape of **Lac Abbé** (p309)

❻ Snorkel amid shoals

of colourful fish around **Moucha Island** (p307)

❼ Unwind on picture-perfect, white-sand **Plage des Sables Blancs** (p311)

❽ Take an unforgettable hike to **Abourma** (p310) and look for some well-preserved petroglyphs

DJIBOUTI DJIBOUTI CITY

businessmen with the latest mobile phones stuck to their ear all jostle side by side.

Djibouti City boasts good infrastructure, including hotels, bars (a note for those who've just come from Somaliland: yes, they're licensed), clubs and restaurants – it's *the* place in the Horn of Africa to treat yourself to a fine meal. Sure, it lacks stand-out sights, and its architecture doesn't have much to turn your head, but stick around this engaging city long enough and you might fall prey to its unexpected charms. It's also the obvious place to organise forays into the fantastic hinterland, or boat excursions.

## ◉ Sights

The centre can be divided into two quarters: the European Quarter, laid out on a grid system to the north, and the African Quarter, which spills out to the south.

Most of the following sights can be reached on foot.

### European Quarter                    NEIGHBOURHOOD
The focal point of the European Quarter is **Place du 27 Juin 1977** (Place Ménélik). With its whitewashed houses and Moorish arcades, this vast square is a strange mix of the Arab and the European. It's lined with cafes, bars, restaurants and shops.

The European Quarter is connected to the Plateau du Serpent to the north by the Blvd de la République, along which many of the principal administrative buildings can be found. In this area you'll also find a smattering of enticing religious buildings, including the eye-catching **cathedral** (Map p302; Blvd de la République). In a street running parallel to Blvd de la République, **Église Éthiopienne Orthodoxe Tewahido St Gabriel du Soleil** (Orthodox Church; Map p302; west of Blvd de la République), which is popular with the Ethiopian community, is well worth a peek.

### African Quarter                     NEIGHBOURHOOD
The vast **Place Mahmoud Harbi** (Place Rimbaud; Map p304), which was being renovated

at the time of writing, is dominated by the minaret of the great **Hamoudi mosque** (Map p304), Djibouti City's most iconic building. Eastward, the chaotic **Quartier 1** is a criss-cross of alleyways where stalls and shops are lined cheek by jowl. Spreading along Blvd de Bender are the stalls of **Les Caisses market** (Map p304). Crammed with every type of souvenir from woodcarvings to clothing, it's a colourful place for soaking up the atmosphere.

### L'Escale                                  MARINA
In the early evening, the walk along the causeway northwest of the centre makes a very pleasant stroll. The Moorish-inspired **presidential palace** (not open to the public) marks one end, the harbour of L'Escale, the other. The little marina is home to a variety of boats, from the traditional and picturesque Arab dhows to the simple local fishing skiffs and ferries to Tadjoura and Obock.

Further north, running almost parallel to L'Escale, is the city's port proper, access to which is restricted. From the marina you can see the imposing cranes and cargo boats.

### Plateau du Serpent &
### Îlot du Héron                      NEIGHBOURHOODS
These adjoining neighbourhoods north of the centre are residential areas where you'll find many of the foreign embassies and residences, as well as lavish villas and Djibouti's swankiest hotels.

### Beaches
For a capital that's surrounded by water, Djibouti City is not well endowed with beaches. The only decent stretch of sand is at the **Djibouti Palace Kempinski**, but there's an entrance fee of DFr3000, and swimming is not *that* tempting, with shallow waters and a profusion of algae. There's also a postage stamp–sized beach at the **Sheraton Djibouti Hotel** (Map p302). For a dip, your best bet is to use the pools at both hotels (DFr2000 at the Djibouti Palace Kempinski; no charge at the Sheraton).

## 🏃 Activities
Diving, kitesurfing, whale-shark spotting and hiking can all be organised from Djibouti City.

### Diving
Most diving takes place off the islands of Maskali and Moucha in the Gulf of Tadjoura (see p307), where you'll find a variety of dive sites for all levels. There's also a handful of

---

### ℹ️ GETTING TO A BEACH

Feeling disappointed by Djibouti City's lack of good beaches? Don't despair. Consider booking a trip to the easily accessible Moucha Island (p307), which features a good stretch of white sand and azure waters – perfect for swimming and evening up your sunburn.

spectacular sites scattered along the shoreline of the Bay of Ghoubbet, furthest west.

You'll find two professional dive centres staffed with qualified instructors who speak English.

**Dolphin**  DIVING, SNORKELLING

(Map p302; ☑21350313, 77825318; www.dolphin services.com; Blvd de la République) This well-organised dive shop offers a full menu of underwater adventures, including introductory dives, day trips to Moucha Island and the Bay of Ghoubbet (from DFr17,700), snorkelling trips and certification courses. From November to March, Dolphin also operates a live-aboard dive boat that schedules regular trips around the Gulf of Tadjoura.

**Le Lagon Bleu**  DIVING, SNORKELLING

(Map p302; ☑21250296, 21325555, 77826119; www. djiboutidivers.com; ⊙closed Aug) The main office is based at Djibouti Palace Kempinski but the dive centre is on Moucha Island (p307).

**Kitesurfing**

The steady winds that buff the Gulf of Tadjoura make kitesurfing hounds go ga-ga – but don't be put off; it's also a great place to learn. For beginners, Île de la Tortue, near the international airport, is a hot favourite, with shallow waters and more manageable breezes (about 15 knots).

**Djibouti Kitesurf**  KITESURFING

(☑77828614, 21357233; www.djiboutikitesurf.com) Chat with Dante Kourallos to get hooked up with the how-to. Tuition and courses for all levels can be arranged, as well as a half-day 'discovery' session (DFr20,000, minimum six people). For experienced kitesurfers, two- to three-day excursions to the Bay of Ghoubbet can be arranged between October and May (from DFr50,000, minimum 12 people).

**Whale-Shark Spotting**

The Bay of Ghoubbet, at the western end of the Gulf of Tadjoura, is one of most dependable locations in the world to swim alongside a massive whale shark (*Rhincodon typus*), the world's largest fish. The peak season runs from November to January. There are between two and 10 individuals, close to the shore, and it's very easy to snorkel with these graceful creatures.

This activity has exploded in recent years, and plenty of unprofessional operators can arrange trips. It's better to stick to Lagon Bleu or Dolphin; at least these two operators are more ecologically sensitive and follow protocols. Give the sharks a berth of at least 4m. Touching is an absolute no-no.

A full-day excursion costs from DFr14,000.

## 🛏 Sleeping

The choice of budget accommodation is limited, and most hotels tend to be dull multi-storey blocks.

**TOP CHOICE Le Héron Auberge**  HOTEL $$

(Map p302; ☑21324343, 21340001; www.au bergeleheron.net; Rue de l'Imam Hassan Abdallah Mohamed; s/d with breakfast DFr10,000/14,000; ❄🖼) An attractive, secure compound in a residential area, Le Héron is Djibouti City's best value hotel. Rooms: well-appointed and clean as a whistle. Facilities: top-notch and free. Staff: competent and friendly. Location: on a peaceful street. Nice extra: a drinking fountain near the reception. A shuttle service is also available to drive you to the centre (by reservation). The slightly off-the-beaten-path location means you can actually get a good night's sleep here. It's within walking distance of a couple of eateries. Credit cards are accepted (no commission). Book ahead.

**TOP CHOICE Sheraton Djibouti Hotel**  RESORT $$$

(Map p302; ☑21328000; www.sheraton.com/dji bouti; Plateau du Serpent; s DFr 29,000-40,000, d DFr35,000-45,000, ste from DFr65,000, incl breakfast; ❄🖼🏊) The Sheraton is back with a vengeance. After an extensive renovation in 2012, it now ranks as one of the best value options in Djibouti City. Sure, the exterior of the hotel looks like a common apartment block, but once you enter the spacious lobby things get much better, with nicely laid-out rooms (some with sensational sea views), enticing bathrooms and a prolific list of facilities, including two restaurants, a bar, a spa, a pool, a gift shop, a fitness centre, a casino and a business centre.

**Hotel Alia**  HOTEL $$

(Map p302; ☑21358222; Ave Maréchal Lyautey; s/d with breakfast DFr16,800/18,800; ❄🖼) Popular with expats, aid workers and business-people, this well-managed establishment gets kudos for its convenient location, immaculate rooms, back-friendly mattresses, squeaky-clean bathrooms and professional service. Some rooms upstairs come with partial sea views. It's within walking distance of Place du 27 Juin 1977. Good value.

**Auberge Sable Blanc**  HOTEL $

(Map p302; ☑21351163; off Rue du Palais du Peuple; d DFr7700; ❄) Tucked away on a quiet street

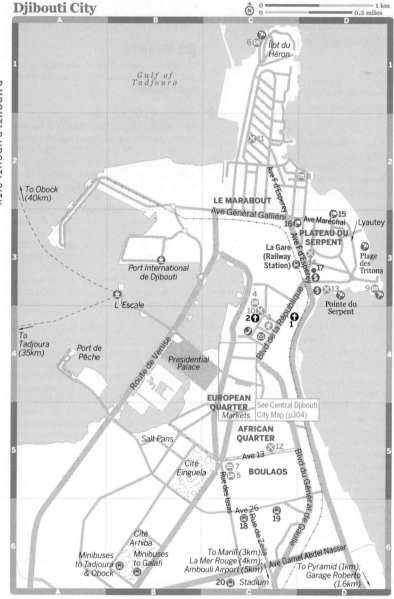

running parallel to Blvd de la République, this little modern construction is a discreet place (sometimes used by adulterous couples) with eight clean, if rather unloved, rooms and salubrious bathrooms. Note that the air-con is on from 7pm to 7am only.

**Djibouti Palace Kempinski** RESORT **$$$**
(Map p302; ☑ 21325555; www.kempinski.com/djibouti; Ilot du Héron; s incl breakfast DFr98,000-113,000, d DFr110,000-125,000, ste from DFr135,000; ☀@☞☎) Well-heeled Arabian businessmen, Western military officers and soldiers, folks

# Djibouti City

from various intelligence agencies and African bigwigs – they all end up here. It's all very 'Bond, James Bond'. Away from 007 fantasies, you know exactly what you'll be getting at the swanky Kempinski: impersonal yet shiny-clean rooms and a host of top-notch facilities, including three restaurants, two swimming pools, a business centre, a dive shop, a spa and a gym. What you won't be getting is any kind of indication that you are in Djibouti but, as you flake out on the (tiny) beach or do laps in the gleaming pool, you probably won't be that bothered. Many guests have found the service a bit lackadaisical.

**Hôtel de Djibouti**  HOTEL $
(Map p302; ☎21356415; Ave 13; s/d DFr6300/8600; ❄️📶) Located in the heart of the African Quarter, this classic, long-standing shoestringer's haunt may not be the most memorable stay of your trip, but it's an economic option for anyone in need of a good night's rest with basic fixings like functioning air-con, TV and reliable internet (or so they claim). Fight tooth and nail to get a room at the back of the hotel; if you don't the road noise will make the idea of sleep a wishful dream.

**Hotel Horseed**  HOTEL $
(☎21352316, 77017804; s without bathroom DFr5000-6000; d without bathroom DFr6000;

❄️📶) Under new management, the Horseed is a reliable choice for unfussy budgeteers, with bare but serviceable rooms. The owner, Kadar Ismael, has lived for 10 years in Canada and speaks excellent English; he's a mine of local information. He has plans to add a floor with better-equipped rooms.

**Dar Es Salam**  HOTEL $
(Map p302; ☎21353334; off Ave 13; s DFr5700, d DFr7400-8400; ❄️📶) Right in the African Quarter, the Dar Es Salam would be a dependable budget choice were it not for its lack of facilities and noisy location. Rooms vary in size, light and noisiness so ask to see a couple before you settle on one. Overall, not a bad deal provided you keep your expectations in check.

**Résidence de l'Europe**  HOTEL $$
(Map p304; ☎21355060; www.hotelresdjibouti.com; Pl du 27 Juin 1977; s/d incl breakfast DFr15,700/19,800; ❄️📶) This venture gets by on its tip-top location, a waddle away from the restaurants, bars and clubs. There's no great luxury involved and some of the furnishings have seen better days, but the 24 rooms are spacious and kept in reasonable nick. Credit cards (Visa only) are accepted here.

**Menelik Hotel** HOTEL **$$**
(Map p304; ☎21351177; menelikhotel@intnet.dj; Pl du 27 Juin 1977; s/d incl breakfast DFr15,500/ 20,200; ❈🛜) It's hard to top the Menelik's location, smack-dab in the centre. Service is acceptable and the rooms provide good levels of comfort and hygiene but, to be honest, you pay for the location. Cash only.

## ✗ Eating

If you've just come from Ethiopia (and you're weary of *injera* flatbread) or Somaliland (and you've had your fill of goat meat), now's your chance to broaden your culinary experiences. The city is endowed with a smattering of restaurants that will please most palates – a testimony to the French presence. No alcohol is served in the cheaper places.

**TOP CHOICE La Mer Rouge** SEAFOOD **$$$**
(off Map p302; ☎21340005; www.lamerrougedj. com; Rte Nelson Mandela, Ambouli; mains DFr2500-4500; ⊘lunch & dinner Mon-Sat) Seafood, seafood and seafood – that's all that matters at the sleek La Mer Rouge, Djibouti City's premier address for crustaceans and fish. The menu is a real sea-sourced smorgasbord, and revolves around whatever happens to flop onto the quayside. If they're on offer, plump for the *gambas feta* (king prawns with feta cheese), oysters or crab – or splash out on a supersized seafood platter. Make sure you leave space for dessert: the homemade *fondue au chocolat* (melted chocolate) is sheer ambrosia. The only drawback is the out-of-the-way location, near the airport – you'll need to get here by taxi.

**La Terrasse** ETHIOPIAN **$**
(Map p304; ☎21350227; Rue d'Ethiopie; mains DFr800-1500; ⊘dinner) Bargain! This place has plenty of character and serves up good Ethiopian food as well as pasta and sandwiches at puny prices. It occupies a rooftop, with a moodily lit dining area and an open kitchen – not to mention the heady scents of incense. For lunch, you can head to the much less atmospheric **Restaurant La Fontaine**, on the 1st floor (same management).

**Moukbasa National** YEMENI **$$**
(Map p302; ☎21351588; Ave 13; fish menu DFr2000; ⊘lunch & dinner Sat-Thu) There are a few good ventures specialising in *poisson yemenite* (oven-baked fish) around town but this one was the most popular at the time of writing, although it's not right in the thick of things. There are no menus; just choose your glisten-

ing beastie (usually sea bream, grouper or barracuda) in the fridge and it's barbecued *a la Yemeni*: the whole thing is sliced in half, smacked against the walls of a fire pit and baked to a black crisp – you're welcome to have a look and take pictures. It's sprinkled with hot pepper and served with a *chapati* (flatbread) and a belt-bustingly good *mokbasa* (purée of honey and either dates or banana). Truly finger-licking.

**Restaurant Saba** YEMENI, SEAFOOD **$$**
(Map p302; ☎21354244; Ave Maréchal Lyautey; mains DFr1000-3000; ⊘breakfast & lunch Sat-Thu, dinner daily) This Yemeni-run institution serves well-prepared fish and meat dishes without fuss. Some reliable choices are skewered fish, fillet of barracuda, camel steak and *poisson yemenite*. There are some good pastas and salads (from DFr800), which will gladden vegetarian hearts, as well as superb fruit juices.

## Central Djibouti City

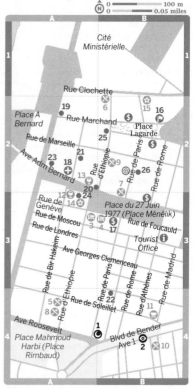

# Central Djibouti City

**Restaurant-Café de la Gare**       FRENCH $$$
(Map p302; ☑21351530; Ave F d'Esperey; mains DFr2500-3600; ☺lunch & dinner Sat-Thu) Alfresco on a little pavement terrace or inside the pretty dining room decorated with earthy tones, dining at this cosy eatery is a treat – a true alchemist, the Senegalese chef here conjures up French-inspired specialities with an African twist. Highlights include fish fillet, king prawns and duck leg preserved in its own fat.

**Mukbassa Central –
Chez Youssouf**       YEMENI $$
(Map p304; ☑21351899; off Ave 1; fish menu DFr2200; ☺lunch Sat-Thu, dinner daily) In business for ages, this Djibouti City icon is famous for one thing and one thing only: *poisson yemenite*. The colourful, wooden building feels a bit ramshackle, but that's part of the experience. Dessert (pancakes) is extra (DFr400).

**Restaurant L'Historil**       FRENCH $$
(Map p304; ☑21341364; off Pl du 27 Juin 1977; mains DFr1800-3000; ☺lunch Sat-Thu, dinner daily) Subdued lighting, cosy surrounds, a soothing blue colour scheme and an ample selection of taste-bud-titillating specialities have made this restaurant one of the most popular in town for a fancy meal. Among the many winners are rib of beef, steak tartare,

fillet of grouper and grilled kingfish. Delicious salads, too.

**Melting Pot**       JAPANESE $$$
(Map p302; ☑21350399; www.meltingpotdj.com; rue Bernard; mains DFr2400-4600; ☺breakfast, lunch & dinner Tue-Sun) If you have a sashimi or yakitori craving that must be met while in Djibouti, head to cute and cosy Melting Pot for authentic Japanese food. The menu also features French classics. The decor is embellished with wood and exotic touches, and there's a wonderfully overgrown garden. It's tucked away on a little side street in Îlot du Héron.

**Blue Nile**       DJIBOUTIAN $$
(Map p304; Rue d'Ethiopie; mains DFr900-1800; ☺breakfast, lunch & dinner Sat-Thu) Frills are sparse, but servings are anything but stingy in this super-cheap Djiboutian restaurant. The menu runs the gamut from fish dishes and salads to pizzas and sandwiches.

**Le Pizzaiolo**       ITALIAN $$
(Map p304; ☑21354439; Rue d'Ethiopie; mains DFr1600-3100; ☺lunch & dinner) Feast on palate-blowing Italian specialities in this zingy trattoria-like venue. The menu roves from faultlessly cooked pizzas to pasta and from salads to meat dishes.

## EATING OUT ON A BUDGET

Some of the cheapest meals in town come from the food stands in front of La Terrasse and Blue Nile restaurants on Rue d'Ethiopie (Map p304). Fork out DFr500 for a good-sized sandwich or a kebab and you'll leave patting your tummy contentedly. They open in the evenings only.

**Tentazioni**                                    ITALIAN $$$
(Map p302; ☑21325555; Djibouti Palace Kempinski, Îlot du Héron; mains DFr2200-4500; ◷lunch & dinner) If pastas, creamy risotto or *piccata de veau* (veal stew) make your stomach quiver with excitement, slide into this great Italian restaurant inside the Djibouti Palace Kempinski. Also part of the hotel, **Restaurant Lac Assal** (buffet DFr6500-7500; ◷lunch & dinner daily) is renowned for its themed buffet meals. Kempinski's third restaurant, **Le Bankoualé** (mains DFr2500-4000; ◷dinner daily) overlooks the beach and is great for a candlelit dinner.

**La Brasserie**                      INTERNATIONAL $$$
(Map p302; ☑21328000; Sheraton Djibouti Hotel, Plateau du Serpent; buffet DFr6000-7500; ◷lunch & dinner) Inside the Sheraton Djibouti Hotel, you'll find a casually elegant restaurant that is noted for its good-value lunch and dinner buffets. Prices include access to the swimming pool.

**La Chaumière**                  FRENCH, CHINESE $$
(Map p304; ☑21357002; Pl du 27 Juin 1977; mains DFr1300-3300; ◷lunch & dinner) This popular joint overlooking the main square serves well-prepared French favourites as well as a good selection of Chinese dishes and sandwiches. The rustic decor is easy on the eye, with exposed beams and stone walls. You can also dine alfresco on the agreeable terrace. Oh, and it's open for lunch on Friday (an exception in Djibouti City).

**Association de la Communauté Ethiopienne à Djibouti**           ETHIOPIAN $
(Map p302; west of Blvd de la République; mains DFr500-1200; ◷lunch & dinner) Also known as 'Club Ethiopien', this simple establishment serves good Ethiopian fare at economical prices.

**Casino**                              SUPERMARKET $
(Map p304; Rue Clochette; ◷7.30am-1pm & 4-8pm Sat-Thu) This well-stocked supermarket has a good selection of wines and beers.

## 🍷 Drinking

If you've come to Djibouti from dry Somaliland, rejoice! There's no shortage of watering holes in Djibouti City, especially around Pl du 27 Juin 1977. Plenty of teahouses are also scattered around the centre.

**L'Historil**                                  BAR
(Map p304; Pl du 27 Juin 1977) Popularly considered to be Djibouti City's most esteemed bar, L'Historil has an appealing terrace that offers excellent people-watching opportunities.

**Association de la Communauté Ethiopienne de Djibouti**              BAR
(Map p302; west of Blvd de la République) This down-to-earth restaurant and bar, with its large outdoor courtyard, is a pleasant place to enjoy a very cheap beer – a bottle of St George costs only DFr350 – and meet locals.

**Chez Mahad**                             JUICE BAR
(Map p304; off Rue de Madrid; juices DFr350-800; ◷7am-noon & 4-8.30pm Sat-Thu, 4-8.30pm Fri) Has a dizzying array of fruity concoctions (over 45 varieties). Also serves tea, coffee and pastries.

**Le Palmier en Zinc**                        PUB
(Map p304; Pl du 27 Juin 1977) This smart-looking pub has a respectably long list of beers and cocktails. It also offers karaoke on selected evenings.

## ☆ Entertainment

Most clubs are on or around Rue d'Ethiopie, in the European Quarter. They are at their liveliest on Thursday and Friday nights. Entrance is free, but a beer costs upwards of DFr1000.

**Bar Menelik – VIP**                         CLUB
(Map p304; Pl du 27 Juin 1977) In the basement of Menelik Hotel, this was the 'most happening' (meaning 'least sleazy') place at the time of research.

**Club Hermes**                               CLUB
(Map p304; Rue de Genève) If there's a constant here, it's the promise that the music, whatever the style, will get you groovin'.

**Le Scotch**                                 CLUB
(Map p304; Rue Clochette) Another of Djibouti City's hot spots. Cosy seats, red lights and the odd full-length mirror surround the dance floor.

# ℹ Information

## Internet Access

There's a slew of internet outlets in the centre. They all offer fast connections. Expect to pay around DFr200 per hour.

**Filga Foire Informatique** (Rue de Paris; per hr DFr200; ⊙7am-12.30pm & 4-10pm Sat-Thu, 7am-12.30pm Fri) Internet access.

## Medical Services

You'll find several well-stocked pharmacies in the centre.

**Pôle Médical** (Map p304; ☑21352724; ⊙8am-noon & 4-7pm Sat-Thu) A well-equipped clinic. It's off Pl du 27 Juin 1977.

## Money

There are banks and two bureaux de change in the centre, as well as a few Visa-friendly ATMs (but only one ATM accepts MasterCard). Both the Djibouti Palace Kempinski and Sheraton Djibouti Hotel have an ATM.

**Bank of Africa** (Pl Lagarde; ⊙7.30am-noon & 4.15-6pm Sun & Wed, 7.30am-noon Mon, Tue & Fri) Changes cash and has one ATM.

**BCIMR** Pl Lagarde (⊙7.30-11.45am Sun-Thu); Plateau du Serpent (Ave F d'Esperey; ⊙7.45-noon & 4-5.15pm Sun-Thu) Changes cash and has ATMs.

**Dilip Corporation** (Map p304; Pl du 27 Juin 1977; ⊙8am-noon & 4-7.30pm Sat-Thu) Authorised bureau de change. Changes cash (no commission) and does cash advances on Visa and MasterCard for a 6% commission and a DFr1000 fee for the service.

**Mehta** (Map p304; ☑353719; Pl du 27 Juin 1977; ⊙7.30am-noon & 4-7.30pm Sat-Thu) Authorised bureau de change. Next door to Dilip, Mehta also changes cash (no commission).

**Saba Islamic Bank** (off Pl du 27 Juin 1977; ⊙7.45-noon & 4-6pm Sun-Thu) Has one ATM, which accepts both Visa and MasterCard.

## Post

**Main post office** (Blvd de la République; ⊙7am-2pm & 4.30-6.30pm Sat-Thu) North of the centre. Also houses a Western Union counter.

## Telephone

The most convenient places to make an international or a local call are the various telephone outlets scattered around the city centre.

**Djibouti Telecom** (west of Blvd de la République; ⊙7.30am-1.30pm Sat-Thu) Sells prepaid SIM cards.

## Tourist Information

**Tourist office** (Map p304; ☑352800; www.office-tourisme.dj; Rue de Foucauld; ⊙7am-1.30pm Sat-Thu, 4-6pm Sat, Mon & Wed) Mildly helpful. Sells a map of the city (DFr1500). To the southeastern side of Pl du 27 Juin 1977.

# ℹ Getting There & Away

## Air

Ambouli airport is 5km south of town. For details of international flights to and from Djibouti City, see p317. **ATTA/Globe Travel** (Map p304; ☑21353036; atta@intnet.dj; off Pl du 27 Juin 1977) and **Agence Le Goubet** (Map p304; ☑21354520; valerie@riesgroup.dj; Blvd Cheikh Osman) represent most international and regional airlines.

## Boat

A ferry plies the Djibouti–Tadjoura and Djibouti–Obock routes two to three times a week (DFr1500 one way, two to three hours for either journey). It doesn't operate from mid-June to mid-September. Boats leave from L'Escale.

## Car

For 4WD rental (from DFr25,000 per day, with driver), contact the following outfits. See also p318 for information on hiring a car.

**Garage Roberto** (off Map p302; ☑21352029; Rte de Boulaos)

**Marill** (☑21329400; www.groupe-marill.com; Rte de l'Aéroport)

**Pyramid** (off Map p302; ☑21358203; www.pyramidrental.com; Rte de Boulaos)

## Local Transport

Minibuses leave from various departure points south of town. They connect Djibouti City to Tadjoura, Galafi (at the Ethiopian border) and Obock. Most minibuses leave early in the morning and only when they are full. Most journeys cost from DFr600 to DFr2000, depending on distance.

# ℹ Getting Around

The central hub for city minibuses (all tickets DFr50) is on Pl Mahmoud Harbi (Map p304). A taxi ride within the centre costs about DFr600 (DFr1000 to or from the airport).

# AROUND DJIBOUTI

## Moucha Island

It ain't the Bahamas, but this island, easily accessible from Djibouti City, is a welcome respite from the hustle and bustle of the capital, with good, uncrowded beaches and warm waters.

# 🏃 Activities

## Diving & Snorkelling

Moucha Island is an excellent underwater playground and a good place to learn to dive, with a couple of very safe dive sites that are less than 15 minutes away by boat. Wreck enthusiasts will head for monster-sized Le Faon, a 120m-long cargo ship that lies in 27m of water on a sandy floor; it's also noted for being heavily overgrown with marine life. Other shipwrecks worthy of exploration include L'Arthur Rimbaud, a tugboat that was scuttled in 2005 (average depth is 25m), and the nearby Nagfa, a small Ethiopian boat that lies in about 32m of water. If you need a break from wreck dives, some excellent reef dives beckon, including Le Tombant Nord (The Northern Drop-Off), blessed with healthy corals and prolific marine life; Tombant Point, where you'll see a smorgasbord of reef fish; and the Canyon, a relaxing site suitable for novices.

Snorkelling is also superb. You can grab a snorkel and splash around near the shore, but to really experience life under the sea it's necessary to sign up with Le Lagon Bleu and go out to further marine wonderlands.

**Le Lagon Bleu**      DIVING, SNORKELLING
(☑21250296, 77826119, 21325555; www.djibouti divers.com; ⊘closed Aug) Professional dive shop run by a French couple. They come with a good reputation for service and instruction, and offer introductory dives (from DFr10,000), single-dive trips (from DFr8000, half day), snorkelling excursions (from DFr6000) and courses. Their day trips to Moucha Island (from DFr24,000 per person, including two dives and lunch) are very popular. They have an office at the Djibouti Palace Kempinski in Djibouti City.

### Kayaking

Kayaking is another popular activity of the DIY variety. Paddling around the island offers the chance to discover hidden coves or just put down the oar, lie back and sunbathe. Lagon Bleu Village rents out sea kayaks (DFr1000 per hour).

## 🛏 Sleeping & Eating

**Lagon Bleu Village**      RESORT $$
(☑21250296; Moucha Island; d incl full board & transport from DFr17,000; ❄) This is a good place to take up a Robinson Crusoe lifestyle without sacrificing comfort, with 19 well-equipped bungalows, a restaurant and a diving centre. Divers should ask for package room-and-scuba deals with the on-site dive centre. One downside: air-con and electricity are on at night only. For bookings, contact ATTA/Globe Travel (p307).

## ℹ Getting There & Away

ATTA/Globe Travel offers various packages that include transfers to/from Djibouti City, accommodation and meals. Day trips are also possible (from DFr8000, including lunch).

---

WORTH A TRIP

## DECAN

Weary of the hustle and bustle of Djibouti City? Have a soft spot for endangered species? The efficiently run wildlife refuge Decan (☑21340119; www.decandjibouti.org; admission DFr1500-2000; ⊘3.30-6.30pm Mon, Thu & Sat Oct-May, 4.30-6.30pm Mon, Thu & Sat Jun-Sep) is about 10km south of Djibouti City (on the road to Somaliland) and makes for an easy two- to three-hour excursion from the capital.

Decan was set up as a rehabilitation centre for various species that have been orphaned or illegally caged for trafficking purposes. You'll see nine endlessly appealing cheetahs (don't forget your camera for that fantastic close-up!), three lions and two striped hyenas, as well as ostriches, turtles, Somali donkeys, caracals, squirrels, antelopes and porcupines. According to Bertrand Lafrance, the French vet who runs Decan, it's not a zoo, but a small nature reserve, with its own ecosystem. There are plans to extend it from 30 acres to 500 acres, down to the coastline, which would encompass a mangrove area. Birders, rejoice: a dedicated birdwatching area was under construction at the time of writing – expect to see flamingos, ibises, herons and spoonbills. Decan also runs education programs for customs officers, the police and school kids. Watching the big cats being fed is just one of the many exhilarating moments at Decan. Volunteers are welcome.

The only practical options for getting here from Djibouti City are by taxi (DFr3000, including waiting time).

# Lac Assal

Just over 100km west of the capital lies one of the most spectacular natural phenomena in Africa: Lac Assal. Situated 155m below sea level, this crater lake is encircled by dark, dormant volcanoes. It represents the lowest point on the continent. The aquamarine water is ringed by a huge salt field, 60m in depth. The salt field has been mined by the Afar nomads for centuries, and they can still be seen loading up their camels for the long trek south to Ethiopia.

##  Getting There & Away

There's no public transport to Lac Assal. Most visitors come with tours (see p318) or hire their own vehicles from the capital (see p318). A tour should set you back about DFr15,000.

# Grand Barra & Petit Barra

The road from Djibouti City to Lac Abbé crosses two spectacular desert plains that are the remnants of an ancient lake: the Petit Barra and Grand Barra, the latter being 27km long and 12km wide. The Grand Barra is basically a plain of white clay, which has dried and cracked in the desert sun. It can be visited en route to Lac Abbé.

# Lac Abbé

You'll never forget your first glimpse of Lac Abbé. The scenery is sensational: the plain is dotted with hundreds of limestone chimneys, some standing as high as 50m, belching out puffs of steam. Located 140km southwest of Djibouti City, it is often described as 'a slice of moon on the crust of earth'.

Though desolate, it is not uninhabited. Numerous mineral-rich hot springs feed the farms of local nomads who graze their camels and goats here. Flamingos also gather on the banks of the lake at dawn.

The best time to visit the lake is in the early morning, when the chimneys appear to belch smoke in the cool morning air. An even better plan is to arrive in the late afternoon, stay the night, and leave after sunrise the following morning. In the evening, when the sun sets behind the chimneys, the landscape can look almost magical.

## ℹ️ LAC ABBÉ GUIDED TOURS

A guide to Lac Abbé is essential (see p318). Not just to get there, but also to steer you clear of the quicksand and pits said to riddle certain areas of the banks. Guides can also give you a proper tour of the site, which should include the chimneys, the boiling, sulphurous-smelling springs and the flamingos. Some of the chimneys can be climbed, if you fancy it. There's a great view of the lake and surrounding plain from *La Grande Cheminée* (The Big Chimney), but you should take care, as the shifting shale can make it a bit treacherous underfoot. Don't forget sunscreen and lots of water.

## 🛏️ Sleeping & Eating

**Campement Touristique d'Asboley**                 HUTS, BUNGALOWS $
(☑77822291, 21357244; houmed_asboley@hotmail.fr; huts/bungalows with full board DFr8000/10,000) This *campement touristique* (traditional huts with shared showers and toilets) is set in the most surreal landscape you've ever imagined. It lies on a plateau that proffers stupendous views of the big chimneys – whatever the time of the day, you're guaranteed to be hypnotised by the scenery. It comprises traditional Afar huts and three simple bungalows made of cement (true, they don't really blend in such a grandiose environment). Prices include a guided walk to the chimneys.

## ℹ️ Getting There & Away

The only way of getting here is by hiring a 4WD with driver (see p318) or by taking a tour (p318). If you are (or can find) a party of four, the *campement touristique* can arrange all-inclusive packages for DFr17,700 per person per day – prices include transfers from Djibouti City, accommodation, meals and guided walks.

# Goda Mountains

Northwest of the Gulf of Tadjoura, the Goda Mountains rise to a height of 1750m and are a spectacular natural oddity. This area shelters one of the rare speckles of green on Djibouti's parched map, like a giant oasis – a real relief after the scorched desert

WORTH A TRIP

## ABOURMA ROCK ART SITE

This superb hike is a must for those with a penchant for archaeology, as it feels like you're catching a time machine into the prehistoric past. It takes you to a site that was uncovered by a team of French archaeologists in 2008, some 30km northeast of Randa. It's a tiring hike but you'll be rewarded with spectacular landscapes consisting of undulating rocky hills, small gorges, barren ridges and vast expanses of chaotic boulders. Reached after about 3½ hours, the site features well-preserved rock engravings dating back to the Neolithic. They're striking both for their rich complexity and their incredible variety; many of the engravings depict animals that are no longer found in the area – giraffes, cows, antelopes, kudus, oryxes and ostriches. Human figures are also represented.

The usual starting point for the hike is the tiny Afar settlement of Giba Gebiley, about 22km north of Randa. You'll need a rented 4WD with driver to get here. From Giba Gebiley, allow eight hours there and back. A knowledgeable guide (usually somebody from Randa who has worked with the archaeologists) is mandatory and can be arranged through Agence Safar (p318) in Djibouti City. Count on DFr5000.

There are no facilities at all, so bring several litres of water, as well as a hat and plenty of sunscreen.

landscapes. A few Afar villages are scattered around and merit at least a couple of days of your time to soak up their charm. It won't be long before you're smitten by the region's mellow tranquillity and laid-back lifestyle.

For outdoorsy types, this area offers ample hiking opportunities.

### ❶ Getting There & Away

The most convenient way to visit the area is on a tour or with a rental 4WD (see p318). Transport can also be organised by the *campements touristiques* if there's a group (usually a minimum of four people). Count on DFr15,000 per person, including transfers and one night's accommodation with full board.

### FORÊT DU DAY

Measuring just 3.2 sq km, this tiny pocket of vegetation is an exceptional ecosystem. Situated at 1500m above sea level, the forest benefits from its proximity to Mt Goda. As rain clouds and mist from the mountain drift into the forest, considerable condensation forms. The soil, as wet as after a storm, releases humidity, which allows the plants and trees to flourish despite the infrequent rains. From December to March, the temperature at night can drop sometimes to just above freezing.

Despite its size, plant life is incredibly diverse (including several endemic and very rare species), and wildlife abundant. The forest is home to the country's only endemic bird species, the Djibouti francolin, and it's one of the few places where leopards are still seen. Common sightings include various species of monkey and deer, and several birds of prey, including Bonelli's eagle. Tree species include ancient juniper, box wood, wild olive and various types of fig.

### 🏃 Activities

Guides from the Campement Touristique de la Forêt du Day can take you on beautiful walks in the forest and the surrounding mountains (about two hours return). You can also walk to Bankoualé or Dittilou (three hours one way).

### 🛌 Sleeping & Eating

**Campement Touristique de la Forêt du Day**          HUTS $
(☎77829774; Day; full board DFr8000) If you like peace, quiet and sigh-inducing views, you'll have few quibbles with this atmospheric *campement* in the village of Day, at an altitude of 1400m, close to the Forêt du Day. The traditional huts are welcoming and the toilet block is kept clean. Other draws include the host of walking options available, and the healthy food.

### BANKOUALÉ

The green and fertile oasis of Bankoualé boasts one of the most spectacular settings in Djibouti, with staggering mountain scenery, impressive canyons and a few scenic waterfalls.

### ◉ Sights & Activities

On the way to Bankoualé – just 2km down the dirt road – you'll pass the little village of Ardo, which has a small craft centre run by

Afar women. It's a great opportunity to see the well-known and highly accomplished Afar basketware. Any purchase you make will directly benefit the community.

A variety of **walks** will take you up to the waterfalls, streams, fruit trees and little gardens around Bankoualé. Don't miss the walk to the Cascade de Bankoualé (Bankoualé Waterfall; about two hours return). It's not the Niagara Falls, though; in the drier months the volume of the falls lessens and can be reduced to a mere trickle. Another enjoyable walk goes to the Grotte de la Chauve-Souris (Bat's Cave; four hours return). It's also possible to walk to Dittilou (four hours one way) and Forêt du Day (4½ hours one way).

A guide is essential because trails are not marked and it's easy to get lost. You can organise a guide through the Campement Touristique de Bankoualé. Costs vary according to the duration of the walk.

**Sleeping & Eating**

**Campement Touristique de Bankoualé** HUTS $
(☎77814115; Bankoualé; full board DFr8000; ☺Oct-May) If you want to get away from it all, look no further. This ecofriendly camp (electricity is solar powered) in a scenic location – it's perched on a hillside and overlooks a deep gorge – is a pleasant place to spend a couple of days, particularly if you're keen on hiking. Many huts have been recently upgraded and are equipped with traditional Afar beds made of wood and goat skin (fear not, there's a mattress, too), and the views of the valley are sensational. The ablution blocks are well scrubbed, and the food gets good reports.

**DITTILOU**

A visit to Dittilou, at the edge of vegetation around the Forêt du Day, should not be missed. Set 700m above sea level on the flank of Mt Goda, it features an enchanted landscape of dripping forest and viewpoints swirling in mist. This explosion of green amid a desert land is extraordinary. You'll find it hard to believe that Dittilou belongs to the same country as the one you left on the burning coastal road just one hour before.

**Activities**

Dittilou is a good base for **hiking**. The owners of Campement Touristique de Dittilou will be happy to suggest guided walks suited to your level of ability. Don't miss the waterfall of Toha (a three- to four-hour return visit). Another lovely walk goes to a plane wreck (a six-hour loop). You can also walk to Bankoualé (four to five hours one way).

**Sleeping & Eating**

**Campement Touristique de Dittilou** HUTS $
(☎27510871, 21354520, 77810488; Dittilou; full board DFr8000) This *campement* has helpful and friendly management offering a series of well-designed *daboytas* (traditional huts) brimful of rustic charm. They are set against a lush and peaceful landscape. The laid-back restaurant is chilled and the food is great. The prices quoted include guided walks.

## Tadjoura
POP 25,000

Nestled in the shadow of the green Goda Mountains with the bright blue sea lapping at its doorstep, Tadjoura is a picturesque little place. With its palm trees, white-washed houses and numerous mosques, it has an Arabian feel to it. There's little to do here besides stroll around and soak up the atmosphere, but it's a great place to spend a few hours.

If you're after sustainably produced local handicrafts, the women-run **Association**

**DON'T MISS**

### PLAGE DES SABLES BLANCS

Plage des Sables Blancs, 7km east of Tadjoura, is tranquillity incarnate and a lovely place to sun yourself, with a good string of white sand and excellent facilities. Your biggest quandary here: a bout of snorkelling, kayaking, or a snooze on the beach? You can lay your head at **Plage des Sables Blancs Campement** (☎21354520; goubet@intnet. dj; Plage des Sables Blancs; beds with full board DFr11,500, r DFr25,000; ❄🖥), right on the beach. Accommodation is simple (beds and mattresses only), or you can opt for a room with all mod cons in the recently built hotel at the western tip of the beach. All rooms face the sea. The on-site restaurant serves up toothsome local dishes. One grumble: although it has only 10 rooms, the hotel feels a bit incongruous in such a scenic setting. You'll need your own wheels to get here. Contact Agence Le Goubet for bookings (p318).

des Femmes de Tadjoura (Tadjoura; ☺7.30am-12.30pm & 4-6pm Sat-Thu) sells colourful Afar basketware.

## 🍽 Sleeping & Eating

### Le Golfe                    HOTEL, RESTAURANT $

(☑27424091, 27424153; http://hotel-restaurant-le-golfe-djibouti-tadjourah.e-monsite.com; bungalows with breakfast DFr10,000; ❄) Under French-Ethiopian management, this low-key but well-kept resort, popular with French soldiers and their families, is situated in a relaxing waterfront setting, about 1.5km from the town centre. The 11 units are not fancy but are functional, and there's a good on-site restaurant (mains DFr1400-2500; ☺breakfast, lunch & dinner) with a terrace facing the sea. The menu concentrates on simply prepared seafood served in generous portions. There's no beach to speak of but the owners can organise transfers to Plage des Sables Blancs (DFr6000 for four people).

### Le Corto Maltese        HOTEL, RESTAURANT $$

(☑77859574, 27510300; r with breakfast DFr12,000; ❄) A modernish and reasonably priced choice, Le Corto Maltese is right on the seashore, about 1.5km west of the town centre. The adjoining 18 rooms are well organised, with good bedding and large bathrooms. The rooftop terrace is a plus, and we hear good things about the on-site restaurant (mains DFr1200-3300; ☺breakfast, lunch & dinner daily). No beach, but transfers to Plage des Sables Blancs can easily be arranged. The owner has plans to build overwater bungalows.

## ℹ Getting There & Away

Regular morning buses ply the route between Djibouti City and Tadjoura (DFr1500, three hours).

A passenger ferry runs two to three times weekly between Djibouti City and Tadjoura (DFr1500 one way, two to three hours).

## Obock

Obock exudes a kind of 'last frontier' feel, light years away from the hullabaloo of Djibouti City. This little town is something of a backwater, and survives primarily from its small fishing industry.

## ◉ Sights

### Governor's House          HISTORIC BUILDING

Obock is where French colonialism all began. In 1862, the Afar sultans of Obock sold their land to the French, and construction of the town began. But it was soon eclipsed by Djibouti City. All that remains of its past glory as the capital is the governor's house (the first official building erected on the site).

### Cimetière Marin                    CEMETERY

The eerily quiet Cimetière Marin (Marine Cemetery), on the western outskirts of town, contains the graves of French soldiers who died from fever on their way to Indochina between 1885 and 1889.

### Ras Bir Lighthouse            LIGHTHOUSE

About 6km east of the centre, this well-kept lighthouse is worth a gander. It's completely isolated, and there's an eerie atmosphere.

## 🍽 Sleeping & Eating

### Campement Oubouky                HUTS $

(☑77816034; full board DFr8000-10,000; ❄) Facilities are fairly run-down at this campement about 5km east of the centre, but the location is ace – it's right on a blissfully quiet beach with excellent swimming and snorkelling. Lovers of seafood will enjoy the cooking here. Fishing trips can be organised.

### Chez Abdou                    GUESTHOUSE $

(☑77816034; r DFr5000-7000; ❄) The owner of Campement Oubouky, Abdou, rents out a comfortable and well-equipped four-bedroom house near the Cimetière Marin. One room has a private bathroom and two rooms have air-con.

## ℹ Getting There & Away

A regular morning minibus service operates between Djibouti City and Obock (DFr2000, about 4½ hours).

There's a twice-weekly passenger ferry service between Djibouti City and Obock (DFr1500 one way, two to three hours).

# UNDERSTAND DJIBOUTI

## Djibouti Today

Djibouti's stability and neutrality, combined with its strategic position, have brought lots of benefits. In an effort to combat piracy off the Somali coast, the Americans have reinforced their military presence. As if this wasn't enough, the Japanese set up a huge military base near the international airport in 2011. The total number of foreign soldiers on the Djiboutian territory is estimated at 7000.

Foreign investors from Asia and the Gulf are increasingly active in Djibouti, and there are building projects springing up all over the capital. There are also plans to build a port in Tadjoura and to upgrade the road system throughout the country.

# History

## From Aksum to Islam

Around the 1st century AD, Djibouti made up part of the powerful Ethiopian kingdom of Aksum, which included modern-day Eritrea and even stretched across the Red Sea to parts of southern Arabia. It was during the Aksumite era, in the 4th century AD, that Christianity first appeared in the region.

As the empire of Aksum gradually fell into decline, a new influence arose that would forever supersede the Christian religion in Djibouti: Islam. It was introduced to the region around AD 825 by Arab traders from Southern Arabia.

## European Ambitions

In the second half of the 19th century, European powers competed to grab new colonies in Africa. The French, seeking to counter the British presence in Yemen on the other side of the Bab al-Mandab Strait, made agreements with the Afar sultans of Obock and Tadjoura that gave them the right to settle. In 1888, construction of Djibouti City began on the southern shore of the Gulf of Tadjoura. French Somaliland (present-day Djibouti) began to take shape.

France and the emperor of Ethiopia then signed a pact designating Djibouti as the 'official outlet of Ethiopian commerce'. This led to the construction of the Addis Ababa–Djibouti City railway, which was of vital commercial importance until recently.

## Throwing off the French Yoke

As early as 1949 there were a number of anticolonial demonstrations that were led by the Issa Somalis, who were in favour of the reunification of the territories of Italian, British and French Somaliland. Meanwhile, the Afars were in favour of continued French rule.

Major riots ensued, especially after the 1967 referendum, which produced a vote in favour of continued French rule – a vote achieved partly as a result of the arrest of opposition leaders and the massive expulsion of ethnic Somalis. After the referendum, the colony's name was changed from French Somaliland to the French Territory of the Afars and Issas.

In June 1977 the colony finally won its sovereignty from France. The country became the Republic of Djibouti.

## Small Country, Adroit Leaders

Despite continuous clan rivalries between the two main ethnic groups, Afars and Issas, who have been jostling for power since the 1970s, Djibouti has learnt to exploit its strategic position.

When the Gulf War broke out in 1990, the country's president, Hassan Gouled Aptidon, while appearing to oppose the military build-up in the Gulf, simultaneously allowed France to increase its military presence in the country, as well as granting the Americans and Italians access to the naval port. And he skilfully managed to retain the support of Saudi Arabia and Kuwait for the modernisation of Djibouti port. During the war between Eritrea and Ethiopia in the 1990s, Djibouti port proved to be strategic when Ethiopia diverted its foreign trade through it (which it still does).

During the Second Gulf War in 2003, Djibouti continued to play an ambivalent role, allowing a US presence in the country – to the great displeasure of France.

In 2006 the first phase of the Doraleh Project, which consists of a large-capacity oil terminal about 8km east of the current seaport, was completed. Thanks to this megaproject, partly financed by Dubai Port International, Djibouti aims to be the 'Dubai of East Africa'.

Djibouti maintains good relations with Ethiopia and Somaliland, which are considered as 'partners'. However, it clashed with Eritrea, its northern neighbour, in June 2008. At the time of writing, the borders between the two countries remained closed.

# The Culture

Djiboutians are charming, respectful and very hospitable people. This has its origins in the traditionally nomadic culture of the two main ethnic groups, the Afars and Issas. Despite an increasing tendency towards a more sedentary lifestyle, most Djiboutians living in towns retain strong links with their nomadic past.

One of the most striking features in Djibouti is the overwhelming presence of *qat* (leaf chewed as a stimulant). The life of most Djiboutian males seems to revolve entirely around the consumption of this mild narcotic. Every day, *qat* consumers meet their circle of friends in the *mabraz* (*qat* den) to *brouter* (graze). Only 10% of women are thought to consume the plant regularly.

Of Djibouti's estimated 900,000 inhabitants, about 35% are Afars and 60% are Issas. Both groups are Muslim. The rest of the population is divided between Arabs and Europeans. The south is predominantly Issa, while the north is mostly Afar. Ethnic tensions between Afars and Issas have always dogged Djibouti. These tensions came to a head in 1991, when Afar rebels launched a civil war in the north. A peace accord was brokered in 1994, but ethnic hostility has not completely waned.

## Arts & Crafts

Dance is arguably the highest form of culture in Djibouti, along with oral literature and poetry. Some dances celebrate major life events, such as birth, marriage or circumcision.

If you are looking for handicrafts, the traditional Afar and Somali knives and the very attractive Afar woven straw mats (known in Afar as *fiddima*) are among the finest products.

## Environment

Djibouti's 23,000 sq km can be divided into three geographic regions: the coastal plains which feature white, sandy beaches; the volcanic plateaus in the southern and central parts of the country; and the mountain ranges in the north, where the altitude reaches over 2000m above sea level. Essentially the country is a vast wasteland, with the exception of pockets of forest and dense vegetation to the north.

Livestock rearing is the most important type of agriculture. As demand for scarce grazing land mounts, the forests of the north are increasingly coming under threat, including the fragile Forêt du Day.

## Food & Drink

Djibouti City is endowed with a plethora of tasty restaurants that will please most palates – a testimony to the French presence. You'll find excellent seafood, rice, pasta, local meat dishes, such as stuffed kid or lamb, and other treats imported from France. In the countryside, choice is obviously more limited, with goat meat and rice as the main staples. Alcohol (wine and beer) is widely available in the capital. You'll also find excellent fruit juices.

# SURVIVAL GUIDE

## Directory A–Z

### Accommodation

Most hotels are in the capital, with few options outside. Hotel categories are limited in range; most of them fit into the upper echelon and are expensive. At the lower end, the few budget hotels that exist tend to be pretty basic. There's a limited choice in between.

A rather popular option that is developing around the major attractions in the hinterland is the *campements touristiques*. These are traditional huts with shared showers and toilets. These quaint, low-key establishments are great places to meet locals and get an authentic cultural experience. They're family-run, which ensures your money goes straight into local pockets. They're also a good budget option, although there's no public transport to get to them.

### Activities

#### Diving & Snorkelling

» Although it's less charismatic than Egypt, Djibouti has its fair share of underwater delights. You'll be positively surprised: there's a wide choice of shallow dives for novices and deeper dives for more experienced divers in the Gulf of Tadjoura. Wreck fans will be spoiled here, too, with a handful of atmospheric shipwrecks.

### EATING PRICE RANGES

In this book, we indicate the prices of mains. Eating places in this chapter have been categorised according to the following price brackets:

$ Less than DFr1000

$$ DFr1000–2500

$$$ More than DFr2500

## ACCOMMODATION PRICE RANGES

Listings in this book quote full board when the accommodation rate includes three meals a day. Accommodation reviews in this chapter are categorised as follows:

**$** Less than DFr10,000

**$$** DFr10,000 to DFr25,000

**$$$** More than DFr25,000

» Although Djibouti is diveable year-round, the best season for diving is from November to March. During July and August, the seas may be too rough for diving.

» Visibility is not the strong point of diving in Djibouti – it rarely exceeds 10m to 15m (and can drop to 5m at certain sites at certain periods of the year). Current conditions vary, but are generally imperceptible to mild. During the coolest months (December through March), water temperatures are usually between 25°C and 27°C. Summer water temperatures range from 27°C to 29°C.

» There are only two dive areas, the Gulf of Tadjoura and the Bay of Ghoubbet. Diving trips to the fantastic Les Sept Frères Archipelago, at the junction between the Red Sea and the Gulf of Aden, were suspended at the time of writing due to the heavy military presence in the area but may be scheduled again when the situation normalises.

» There are only two professional dive operators in Djibouti, both based in Djibouti City (p300). They are affiliated with CMAS and PADI, two internationally recognised certifying agencies. In general, equipment is well-maintained, facilities are well equipped and staff are friendly and knowledgeable.

» There's also one live-aboard operating from Djibouti City.

» Diving in Djibouti is rather expensive, especially if you compare it with other Red Sea destinations.

» Snorkelling is also superlative. Dive shops run snorkelling trips in parallel with their dive excursions.

### Hiking

Hiking is popular in the Goda Mountains. From canyons and valleys to waterfalls and peaks, the mountainscape is fantastic and you'll be rewarded with lovely vistas. Most *campements touristiques* can organise guided nature walks, from one-hour jaunts to more challenging day hikes.

Various treks led by Afar nomads can also be arranged along ancient salt routes in western Djibouti. It's the best way to immerse yourself in traditional nomadic culture. Duration varies from two-day hikes near Lac Assal to 10-day expeditions as far as Ethiopia. Contact tour operators in Djibouti City.

### Kitesurfing

The combination of constant, strong breezes, protected areas with calm water conditions and the lack of obstacles make Djibouti a world-class destination for kitesurfers. In the Bay of Ghoubbet, winds can reach 35 knots and blow about 300 days a year.

### Whale-Shark Spotting

The Bay of Ghoubbet is one of the best places in the world to snorkel near a massive whale shark. During the peak season (November to January), the question isn't whether you will see a shark, but how many you will see.

## Business Hours

The following are common business hours in Djibouti. Friday is the weekly holiday for offices and most shops.

**Banks** 7.30am to 12.30pm and 4pm to 6pm Sunday to Thursday

**Businesses** 7.30am to 1.30pm and 4pm to 6.30pm Saturday to Thursday

**Government offices** 8am to 12.30pm and 4pm to 6pm Saturday to Thursday

**Restaurants** Breakfast from 6.30am, lunch from 11.30am, dinner 6.30pm to 9pm

## Embassies & Consulates

Djiboutian diplomatic representation abroad is scarce, but there are embassies in Ethiopia,

## PRACTICALITIES

» **Newspapers & Magazines** The most widely read newspaper is *La Nation* (www.lanation.dj), published weekly in French.

» **Weights & Measures** Metric system.

» **Electricity** 220V, 60Hz, with two-round-pin plugs.

as well as in France, Egypt and the USA. In countries without representation, travellers should head for the French embassy, which acts for Djibouti in the issuing of visas.

The following is a list of nations with diplomatic representation in Djibouti City.

**Canadian Honorary Consulate** (Map p304; ☎21353950; Pl Lagarde; ☺8am-noon Sun-Thu)

**Ethiopian Embassy** (Map p302; ☎21350718; Ave Maréchal Lyautey; ☺8am-noon Sat, 8am-12.30pm & 4.30-6pm Sun-Thu)

**French Embassy** (☎21350963; www.ambafrance-dj.org; Ave F d'Esperey; ☺7am-1.30pm & 3-6pm Mon & Wed, 7am-1.30pm Sun, Tue & Thu)

**Somaliland Bureau de Liaison** (Somaliland Liaison Office; ☎21358758; Ave F d'Esperey; ☺7.30am-1pm Sat-Thu)

**US Embassy** (☎21453000; djibouti.usembassy.gov; Lotissement Haramous)

## Internet Access

Establishments with wireless are identified in this book with a ☎ icon.
» Internet cafes are found only in Djibouti City.
» Wireless is widespread and free in most hotels in Djibouti City.
» If you will be in Djibouti for a while, consider buying a USB stick ('dongle') from the local mobile provider, which you can then load with airtime and plug into your laptop.

## Maps

The best map is the 1:200,000 Djibouti map published in 1992 by the IGN (French Institut Géographique National; www.ign.fr).

## Money

» The unit of currency is the Djibouti franc (DFr), which is divided into 100 centimes. Coins are in denominations of DFr1, 2, 5, 10, 20, 50, 100 and 500. Notes are available in DFr1000, 2000, 5000 and 10,000.
» You'll find a few ATMs in Djibouti City. All ATMs accept Visa. At the time of research, only one ATM accepted MasterCard.
» Visa credit cards are accepted at some upmarket hotels and shops, and at some larger travel agencies. Some places levy a commission of about 5% for credit-card payment.
» There are several banks and a couple of authorised bureaux de change in the capital. Outside the capital, banking facilities are almost nonexistent.
» The euro and the US dollar are the favoured hard currencies. Travellers cheques are not useful; euros and dollars in cash and an ATM card are the way to go.

## Post

The cost for a letter is DFr170 to Europe and DFr190 to North America or Australia.

## Public Holidays

As well as Islamic holidays, which change dates every year, these are the principal public holidays in Djibouti:
**New Year's Day** 1 January
**Labour Day** 1 May
**Independence Day** 27 June
**Christmas Day** 25 December

## Telephone

» The country code for Djibouti is +253. There are no area codes in Djibouti.
» Phone numbers have 10 digits. Mobile numbers start with 77; landline numbers start with 21 or 27.
» International and local calls are best made from the post office or from one of the numerous phone shops (look for the *cabine telephonique* signs).
» Mobile (cell) phone coverage is pretty good across Djibouti. Depending on which mobile network you use at home, your phone may or may not work while in Djibouti – ask your mobile network provider. You can also bring your phone and buy a local SIM card (DFr2000). You can buy credit at some shops in the form of scratch cards (DFr500 to DFr5000).
» The only mobile network is Djibouti Telecom (www.adjib.dj).

## Tourist Information

The only tourist office in the country is found in Djibouti City (see p307). Tour agencies are also reliable sources of travel information; see p318.

Information for travellers is hard to come by outside the country. In Europe, contact **Association Djibouti Environnement Nomade** (ADEN; ☎01 48 51 71 56; www.aden-asso.com; 64 rue des Meuniers, 93100 Montreuil-sous-Bois, France), which functions as a kind of tourist office abroad. Run by Dominique Lommatzsch, a French national, it promotes sustainable tourism and can help with bookings in the *campements touristiques*.

## Visas

» All visitors, including French nationals, must have a visa to enter Djibouti. Tourist visas cost from US$30 to US$60 depending on where you apply, and are valid for one month. Visas can be obtained at the nearest Djibouti embassy (including Addis Ababa if you're in the Horn) or, where there is none, from the French embassy.

» Travellers from most Western countries can also obtain a single-entry tourist visa on arrival at the airport; it's issued on the spot. It costs DFr5000 for three days and DFr10,000 for one month. Payment can also be made in US dollars or in euros.

» You must have a valid visa to enter overland as none are available at borders. That said, we've heard from travellers coming from Somaliland that visas can also be purchased at the Loyaada border for DFr15,000 or the equivalent in US dollars.

### VISAS FOR ONWARD TRAVEL

For information on embassies and consulates, see p315.

**Ethiopia** A one-month single-entry visa costs DFr3600 (DFr12,600 for US nationals). You need to supply two photos. It takes 24 hours to process. Visas are also easily obtained at Bole International Airport in Addis Ababa.

**Somaliland** A two-week single-entry visa costs DFr5400. You need to supply one photo and it's issued on the spot.

## Getting There & Away
### Entering Djibouti

You'll need a valid passport and a visa to enter Djibouti. Disembarkation at the airport is usually simple. You might be asked for an address or contact in the country; in this case, mention a hotel in Djibouti City. Crossing at land borders is relatively easy, too, but be sure to have your passport stamped with an entry/exit stamp if you enter/leave the country.

## Air
### AIRPORTS & AIRLINES

Djibouti has one international gateway for arrival by air, **Ambouli Airport** (JIB), about 5km south of Djibouti City. All airlines flying to/from Djibouti have an office or a representative in Djibouti City.

**Air France** (Map p304; ☑21351010; www.airfrance.com; Pl du 27 Juin 1977) Three flights a week to/from Paris.

**Daallo Airlines** (Map p304; ☑21353401; www.daallo.com; Rue de Paris) Two flights a week to/from Somaliland and on to Dubai. Also flies to/from Mogadishu.

**Ethiopian Airlines** (Map p304; ☑21351007; www.flyethiopian.com; off Blvd Cheikh Osman) Daily flights to/from Addis Ababa and to/from Dire Dawa.

**FlyDubai** (Map p304; ☑21350964; www.flydubai.com; off Pl du 27 Juin 1977) Operates three flights a week to/from Dubai. Same location as the ATTA/Globe Travel office.

**Jubba Airways** (Map p304; ☑21356264; www.jubba-airways.com; Pl du 27 Juin 1977) Three flights a week to/from Hargeisa.

**Kenya Airways** (Map p304; ☑21353036; www.kenya-airways.com; Pl Lagarde) Daily flights to/from Nairobi.

**Turkish Airlines** (☑21340110; www.turkishairlines.com) Daily flights to/from Istanbul.

**Yemenia** (Map p304; ☑21355427; www.yemenia.com; Rue de Paris) Three flights a week to/from San'a.

### TICKETS

Expect to pay at least DFr100,000 for a return ticket to Dubai (UAE), DFr39,000 to Somaliland, DFr57,000 to San'a (Yemen), DFr101,000 to Nairobi (Kenya) and DFr60,000 to Addis Ababa (Ethiopia).

If you're coming from Europe or North America, your best bet is to fly to Dubai, Addis Ababa, Istanbul or Nairobi and find an onward connection to Djibouti. You can also fly direct from Paris.

From Australasia, fly to Dubai and then continue to Djibouti with FlyDubai or Daallo Airlines.

## Land
### ERITREA

The border with Eritrea was indefinitely closed at the time of writing, and travel overland between Djibouti and Eritrea was not possible.

### ETHIOPIA

#### Bus

» There is a daily service between Djibouti City and Dire Dawa – a strenuous 10- to 12-hour ride on a gravel road. Take your first bus to the border town of Gelille, then another bus to Djibouti City; see p288. Bring plenty of water.

» From Djibouti City, buses leave at dawn from Ave Gamel Abdel Nasser. The company is called Société Bus Assajog (Map p302; ☑77846670). Buy your ticket (DFr3000) at least a day in advance to be sure of getting a seat.

## Hitching

Hitching is never entirely safe in any country, and we don't recommend it. Still, if you want to enter Djibouti from Ethiopia via the border town of Galafi, you can hitch a lift (front seats only) with one of the legions of trucks that ply the route between Addis Ababa and Djibouti City via Awash, Gewane, Logiya and Dikhil. This option is best avoided by women.

## Train

There are plans to resurrect the old Djibouti City–Addis Ababa train.

### SOMALILAND

From Ave 26, 4WDs depart daily to Hargeisa and Borama. They usually leave around 3pm (it's wise to buy your ticket in the morning). The border crossing is at Loyaada. It costs from DFr6000 (back seat) to DFr9000 (front seat). Be warned: it's a taxing journey. Bring plenty of water.

# Getting Around

## Boat

A passenger boat operates between Djibouti City and Tadjoura and between Djibouti City and Obock (see p318).

## Car

» The Route de l'Unité, a good sealed road, covers the 240km from the capital around the Gulf de Tadjoura, as far as Obock.
» Off-road excursions into the interior are usually off limits to anything other than a 4WD.
» Most rental agencies make hiring a driver compulsory with their vehicles.
» There are several car-hire agencies in Djibouti City (p318), but the prices really don't vary much. For a 4WD with driver

expect to pay around DFr25,000 a day. Fuel is generally extra, although not always.

## Local Transport

Public transport is available between Djibouti City (see p318) and major towns. It's a cheap way to get around but services are infrequent in remote areas.

## Tours

Djibouti is not properly geared up for DIY tourism. The only way of getting to some of the country's principal attractions is by joining an excursion. Tours are expensive (from DFr15,000 per person), but the price includes food and accommodation. Try to be part of an existing group – the more people, the less you pay. Your chances of joining an existing tour group are decidedly greater at weekends.

**Agence Le Goubet** (☑21354520; valerie@riesgroup.dj; Blvd Cheikh Osman) Can make bookings to Plage des Sables Blancs and in the *campements touristiques*. It sometimes organises kayaking trips on Lac Assal. Also sells flight tickets. Ask for Valerie, who can get by in English.

**Agence Safar** (☑77814115; safar.djibouti@gmail.com) Friendly and professional, this operator seems to go the extra mile for their customers. It organises all kinds of customised tours throughout the country, including multiday guided treks and excursions to Lac Abbé and Lac Assal. Can also make bookings in the *campements touristiques*. The owner, Houmed Ali, knows everything about the Afar culture.

**Dolphin** (☑21350313, 77718034, 77825318; www.dolphin-excursions.com; Blvd de la République) This well-established operator can organise all kinds of tours throughout the country, on land and at sea, as well as live-aboard dive boats to the Gulf of Tadjoura.

**Houmed Loita** (☑77822291, 21357244; houmed_asboley@hotmail.fr) Friendly Houmed Loita runs the Campement Touristique d'Asboley and can organise all kinds of cultural trips and excursions.

# Somaliland

## Best of Culture

» Las Geel (p326)
» Berbera (p328)
» Zeila (p330)
» Dhagax Khoure (p333)
» Maydh (p332)

## Best of Nature

» Daallo Forest (p332)
» Giriyad Plains (p330)
» Saadedin Islands (p330)

## Why Go?

For seasoned travellers in search of a totally unusual travel experience, Somaliland is a must. Where else in the world can you visit a country that doesn't officially exist? While the rest of Somalia has been a no-go zone for travellers for two decades, the self-proclaimed Republic of Somaliland has restored law and order within its boundaries. Here the safety of Westerners is taken very seriously and foreigners are welcome.

Somaliland offers plenty of unexpected and wonderful surprises. Admire some exceptional rock paintings, feel the pulse of the fast-growing capital, walk along deserted beaches, visit bustling market towns, be awed by stunning landscapes, and blaze a trail of your own in the far east and west of the country – wherever you go, you'll feel like a pioneer. More than anything, though, it is the Somali people who make a visit to the country so memorable, with their legendary sense of hospitality.

## When to Go
### Hargeisa

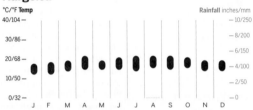

| **Apr-Sep** Rainy months make travel tough. July/August is very hot along the coast. | **Oct & Nov** Comfortable temperatures make the shoulder season good for travelling. | **Dec-Mar** Best weather: very few rains and cool temperatures. |

SOMALILAND

## AT A GLANCE

» **Currency** Somaliland shilling (SISh); US dollars (US$)

» **Language** Somali

» **Money** Bring cash (US dollars). One ATM in Hargeisa (not working at time of writing); credit cards generally not accepted.

» **Visas** Single-entry tourist visas; see p337.

» **Mobile phones** Local SIM cards (and top-up credits) OK in unlocked GSM-compatible phones. Other phones must be set to roaming.

## Fast Facts

» **Area** 637,657 sq km
» **Capital** Hargeisa
» **Country Code** ☑2522
» **Population** 3.5 million

## Exchange Rates

| Australia | A$1 | US$1.04 |
|---|---|---|
| Canada | C$1 | US$0.99 |
| Euro Zone | €1 | US$1.36 |
| Japan | ¥100 | US$1.10 |
| New Zealand | NZ$1 | US$0.84 |
| UK | UK£1 | US$1.58 |

US$1 = SISh6500

For current exchange rates see www.xe.com.

## Set Your Budget

» Budget hotel room: US$10
» Local-style meal: US$2
» 4WD hire per day: US$150
» Police escort per day: US$20

# Entering Somaliland

Somaliland has one primary international airport in Hargeisa, while Berbera receives some flights from nearby countries. At the time of writing, Hargeisa airport was closed for renovation and expansion, and all Hargeisa-bound flights were diverted to Berbera, with a free bus connection provided to Hargeisa. There are regular flights to/from Addis Ababa (Ethiopia), Djibouti City (Djibouti), Dubai (UAE), Mogadishu (Somalia) and Nairobi (Kenya). Land borders with Ethiopia (Tog Wajaale) and Djibouti (Loyaada) are open.

## ITINERARIES

### Three Days

Arriving in Hargeisa, spend your first day getting oriented and soaking up the atmosphere. On your second day visit the livestock market early in the morning and take an overnight trip via Las Geel – Somaliland's touristic *pièce de résistance* – to the port of Berbera. Wander the streets of Berbera's character-filled old town, check out Baathala beach and end the day feasting on fresh fish. Day three should see you returning to the capital.

### Ten Days

Having enjoyed Hargeisa, Las Geel and Berbera at a more relaxed pace, go where few are bold enough to attempt and book a trip to the Sanaag province. Devote at least four days to Erigavo, Daallo Forest and Maydh. Alternatively, you could explore the far west of the country and arrange a 4WD trip to the historic port of Zeila, taking in the rock art sites of Dhagax Khoure and Dhagax Marodi, Borama and the Giriyad Plains before reaching the coast – from Hargeisa, this is a five-day expedition (return).

# Safe Travel

Somaliland was safe at the time of writing, and our on-the-ground research included Hargeisa, Las Geel, Berbera, Borama, Zeila, Tog Wajaale, Sheekh, Burao, Erigavo and Maydh. However, despite what officials claim, there is an element of uncertainty regarding the security situation. The Somalilanders have established law and order in their separatist territory, but as long as their unruly brothers from Puntland and Southern Somalia don't settle for peace, there will be an element of risk – borders are not terrorist-proof. Prospective travellers should carefully monitor the situation before setting off. In late January 2013, after French troops liberated Saharan cities in northern Mali from fundamentalist rebels, the Foreign & Commonwealth Office (FCO) issued an advice against all travel to Somaliland.

Although security has improved in previously high-risk areas such as the Sanaag province, check the situation locally before heading there. Travel in the Sool region is currently unsafe due to conflict in Puntland, which claims this province.

# HARGEISA

POP 1.2 MILLION

On a global index of odd capitals, Hargeisa would be a strong contender for one of the top spots. It's a down-to-earth, friendly place that's undergoing a rapid transformation. The streets are alive, the roads are busy and the air is thick with a very bearable cacophony of mobile phones, vehicle horns and calls to prayer. Sure, the capital of Somaliland still bears the scars of the civil war that destroyed the country in the past decades, but look past the makeshift shops and housing and you will see Hargeisa's unmistakable pep and determination to rebuild. As with any city in transition, it offers plenty of contrasts: donkey carts jostle for road space with 4WDs and battered minibuses, goats and sheep roam through the dusty side roads, elegant Somali ladies stroll down the main drag, turbaned clan elders relax over a cup of sweet Somali tea and youngsters from the diaspora watch Manchester United on Al-Jazeera at a modern cafeteria or update their Facebook page at an internet cafe.

Hargeisa has all the conveniences a traveller could hope for: good-value hotels with English-speaking staff, a couple of tasty restaurants, internet cafes, electronics stores, shopping malls, tea shops, markets, bus stations, taxis...but no alcohol (that would be too good to be true!).

Hargeisa lacks standout sights but if you enjoy the feeling of being the only tourist wandering its streets, it might just get under your skin.

## ◉ Sights

Visually, Hargeisa is fairly underwhelming; it's the ambience and the sense of exploration that are the pull here. Most places of interest to travellers, including shops, businesses and hotels, are on or around the main thoroughfare, Independence Rd, which snakes for several kilometres from the western outskirts of town to the east.

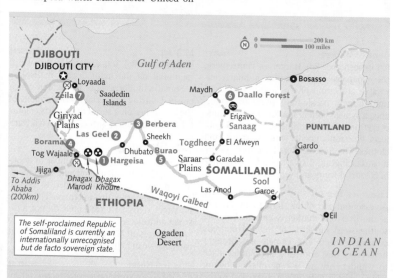

## Somaliland Highlights

**1** Dream of purchasing your own ship of the desert at **Hargeisa's livestock market** (p321)

**2** Visit one of the world's finest open-air galleries of prehistoric rock art at **Las Geel** (p326)

**3** Nurse a soft drink, feast on fresh fish and relax on deserted beaches in **Berbera** (p328)

**4** Soak up the atmosphere of laid-back **Borama** (p332)

**5** Immerse yourself in the bustling provincial town of **Burao** (p330)

**6** Explore the escarpment around the **Daallo Forest** (p332), home to magnificent birdlife and unparalleled panoramas

**7** Spend a couple of days in the remote and otherworldly fishing village of **Zeila** (p330)

The self-proclaimed Republic of Somaliland is currently an internationally unrecognised but de facto sovereign state.

SOMALILAND HARGEISA

# Hargeisa

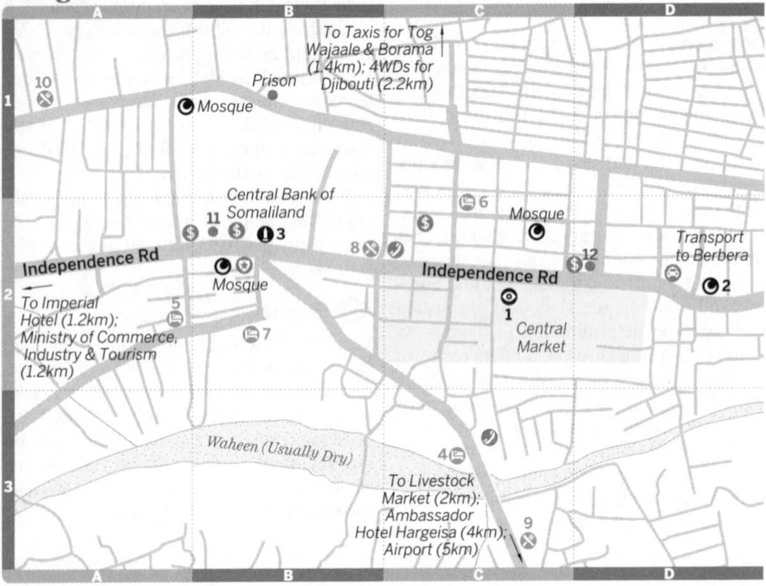

**Central Market** MARKET

(off Independence Rd) Hargeisa's centrepiece, the expansive central market is hugely enjoyable and atmospheric, and a wonderful (and largely hassle-free) place to experience a typical Somali market. Its lanes hide everything from perfume to household objects, electronic goods, wind-up radios and clothes. The food vendors have some of the most fascinating displays – think pyramids of colourful fruits and vegetables.

**Livestock Market** MARKET

An essential part of the Hargeisa experience is the livestock market, which lies on the southeastern outskirts of town. Hundreds of goats, sheep and camels are brought here every day, and it's a fascinating place to wander. Always ask permission before taking photographs. It's at its busiest in the morning.

**Jama Mosque** MOSQUE

(Independence Rd) East of the market area, the modern Jama Mosque hosts Hargeisa's main Friday prayers around noon, attracting hundreds of worshippers – it is an amazing sight. Though not permitted to enter the mosque, you can admire its whitewashed facade, domed roof and tall twin minarets.

**MiG Jet** MEMORIAL

(Independence Rd) You can't miss this weird memorial on the main drag – it displays a Somali Air Force MiG jet fighter which crashed during an aerial bombardment of the city. It lies on a stand that sports colourful murals depicting scenes of the civil war.

## 🛏 Sleeping

Hargeisa has a surprising number of good-value options to suit all budgets. The following options come recommended as they're used to dealing with foreigners. There are no street signs, so most hotels do not have street addresses.

All hotels in the midrange and top-end categories can help you with logistics.

**Oriental Hotel** HOTEL **$$**

(☑514999; www.orientalhotelhargeisa.com; off Independence Rd; s/d with breakfast US$15/30; ☎) The closest Hargeisa comes to a travellers' hang-out, the Oriental can't be beaten for convenience. Its ultracentral location is ideal if you want to immerse yourself in Hargeisa; from your room you can feel the heartbeat of the city. It's nicely laid out, with the reception area opening onto the pleasant sun-filled patio. Rooms are medium-sized and functional, with satellite TV, hot shower

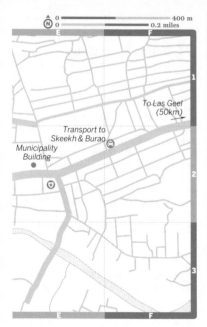

To Las Geel
(50km)

Transport to
Skeekh & Burao

Municipality
Building

SOMALILAND HARGEISA

Staff do an excellent job with car rental, tour guides, police escort and visa matters. Its single drawback is its location away from the central buzz – it feels like an isolated fortress, about 4km from the centre, near the airport. Not very Hargeisa, but it's quiet.

**Safari Hotel**     HOTEL **$$**
(☏570000; www.safarihotelhargeisa.com; off Jijiga Yer Rd; incl breakfast s US$21, d US$25-42; 🛜) Drop anchor here for a night or two if you need to reassure your family at home that you're looking after yourself. Popular with Somali businessmen, this modern multistorey venture boasts comfortable rooms with sparkling bathrooms and a well-regarded restaurant at the back. Just one grumble: you'll need a taxi to get to the centre, as it's positioned on the northwestern outskirts of Hargeisa.

**Hadhwanaag**     HOTEL **$$**
(☏521820; s/d US$10/15) As far as Hargeisa prices go, the Hadhwanaag is good value. The low-slung building occupies a leafy compound and is a five-minute walk away from the main drag. The staff's attention to detail could be sharper (you'll have to ask for a fan), but the tiled rooms are serviceable and you can eat well here at the restaurant.

**Maan-soor Hotel**     HOTEL **$$$**
(☏527000; maan-soor.com; off Jijiga Yer Rd; incl breakfast s US$35, d US$45-60, ste US$80; @🛜)

and a standing fan. There's an on-site restaurant, but the food is only so-so and service is a bit lackadaisical. Light sleepers, take note: the Oriental is right beside a mosque, so be prepared for an early morning wake-up call.

**Imperial Hotel**     HOTEL **$$**
(☏520524; imperialhotelhargeisa@hotmail.com; off Independence Rd; s US$20-25, d US$30; 🛜) A good, quality choice, the modernish Imperial Hotel is in a calm neighbourhood, but within walking distance of the centre. Expect well-appointed rooms, good bedding, working fans, salubrious bathrooms and a good restaurant in a courtyard at the back. Rooms upstairs get more natural light. It's west of the town centre, near the Presidential Palace.

**Ambassador Hotel Hargeisa**     HOTEL **$$$**
(☏526666; www.ambassadorhotelhargeisa.com; Airport Rd; s/d incl breakfast US$53/95; @🛜) With its efficient, English-speaking reception staff, prolific facilities and surgical cleanliness, the Ambassador exudes an international confidence. The squeaky-clean rooms are equipped with everything to ensure a comfortable stay, including satellite TVs, glittering bathrooms, a gym, a business centre, a restaurant and a bar (not licensed).

This classic, well-managed establishment is a perennial favourite for its quiet location, green surrounds, well-furnished yet un-spectacular rooms and professional service. Popular with African politicians, Somali clan elders and aid workers, it can't quite shake that just-a-motel feeling, despite its verdant setting. Its trump card is its wide array of facilities (a restaurant, a business centre, a gym and a conference hall). Northwest of the centre.

### Jirdeh Hotel Hargeisa HOTEL $$

(🕿528792; off Independence Rd; s/d US$12/17; 🗐) A saunter from the main drag, this concrete lump is certainly not a paean to design but the prices are competitive, the rooms present-able and the location peerless. Enough for a night's kip. You'll have to forgo breakfast.

### Sugal Hotel HOTEL

(south of Independence Rd) This hotel was be-ing built at the time of writing, and it looked promising, with well-equipped rooms with private bathrooms. It's in a street running parallel to Independence Rd.

## 🍴 Eating & Drinking

Hargeisa features a string of decent eateries. No alcohol is served, but you'll enjoy superb Somali tea and fresh fruit juices.

### TOP CHOICE Summer Time Restaurant SOMALI $$

(Jijiga Yer Rd; mains US$2-6; ⏱breakfast & dinner) This trendy (for Hargeisa) outfit was the fla-vour of the month at the time of writing. It gets kudos for its expansive menu (written in English) that will satisfy even the picki-est eater. You can have omelettes, corn flakes and scrambled eggs at breakfast. The leaf-dappled outdoor terrace is perfect for escap-ing sticky Hargeisa on a hot day. Northwest of the centre.

### TOP CHOICE Saba YEMENI $$$

(Independence Rd; mains US$4-6; ⏱lunch & din-ner) You'll leave this excellent restaurant,

## ORGANISING A POLICE ESCORT

Independent travel is possible in Somaliland, but there are restrictions. Since the murder of three aid workers by Somali terrorists from Mogadishu in 2003, local authorities have taken the safety of Westerners very seriously, to the point of being overprotective. But no wonder: if foreigners were to encounter a 'problem', Somaliland's diplomatic efforts to gain international recognition would be ruined. In fact, petty crime is almost unheard of and Somalilanders welcome travellers in their country.

In principle, foreigners are required to travel accompanied by a member of the Special Protection Unit (SPU) outside Hargeisa, whether you travel on public transport or private car with driver. If you don't have a soldier with you, you'll be turned back at checkpoints. That said, this rule is ambiguous and erratically enforced, as local authorities seem to change policies on a regular basis. At the time of research, we were told that foreigners are permitted to travel without an SPU officer between Hargeisa, Berbera, Burao and Borama, and between Hargeisa and the Ethiopian and Djiboutian borders. In theory, you are allowed to use public transport between these towns. However, prior to leaving Hargeisa, it's a good idea to meet the Police Commissioner Secretary at the Somaliland Police Force Headquarters, who will either issue a waiver letter on the spot or give a call to the soldiers at checkpoints so that they let you through. If you don't have an escort or a waiver letter, you might be turned back at checkpoints.

For all parts of the country east of Burao, you must have SPU protection (two armed soldiers, though one may be considered enough – again, check the situation with the Somaliland Police Force Headquarters) and travel in a private vehicle. It also helps at checkpoints if you have an official form from the Ministry of Commerce, Industry & Tour-ism that lists all the places you intend to visit in the country (see p326).

All hotels can arrange SPU protection. It costs about US$20 per day for a soldier, plus food. Having a soldier can sometimes be fun, and soldiers can also act as interpret-ers and de facto guides. It's a good idea to buy a few bunches of *chat* (leaf chewed as a stimulant) to facilitate things at the various checkpoints.

Keep your ears to the ground and seek local advice before setting off, and read the Safe Travel section, p320.

specialising in Yemeni dishes, as full as an egg, and whatever you opt for is certain to tickle your taste buds in just the right way. The *mendi* (lamb) and *hanid* mutton or goat (slow-cooked in a beehive oven) are tasty and filling, but leave room for the Yemeni desserts – the *fata mus* (a concoction with banana) and the *fata timir* (a concoction with dates) will satisfy everyone except your personal trainer. West of the centre.

**TOP CHOICE** **Kulan Art Cafe**  CAFETERIA $$
(Jijiga Yer Rd; mains US$2-5; ⊗breakfast & dinner) Ease into low gear sinking a fruit juice or a Somali tea at this atmospheric lounge bar owned by Kulan, a fashion designer whose shop is just across the street. It's genteel and civilised, and a popular hang-out for well-heeled diaspora Somalilanders. The walls lined with vivid paintings by local artists are a nice touch. It serves burgers, pastas, kebabs and mouth-watering cakes.

**African Village**  SOMALI, INTERNATIONAL $$
(mains US$3-6; ⊗8.30am-3pm & 4.30pm-midnight) Opposite Maan-soor Hotel, this large compound is one of the favourite haunts of diaspora Somalilanders, who come here to relax and sample excellent fare, including Ethiopian specialities, pastas, fish dishes, burgers and a few Djiboutian classics.

**Fish & Steak House**  PIZZERIA, SOMALI $$
(mains US$3-6; ⊗breakfast, lunch & dinner) Belying its name, this venture is regarded as the best place in town for a fresh pizza. If pizzas aren't doing it for you, delve into fish and meat dishes. The outdoor tables are pleasant and the service is good. It's in a street running parallel to Independence Rd.

**Ethiopian Restaurant**  ETHIOPIAN $$
(Jijiga Yer Rd; mains US$2-4; ⊗lunch & dinner) True to its name, this authentic Ethiopian eatery serves good honest Ethiopian fare in intimate, low-key surrounds. Be sure to get your caffeine fix served in the traditional style. Opposite Kulan Art Cafe.

**Ambassador Hotel Hargeisa**  SOMALI, INTERNATIONAL $$$
(Airport Rd; mains US$4-11; ⊗breakfast, lunch & dinner) Though there's something on the menu for everyone, the in-house restaurant at the Ambassador Hotel is highly rated for its choice of camel dishes, including camel steaks and camel burgers.

**ⓘ HARGEISA ADDRESSES**

Most streets in Hargeisa don't have names; places are often identified by their proximity to landmarks – bear this in mind when taking taxis or asking for directions.

**Imperial Hotel**  SOMALI, DJIBOUTIAN $$
(off Independence Rd; mains US$3-4; ⊗breakfast, lunch & dinner) The Imperial's on-site restaurant serves an assortment of well-prepared Djiboutian, Somali and Yemeni dishes. Don't miss its delicious *anbabur* (pancake with egg, milk curd and sugar), served on Mondays and Thursdays at breakfast.

**Safari Hotel**  SOMALI $$
(off Jijiga Yer Rd; mains US$2-6; ⊗breakfast, lunch & dinner) Inside the Safari Hotel, you'll find a welcoming garden restaurant offering an array of belly-filling dishes, including lamb, chicken, goat, beef, burgers, salads and pasta.

**Man-soor Hotel**  SOMALI, INTERNATIONAL $$$
(off Jijiga Yer Rd; mains US$3-9; ⊗breakfast, lunch & dinner) This hotel restaurant has a good repertoire of palate-pleasing dishes. Choosing the main course is a real nail-biter – should it be salads, burgers, pizzas, pasta, fish or meat dishes?

**Hadhwanaag**  SOMALI $$
(mains US$3-5; ⊗breakfast, lunch & dinner) Located at the hotel of the same name, Hadhwanaag is a great place to sample Somali specialities like *loxox* (a pancake-like flatbread with butter and honey), fish, goat, chicken and pasta. Enjoy your plunder under a gazebo in the garden.

**Cadaani**  CAFETERIA $
(Independence Rd; mains US$1-3; ⊗breakfast, lunch & dinner) You can't miss this bustling cafeteria – look for the red-and-white building near Telesom. It rustles up simple dishes such as spaghetti and sandwiches. The outdoor terrace is ideal for honing people-watching skills.

**Dalxiis Restaurant**  SOMALI $$
(mains US$3-5; ⊗breakfast & dinner) The Dalxiis is an enticing 'park restaurant', with a garden-like setting. Get your fingers dirty experimenting with the wide range of Somali dishes, including *geel hanid* (roast camel), basmati rice, goat and grilled fish.

Order *ber geel* (camel's liver) or *loxox* at breakfast.

### Maka Al Mukarama
CAFETERIA $

(fruit juices US$1, sandwiches US$1; ☺7am-9pm, lunch & dinner) Put some bounce in your step with a glass of mango or orange juice at this unpretentious supermarket-cum-cafeteria. Cakes, samosas and sandwiches are available.

### Al Baraka
CAFETERIA $

(off Independence Rd; cakes US$1; ☺8am-8pm) This is the closest thing Hargeisa has to a Western cafeteria. It's popular with 20-somethings here to enjoy the atmosphere, chat over a cappuccino and nosh on calorie-busting cakes.

## ℹ Information

### Dangers & Annoyances

Hargeisa is a safe city, but the usual precautions apply. Avoid walking alone at night, don't be ostentatious with valuables, and beware of pickpockets in crowded areas.

### Internet Access

There's a profusion of internet cafes in the centre, most of them tucked away in anonymous buildings. Connection speed is decent assuming you're not streaming YouTube, though machine quality varies wildly. Rates range from US$0.50 to US$1 per hour.

### Medical Services

There are lots of well-stocked pharmacies around town. For medical treatment, **Edna Adan Hospital** (☎4426922; www.ednahospital.org) offers excellent facilities. It's staffed by qualified, English-speaking doctors (mostly volunteers).

### Money

Most transactions can be conducted using US dollars, but if you want to change money, head to one of the **Dahabshiil** (www.dahabshiil.com; Independence Rd; ☺7am-noon & 1-5.30pm Sat-Thu) branches. You'll also find plenty of foreign exchange stalls near the central market; you can't miss them – they're piled high with blocks of notes held together with elastic bands. Most hotels also change money and don't take commission. Somaliland is a strictly cash economy – forget about travellers cheques and credit cards. One ATM had just been introduced at the time of research (in the same street as Oriental Hotel) but it didn't accept foreign cards – check while you're there. Money transfers from a number of countries (see p336) are possible.

### Post & Telephone

There's no post office in Hargeisa. You'll have to use courier services, such as DHL (hotel staff can assist with this).

Making phone calls is easy and cheap. You can also bring your mobile phone and buy a local SIM card from **Telesom** (Independence Rd) or any other mobile phone company.

## Tourist Information

Hotel owners (especially at the Ambassador and the Oriental Hotel, among others) are the best sources for travel information and can also help with visa matters, escorts and car rentals. You can also head to the **Ministry of Commerce, Industry & Tourism** (☎440148, 4014801; south of Independence Rd; ☺7am-noon Sat-Thu), which is in the vicinity of the Imperial Hotel.

## ℹ Getting There & Away

### Air

See p337 for details on flights to/from Somaliland. **Sagal Travel Agency** (☎2514480; Independence Rd) sells air tickets.

The **airport** (Airport Rd) is about 5km south of the centre.

### Land

Regular shared taxis travel between Hargeisa, Berbera, Sheekh, Burao, and Tog Wajaale at the Ethiopian border. They leave from various departure points (north of town for Borama, Tog Wajaale and Djibouti; three blocks east from the Oriental Hotel for Berbera; and near the Municipality building for Sheekh and Burao). They cost from US$6 to US$12 depending on the destination. There are also daily services to Djibouti (see p338).

## ℹ Getting Around

A taxi ride in the centre should cost no more than US$3, and about US$10 to the airport. Two taxi companies were operating in Hargeisa at the time of writing.

**Hargeisa Taxi** (☎4443444)

**Raaxo City Taxi** (☎9722666, 4425810, 4834200) Same location as the Oriental Hotel.

# AROUND SOMALILAND

## Las Geel

Is this Africa's best-kept secret? Las Geel features one of the most impressive collections of ancient rock art on the African continent. It's a must-see, even if you're not an archaeology buff. The poignant paintings, the typical Somali landscape of dry plains covered in acacia shrub, the spectacular granite outcrops and the total lack of crowds make for an eerie ambience that is unforgettable.

## History

This archaeological wonder was only brought to light in 2003, following research conducted by a team of French archaeologists. Despite a number of studies, the history of the site remains shrouded in mystery, with little known about either its artists or even its age. Experts believe that the rock paintings date back around 5000 years to the neolithic era and were the work of pastoralists. In the ancient past, the two *wadis* (dry watercourses) nearby – Las Geel means 'camel's well' in Somali – most likely created a paradise for the cattle herders who eventually left their marks on the surrounding rocks. To date, over 20 shelters containing painted panels have been discovered.

Despite its exceptional historical significance, the site has received minimal formal protection.

##  Sights

Hundreds of magnificent neolithic rock art paintings adorn the walls of several

---

## VOLUNTEER OPPORTUNITIES IN SOMALILAND

While researching this book, we've unearthed a number of locally run programs. There's no language barrier – English is the lingua franca. Male and female volunteers are welcome. Board and lodging are provided but you'll have to pay for your international airfares.

All the people we met told us they could ensure the safety of volunteers, but it's wise to review the local security situation before settling in.

**Edna Adan Hospital** (Edna Adan, Director; ☑4426922; www.ednahospital.org) The best-resourced hospital in Hargeisa (and Somaliland) welcomes health professionals, including general practitioners, gynaecologists, paediatric surgeons, midwives, pharmacists, radiologists and microbiologists. Students are accepted if they've completed at least four years of study.

**University of Hargeisa** (Mohamoud Hussein Farah, Dean, Faculty of Law; ☑4423533; salin100@hotmail.com) With 3400 students in 2009, the University of Hargeisa is quickly expanding. Foreign lecturers in law (with a specialisation in constitution law, judiciary reform, civil law systems and civil procedures) are in hot demand. One semester minimum.

**Havoyoco** (Ahmed Muhamad, Executive Director; ☑4428854; havoyoco@hotmail.com) or (Ifrah Rashid Mohamed, Human Resources Assistant; ☑4418288; ifrahrashid@yahoo.com) The Horn of Africa Voluntary Youth Committee (Havoyoco) is an NGO that was founded in 1992 in Hargeisa. Its objectives include raising awareness on social issues (such as HIV or family life education through an itinerant circus in remote settlements), capacity building and youth training (especially street children who were members of militia). Volunteers who can train youth in masonry, carpentry, cooking, sewing and mechanics are welcome. Minimum three months.

**Sheekh Secondary School** (Mohamed Ibrahim Abdilahi, District Education Officer; ☑730148; sheekhdeo@yahoo.com) The small town of Sheekh is a major educational centre, and a welcoming place where you'll quickly be made to feel at home. There's a shortage of teachers in the following subject matters: English, biology, chemistry, history and geography. Pupils are from 10 to 22 years old.

**Sheekh Technical Veterinary School** (Thomas Bazarusanga, Project Manager; ☑4261665; tbazar05@yahoo.fr) Somaliland is heavily reliant on livestock farming for its foreign exchange earnings and needs more professionals to sustain livestock export and meet the demands of the livestock industry, especially livestock product inspection and animal health. The state-of-the-art Sheekh Technical Veterinary School seeks volunteers in the following fields: veterinary epidemiology, quality management, food safety and standards and library management. Minimum one semester.

**Abaarso Tech** (www.abaarsotech.com) Founded in 2008, this nonprofit secondary school located in a village about 18km outside of Hargeisa admits the top 1% of 8th grade students in Somaliland. Welcomes volunteers in the following fields: English, maths, science and computer science. No minimum stay required.

## LAS GEEL ETIQUETTE

» Don't touch the paintings, as they are very fragile.

» Don't use the flash of your camera.

» Don't get too close to the paintings; humidity contained in your breath may damage them.

interconnected shelters and overhangs on the eastern face of a massive granite outcrop. The paintings contain stylised polychromatic depictions of humans and various animals, notably cows, dogs and a few antelopes, goats and giraffes. The ceiling of the most important shelter is blanketed with 350 individual paintings, which resembles a giant fresco. The colours are mostly shades of red, ochre, yellow and white. Some paintings exceed 1m in length and their state of preservation is exceptional. The bovine figures are particularly colourful and elaborate; they are painted in profile, with a white-and-ochre-striped plastron around the neck, majestic U-shaped or lyre-shaped horns and a prominent udder with clearly outlined teats. Although much less numerous than the animals, the human figures, usually placed under the udder, are also visually striking, with a wide thorax draped in a white tunic, outstretched filiform arms, a minuscule head and spindly lower limbs. They are sometimes shown carrying a bow and accompanied by hunting dogs, which indicates that cattle herders were also hunters.

There's a small **museum** at the entrance of the site, immediately below the main rock shelters. It has panels in English.

There aren't any tourist facilities in the Las Geel area. Most travellers come on a day trip from Hargeisa. Bring plenty of water as there's little shade. Allow at least two hours at the site.

### ❶ Getting There & Away

Las Geel is about 50km from Hargeisa, along the road to Berbera (the turn-off is at Dhubato village and Las Geel is about 6km down the road).

There's no public transport to Las Geel. Most travellers visit the site on a half-day trip from Hargeisa or en route to Berbera. Your best bet is to arrange such a trip through your hotel. Hotels charge from US$80 to US$120 per vehicle (with driver), which usually includes the cost of the mandatory armed guard (it's wise to double check, though). If you're travelling solo, try to share costs with other travellers. You'll also need a permit (US$25) from the Ministry of Commerce, Industry & Tourism to present to the guard at the entrance of the site.

## Berbera

POP 35,000

The name alone sounds impossibly exotic, conjuring images of tropical ports, spices and palm oil. If the reality is a little more prosaic, Berbera is a real gem that oozes ambience and soul and should definitely be on your itinerary. It's hard to believe when you see it, but Berbera was once a busy town. Lying on the Gulf of Aden opposite Yemen, it has been a centre of maritime trade since ancient times. Today this shady town consists mostly of crumbling buildings and mud-and-thatch houses. Various restorations schemes are under investigation but nothing has been done yet.

Berbera's potential is immense, though, with superb beaches and a relaxed atmosphere. If, one day, Somaliland appears on tourist brochures, Berbera will probably top the bill. Meanwhile, it's a nice little earner for Somaliland thanks to land-locked Ethiopia's need for a cheap, friendly port.

### ◉ Sights

Berbera is one of those places where the real attraction is just the overall feel of the place – it's shrouded with a palpable historical aura – and there actually aren't all that many 'sights' to tick off. Having said that, there is an array of pre-20th-century buildings dotted around the historic centre. You'll see a few remarkable examples of **mansions** dating back to the Ottoman era as well as venerable old **mosques**, though these fragile architectural beauties are gradually disintegrating due to a lack of funds.

You can also delve into the small **market** area and soak up its atmosphere. Not far from Al Xayaat Restaurant, the tiny **fishing harbour** deserves a few photo snaps (but ask permission first).

Towards the commercial port, the **Ottoman Mosque**, with its balconied minaret, is worth a peek. Forget about visiting the **port** if you don't have permission from the Municipality and the harbourmaster.

Berbera is also bound by sweeping beaches, about 3km from the centre, including **Baathela Beach**, just in front of Maan-soor Hotel. At dawn, dolphins can be seen frolicking in the bay.

## Sleeping

**Yaxye Hotel**                                    HOTEL **$$**
(☎4410098, 740577; s with/without bathroom & fan US$10/7, d with air-con US$25; ❄️🖢🛜) The Yaxye feels a little more modern than its equivalents elsewhere in the centre. Rooms are simple but tidy and quite spacious considering the price. The upstairs rooms catch cool breezes and salty scents.

**Maan-soor Hotel**                          HOTEL **$$$**
(☎4244240, 4419423; maan-soor.com; s/d with breakfast US$50/60; ❄️🛜) This venture consists of a handful of square 'cottages' scattered around a large property just spitting distance from Baathela Beach. Rooms are impersonal but crisp and comfortable. Note that they don't face the sea. Amenities include an attached restaurant, satellite TV and a so-called 'diving centre' (not professionally run; the 'divemaster' is a hotel employee who speaks minimal English, and safety procedures are lackadaisical). So, what's wrong with this hotel? Nothing, but it struggles to find much of a personality beyond a slightly dour exterior. It's about 3km away from the centre.

**Al Madiina Hotel**                              HOTEL **$**
(☎740254, 4448291; r with/without bathroom & with fan US$6/3, r with bathroom & air-con US$30; ❄️) Right in the centre, this venture doesn't feel the need for fancy touches and what you see is what you get, which in this case is a bed plonked in a threadbare room. The shared bathrooms are OK. All rooms are fan-cooled and a few singles have air-con.

**Esco Hotel**                                    HOTEL **$**
(☎740121, 4016425; r without bathroom & with fan US$7, r with bathroom & air-con US$30; ❄️🖢🛜) Fine in a pinch, the Esco has sparse but acceptable rooms with furniture you would be happy to find at a flea market. Rooms vary in size, layout and plumbing quality so scope out a few before committing yourself. The better rooms have air-con. It's a coin's toss from Al Xayaat Restaurant.

## Eating

**Al Xayaat Restaurant & Fish House**                          SEAFOOD **$$**
(☎740224; mains US$3-5; ⊙breakfast, lunch & dinner) Lap up a reviving fruit juice and scoff a grilled fish at this colourful eatery overlooking the bay, and you'll leave with a smile on your face. While eating you'll be surrounded by a menagerie of cats, crows and seagulls

expecting a titbit. Ali, the amiable owner, speaks good English.

**Xeeb Soor**                                    SEAFOOD **$$**
(mains US$3-5; ⊙breakfast, lunch & dinner) Facing the bay, the Xeeb Soor enjoys pleasant outdoor seating. There are good rice dishes and a variety of tasty fishes straight from the fishing harbour.

## 🛈 Getting There & Away

Regular shared taxis travel between Hargeisa and Berbera (US$6, 150km) and between Burao and Berbera (US$4). There's no public transport to Zeila.

# Sheekh

POP 15,000
From Berbera and the coastal plain, you can make a beautiful journey along the switchback ascent to the central plateau on the Berbera–Burao road and stop at the hill town of Sheekh, a welcome refuge from the heat of the lowland areas. This is one of the main educational centres in the country, with a well-established veterinary school and various colleges, including the Sheekh Secondary School, which give the town a surprisingly dynamic feel. (See the boxed text, p327, for information on volunteering opportunities.)

Sheekh boasts a small necropolis, called **Ferdusa**, which dates from the 13th century. There's not much to be seen, as the site has not been excavated yet. It's a five-minute walk from the Maanshaalah Hotel.

You'll find a few eateries along the main road.

## Sleeping

**Sheekh Guesthouse**                     GUESTHOUSE **$$**
(☎4418664; bungalows US$50) A good safe bet well worth bookmarking if you intend to break up your journey in Sheekh. This venture comprises two three-bedroom bungalows that are well furnished and as neat as a pin. The major drawback is the tariff; Sheekh Guesthouse is nice enough, but rates are, frankly, overpriced.

**Maanshaalah Hotel**                             HOTEL **$**
(☎730167, 4804729; s/d US$10/15, s/d without bathroom US$5/10) The Maanshaalah won't hurt the hip pocket but the plumbing seems on the brink of collapse, mattresses are saggy and the bathrooms are a few scrubs short of being considered clean. It's manageable for a night's kip.

**WORTH A TRIP**

## ZEILA

It's hard to believe today that the fishing village of Zeila was once a thriving port town. Despite being only 28km south of the Djibouti border, it really feels like the end of the line. Few places in the Horn feel so gloriously remote and inhospitable, and equally utterly beguiling. Zanzibar it ain't, but Zeila is still a fascinating place to explore because of its exotic (and melancholic) character. It was occupied by the Portuguese, Arabs, Turks and Egyptians. Trade in Zeila flourished throughout these occupations; everything – slaves, pearls, incense and myrrh – passed through the port. Remnants of this glory are the two **mosques** in the centre as well as a big Islamic **mausoleum** in the southern part of the town. Even if the older mosque is in a very bad shape, it boasts a dilapidated charm that is uniquely unforgettable. Pity about the telecom towers that were installed a few years ago – they *do* mar the great vista.

You can lay your head at the **Kaboode Guesthouse** (☑4580020; d without bathroom & with fan US$10), which has three ultrabasic rooms with shared (bucket) showers. Zeila has no formal restaurant, but you'll find a couple of simple eateries near the guesthouse.

If you've got this far, it's worth making the simple 20-minute boat trip to the **Saadedin Islands**. These six uninhabited islands are ringed by sandy beaches, mangrove swamps and mud flats. There's potential for snorkelling and diving, but there aren't any facilities. The owner of the Kaboode Guesthouse can arrange boat excursions there for US$100 for the boat and another US$10 for a coast guard.

Because Zeila is so isolated, getting here by public transport isn't straightforward – services from Borama or Hargeisa are infrequent (and nonexistent from Berbera). Your best bet is to hire a 4WD with a knowledgeable driver in Hargeisa. From the capital, you really need at least four days for the round trip via Borama and the vast desert-like expanses of the **Giriyad Plains**.

### ❶ Getting There & Away

Sheekh is approximately halfway between Berbera and Burao. Shared taxis connect Sheekh to Berbera (US$4) and Burao (US$4).

## Burao

POP 200,000

The capital of Todgheer province and the second-largest city in the country, Burao feels a bit rougher around the edges than Berbera or Hargeisa, but that's part of the adventure. There's nothing of tangible interest here, but you can soak up the atmosphere at the **livestock market** and enjoy being the focus of attention – as a tourist, you'll be something of a novelty here! On a more practical note it's also a staging point for travel east to Erigavo.

### 🛏 Sleeping & Eating

**City Plaza Hotel**　　　　　　　HOTEL **$$**
(☑710658, 4315217; www.buraocityplazahotel.com; s/d US$21/23, ste US$35; ❉🕿) The City Plaza is a low-slung compound of cottages scattered amid a leafy garden full of birdsong. Service is professional, rooms are well appointed and cleaned with soldierly precision and an expansion wing should only add to the goodness. It's located in a quiet area, about 3km out of town along the road to Erigavo, so while the vibe is mellow, you're sort of stuck here amid on-site amenities...which, on the plus side, include a kick-butt restaurant (mains US$3 to US$5).

**Deero Hotel & Restaurant**　　　　HOTEL **$**
(☑714499, 712299; s/d US$10/15; 🕿) This multistorey building gets an A+ for its clean rooms, ultra-central location, good beds and hygienic bathrooms. Another bonus is the rooftop restaurant (mains US$2 to US$5), which trots out fish and meat dishes with the added treat of splendid views over Burao.

**Barwaaqo Hotel**　　　　　　　HOTEL **$**
(☑715700, 4140427; s/d US$10/15; 🕿) Cheap, well-maintained rooms with itty-bitty bathrooms. However, most of the singles have only interior windows. Cold water only. It's close to the centre.

**Shamaxle Restaurant**　　　　　　SOMALI **$**
(mains US$3-6; ⊘breakfast, lunch & dinner) The location, in a leafy compound right by the Todgheer River, is top-notch. And the juicy *hanid* (roast lamb) will have your taste buds leaping for joy.

## ℹ Getting There & Away

Shared taxis leave for Hargeisa (US$12, 260km) via Sheekh (60km) and Berbera (120km).

# Sanaag

Welcome to what is possibly the most special province in the country. Now is your chance to leave behind all that is familiar and to fall completely off the radar. This part of the country is largely cut off from the rest, and from itself, by a degraded transportation network, including some roads out of an engineer's nightmare. This inaccessibility results in isolated communities and, for the travellers, a constant sense of coming upon undiscovered locales. Birdwatchers will be rubbing their hands in anticipation: the Sanaag province is one of Somaliland's finest birdwatching venues.

From Burao, allow at least four days to do the region justice.

### FROM BURAO TO ERIGAVO

The main gateway to the Sanaag province is Burao. From here, a tarred road leads to the junction village of Inaafmadaw, about 65km south of Burao, where the real wilderness of the far east begins to unfold. Here you turn left onto a sandy track that runs southeast through a series of rickety settlements, including Garadak, El Afweyn, Calsheikh and Yulfe before reaching Erigavo. This stretch takes you through the hauntingly beautiful Saraar Plains; these vast arid expanses of stone and sand populated by nomadic pastoralists and hemmed in by bulky rocky outcrops are a magical sight. Count on a good full day to cover the daunting but fascinating 350km trip from Burao to Erigavo.

### ERIGAVO

The first major stop in the east after leaving Burao, Erigavo has the feeling of a frontier town. Perched on an arid plateau at an altitude of 1770m, the capital of the Sanaag region has little tourism value of its own, but it has a pleasant enough atmosphere and it's the only place with decent facilities in the far east. It's also the perfect base from which to head out to Daallo Forest and Maydh.

### 🍴 Sleeping & Eating

**Sanaag Hotel** HOTEL $
(☑4414507, 4200484; s/d US$10/20, s/d without bathroom US$4/8; 🛜) Accommodation options are thin on the ground here. Sanaag

SOMALILAND SANAAG

---

### NIGEL REDMAN: BIRD TOUR LEADER

Nigel Redman is the author of *Birds of the Horn of Africa* (Princeton Field Guides) and leads birdwatching tours in Africa.

**How would you characterise birdlife in Somaliland?** Many of the birds in Somaliland are typical of those found in the drier eastern parts of East Africa, but a suite of endemic species are of considerable interest to birders. Top targets include the little brown bustard, Somali pigeon, Somali wheatear, Philippa's Crombec and Warsangli Linnet.

**Where are the best birdwatching spots in Somaliland?** Half of Somaliland's special birds are found on the extensive, semi-arid plains and bushland that cover most of the country. The rest are in the hills of the escarpment, which rises to 2400m and runs east to west, close to the coast. The best and most scenic area is the magnificent Daallo Forest which holds all of the highland specialities.

**What makes birdwatching in Somaliland different from other birdwatching destinations in Africa?** The 15 or so species that can only be seen in the Somali region; all but two of these endemics occur in Somaliland. Somaliland is perhaps best known for its profusion of larks (20 species).

**Is it safe to sign up for a birdwatching tour in Somaliland?** Yes, at present it is. Somaliland has a stable and democratically elected government. The authorities require visitors to be escorted by armed soldiers, just to be on the safe side.

**What about mammals?** Although not as rich in mammals as East Africa, Somaliland has a wide variety of mammals. Most interesting is probably the beira, a small, unique species of antelope that is only found in Somaliland and Djibouti. Speke's gazelle is another Somali endemic and quite easy to see.

is a modest venture where you can relax in peace. It has spartan rooms with dank bathrooms. With notice staff can prepare meals. The owner, Abdirahman Farah, has lived in the US and speaks excellent English.

### Beder Restaurant                    SOMALI $
(mains US$1-3; ☺breakfast, lunch & dinner) A cheerful little place with a strikingly colourful facade. Good spot for a comforting breakfast (superb *loxox*!) or a quick meal later in the day.

### Goljano Brothers Restaurant       SOMALI $
(mains US$1-3; ☺breakfast, lunch & dinner) Next door to Beder, the Goljano offers the usual selection of pastas and goat meat dishes.

#### DAALLO FOREST
Some 16km northeast of Erigavo lies the village of **Karin**, which is the gateway to the majestic Daallo Forest. It's one of the best places in Somaliland to see **birds**, including a host of endemics, and mammals. From Karin, a dirt track leads through the forest to a **lookout**, reached after 5km. The lookout is perched on the edge of a vast canyon that plummets dramatically and offers hallucinogenic views down into the valley, more than 2000m below. On a clear day you can see all the way to the Gulf of Aden, some 30km away.

#### KARIN TO MAYDH
Back to Karin, be prepared for a dizzying downhill trip. The journey from Karin to Maydh is one of the most dramatic in Somaliland. In just 30km, a spectacular dirt road descends nearly 2200m, plummeting through tall limestone cliffs often clad in mist, around numerous hairpin bends, before reaching the village of **Rugay**. The gradual change of scenery is mind-boggling. The forested slopes progressively change to scrubby thorn bushes and stunning Marscape. The stretch of road between Rugay and Maydh offers a few sites of interest that are worth checking out – be on the lookout for huge **tumuli** (stone burial cairns) just metres from the road and the shining white **tomb of Sheikh Issa**, about 400m east of the main road.

About 77km north of Erigavo, the coastal village of **Maydh** appears like a mirage. It is little more than a few undistinguished buildings, but it was once a harbour of some significance. The setting is astounding: it lies in a sheltered bay fringed with a yellow scimitar of sand and framed with barren hillsides.

Most villagers make a living from the sea, although smuggling with Yemeni merchants has proved a more lucrative means of income. A particular highlight in Maydh is the whitewashed **tomb of Sheikh Isaq**, which is located near the beach about 3km south of Maydh. The Isaq clan is the most politically important clan in Somaliland, and the tomb attracts pilgrims from all over the country.

Feeling peckish? In the centre, the modest Maansor dishes up basic fish and pasta dishes.

## ❶ Getting There & Away
Although improved security meant the Sanaag province was accessible to foreigners during our research, it's still wise to get the latest security information from the Ministry of Commerce, Industry & Tourism (p326) in Hargeisa before setting off. The official requirement for travel east of Burao is that foreign visitors must travel in a private 4WD with at least one Special Protection Unit (SPU) guard (although a second one may be required). It's also sensible to hire a guide/interpreter. This can be arranged through travel agencies and larger hotels in Hargeisa. Make sure to have a driver who is familiar with the region.

You'll also need a letter of permission from the Ministry of Commerce, Industry & Tourism – you'll be asked to show this permit at the various checkpoints on the road between Erigavo and Maydh. It's also wise to inform the Ministry of Interior of your itinerary. Once in Erigavo, it's advisable to meet with the governor and the mayor and let them know about your itinerary in the area.

## Borama
POP 190,000
The provincial capital of Borama feels different from other urban centres in Somaliland, not least because of its sizable student population – approximately 2500 students are enrolled at **Amoud University** (www.amouduniversity.org) in the Amoud Valley, some 5km east of the centre. It's certainly not hedonistic, but there's a fluid, lively energy to the city.

The setting is alluring – Borama lies at an altitude of 1450m amid mildly undulating hills, and it's greener than most other areas in the country. That said, there's little in the way of sightseeing, the one exception being the sprawling **market** in the centre.

Overall it's a pleasant spot, with a decent selection of places to stay and good trans-

## ROCK ART SITES BETWEEN HARGEISA & BORAMA

There are two ancient rock art sites off the main road between Hargeisa and Borama. Though playing second fiddle to Las Geel, they're worth stopping at on the way to Borama if you have your own vehicle with driver – a 4WD is recommended. It's also advisable to hire a guide who knows the exact location of the sites, as there are no signs.

Coming from Hargeisa, the first rock art site, **Dhagax Khoure**, lies about 45km northwest of the capital and 15km off the main road. It comprises several individual painted shelters scattered on a rocky hill. According to archaeologists, they may be more than 5000 years old.

The main shelter has an inclined ceiling which is decorated with an assemblage of bovid figures as well as one giraffe and one anthropomorphic figure. The second most important shelter, which lies at the base of the granite outcrop, is adorned with panels representing sheep (or goats) and a few human figures holding a bow. The colours and the complexity of the paintings are much less striking than those at Las Geel, but they're interesting nonetheless. The eerie landscape is another draw.

You'll be met by the local caretaker, who'll be happy to show you the main panels in exchange for a tip.

Back to the main road, continue further west until you reach the town of **Gebiley**. **Dhagax Marodi** lies about 2.5km north of Gebiley and features a huge cow, perhaps 1.5m tall, inscribed on a big slab. Sadly, it has been badly damaged by vandals.

port facilities. It's also a good base to lay over between Hargeisa and Djibouti.

### 🛏 Sleeping & Eating

**Rays Hotel**                               HOTEL **$$**
(📞614370, 350313; s/d US$20/25; ❄🛜) The Rays is the pick of Borama's accommodation, and has neat rooms with excellent bathrooms and crisp, clean bedding. A huge drawcard is the quiet garden, where you can enjoy a cup Somali tea or a meal – the on-site **restaurant** (mains US$2-5; ⊙breakfast, lunch & dinner) serves up local specialities, burgers and salads. It's on the northern outskirts of town.

**Gallad Hotel**                              HOTEL **$**
(📞617480, 4405290; r US$10) Don't be fooled by the drab exterior of this multistorey building. Inside it's much more appealing, with 18 well-scrubbed rooms (with or without bathrooms), hot showers and an inviting rooftop TV room that proffers unabashed views of the town. Location is ace – it's smack dab in the centre. One negative: a thigh-burning number of stairs.

**Borama Hotel**                              HOTEL **$**
(📞4457608; s/d without bathroom US$3/4) Rooms here are utterly simple (a bed and a mosquito net) and cleanliness is only just OK in the bathrooms – wear flip-flops to shower – but it's a worthwhile backup if you're seriously strapped for cash. Its best

asset is the quiet location, a little way from the action.

**Awdal**                                  SOMALI **$$**
(mains US$2-4; ⊙lunch & dinner) The restaurant of choice for locals. Simple Somali standards, including camel meat.

**Goljano Cafeteria**                     CAFETERIA **$**
(mains US$1-3; ⊙breakfast, lunch & dinner) Grab a burger and get filled for minimal coinage at this undeniable favourite. Superb fruit juices, too.

## UNDERSTAND SOMALILAND

## Somaliland Today

While the self-proclaimed Republic of Somaliland remains unrecognised by the international community, expat Somalilanders continue to do their best to influence diplomatic corps in Europe, East Africa and North America – in vain, so far. Somaliland's leaders have nurtured good relations with Kenya, Ethiopia, France, the UK, Germany and Norway, and seem to be backed by the African Union.

Somaliland has a fragile economy that is based on agriculture and pastoralism – the fragility is compounded by the fact that the diplomatic isolation of the country and its nonrecognition restrict foreign investment and access to loans. However, expat Somalilanders have started to invest massively in the capital in recent years. Well over a million Somalis are scattered across Europe, North America and the Middle East; together they send hundreds of millions of dollars back to Somaliland each year.

But what could really give a new impetus to the country is the oil exploration; eastern Somaliland is said to be rich in oil resources. There are plans to start prospecting with the help of foreign companies.

## History

Originally, Somalis probably hail from the southern Ethiopian highlands, and have been subject to a strong Arabic influence ever since the 7th century when the Somali coast formed part of the extensive Arab-controlled trans–Indian Ocean trading network.

In the 19th century much of the Ogaden Desert – ethnically, a part of Somalia – was annexed by Ethiopia (an invasion that has been a source of bad blood ever since) and then in 1888 the country was divided by European powers. The French got the area around Djibouti, Britain much of the north, while Italy got Puntland and the south. Sayid Maxamed Cabdulle Xasan (known affectionately as 'the Mad Mullah') fought the British for two decades, but it wasn't until 1960 that Somaliland, Puntland and southern Somalia were united.

Sadly, interclan tensions, radical socialism, rearmament by the USSR and the occasional (often disastrous) war with Ethiopia helped tear the country apart. Mohammed Siad Barre, Somalia's last recognised leader, fled to Nigeria in 1991 after the forces of General Aideed took Mogadishu. At the same time the Somali National Movement (SNM) moved quickly and declared independence for Somaliland. Puntland also broke away.

While fierce battles between warring factions plagued southern Somalia throughout the 1990s, Somaliland has remained largely peaceful and stable since 1991, thanks mainly to the predominance of a single clan (the Isaq). It has great oil and gas potential and voted for complete independence in 1997 before holding free presidential elections in 2003. However, Somaliland is not officially recognised as a separate state by the international community. The main reason why the world is reluctant to accept Somaliland's independence is that the UN still hopes for a peace agreement covering all of Somalia, and its other neighbours are wary of an independent Somaliland, fearing a potential 'Balkanisation' of the Horn. For Somalilanders, this seems profoundly unfair. Unlike the rest of Somalia, they have managed to establish law and order in their own country.

In 2003, terrorists from Mogadishu illegally entered Somaliland and shot dead several aid workers with the aim of destabilising the fledgling country and causing it to lose its credibility on the international scene. This explains why the local authorities tend to be overprotective of foreigners once they venture outside the capital. In October 2008, another group of terrorists from Mogadishu carried out suicide bombings in Hargeisa. The targets included the presidency, the Ethiopian Liaison Office and one UN office.

The second presidential elections took place in 2010, after having been delayed a few times. Municipal elections were held in late 2012 without trouble.

## The Culture

The clan structure is the main pillar of Somali culture. Somalis all hail from the same tribe, which is divided into six main clans and loads of subclans. The nomadic lifestyle also exerts a major influence on Somali culture.

Somalis can be quiet and dignified, with a tendency to ignore strangers, but have a tremendous oral (often poetic) tradition. Written Somali is a very young language (the Somali Latin script was established in 1973), and spelling variation, especially of place names, is very common. English is widely used in Somaliland.

All Somalis are Sunni Muslims and Islam is extremely important to the Somali sense of national identity. Most women wear headscarves, and arranged marriage is still the norm in rural areas.

## Food & Drink

Goat and camel meat are popular dishes in Somaliland. The standard breakfast throughout the country is fried liver with

## EATING PRICE RANGES

The following price ranges used for restaurants and eateries in this guide refer to a standard main course.

**$** Less than US$2

**$$** US$2 to US$4

**$$$** More than US$4

onions and *loxox,* a flat bread similar to the Ethiopian *injera* served with honey, sugar and tea. Rice and noodles are also common staples. Camel and goat are the preferred sources of meat.

Tea is the favourite drink. Goat's or camel's milk are also widespread. Alcohol is strictly prohibited and not available.

# SURVIVAL GUIDE

## Directory A–Z

### Accommodation

» Owing perhaps to its undeveloped tourist industry, accommodation in Somaliland is generally good value compared to neighbouring countries. Not surprisingly, Hargeisa has the widest choice of available options.

» Budget rooms are no-frills, with a narrow double bed (or twin beds), neon lights, a fan and shared showers. The shower is usually a bucket-and-scoop affair in the bathtub. Towels and soap are usually not provided.

» In larger towns you can find at least one comfortable midrange option with reliable hot shower, air-con and wireless internet.

» Upmarket hotels are confined to the capital and are mainly aimed at aid workers and other NGO and UN employees travelling in the country, as well as businesspeople. Although basic by international standards, these hotels have rooms with private shower, air-con and satellite TV. They also have restaurants and offer wi-fi, and breakfast is sometimes included in the room price. The better hotels are typically found on the outskirts of town to offer calm and security. They can organise tours and can help with visa matters and organising an armed guard.

» A room with a double bed is usually called a 'single', and a room with twin beds

a 'double'. In our reviews we've used the Western interpretation of singles, doubles and twins. In some places you'll just be quoted a flat rate for the room irrespective of occupancy.

» There are no campsites.

» All places to stay quote their prices in US dollars. Note that payment is by cash only – even larger hotels don't take credit cards.

### Activities

Somaliland has great potential for outdoor pursuits but there are no proper facilities. Because of the lack of funds, nothing has been really developed yet.

#### Birdwatching

Although it's still relatively poorly known in ornithological terms, Somaliland is a great destination for adventurous birdwatchers. The best birdwatching opportunities can be found near Sheekh, around Burao and in the vicinity of Daallo Forest. Contact the following outfits:

**Birding Africa** (✆ in South Africa +27 (0)21 531 9148; www.birdingafrica.com) This highly regarded company runs ornithological expeditions in Somaliland in combination with Djibouti.

**Birdquest** (✆ in the UK +44 1254 826317; www.birdquest-tours.com) This well-established tour operator arranges trips for dedicated birders. Trips combine Djibouti and Somaliland.

**Nature Somaliland** (✆4138813; abdi.jama@ymail.com) The owner, Abdi Jama, is passionate about birdwatching and can organise tailor-made birdwatching trips on request.

#### Diving & Snorkelling

The reefs off Berbera and the islands off Zeila have potential for diving and snorkelling, but they can't compare with the Gulf of Tadjoura in Djibouti. At the time of writing there was no professional dive operator.

## ACCOMMODATION PRICE RANGES

Accommodation reviews in this chapter are categorised as follows:

**$** Less than US$10

**$$** US$10 to US$50

**$$$** More than US$50

### Hiking

In theory hiking is possible around Mt Wagar and Daallo Forest but you'll need a guide. Organised hiking is still embryonic and much has to be done to promote this activity.

## Business Hours

The following are common business hours in Somaliland; exceptions are noted in individual reviews. Friday is the weekly holiday for offices and most shops.

**Banks** 7.30am to 12.30pm and 4pm to 6pm Saturday to Thursday

**Businesses** 7.30am to 1.30pm and 4pm to 6.30pm Saturday to Thursday

**Government offices** 8am to 12.30pm and 4pm to 6pm Saturday to Thursday

**Restaurants** breakfast from 6.30am, lunch from 11.30am, dinner 6.30pm to 9pm

## Embassies & Consulates

The only official foreign representation in Somaliland is the **Ethiopian Liaison Office** (south of Independence Rd, Hargeisa; ⊘8.30am-noon Mon-Thu & Sat), which acts as a de facto embassy. It's not signed; it's on a backstreet not far from the Ministry of Finance and the Ministry of Commerce, Industry & Tourism.

Somaliland Liaison Offices abroad include the following:

**Djibouti** (Map p302; ☑21358758; Ave F d'Esperey, Djibouti City)

**Ethiopia** (Map p46; ☑0116-635921; btwn Bole Rd & Cameroon St, Addis Ababa)

**France** (☑09 50 81 50 94, 06 17 67 70 75; wakiil_sl_fr@hotmail.fr; 19 rue Augustin Thierry, 75019 Paris)

**UK** (☑0207 7027064; 319 Waterlily Business Centre, 10 Cleveland Way, London E1 4UF; contact@somaliland-mission.com)

**USA** (☑202 587-5743; www.somaliland.us; 1425 K Street, NW, Washington DC 20005)

## Insurance

» It's worth checking with your insurance company if you're covered in case of emergency while travelling around Somaliland.

## Internet Access

» Establishments with wireless are identified in this book with a 🛜 icon.
» Internet cafes can be found in all major towns.

» An increasing number of hotels, including budget and midrange places, have complimentary wi-fi.
» Connection speeds vary from pretty good to acceptable.

## Money

» Somaliland's currency is the Somaliland shilling (SISh). There are bills of SISh500 and SISh1000.
» Your best bet is to carry considerable amounts of US dollars (vastly preferable to euros) that can be exchanged for shillings in hotels, shops and bureaux de change; payment in US dollars is accepted everywhere. Bring a good stash of smaller denomination bills.
» At the time of writing one ATM was being installed in Hargeisa, and there were plans to introduce more ATMs in the city. Don't get too excited, though – there's no guarantee that they will work with foreign credit cards; check while in Hargeisa.
» There's no chance of changing your travellers cheques.
» If you need to wire money, you'll find **Dahabshiil** (www.dahabshiil.com), **Western Union** (www.westernunion.com) and **WorldRemit** (www.worldremit.com) offices in Hargeisa.

## Public Holidays

As well as major Islamic holidays, these are the principal public holidays in Somaliland:

**Restoration of Somaliland Sovereignty** 18–19 May

**Independence Day** 26 June

## Telephone

» The international dialling code for Somaliland is +2522.
» There are several private telephone companies including Telesom and Somtel in Somaliland.
» International telephone calls made from Somaliland are the cheapest in Africa (less than US$0.20 per minute).

---

### PRACTICALITIES

» Electricity is 220V, 50Hz, with square three-pin sockets as used in the UK.

» The metric system is used for weights and measures.

» Mobile-phone coverage is good and being continuously expanded as new phone towers are built. Mobile-phone users can use their phones in Somaliland. If you have a GSM phone that is unlocked you can purchase a new SIM card from any Telesom or Somtel branch – this gives you a local number to call from and is much cheaper in the long run compared to global roaming.

## Visas

» You will need a visa to enter Somaliland. Visas are *not* issued at the airport.

» The most convenient place to get a visa is Addis Ababa. They are issued while you wait through the Somaliland Liaison Office (see p336) and cost US$40 for a one-month visa. Visas can also be obtained in Djibouti, the UK, the USA and France; visa fees cost about US$40, although requirements tend to vary arbitrarily from one Liaison Office to another (US$80 in the USA).

» Another option is to go through a local sponsor, such as the Oriental Hotel, the Ambassador Hotel or the Maan-soor Hotel. Email them the (scanned) ID pages of your passport and give them at least three days to organise the visa. They will email a visa certificate back to you as an attached document. Print it and present it upon arrival at the airport (or at any land border). Note that this is a certificate; the original visa should have been deposited at the immigration office at the airport (or at the border post, if you arrive by land) by your sponsor. In many cases your sponsor will be waiting for you at the airport with the original visa. If you plan to enter Somaliland at Tog Wajaale (from Ethiopia), ask your sponsor to send the original visa to the Somaliland border post (your sponsor will put it in an envelope and give it to a reputable taxi driver heading to Tog Wajaale). Hotels charge US$20 to US$50 for the service, and expect that you spend a couple of nights with them.

### VISAS FOR ONWARD TRAVEL

The Ethiopian Liaison Office (see p336) can issue Ethiopian visas. You'll need two photos, US$20 and a letter from the **Immigration Department Office Headquarters** (north of Independence Rd, Hargeisa; ☉8am-noon Sat-Thu), though this letter is not always required by the Ethiopian

### MINISTRY OF COMMERCE, INDUSTRY & TOURISM

It helps at checkpoints if you have an official form from the **Ministry of Commerce, Industry & Tourism** (Map p322; ☑440148, 4014801; south of Independence Rd; ☉7am-noon Sat-Thu) that lists all the places you intend to visit in the country (be extensive). For Las Geel, Zeila and all travel east of Burao, this form is mandatory. Get there in the morning, fill in the form, fork out US$25 and it's issued on the spot. It's on a side street near Imperial Hotel.

officer. The whole process should take less than a day provided you arrive early in the morning.

## Getting There & Away
### Entering Somaliland

Entering Somaliland, whether by air or land, is a surprisingly painless process, provided you have your visa ready (or prearranged) and your passport at hand.

### Air
#### AIRPORTS & AIRLINES

Somaliland has two international gateways for arrival by air: **Hargeisa Egal International Airport** (HGA) and **Berbera International Airport** (BBO). Hargeisa is the busiest. Note that Hargeisa airport was closed for renovation at the time of writing – all international flights were landing at Berbera, from where passengers were being bussed to Hargeisa.

The following airlines fly to/from Somaliland and have offices in Hargeisa:

**African Express Airways** (Map p322; ☑523646; www.africanexpress.co.ke; Independence Rd) Has two to four flights a week to/from Dubai and four flights a week to/from Nairobi (via Mogadishu).

**Daallo Airlines** (☑523003, 300063; www.daallo.com; Independence Rd) The national carrier. Operates two flights a week to/from Dubai and three flights a week to/from Djibouti. Also serves Mogadishu (Somalia), Jeddah (Saudi Arabia) and Nairobi

(Kenya), and should have started services to Addis Ababa by the time you read this.

**Ethiopian Airlines** (www.flyethiopian.com) Daily flights to/from Addis Ababa and four weekly flights to/from Dire Dawa. The office was about to reopen at the time of research – most probably somewhere on Independence Rd.

**Jubba Airways** (Map p322; ☑524022; www. jubba-airways.com; Independence Rd) Two flights a week to/from Dubai and to/from Mogadishu, as well as three flights a week to/from Djibouti.

### TICKETS

Expect to pay US$450 to US$500 for a return ticket to Dubai, at least US$250 from Djibouti and at least US$430 from Addis Ababa. For Nairobi, a return ticket costs around US$470.

If you're coming from Europe or North America, your best bet is to fly to Dubai or Addis Ababa and find an onward connection to Hargeisa or Berbera. From Australasia, fly to Dubai and find an onward connection to Hargeisa or Berbera.

## Land

### DJIBOUTI

The land border between Somaliland and Djibouti is open. Shared taxis (usually 4WDs) ply the route on a daily basis from Hargeisa to Djibouti City – a strenuous 16- to 20-hour journey on a dirt road (US$30 to US$40 for the front seat). Taxis usually leave Hargeisa around 4pm so as to travel by night and avoid the scorching heat. They drive in convoy – a matter of survival in case of a breakdown in this desolate area. Bring food and plenty of water. The border crossing is at Loyaada.

### ETHIOPIA

A significant proportion of visitors to Somaliland travel overland from Ethiopia. From Jijiga in eastern Ethiopia there's regular bus traffic to the border town of Tog Wajaale (Togo-Wuchale on Ethiopian side; see p290). In Tog Wajaale, take a shared taxi (about US$7, two hours) to Hargeisa, about 90km to the southeast. Ask to be dropped in front of your hotel. Expect a couple of checkpoints, but no hassle.

## Getting Around

Somaliland has a few sealed roads (like from Hargeisa to Berbera and from Berbera to Burao). Medium-sized buses and crowded 4WDs service routes between Hargeisa and major settlements, including Berbera, Borama, Sheekh and Burao. For Zeila and the Sanaag region, you'll need to hire a 4WD with driver.

You can hire a taxi for about US$70 per day (fuel and escort are extra) or a 4WD with driver for about US$150. Hotels can help with logistics.

## Tours

There are a few tour operators in Hargeisa. Don't expect fully fledged outfits or Kenya-style safari companies, though – you'll be most likely dealing with a one-person operation or a freelance guide who will arrange car rental and SPU protection when required, and will accompany you to the Somaliland Police Force Headquarters and the Ministry of Commerce, Industry & Tourism.

Recommended operators:

**Dalmar Tours** (☑514999, 4129334; www.dalmartours.com) Based at the Oriental Hotel, this operator is quite used to dealing with foreign visitors. Uses selected 4WDs with drivers and can organise day trips to Las Geel (US$125) as well as longer expeditions.

**Safari Somaliland Travel Tourism and Culture** (☑4478201, 79152047; www.safarisomalilandtour.com) Friendly Mohamed Abdirizak works as a freelance guide and can help with logistics.

**Nature Somaliland** (☑4138813; abdi.jama@ymail.com) Specialises in birdwatching expeditions, but can also arrange all kinds of trips in the country.

# Health

One who hides his illness has no medicine; one who hides his problem has no remedy.
*Ethiopian proverb*

As long as you stay up to date with your vaccinations and take some basic preventive measures, you'd have to be pretty unlucky to succumb to most of the health hazards covered in this chapter. Africa certainly has an impressive selection of tropical diseases on offer, but you're much more likely to get a bout of diarrhoea (in fact, you should bank on it), a cold or an infected mosquito bite than an exotic disease such as sleeping sickness.

## BEFORE YOU GO

A little planning before departure, particularly for vaccinations or if you have a pre-existing illness, will save you a lot of trouble later. Before a long trip get a checkup from your dentist, and from your doctor if you have any regular medication or chronic illness, eg high blood pressure or asthma. You should also organise spare contact lenses and glasses (and take your optical prescription with you); get a first-aid and medical kit together; and arrange necessary vaccinations.

It's tempting to leave it all to the last minute – don't! Many vaccines take several doses over a period of up to six weeks, so you must visit a doctor six to eight weeks before departure. Ask your doctor for an International Certificate of Vaccination (otherwise known as the yellow booklet), which will list all the vaccinations you've received. This is necessary, as proof of yellow-fever (and possibly cholera) vaccination is mandatory in Ethiopia.

Travellers can register with the **International Association for Medical Advice to Travellers** (IMAT; www.iamat.org). Its website can help travellers to find a doctor who has recognised training. Those heading off to very remote areas might like to do a first-aid course (contact the Red Cross or St John's Ambulance) or attend a remote-medicine first-aid course, such as that offered by the **Royal Geographical Society** (www.wilderness medicaltraining.co.uk).

If you're bringing medications with you, carry them in their original containers, clearly labelled. A signed and dated letter from your physician describing all medical conditions and medications, including generic names, is also a good idea. If you're carrying syringes or needles be sure to have a physician's letter documenting their medical necessity.

## Insurance

Medical insurance is crucial, but policies differ. Check that the policy includes all the activities you want to do. Some specifically exclude 'dangerous activities' such as white-water rafting, rock climbing and motorcycling. Sometimes even trekking is excluded. Also find out whether your insurance will make payments directly to providers or will reimburse you later for overseas health expenditures (in Ethiopia, Djibouti and Somaliland many doctors expect payment in cash).

Ensure that your travel insurance will cover the emergency transport required to get you to a hospital in a major city, to better medical facilities elsewhere in Africa, or all the way home, by air and with a medical attendant if necessary. If you need medical help, your insurance company might be able to help locate the nearest hospital or clinic, or you can ask at your hotel. In an emergency, contact your embassy or consulate.

Membership of the **African Medical & Research Foundation** (Amref; www. amref.org) provides an air evacuation service in medical emergencies in many African countries, including Ethiopia and Djibouti. It also provides air-ambulance transfers between medical facilities. Money paid by members for this service goes into providing grass-roots medical assistance for local people.

## Recommended Vaccinations

The **World Health Organization** (www.who.int) recommends that all travellers be covered for diphtheria, tetanus, measles, mumps, rubella and polio, as well as for hepatitis B, regardless of their destination. The consequences of these diseases can be severe, and outbreaks of them do occur.

According to the **Centers for Disease Control & Prevention** (www.cdc.gov), the following vaccinations are recommended for all parts of Africa: hepatitis A, hepatitis B, meningococcal meningitis, rabies and typhoid, and boosters for tetanus, diphtheria and measles. Proof of yellow-fever vaccination is mandatory for travel to Ethiopia. Depending on where you've travelled from, cholera vaccination may also be required.

## Medical Checklist

It's a very good idea to carry a medical and first-aid kit with you, to help yourself in the case of minor illness or injury. Following is a list of items you should consider packing.

» Acetaminophen (paracetamol) or aspirin
» Acetazolamide (Diamox) for altitude sickness (prescription only)
» Adhesive or paper tape
» Antibacterial ointment (eg Bactroban) for cuts and abrasions (prescription only)
» Antibiotics (see your medical-health professional for the most useful ones to bring)
» Antidiarrhoeal drugs (eg loperamide)
» Antihistamines (for hay-fever and allergic reactions)
» Anti-inflammatory drugs (eg ibuprofen)
» Antimalaria pills
» Bandages, gauze, gauze rolls

» DEET-containing insect repellent for the skin
» Iodine tablets (for water purification)
» Oral rehydration salts
» Permethrin-containing insect spray for clothing, tents, and bed nets
» Pocket knife
» Scissors, safety pins, tweezers
» Sterile needles, syringes and fluids if travelling to remote areas
» Steroid cream or hydrocortisone cream (for allergic rashes)
» Sunblock
» Syringes and sterile needles
» Thermometer

Since falciparum malaria predominates in Ethiopia, consider taking a self-diagnostic kit that can identify malaria in the blood from a finger prick.

## Internet Resources

There's a wealth of travel-health advice on the internet. For further information, lonely planet.com is a good place to start. The World Health Organization publishes a superb book called *International Travel and Health*, which is revised annually and is available online at no cost at www.who.int/ith. Other websites of general interest:

**Centers for Disease Control and Prevention** (www.cdc.gov)
**Fit for Travel** (www.fitfor travel.scot.nhs.uk) Up-to-date information about outbreaks and is very user-friendly for travellers on the road.
**MD Travel Health** (www. mdtravelhealth.com) Provides complete travel health recommendations for every country, updated daily, at no cost.

It's also a good idea to consult your government's travel

health website before departure, if one is available.
**Australia** (www.dfat.gov.au/travel)
**Canada** (www.hc-sc.gc.ca/english/index.html)
**UK** (www.doh.gov.uk/travel advice/index.htm)
**USA** (www.cdc.gov/travel)

## Further Reading

» *A Comprehensive Guide to Wilderness and Travel Medicine* by Eric A Weiss (1998)
» *Healthy Travel* by Jane Wilson-Howarth (1999)
» *Healthy Travel Africa* by Isabelle Young (2000)
» *How to Stay Healthy Abroad* by Richard Dawood (2002)
» *Travel in Health* by Graham Fry (1994)
» *Travel with Children* by Cathy Lanigan (2004)

# IN TRANSIT

## Deep Vein Thrombosis (DVT)

Blood clots can form in the legs during flights, chiefly because of prolonged immobility. This formation of clots is known as deep vein thrombosis (DVT), and the longer the flight, the greater the risk. Although most blood clots are reabsorbed uneventfully, some might break off and travel through the blood vessels to the lungs, where they could cause life-threatening complications.

The chief symptom of DVT is swelling or pain of the foot, ankle or calf, usually but not always on just one side. When a blood clot travels to the lungs, it could cause chest pain and breathing difficulty. Travellers with any of these symptoms should immediately seek medical attention.

To prevent the development of DVT on long flights

you should walk about the cabin, perform isometric compressions of the leg muscles (ie contract the leg muscles while sitting), drink plenty of fluids, and avoid alcohol.

# IN ETHIOPIA, DJIBOUTI & SOMALILAND

## Availability & Cost of Health Care

Health care in Ethiopia, Djibouti and Somaliland is varied: Addis Ababa, Djibouti City and Hargeisa have good facilities with well-trained doctors and nurses, but outside the capitals health care is patchy at best. Medicine and even sterile dressings and intravenous fluids might need to be purchased from a local pharmacy by patients or their relatives. The standard of dental care is equally variable, and there's an increased risk of hepatitis B and HIV transmission via poorly sterilised equipment. By and large, public hospitals in the region offer the cheapest service, but will have the least up-to-date equipment and medications; mission hospitals (where donations are the usual form of payment) often have more reasonable facilities; and private hospitals and clinics are more expensive but tend to have more advanced drugs and equipment and better trained medical staff.

Most drugs can be purchased over the counter in the region, without a prescription. Try to visit a pharmacy rather than a 'drug shop' or 'rural drug vendor', as they're the only ones with trained pharmacists who can offer educated advice. Many drugs for sale in Africa might be ineffective: they might be counterfeit or might not have been stored under the right conditions. The most common examples of counterfeit drugs are malaria tablets and expensive antibiotics, such as ciprofloxacin. Most drugs are available in larger towns, but remote villages will be lucky to have a couple of paracetamol tablets. It's strongly recommended that all drugs for chronic diseases be brought from home.

Although condoms are readily available (sometimes boxes – yes boxes! – are in hotel rooms), their efficacy cannot be relied upon, so bring all the contraception you'll need. Condoms bought in Africa might not be of the same quality as in Europe or Australia, and they might have been incorrectly stored.

There's a high risk of contracting HIV from infected blood if you receive a blood transfusion in the region. The **BloodCare Foundation** (www.bloodcare.org.uk) is a useful source of safe, screened blood, which can be transported to any part of the world within 24 hours.

# Infectious Diseases

It's a formidable list but, as we say, a few precautions go a long way...

## Cholera

Cholera is usually only a problem during natural or artificial disasters, eg war, floods or earthquakes, although small outbreaks can also occur at other times. Travellers are rarely affected. It's caused by a bacteria and spread via contaminated drinking water. The main symptom is profuse watery diarrhoea, which causes debilitation if fluids are not replaced quickly. An oral cholera vaccine is available in the USA, but it's not particularly effective. Most cases of cholera could be avoided by close attention to good drinking water and by avoiding potentially contaminated food. Treatment is by fluid replacement (orally or via a drip), but sometimes antibiotics are needed. Self-treatment isn't advised.

## Dengue Fever (Break-Bone Fever)

Spread through the bite of the mosquito, dengue fever causes a feverish illness with headache and muscle pains similar to those experienced with a bad, prolonged attack of influenza. There might be a rash. Mosquito bites should be avoided whenever possible. Self-treatment: paracetamol and rest. Aspirin should be avoided.

## Diphtheria

Found in all of Africa, diphtheria is spread through close respiratory contact. It usually causes a temperature and a severe sore throat. Sometimes a membrane forms across the throat, and a tracheotomy is needed to prevent suffocation. Vaccination is recommended for those likely to be in close contact with the local population in infected areas. More important for long stays than for short-term trips. The vaccine is given as an injection alone or with tetanus, and lasts 10 years.

## Filariasis

Tiny worms migrating in the lymphatic system cause filariasis. The bite from an infected mosquito spreads the infection. Symptoms include localised itching and swelling of the legs and/or genitalia. Treatment is available.

## Hepatitis A

Hepatitis A is spread through contaminated food (particularly shellfish) and water. It causes jaundice and, although it's rarely fatal, it can cause prolonged lethargy and delayed recovery. If you've had hepatitis A, you shouldn't drink alcohol for up to six months afterwards, but once you've recovered, there won't be any long-term problems. The first symptoms include dark urine and a yellow colour to the whites of the eyes. Sometimes a fever and abdominal pain might be present. Hepatitis A vaccine (Avaxim, VAQTA, Havrix) is given as an injection: a single dose will give protection for up to a year, and a booster after a year gives 10-year protection. Hepatitis A and typhoid vaccines can also be given as a single-dose vaccine, hepatyrix or viatim.

## Hepatitis B

Hepatitis B is spread through infected blood, contaminated needles and sexual intercourse. It can also be spread from an infected mother to the baby during childbirth. It affects the liver, causing jaundice and occasionally liver failure. Most people recover completely, but some people might be chronic carriers of the virus, which could lead eventually to cirrhosis or liver cancer. Those visiting high-risk areas for long periods or those with increased social or occupational risk should be immunised.

Many countries now give hepatitis B as part of the routine childhood vaccinations. It's given singly or can be given at the same time as hepatitis A (hepatyrix). A course will give protection for at least five years. It can be given over four weeks or six months.

## HIV

HIV, the virus that causes AIDS, is an enormous problem throughout Ethiopia and Djibouti. It's also an issue in Somaliland, though on a smaller scale. The virus is spread through infected blood and blood products, by sexual intercourse with an infected partner and from an infected mother to her baby during childbirth and breast-feeding. It can be spread through 'blood to blood' contacts, such as with contaminated instruments during medical, dental, acupuncture and other body-piercing procedures, and through sharing used intravenous needles. At present there's no cure;

medication that might keep the disease under control is available, but these drugs are too expensive for the overwhelming majority of Africans, and are not readily available for travellers either. If you think you might have been infected with HIV, a blood test is necessary; a three-month gap after exposure and before testing is required to allow antibodies to appear in the blood.

## Leishmaniasis

This is spread through the bite of an infected sandfly. It can cause a slowly growing skin lump or ulcer (the cutaneous form) and sometimes a life-threatening fever with anaemia and weight loss. Dogs can also be carriers of the infection. Sandfly bites should be avoided whenever possible.

## Leptospirosis

It's spread through the excreta of infected rodents, especially rats. It can cause hepatitis and renal failure, which might be fatal. It's unusual for travellers to be affected unless living in poor sanitary conditions. It causes a fever and sometimes jaundice.

## Malaria

Malaria is a serious problem in Ethiopia, with one to two million new cases reported each year. Though malaria is generally absent at altitudes above 1800m, epidemics have occurred in areas above 2000m in Ethiopia. The central plateau, Addis Ababa, the Bale and Simien Mountains, and most of the northern Historical Circuit are usually considered safe areas, but they're not risk-free.

For short-term visitors, it's probably wise to err on the side of caution. If you're thinking of travelling outside these areas, you shouldn't think twice – take prophylactics.

Self-treatment: see standby treatment if you're more than 24 hours away from medical help.

### CAUSE

The disease is caused by a parasite in the bloodstream spread via the bite of the female Anopheles mosquito. There are several types of malaria – falciparum malaria is the most dangerous type and makes up 70% of the cases in Ethiopia. Infection rates vary with season and climate, so check out the situation before departure. Unlike most other diseases regularly encountered by travellers, there's no vaccination against malaria (yet). However, several different drugs are used to prevent malaria, and new ones are in the pipeline. Up-to-date advice from a travel-health clinic is essential as some medication is more suitable for some travellers than others. The pattern of drug-resistant malaria is changing rapidly, so what was advised several years ago might no longer be the case.

### SYMPTOMS

Malaria can present in several ways. The early stages include headaches, fevers, generalised aches and pains, and malaise, which could be mistaken for flu. Other symptoms can include abdominal pain, diarrhoea and a cough. Anyone who develops a fever in a malarial area should assume they have a malarial infection until a blood test proves negative, even if they have been taking antimalarial medication. If not treated, the next stage could develop within 24 hours, particularly if falciparum malaria is the parasite: jaundice, then reduced consciousness and coma (also known as cerebral malaria) followed by death. Treatment in hospital is essential, and the death rate might still be as high as 10%, even in the best intensive-care facilities in the country.

### MEDICATION

Many travellers are under the impression that malaria is a mild illness, that treatment is always easy and successful, and that taking antimalarial drugs causes more illness through side effects than actually getting malaria. In Africa, this is unfortunately not true. Side effects of the medication depend on the drug being taken. Doxycycline can cause heartburn, indigestion and increased sensitivity to sunlight; mefloquine (Larium) can cause anxiety attacks, insomnia and nightmares, and (rarely) severe psychiatric disorders; chloroquine can cause nausea and hair loss; and atovaquone and proguanil hydrochloride (malarone) can cause diarrhoea, abdominal pain and mouth ulcers.

These side effects are not universal, and can be minimised by taking medication correctly, eg with food. Also, some people should not take a particular antimalarial drug, eg people with epilepsy should avoid mefloquine, and doxycycline should not be taken by pregnant women or children younger than 12.

If you decide that you really do not wish to take antimalarial drugs, you must understand the risks, and be obsessive about avoiding mosquito bites. Use nets and insect repellent, and report any fever or flulike symptoms to a doctor as soon as possible. Some people advocate homeopathic preparations against malaria, such as Demal200, but as yet there's no conclusive evidence that this is effective, and many homeopaths don't recommend their use.

**STAND-BY TREATMENT**

If you're planning a journey through a malarial area, particularly where falciparum malaria predominates, consider taking stand-by treatment. Emergency stand-by treatment should be seen as emergency treatment aimed at saving the patient's life and not as routine self-medication. It should be used only if you'll be far from medical facilities and have been advised about the symptoms of malaria and how to use the medication. Medical advice should be sought as soon as possible to confirm whether the treatment has been successful.

The type of stand-by treatment used will depend on local conditions, such as drug resistance, and on what antimalarial drugs were being used before stand-by treatment. This is worthwhile because you want to avoid contracting a particularly serious form such as cerebral malaria, which affects the brain and central nervous system and can be fatal in 24 hours. As mentioned earlier, self-diagnostic kits, which can identify malaria in the blood from a finger prick, are also available in the West.

## Meningococcal Meningitis

Meningococcal infection is spread through close respiratory contact and is more likely in crowded situations, such as buses. Infection is uncommon in travellers. Vaccination is recommended for long stays and is especially important towards the end of the dry season. Symptoms include a fever, severe headache, neck stiffness and a red rash. Immediate medical treatment is necessary.

The ACWY vaccine is recommended for all travellers in sub-Saharan Africa. This vaccine is different from the meningococcal meningitis C vaccine given to children and adolescents in some countries; it's safe to be given both types of vaccine.

## Onchocerciasis (River Blindness)

This is caused by the larvae of a tiny worm, which is spread by the bite of a small fly. The earliest sign of infection is intensely itchy, red, sore eyes. Travellers are rarely severely affected. Treatment in a specialised clinic is curative.

## Poliomyelitis

Generally spread through contaminated food and water. It's one of the vaccines given in childhood and should be boosted every 10

## THE ANTIMALARIAL A TO D

» A – Awareness of the risk. No medication is totally effective, but protection of up to 95% is achievable with most drugs, as long as other measures have been taken.

» B – Bites are to be avoided at all costs. Sleep in a screened room, use a mosquito spray or coils, sleep under a permethrin-impregnated net at night. Cover up at night with long trousers and long sleeves, preferably with permethrin-treated clothing. Apply appropriate repellent to all areas of exposed skin in the evenings.

» C – Chemical prevention (ie antimalarial drugs) is usually needed in malarial areas. Expert advice is needed as resistance patterns can change, and new drugs are in development. Not all antimalarial drugs are suitable for everyone. Most antimalarial drugs need to be started at least a week in advance and continued for four weeks after the last possible exposure to malaria.

» D – Diagnosis. If you have a fever or flulike illness within a year of travel to a malarial area, malaria is a possibility, and immediate medical attention is necessary.

years, either orally (a drop on the tongue) or as an injection. Polio can be carried asymptomatically (ie showing no symptoms) and could cause a transient fever. In rare cases it causes weakness or paralysis of one or more muscles, which might be permanent.

## Rabies

Rabies is spread by receiving the bites or licks of an infected animal on broken skin. It's always fatal once the clinical symptoms start (which might be up to several months after an infected bite), so postbite vaccination should be given as soon as possible. Postbite vaccination (whether or not you've been vaccinated before the bite) prevents the virus from spreading to the central nervous system. Animal handlers should be vaccinated, as should those travelling to remote areas where a reliable source of postbite vaccine isn't available within 24 hours. Three preventive injections are needed over a month. If you have not been vaccinated you'll need a course of five injections starting 24 hours or as soon as possible after the injury. If you have been vaccinated, you'll need fewer postbite injections, and have more time to seek medical help.

## Schistosomiasis (Bilharzia)

This disease is spread by flukes (minute worms) that are carried by a species of freshwater snail. The flukes are carried inside the snail, which then sheds them into slow-moving or still water. The parasites penetrate human skin during paddling or swimming and then migrate to the bladder or bowel. They're passed out via stool or urine and could contaminate fresh water, where the cycle starts again. Paddling or swimming in suspect freshwater lakes or slow-running rivers should be

avoided. There might be no symptoms; there might be a transient fever and rash; and advanced cases might have blood in the stool or in the urine. A blood test can detect antibodies if you might have been exposed, and treatment is then possible in specialist travel or infectious-disease clinics. If not treated the infection can cause kidney failure or permanent bowel damage. It's not possible for you to infect others.

## Tuberculosis (TB)

TB is spread through close respiratory contact and occasionally through infected milk or milk products. BCG vaccination is recommended for those likely to be mixing closely with the local population, although it gives only moderate protection against TB. It's more important for long stays than for short-term stays. Inoculation with the BCG vaccine isn't available in all countries. It's given routinely to many children in developing countries. The vaccination causes a small permanent scar at the site of injection, and is usually given in a specialised chest clinic. It's a live vaccine and should not be given to pregnant women or immunocompromised individuals.

TB can be asymptomatic, only being picked up on a routine chest X-ray. Alternatively, it can cause a cough, weight loss or fever, sometimes months or even years after exposure.

## Trypanosomiasis (Sleeping Sickness)

Spread via the bite of the tsetse fly. It causes a headache, fever and eventually coma. There's an effective treatment.

## Typhoid

This is spread through food or water contaminated by infected human faeces. The first symptom is usually a fever or a pink rash on the abdomen. Sometimes septicaemia (blood poisoning)

can occur. A typhoid vaccine (typhim Vi, typherix) will give protection for three years. In some countries, the oral vaccine Vivotif is also available. Antibiotics are usually given as treatment, and death is rare unless septicaemia occurs.

## Yellow Fever

Yellow fever is spread by infected mosquitoes. Symptoms range from a flu-like illness to severe hepatitis (liver inflammation), jaundice and death. The yellow-fever vaccination must be given at a designated clinic and is valid for 10 years. It's a live vaccine and must not be given to immunocompromised or pregnant travellers.

Travellers must carry a certificate as evidence of vaccination to obtain a visa for Ethiopia. You may also have to present it at immigration upon arrival. There's always the possibility that a traveller without a legally required, up-to-date certificate will be vaccinated and detained in isolation at the port of arrival for up to 10 days or possibly repatriated.

## Travellers' Diarrhoea

Although it's not inevitable that you'll get diarrhoea while travelling in the Horn, it's certainly very likely. Diarrhoea is the most common travel-related illness: figures suggest that at least half of all travellers will get diarrhoea at some stage. Sometimes dietary changes, such as increased spices or oils, are the cause. To help prevent diarrhoea, avoid tap water. You should also only eat fresh fruits or vegetables if cooked or peeled, and be wary of dairy products that might contain unpasteur-ised milk. Although freshly cooked food can often be a safe option, plates or serving utensils might be dirty, so you should be highly selec-tive when eating food from street vendors (make sure that cooked food is piping hot all the way through).

If you develop diarrhoea, be sure to drink plenty of fluids, preferably an oral rehydration solution contain-ing water (lots), and some salt and sugar. A few loose stools don't require treat-ment, but if you start having more than four or five stools a day you should start tak-ing an antibiotic (usually a quinoline drug, such as cip-rofloxacin or norfloxacin) and an antidiarrhoeal agent (such as loperamide) if you're not within easy reach of a toilet. If diarrhoea is bloody, per-sists for more than 72 hours or is accompanied by fever, shaking chills or severe ab-dominal pain, seek medical attention.

## Amoebic Dysentery

Contracted by eating con-taminated food and water, amoebic dysentery causes blood and mucus in the faeces. It can be relatively mild and tends to come on gradually, but seek medical advice if you think you have the illness as it won't clear up without treatment (which is with specific antibiotics).

## Giardiasis

This, like amoebic dysentery, is also caused by ingesting contaminated food or water. The illness usually appears a week or more after you have been exposed to the offend-ing parasite. Giardiasis might cause only a short-lived bout of typical travellers' diar-rhoea, but it can also cause persistent diarrhoea. Ideally, seek medical advice if you suspect you have giardiasis.

# Environmental Hazards

## Heat Exhaustion

This condition occurs fol-lowing heavy sweating and excessive fluid loss with inadequate replacement of fluids and salt, and is particu-larly common in hot climates when taking unaccustomed exercise before full acclima-tisation. Symptoms include headache, dizziness and tiredness. Dehydration is al-ready happening by the time you feel thirsty; aim to drink sufficient water to produce pale, diluted urine.

Self-treatment: fluid re-placement with water and/or fruit juice, and cooling by cold water and fans. The treatment of the salt-loss component consists of consuming salty fluids as in soup, and adding a little more table salt to foods than usual.

## Heatstroke

Heat exhaustion is a precursor to the much more serious condition of heatstroke. In this case there's damage to the sweating mechanism, with an excessive rise in body temperature; irrational and hyperactive behaviour; and eventually loss of conscious-ness and death. Rapid cool-ing by spraying the body with water and fanning is ideal. Emergency fluid and electro-lyte replacement is usually also required by intravenous drip.

## Insect Bites & Stings

Mosquitoes might not always carry malaria or dengue fever, but they (and other insects) can cause irritation and in-fected bites. To avoid these, take the same precautions as you would for avoiding ma-laria. Use DEET-based insect repellents. Excellent clothing treatments are also available; mosquitoes that land on treated clothing will die.

Bee and wasp stings cause real problems only to those who have a severe allergy to the stings (anaphy-laxis). If you're one of these people, carry an 'epipen': an adrenaline (epinephrine) injection, which you can give yourself. This could save your life.

Scorpions are frequently found in arid or dry climates. They can cause a painful bite that is sometimes life-threatening. If bitten by a scorpion, take a painkiller. Medical treatment should be sought if collapse occurs.

Fleas and bed bugs are often found in cheap hotels. Fleas are also common on lo-cal and long-distance buses and in the rugs of some remote churches. They lead to very itchy, lumpy bites. Spraying the mattress with crawling-insect killer after removing bedding will get rid of them.

Scabies is also frequently found in cheap accommoda-tion. These tiny mites live in the skin, particularly between the fingers. They cause an in-tensely itchy rash. The itch is easily treated with malathion and permethrin lotion from a pharmacy; other members of the household also need treating to avoid spreading scabies, even if they do not show any symptoms.

## Snake Bites

Basically, do all you can to avoid getting bitten! Do not walk barefoot, or stick your hand into holes or cracks. However, 50% of people bitten by venomous snakes are not actually injected with poison (envenomed). If you are bitten by a snake, do not panic. Immobilise the bitten limb with a splint (such as a stick) and apply a band-age over the site, with firm pressure, similar to bandag-ing a sprain. Do not apply a tourniquet, or try to cut or suck the bite. Get medical help as soon as possible so you can get treated with an antivenene if necessary.

## Water

Never drink tap water unless it has been boiled, filtered or chemically disinfected (such as with iodine tablets). Never drink from streams, rivers and lakes. It's also best to avoid drinking from pumps and wells: some do bring pure water to the surface, but the presence of animals can still contaminate supplies.

Bottled water is available everywhere, though it's better for the environment if you treat/filter local water.

## WANT MORE?

For in-depth language information and handy phrases, check out Lonely Planet's *Ethiopian Amharic Phrasebook*. You'll find it at **shop.lonelyplanet.com**, or you can buy Lonely Planet's iPhone phrasebooks at the Apple App Store.

# Language

Amharic is Ethiopia's national language. It belongs to the Semitic language group of the Afro-Asiatic language family, along with Arabic, Hebrew and Assyrian.

While regional languages such as Oromo, Somali and Tigrinya are also important, Amharic is the most widely used and understood language throughout the country. It is the mother tongue of the 12 million or so Amhara people in the country's central and north-western regions, and a second language for about one third of the total population.

If you read our pronunciation guides as if they were English, you'll be understood. The apostrophe ( ' ) before a vowel indicates a glottal stop, which sounds like the pause in the middle of 'uh-oh'. Amharic's 'glottalised' consonants (ch', k', p', s' and t' in our pronunciation guides), are pronounced by tightening and releasing the vocal cords, a bit like combining the sound with the glottal stop. Note also that ai is pronounced as in 'aisle', ee as in 'see', ow as in 'now', uh as the 'a' in 'ago', ny as in 'canoyn', sh as in 'shot', zh as the 's' in 'pleasure', and that r is trilled.

Amharic word endings vary according to the gender and number of people you're speaking to. Gender is indicated in this chapter where relevant by the abbreviations 'm' (for speaking to a male) and 'f' (for addressing a female).

## BASICS

| | | |
|---|---|---|
| Hello. | ሰላም | suh·lam |
| Goodbye. | ደህና ሁን | duh·na hun (m) |
| | ደህና ሁኚ | duh·na hun·yee (f) |
| Yes. | አዎ | 'a·wo |
| No. | አይደለም· | 'ai·duh·luhm |
| Please. | እባክህ | 'i·ba·kih (m) |
| | እባክሽ | 'i·ba·kish·(f) |
| Thank you. | አመሰግናለሁ | 'a·muh·suh·gi·na·luh·hu |
| Sorry. | ይቅር | yi·k'ir·ta |

### How are you?

| | |
|---|---|
| እንዴት ነህ? | 'in·det nuh·hi (m) |
| እንዴት ነሽ? | 'in·det nuhsh (f) |

### Fine, and you?

| | |
|---|---|
| ይመስገነው | yi·muhs·guh·nuhw |
| አንተስ/አንቺስ? | 'an·tuhs/'an·chees (m/f) |

### What's your name?

| | |
|---|---|
| ማን ትባላለህ? | man ti·ba·la·luh (m) |
| ማን ትባያለሽ? | man ti·ba·ya·luhsh (f) |

### My name's ...

| | |
|---|---|
| ... ነኝ | ... nuhny |

### Do you speak English?

| | |
|---|---|
| እንግሊዘኛ | 'in·glee·zuh·nya |
| ትችላለህ/ | ti·chi·la·luh·hi/ |
| ትችያለሽ? | ti·chia·luhsh (m/f) |

### I don't understand.

| | |
|---|---|
| አልገባኝም | 'al·guh·bany·mi |

### Can I take a photo (of you)?

| | |
|---|---|
| ፎቶ ላነሳ(ህ)/ | fo·to la·nuh·sa(h)/ |
| ላነሳ(ሽ) | la·nuh·sa(sh) |
| እችላለሁ? | 'i·chi·la·luh·hu (m/f) |

## ACCOMMODATION

**Can you recommend somewhere (cheap/good)?**

| | | |
|---|---|---|
| (ርካሽ/ጥሩ) ቦታ | ri·kash/t'i·ru) bo·ta |
| ልታጠቁመኝ | li·ti·t'uh·k'u·muhny |
| ትችላለህ/ | ti·chi·la·luh·hi/ |
| ትችያለሽ? | ti·chi·ya·luhsh (m/f) |

| **Where's a ...?** | ... የት ነው? | ... yuht nuhw |
|---|---|---|
| campsite | የድንኩዋኑ ቦታ | yuh·din·ku·wa·nu bo·ta |
| guesthouse | የእንግዳ ማረፊያ | yuh·'in·gi·da ma·ruh·fee·ya |
| hotel | ሆቴሉ | ho·te·lu |
| youth hostel | ሆስቴሉ | hos·te·lu |

| **Do you have a ... room?** | ... ክፍል አላችሁ? | ... ki·fil 'a·la·chi·hu |
|---|---|---|
| single | አንድ | and |
| double | ሁለት | hu·luht |
| twin | ሁለት አልጋ ያለው | hu·luht 'al·ga ya·luhw |

**How much is it per night/person?**

በቀን/በሰው ዋጋው ስንት ነው? — buh·k'uhn/buh·suhw wa·gow sint nuhw

## DIRECTIONS

| **Where's the (nearest) ...?** | (ቅርብ) ያለ ... የት ነው? | (k'irb) ya·luh ... yuht nuhw |
|---|---|---|
| internet cafe | ኢንተርኔት ካፌ | 'een·tuhr·net ka·fe |
| market | ገበያ | guh·buh·ya |

**Is this the road to (the museum)?**

ይህ መንገድ ወደ (ሙዚየም) ይወስዳል? — yih muhn·guhd wuh·duh (mu·zee·yuhm) yi·wuhs·dal

**Can you show me (on the map)?**

(ካርታ ላይ) ልታሳየኝ ትችላለህ/ ትችያለሽ? — (kar·ta lai) li·ta·sa·yuhny ti·chi·la·luh/ ti·chi·ya·luhsh (m/f)

**What's the address?**

አድራሻው የት ነው? — 'ad·ra·show yuht nuhw

**How far is it?**

ምን ያህል ይርቃል? — min yahl yir·k'al

**How do I get there?**

እዚያ እንዴት መሄድ ይቻላል? — 'i·zee·ya 'in·det muh·hed yi·cha·lal

### Numbers

Although there are Amharic script numerals, Arabic numerals (ie those used in English) are now commonly used in writing throughout Ethiopia. Amharic words are used to refer to numbers in speech.

| 1 | አንድ | and |
|---|---|---|
| 2 | ሁለት | hu·luht |
| 3 | ሶስት | sost |
| 4 | አራት | 'ar·at |
| 5 | አምስት | 'am·mist |
| 6 | ስድስት | si·dist |
| 7 | ሰባት | suh·bat |
| 8 | ስምንት | si·mint |
| 9 | ዘጠኝ | zuh·t'uhny |
| 10 | አስር | a·sir |
| 20 | ሃያ | ha·ya |
| 30 | ሰላሳ | suh·la·sa |
| 40 | አርባ | 'ar·ba |
| 50 | ሃምሳ | ham·sa |
| 60 | ስልሳ | sil·sa |
| 70 | ሰባ | suh·ba |
| 80 | ሰማንያ | suh·ma·nia |
| 90 | ዘጠና | zuh·t'uh·na |
| 100 | መቶ | muh·to |
| 1000 | ሺ | shee |

**Turn left/right.**

ወደ ግራ/ቀኝ ታጠፍ — wuh·duh gi·ra/k'uhny ta·t'uhf

| **It's ...** | ... ነው | ... nuhw |
|---|---|---|
| behind ... | ... ከጀርባ | ... kuh·juhr·ba |
| in front of ... | ... ፊት ለፊት | ... feet luh·feet |
| near ... | ... አጠገብ | ... 'a·t'uh·guhb |
| next to ... | ... ቀጥሎ | ... k'uh·t'i·lo |
| on the corner | መታጠፊያው ላይ | muh·ta·t'uh·fee·yow lai |
| opposite ... | ... ትይዩ | ... ti·yi·yu |
| straight ahead | ቀጥታ | k'uh·t'i·ta |
| there | እዚያ | 'i·zee·ya |

# EATING & DRINKING

| Can you | ጥሩ ... | t'i·ru ... |
| recommend | ልትጠቁመኝ | li·ti·t'uh·k'u·muhny |
| a ...? | ትችላለህ? | ti·chi·la·luh |
| bar | ቡና ቤት | bu·na bet |
| dish | ምግብ | mi·gib |
| place to eat | ምግብ ቤት | mi·gib bet |

Do you have vegetarian food?
የጾም ምግብ    yuh·s'om mi·gib
አላችሁ?    'a·la·chi·hu

Could you prepare a meal without (eggs)?
ምግብ ያለ (እንቁላል)    mi·gib ya·luh ('in·k'u·lal)
ልታዘጋጂልኝ    li·ta·zuh·ga·jee·lin
ትችያለሽ?    ti·chi·ya·luhsh (f)
ምግብ ያለ (እንቁላል)    mi·gib ya·luh ('in·k'u·lal)
ልታዘጋጅልኝ    li·ta·zuh·gaj·lin
ትችላለህ?    ti·chi·la·luh·hi (m)

| I'd like ..., | እባክህ/ | 'i·ba·kih/ |
| please. | እባክሽ ... | 'i·ba·kish ... |
| | እፈልጋለሁ· | 'i·fuh·li·ga·luh·hu (m/f) |
| a table for | ጠረጴዛ | t'uh·ruh·p'e·za |
| (two) | (ለሁ·ለት) | (luh·hu·luht) |
| | ሰው | suhw |
| that dish | ያንን ምግብ | ya·nin mi·gib |
| the bill | ቢል | beel |
| the menu | ሜኑ | me·nu |

| coffee ... | ቡና ... | bu·na ... |
| tea ... | ሻይ ... | shai ... |
| with milk | በወተት | buh·wuh·tuht |
| without | ያለ | ya·luh |
| sugar | ስኩዋር | si·ku·war |

| beer | ቢራ | bee·ra |
| bottle | ጠርሙ·ስ | t'uhr·mus |
| breakfast | ቁርስ | k'urs |

| cold | ጉንፋን | gun·fan |
| dairy | የወተት | yuh·wuh·tuht |
| products | ተዋጽኦ | tuh·wa·s'i·'o |
| dinner | እራት | i·rat |
| drink | መጠጥ | muh·t'uht' |
| fish | አሳ | 'a·sa |
| food | ምግብ | mi·gib |
| fork | ሹካ | shu·ka |
| fruit | ፍራፍሬ | fi·ra·fi·re |
| glass | ብርጭቆ | bir·ch'i·k'o |
| gluten | አንጸባራቂ | 'an·s'uh·ba·ra·k'ee |
| hot | ሙ·ቅ | muk' |
| knife | ቢላዋ | bee·la·wa |
| lunch | ምሳ | mi·sa |
| meat | ስጋ | si·ga |
| nuts | አቾሎኒ | 'o·cho·lo·nee |
| plate | ሳህን | sa·hin |
| restaurant | ሬስቶራንት | res·to·rant |
| seafood | የባህር | yuh·ba·hir |
| | ምግቦች | mi·gib·och |
| spoon | ማንኪያ | man·kee·ya |
| vegetable | አትክልት | 'at·kilt |
| waiter | አስተናጋጅ | as·tuh·na·gaj |
| (boiled) | (የፈላ) | (yuh·fuh·la) |
| water | ውሃ | wi·ha |
| wine | ወይን | wuh·yin |
| with | ጋር | gar |
| without | ያለ | ya·luh |

# EMERGENCIES

Help!
እርዳታ እርዳታ!    'ir·da·ta 'ir·da·ta

I'm lost.
ጠፋብኝ    t'uh·fa·biny

Where are the toilets?
ሽንት ቤት የት ነው?    shint bet yuht nuhw

| Call ...! | ... ጥራልኝ | ... t'i·ra·liny (m) |
| | ... ጥሪልኝ | ... t'i·ree·liny (f) |
| a doctor | ዶክተር | dok·tuhr |
| an ambulance | አምቡላንስ | 'am·bu·lans |
| the police | ፖ·ሊስ | po·lees |

## Question Words

| when | መቼ | muh·che |
| where | የት | yuht |
| who | ማን | man |
| why | ለምን | luh·min |

| My ... was/ | የኔ ... | yuh·ne ... |
| were stolen. | ተሰረቀ | tuh·suh·ruh·k'uh |
| bags | ሻንጣ | shan·t'a |
| credit card | ክሬዲት ካርድ | ki·re·deet kard |
| handbag | የጅ ቦርሳ | yuhj bor·sa |
| money | ገንዘብ | guhn·zuhb |
| passport | ፓስፖርት | pas·port |
| wallet | የኪስ ቦርሳ | yuh·kees bor·sa |

**It hurts here.**

| እዚህ ጋ ያመኛል | 'i·zeeh ga ya·muhn·yal |

**I'm allergic to (penicillin).**

| ለ(ፔኒሲሊን) | luh·(pe·nee·see·leen) |
| አለርጂ ነኝ | 'a·luhr·jee nuhny |

| asthma | አስም | as·m |
| constipation | ድርቀት | dir·k'uht |
| diarrhoea | ተቅማጥ | tuh·k'i·mat' |
| fever | ትኩሳት | ti·ku·sat |
| headache | ራስ ምታት | ras mi·tat |
| heart condition | የልብ ሁናቴ | yuh·lib hu·na·te |
| nausea | ማጥወልወል | mat'·wuhl·wuhl |
| pain | ህመም | hi·muhm |
| pregnant | እርጉዝ | 'ir·guz |
| sore throat | የቆሰለ | yuh·k'o·suh·luh |
| | ጉሮሮ | gu·ro·ro |
| toothache | የጥርስ | yuh·t'irs |
| | ህመም | hi·muhm |

# SHOPPING & SERVICES

**I'm looking for ...**

| ... እፈልጋለሁ | ... 'i·fuh·li·ga·luh·hu |

**How much is it?**

| ዋጋው ስንት ነው? | wa·gow sint nuhw |

**Can you write down the price?**

| ዋጋውን ልትጥፍልኝ | wa·gown li·ti·s'if·liny |
| ትችላለህ? | ti·chi·la·luh |

**What's your lowest price?**

| መጨረሻውን | muh·ch'uh·ruh·sha·win |
| ስንት ትለዋለህ? | sint ti·luh·wa·luh·hi |

**I'll give you (five) birr.**

| (አምስት) ብር | ('am·mist) bir |
| እከፍላለሁ | 'i·kuhf·la·luh·hu |

**Do you accept credit cards?**

| ክሬዲት ካርድ | ki·re·deet kard |
| ትቀበላላችሁ? | ti·k'uh·buh·la·la·chi·hu |

**There's a mistake in the bill.**

| ቢሉ ላይ | bee·lu lai |
| ስህተት አለ | sih·tuht 'a·luh |

**I'd like a receipt/refund, please.**

| እባክህ/እባክሽ | i·ba·kih/'i·ba·kish |
| ደረሰኝ/ገንዘቤ | duh·ruh·suhny/guhn·zuh·be |
| እንዲመለስልኝ | 'in·dee·muh·luhs·liny |
| እፈልጋለሁ | 'i·fuh·li·ga·luh·hu (m/f) |

**Can I have my ... repaired?**

| ... ማስጠገን | ... mas·t'uh·guhn |
| እችላለሁ? | 'i·chi·la·luh·hu |

**When will it be ready?**

| መቼ ይደርሳል? | muh·che yi·duhr·sal |

| closed | ዝግ | zig |
| currency | የውጭ | yuh·wich' |
| exchange | ምንዛሪ | mi·ni·za·ree |
| email | ኢ.ሜይል | 'ee·me·yil |
| exchange | የውጭ | yuh·wich' |
| rate | ምንዛሪ ዋጋ | min·za·ree wa·ga |
| open | ክፍት | kift |
| post office | ፖስታ ቤት | pos·ta bet |
| shop | ሱቅ | suk' |
| telephone | ስልክ | silk |
| travel agency | የጉዞ | yuh·gu·zo |
| | ወኪል | wuh·keel |

# TIME & DATES

**What time is it?**

| ስንት ሰአት ነው? | sint suh·'at nuhw |

**It's (two) o'clock.**

| (ስምንት) ሰአት ነው | (si·mint) suh·'at nuhw |

**Quarter past (one).**

| (ሰባት) ከሩብ ነው | (suh·bat) kuh·rub nuhw |

**Half past (one).**

| (ሰባት) ተኩል ነው | (suh·bat) tuh·kul nuhw |

**Quarter to (eight).**

| ለ(ሁለት) ሩብ | luh·(hu·luht) rub |
| ጉዳይ ነው | gu·dai nuhw |

**At what time ...?**

| በስንት ሰአት...? | buh·sint suh·'at ... |

**At ...**

| በ ... | buh ... |

# LANGUAGES OF DJIBOUTI & SOMALILAND

Somaliland's official language is Somali, but English is widely used and will see you through.

Djibouti's languages are Afar, Somali, Arabic and French. In Djibouti town you should also get by with English, and some French basics (included below) might prove helpful too during your visit to this country.

| | | |
|---|---|---|
| **Hello.** | *Bonjour.* | bon·zhoor |
| **Goodbye.** | *Au revoir.* | o·rer·vwa |
| **Excuse me.** | *Excusez-moi.* | ek·skew·zay·mwa |
| **Sorry.** | *Pardon.* | par·don |
| **Yes./No.** | *Oui./Non.* | wee/non |
| **Please.** | *S'il vous plaît.* | seel voo play |
| **Thank you.** | *Merci.* | mair·see |

**Where's ...?**
*Où est ...?* oo ay ...

**What's the address?**
*Quelle est l'adresse?* kel ay la·dres

**Can you show me (on the map)?**
*Pouvez-vous* poo·vay·voo
*m'indiquer* mun·dee·kay
*(sur la carte)?* (sewr la kart)

**Help!**
*Au secours!* o skoor

**I'm lost.**
*Je suis perdu/* zhe swee·
*perdue.* pair·dew (m/f)

**Call a doctor.**
*Appelez un médecin.* a·play un mayd·sun

**Call the police.**
*Appelez la police.* a·play la po·lees

**Where are the toilets?**
*Où sont les toilettes?* oo son lay twa·let

**Can I see the menu, please?**
*Est-ce que je peux voir* es·ker zher per vwar
*la carte, s'il vous plaît?* la kart seel voo play

**What would you recommend?**
*Qu'est-ce que vous* kes·ker voo
*conseillez?* kon·say·yay

**I don't eat ...**
*Je ne mange pas ...* zher ner monzh pa ...

**Please bring the bill.**
*Apportez-moi* a·por·tay·mwa
*l'addition,* la·dee·syon
*s'il vous plaît.* seel voo play

| | | |
|---|---|---|
| **Cheers!** | *Santé!* | son·tay |
| **eat/drink** | *manger/boire* | mon·zhay/bwar |
| **local speciality** | *spécialité locale* | spay·sya·lee·tay lo·kal |
| **market** | *marché* | mar·shay |

**I'd like to buy ...**
*Je voudrais acheter ...* zher voo·dray ash·tay ...

**How much is it?**
*C'est combien?* say kom·byun

**It's too expensive.**
*C'est trop cher.* say tro shair

| | | |
|---|---|---|
| **post office** | *bureau de poste* | bew·ro der post |
| **tourist office** | *office de tourisme* | o·fees der too·rees·mer |
| **morning** | *matin* | ma·tun |
| **afternoon** | *après-midi* | a·pray·mee·dee |
| **evening** | *soir* | swar |
| **yesterday** | *hier* | yair |
| **today** | *aujourd'hui* | o·zhoor·dwee |
| **tomorrow** | *demain* | der·mun |
| **1** | *un* | un |
| **2** | *deux* | der |
| **3** | *trois* | trwa |
| **4** | *quatre* | ka·trer |
| **5** | *cinq* | sungk |
| **6** | *six* | sees |
| **7** | *sept* | set |
| **8** | *huit* | weet |
| **9** | *neuf* | nerf |
| **10** | *dix* | dees |
| **boat** | *bateau* | ba·to |
| **bus** | *bus* | bews |
| **plane** | *avion* | a·vyon |
| **train** | *train* | trun |

**Does it stop at ...?**
*Est-ce qu'il s'arrête à ...?* es·kil sa·ret a ...

**At what time does it leave/arrive?**
*À quelle heure est-ce* a kel er es
*qu'il part/arrive?* kil par/a·reev

**Can you tell me when we get to ...?**
*Pouvez-vous me dire* poo·vay·voo mer deer
*quand nous arrivons à ...?* kon noo za·ree·von a ...

**I want to get off here.**
*Je veux descendre* zher ver day·son·drer
*ici.* ee·see

| morning | ጠዋት | t'uh·wat |
| night | ምሽት | mi·shit |
| today | ዛሬ | za·re |
| tomorrow | ነገ | nuh·guh |
| tonight | ዛሬ ማታ | za·re ma·ta |
| yesterday | ትላንትና | ti·lan·ti·na |
| | | |
| Monday | ሰኞ | suh·nyo |
| Tuesday | ማክሰኞ | mak·suh·nyo |
| Wednesday | ሮብ | rob |
| Thursday | ሀሙስ | ha·mus |
| Friday | ኣርብ | 'a·rib |
| Saturday | ቅዳሜ | k'i·da·me |
| Sunday | እሁድ | 'i·hud |

## TOURS & SIGHTSEEING

| When's the next ...? | የሚቀጥለው ... መቼ ነው? | yuh·mee·k'uh·t'i·luhw ... muh·che nuhw |
| | | |
| day trip | ውሎ ገባ ጉዞ | wi·lo guh·ba gu·zo |
| tour | ሽርሽር | shi·ri·shir |
| | | |
| Is (the) ... included? | ... ይጨምራል? | ... yi·ch'uh·mi·ral |
| | | |
| admission charge | የኣገልግሎት ዋጋን | yuh·'a·guhl·gi·lot wa·gan |
| food | ምግብን | mi·gib·n |
| transport | ትራንስፖርትን | ti·rans·por·tin |

### How long is the tour?
| ሽርሽሩ ምን ያህል ጊዜ ይፈጃል? | shi·ri·shi·ru min ya·hil gee·ze yi·fuh·jal |

### What time should we be back?
| በስንት ሰአት እንመለሳለን? | buh·sint suh·'at 'in·muh·luh·sa·luhn |

| game park | ፓርክ | park |
| guide | መሪ | muh·ree |
| museum | ሙዚየም | mu·zee·yuhm |
| national park | ብሄራዊ ፓርክ | bi·he·ra·wee park |
| palace | ቤተ መንግስት | be·tuh muhn·gist |

## TRANSPORT

| A ... ticket (to Bahir Dar), please. | አንድ ... ትኬት (ወደባህር ዳር) እባክህ/ እባክሽ? | and ... ti·ket (wuh·duh ba·hir dar) 'i·ba·kih/ 'i·ba·kish (m/f) |
| | | |
| one-way (going) | የአንድ ጉዞ (መሄጃ) ብቻ | yuh·and gu·zo (muh·he·ja) bi·cha |
| one-way (returning) | የአንድ ጉዞ (መመለሻ) ብቻ | yuh·and gu·zo (muh·muh· luh·sha) bi·cha |
| return | ደርሶ መልስ | duhr·so muh·lis |
| | | |
| airport | አይሮፕላን ማረፊያ | ai·rop·lan ma·ruh·fee·ya |
| bus stop | ፌርማታ | fer·ma·ta |
| first class | አንደኛ ማእረግ | 'an·duh·nya ma·'i·ruhg |
| train station | ጣቢያ | t'a·bee·ya |
| | | |
| Is this the ... to (Dire Dawa)? | ይህ ... ወደ (ድሬዳዋ) የሚሄደው ነው? | yih ... wuh·duh (di·re da·wa) yuh·mee·he· duhw nuhw |
| boat | ጀልባ | juhl·ba |
| bus | አውቶቢስ | 'ow·to·bees |
| plane | አውሮፕላን | ow·rop·lan |
| train | ባቡር | ba·bur |

### I'd like a smoking/nonsmoking seat, please.
| መቀመጫ የሚጨስበት/ የማይጨስበት ቦታ ጋ እፈልጋለሁ | muh·k'uh·muh·ch'a yuh·mee·ch'uhs·buht/ yuh·mai·ch'uhs·buht bo·ta ga 'i·fuh·li·ga·luh·hu |

### How long does the trip take?
| ጉዞው ምን ያህል ይፈጃል? | gu·zo·wi min ya·hil yi·fuh·jal |

### Is it a direct route?
| ይሄ ዋናው መንገድ ነው? | yi·he wa·now muhn·guhd nuhw |

### How long will it be delayed?
| ምን ያህል ይዘገያል? | min ya·hil yi·zuh·guh·yal |

### How much is it to ...?
| ወደ ... ለመሄድ ዋጋው ስንት ነው? | wuh·duh ... luh·muh·hed wa·gow sint nuhw |

| | | |
|---|---|---|
| **Please take me to (the museum).** | | |
| እባክህ/እባክሽ | 'i·ba·kih/'i·ba·kish | |
| ወደ (ሙ·ዚየም) | wuh·duh (mu·zee·yuhm) | |
| ው·ሰደኝ/ | wi·suh·duhny/ | |
| ው·ሰጂኝ | wi·suh·jeeny (m/f) | |
| **I'd like to hire a car.** | | |
| እባክህ/እባክሽ | 'i·ba·kih/'i·ba·kish | |
| መኪና መከራየት | muh·kee·na muh·kuh·ra·yuht | |
| እፈል.ጋለሁ? | 'i·fuh·li·ga·luh·hu (m/f) | |

| bicycle | ብስክሌት | bisk·let |
|---|---|---|
| brakes (car) | ፍሬን | fi·ren |
| oil (engine) | የሞተር | yuh·mo·tuhr |
| | ዘይት | zuh·yit |
| park (car) | ማቆም | ma·k'om |
| petrol | ቤንዚን | ben·zeen |
| road | መንገድ | muhn·guhd |
| tyre | ጎማ | go·ma |

# GLOSSARY

Ethiopian culinary terms are found in the Ethiopian Cuisine chapter, p259.

**abba** – a prefix used by a priest before his name; means 'father'

**abuna** – archbishop of the Ethiopian Orthodox church, from the *Ge'ez* word meaning 'our father'

**agelgil** – round, leather-bound lunch boxes carried by locals

**amba** (also *emba*) – flat-topped mountain

**azmari** – itinerant minstrel (Ethiopia)

**asmat** secret name of God; if invoked it provides protection from illness and misfortune

**bajaj** –auto-rickshaw

**bet** – Amharic word meaning 'place' that is attached to the end of other words, eg *azmari bet* (Ethiopia)

**buna** – coffee (Ethiopia)

**campement touristique** – traditional huts with shared showers and toilets (Djibouti)

**chat** – mildly intoxicating leaf that's consumed primarily in eastern Ethiopia and Djibouti

**cheka** – home-brewed sorghum beer

**contract taxi** – private, or nonshared, taxi

**Derg** – Socialist military junta that governed Ethiopia from 1974 to 1991; derived from the *Ge'ez* word for 'committee'

**dula** – wooden staff carried by many Ethiopian highlanders

**emba** – see *amba*

**enset** – false-banana tree found in much of southern Ethiopia, used to produce a breadlike staple also known as *enset*

**EPLF** – Eritrean People's Liberation Front; victorious guerrilla army in the 'Struggle for Independence'

**etan** – incense used in coffee ceremonies

**Falasha** – Ethiopian Jew

**faranji** – foreigner, especially Western ones (Ethiopia)

**gada** – age system of male hierarchy among the Oromo

**gari** – horse-drawn cart used for transporting passengers and goods in the towns

**Ge'ez** – a forerunner of modern Amharic

**gegar** – a rectangular, two-storey structure with a flat roof

**genna** – a game like hockey, without boundaries

**gommista** – tyre-repair shop (Italian)

**habesha** – Ethiopian

**injera** – an Ethiopian pancake upon which sits anything from spicy meat stews to colourful dollops of boiled veg and cubes of raw beef

**jile** – the curved knife that is carried by Afar nomads

**katickala** – a distilled alcohol

**Kiddus** – Saint, eg Kiddus Mikael translates to St Michael

**maqdas** – inner sanctuary of a church (holy of holies)

**mesob** – hourglass-shaped woven table from which traditional food is served (Ethiopia)

**qat** – see *chat*

**ras** – title (usually of nobility but given to any outstanding male) similar to duke or prince

**shamma** – a white, light cotton toga

**shifta** – traditionally a rebel

or outlaw; today a bandit or roadside robber

**tabot** – replica of the Ark of the Covenant, kept in the *maqdas* of every Orthodox church

**tankwa** – traditional papyrus boat used on Lake Tana and elsewhere (Ethiopia)

**tef** – an indigenous grass cultivated as a cereal grain; the key ingredient of injera

**tej** – wine made from honey, popular in Ethiopia

**tella** – home-brewed beer made from finger millet, maize or barley, popular in Ethiopia

**tilapia** freshwater fish

**tukul** – traditional cone-shaped hut with thatched roof; like South Africa's rondavel

**wadi** – a river that is usually dry except in the rainy season

**waga** – carved wooden sculptures raised in honour of Konso warriors after their death

**behind the scenes**

## SEND US YOUR FEEDBACK

We love to hear from travellers – your comments keep us on our toes and help make our books better. Our well-travelled team reads every word on what you loved or loathed about this book. Although we cannot reply individually to postal submissions, we always guarantee that your feedback goes straight to the appropriate authors, in time for the next edition. Each person who sends us information is thanked in the next edition – the most useful submissions are rewarded with a selection of digital PDF chapters.

Visit **lonelyplanet.com/contact** to submit your updates and suggestions or to ask for help. Our award-winning website also features inspirational travel stories, news and discussions.

Note: We may edit, reproduce and incorporate your comments in Lonely Planet products such as guidebooks, websites and digital products, so let us know if you don't want your comments reproduced or your name acknowledged. For a copy of our privacy policy visit lonelyplanet.com/privacy.

## OUR READERS

**Many thanks to the travellers who used the last edition and wrote to us with helpful hints, useful advice and interesting anecdotes:**

Justin Ames, Claude Armstrong, Merav Batgil, Patrick Beatty, Fabio Bergamin, Abdiisee Bersissa, Joachim Bertele, Andrzej Bielecki, Piroska Bisits Bullen, Stephanie Bleyer, Bernhard Bouzek, Pankaja Brooke, Yuliono Budianto, Mark Buzinkay, Sergio Cacopardo, Andrew Craig, Nick Crane, Laure Curt, Noah Daniels, Eva-Marije De Boer, Carlo De Pietro, Nadege Debax, Yirmed Demeke, Cornelie Den Outer, Lothar Dieterich, Kay Durden, Jana Ehrler, Heike Faber, Christina Feldt, Georgina Fenton, Daniela Feuchtmayr, Pol Font, Chesney Fowler, Andrew Gebhardt, W Hendricks, Eliza Jarl Estrup, Caley Johnson, David Killick, Dan Klein, Michael Kleiner, Dominika Kratochvilova, Sally May, Colin Mckenna, Markus Merz, Wayne Mikkelsen, Thomas Miller, Emily Milner, Aryk Moore, Eugenia Morlans, Arthur Neslen, Karen Nicholson, Eva-Maria Niedermeier, Karen Obling, Marco Pagliani, Nicolas Pestiau, Jan Polatschek, Yves Ramonet, Karlheinz Rieser, José Luis Romero, Cathy Routhier, Michal Rudziecki, Mridu Thanki, Dana Trytten, Adriana Valencia, Leo Van Riemsdijk, Sara Weisdorf, Chris Weseloh

## AUTHOR THANKS
### Jean-Bernard Carillet

A huge thanks to everyone who made this trip a pure joy, including Dominique, Najiib, Nigel, Mohammed, Ramadan, Adam, Masso, Baragoïta, the two Houmeds, Dimbio, Nicolas and his team, and Vicente – you were all great! At Lonely Planet, a big thanks to Will, Glenn, Annelies, Brigitte and the carto team for their support. I'm also grateful to my fellow authors, Stuart and Tim, for their dedication throughout the process. And, finally, once again a *gros bisou* to Christine and Eva.

### Tim Bewer

Thanks to all the people of Ethiopia who took time to answer my incessant questions. There are too many to thank, but Aseged Alemu, Tony Hickey, Tania O'Connor, Abayneh Temesgen and Dereje Yelma were especially helpful. And to Stuart, Jean-Bernard and Will at Lonely Planet: it was a pleasure, as always. Finally, a special thanks to Cookkai for so many things.

### Stuart Butler

First and foremost I would like to thank my son, Jake, for putting up with his daddy disappearing for so long, and likewise to my wife, Heather, who, being heavily pregnant while I was away, had even more than normal to deal with! Thank you also to Tania O'Connor, Cheru Alemu, Shemels Taye, Abayneh Temesgen, Blen Mandefro, Yasmin Abdulwassie, Pete Diston, Praveen Wignarajah, Teddy Yo, Yoni Yoyi and Barkugura Welerege, and, finally, Toby Adamson for once again enduring the *injera*.

## ACKNOWLEDGMENTS

Climate map data adapted from Peel MC, Finlayson BL & McMahon TA (2007) 'Updated World Map of the Köppen-Geiger Climate Classification', *Hydrology and Earth System Sciences*, 11, 163344.

Cover photograph: Hamer girls, southern Ethiopia, Jesus Jaime Mota/Getty Images ©.

## THIS BOOK

This 5th edition of Lonely Planet's *Ethiopia, Djibouti & Somaliland* guidebook was researched and written by Jean-Bernard Carillet, Tim Bewer and Stuart Butler. The previous edition was written by Jean-Bernard Carillet, Stuart Butler and Dean Starnes, and the 3rd edition was written by Matt Phillips and Jean-Bernard Carillet. This guidebook was commissioned in Lonely Planet's Melbourne office, and produced by the following:

**Commissioning Editors** Will Gourlay, Glenn van der Knijff

**Coordinating Editors** Carolyn Boicos, Fionnuala Twomey

**Coordinating Cartographer** Jacqueline Nguyen

**Coordinating Layout Designer** Wibowo Rusli

**Managing Editor** Annelies Mertens

**Senior Editors** Andi Jones, Martine Power

**Managing Cartographer** Adrian Persoglia

**Managing Layout Designer** Jane Hart

**Assisting Editors** Helen Koehne, Joanne Newell, Rosie Nicholson, Monique Perrin, Erin Richards

**Assisting Cartographer** James Leversha

**Cover Research** Naomi Parker

**Internal Image Research** Aude Vauconsant

**Language Content** Branislava Vladisavljevic

**Thanks to** Brigitte Ellemor, Ryan Evans, Larissa Frost, Genesys India, Chris Girdler, Laura Jane, Tania O'Connor, Trent Paton, Kirsten Rawlings, Raphael Richards, Laura Stansfeld, Navin Sushil, Gerard Walker, Juan Winata

# index

NOTES

NOTES

# how to use this book

**These symbols will help you find the listings you want:**

- 👁 Sights
- 👉 Tours
- 🍷 Drinking
- 🏄 Beaches
- 🎎 Festivals & Events
- ☆ Entertainment
- 🏃 Activities
- 🛏 Sleeping
- 🛍 Shopping
- 🥢 Courses
- 🍴 Eating
- ℹ Information/Transport

**These symbols give you the vital information for each listing:**

- ☎ Telephone Numbers
- ☎ Wi-Fi Access
- 🚌 Bus
- ☻ Opening Hours
- ▣ Swimming Pool
- ☻ Ferry
- Ⓟ Parking
- ◢ Vegetarian Selection
- Ⓜ Metro
- ☻ Nonsmoking
- ▣ English-Language Menu
- Ⓢ Subway
- ✳ Air-Conditioning
- ♦ Family-Friendly
- ☻ Tram
- @ Internet Access
- ☻ Pet-Friendly
- ▣ Train

**Reviews are organised by author preference.**

## Look out for these icons:

- **TOP** Our author's recommendation
- **FREE** No payment required
- 🍃 A green or sustainable option

*Our authors have nominated these places as demonstrating a strong commitment to sustainability – for example by supporting local communities and producers, operating in an environmentally friendly way, or supporting conservation projects.*

## Map Legend

### Sights
- 🏖 Beach
- 🛕 Buddhist
- 🏰 Castle
- ✝ Christian
- ☪ Hindu
- ☾ Islamic
- ✡ Jewish
- 🏛 Monument
- 🏛 Museum/Gallery
- 🏚 Ruin
- 🍷 Winery/Vineyard
- 🐾 Zoo
- ⦿ Other Sight

### Activities, Courses & Tours
- 🤿 Diving/Snorkelling
- 🛶 Canoeing/Kayaking
- 🎿 Skiing
- 🏄 Surfing
- 🏊 Swimming/Pool
- 🚶 Walking
- 🏄 Windsurfing
- ⊕ Other Activity/Course/Tour

### Sleeping
- 🛏 Sleeping
- ⛺ Camping

### Eating
- 🍴 Eating

### Drinking
- ☕ Drinking
- ☕ Cafe

### Entertainment
- 🎭 Entertainment

### Shopping
- 🛍 Shopping

### Information
- 💲 Bank
- 🏦 Embassy/Consulate
- ➕ Hospital/Medical
- @ Internet
- 👮 Police
- ✉ Post Office
- ☎ Telephone
- 🚻 Toilet
- ℹ Tourist Information
- • Other Information

### Transport
- ✈ Airport
- ⊗ Border Crossing
- 🚌 Bus
- ⊹⊕⊹ Cable Car/Funicular
- -⊛- Cycling
- -⊖- Ferry
- =⊕= Monorail
- Ⓟ Parking
- ⊖ Petrol Station
- ⊖ Taxi
- +⊕+ Train/Railway
- =⊕= Tram
- Ⓜ Underground Train Station
- • Other Transport

### Routes
- Tollway
- Freeway
- Primary
- Secondary
- Tertiary
- Lane
- Unsealed Road
- Plaza/Mall
- Steps
- )==( Tunnel
- Pedestrian Overpass
- Walking Tour
- Walking Tour Detour
- Path

### Geographic
- 🏠 Hut/Shelter
- 💡 Lighthouse
- 👁 Lookout
- ▲ Mountain/Volcano
- 🌴 Oasis
- 🌳 Park
- )( Pass
- 🌲 Picnic Area
- 💧 Waterfall

### Population
- ⊙ Capital (National)
- ◉ Capital (State/Province)
- ● City/Large Town
- • Town/Village

### Boundaries
- — — — International
- - - - - State/Province
- —— - Disputed
- — - - Regional/Suburb
- Marine Park
- Cliff
- Wall

### Hydrography
- River, Creek
- Intermittent River
- Swamp/Mangrove
- Reef
- Canal
- Water
- Dry/Salt/Intermittent Lake
- Glacier

### Areas
- Beach/Desert
- + + + Cemetery (Christian)
- × × × Cemetery (Other)
- Park/Forest
- Sportsground
- Sight (Building)
- Top Sight (Building)

# OUR STORY

A beat-up old car, a few dollars in the pocket and a sense of adventure. In 1972 that's all Tony and Maureen Wheeler needed for the trip of a lifetime – across Europe and Asia overland to Australia. It took several months, and at the end – broke but inspired – they sat at their kitchen table writing and stapling together their first travel guide, *Across Asia on the Cheap*. Within a week they'd sold 1500 copies. Lonely Planet was born.

Today, Lonely Planet has offices in Melbourne, London, Oakland and Delhi, with more than 600 staff and writers. We share Tony's belief that 'a great guidebook should do three things: inform, educate and amuse'.

# OUR WRITERS

### Jean-Bernard Carillet

Coordinating Author; Plan Your Trip, Djibouti, Somaliland A Paris-based journalist and photographer, Jean-Bernard is a die-hard Africa lover who never misses an opportunity to explore the continent. He has travelled the breadth and length of Africa for more than two decades now and has been thoroughly enlightened by 23 of its amazing countries. Highlights researching for this edition included exploring the far-flung provinces of Somaliland, drinking fresh camel milk with Somali friends in the bush around Hargeisa, getting up close and personal with a massive guitar shark off Moucha Island and following the steps of archaeologists in northern Djibouti. Jean-Bernard's wanderlust has taken him to six continents, inspiring numerous articles and some 30 guidebooks, including Lonely Planet's *Africa* and *West Africa*.

### Tim Bewer

Northern Ethiopia, Southern Ethiopia, Eastern Ethiopia Growing up, Tim didn't travel much except for the obligatory pilgrimage to Disney World and an annual lake-side summer week. He's spent most of his adult life making up for this, and has since visited over 80 countries. After university he worked as a legislative assistant before quitting capitol life to backpack around West Africa. During this trip the idea of becoming a travel writer/photographer was hatched, and he's been at it ever since, returning to Africa 10 times in the process. When he isn't shouldering a backpack somewhere for work or pleasure, he lives in Khon Kaen, Thailand, where he runs a tour company.

Read more about Tim at:
lonelyplanet.com/members/timbewer

### Stuart Butler

Addis Ababa, Western Ethiopia, Understand Ethiopia, Ethiopia Directory A–Z, Ethiopia Transport Stuart first visited Ethiopia in the early 1990s shortly after the fall of the Derg. He was utterly infatuated with what he saw and has returned to Ethiopia many times since; each time the country has woven its spell on him a little more. Stuart's travels, both for Lonely Planet and various surf magazines, have taken him beyond Ethiopia, from the coastal deserts of Pakistan to the jungles of Colombia. He now lives in southwest France with his wife and young son. Find Stuart at www.stuartbutlerjournalist.com.

Read more about Stuart at:
lonelyplanet.com/members/stuartbutler

**Published by Lonely Planet Publications Pty Ltd**
ABN 36 005 607 983
5th edition – June 2013
ISBN 978 1 74179 796 1
© Lonely Planet 2013    Photographs © as indicated 2013
10 9 8 7 6 5 4 3 2
Printed in China